Native Peoples of the Southwest

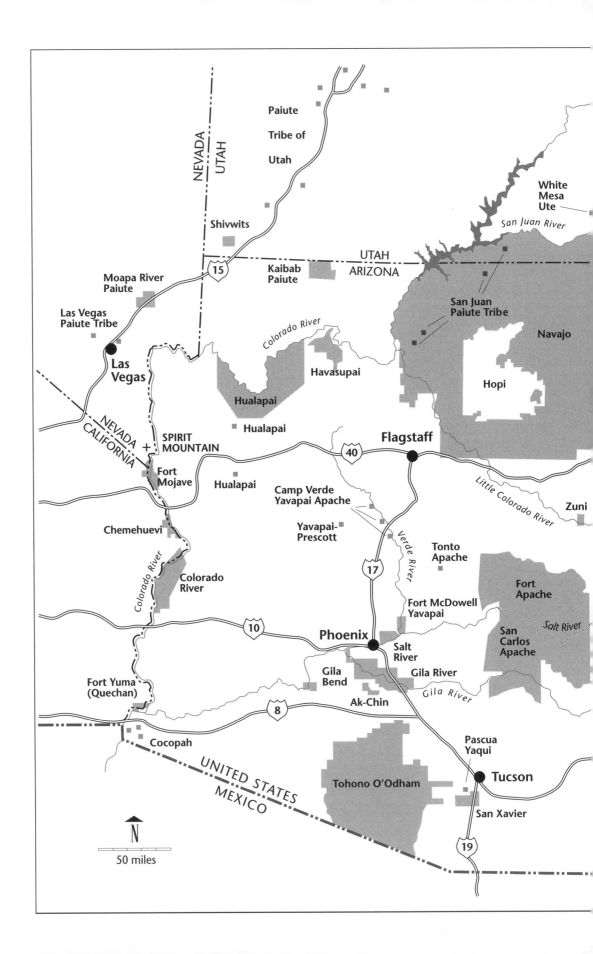

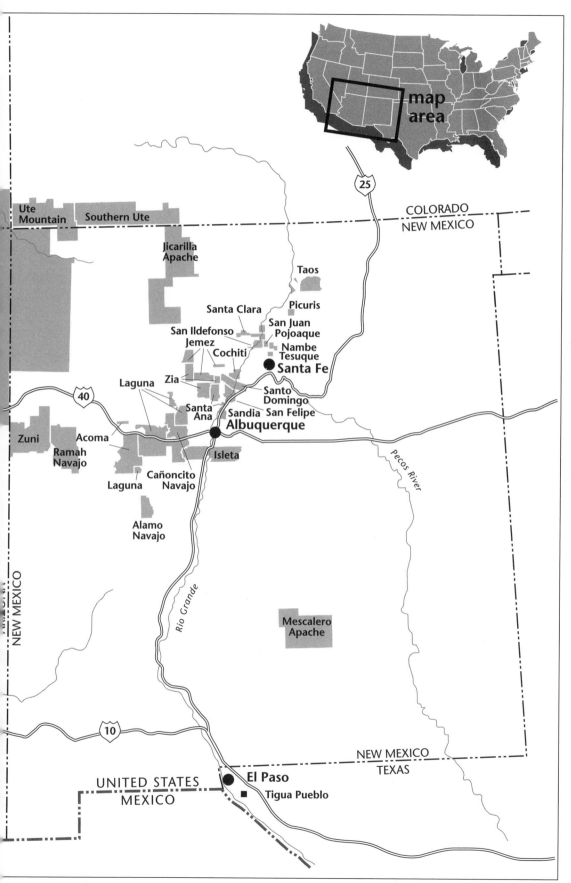

map area

25

COLORADO
NEW MEXICO

Ute Mountain

Southern Ute

Jicarilla Apache

Taos

Picuris

Santa Clara

San Juan
Pojoaque

San Ildefonso
Jemez

Cochiti

Nambe
Tesuque

Santa Fe

Zia

Laguna

Santo
Domingo

Santa
Ana

San Felipe

Sandia

Albuquerque

40

Zuni

Acoma

Isleta

Ramah
Navajo

Pecos River

Laguna

Cañoncito
Navajo

Alamo
Navajo

NEW MEXICO

Rio Grande

Mescalero
Apache

10

NEW MEXICO
TEXAS

UNITED STATES
MEXICO

El Paso

Tigua Pueblo

Map by Carol Cooperrider

Native Peoples of the Southwest

Trudy Griffin-Pierce

University of New Mexico Press   Albuquerque

Frontispiece: Wave clouds over Baboquivari, Tohono O'odham Reservation, 1966.
Photograph: Keith Pierce

Design and composition by Julie Allred, B. Williams & Associates

First edition

Library of Congress Cataloging-in-Publication Data
Griffin-Pierce, Trudy, 1949–
Native peoples of the Southwest / Trudy Griffin-Pierce.—1st ed.
     p.   cm.
ISBN 0-8263-1907-6 (cloth)
1. Indians of North America—Southwest, New—History.   2. Indians of
North America—Southwest, New—Social life and customs.   3. Indians
of North America—Southwest, New—Government relations.   I. Title.
E78.S7 G76 2000
979.004'97—dc21
00-008872

To Emory Sekaquaptewa, Octaviana Trujillo,
Lucille Watahomigie, and Ofelia Zepeda

Contents

Acknowledgments

I would like to thank the many individuals who have helped me in countless ways, beginning with friends and colleagues who have read all or a portion of the manuscript and have provided suggestions. This includes Emory Sekaquaptewa, Ofelia Zepeda, Octaviana Trujillo, Lavonne Honyouti, Karl Hoerig, Claire Farrer, and Louise Lamphere. I also want to extend my gratitude to those who contributed suggestions and support in the development of my ideas: in Peach Springs, Lucille Watahomigie; in Supai, Matthew Purtesoy and Bernadine Jones; at Kitt Peak, Ron Miguel, Sharmain Garcia, Richard Green, Suzanne Jacoby, and Larry Dunlop; in Santa Fe, Luana Ortiz; in Whitetail, Jordan Torres; in Tucson, R. Carlos Nakai, Pam Hyde-Nakai, Alicia Delgadillo, and Rich Stoffle; at Zuni, Alex Seowtewa; in Chinle, Edwin and Norma Irvin and their three daughters (Michelle, Malynda, and Natalie); in Fruitland, Lorraine and Samantha Sammons; in Low Mountain, Loretta Denny Bahe and the Denny family; in Phoenix, Andrew Means; in Boulder, Thomas Windham; in Albany, New York, Helmut Hirsch and Helen Ghiradella; in Tsaile, Harry Walters and Avery Denny; at Canyon de Chelly, Lupita Litson; and on Maui, Sam Ako and Dee Coyle. Several colleagues have provided inspiration, including Keith Basso, Bernard Fontana, Jane Young, Barbara Tedlock, Alice Schlegel, Carolyn Smith, Gary Nabhan, Stephen Trimble, and my mentor, the late Jim Officer. Special thanks go to Helga Teiwes, for her wonderful photographs, and to Kathy Hubenschmidt of the Arizona State Museum and Susan Sheehan of the Arizona Historical Society.

Barbara Guth, my editor at the University of New Mexico Press, has contributed both her considerable expertise and encouragement; I greatly appreciate her steadfast belief in this book. I also want to thank Lys Ann Shore, my copy editor, and Emmy Ezzell, production manager, for their painstaking attention to detail. Dirk Harris provided invaluable computer support. Margaret von Kuegelgen, Brenda Brandt, Marc Severson, Sue Southern, and my husband, Keith Pierce, have been wonderful traveling companions during the many miles logged in researching this book. I especially extend heartfelt thanks to Keith for his encouragement and support throughout the long process of writing this book.

Preface

The Navajos brought me to Arizona in 1970 and have kept me here ever since. Near the end of my first stay with my Navajo family, we went to a rodeo at a remote spot only a few miles from where Arizona, New Mexico, Utah, and Colorado meet. My skin was brown from weeks of herding sheep in the summer sun, my long hair held back in a Navajo bun, and I wore the long, full skirts of the Navajo. Sitting in the back of a pickup truck with my Navajo friends and family, I shared their laughter, despite a language barrier. When we parked next to a Winnebago driven by the only Anglos at the rodeo, I overheard one of them whisper to another, "Do you think she was captured by the Indians when she was a little girl?" My Navajo friends and I had a great laugh over their comment, but those Anglos were remarkably close to the truth. The Navajos captured my heart and my imagination from an early age.

Since my earliest childhood—I was a military nomad who grew up in Hawaii, California, England, Florida, and Illinois—I had always known that someday I would live with the Navajos, but I might not have followed through on this dream had my mother not died when I was in high school. The sudden death of the person who was my whole world shattered my core beliefs about reality and sent me searching for meaning. The only thing in my life to which I was truly connected was the Navajo and their way of being in the world.

Two years later, I wrote to Tribal Chairman Raymond Nakai, asking him "to find me a traditional family whom I could join," not as an observer but as a daughter. And so I came to live with a non-English-speaking older couple who lived in a hogan between Many Farms and Round Rock, Arizona. The couple's nephew met me at the El Rancho Hotel in Gallup, where friends had deposited me before resuming their cross-country honeymoon. The nephew approached me in the hotel lobby and simply asked, "Are you the girl?" I barely got out, "I think I am," before he asked where my things were, grabbed my sleeping bag and suitcase, and was out the door. We were soon bouncing along Highway 264 in his Ford truck; every time a pickup passed us, Navajo wives turned around to see who the Anglo woman was with the Navajo man.

This was my initiation into Athapaskan silence, for over the course of the two-hour drive, he uttered only a handful of words. My anxiety reached a fever pitch when he turned off the road, got out of the pickup, and reached into the bed of the truck to wind a rope into a tight coil. Convinced that he was about to tie me up and leave me for dead, I tried to keep from glancing in the rearview mirror. A few minutes later, he climbed back into the cab, explaining, "Late meeting at the chapter house last night. I was about to fall asleep, just needed some air." Flooded with relief, I finally exhaled as we pulled back onto the highway to resume our journey.

After a long bumpy ride over a deeply rutted dirt road, we arrived at the hogan, and my new way of life began. Without electricity or running water, we got up at dawn to chop firewood, fix breakfast, and pack food for lunch before we ushered the flock of sheep and goats out of their corral and over the hill. All day long we herded them, occasionally resting beneath the spotty shade of a lone juniper, where my Navajo mother spun carded wool into yarn with her wooden spindle. We returned home with just enough sunlight to chop firewood and prepare dinner; I usually finished drying the dishes by the light of an oil lamp.

The highlight of my first visit was the sheep dip, for it took all day to herd the flock to and from the pens near the highway where they were inoculated against a host of diseases. I herded the flock with two young nephews, who delighted in mistranslating my Navajo father's directions; they doubled up with laughter when I got in trouble for herding the sheep to the wrong side of the wash. Coming home, I got to ride in the buckboard, probably because my father realized how much more expedient it would be for everyone.

Nevertheless, the day before my departure they left me with the flock when their niece came by to take them to the trading post in her pickup truck. Before they left, she translated their instructions to take the sheep and goats out just over the first hill to graze for the morning; they'd be back in a couple of hours. Those Navajo sheepdogs, as wily as the young nephews, refused to obey my directions and soon scattered the flock. After my initial panic—I'd just lost the family's life savings and I knew I would have to abandon college for a career of hamburger flipping at McDonald's to buy back all those sheep and goats!—I managed to get my bearings by climbing a hill and locating Tsaile Lake on the horizon. Eventually, I heard the distant clank of the ram's bell, which led me to the cluster of ewes grazing around him; the rest of the sheep were grazing placidly nearby. But the goats were nowhere to be found; the specter of McDonald's began to loom once more in my future. The family found me just as I returned with the sheep; they were worried about how they would explain my disappearance. When they allayed my fears over the goats—which had followed the trail to their winter home, as the family predicted—I was overjoyed.

After returning to Florida State University to complete my final semester, I moved to Arizona for good to be close to my Navajo parents and began graduate school at the University of Arizona. At the time, I did not really know where I was going, but I knew I had begun. I was only following what sustained me and what was most alive in me; little did I dream then that the Navajos would lead me to a career of writing and university teaching in anthropology.

Introduction

August 1994 Projected downward from the mirrors of the solar telescope, the sun sails across the viewing table, a simmering molten ball with wavering edges of green and blue and violet on one side and frayed filaments of red and orange and yellow on the other side. The earth's atmosphere distorts the sun into an oblate egg, dancing and shimmering, until at last, the sun is swallowed by the mountains. Huge chunks of boiling sun appear to float off at both ends—jewel-like pieces of lapis and turquoise, ruby and topaz.

Everyone is silent, joined in shared reverence at the wonder of humankind's place in the universe. The astronomers, who have seen this sight countless times, are as captivated as the Tohono O'odham families—feeble grandmothers, fathers with thick black ponytails, plump mothers holding babies, self-absorbed teenagers, even bubbling grade-schoolers—who are viewing sunset on the world's largest solar telescope for the first time. This is Tohono O'odham Family Night at Kitt Peak, and the scientists and families are about to share an even more distant glimpse through time and space as they look through telescopes at stars hundreds of light years away.

Earlier, some of these children had danced in front of the telescope, their bare feet shuffling across the pavement, their arms outstretched, and their hands bearing dance wands mounted by white seagulls, gray geese, black swallows, clouds, lightning superimposed on clouds, and rainbows. Once performed following the harvest to show gratitude for the earth's bounty, the *celkona* was danced this evening as an expression of Tohono O'odham culture. The sleek angularity and scientific precision of the solar telescope presented a striking contrast to the stark simplicity and nature-inspired imagery of the children's dance. As the dancers skipped across the blacktop, they could look across the valley and see *Waw kiwulk*, Baboquivari Peak—home to *I'itoi*, the creator of human beings—a sacred mountain that has withstood the comings and goings of many generations and many cultures.

The dynamic and interconnected nature of cultures is evident in the faces in the audience: in addition to O'odham, there are scientists who have come from all parts of the world to look through the telescopes of the national observatory, which lies on land leased from the Tohono O'odham Nation. Many will take home O'odham baskets and other crafts bought at the visitors' center on the mountaintop or at a store in Tucson specializing in Native American arts. The Tohono O'odham people, whose government is dependent on funding from the Bureau of Indian Affairs, are at the mercy of decisions made in Washington regarding the balancing of the national budget and, ultimately, of the boom-and-bust cycles of international markets. Today such interrelationships are explicitly acknowledged because of what Immanuel Wallerstein (1974) calls the modern world system; however, it is important to remember that Tohono O'odham communities never existed in isolation nor were they unchanging.

Our heightened awareness of change in today's world—due not only to its accelerated rate, but also to the rapid dissemination of this information—makes cultures as they existed in the past seem static, when, in reality, they were simply changing more slowly. The unbroken continuity of Southwestern cultures, in contrast to those in the rest of the continent, also obscures the fact that new ideas and cultural patterns were constantly being introduced and that groups were moving, interacting with other groups, and responding to changing conditions on a continuous basis. Creative risk-takers within each group broke from the traditions of the past; even within bands that did not permit full-time specialization, each individual had unique abilities, preferred activities, and a distinct personality shaped by the family's style of child raising.

In writing this book, I have tried to convey the great cultural vitality and dynamic nature of Southwestern Indian cultures, including their contemporary nature. Many books about the native peoples of the Southwest are so specialized that they do not convey a sense of the region as a whole, while others are so general that they do not portray these cultures as dynamic and ever changing. When I teach the course of the same name at the University of Arizona, I begin by gathering the students into a circle and explaining the significance of a Navajo ceremonial basket, before passing it to the student on my left, who explains what he or she hopes to get from the class. In the tradition of the talking circle, each person is empowered to speak when he or she is holding the basket, while everyone else listens in a respectful silence. Many Anglo students are amazed at the number of Native Americans in the class, and many confide later that they did not realize the strength of these cultures today; the Native American students usually say that they hope to learn about "the other" Indians of the Southwest. I hope that this book brings to life Southwestern Indian peoples, communicating their spirit and their vitality. This is why I visited each group, conducting interviews and asking individuals what they would like to have included in this book.

To portray the living, dynamic nature of these cultures, I introduce each chapter with a present-day account to show how the people are continuing important cultural traditions as they deal with ongoing influence from Anglo-American culture. Immediately after this vignette is an abbreviated version of the people's Creation/Emergence story, followed by a section detailing the group's linguistic affiliation, territory, prehistory, and history. The next sections cover the group's subsistence pattern, material culture, social organization, political organization, and religion and world view. Contemporary issues, such as the development of mineral resources and the introduction of reservation gaming, follow; sidebars further emphasize the dynamic nature of Southwestern cultures, including examples of how individuals are not only keeping their cultures alive but also infusing them with new ideas and practices. Finally, for readers who want to learn more about each group, there is a list of additional resources, including videos, films, articles, and books.

Immediately following this introduction is a description and chart of Native American languages in the Southwest. The survival of these languages—and the cultures they reflect—is a major issue among contemporary indigenous peoples, as more and more languages are becoming extinct.

Although the book's length limits the depth to which I can explore the impact that various ethnic groups have had on the indigenous peoples of the Southwest—as well as the impact that Native Americans have had on Anglo-Europeans—it is essential to keep in mind that Southwestern peoples were constantly responding in many different ways to changing conditions. Sometimes, they accommodated to the intrusion by interacting with outsiders; at other times, they resisted the changes forced upon them. Never were they passive bystanders. Thus, the first chapter presents a background of the larger historical, political, and economic movements to establish the context within which later chapters are set.

Finally, I want to point out that the divisions within each chapter are a heuristic device, meant to help students better understand and compare the cultures of native Southwestern peoples. This presentation violates the sense of connectedness that is a basic tenet of American Indian world views. The perspective of oneness and interconnection, more flexible than holism, which still contains a sense of separation from other entities, emphasizes the danger of treating any one phenomenon in isolation. The spiritual permeates all aspects of life, including the planting of corn, the hunting of animals, the relationships of people, ceremonial performances, public oratory, creative processes, and, especially, stories that recount how the world came to be as it is. My intent in writing this book is to make an understanding of this sense of interconnectedness accessible to a wider audience. I hope that such an understanding will enrich the lives of those who read this book, so that they will take with them a greater respect not only for the cultures and peoples of the Southwest but also for the world we all share.

Native American Languages in the Southwest

Native American languages within the Americas display enormous variation in grammar and phonology. For example, the tonal distinctions found in Navajo, an Athapaskan language, are reminiscent of Mandarin, while other languages, such as Karuk (California) and Seneca (New York), have structures found in American Indian languages but nowhere else in the world (Golla 1994:310). Scholars agree that such a vast range of structural differences attests to considerable time depth. This is especially evident in the Southwest, where different Puebloan peoples live a relatively similar lifestyle but speak such dissimilar languages as Zuni, Keresan, Tanoan, and Hopi. (Zuni and Keresan are language isolates, which means that they are unrelated to any other known languages.)

Over 300 distinct languages were spoken by Native Americans in 1900. Tragically, by 1995, 120 of these had become extinct, 72 were only spoken by a few elders, 91 were spoken by adults but by no or very few children, and only 46 were still spoken by a significant number of children (Goddard 1996:3). Linguists Ofelia Zepeda and Jane Hill describe "this vastly reduced reservoir of linguistic diversity" as "one of the great treasures of humanity, an enormous storehouse of expressive power and profound understandings of the universe," and call the loss of the hundreds of now extinct Native American languages "an intellectual catastrophe in every way comparable in magnitude to the ecological catastrophe" we are now facing (1991:135).

This situation developed around 1880 during the reservation period, when federal education policy favored the removal of Indian children from their communities to boarding schools where the use of Native American languages was absolutely forbidden. Children who dared to speak their native languages received "shockingly abusive treatment and humiliation," a situation that continued in some areas until the early 1970s (Zepeda and Hill 1991:138). Although the punishment no longer continues, it is still common for teachers and school administrators to urge parents to discourage their children from speaking their own languages; furthermore, schools are heavily dominated by English, implying that native languages are inferior. Another linguistically destructive force has been evangelical missionary efforts, which oppose indigenous languages as "reservoirs of paganism and satanic influence" (ibid., 139). On the San Carlos Apache Reservation in Arizona and the Alamo Navajo Reservation in New Mexico, some fundamentalist churches still forbid their members to speak their native languages or even to attend any event at which these languages are spoken (Brandt 1988:324). Even those evangelical groups which do not forbid the use of native languages still discourage members from attending indigenous religious events, including healing, which is the context for some of the most complex and creative language use.

Another major influence today is the mass media which, through the use of English in television, radio, videos, and books, constantly reinforces the dominance and prestige of English to susceptible young people. Many parents, forced to work two jobs to support their families, have no choice but to spend less time with their children, who may then be exposed to a greater amount of English-language television (Zepeda and Hill 1991:140–41). To increase their children's chances of academic success, parents may decide not to bring their children up bilingually. Finally, although the 1960s and 1970s brought a political climate receptive to indigenous–language programs, the backlash of conservatism in the 1980s favored total immersion in English from the earliest grades and a constitutional amendment to make English the official language in the United States.

Cocopah, Keresan, Havasupai-Hualapai-Yavapai, Hopi, Towa, Mescalero Apache, Tiwa, Navajo, Piman, Yaqui, and Zuni are among only 20 American Indian languages that linguist Victor Golla estimates will definitely survive into future generations because they continue to be learned by children (Golla 1994:311). Among the Navajo and Pueblos, ceremonial life has helped to keep the vitality of the languages; other tribes, most notably, the Hualapai, have used the 1968 Bilingual Education Act (Title VII) to create a consistently high quality of bilingual/bicultural teaching materials and teaching efforts. (For a further description of this program, see the Hualapai section of chapter 8. See also the sidebar in chapter 6, "A Yaqui Approach to Cultural and Linguistic Survival," based on the work of Octaviana Trujillo [Yaqui].) Many Native American linguists, such as Emory Sekaquaptewa (Hopi), Lucille Watahomigie (Hualapai), and Ofelia Zepeda (Tohono O'odham) are documenting their languages by creating exhaustive dictionaries, developing strategies for preservation, and collecting and analyzing oral literature.

The American Indian Language Development Institute (AILDI), which celebrated its twentieth year in 1999, is a major force for the continuing vitality of Native American languages. Lucille Watahomigie, a group of academic linguists, and eighteen Native American parents interested in learning to read and write in their own languages, created the institute, which is codirected by Ofelia Zepeda. They held workshops in various tribal communities and campuses throughout the Southwest; since 1990, AILDI has been based at the University of Arizona. The institute's annual workshops draw educators to the UA campus each summer, where they learn how to combine Native American traditions with modern teaching methods to help their students succeed. All of its courses lead toward regular UA degrees, as well as bilingual and English as a second language (ESL) endorsements; thus, the institute helps Native Americans obtain degree certification as teachers.

In 1990, by passing SB 1781, the Native American Language Act, the U.S. government officially recognized the special status of indigenous languages and cultures, and the federal government's responsibility to cooperate with Native Americans to ensure their survival (Zepeda and Hill 1991:148–51). Despite this encouraging step, Native Americans still struggle against enormous odds to save languages that are fundamental to the personal, social, and spiritual identities of their speakers. As Zepeda and Hill emphasize, this is a struggle that affects us all, for these languages and the cultures that they frame not only enrich the lives of their speakers but also "enlarge the cultural wealth of all humanity" (ibid., 150).

References and Further Reading

Bills, Garland D. 1974. "Apachean Language Maintenance." *International Journal of the Sociology of Language* 2:91–100.

Brandt, Elizabeth. 1981. "Native American Attitudes toward Literacy and Recording in the Southwest." *Journal of the Linguistic Association of the Southwest* 4:2:185–95.

———. 1988. "Applied Linguistic Anthropology and American Indian Language Renewal." *Human Organization* 47, no. 4:322–29.

Goddard, Ives, ed. 1996. *Languages*, vol. 17 of *The Handbook of North American Indians*.

Golla, Victor. 1994. "Languages." In *Native America in the Twentieth Century, An Encyclopedia*, pp. 310–12, ed. Mary B. Davis. Garland Publishing, New York.

Hill, Jane H. 1978. "Language Death, Language Contact, and Language Function." In *Approaches to Language*, pp. 44–78, ed. William McCormack and Stephen Wurm. Mouton, The Hague.

———. 1983. "Language Death in Uto-Aztecan." *International Journal of American Linguistics* 49:258–76.

Leap, William L. 1981. "American Indian Language Maintenance." *Annual Review of Anthropology* 10:209–36.

———. 1988. "Applied Linguistics and American Indian Language Renewal: Introductory Comments." *Human Organization* 47:283–91.

Reyhner, J. 1997. *Teaching Indigenous Languages.* Northern Arizona University, Flagstaff.

Silver, Shirley, and Wick R. Miller. 1997. *American Indian Languages: Cultural and Social Contexts.* University of Arizona Press, Tucson.

Spolsky, Bernard. 1975. "Prospects for the Survival of the Navajo Language." In *Linguistics and Anthropology in Honor of C. F. Voegelin,* pp. 597–606, ed. Dale Kinkade, Kenneth Hale, and Oswald Werner. Peter de Ridder Press, Lisse.

Trujillo, Octaviana. 1998. "The Yaqui of Guadalupe, Arizona: A Century of Cultural Survival through Trilingualism." *American Indian Culture and Research Journal* 22:1:67–88.

U.S. Senate. 1989. *Joint Resolution on Native American Languages.* S.J. Res. 379.

———. 1990. *The Native American Language Act.* S.B. 1781.

Watahomigie, Lucille, and Yamamoto Akira. n.d. [1983]. "Action Linguistics with the Hualapai Bilingual/Bicultural Program." Peach Springs Bilingual Program (manuscript).

Zepeda, Ofelia, and Jane Hill. 1991. "The Condition of Native American Languages in the United States." In *Endangered Languages,* pp. 135–55, ed. R. H. Robbins and E. M. Uhlenbeck. Berg, Oxford, England.

Native American Languages in the Southwest

I. COCHIMÍ-YUMAN
    YUMAN
        PAI Upland Yuman (Havasupai, Hualapai, Yavapai)
        RIVER Mojave
            Quechan
            Maricopa
        DELTA Cocopah

II. UTO-AZTECAN
    NUMIC
        SOUTHERN NUMIC Ute (Chemehuevi, Southern Paiute)
    Hopi
    TEPIMAN
        Upper Piman (Pima, Tohono O'odham)
    TARACAHITAN
        Cahitan(Yaqui)

III. KIOWA-TANOAN
    Towa Jemez
    TIWA
        NORTHERN TIWA
            Taos
            Picuris
        Southern Tiwa (Isleta and Sandia)
    Tewa (Rio Grande Tewa [San Juan, Santa Clara, San Ildefonso, Pojoaque, Nambe, Tesuque] and Tano [Arizona Tewa])

IV. KERESAN
    Western Keresan (Acoma, Laguna)
    Eastern Keresan (Zia, Santa Ana, San Felipe, Santo Domingo, Cochiti)

V. ZUNI

VI. NADENE
    ATHAPASKAN
        APACHEAN
            WESTERN APACHEAN
                Navajo
                Western Apache (Northern and Southern Tonto, Cibicue, San Carlos, White Mountain)
                Mescalero, Chiricahua
            EASTERN APACHEAN
            Jicarilla
            Lipan
         Kiowa-Apache

This chart is not inclusive; only those groups discussed in this book are included. Language names are in normal type; greater linguistic divergence is implied by the listing of groups on separate lines; and the names of families that contain more than one language, subfamilies, and intermediate branches are in all capital letters. The indentations indicate the degree of ramification in the subclassification of language families (adapted from Goddard 1996:5–7).

Chapter 1

Connections

The Chiricahua Apache sculptor Allan Houser (1914–94) embodies the idea of interconnecting cultures as well as the vitality of his own culture. His father was a nephew of Geronimo, and Houser was one of the first children born after the Chiricahua were released from captivity. He grew up attending powwows in Oklahoma, where Indians from many tribes came together; attended the Santa Fe Indian School; and, during World War II, worked in Los Angeles as a pipefitter's helper. Through time, he became known for his monumental bronze, steel, and stone sculptures of Plains warriors, Navajo and Pueblo shepherds, and Apache mothers and children, works that express universal qualities. He once said, "Human dignity is very important to me. I feel that way toward all people, not just Indians . . . in my work, this is what I strive for—this dignity, this goodness that is in man." His legacy transcends ethnic boundaries: Houser's sculptures are owned by such varied institutions as the Pompidou Museum in Paris, the U.S. Mission to the United Nations, the British Royal Collection, and the National Portrait Gallery, part of the Smithsonian Institution.

In much the same way that Houser drew inspiration from many cultures and experiences, which allowed his work to serve as a bridge linking ancient Apache values to the modern world, his homeland, the American Southwest, is best understood within the greater context of interconnecting cultures and global processes. Each nation that conquered the Southwest was driven by its own economic, political, and cultural goals, which, in turn, were the product of its own culture history and position on the world stage.

While military force explains how these nations overcame the native populations of the Southwest, military strength tells us only how, rather than why, such changes occurred (White 1983:xv). The unifying thread that connects the histories of the conquering nations is their attempt to bring Indian resources, land, and labor into the market for the benefit of the conquering nation. Often, economic interests blended with other imperial, religious, and cultural aims. For example, the Spanish pressed northward to Zuni from Mexico because they needed gold and silver to support large-scale military operations and an ever expanding royal bureaucracy, and to reestablish their economy after ousting the Moors and the Jews. Although their search for the fabled Seven Cities of Cibola proved fruitless, it nevertheless had far-reaching effects on the Pueblo peoples of the Rio Grande area.

Until Europeans set foot on the North American continent in 1492, the peoples of the Americas, Australia, and Oceania had existed in isolation, outside the enormous trade network of the so-called Old World, which consisted of Europe, Africa, and Asia. Rather than being an isolated adventure, Columbus's arrival was only a late manifestation of what had begun at least 500 years previously with Icelanders and Greenlanders; in time, this unifying wave would grow and spread to encompass both hemispheres. Motivated by powerful forces of empire building and trade, European expansion eventually resulted in wide-ranging linkages far beyond anything the world had ever known.

The Southwest is remarkable for the range of ethnic groups to which its indigenous peoples were exposed and the variety of ways in which Native Americans responded to such contact. Although Spaniards, Mexicans, and Anglo-Americans were unsuccessful in their attempts to exterminate and absorb native peoples, they still had an immense impact on indigenous cultures. Cultural interaction sometimes led to creative outcomes, such as the Yaqui fusion of two religions through attributing native meanings to Catholic symbols. But, more often than not, the clash of cultures led to the oppression of native peoples, such as the treatment of the people of the Rio Grande Pueblos at the hands of the Spaniards, who whipped and executed native leaders.

But long before the Spanish set foot in the "New World," Southwestern peoples were passing on to each other rituals, traits, ideas, commodities, and genes. Despite long periods of apparent stability, their cultures continued to change through time in response to trading, raiding, and environmental changes. It is important to keep the bigger picture in mind and to remember that long before recorded history, regional and global events had an impact on the peoples of the Southwest.

Frequent movement among the peoples of adjoining areas led to the sharing of many traits. To the east, the peoples of the Great Plains, who depended upon the bison as a major food source, influenced nearby Southwestern groups, such as the Jicarilla Apache and the people of Taos Pueblo, who borrowed aspects of Plains dress as well as the hunting of bison. (Until it was abandoned in the 1830s, the pueblo of Pecos was also a major Southwest-Plains link.) Mesoamerican peoples, who domesticated corn over 7,000 years ago, shared this knowledge with their northern neighbors in the Southwest. West of the Colorado River, the western boundary of the Southwest, the peoples of southern California borrowed many elements from Puebloan cultures. To the north, Great Basin peoples lived between the Rocky Mountains and the Sierra Nevada, two natural barriers that isolate the area geographically as moisture flows back into the basin, where it accumulates in shallow lakes, evaporates slowly, and increases in salt content. Considerable cultural unity, along with this isolation, helped to bring about linguistic uniformity: nearly every group in the Great Basin area speaks a Numic language, as do the Southern Paiute, some of whom live in Arizona; the Hopi of northern Arizona speak a related language.

The Land

The Southwest is a harsh and beautiful land with open spaces, brilliant light, and high elevations that make possible great clarity of vision. Little wonder that the native peoples of this region named every mesa, mountain, and river, giving each its own story to mark its sacredness. The spirit of the land is impossible to ignore.

Water makes the difference between life and death in the arid Southwest. Two major rivers sculpt and shape the land and the lives of those who live there. Plunging southwestward from the Rocky Mountains to the Gulf of California, the Colorado River created the Grand Canyon. The Rio Grande tumbles down from the Rockies as well, but takes a southward and then an eastward route to the Gulf of Mexico, forming a natural boundary between the United States and Mexico. In addition to these two great river systems, the Pecos River leads south near the eastern boundary of the Southwest, eventually joining the Rio Grande, and the Salt and Gila Rivers flow through southern Arizona.

Four major environmental zones, each with its own distinctive geologic features, climate, flora, and fauna, are found in the Southwest. The peoples of this area had to adapt to the specific characteristics of the zone or zones in which they lived, learning what plants and animals were best for food, shelter, and clothing.

The Colorado Plateau surrounds the Four Corners area, where the states of New Mexico, Arizona, Utah, and Colorado meet. This is the homeland of many of the village-dwelling Pueblo peoples, who are the genetic and cultural descendants of people who settled in the Southwest many millennia before the time of Christ. The Colorado Plateau is also home to two groups of Upland Yumans—the Hualapai and the Havasupai, who lived along the southern rim and in a side branch of the Grand Canyon, respectively. The Navajo, relative latecomers to the Southwest, also share the Colorado Plateau.

The outstanding geological features of the Colorado Plateau include mesas, buttes, valleys, and canyons cut by rivers, most notably the Grand Canyon. The terrain of the plateau is rugged, ranging between 5,000 feet and 6,750 feet in elevation, with many mountains and canyons and piñon and juniper forests. Sage, greasewood, saltbush, blackbush, and other shrubs and grasses cover the land below 5,000 feet.

The Rocky Mountain zone lies just east of the Colorado Plateau in the north-central portion of New Mexico and reaches south of Santa Fe. Rugged mountain chains, covered with heavy forests of piñon and juniper, pine and fir, receive precipitation in the form of snow and rain. The higher elevations have short growing seasons and cool temperatures, which make these areas unsuitable for farming. Fortunately, the forests supplied abundant plant foods and wild game, timber, and firewood for the peoples who lived nearby. Many of the Pueblo peoples lived here, as well as the Jicarilla Apache, who moved into this region much later.

The Central Mountains, which cut across the middle of Arizona and western New Mexico, follow the Mogollon Rim, an escarpment where the highlands meet the plateau. An area with a few broad valleys or mesas, this zone consists primarily of sloping land. Most of this area lies above 6,750 feet. The steep terrain, along with the short growing season created by the altitude, made farming difficult in this zone. As in the Rocky Mountain zone, the pine and fir forests of this area provide a supply of wild plant and animal foods, which once formed the basis for subsistence for the Yavapai and the Western Apache.

The largest of the four zones, the **Desert Basin and Range**, lies south of the other areas, curving around them in a crescent. The zone gets its name from its parallel mountain ranges separated by the alluvial material that washes off the mountains during rainstorms to form basins. From the southernmost point of Nevada in the west, this zone reaches across both states and up the eastern boundaries of the three other zones. Most of this area is low desert, covered with creosote, bursage, and other shrubs, along with cactus, mesquite, and palo verde. The Sonoran desert region of this zone contains the giant saguaro, organ pipe, and barrel cactus, which are highly valued by the Pimans (O'odham) who live there. Rainfall in this area varies with temperature and altitude: the west, home to the River Yuman peoples who live along the lower Colorado River, receives less than 5 inches of precipitation annually, while the east receives about twice that amount. Agriculture is also limited in this area; although the growing season is much longer than in the higher zones, there are few permanent sources of water. The people who live in this zone once relied primarily on game they caught in mountainous areas and on wild plants, including the agave, mesquite, and tepary beans, and the fruits and buds of various cactus.

The First People

Thousands of years before Europeans dreamed of exploring this region, the ancestors of Southwestern peoples were living here. Although archaeologists continue to debate when the peopling of the Americas occurred, it is known that the Clovis people, who were Paleo-Indians, were hunting elephants in southern Arizona along the San Pedro River and its tributaries 12,000 years ago (Reid and Whittlesey 1997:29). More locally adapted groups known as Archaic cultures replaced these peoples, followed by cultures that roughly correspond to three of the four geographic zones previously described.

The Colorado Plateau region was home to the *Ancestral Pueblo* people (a term that is gaining more common usage and is replacing *Anasazi,* which is a Navajo word); they are known in Hopi as the *Hisatsinom.* The *Mogollon,* who lived in the Central Mountains, were also ancestral to the present-day Puebloans. The Desert Basin and Range was associated with both the *Hohokam* of southern Arizona and the *Patayan* of the Colorado River region. The Hohokam are assumed to be ancestral Piman speakers, and the Patayan were the ancestors of the Yuman-speaking peoples. The Athapaskan speakers—the Navajo and the various Apache tribes—entered the Southwest much later and are not related to any of these prehistoric groups.

Adaptation in 1600

When Spanish missionaries and explorers began their expeditions into what is now the southwestern United States in 1540, they became increasingly aware of vast cultural differences between the people they found there and the Aztecs and other peoples of Mexico with whom they were familiar. Clearly, the new cultural region to the northwest was quite unlike central Mexico, where domination over the Indians had been facilitated by their centralized governments and organization into states. The density of Indian settlements, depending upon the intensity of agricultural activities, varied widely, ranging from permanent, compact villages to temporary places of residence occupied for a brief period once a year.

The Pueblos practiced *village farming,* the most intensive form of agriculture in the Southwest. Using irrigation and dry-farming techniques, they were able to produce enough food to support their small, compact villages composed of contiguous, apartment-style houses of masonry or sun-dried mud. Life in permanent villages gave them more time to develop complex ceremonial systems and elaborate forms of material culture, such as pottery and *kivas* (the permanent ceremonial structures of the Pueblo Indians). Each village was an autonomous unit. With so many people living side by side, it was necessary to develop complex sociopolitical organizations to handle governmental responsibilities, land inheritance, postmarital residence, and other aspects of their culture. Many of the Eastern Pueblos lived along the Rio Grande in New Mexico, while the Western Pueblos lived away from the river on the Colorado Plateau. (The Zuni area is situated primarily in the southeastern section of the Colorado Plateau [Ferguson and Hart 1990:5].)

In the 1600s, three-quarters of Southwestern peoples practiced *rancheria farming* (Spicer 1981 [1962]:13), a subsistence strategy that relies on agriculture but results in a much more dispersed settlement pattern. Instead of contiguous apartments, a rancheria settlement would have houses that were separated by as much as half a mile; rancheria peoples often shifted the location of their settlements during the year when a nearby river flooded its banks. They, too, had to develop forms of leadership, effective work groups, and ceremonial practices suited to their lifestyle. The rancheria adaptation varies in the concentration of settlements. The most widely dispersed communities were those of the Tarahumara in Mexico, who occupied ridges and mountain valleys in summer, lowlands and gorges in winter. (The groups of northern Mexico are not discussed in this book, even though the Southwest culture area extends into Mexico.) The O'odham (Pimans) of southern Arizona lived in somewhat more compact settlements, but many O'odham also moved from winter mountain villages to summer valley settlements. The Yumans of the lower Colorado River had rancherias that were more permanent than those of the O'odham. Finally, the Yaquis, who lived near the mouths of large rivers in northern Mexico, had the most concentrated settlements of all subtypes of rancheria farmers.

At the time of Spanish arrival in the Southwest, some Southwestern peoples practiced *foraging with some or no farming*. Some groups planted small plots of corn, beans, and squash, which supplied about one-fourth of their food; with no fixed settlement locations, they ranged over great expanses but returned seasonally and annually to plant and harvest at their temporary places of residence. Some Apache tribes, as well as the Upland Yumans and Southern Paiutes, did some farming and lived in bands. The leadership of these loosely organized groups varied, depending upon the situation. Such small groups, which could easily be organized into larger groups when needed, were ideally suited to the needs of hunters and gatherers for mobility, and individuals with outstanding skills took charge when their expertise was required. Though there was an informal overall leader, he led more through influence than absolute authority, for he had no powers to coerce his followers, and band members came and went at will. Such flexibility in changing band membership was ideal because of year-to-year fluctuations in the abundance of particular areas.

A more nomadic lifestyle also had an impact on material culture, as well as on the form of ceremonies. While agriculturalists tended to develop a more complex ceremonial system led by priests, nomadic groups relied more on shamans for healing and hunt magic. The distinction between priests and shamans is especially useful in discussing the cultures of the Southwest: while a shaman learns rituals through personal revelation, a priest learns the ritual procedures from other ceremonial practitioners. These ceremonial practitioners are not necessarily called "priest" or "shaman." For example, among the Navajo, singers (chanters) are priests because they must go through an apprenticeship to learn a codified body of standardized ritual. Navajo handtremblers, stargazers, crystalgazers, and listeners follow the shamanistic tradition. Shamans are more common among loosely structured food-gathering societies, where most ceremonies are crisis rituals or else curing rites performed for one or more patients within the context of an extended family group; such rites usually take place according to individual need, rather than on a calendrical basis. In contrast, priests and priesthoods are more prevalent in tightly structured food-producing (usually agricultural) societies, where most ceremonies are communal and calendrical, performed for the well-being of the entire village.

The Spanish Colonial Period (1540–1821)

The first wave of hegemonic force to engulf the Indians of the Southwest came in the mid-sixteenth century when Spaniards in the Rio Grande drainage moved quickly to add New Mexico to their empire by integrating the Indians into European trade lines and political systems, and the Catholic religion. The domination of the western Southwest came much later: after 200 years of steady northward advance from the Valley of Mexico, the Spanish conquest spent itself in the face of Apache resistance in the last half of the eighteenth century.

Driven by imperial, economic, and religious goals, the Spaniards sought to claim the deserts and mountains of the Southwest to finance their newly created polity. Spain had achieved political unity less than a century before, in 1469, with the union of the crowns of Castile and Aragon. The military nobles who drove out the Moors were paid in land, thus establishing both a system of land grants as reward for military conquest and a pattern of land ownership in which 2–3 percent of the population owned 97 percent of the land (Elliott 1966:111). Unfortunately for the future of Spain, instead of commercial and industrial development, warfare and the seizure of people and resources became the primary means of growth (Wolf 1997 [1982]:113).

Iberians came seeking treasure in the form of gold, but it was silver that became the mainstay of Spanish wealth. In 1545, in Bolivia, the Spaniards discovered the first silver deposits in the New World. But even though the supply of silver that reached Seville was so vast that it tripled the European supply of this precious metal (Elliott 1966:180), it was not enough to pay for the excesses of the Spanish Crown. Spain was so overextended in its global and European military pursuits, and so dependent upon the importation of foreign manufactured goods, that at the end of the sixteenth century, three-fifths of all the bullion that entered Spain went abroad in payment of royal and foreign debts (Wolf 1997 [1982]: 139–40). In addition to pursuing their economic and imperial goals, the Spaniards considered themselves to have been charged with the mission of "civilizing" the Indians.

Lured by tales of legendary riches in Cibola's golden cities, the Spaniards pushed north to New Mexico, with a systematic plan for colonizing the Rio Grande valley. In contrast to their more haphazard approach to settlement in the Chihuahua-Sonoran region, with the Tarahumara, Yaqui, and Piman Indians, the Spaniards entered the Rio Grande region with a three-point program that included systematic colonization, the institution of firm political control, and Franciscan rather than Jesuit control of the missionary program (Spicer 1981 [1962]:152).

Spanish contact began poorly: in 1540 the Zuni executed Esteban, the boastful, swaggering African who scouted for Fray Marcos de Niza, after Esteban demanded tribute and raped Zuni women. Several expeditions later, in 1598, Juan de Oñate arrived in the Rio Grande valley prepared to establish a full-fledged community with 400 soldiers, settlers, Franciscan missionaries, and Mexican Indian servants. Extracting what he believed to be a pledge of submission to his authority from a group of Pueblo leaders, Oñate proclaimed New Mexico a missionary province of the Franciscan Order. When the silver and gold he had counted on to provide the economic base for his colony was not found in nearby mountains, the Indians were forced to bear even more of the burden of supporting the Spaniards.

Later that year, the people of Acoma Pueblo began to show signs of hostility after they had vowed submission. According to some accounts, after Acomans killed some Spanish soldiers (including Oñate's nephew) in battle and by tossing them off the mesa, Oñate retaliated by capturing 500 Acomans whom he sentenced to amputation of one foot and to twenty years of servitude.

In 1610 Pedro de Peralta, the new governor, founded Santa Fe as the colonial capital, forcing Indian workers to build the governor's palace and other municipal buildings, thus ushering in a seventy-year period of Indian servitude. In most areas of New Spain, new policies against abuses of the Indian population were enforced, but here, on the distant northern frontier, oppression based on the rendering of tribute (*encomienda*) and forced labor (*repartimiento*) continued.

The efficiency of the Spanish program deteriorated as each of the three groups—the missionaries, the civil government, and the military—fought over plans and policies and the best use of the available resources. Competition among the three groups for the produce and forced labor of the Indians became increasingly bitter, tearing apart the new settlement. The missionaries wanted to build peaceful agricultural communities with Indian workers to supply labor and to produce tribute in support of the Church. The governors resented this appropriation of Indian labor and natural resources, considering the missionaries to be constructing little kingdoms of their own. As a reward for living in the isolation and cultural austerity of such a remote outpost, the governors had been granted the privilege of engaging in trade and manufacturing; they wanted to use Indian labor to further their personal interests as well as those of the civil authority. Finally, the military nobility—who had been awarded land for contributing to the conquest, following the pattern earlier established in Spain—felt that the Indians should be forced to devote more time to labor on Spanish farms and haciendas.

The Pueblos grew increasingly resentful as they faced a growing crisis in their subsistence. Pueblo agriculture was no longer viable, for several reasons. The Spaniards were exerting increasing pressure to force the Indians to tend their crops, which meant that the Pueblos had to leave their own unfenced plots to be ravaged by livestock. At the same time the Apache were becoming more predatory, for they had developed an equestrian hunting economy and had increased in strength and numbers. The Pueblos, forced to bear the brunt of Apache raids because their villages lay exposed on the frontier, became afraid to work in their fields. A series of droughts resulting in widespread famine combined with European disease to take a devastating toll on the Pueblo population. Had the Pueblos remained well nourished, they might not have succumbed in such high numbers: in 1640 alone 3,000 Indians died; thousands more died between 1663 and 1669 (Simmons 1979: 184).

At the same time the Franciscans, caught up in a frenzy to save souls, raided kivas, destroying hundreds of katsina friends and altarpieces. According to Pueblo belief, their ceremonies were what ensured that the corn grew and that their communities prospered. Spanish actions were an abomination that cut to the very heart of the Pueblo way of life. When forty-three Pueblo leaders were publicly whipped and three were hanged in 1675, Spanish rule became intolerable. Pueblo religious leaders and their war captains began to discuss the possibility of a unified revolt against the Spaniards.

In 1680 the Pueblos staged a revolt that remains the most spectacular victory achieved by Native Americans within what is now the United States. Killing colonists and missionaries and laying siege to Santa Fe, the Indians threw out the Spaniards and kept their independence until the Spanish reconquest, which occurred in 1693–94. The Spaniards, who had suffered a severe blow to their empire, moderated their program considerably: the *encomienda* system was not reestablished; the missionary program was tempered by moderation; and a new generation of colonists from northern Mexican provinces established small farms on which they performed their own work with the help of *genizaros* (Indians descended from those who were purchased or captured from nomadic tribes and who adopted a Hispanicized way of life in New Mexico). These Hispanos and the Pueblos united against their common enemies, the Apaches and Navajos. By 1725 the Ute and, even more, the Comanche had become the principal raiders. During the last fifty years of Spanish administration, the colonial governors formed an alliance with the Comanche, Ute, Navajo, and Jicarilla Apache by liberally distributing gifts and rations in return for a cessation of raiding.

The Mexican Period (1821–48)

When Mexico gained its independence from Spain in 1821, the change in government meant relief for the Pueblos from outside interference. Although the Treaty of Córdoba, a proclamation of Mexican independence, guaranteed racial equality, the preservation of private property, and personal rights, there were few changes in the ethnic relations in New Mexico. Indians resisted attempts to remove land from their collective ownership so that it could be redistributed with leftover land going to Mexican settlers. Although the Mexican government still recognized grants of land that had been conceded to the Pueblos by the Spanish Crown, government officials did not always support the villagers' title. An expanding Hispano population frequently trespassed on Pueblo grants in the desire for farmland.

The carefully cultivated peace agreement with the Comanche, Ute, Navajo, and Jicarilla Apache disintegrated when the Mexican administration lacked the funds and the desire to continue distributing gifts or food to the raiders. Mexican citizens raided Navajo settlements for slaves, and this, in turn, led to increased raiding on the part of the Indians. Infuriated New Mexicans massacred a delegation of Navajo chiefs who had been summoned for peace talks. Pueblos joined Mexican soldiers in expeditions against the Apache and Navajo. The major impact of the shift in government was felt further south, by the Yaqui and the O'odham. On the southern frontier, Mexican settlers surged into the fertile Rio Yaqui area and vied with the O'odham for farmland.

The American Period (1848–Present)

In 1848 with the Treaty of Guadalupe Hidalgo, the United States assumed control of the region. Slowed by their conquest of the Navajo, Apache, and Yuman-speaking peoples, the Anglo-Americans saw their first goal as ensuring the protection of settlers from the Indians. Over time, they implemented this by isolating the Indians on reservations, thus giving settlers access to what was once Indian territory.

Anglo-Americans had long been interested in the West. Lewis and Clark's groundbreaking expedition (1804–6) had ignited the imagination of all Americans, leading popular writers to portray the country beyond the Mississippi and Missouri Rivers in romantic terms. Despite lurid accounts of vast treeless expanses of wilderness peopled only by bloodthirsty savages, Americans were drawn to the West. American ideals of opportunity, rugged idealism, and manifest destiny made the push westward inevitable.

By the 1830s Anglo-Americans were settling in eastern Texas, and Missouri pack trains were hauling trading goods to Santa Fe. Within a decade Mormons were farming in Utah, and settlers were carrying their possessions in covered wagons to Oregon. Gold and silver rushes throughout the West, including present-day Arizona and New Mexico, impelled adventurers westward to seek new lives, and by the 1850s much of the previously unexplored expanses had been mapped.

However, when Abraham Lincoln began his presidency, only 14 percent of the population of the United States—fewer than 5 million people—lived west of the Mississippi River, with four-fifths of them concentrated in Missouri and nearby states east of the great plains

(Josephy 1991:7). To protect settlers, miners, and the transportation routes that formed the lifeline between the West and East, almost three-quarters of the peacetime army—some 10,000 soldiers—was scattered at more than sixty army posts and forts from Puget Sound to the Rio Grande.

The Santa Fe Trail, a major trunk route, ran westward from present-day Kansas City, Missouri, across Kansas to Bent's Fort in Colorado Territory, before turning southwestward to Santa Fe. Farther north ran the Oregon Trail. New trails, as well as border towns eager for commerce, proliferated during the 1850s. Other routes linked Santa Fe, Albuquerque, and El Paso with southern California, including the route adopted by John Butterfield's stage line in 1858, the first transcontinental stage line.

Western Americans, eager to have their region gain statehood, had to contend with the balance of power between the North and South; as early as 1820 representatives of free and slave states were arguing over the extension of slavery into the West. The Compromise of 1850 temporarily quelled the crisis by creating the territories of New Mexico (which included most of present-day Arizona) and Utah, allowing their inhabitants to decide whether they would be free or slave, and balancing their choice with the admission of California as a free state. Secretary of War Jefferson Davis (under President Pierce) recognized the strategic importance of the territory of New Mexico: stretching from Texas to California, this territory could allow Southern slave power to reach the Pacific Ocean and even expand into Mexico. Davis won support for a Southwestern railroad. Such a transcontinental railroad would greatly strengthen the South by linking the major Southern cities of New Orleans and Memphis with California's ports and growing population (Josephy 1991: 10–11). In 1853, Pierce chose South Carolinian James Gadsden to negotiate with Mexico for the acquisition of land that thousands of miners had used during the California Gold Rush. This strip of land—the Gadsden Purchase—added the rest of what is now Arizona to the United States, as well as other territory; this was also the route the Butterfield stage line would follow. Although Davis's dream of a Southern route for the transcontinental railroad was never realized, the surveys conducted under Davis's direction by the Army Topographical Engineers were rich with information about Southwestern geography.

The outbreak of the Civil War in 1861 made the West even more important to southerners, both as land for the expansion of slavery and as a source of wealth in the form of gold and silver. California would provide alternate coastal ports too distant for Northern blockades. Many Southern officers commanded Western forts, but as slave states seceded, many of these officers, with strong emotional ties to their home states, resigned their commissions in the army to fight for the South. The frontier army was thrown into a crisis by the rash of resignations, the need to redeploy regular soldiers from the West, and the threat of Southern sympathizers. When soldiers evacuated and burned Fort Breckenridge north of Tucson and Fort Buchanan east of Tubac, local ranchers and miners were enraged to be left to deal with the Apaches on their own. The federal government raised a call for volunteers, most of whom were dispatched to serve in Union armies; only a few units remained in the West throughout the war.

The Chiricahua and Mimbreño Apaches, convinced that their resistance had led to the withdrawal of federal troops and the abandonment of the Butterfield stage line, intensified their raids. Mescalero Apaches, Utes, Comanches, and Kiowas swept across northern New Mexico, while in Tucson, Apaches, as well as groups of Mexican and Anglo bandits, took control of desert roads, looting abandoned ranches and murdering miners and settlers. Under the pressure of daily raids, the citizens of Mesilla organized a company of Arizona Rangers, while miners and settlers in the Pinos Altos region formed the Arizona Guards. Farther north, New Mexicans ignored the prewar truce with the Navajos to continue their old practice of raiding Navajo bands for slaves, leading the Navajos to renew their counter-attacks. The members of these volunteer forces differed greatly from the soldiers of the prewar army because they were less disciplined and more aggressive in their eagerness to kill Indians.

Although the Civil War forever silenced the debate over whether new territories would be admitted as free or slave states, it was not until the late 1880s, when the New Mexico and Arizona territories grew in population with the development of the railroads and mining, that a call for statehood became stronger. The Republican majority in Congress proposed that the two become a single state because both were overwhelmingly Democratic, while the inhabitants of Arizona wanted separate statehood so that they would not be dominated by New Mexico's larger Indian and Mexican American population (Wexler 1995:212–13). In 1912, after Democrats gained a stronger position in Congress, both states were admitted, a month apart.

Western expansion resumed almost immediately after the Civil War; without Southern opposition, the Great Plains was transformed into a land of free-soil farmers. At the same time, many southerners migrated into the Southwest and West to make a new life for themselves. White policymakers justified their actions toward Indians by saying that Indians had no title to the land on which they lived and that any land which was not inhabited year-round was unused. The religious claimed that God demanded the spread of Christianity; the secular-minded justified the seizure of Indian lands as the next step toward the realization of manifest destiny and pointed to the technical progress of the United States and social evolutionary theory to support their doctrine.

Federal law generally treated the Indian as a ward to supposedly protect him from his own incompetency in handling civilizing institutions and the vices of Anglo-American civilization; this rationale formed the basis for legislation restricting trade and land transactions as well as citizenship, with its attendant voting privileges. After 1871 U.S. Indian policy dealt with Indians as separate nations with which formal treaties were negotiated. However, Indian sovereignty was limited by the treaties themselves and by the Indian trade and intercourse laws that supported the treaty provisions. The desire to expand

Anglo-American settlement underlay government policy toward the Indians, exemplified by the Removal Act of 1830 under which tribes east of the Mississippi River were intimidated into moving westward.

By the early 1860s the idea of reservations had been conceived; reservations were thought of as temporary expedients until Indians could be assimilated into Anglo-American society. Indians were to cede their land holdings and relocate on reservations, which would gradually be reduced in size as Indians made the transition from hunting to farming and animal husbandry. Thus, their land could be opened to Anglo-American settlement, with proceeds from the sale of Indian land used to buy cattle and farm implements for the Indians, relieving taxpayers of a financial burden. Education—in the form of manual-labor schools where boys would learn agricultural techniques and girls, household skills and dairying, along with minimal reading, writing, and arithmetic—was considered to be the most important vehicle for assimilation (Harlan 1865).

In 1862 Brigadier General James Carleton hoped to develop a self-sufficient agricultural community on the Pecos River in eastern New Mexico at Bosque Redondo, but he had no idea that in addition to the 400 Mescalero Apache, there were over 8,000 Navajos. Carleton represented the War Department; had his attempt been successful, Indian affairs might have been transferred back to the Department of War, which had held control before the Department of the Interior was established in 1849 (Utley 1988:171; Prucha 1988:47). The debate over administrative responsibility for the Indians continued after the Civil War. Army advocates pointed to corruption among civilian Indian agents and argued that army Indian agents would be cheaper and would command greater respect from the Indians, who were warriors themselves. Civilian proponents, meanwhile, claimed that military officers were ill equipped to instruct the Indians in peaceful pursuits. Before 1871 reservations were created by treaty arrangements; after that date, it took acts of Congress and executive orders of the president to set aside land for reservations. The Yavapai and Apache were the last Indians to be subdued in the Southwest. After the Civil War, war-tested troops equipped with technically advanced weapons mounted better organized campaigns against them.

The Impact of the Railroad

The first transcontinental railroad, once delayed by debates between the North and the South over its route, was completed in 1869, four years after the end of the Civil War. Now the West was linked to the rest of the nation physically as well as economically, and a journey that once took months was reduced to less than ten days. During the thirty years following its construction, the railroad brought millions of pioneers to the West; eager to recoup their investment, railroad companies mounted an advertising campaign throughout the eastern United States and also in Europe. As a result, hundreds of thousands of overseas emigrants poured into the West, creating one of the largest mass movements of people in history; towns began to grow up rapidly along railroad lines.

By 1883 the Atchison, Topeka, and Santa Fe railroad linked Kansas City, Missouri, to Lamy and Deming, New Mexico, where it connected with the Southern Pacific and continued west to Los Angeles by way of Yuma, Arizona. The railroad also brought tourists fascinated by a romanticized conception of Indian peoples, a legacy of the recent military defeat of the Plains tribes. At the same time, many people reacted to growing industrialization with a deeper sense of appreciation of handmade artifacts (Brody 1979:604), which transformed the cultures of Southwestern native peoples into a marketable commodity. Enterprising individuals such as Fred Harvey arranged for Indian women to sell their pottery, silverwork, baskets, and rugs in railroad stations, with employees of his company present to explain Indian cultures.

Even before the influx of tourists, the railroads had had a major impact on the Indians of the Southwest by supplying goods to newly created trading posts; for groups such as the Navajo, who lived in scattered family settlements, this was particularly important. Traders also encouraged Navajo women to make their weaving more marketable with the introduction of new designs and aniline dyes that complemented Victorian drawing rooms in the East. For Eastern markets, Navajo women began to weave rugs instead of blankets; they had already replaced the blankets they wove for their own use with machine-made blankets from mills in Pendleton, Oregon.

The Twentieth Century

Despite the railroad, the Southwest continued to be a marginal area in terms of population in comparison to the rest of the country. Before World War II and the postwar boom, this region remained sparsely settled, an area devoted primarily to mining, agriculture, and ranching. The government, which had subsidized agribusiness in the West, began to establish defense plants, military bases, and research laboratories in the Southwest in an all-out effort to win the war. Arizona and New Mexico became a contrast between isolated urban centers and the vast countryside that surrounded them, the domain of miners, ranchers, and farmers. After the war, with the introduction of evaporative coolers (more commonly known as "swamp coolers") and then air-conditioning, the population of the Southwest exploded. Engineers and skilled employees were eager to work here because of the sunny climate, and manufacturing companies had no difficulty in the recruitment of labor.

U.S. Indian policy in the twentieth century continued the policy of forced assimilation, characterized by the Dawes Severalty Act of 1887, under which the president was authorized to allot the lands of most reservations to individual Indians, with surplus land being sold to settlers. Ironically, convinced that allotment was the best way to promote farming and the assimilation of Indians into Anglo-American society, the humanitarian reformers who pushed for the passage of the General Allotment Act (the Dawes Act) and the commissioners of Indian affairs who carried out the policy were sincere in their desire to help the Indians. However, both groups failed to understand the richness of Indian institutions and societies, and the right of Native Americans to shape their own destinies. Once this legislation was in place, the bureaucracy of the Office of Indian Affairs and outside interests affected how allotment policies were implemented, with a wide range of negative consequences. So much land was ceded by Indians or sold without their consent as a result of allotment that this policy appeared to be a scheme to deliberately deprive them of their land. Allotment reduced the resources available to tribes, checkerboarded reservations into such small parcels that reservation resources became even more difficult to use, and divided land into heirship allotments that had too many owners and were too small to operate economically (Carlson 1994:29).

The Indian Reorganization Act of 1934 (IRA) heralded a major change in federal Indian policy. In fifty years of allotment, Indians had lost nearly 90 million acres of their 138 million acres of land (Hauptman 1994:263). Now, this far-reaching piece of legislation led to the acquisition of additional land for Indians, which was then placed under federal control. John Collier, commissioner of Indian affairs between 1934 and 1944, was an idealistic man dedicated to social justice. He embodied the spirit of the IRA, which was based upon the idea of self-determination for Indians through self-government, including the formation of tribal councils, and communal enterprises as a means to economic improvement. For some tribes, such as the Oneida Nation in Wisconsin, who had lost nearly their entire reservation through the allotment act, the act provided tribal economic restoration and meaningful self-government, but for others, such as the Lakota, the new system brought increased tribal factionalism (ibid., 262–63). After a century of mismanagement, the act sought to reorganize the Bureau of Indian Affairs (BIA) and its mistaken policies, but instead of fostering true self-government, the act actually increased the powers of the secretary of the interior (who supervised the BIA) and failed to correct the abuses of authority among BIA reservation superintendents (ibid., 264).

Between World War II and the early 1960s, the government moved back toward assimilationist policies that favored the termination of the special federal tribal relationship, by doing away with tribal sovereignty, treaty rights, the nontaxable status of reservation lands, and the provision of federal services. World War II had generated a spirit of intense nationalism among Anglo-Americans and Native Americans alike; the threat of communism and the Cold War that followed united Americans against a common enemy. At the same time, private economic interests wanted access to the untapped natural resources on Indian trust lands, and state and local governments were eager to tax Indian land for additional revenue to support the growing population of the West, stimulated by the postwar economic boom (Burt 1994:221).

Congressional conservatives who advocated the most extreme form of nationalism—that Native American sovereignty was a threat to U.S. sovereignty—were the most vigorous proponents of termination, for they believed this policy would extend U.S. citizenship rights to Indians and free them to compete individually in a private enterprise system (Burt 1994:221). The Indian Claims Commission Act of 1946 gave tribes the power to sue the government for inadequate compensation in past land transactions, as a prelude to termination. The following year, the Senate Civil Service Committee directed the commissioner of Indian Affairs to identify and classify tribes according to their readiness for termination. Dwight Eisenhower's election to the presidency in 1952 brought even more conservatives into positions of influence in Indian affairs. These men were committed to phasing out the BIA and passed legislation that gave certain states law-and-order jurisdiction on reservations within their borders without Indian consent.

By the late 1950s, however, support for termination had begun to fade as the social and political atmosphere of the country began to change from one of nationalism against communism to a spirit that was more supportive of ethnic minorities and cultural diversity. The national civil rights movement and the international indigenous peoples movement popularized ethnic awareness. At the same time, the National Congress of American Indians (founded in 1944) mobilized tribes into effective opposition, church groups protested the social injustice inherent in the termination policy, and state and local governments realized that the cost of providing social services to Native Americans would outweigh the revenue gained from taxing Indian land. The Democrats who regained power in Congress considered termination to be a violation of Native American sovereignty. Opposition to this policy continued to mount as its devastating effects became evident for the tribes that experienced termination, such as the Menominees of Wisconsin. The surge of pride in Indian identity generated by the American Indian Movement (AIM) of the late 1960s led to greater demands for tribal sovereignty. Presidents Kennedy, Johnson, and Nixon all rejected termination and supported self-determination.

Since the 1960s self-determination has been the prevailing government policy, as embodied in the 1975 Indian Self-Determination and Education Assistance Act, which encouraged tribes to enter into contracts to provide services previously provided by the federal government. This legislation resulted from investigations by national task forces and commissions into reservation poverty and low standards of health, education, and income. Further, AIM's activism increased national awareness, which spurred Congress to action. The 1990 Native American Graves Protection and Repatriation Act (which did not take effect until the following year) established a congressional policy for the return to tribes of aboriginal human remains, associated funerary objects, and items of cultural significance. Federal policy shifted once more with severe budget cuts initiated by the Reagan administration; today, big businesses, fish and game lobbies, and state and local interests try to erode Indian rights as government policies continue to fluctuate between assimilation and the preservation of Indian heritage.

Southwestern Indians in Perspective

Indians in the Southwest experienced European contact much differently from those east of the Rocky Mountains. Europeans or Indians armed with European weaponry destroyed or weakened Eastern tribes; many of these native populations had already been decimated by epidemics of European disease, to which they had no immunity. Anglo-European settlement led to the loss of Indian lands and forced removal, often to areas ecologically different from their homelands, while the destruction of wildlife, most notably the bison herds, weakened economic stability. Tribal communities collapsed as population loss led to the disappearance of rituals, social institutions, languages, and political structures. Some tribes were absorbed into larger ones, while other tribes became so fragmented that their survivors were assimilated into non-Indian communities.

In contrast, groups in the Southwest were somewhat protected by their isolation and by the fact that their land was less desirable for settlement. Except for the Pueblos of the Rio Grande area, who experienced the brunt of Spanish contact, most groups remained free of European control much longer than did the Indians farther east. However, each wave of European immigrants, beginning with the Spaniards in the sixteenth century, carried its own set of Old World pathogens, which decimated Native American populations in the Southwest. Records show that the Pueblo peoples lost much of their population during the smallpox pandemic of 1520–24; nearly every decade was marked by another epidemic episode, often recurrences of smallpox (1564, 1704, 1719, 1738, 1748, 1759, 1780–81, 1799–1800, 1816), measles (1531–33, 1592, 1635, 1728–29, 1826), and the bubonic plague (1545–48, 1613–17) (Stoffle, Jones, and Dobyns 1995:196). By the time ethnographers were recording the cultures of Southwestern Indians in the nineteenth century, the native populations had been so decimated that there was no way to determine accurately how complex their social organization and cultures had been in precontact times.

Government policy until the late 1880s favored removal to remote regions in response to the fear of Native Americans felt by most Anglo-American settlers. Although settlers and ranchers pressured the government to control the Indians in the Southwest and to isolate them on reservations, with a few exceptions, such as the Chiricahua Apache, Southwestern Indians were not forced to relocate in areas far removed from their homelands. They were able to remain on their sacred lands, and they did not experience the major population losses suffered by the eastern tribes. This meant that native peoples in the Southwest were able to retain many more of their cultural institutions over time.

World War II did more to expose Southwestern Indians to the dominant culture than any other, previous event. Their isolation, relative to Indians elsewhere in the country, ended when they returned from the war to take wage-labor jobs outside their reservations. When government policy favored urban relocation, many moved to Los Angeles and other urban areas; however, many later returned to the Southwest. Unlike Indians in other areas, whose cultural traditions have not remained intact, many Southwestern Indians work in cities but return to reservations to participate in ceremonies.

Since World War II, a new sense of national consciousness and common purpose has emerged among all Native Americans in a struggle to achieve the social and cultural reintegration of Indian institutions within the context of contemporary society. In response to assimilation pressures, including boarding schools, a pan-Indian social identity has developed for many urban Indians. The pan-Indian movement has had less effect on peoples of the Southwest, compared to Native Americans in other areas of the country, because native peoples here have maintained their cultural identities and community cohesiveness to a much greater extent.

References and Further Reading

Volumes 9 (1979) and 10 (1983) of the Smithsonian Institution's *Handbook of North American Indians* contain chapters about the Southwest. In addition, these volumes also contain useful bibliographies. Volume 4, *History of Indian-White Relations* (1988), subsumes specific aspects of Indian-white history under several basic themes: national policies, military relations, political relations, economic relations, religious relations, and conceptual relations, and discusses how Indians have affected non-Indian cultures. Various journals, magazines, and newspapers present historical and contemporary issues that affect Native American peoples. These include *Akwesasne Notes, American Indian Culture and Research Journal, American Indian Quarterly, Ethnohistory, Native Peoples, News from Indian Country,* and *Winds of Change Magazine.* In addition, many groups have tribal newspapers, such as *The Cherokee One Feather* and *The Navajo Times.* In the following list, and in the end-of-chapter reference lists throughout this book, a few references of particular interest and importance are marked with an asterisk and briefly annotated.

Brody, J. J. 1979. "Pueblo Fine Arts." In *Handbook of North American Indians,* vol. 9: *The Southwest,* pp. 603–8.

Bryant, Keith. 1974. *History of the Atchison, Topeka and Santa Fe Railroad.* Macmillan, New York.

Burt, Larry W. 1982. *Tribalism in Crisis: Federal Indian Policy, 1953–1961.* University of New Mexico Press, Albuquerque.

———. 1994. "Termination and Restoration." In *Native America in the Twentieth Century: An Encyclopedia,* pp. 221–23. Garland Publishing, New York.

Carlson, Leonard A. 1981. *Indians, Bureaucrats, and Land: The Dawes Act and the Decline of Indian Farming*. Greenwood Press, Westport, Conn.

———. 1994. "Allotment." In *Native America in the Twentieth Century: An Encyclopedia*, pp. 27–29. Garland Publishing, New York.

*Champagne, Duane, ed. 1994. *Native America: Portrait of the Peoples*. Visible Ink Press, Detroit. [This is a good overall reference that covers a wide range of topics, including regional and national issues, by Native American scholars.]

Cordell, Linda S. 1984. *Prehistory of the Southwest*. Academic Press, New York.

Cordell, Linda S., and George J. Gummerman, eds. 1989. *Dynamics of Southwest Prehistory*. Smithsonian Institution Press, Washington, D.C.

*Deloria, Vine, Jr., and Clifford Lytle. 1984. *The Nation Within: The Past and Future of American Indian Sovereignty*. Pantheon Books, New York. [Deloria, a Standing Rock Sioux, is an attorney, professor, and writer who is outstanding at addressing legal issues involving American Indians.]

Elliott, J. H. 1966. *Imperial Spain 1469–1716*. Mentor Books, New American Library, New York.

Ferguson, T. J., and E. Richard Hart. 1990. *A Zuni Atlas*. University of Oklahoma Press, Norman.

Fixico, Donald L. 1986. *Termination and Relocation: Federal Indian Policy, 1945–1960*. University of New Mexico Press, Albuquerque.

*Fontana, Bernard L. 1999. *A Guide to Contemporary Southwest Indians*. Southwest Parks and Monuments Association, Tucson. [A comprehensive guide to points of interest on each reservation in the Southwest, written for the layperson by a well-known Southwestern scholar.]

Grove, Noel. 1997. *Atlas of World History*. National Geographic Society, Washington, D.C.

Hall, Thomas. 1989. *Social Change in the Southwest, 1350–1880*. University Press of Kansas, Lawrence.

Harlan, James. 1865. Letter to William P. Dole, Dated June 22, 1865, re Renewal of Talks with Indians Following the Civil War. Letters Sent by the Indian Division of the Office of the Secretary of the Interior, 1849–1903, 5:262–63, M606, Record Group 48, Natural Resources Branch, National Archives, Washington, D.C.

Hauptman, Laurence, M. 1994. "Indian Reorganization Act." In *Native America in the Twentieth Century: An Encyclopedia*, pp. 262–64. Garland Publishing, New York.

Josephy, Alvin M., Jr. 1991. *The Civil War and the American West*. Alfred A. Knopf, New York.

———. 1994. *500 Nations: An Illustrated History of North American Indians*. Alfred A. Knopf, New York.

Kirk, Ruth. 1973. *Desert: The American Southwest*. Houghton Mifflin, Boston.

Leacock, Eleanor B., and Nancy Oestreich Lurie, eds. 1988 [1971]. *North American Indians in Historical Perspective*. Waveland Press, Prospect Heights, Ill.

Marshall, James. 1945. *Santa Fe: The Railroad That Built an Empire*. Random House, New York.

McDonnell, Janet A. 1991. *The Dispossession of the American Indian, 1887–1934*. Indiana University Press, Bloomington.

Nabhan, Gary Paul. 1985. *Gathering the Desert*. University of Arizona, Tucson.

Nash, Gerald. 1973. *The American West in the Twentieth Century: A Short History of an Urban Oasis*. Prentice-Hall, Englewood Cliffs, N.J.

———. 1985. *The American West Transformed: The Impact of the Second World War*. Indiana University Press, Bloomington.

———. 1990. *World War II and the West: Reshaping the Economy*. University of Nebraska Press, Lincoln.

Noble, David Grant. 1981. *Ancient Ruins of the Southwest: An Archaeological Guide*. Northland Publishing, Flagstaff.

Officer, James. 1987. *Hispanic Arizona, 1536–1856*. University of Arizona Press, Tucson.

Oswalt, Wendell H., and Sharlotte Neely. 1996 [1988]. *This Land Was Theirs: A Study of North American Indians*. Mayfield Publishing, Mountain View, Calif.

Philp, Kenneth R., ed. 1986. *Indian Self-Rule: First-Hand Accounts of Indian-White Relations from Roosevelt to Reagan*. Howe Brothers, Salt Lake City, Utah.

Pommersheim, Frank. 1995. *Braid of Feathers: American Indian Law and Contemporary Tribal Life*. University of California Press, Berkeley.

*Prucha, Francis Paul. 1984. *The Great Father: The United States Government and the American Indians*. University of Nebraska Press, Lincoln. [This two-volume work is one of the most comprehensive histories of Indian relations with the United States.]

———. 1985. *The Indians in American Society*. University of California Press, Berkeley.

———. 1988. "United States Indian Policies, 1815–1860." In *Handbook of North American Indians*, vol. 4: *History of Indian-White Relations*, pp. 40–50.

Reid, J. Jefferson, and David E. Doyel, eds. 1986. *Emil W. Haury's Prehistory of the American Southwest*. University of Arizona Press, Tucson.

Reid, J. Jefferson, and Stephanie Whittlesey. 1997. *The Archaeology of Ancient Arizona*. University of Arizona, Tucson.

Reisner, Marc. 1986. *Cadillac Desert: The American West and Its Disappearing Water*. Penguin Books, New York.

Sheridan, Thomas E. 1995. *Arizona: A History*. University of Arizona Press, Tucson.

Sheridan, Thomas E., and Nancy J. Parezo. 1996. *Paths of Life: American Indians of the Southwest and Northern Mexico*. University of Arizona Press, Tucson.

Simmons, Marc. 1979. "History of Pueblo-Spanish Relations to 1821." In *Handbook of North American Indians*, vol. 9: *Southwest*, pp. 178–93.

*Spicer, Edward H. 1981 [1962]. *Cycles of Conquest: The Impact of Spain, Mexico, and the United States on the Indians of the Southwest, 1533–1960*. University of Arizona Press, Tucson. [A classic work on the peoples and cultures of the Southwest.]

Spicer, Edward H., and Raymond H. Thompson, eds. 1972. *Plural Society in the Southwest*. University of New Mexico Press, Albuquerque.

Stefon, Frederick J. Summer, 1978. "The Irony of Termination: 1943–1958." *The Indian Historian* 11:3–14.

Stoffle, Richard W., Kristine L. Jones, and Henry F. Dobyns. 1995. "Direct European Immigrant Transmission of Old World Pathogens to Numic Indians during the Nineteenth Century." *American Indian Quarterly* 19:2:181–203.

*Trimble, Stephen. 1993. *The People: Indians of the American Southwest*. School of American Research Press, Santa Fe, N.M. [A nonanthropologist presents a vivid portrayal of Southwestern Indians for the layperson with an emphasis on contemporary issues and native voices.]

Utley, Robert. 1988. "Indian–United States Military Situation, 1848–1891." In *Handbook of North American Indians*, vol. 4: *The History of Indian-White Relations*, pp. 163–84.

Waldman, Carl. 1985. *Atlas of the North American Indian*. Facts on File, New York.

*Wallerstein, Immanuel. 1974. *The Modern World-System I: Capitalist Agriculture and the Origins of the European World-Economy in the Sixteenth Century*. Academic Press, New York. [A classic work on the origins of the capitalist world economy.]

Washburn, Wilcomb E. 1984. "Fifty-Year Perspectives on Indian Reorganization Act." *American Anthropologist* 86 (June): 279–89.

Weber, David. 1982. *The Mexican Frontier, 1821–1846: The American Southwest under Mexico*. University of New Mexico Press, Albuquerque.

———. 1992. *The Spanish Frontier in North America*. Yale University Press, New Haven.

Wexler, Alan. 1995. *Atlas of Westward Expansion*. Facts on File, New York.

White, Richard. 1983. *The Roots of Dependency: Subsistence, Environment, and Social Change among the Choctaws, Pawnees, and Navajos*. University of Nebraska Press, Lincoln.

———. 1991. *It's Your Misfortune and None of My Own: A History of the American West*. University of Oklahoma Press, Norman.

Wilkinson, Charles, and Eric R. Biggs. 1977. "The Evolution of the Termination Policy." *American Indian Law Review* 5, no. 1: 139–284.

*Wolf, Eric R. 1997 [1982]. *Europe and the People without History*. University of California Press, Berkeley. [An anthropologist examines the effects of European expansion on tribal peoples and presents a world-system approach to anthropology.]

Worster, Donald. 1985. *Rivers of Empire: Water, Aridity, and the Growth of the American West*. Pantheon Books, New York.

Part 1   Village Farming

Luana Ortiz of San Felipe Pueblo at the Palace of the Governors, 1999. Luana designs and makes contemporary jewelry with her partner, Navajo Marvin Slim. Author photograph

Chapter 2 The Pueblos

Po-wa-ha ('water-wind-breath') is the creative energy of the world, the breath that makes the wind blow and the water flow. Within Mimbres pots . . . wonderful, billowing cloud forms swirl with the wind around the mountains. You can . . . sense the breath that gives everything its energy.—Rina Swentzell, Ph.D., contemporary Tewa–Santa Clara educator and writer (1994:34–35)

The sense of unbroken cultural continuity, from prehistoric peoples to the present-day Puebloans, is a major part of what makes Pueblo societies so strong and vital in today's world. The dwellings of their ancestors lie scattered throughout the canyons and valleys of the Four Corners area. Living in two- and four-storied, apartmentlike homes, Ancestral Pueblo (Anasazi) women made elaborate pottery, decorated with elegant black-on-white Mesa Verde zigzags; hatched Tularosa spirals; bold, asymmetric, birdlike Sikyatki designs; and fine-line, black-on-white Chaco hatching.

The Ancestral Pueblo developed a rich culture in an unforgiving environment. As master farmers on the mesas and in the desert, they were superbly ingenious. They were also artisans and artists who created a vast inventory of household tools, utensils, and furnishings: corrugated cooking and storage pots; wood-handled flint knives; stout bows with specialized arrows; hundreds of different bone, string, and cord tools; decorated ladles, mugs, and bowls; cotton blankets; feather robes; sandals and belts; and wristlets, necklaces, and pendants made of turquoise, coral, and Pacific shell. Ancestral Pueblo architects left behind cliff dwellings tucked into canyon ledges and stunning multistoried pueblos atop sandstone mesas. They built permanent ceremonial structures (called *kivas*) and plazas in their towns to hold religious ceremonies that probably focused on crop fertility and the bringing of rain.

When the Spaniards arrived in 1540, however, they found these villages deserted and over 40,000 Pueblo people living in about ninety villages on the Colorado Plateau. Even the ethnocentric Spaniards were impressed by their distinctive stone and adobe, multi-chambered houses and settled village lifestyle, and named them "town-dwellers" or Pueblo Indians. Today, the term *Pueblo* is used to refer to Puebloan peoples collectively, an individual person, the people of a single Pueblo village, and the village itself. The Pueblo Indians have never constituted a single tribe, for each Pueblo village has its own culture and functions as an autonomous political entity. But this autonomy does not mean that they lived in isolation, because Puebloans recognized their common ancestry and traded, visited, and intermarried with each other.

These descendants of the Anasazi—and of the Mogollon, who by 1400 had blended with the Anasazi—inherited from their prehistoric ancestors an encyclopedic knowledge of their lands, as well as sophisticated agricultural techniques. This highly specialized knowledge enabled them to live in the same area over a very long period of time without depleting its resources. Along with sustainable subsistence patterns and architecture, they inherited elements of the Anasazi world view and ritual system. The central value of the Puebloan world view is that people must live in harmony with nature and with each other. This is expressed in their architecture, ceremonies, dances, poetry, pottery, songs, and legends. In the kiva, the ceremonial chamber located at the spiritual and physical heart of the pueblo, men continue to fulfill ritual responsibilities on a daily and annual basis to ensure the continuation of human, plant, and animal life. Puebloan peoples perform ceremonial dances in their plazas much as their ancestors probably did centuries ago.

Unlike many native nations in the United States, the Pueblos still reside today where the invading Europeans found them. Considering that they have lived under three different flags—those of Spain, Mexico, and the United States—within the space of 200 years, this cultural continuity in architecture, religion, art, society, and government is especially remarkable. A major reason for their cultural persistence is that these three nations had only marginal interest in the Puebloan homeland.

The Pueblos experienced intense assimilative pressure from the Spanish, who established their headquarters first near San Juan Pueblo and later in Santa Fe. The Pueblos experienced the brunt of Spanish efforts to Christianize and reduce their populations when Spanish friars tried to root out all aspects of native religion by whipping, torturing, and publicly executing native priests and medicine men. By compartmentalizing the native ceremonial system—practicing it underground in their kivas to keep it alive and uncontaminated by Catholicism—the Pueblos managed to sustain their ancient practices and beliefs. Today, the Pueblos of the Rio Grande area do not allow non-Indians to observe religious dances in the pueblos, nor do they allow sketching or photography.

As time went on and the Church relaxed pressure for conformity, the Pueblos accepted certain elements of Catholic rituals. Today, most Pueblos practice and believe both their traditional religion and Catholicism, which they consider to be different ways of worshipping the same god. (This will be especially evident in the description of the Katsina murals in the Catholic church, in chapter 4.) Among the Christian concepts and practices accepted by the Pueblos are Sunday worship and such sacraments as confirmation, baptism, and weddings. Nearly every pueblo also has a feast day for the patron saint of the pueblo: for example, the patron saint of San Juan Pueblo is honored on San Juan's (St. John's) Feast Day, which is celebrated annually on June 24. (The Catholic church in the pueblo is named after the patron saint.) The feast day begins with mass, followed by the first dance, which is performed in front of the church. The saint's statue is carried in a procession to the plaza, where it is placed in an evergreen-covered bower. Throughout the day dances are performed in the plaza, and at the end of the day a procession returns the saint's statue to the church (Sando 1992:33).

Many of the names of these pueblos came from the Spanish missions founded there, but the people in each pueblo identify themselves by their own name in their language. In comparison with other Southwestern groups, the Pueblos form a unit because they share a distinctive world view, ceremonial system, agricultural subsistence pattern, social organization, and history, as well as material culture, including architecture, pottery, and dress.

Yet beyond these similarities, there are significant differences, beginning with geography: New Mexico's All Pueblo Indian Council divides its twenty members into eight Northern Pueblos and twelve Southern Pueblos. Since 1965 the pueblos located north of Santa Fe have been organized under the Eight Northern Indian Pueblos Council, which has its headquarters in San Juan Pueblo; these pueblos include Taos, Picuris, San Juan, Santa Clara, San Ildefonso, Nambe, Pojoaque, and Tesuque. The Southern Pueblos are Isleta, Sandia, Santa Ana, San Felipe, Santo Domingo, Cochiti, Zia, Jemez, Zuni, Acoma, Laguna, and Ysleta del Sur.

The Pueblos

June 1999

The early-morning sunlight seems to shine with greater clarity in Santa Fe. The high altitude, nearly 7,000 feet above sea level, along with fewer dust particles and less moisture, makes the air appear to be suffused with brilliant light. This luminous quality is especially noticeable as the sun strikes the roof of the Palace of the Governors on the north side of the Santa Fe plaza.

A young woman from Santa Clara Pueblo calls out a greeting to brothers from Jemez and Laguna as she carries a large box from her pickup truck to the porch of the Palace of the Governors. The two men are already spreading blankets and taping them to the brick floor of the portal. Wearing a windbreaker to fend off the morning chill, the woman carefully arranges her polished black pots, while the younger brother places bracelets, rings, and necklaces at even intervals and then finishes unloading. Soon the portal will be filled with vendors from other pueblos and other tribes. After setting out their work, they relax with cups of coffee, enjoying a few moments of quiet. Others chat, catching up on the health and activities of their respective families before the arrival of the first customers.

It is not long before a boy and his parents from Iowa, on their first trip to the Southwest, emerge from a cafe and walk across the plaza to the portal. Drawn by the activity they had watched as they ate breakfast, they are eager to discover what kinds of articles might be for sale. As they amble along the shaded portal, they have not yet realized what a rare opportunity they have to talk to the artists themselves and to pay them directly for the time, materials, and creativity invested in their work. The portal is unique in this respect, for it is one of the few places where tourists can converse with Indian people about their cultures and their lives, free from the sense of intrusion so common to reservation settings. Seated against the wall on milk crates, plastic lawn chairs, and pillows, the artists pride themselves on their ability to educate outsiders about their cultures and their work. They have much to be proud of in the work they display on black jewelers' trays and blankets, for it is of the highest quality.

While strolling the length of the portal, I spot a series of unusual rings. One in particular catches my eye, and I pick it up, delighted with its setting of an oval of lapis lazuli and narrow sliver of turquoise matrix in silver. An attractive woman in her twenties explains, "I stamped the band on the ring you're holding with a rising sun design to symbolize a new dawn and a new awakening. My partner and I make each one different so no two are exactly alike. You can try it on if you want to." The elegant ring slides on my finger, too beautiful to resist, and I dig out my wallet. I can't help but ask her where she lives. She says, "Oh, I'm from San Felipe Pueblo, but my partner is Navajo."

The Cultural Center in Albuquerque is our next destination today, and when I see the building that afternoon, a flood of memories takes me back to the mid-1970s, when I served as curator of collections there. It was my job to select a series of historic bowls and ollas from the Smithsonian Institution in Washington, D.C., for display and to help with the accessioning of pottery that Pueblo artists brought to the museum.

The distinctive D-shaped building is a tribute to the Ancestral Pueblo who built Pueblo Bonito in Chaco Canyon. Owned and operated by the nineteen Pueblo tribes of New Mexico, the Indian Pueblo Cultural Center provides an opportunity to learn about New Mexico's Pueblo Indians. (The Hopi, who live in Arizona, have their own cultural center.) Inside, each Pueblo has its own exhibit, which traces its history and displays its distinctive arts and crafts. The upstairs area includes gift shops that sell Indian-made kachinas, drums, paintings, sandpaintings, rugs, pottery, and contemporary and traditional jewelry, and a curio shop that sells souvenirs. Tourists can sample traditional Pueblo and Hispanic food at the restaurant and, on weekends, watch traditional Indian dances and arts and crafts demonstrations. Two-story-high murals, painted by Pueblo artists, decorate the walls facing the plaza. The overview of the different Pueblo tribes provided by the center makes it the ideal introduction to Puebloan culture.

Locations and Languages

Puebloan peoples speak languages from four different linguistic stocks: Uto-Aztecan, Zuni, Keresan, and Kiowa-Tanoan. The Tanoan language is further divided into three dialects: Tiwa, Tewa, and Towa. An overview of these divisions helps clarify the situation:

A. Uto-Aztecan is spoken by the Hopi.
B. The Zuni language is spoken only by the Zunis.
C. Keresan is spoken, with some differences, by the people of Acoma, Cochiti, Laguna, San Felipe, Santa Ana, Santo Domingo, and Zia pueblos.
D. The Tanoan language includes three subgroups, Tiwa, Tewa, and Towa.
    1. Tiwa is spoken by the people of Taos, Picuris, Sandia, and Isleta (and the Tigua Indians of Ysleta del Sur Pueblo).
    2. Tewa is spoken by the people of San Juan, Santa Clara, San Ildefonso, Nambe, Tesuque, and Pojoaque pueblos.
    3. Towa is spoken only by the people of Jemez Pueblo.

The Hopi people, who live on and around three mesas in northern Arizona, speak a Uto-Aztecan language that is closely related to the Numic languages of the Great Basin. The Zuni of western New Mexico speak a language of their own that is unrelated to any other language. (A few linguists think that Zuni may be related to Penutian languages in California, but this has not been proven.)

All Keresan villages are in New Mexico; Keresans have no known linguistic relatives. The Keresan-speaking pueblos of Cochiti, Santo Domingo, and San Felipe are located along the Rio Grande, while Santa Ana and Zia are situated west and north along the banks of the Jemez River. Acoma and Laguna are in the western part of the state.

The three Tanoan subgroups, which represent the Kiowa-Tanoan language family, are located in the Rio Grande valley. The northernmost pueblos, Taos and Picuris, are Tiwa-speaking pueblos, as are Sandia and Isleta, located just north and south, respectively, of present-day Albuquerque. Ysleta del Sur ("Ysleta of the South") in El Paso, Texas, is home to the descendants of Puebloan Indians, primarily Tiguas (Tiwas) who came with Spaniards when they fled from New Mexico during the Pueblo Revolt of 1680. Clustered north of modern Santa Fe, along the Rio Grande, are the Tewa-speaking pueblos: San Juan, Santa Clara, Nambe, Pojoaque, San Ildefonso, and Tesuque. After the Spaniards reconquered New Mexico in 1693, a Tewa-speaking group left New Mexico to live with the Hopi; they founded the village of Hano on First Mesa. The only remaining Towa-speaking pueblo is Jemez, situated north of Albuquerque.

Although the pueblos are located near each other, each remains a distinctive entity with political autonomy. Not surprisingly, Pueblo peoples were multilingual. In past times many Keresans could speak Tanoan, Zuni, and Hopi, and vice versa; they also acquired Apache, Navajo, Kiowa, and Comanche. Once the Spaniards arrived, they learned to speak Spanish, and later, when the American Territorial Government moved into the area, they learned English. Today most Pueblo people speak English and their native language.

Native Americans at the Palace of the Governors

Nearly every day of the year finds Native American artists from Pueblo villages and native communities in New Mexico selling their work beneath the portal of the Palace of the Governors. The Santa Fe plaza has a long history, from the days when it was a marketplace for Hispano, Anglo, and Native American farmers, ranchers, craftspeople, and merchants selling their produce and wares. Until 1950 the plaza and portal continued as a bustling multiethnic marketplace that featured everything from Indian art to goats and bubble gum. The brick-paved porch of the Palace of the Governors, which spans the north side of the plaza, provides an ideal space for displaying jewelry, pottery, and other wares made by Native American artists. The present form of the Portal Program goes back to 1936, when the New Mexico Association on Indian Affairs (now the Southwestern Association on Indian Affairs) invited members of different pueblos to sell their work under the palace portal. By the mid-twentieth century, the portal had become a daily market for Native American artists. The increased popularity of Native American art in the 1970s brought a greater demand for space. This led the Museum of New Mexico's board of regents to limit sales to Indian vendors in 1972; the board later made the market an official museum program and established guidelines for its daily operation. As the program evolved, rules

The portal in front of the Palace of the Governors on the Santa Fe plaza, 1999. Author photograph

were developed to ensure the quality and authenticity of the goods sold; for example, only sterling silver and natural or stabilized stones are acceptable for jewelry, and pottery must be made of earth clays from the potter's reservation and traditionally fired in an open fire. An administrative committee regularly checks vendors' pieces to ensure the continued quality of items sold on the portal, and artists must demonstrate their crafts to members of the program's committee before they are allowed to sell there.

Today, the Portal Program continues to grow and change. In 1998 it included over 850 artists from some 400 households from all federally recognized Native American tribes in New Mexico, as well as Hopi and Navajo from Arizona and representatives from other Native American groups that have ties to New Mexico. Each day, thousands of visitors from all over the world come into direct contact with Native

Americans from at least a dozen communities. Program participants/vendors enjoy spending time with their friends and fellow artists, as well as sharing their art directly with customers—something they could not do as easily if they sold their work from their homes or through shops. There are no set schedules, and artists may sell on the portal as often or seldom as they like. The freedom of choosing the days when they come to the portal enables deeply traditional people to fulfill their social and religious responsibilities in their home communities while still supporting their families through their art. Younger artists also benefit by being able to sell their work even as they are learning. As it has for over sixty years, the Portal Program continues to thrive, bringing together not only the cultures of New Mexico but also the cultures of the world. (Based on Hoerig, forthcoming).

Regional Variations

Even though each pueblo has its own cultural identity, they may be grouped into three regional divisions on the basis of similarities in social organization, political organization, ceremonial organization, religion, and world view. (This comparison is based in the nineteenth century, before reservations were established.) It is important to keep in mind that these three groups form a continuum, shifting gradually into each other as one moves from west to east. The three regional groups are the *Western Pueblos* of the more arid mesa and canyon country; the *Keresan Bridge Pueblos*—so called because they are intermediate geographically and share characteristics of both the Western Pueblos and the Eastern Tanoans—of the central area; and the *Eastern Tanoan Pueblos* of the Rio Grande valley.

None of the three major divisions corresponds precisely to the four linguistic groupings. Thus, some Keresan pueblos—Acoma and Laguna—have more in common with Zuni, Hopi, and Hano than they do with their fellow Keresans on the Rio Grande. The following discussion, therefore, centers on regional rather than linguistic groupings. The dominant features of Western, Keresan Bridge, and Eastern Tanoan Pueblo organization may be summarized as follows:

The Western Pueblos include Hopi, Hano, Laguna, Acoma, and Zuni. Their key features are strong matrilineal clans, matrilocal residence, female ownership of house and garden plots, a strong Katsina Cult, and dispersed political authority. Their ceremonies emphasize weather control and rainmaking.

The Keresan Bridge Pueblos—Zia, Santa Ana, San Felipe, Santo Domingo, and Cochiti —emphasize medicine societies, which provide the most centralized political authority of the three regional groups. They have weak matrilineal clans, matrilocal residence, and moieties (a dual division of the village) whose membership is essentially patrilineal. Their ceremonies emphasize curing and warfare.

The Eastern Tanoan Pueblos—the Tewa pueblos of Tesuque, Nambe, Pojoaque, San Ildefonso, Santa Clara, and San Juan, and the Tiwa pueblos of Taos, Picuris, Sandia, and Isleta—have a dual chieftainship based on their moiety division, so that each moiety governs for six months of the year. This makes the Tanoan form of government less centralized than that of the Keresans but much more so than that of the western pueblos. Sodalities (non–kinship-based associations) crosscut the moiety division, thus uniting each pueblo. They have bilateral extended family structure (with patrilineal recruitment into moieties in some pueblos and matrilineal recruitment in others). Men own the houses and land, and there are no matrilineal clans among most eastern Tanoans. (Jemez, the Towa pueblo, has matrilineal exogamous clans and two kiva groups with patrilineal affiliation.) Their ceremonies emphasize hunting and warfare, and the Katsina Cult is weak, if it is present at all.

Social Organization

Western Pueblos. Kinship is matrilineal among the Western Pueblos, and all people belong to their mothers' clans. Families live in extended matrilocal households. A single house, with a series of adjoining rooms, is home to a woman and her husband, their unmarried sons, and their married daughters, the daughters' husbands, and the daughters' children.

Of the three groups, the Western Pueblos have the strongest clan organization. Here, the clan has a name and a central residence, known as the clan house. Marriage between clan members is prohibited (clan exogamy). Clans at Hopi are corporate: like business corporations, they exist in perpetuity despite the death of individual members, and they own property, consisting of ritual knowledge, ceremonial paraphernalia, land, and economic goods, which they hold in trust for future generations. (For more extensive treatment of Hopi clanship, see chapter 3.) The major contrast between Western and Eastern Pueblos is the dominant role of clans among the Western Pueblos.

Keresan Bridge Pueblos. Although the Keresan kinship system is matrilineal, both kinship behavior and terminology are moving toward bilaterality. There is a definite shift away from the overriding importance of matrilineal kin, and matrilineal and patrilineal relations tend to have equal importance in a person's life. For example, the father disciplines his children, while among the Western Pueblos the mother's brother is the disciplinarian. Children—though reared in the context of matrilineal kin because Keresan pueblos tend to be matrilocal—join their fathers' kiva organization. The nuclear family appears to be emerging as the important social unit.

Clan exogamy is the only important and consistent clan function today: the clan is a kinship group rather than a political and ceremonial organization, as it is farther west. Medicine societies, whose membership cuts across kinship lines, appear to have taken on the functions assumed by clans among the Western Pueblos.

Eastern Tanoans. Tanoan kinship terms are bilateral, and the bilateral extended family is the social and economic unit. At Taos and Picuris (which are Tiwa pueblos), households consist of the members of a nuclear family, but at Tewa pueblos they include a husband and wife, one or more married daughters and their husbands, and all unmarried sons and daughters of the married members of the household. Some daughters may choose to live in the households of their husbands. The bilateral kin group plants, tills, and harvests fields together. Land-use rights may be passed on to either the daughter or son, and the head of the household is the oldest member. There is no evidence of a clan system in the kinship terms, and clan names seem to be only sacred words uttered in a ceremonial context, having nothing to do with governmental or ceremonial organizations or with the regulation of property or marriage (Dozier 1970:166). (Jemez, perhaps because of its proximity to and intermarriage with the Keresans, has exogamous clans.)

Political Organization

All pueblo villages have separate organizations to deal with secular and religious matters. Although the Western Pueblos are more tightly structured theocracies, the Eastern Pueblos also have religious leaders who direct the elaborate ceremonial life of the pueblo. The secular political structure is more visible to the outside world. A governor heads the secular organization and protects the spiritual leaders by dealing with all tribal business of the modern world. The office of pueblo governor was introduced by the Spaniards, who created it to facilitate Spanish domination, but the Pueblos themselves converted it into a bulwark against foreign intrusion (Sando 1992:14). The governor's staff consists of a first and second lieutenant governor, five aides, a sheriff, and the *fiscales,* or church officers, who maintain church property and oversee activities involving the Catholic Church. In some pueblos, these officials are selected annually by the *cacique* (supreme village or town priest) and his staff, while in others the people cast ballots for their officers.

Although each New Mexico pueblo is autonomous, today each one also belongs to the All Indian Pueblo Council, which gives it greater political power in dealing with the state and federal governments. Each pueblo's governor is the official representative for that pueblo to the council and has the power to vote for the council officers (chairman, vice chairman, secretary, and treasurer). Attendance of ten pueblo delegates is sufficient for a quorum at a meeting.

The Pueblo Indians have a unique relationship, among Indian nations, with the U.S. government because of Pueblo relationships with the Spanish and Mexican governments. Today international treaties, land grants, and court decisions with international ramifications continue to complicate this relationship. The Spaniards, recognizing the rights of the Indians to the lands on which they lived, set aside blocks of land for each Pueblo group, areas that came to be known as land grants.

The following descriptions deal with the traditional leadership and political organization of pueblos in the three regions.

Western Pueblos. Clans dominate government, religious, subsistence, and community affairs, and government is essentially theocratic. Social control is maintained through gossip and "enforcement" by special katsinam, as well as through avoidance of an offender by other members of the pueblo. (Katsinam are ancestral beings who have the power to bring rain and well-being. Men bring these spirits to life by representing them in physical form.) Political control is dispersed among clan and/or lineage leaders, and sodalities are clan-owned. Even though the village chief does not have the authority of his counterpart among the Eastern Pueblos, he comes from a specific clan among the Western Pueblos: the Bear Clan at Hopi and Hano, the Dogwood Clan at Zuni, and the Antelope Clan at Acoma and perhaps Laguna (Eggan 1950:303).

At Zuni and Acoma power is more centralized than at other Western Pueblos. Zuni is a theocracy with the ultimate control residing in the Council of Priests, for which the Bow Priests act as an executive arm; here, tribal organization is emphasized over clan organization. (For more extensive treatment of Zuni priesthoods, see chapter 4.) At Acoma the town chief (chosen from the Antelope Clan) works with Antelope Clan leaders to "exercise virtually absolute control" over lineage and clan heads, the Katsina Cult, and the ceremonial associations (Dozier 1970:142).

Keresan Bridge Pueblos. Of the three Pueblo groups, authority is most centralized among the Keresans, whose medicine societies are so powerful that they have been described as an embryonic ruling class (White 1942:187). The medicine societies have the functions that clans have farther west (except for the regulation of marriage), resulting in the consolidation of authority in a small, powerful group of officers. As directors and coordinators of tasks that concern the entire village, the medicine associations also have the role of maintaining morale and preserving tradition. Without exception, they tend to champion the old ways, thus exerting "a powerful influence in the pueblo on the side of conservatism if not reaction" (ibid., 124). They also choose the cacique, which not only adds to their power but also strengthens the conservatism of the pueblo. Ultimately, it is the strongly developed medicine societies that make Keresan pueblos highly centralized communities, even more so than Tewa pueblos.

In most Keresan villages, the cacique comes from the Flint medicine association and belongs to the Koshare clown association, which means that the clown and medicine societies are closely allied in forming the sociopolitical and ceremonial authority structure of the Keresan pueblos (Dozier 1970:155). In addition to working with the medicine societies to coordinate communal projects, clowns also provide social control by pointing out deviant behavior through public ridicule of individuals who have defied the authority of the medicine societies.

The two large kivas in a Keresan village serve as the basis for a dual ceremonial division. The only thing that Keresan kiva membership has in common with Tanoan moieties is its dual nature, because everyone in the pueblo belongs to one kiva or the other. However, the two Keresan kiva groups do not govern the pueblo. (As ceremonial groups, Keresan kiva groups are discussed under ceremonial organization, below.)

Eastern Tanoans. Moieties—the dual organization of society—are the most important unit of social and ceremonial organization among the Eastern Tanoans, and all members of the pueblo belong to one of the two moieties. These government divisions manage and conduct both secular and sacred activities. The Tewas have a double chieftainship: each cacique belongs to one of the moiety sociopolitical associations and rules the pueblo for half a year. Each cacique has his own staff, headed by a war captain, whose function, besides his military duties at times of warfare in the past, has been executive and disciplinary in both sacred and secular affairs. The war captain disciplines members of the pueblo who harvest and plant out of season, refuse to work on cleaning irrigation ditches, or refuse to participate in communal ceremonial activities.

Tanoan pueblos do not split apart into two factions based on moiety membership because they also have sodalities that draw their members from both moieties. Thus, the sodalities help unite the pueblo. They consist of three specialized types of social and ceremonial organizations: associations with special functions, such as war, hunting, and clowning (discussed under ceremonial organizations); medicine associations that conduct curing rituals (discussed under ceremonial organizations); and associations whose government and religious functions are associated with the moieties. Among the many responsibilities of this third type of organizations are the maintenance of the solar calendar, the coordination of purificatory rites for the pueblo, the organization of large communal dances and ceremonies, the coordination of warfare ceremonies, the coordination of communal hunts, the organization of planting and harvesting activities, the cleaning and construction of irrigation ditches; the repairing of the communal kiva and the cleaning of the plaza for communal ceremonies; and the nomination and installation of secular officials (Dozier 1970:169).

Ceremonial Organization, Religion, and World View

Spirituality is inseparable from all other aspects of life in Native American thought, so much so that Indian languages have no word that translates specifically as "religion." Transcending and permeating all aspects of Pueblo life, religion governs interaction with the land, other peoples, and the supernatural. Edward Dozier (1970:151), an anthropologist and Santa Clara Indian, considered the reciprocal relationship between humankind and nature to be the foundation of the Pueblo world view. From these central values, the Pueblo peoples have developed rich cultural traditions that are expressed in song, stories, poetry, dance, and art.

Through their thoughts, words, and deeds, humans can disrupt the equilibrium in the universe, resulting in imbalance, which manifests itself in drought, disaster, illness, and other misfortune. When people perform ceremonies in a spirit of joy and faith, nature responds in kind by "keeping the universe moving." When properly performed, ceremonies and rites "keep the seasons moving, allow the sun to rise and set properly, bring rain and snow, quell the winds, and insure a well-ordered physical environment and society" (Dozier 1970:151). Dozier summarized the five basic concerns of Pueblo society as follows (ibid., 133): "(1) weather, (2) illness, (3) warfare, (4) control of flora and fauna, and (5) village harmony."

As we will see, the Western Pueblos, the Keresan Bridge Pueblos, and the Eastern Tanoans place varying amounts of emphasis on each of the five concerns. They also differ in the organizations they have developed to deal with these concerns. In general, the Western Pueblos tend to be concerned more with weather control and rain, while the Eastern Pueblos focus more on health and government concerns. All Pueblos are concerned with village harmony, the natural outcome of personal and communal spiritual practices.

Western Pueblos. The dominant role of clans and lineages in these theocratic societies is evident in their role as the repositories of ceremonial lore and ritual paraphernalia. Each lineage or lineage segment in a Hopi village has a ceremonial room, and its female head, the Clan Mother, usually the oldest woman of the lineage, cares for the ritual paraphernalia stored in this room. The lineage in a Hopi village stages and directs at least one ceremony; the male head of the lineage (the female head's brother) erects the lineage's altar in the lineage ceremonial room, and clan members from the village (as well as those from other villages) visit this ceremonial room, where they smoke the ceremonial pipe and pray. The clan fetish—an ear of corn wrapped in feathers and cloth—and other clan ceremonial objects are displayed on the altar.

The Katsina Cult and several religious sodalities separately carry out the religious life of the village. In all Western Pueblos except Zuni, where membership is generally restricted to males, all children join the Katsina Cult. This cult is associated with the kivas, ceremonial structures that serve as theaters, dormitories for unmarried men, and workshops for men. Depending upon the number of men who belong to a particular kiva, the number of katsina dancers varies. Each of the Western Pueblos also has a series of ceremonial associations for curing (medicine associations), hunting, warfare, social control (clown), and rainmaking. (For a more detailed discussion of Western Pueblo ceremonial organization and world view, see chapters 3 and 4.)

Keresan Bridge Pueblos. The Keresans of the Rio Grande focus their ceremonial institutions and rituals on curing, which is consistent with the prominence of medicine associations in their pueblos. These medicine associations, whose members specialize in the treatment of specific kinds of illnesses, have additional functions as well. They conduct communal ceremonies to bring rain and to control the sun, seasons, and weather. They also coordinate communal tasks, thus fostering unity in the pueblo.

Everyone in a Keresan pueblo is a member of one of the two kivas, which are ceremonial rather than kinship organizations. The Katsina Cult, which is strongest in the Western Pueblos, is less developed among the Keresans. Associated with the kivas, the Katsina Cult is controlled by the medicine associations and the clown organizations—the Koshare and the Kwirena—which also manage its activities. The cacique and his assistants, who are associated with the mythical war gods, lead katsina ceremonies. The clown organizations in nearly all Rio Grande pueblos, Keresan and Tanoan alike, are very powerful and belong to the authority system. They serve many functions, such as retrieving dropped costume parts, leading the dancers, exposing individuals suspected of discrediting Pueblo culture, and providing humor.

The Warriors' Association (the Opi, or "scalptakers") is now extinct. It was once so important that at Cochiti it was subordinate only to the cacique. Today the cacique and the Flint Medicine Society (to which the cacique usually belongs) keep the scalps that were once required for joining the Opi. The village chief has absorbed the position of the war chief and his functions.

The Caiyaik (the Keresan's Hunters' Association) was believed to have acquired, from the spirits of the beasts of prey (the mountain lion, coyote, eagle, and bear), the power to kill game animals, which it could bestow on Indian hunters. The priest who headed the Caiyaik prayed for the success of all hunting ventures, including both communal and individual efforts. To ensure the magical increase of game and the success of individual and group hunts, the Hunters' Association performed private and public rituals, such as animal dances.

Eastern Tanoans. The Rio Grande Tanoans developed the dual organization of society and ceremony into its most comprehensive form, the moieties. The late Alfonso Ortiz, an anthropologist and Tewa from San Juan Pueblo, in his account of the Tewa world view (1969), documented this complex system of human and spiritual categories of existence, showing the intimate relationship between these categories and the Tewa world of sacred mountains, hills, and shrines that surround the village. These contrasting sets also have associated symbols and concepts related to the dual organization, which tie the human categories into a larger structure.

For the Tewa, winter represents qualities of maleness and strength, and is associated with hunting and meat, the directions of north and east, hard substances, and the colors blue and white. Summer represents femaleness and gentleness, and is associated with planting, plants, and flowers; the directions of west and south; soft substances; and the colors yellow and red. Instead of either half—winter or summer—being superior, each is necessary to the totality of the year and takes its meaning through its contrast to the other; thus, it is more appropriate to describe them as complementary halves rather than as opposites.

Maleness and femaleness are also associated with areas in the physical world of the Tewa: the innermost domain, which belongs to women; the farthest domain, which belongs to men; and a mediating environment between the two. The first, consisting of the village, farmlands, and other lowlands near the village, is the women's domain because it contains the homes and the major subsistence areas. Four shrines dedicated to the spirits of departed ancestors lie at the outer periphery of the village and give this innermost realm its spiritual dimension. The second realm, which consists of hills, mesas, and washes around the village, is a middle, mediating area where both men and women may be and where they may both hunt and gather; four sacred mesas define its spiritual essence. The third and most distant realm, demarcated by four sacred mountains, is the domain of men, the destination of male religious pilgrimages, and an area of male hunting and gathering of medicinal plants. The four sacred peaks that bound the outermost limits of the Tewa world are Tse Shu Pin ("Hazy or Shimmering Mountain," more commonly known as Conjilon Peak), located 60 miles north of San Juan; Tsikomo ("Obsidian Covered Mountain," also known as Sandia Crest, northeast of Albuquerque), some 15 miles west of San Juan; Oku Pin ("Turtle Mountain," more commonly identified as Truchas Peak), which lies 80 miles south; and Ku Sehn Pin ("Stone Man Mountain"), which is 20 miles east of San Juan. Each of the three realms is also the domain of special classes of spiritual beings, the supernatural counterparts of three classes of humans (that is, their souls after they die). The Dry Food People constitute the first and lowest dimension of Tewa society; these common Tewa serve in no official capacity in the political or ritual system. The second level consists of the Towa é, the social counterparts of the six pairs of sibling deities who were with the Tewa before emergence; they constitute the core of the political organization of the Tewa. The third level is the Made People, who are active in special societies, such as the Hunt, Scalp, and Women's societies.

Ortiz (1969:283) summarized the significance of the order that permeates all aspects of the Tewa world by explaining that his people, "when first informing their world with meaning . . . took their . . . social order and projected it outward and upward to encompass the whole of their physical world as well by imbuing that world with . . . spiritual meaning, one both reflecting and reinforcing their social order." In the Tewa world, "the fit among their ideas of order in society, in the physical world, and in the spiritual realm is ingenious, for these three orders interlock and render order into everything in the Tewa world" (ibid., 283). The Tewa world is indeed well ordered and well bounded, with concepts of complementary pairing and mediation between the two that embrace social, physical, and spiritual domains of existence. By giving ideological pairing and mediation physical reality in the natural world and social world, the Tewa reflected and reinforced the pairing and mediation of the spiritual world.

Tanoan pueblos tend to have one communal kiva and one or more kivas for each moiety. The Tewa Katsina Cult, whose primary role is the bringing of rain, is also organized along dual lines. Tanoan villages also have several esoteric associations: a hunters' association, a warriors' association, and one or two clown associations. When medicine associations are present, they exist purely for curing and exorcism, instead of having the broad range of functions they have among the Keresans.

The Tanoans emphasize hunting and war. The Tanoan Hunters' Association performs or directs small-group animal dances and, in cooperation with the moiety associations, leads a communal rabbit hunt for the entire pueblo before important kiva ceremonials. The importance of hunting is evident in the installation ceremony of the new cacique, which is led by the chief of the Hunters' Association in Tanoan pueblos, in contrast to medicine society leaders in Keresan pueblos.

War rituals are especially highlighted among the Tanoans, with their Women's Scalp Association and Men's Warriors' Association. The latter directs small-group war dances as well as communal rituals, which include relay races (once essential to physical conditioning for warfare). Both men's and women's scalp associations conduct rites, such as feeding and caring for scalps brought back from campaigns against enemy Indians. The emphasis on warfare is embodied in the term *war captain*, by which the assistants to the town chiefs are known; their supernatural counterparts are considered to be the mythological war gods.

Why Have Such Regional Differences Developed?

How can we explain such variation in social, political, and ceremonial organization among the Pueblos? Before we look at possible reasons for these differences, it is helpful to summarize the differences: in the Western Pueblos, political power is dispersed among matrilineal clans and lineages that are social, political, and ceremonial units; here, even sodalities are clan-owned. In the Eastern Pueblos, political authority is much more centralized in a cacique and his officers, even though each moiety (led by its own cacique and set of officers) alternates government control every six months. Kinship is bilateral, and sodalities are village-owned. Political authority is most centralized in the Keresan Bridge Pueblos, where it is vested in the medicine societies that select the cacique.

One possible explanation for these variations centers on the use of intensive irrigation. Dozier (1970:131–33) theorized that because kinship units were insufficient to mobilize the large numbers of people needed to operate a complex irrigation society, the Eastern Pueblos developed a political system based on sodalities. He felt that intensive irrigation explained the strong, centralized political control invested in the cacique and his council, including the powerful war captains who could revoke permission to live in the pueblo if a person refused to join communal work on the irrigation system. Social control also was much stricter in the east, and deviants were either banished or executed. In the Western Pueblos, smaller work groups based on clans and lineages were sufficient to practice dry and flood farming. Government was essentially theocratic, with social control handled through gossip and avoidance. Most Keresan Bridge Pueblos were irrigation-based societies that had clans and lineages, but put government duties in the hands of sodality and association members. Medicine men and medicine associations wielded considerable power, including the responsibility for communal tasks.

The Pueblos of the Rio Grande, who lived along a permanently flowing river and used government control to deal with issues related to irrigation, concentrated their ceremonial activities on issues of hunting and warfare. Although magical rites were by no means absent among the Eastern Pueblos, they did not emphasize them as much as did the Western Pueblos. In the unpredictable environment of the west, droughts were commonplace and famine was never far away in the memories of the people. Because success of the crops, their basic means of livelihood, was never certain, the people focused their ceremonial activity on ensuring the bounty of nature. The successful observance of a ceremony was believed to result in sufficient precipitation and a good harvest.

Despite the appeal of the irrigation hypothesis, other factors have clearly been operating. Environmental determinism is not sufficient to explain why the Rio Grande Pueblos concentrated on hunting and warfare in their ceremonies, while the Keresans focused on healing. Other factors must be involved, such as the ethnic and linguistic differences that existed among the Western Pueblos, the Keresans, and the Eastern Tanoans long before the arrival of the Spanish. The Uto-Aztecan proto-Hopi may have arrived in the Four Corners area early enough to participate in the Basketmaker-Anasazi transformation of the Desert culture (Hale and Harris 1979:177), while the Keresans and Tanoans were probably descended from the Anasazi, although their location is uncertain before the abandonment of the San Juan Anasazi area, and the Zuni are considered to be a mixture of Anasazi and Mogollon. Clearly, at least four groups—which represent the four Puebloan linguistic stocks—were directly involved in the development of the Ancestral Pueblo.

A third factor is warfare, which was more important in the east, where the people had to protect their villages from raids by nomadic Indians, including Apaches, Comanches, and Navajos. The Apaches, who had acquired horses by the early 1600s, were formidable warriors. Those Pueblo groups most subject to raiding, especially those in the so-called Apache corridor where Apache raiding was most prevalent, developed an emphasis on warfare, such as the war captains and Warriors' Association of the Eastern Tanoans. Spanish documents reveal that although many auxiliary Pueblo warriors served under Spanish control, they remained directly under their own captains of war in "campaigns against the hostile tribes which surrounded the province . . . in the century following the reconquest" (Jones 1966:176, 178). The Pueblos were such superb warriors, in fact, that Spanish authorities tolerated what they considered to be disturbing Pueblo practices, such as body painting in preparation for warfare, the taking of enemy scalps, and scalp dances following the return of a successful war party (ibid., 87–90). Spanish historians in New Mexico remarked on the equestrian skills of the Comanche early in the eighteenth century. Still visible today are the remains of a wall around Taos Pueblo that was constructed for defense and served as a valuable bastion during the Comanche raids of the 1700s.

There was also peaceful exchange with other Indians, especially for the people of the eight Northern Pueblos, who lived in the greatest proximity to the southern Plains Indians. Until recently, it was common to see the men at these pueblos wearing beaded moccasins, vests, and braids, characteristic of Plains Indians (Sando 1992:12). When the Pueblos traveled to the Llano Estacado each year to hunt bison and antelope, they traded with Comanches, Kiowas, and Plains Apaches, and Pueblos still perform the Comanche Dance, a social dance that simultaneously honors the Comanche and attempts to borrow power from them. Within the Southwest, Taos, Picuris, and the Jicarilla Apache continue to share some traditions, such as the footrace all three hold each year on their feast days.

The final differentiating factor was the nature and extent of Spanish influence, which was slowly transforming the Eastern Pueblos toward a more European model. Most evident in Catholicism, this influence was also especially pronounced in the secular governments of the Eastern Pueblos, where the Spaniards introduced the office of pueblo governor and his staff. (The governor's staff includes a first and second lieutenant governor, each with five aides to serve as messengers, a fiscale who has a lieutenant and five aides to oversee the maintenance of church property and activities, and a sheriff.) The impact of the market economy was also much stronger among the Eastern Pueblos, whose relations with Spanish settlers, missionaries, and military and civil officials were far more intense than those experienced by the Puebloans who lived farther west.

Although none of these explanations is sufficient by itself, the differences among the Eastern, Western, and Keresan Bridge Pueblos probably developed over time as a result of the interactions of all the factors. The stage had already been set for variation by long-standing ethnic and linguistic differences when the Eastern Pueblos developed irrigation societies that necessitated greater centralization in political authority. Then the impact of non-Puebloan peoples on the Rio Grande Pueblos brought about further differentiation: increased raiding from nomadic Indians led them to develop a greater emphasis on warfare, while Spanish influence affected their economies and secular governments, slowly transforming their societies toward a more European model.

In more recent times, further differences have developed. The Puebloans in New Mexico, especially those of the Rio Grande area, once experienced much greater Spanish influence because of their location than did the Hopi and their Tewa neighbors in Arizona.

Similarly today the New Mexico Puebloans live close to the cities of Santa Fe and Albuquerque, while the Hopi and the Hopi-Tewa continue to live in rural isolation. The Hopi and the Hopi-Tewa have had a far different relationship to the U.S. government as well and did not have reservation land set aside for them until 1882. The Santa Fe railroad had the strongest impact on the peoples of Laguna and Acoma who took jobs with the railroad, often moving with their families to Gallup, New Mexico; Winslow, Arizona; or Barstow or Richmond, California.

Glass-Blowing at Taos Pueblo

The first joint venture in the history of the Taos tribe, a $1.5 million glass-blowing project, was recently created with the help of, and modeled after, the Hilltop Artists program in Tacoma, Washington. The Hilltop program, which has been featured in documentaries, has received national recognition because of its success in keeping at-risk young people in school. Glass-blowing has changed the lives of many disadvantaged, disenfranchised youth who find creative purpose for the first time in learning this craft. Hundreds of primarily African American middle-school students have attended classes five days a week for the past five years, showing their work in exhibitions and accepting commissions from Tacoma businesses.

Despite its serene setting in the Sangre de Cristo Mountains of northern New Mexico, Taos Pueblo shares many of the same problems as Tacoma's inner city—drugs, gangs, lack of opportunity, and general apathy. One of the most traditional of the nineteen Pueblo tribes, the people of Taos have electricity and running water but have deliberately kept these modern conveniences out of the original North Pueblo and South Pueblo structures. In June 1998 Taos Pueblo leaders approved "a glass art venture to train and direct tribal youth and adults in the production and marketing of blown glass and related glass products," because of their concern about the problems of their young people and the future of the pueblo (Raether 1999:30).

The artistic tradition at Taos is based on micaceous pottery and drum-making. Although glass-blowing is practically unknown among native artists, former tribal secretary Richard Deertrack considers it an expansion of their cultural traditions because "fire . . . a crucial element in glass-blowing . . . [has] always been an essential element in our tradition" (Raether 1999:30). Deertrack explains that the 80 percent unemployment rate at Taos Pueblo is not the primary motivation for establishing the program. "There is an element of the glass project that Western profiteers may not understand. The money isn't our first interest. The preservation and advancement of our culture and its artistic traditions is our first priority" (ibid., 28). The glass-blowing project, when completed, will feature a 15,000-square-foot studio glass center, production shop, exhibit area, and plaza on 2 acres of reservation land, intended to serve the entire Pueblo community. The artwork will be sold and marketed nationwide with a percentage of the sales going to the artists and the rest to a fund for community programs, such as the preservation of the Tiwa language and organic agriculture.

The Pueblos Today

This section provides a brief present-day account of the Pueblos and is drawn from Bahti and Bahti (1997), Barry (1994), Bodine (1994), Brandt (1994), Ellis (1994), Fogelman Lange (1994), Fontana (1999), Goodman (1994), Hyer (1994), Lange (1994), Minge (1994), Tisdale (1994), Toya (1994), and Whatley (1994).

The Western Pueblos

Hopi, Hano, and Zuni are described in chapters 3 and 4.

Laguna. The name Laguna, Spanish for "lake," is a translation of the Keresan name Kawaik. Located 45 miles west of Albuquerque, Laguna carries on its ceremonial traditions with feast days and sacred dances throughout the year. Its white church, San Jose de la Laguna, visible from the nearest rest stop on Interstate 40, draws many people to the reservation. The interior of the church, with its decorative altar screen and ceiling, incorporates Catholic and Indian motifs in brilliant colors and folk baroque designs. Many of the old buildings are still standing in Old Laguna, the center of the reservation, which also includes the villages of Paguate, Mesita, Paraje, Encinal, and Seama. Uranium leases provided significant income for many years, and the tribe invested this money in scholarship programs, as well as other local projects and individual disbursements; however, uranium mining also resulted in radioactive pollution. Laguna Industries and a construction company provide employment on the reservation. Paguate Reservoir offers bass and trout fishing, while Casa Blanca Market Plaza on the interstate sells Laguna pottery, which was revived in the 1970s. Laguna is located west of Albuquerque, on Interstate 40.

Acoma. Ah'-ku-me ("place that always was" in Keresan) is nicknamed Sky City because it is situated atop a 357-foot mesa that rises abruptly from the valley floor, a location that has provided protection from enemies for over 400 years. Under the ancient theocratic system that continues to govern the pueblo, clan members hold authority over appointments and land allocations. Acoma Pueblo, located about 60 miles west of Albuquerque on Interstate 40, with its massive mission church, San Estevan del Rey, is a national historic landmark and may be seen only by guided tour. Visitors can buy the finely painted, thin-walled pottery for which Acoma is famous from vendors who sell their wares outside their homes. There is also a visitors' center with a museum, restaurant, and native crafts shop. The Acoma Sky City Casino, north of Interstate 40, provides revenues.

The Keresan Bridge Pueblos

Zia. Zia Pueblo (from the Keresan name Tseya), 17 miles northwest of Bernalillo, is best known for its sun symbol, which was adopted by the state of New Mexico as its official emblem and appears on the state flag. Classic Zia pottery features black-and-red designs on a cream-colored slip with long-legged birds, plants, clouds, and wide ribbonlike rainbow bands. Zia potters continue a tradition from prehistoric times, and now sell their work in the Zia Cultural Center, where they also give demonstrations. As with their pottery tradition, the people of Zia continue their centuries-old ceremonial practices. They have renovated traditional ceremonial buildings to accommodate population increases, and over the last fifty years their eleven religious societies have either remained stable or increased in size. Zia Lake, about 2.5 miles from the pueblo, is open year-round and features catfish and trout fishing.

Santa Ana. Named in Spanish for St. Anne, Santa Ana is called Tamaya in Keresan and is located near Bernalillo. Today most of the tribe lives at Ranchitos (Ranchos de Santa Ana), a farming community on the Rio Grande at Bernalillo, because the pueblo itself lacks agricultural land and water for irrigation; they return to their village to continue their active ceremonial life. The heads of the medicine societies still compose the Religious Council, and each society contributes toward the welfare of the tribe. The people of Santa Ana revived dormant farmlands by using organic and xeriscopic technology, and with the establishment of the Blue-Corn Mill and commercial blue corn fields, they have expanded their farming from a local market to an international one. The tribe has also developed other means of revenue and employment, including the Santa Ana Star casino. Their country club and golf resort, which overlooks the ancient pueblo, provides for the tribe's economic future. The landscape, where the desert meets the Jemez Mountains, provides spectacular views, and many people picnic at Jemez Canyon Reservoir. Jewelry and other crafts are sold at the Ta-Ma-Ya Cooperative Association.

San Felipe. Known in Keresan as Katishtya, San Felipe was named for St. Philip. Located on Interstate 25 halfway between Albuquerque and Santa Fe, San Felipe Pueblo lies on the banks of the Rio Grande at the foot of the Santa Ana Mesa. One of the most conservative Keresan pueblos, San Felipe continues to practice its traditional religion, guarding it closely; the tribe does not promote itself as a tourist attraction, although some individuals sell their arts and crafts from their homes. San Felipe is well known for its spectacular Green Corn Dance with hundreds of participants, which is held on the village feast day,

May 1. East of Interstate 25, tribal members have built their Casino Hollywood, with its own restaurant.

Santo Domingo. The largest eastern Keresan pueblo, conservative Santo Domingo Pueblo is located about 35 miles southwest of Santa Fe. Called Giuwa in Keresan, Santo Domingo was named for St. Dominic. The ceremonial leader of the tribe, the cacique, continues to be chosen from the Flint Medicine Society, and the two medicine societies still designate tribal officers each year. The pueblo's economy is based on subsistence farming, cattle raising, wage work, and fire fighting, as well as economic development programs. Its modern cultural center and tribal gift shop feature the *heishe* (Keresan for "shell") necklaces and bracelets for which Santo Domingo artists are famous, as well as their distinctive black-and-cream pottery and other crafts. Located just west of Interstate 25 before the entrance to the pueblo, the cultural center was designed to display the culture and crafts of Santo Domingo while relieving the pueblo itself of tourist traffic.

Cochiti. Cochiti is the Spanish version of Kotyete, the Keresan name for the pueblo. This northernmost Keresan pueblo is located about 25 miles southwest of Santa Fe, and its ceremonial leadership still comes from the headmen of the medicine or other secret societies or the headmen of the kiva groups. Cochiti is famed among all the pueblos for its drums because of their superior workmanship and fine tone. Used for ritual plaza dances and for ceremonies in the kivas, the drums are also sold to non-Indians. The craft of drum-making involves an extended apprenticeship and is generally passed down through the generations. After Helen Cordero made the first pottery storyteller to honor her grandfather, Cochiti became famous for these popular figurines. The pueblo leases land to the non-Indian community of Cochiti Lake, which boasts a shopping center, an eighteen-hole golf course, swimming pool, marina, commercial center, tennis courts, and bingo parlor. Many Cochitis live in single-family homes outside the old village, but continue to participate in the ceremonial life of the pueblo, which centers on the two kivas. Traditional houses and San Buenaventura Church also line the central plaza.

The Eastern Tanoan Pueblos

Tesuque. Tesuque is the Spanish rendition of Tecuge (Tewa for "structure at a narrow place"). Tesuque Pueblo, located about 9 miles north of Santa Fe, is one of the most culturally conservative of the northern pueblos, with an active ceremonial life. Tesuque owes its present economic success to the Camel Rock Resort Casino, as well as the Camel Rock Campground, gift shops, and Tesuque Natural Farms, which raises organically grown crops for use in the pueblo and for sale in nearby markets. Listed on the National Register of Historic Places, Tesuque Pueblo is bordered on the south by the open-air site of the Santa Fe Opera.

Nambe. The Tewa name invokes "earth" (*nan*) and "roundness" (*be*). Nambe is the Spanish version of the Tewa name. The only ceremony celebrated at Nambe is its feast day; there is also a tourist-oriented dance in July at Nambe Falls. Located roughly 15 miles north of Santa Fe, in the foothills of the Sangre de Cristo Mountains, Nambe Pueblo still has many of its original structures. Nambe Falls, about 5 miles from the village, is a series of three waterfalls, especially dramatic after snow melt or heavy rain. Nambe Lake is a favorite recreation area, with picnicking and camping facilities for boating, fishing, and hiking. The tribe also has a small bison herd. Nambe potters and jewelry-makers sell their wares in the village in shops and stores, as well as along the road that leads to Nambe and at the nearby Cloud Eagle Studios-Gallery.

Pojoaque. Known in Tewa as Posuwae geh ("water drinking place"), Pojoaque is the smallest pueblo in New Mexico, and its people maintain their cultural identity through participating in religious events at other Tewa pueblos. A handful of Pojoaque Indians reclaimed their pueblo in 1934; it was described in 1909 as having been abandoned when epidemics and economic problems decimated the population, making social and religious activities no longer viable. Since this time Pojoaque, in spite of its small size, has become one of the more prosperous pueblos because of its commercial enterprises. The pueblo now celebrates its feast day and holds ceremonial dances. Pojoaque's Cities of Gold Casino, on U.S. 84/285, generates considerable revenues through gambling and dining. The Poeh Cultural Center and Museum, with a multistoried tower, features a permanent collection and temporary displays of sculpture, textiles, and pottery made by its Tewa students. Hundreds of Tewa artists and craftspeople sell their work at the Pojoaque Pueblo Visitors' Center; the pueblo is located about 16 miles north of Santa Fe.

San Ildefonso. Spanish for St. Ildefonsus, San Ildefonso is known in Tewa as Powhoge ("where the water cuts down through"). The small pueblo, which is located 25 miles northwest of Santa Fe, has three kivas and a cacique who acts as a religious head, assisted by two lifetime assistants, the righthand and lefthand man. There is a tribal museum and several outlets for the matte-painted black-on-black pottery for which the pueblo is famous. About 1919 Maria Martinez and her husband Julian began to make pottery using this technique. Potters, including the direct descendants of Maria and Julian, continue to create world-renowned pottery in this style. Tourists can buy pottery at Sunbeam Indian Arts, the Popovi Da Studio of Indian Arts, Juan Tafoya Pottery, and Babbitt's Cottonwood Trading Post, all located at San Ildefonso Pueblo.

Santa Clara. Known as Kah'P'o ("wild rose place") in Tewa, Santa Clara was named by the Spanish for St. Claire. The Summer and Winter kiva groups, which are moieties, continue to serve as governing bodies, managing civil and ceremonial activities. Santa Clara potters, known for their carved, highly polished blackware, make miniatures as well as full-sized jars, plates, bowls, and figurines, which they sell from their homes as well as at the gift shop that is part of the Puye Café. Santa Clara Pueblo owns the Puye Cliff Ruins, a National Historic Landmark, where visitors can climb ladders to reach rooms carved into the sides of cliffs and on top of the mesa. Another popular recreation area is the deep ravine known as Santa Clara Canyon, which is surrounded by forests of aspen and spruce. Santa Clara is located about 1.5 miles south of Española.

San Juan. Named by the Spanish for St. John, San Juan Pueblo is known in Tewa as Okeh Owinge and is called the Mother Village of the Tewas in creation stories. In 1598 Juan de Oñate made San Juan Pueblo the first Spanish capital in the American Southwest. Many of San Juan's old traditions have survived, and its people continue to celebrate their age-old ceremonies. Located about 5 miles north of Española, at the junction of major highways, San Juan has many tribal enterprises. These include the Ohkay Casino; fishing, picnicking, and camping facilities; the Ohkay T'owa Gardens Cooperative, which grows and processes dried New Mexico native food products; and the Tewa Indian Restaurant. The Oke Oweenge Crafts Cooperative supports high-quality contemporary and traditional handmade crafts and is the site of a training center, as well as a sales area and gallery.

Taos. Tua-tah ("in the village" in Tiwa) was called Taos by the Spanish. It is the northernmost pueblo and continues to draw artists, photographers, and tourists, attracted by its multistoried structures set against the Sangre de Cristo Mountains, its beehive-shaped ovens, and a stream that separates the two halves of the village. Designated a World Heritage Site by the United Nations, the pueblo has become a kind of living museum for the small percentage of Taos Indians who still live in the old pueblo. Once a great trading center because of its location as a crossroads for Comanches, Hispanos, Utes, Navajos, Apaches, and other Puebloans, Taos is located 70 miles north of Santa Fe. The people of Taos continue their kiva-based religion as well as their annual pilgrimage to Blue Lake; in recent years many younger people have shown a renewed commitment to their tribal identity. The tribe operates the Taos Mountain Casino, as well as a glass-blowing enterprise.

Picuris. Picuris Pueblo, 50 miles northeast of Santa Fe, is located in a secluded mountain valley on the western slope of the Sangre de Cristo Mountains. Its setting is reflected in its Tiwa name, Piwwetha, which means "pass in the mountains." (Picuris is probably the Spanish version of Pikuria, the Keresan name for this pueblo.) Surrounded by the Carson National Forest, Picuris is situated at an elevation of 7,300 feet. When lapses in ceremonial activities reduced their importance, the cacique and ceremonial leaders were replaced by a governor as head of the pueblo. The ceremonies have since been restored, and now four kivas are in seasonal use. Potters continue to make unpainted vessels from micaceous clay, which they sell at the visitors' center, where a restaurant and museum are also located. With permits, visitors can fish at one of the two trout fishing ponds or take a self-guided tour through the pueblo.

Sandia. Sandia's name in Tiwa is Nafiat ("sandy place"), but the Spanish called it and the nearby mountains, which turn a watermelon color at sunset, Sandia ("watermelon"). The people of Sandia belong to one of the two moiety groups, Turquoise and Pumpkin, and the pueblo's five Corn groups have important religious, curing, and personal roles. Sandia still celebrates its traditional dances and ceremonies. Located just north of Albuquerque, the pueblo has a recreation area, a gaming facility, and the largest reservation-based retail outlet for Indian arts and crafts in the Southwest. Sandia Lakes Recreation Area features fishing, picnicking, hiking, and volleyball, while horseback riding is also available on the reservation. Sandia Indian Bingo is open twenty-four hours a day, every day. Bien Mur Indian Market Center sells kachinas, jewelry, textiles, and pottery, as well as other Indian-made crafts.

Isleta. Isleta ("Little Island" in Spanish) received its name because it becomes an island when the Rio Grande floods. Known in Tiwa as Cheh-wib-ahg ("flint kick-stick place"), Isleta has a moiety organization and has experienced a recent revival of ceremonialism. The Corn groups, which are similar to clans, choose their own captains, who are responsible for ceremonies and dances; the captains are confirmed by the governor and council of Isleta. Located 13 miles south of Albuquerque, Isleta Pueblo has a broad plaza with historic Saint Augustine Church on its north side. Margaret Jojola's arts and crafts shop, the Shirpoyo Art Gallery, and the Isleta Pueblo Indian Market Center provide outlets for arts and crafts. The tribe operates the Isleta Gaming Palace, the Isleta Eagle Golf Course, and Isleta Lakes and Recreation Area, which offers channel catfish and trout fishing as well as picnicking, camping, and softball.

Jemez. Jemez is the Spanish spelling of Hemish, which means "the people" in Towa. Most tribal members reside in Walatowa (Towa for "this is the place"), a village within the southern end of majestic San Diego Canyon. Despite outside pressures, the people of Jemez have preserved their traditional religion, including the Supreme Council, with a cacique and other spiritual and society leaders. The population of Jemez Pueblo includes the descendants of Pecos Pueblo, who joined their Towa-speaking relatives in 1838 after disease, warfare, and raiding had decimated their population. (The abandoned ruins of Pecos Pueblo, east of Jemez, can be visited in Pecos National Historic Park.) Today the second lieutenant governor at the Pueblo of Jemez is always a descendant of the Pecos immigrants. Jemez Pueblo, 42 miles northwest of Albuquerque on Highway 44, is located where the Jemez Mountains slope to meet the desert and is surrounded by wilderness. Fishing and hunting are available with permits, and the Walatowa Visitor Center features a reconstructed field house, which was used near the communal fields or hunting and gathering areas, as well as exhibits, artists' demonstrations, traditional dancing, and a gift shop.

The Living Traditions of Pueblo Art

Just as native languages have no word for religion, so, too, they have no word for art because it is integral to their way of being in the world, permeating all aspects of life. Pueblo peoples have always been aware of their fundamental connection with the creative forces of life. In the words of Rina Swentzell, Santa Clara educator, writer, and historian, "That thing which connects us is the breath. That's why everything takes on life. . . . We all breathe of the same breath the plants do, the rocks do" (Trimble 1993:97).

The railroad opened the Southwest to tourism at roughly the same time that the military defeat of the Plains tribes created an atmosphere of romance about American Indians among the American public. Fascinated by Indian cultures, Americans and Europeans wanted to purchase small, painted pieces of pottery as souvenirs, and impoverished Pueblo potters began to create curio items, such as cups, ashtrays, and pitchers. Although demand from the tourist market led to a decline in the quality of some Pueblo pottery, such interest also was responsible for keeping Pueblo arts alive and vital. Concerned about the level of workmanship, traders, collectors, and anthropologists helped encourage a revival in the quality of pottery-making.

The Hopis and other Puebloan peoples traded their handcrafted goods for inexpensive china dishes and metal cooking wares brought in by the railroad. By 1890 Hopi-Tewa potter Nampeyo had begun to produce art pottery, modeling her designs after Sikyatki Polychrome and other late prehistoric wares to create stunning designs of stylized birds, butterflies, and animals in red and brown on a yellow background. In contrast to Hopi, where patrons bought work through a trader, such as Thomas Keam at his trading post, the Rio Grande Pueblos had more direct contact between craftspeople and patrons. This situation led to greater competition among museums and other marketing agents. At first tourist wares dominated, but by 1920 artists such as Maria and Julian Martinez of San Ildefonso were creating pottery for a specialized audience, wares that were marketed through fine arts institutions. After rediscovering how to fabricate matte-black-on-polished-black pottery, they began a flourishing industry that soon enabled as many as one-third of the families at this pueblo to make their living from the creation of pottery. Their success encouraged other Pueblo potters to make art pottery, and such artists as Margaret Tafoya from Santa Clara and Lucy Lewis of Acoma kept the tradition of pottery-making alive. By the 1960s a resurgence of Pueblo pottery had begun, and today hundreds of women and men make pottery bowls and figurines. A new tradition began in 1964 when Cochiti potter Helen Cordero made her first storyteller, a group of five children hanging from a seated grandfather with closed eyes "because he's thinking" and an open mouth "because he's singing" (Trimble 1993:99).

The creative vitality of Pueblo artists also finds expression through jewelry-making. Santo Domingo craftsmen favor minuscule, pump-drilled heishi beads with equally tiny turquoise, coral, or jet decoration. Zuni silversmiths use silver to frame an intricate pattern of many small turquoise, coral, and jet stones, while Hopi silverwork is distinguished by the use of overlay with little, if any, turquoise. (See chapters 3 and 4.)

The closest equivalent to easel painting, which is not native to the Southwest, are kiva mural paintings, a tradition that goes back to prehistory and continues today. Native

American secular depictions of customs and ceremonies are relatively recent, an outgrowth of the Anglo-American demand for Indian art that also prompted the revival of Pueblo pottery-making. Jesse Walter Fewkes commissioned Hopi artists to make some 200 paintings and drawings of katsinam for the Bureau of American Ethnology at the turn of the century. Around 1909 Edgar Hewett and Kenneth Chapman of the School of American Research in Santa Fe encouraged men from San Ildefonso to paint a series of ceremonial dancers. Alfred Montoya, Crescencio Martinez, and Alfonso Roybal (Awa Tsireh), all of San Ildefonso, became well known as early Pueblo artists. Roybal excelled at placing finely delineated figures in a setting of highly stylized geometric designs, creating a satisfying composition.

In the fall of 1918 Elizabeth DeHuff, who was married to the superintendent of the Santa Fe Indian School, asked several talented students to paint dances. Among those students were Velino Herrera of Zia, and Otis Polelonema and Fred Kabotie, both of Hopi. Polelonema became known for the quiet, powerful dignity with which he depicted ordinary people, while Kabotie's work portrayed an entire village with katsinam in the plaza, with houses framed by the sky, making nature—and the clouds the katsinam sought to bring— an integral part of the painting. Following the success of the first generation of Pueblo painters, other Pueblo artists began to sell their work, including Encarnacio Peña, Julian Martinez, Abel Sanchez (Oqwa Pi), Wo-Peen, Richard Martinez, Romando Vigil, and Tonita Peña (Quah Ah), all of San Ildefonso. Peña, one of the few female artists, used watercolors to portray single figures and groups of dancers with fluid lines that united self-contained groups into a single composition.

By the 1930s the shift in government policy toward encouraging the expression of Native American cultures created an atmosphere conducive to the painting of native subject matter on a wider scale. While previous programs at the Santa Fe Indian School had been short-lived and informal, involving only a few painters, the studio program begun by Dorothy Dunn in 1932 was part of the official curriculum in an institution that served as many as 300 students who lived together for an extended period of time. During the five years that Dunn led the studio, many fine artists developed their work, including Pablita Velarde of Santa Clara. One of Dunn's students, Gernónima Montoya of San Juan, then became the director, fostering the work of Gilbert Atencio and Joe Herrera, both of San Ildefonso, and Ben Quintana of Cochiti. Other well-known Pueblo artists include Jose Rey Toledo of Jemez and Pablita Velarde's daughter, Helen Hardin, who used an abstract and symbolic approach to native subject matter.

Today some Pueblo artists have turned to sculpture to produce work that stands as a spiritual tribute to tribal values. In 1999 a major exhibition at the Wheelwright Museum of the American Indian in Santa Fe explored the tradition of Pueblo figurative pottery and presented the work of Nora Naranjo-Morse (Santa Clara), Virgil Ortiz (Cochiti), and Roxanne Swentzell (Santa Clara). Naranjo-Morse used the traditional coiling method to create

Our Home, Ourselves, an architectural work with seven vertical pieces, each between 6 feet and 6 feet, 6 inches high. Reflecting the Pueblo sense of home achieved through earthen architecture is important to Naranjo-Morse, who explains, "I'm making pieces that will go into the next millennium from this very old, traditional process. [This] says something about the longevity of our culture" (Fauntleroy 1999:29). Virgil Ortiz adds a modern interpretation to the Cochiti tradition of making amusing, exquisitely painted figurines, with his pierced figures dressed in tight black garments (ibid., 28). Swentzell explains the dazed expression of her piece *Remote Woman* who leans on her side, TV remote control in one hand: "We're killing ourselves with things like television. This is a sneaky way to get that message in, but it works because people go for the humor" (ibid., 27). Swentzell's work exemplifies a quality in Native American art today that transcends native cultures. She believes that "the need to be gently nudged into remembering reverence and a deep connection with the earth is something that cuts across all cultures" (ibid., 30).

Tourism in Indian Country

As world travelers seek out the last places on the globe that have indigenous peoples to visit—so-called ethnic tourism—tribes must decide how they want to entertain, educate, lodge, feed, and sell goods to their visitors. Indian gaming has led to increased interest in Native American cultures, but even tribes that have decided against allowing gaming must decide on the degree of tourism they want to develop on their land. Tribes with few resources may need tourism to stimulate their economy, while other tribes choose not to promote tourism at all.

Many Southwestern tribes supplement the attractions of casino gambling with RV parks, golf courses, guided tours, museums, visitor centers, and hotels. The New Mexico Indian Tourism Association and the Arizona American Indian Tourism Association provide tribes with assistance in tourism planning, development, management, and marketing. Their workshops teach tribal employees the basics of development. New Mexico is the only state in the country that staffs a full-time position of Indian tourism, an indication of the importance attached to the Indian contribution to tourism in that state.

In 1999 the newly created National Indian Tourism Network held its first national conference in Albuquerque. Lalio and Ben Sherman (Oglala Lakota) cochaired the meeting, which considered a need for a national Indian tourism organization. Such an organization could develop working relationships with federal and state agencies, cultural institutions, colleges and universities, chambers of commerce, domestic and international tour businesses, and visitors' bureaus to help support development, marketing, and presentation of American Indian tourism attractions (Sherman 1999: 75).

Navajo Faith Roessel, who grew up on the Navajo Reservation, worked as special assistant to secretary of the interior Bruce Babbitt in 1979. She feels ambivalent about seeing Monument Valley become a product peddled by Madison Avenue; while she is proud of her homeland and her people, she does not want "its uniqueness and sacredness to be marred by outsiders" (1997:5). By deciding how and what they wish to tell non-Indians about themselves and their lands, tribes embody three essential goals, says Roessel, "self-determination, empowerment, and survival. Self-determination is being able to set your own direction on tourism through policies, laws, and programs. Empowerment is having tribal members carrying out those tourism policies and programs for the benefit of the members and the community. Survival is knowing that the choices made will ensure that a tribe's culture, language, and traditions are practiced, respected, and continued" (ibid.).

Contemporary Issues Facing the Pueblos

The basic issues facing the Pueblo Indians today center on land, water, and economics. The critical task is the development of a sustainable economy in the face of a lack of capital and the complexity in tribal-state jurisdictional issues, which discourages on-reservation investment (Sando 1992:105). Without a doubt, Pueblo communities contribute to the cultural and economic life of New Mexico by bringing thousands of tourists to the state. These communities, located in such close proximity to Santa Fe, Albuquerque, and Taos, must balance openness to outsiders with the preservation of their own cultural traditions by closing certain ceremonies. Many issues challenge the ongoing life of the Pueblos today, and the following discussion is meant to be representative rather than exhaustive.

Land

Pueblo land holdings have diminished through time despite the establishment by Congress in 1891 of the Court of Private Land Claims, which has been responsible for confirming the grants of several pueblos and most of the Pueblo tribally held lands outside the original grants (Sando 1992:113). At the end of the nineteenth century, one method of acquiring Pueblo land, favored by land speculators, began with purchasing privately owned land near the pueblos at higher prices than Indians could afford to pay. After the speculators sold the land to a Spanish stockman for grazing purposes, the stockman approached the Pueblo governor, who was usually a friend, asking if he could graze his sheep or cattle on Pueblo land for a couple of years. For the sake of their friendship, the governor agreed to this arrangement. As time passed far beyond a "couple of years," the stockman became so firmly established on Pueblo land that no one remembered how he came to be there. The Spanish stockman or his children paid taxes on the land after New Mexico became part of the United States, and payment was duly recorded in the land office in Santa Fe under the man's name, which also listed him as the landowner. If the Spaniard lapsed in the payment of his taxes, someone connected with the land office moved in to accept ownership (ibid., 113).

During the last quarter of the nineteenth century the Pueblos lost a long line of lawsuits, and in 1913 the Supreme Court decided a case that clearly shifted the center of control over the Pueblo Indians from the state to the federal government; until this time, the Pueblos had been in the same legal category as municipal corporations. In the landmark case *United States v. Sandoval,* the Supreme Court stepped in to overrule a decision by the territory of New Mexico, demonstrating that the federal government—and not the territorial government—had jurisdiction over the Pueblos.

Afraid of losing their holdings within Pueblo land grants, New Mexicans pushed their senator, Holm Bursum, to legalize their title to Indian lands as well as to provide the water to irrigate the land. Leaders from all the New Mexico pueblos opposed the Bursum Bill, declaring, "We the Pueblo Indians, have always been self-supporting and have not been a burden on the government. . . . This bill will destroy our common life and will rob us of everything we hold dear, our lands, our customs, our traditions. Are the American people willing to see this happen?" (Sando 1992:117–18). Fortunately, the social climate in the United States had shifted in favor of Indian rights, and a rising tide of public indignation against the harsh conditions experienced by Indians on reservations joined a wave of new interest and respect for Indian cultures. Many organizations—the Federation of Women's Clubs, the Indian Rights Association, and other national and state organizations with social and cultural interests—as well as nationally prominent individuals came to the support of the Pueblos. Instead of the Bursum Bill, Congress passed the Pueblo Lands Act in 1924, which created a lands board with the authority to confirm title to all Pueblo grants.

One of the most dramatic battles for land was waged at Taos Pueblo over the return of Blue Lake, the pueblo's most important religious shrine, located 20 miles above the pueblo behind Taos Mountain. In 1906 the federal government incorporated Blue Lake and 48,000 adjacent acres into the Carson National Forest, and for the next sixty-four years the people of Taos, along with a nationwide coalition of Indians and non-Indians, struggled to regain control of this area, which the Taos Indians consider to be their place of emergence. Leading the fight were the governor of Taos Pueblo for three terms, Querino Romero, and his wife Daisy. In 1971 the U.S. government returned the land, the first time that it had returned land instead of monetary compensation to an American Indian tribe. Each year the people of Taos Pueblo walk to Blue Lake, where they pray for the welfare and harmony of all people. The slogan for the twenty-year commemoration of the return of Blue Lake is appropriate for all Pueblo people: "Blue Lake—a Symbol of Perseverance."

Water

Today the greatest threat facing the Pueblos is the loss of water through illegal seizure by non-Indians. The Winters Doctrine—which came out of a Supreme Court decision in a 1908 Montana case, *Winters v. United States*—forms the basis for Indian water rights. This key piece of legislation holds that Indian tribes residing on reservations have paramount and prior rights to the waters of their land as well as underground water that crosses their land and water adjacent to their land. Unfortunately, during the first half of the twentieth century the federal government did not assert tribal Winters Doctrine rights on behalf of Indian tribes but instead allowed much of the West's remaining water to be distributed to non-Indian ranchers and farmers and to cities under the auspices of the Reclamation Act (Burton 1994:691).

The issue of water rights is extremely complex. The Middle Rio Grande Conservancy District was created in 1925 as a political subdivision of the state of New Mexico with the intent of planning, constructing, and operating a modern irrigation and flood-control project. The Bureau of Indian Affairs undertook the financial responsibility for the cost of land rehabilitation and efficient water distribution for those pueblos within this district, which included Cochiti, Santo Domingo, San Felipe, Santa Ana, Sandia, and Isleta. These pueblos agreed to redistribute their land into revenue-producing farms, an agreement only Isleta and Sandia fulfilled, while the people in the other pueblos were understandably reluctant to relinquish good land that had been in their families for many generations, without a guarantee that they would get good land in return. Tribal officials were unwilling to force these families to comply. Another concern centered on the wording of the agreement: "The cultivated area of the Pueblo Indian lands . . . has water rights . . . prior and paramount . . . in regard to the newly reclaimed Pueblo Indian lands . . . the District . . . grants a proper share of water" (Clause 20). This meant that newly reclaimed land was only granted a share of the water on the same basis as non-Indian land in the same conservancy district. Jemez scholar Joe Sando (1992:124) pointed out that failure to recognize that the newly reclaimed land—which was nearly double the amount of cultivated land—also had "prior and paramount rights" to water "resulted in a gross seizure of Indian water rights."

New cases continue to arise in the struggle for Indian water rights. Having discovered the effectiveness of concerted action, the Pueblo people work through the All Indian Pueblo Council to defend Indian water rights. The council also funds Pueblo students' tuition through scholarship programs, and spearheads endeavors that will determine the kind of life Pueblo people will have in the next century. The council continues to grow stronger each year as more young Pueblo people undertake the responsibilities of leadership.

Continuity and Change

Although all Indian tribes have experienced rapid changes in their traditional societies, the Pueblo response to social and economic change has been remarkable. The Pueblos have been able to maintain the core of their religion and world view in the face of intense pressure to assimilate. In addition to the work being done by the All Indian Pueblo Council, each pueblo has its own issues. Many pueblos are purchasing ranches and properties bordering their reservations as a means of restoring their aboriginal lands. The people of Acoma Pueblo were discouraged by their repeated attempts to regain land through the courts: first in the 1890s before the Court of Claims, then in 1924 before a Pueblo Lands Board, and finally before the Indian Claims Commission in 1948, 1951–54, 1957, and 1961. In 1970 they received a cash settlement but no land, so in 1977 the tribe began purchasing ranches, beginning with the Berryhill ranch that included 13,860 acres to the west of the reservation. Other land purchases followed, with the largest purchase, the Red Lake ranch purchase of 114,342 acres to the south of the reservation, in 1988. Acoma has also expanded its enterprises and human services. The pueblo's new government complex not far from Acomita includes a large visitors' center, museum, and lunchroom at the base of Acoma, with bus service for visitors to the pueblo. In 1978 Acoma's Tribal Council created the pueblo's first school board to oversee programs at the Sky City Community School, Acomita Day School, and Laguna-Acoma High School. Community programs have made significant progress toward the elimination of illiteracy, and scholarship programs have been established to support university education. Acoma now has a senior center, individual and family counseling, child welfare and protective services, health care, and drug and alcohol programs. In 1976 Acoma opened its first hospital, which is located on the reservation and operated jointly by the people of Acoma and Laguna pueblos and the Cañoncito Navajo. From a population of fewer than 500 in 1900, Acoma has grown to about 4,000 in 1990 (Minge 1994:489–91).

Many pueblos have been able to take advantage of the economic and commercial opportunities provided by their proximity to Albuquerque and Santa Fe. Isleta is only 12 miles south of Albuquerque, where many tribal members work. People from Jemez Pueblo work in high-technology fields at Los Alamos Laboratories and at computer companies in Albuquerque and Santa Fe; others hold government positions with the Bureau of Indian Affairs and the U.S. Forest Service (Whatley 1994:495). Some pueblos have turned to gambling for revenue and employment. Sandia's proximity to Albuquerque, and an exit from Interstate 25 that allows access to Sandia's bingo parlor, has enabled the pueblo to make its bingo enterprise successful. It has created 135 jobs for the community at all levels of ability and education (Brandt 1994:511). Sandia has a remarkably low unemployment rate, just 2 percent. Many tribal members hold college and graduate degrees and are employed by the federal government and in the private sector in Albuquerque. Hoping to meet Albuquerque's expanding metropolitan area, the people of Sandia plan to increase their economic base by developing commercial and industrial facilities on the reservation's southern boundary.

Young, educated Pueblo people are concerned about how they can retain the values of the old ways, while acquiring an education and an understanding of the non-Pueblo world in which they must earn a living. This is a concern shared by all young Native Americans, who continue to struggle to find a balance between two very different worlds with conflicting values and beliefs.

References and Further Reading

Volume 9 of the Smithsonian's *Handbook of North American Indians* (1979) is devoted to the Pueblo Indians.

*Bahti, Tom, and Mark Bahti. 1997. *Southwestern Indians*. KC Publications, Las Vegas. [A beautifully illustrated guide to the arts of the Indians of the Southwest by a father and son who are well known in this field.]

Barry, John W. 1994. "Pojoaque." In *Native America in the Twentieth Century: An Encyclopedia*, pp. 500–501. ed. Mary Davis. Garland Publishing, New York.

Bodine, John J. 1994. "Picuris" and "Taos." In *Native America in the Twentieth Century: An Encyclopedia*, pp. 498–500 and 516–17. Garland Publishing, New York.

Brandt, Elizabeth A. 1994. "Sandia." In *Native America in the Twentieth Century: An Encyclopedia*, pp. 509–12. Garland Publishing, New York.

Brody, J. J. 1971. *Indian Painters and White Patrons*. University of New Mexico Press, Albuquerque.

Burton, Lloyd. 1994. "Water Rights." In *Native America in the Twentieth Century: An Encyclopedia*, pp. 690–92, ed. Mary Davis. Garland Publishing, New York.

*Dozier, Edward P. 1970. *The Pueblo Indians of North America*. Holt, Rinehart, and Winston, New York. [A distinguished anthropologist from Santa Clara Pueblo examines how Pueblo cultures have adapted through time to changing physical, socioeconomic, and political environments.]

DuMars, Charles, Marilyn O'Leary, and Albert Utton. 1984. *Pueblo Indian Water Rights: Struggle for a Precious Resource*. University of Arizona Press, Tucson.

Dunn, Dorothy. 1968. *American Indian Painting of the Southwest and Plains Areas*. University of New Mexico Press, Albuquerque.

Eggan, Fred. 1950. *Social Organization of the Western Pueblos*. University of Chicago Press, Chicago.

——. 1966. "The Pueblo Indians in Modern Perspective: Unity in Diversity." In *The American Indian: Perspectives for the Study of Social Change*, pp. 112–41. Aldine, Chicago.

Ellis, Andrea Hawley. 1994. "Santa Ana" and "Zia." In *Native America in the Twentieth Century: An Encyclopedia*, pp. 512–13 and 519–20. Garland Publishing, New York.

Farrah, Phillip, and Brian McDonald. 1983. "Economic Impact of Alternative Resolutions of New Mexico Pueblo Indian Water Rights, Vol. 2, Final Report." WRRI Project No. B-064-NMEX. Bureau of Business and Economic Research, Institute for Applied Research Services, University of New Mexico, Albuquerque.

Fauntleroy, Gussie. 1999. "Clay People." *Native Peoples* 12, no. 4 (summer): 26–30.

Fogelman Lange, Patricia. 1994. "San Ildefonso" In *Native America in the Twentieth Century: An Encyclopedia*, pp. 503–5. Garland Publishing, New York.

Fontana, Bernard L. 1999. *A Guide to Contemporary Southwest Indians*. Southwest Parks and Monuments Association, Tucson.

Goodman, Linda J. 1994. "San Juan." In *Native America in the Twentieth Century: An Encyclopedia*, pp. 505–9. Garland Publishing, New York.

Hale, Kenneth, and David Harris. 1979. "Historical Linguistics and Archeology." In *Handbook of North American Indians*, vol. 9: *Southwest*, pp. 170–77.

Hoerig, Karl A. 1998. "'Here, Now, and Always.' Museum of Indian Arts and Culture. Santa Fe, New Mexico, Permanent Installation." *American Anthropologist* 100, no. 3 (September): 768–69.

——. Forthcoming. "'This Is My Second Home': The Native American Vendors Program of the Palace of the Governors, Santa Fe, New Mexico." Ph.D. diss., University of Arizona.

Hyer, Sally. 1994 "San Felipe." In *Native America in the Twentieth Century: An Encyclopedia*, pp. 501–3. Garland Publishing, New York.

Jones, Oakah L., Jr. 1966. *Pueblo Warriors and Spanish Conquest*. University of Oklahoma Press, Norman.

Lange, Charles H. 1959. *Cochiti: A New Mexico Pueblo, Past and Present*. University of Texas Press, Austin.

——. 1994. "Cochiti," "Santa Clara," "Santo Domingo." In *Native America in the Twentieth Century: An Encyclopedia*, pp. 491–92, 513–15, 515–16. Garland Publishing, New York.

Minge, Ward A. 1976. *Acoma: Pueblo in the Sky*. University of New Mexico Press, Albuquerque.

——. 1994. "Acoma." In *Native America in the Twentieth Century: An Encyclopedia*, pp. 489–91. Garland Publishing, New York.

*Ortiz, Alfonso. 1969. *The Tewa World: Space, Time, Being, and Becoming in a Pueblo Society*. University of Chicago Press, Chicago. [A penetrating analysis of the belief systems of the Tewa by a well-known anthropologist from San Juan Pueblo.]

Ortiz, Alfonso, ed. 1972. *New Perspectives on the Pueblos.* University of New Mexico Press, Albuquerque.

Parsons, Elsie Clews. 1936. "Taos Pueblo." General Series in Anthropology 2. Menasha, Wisconsin.

Raether, Keith. 1999. "Through a Glass Brightly: New Tradition of Transparent Artwork Dawns at Taos Pueblo." *Native Peoples* 12, no. 3 (spring): 26–32.

Roessel, Faith. 1997. "Guest Essay." *Native Peoples* 10, no. 2 (February–April): 5.

*Sando, Joe S. 1992. *Pueblo Nations: Eight Centuries of Pueblo Indian History.* Clear Light Publishers, Santa Fe. [An eminent scholar from Jemez Pueblo traces the history of the Pueblo peoples.]

Sherman, Ben. 1999. "Tourism in Indian Country—Preserving Our Past, Sharing Our Future." *Winds of Change* 14, no. 3 (summer): 71–76.

Silverberg, Robert. 1994 [1970]. *The Pueblo Revolt.* University of Nebraska Press, Lincoln.

Swentzell, Rina. 1988. "Bupingeh: The Pueblo Plaza." *El Palacio* 94, no. 2: 14–19.

———. 1989. "The Butterfly Effect: A Conversation with Rina Swentzell." *El Palacio* 95, no. 1: 24–29.

———. 1994. "The Sense of Process." In *All Roads Are Good: Native Voices on Life and Culture,* pp. 28–37. Smithsonian Institution Press, Washington, D.C.

Thompson, Raymond H. 1996. "Foreword." In *Paths of Life: American Indians of the Southwest and Northern Mexico,* pp. xvii–xxii. University of Arizona Press, Tucson.

Tisdale, Shelby J. 1994. "Isleta," "Nambe," "Tesuque." In *Native America in the Twentieth Century: An Encyclopedia,* pp. 493–94, 497–98, 517–18. Garland Publishing, New York.

Toya, Debra. 1994. "Laguna." In *Native America in the Twentieth Century: An Encyclopedia,* pp. 496–97, ed. Mary Davis. Garland Publishing, New York.

Trimble, Stephen. 1993. *The People: Indians of the American Southwest.* School of American Research Press, Santa Fe.

U.S. Claims Commission. 1974. *Commission Findings on the Pueblo Indians.* Garland Publishing, New York.

Van Ness Seymour, Tryntje. 1988. *When the Rainbow Touches Down.* Heard Museum, Phoenix.

Whatley, William J. 1994. "Jemez." In *Native America in the Twentieth Century: An Encyclopedia,* pp. 494–96, ed. Mary Davis. Garland Publishing, New York.

White, Leslie. 1935. "The Pueblo of Santo Domingo." Memoirs of the American Anthropological Association 43. Menasha, Wisconsin.

———. 1942. "The Pueblo of Santa Ana, New Mexico." Memoirs of the American Anthropological Association 60. Menasha, Wisconsin.

Whitman, William. 1947. *The Pueblo Indians of San Ildefonso: A Changing Culture.* Columbia University Press, New York.

Petra Lamson with katsina coiled plaque she made, 1987. Photograph: Helga Teiwes, courtesy of Arizona State Museum

Chapter 3   The Hopi

June 1997

The Hopi village bustles like an anthill. Hopi residents, friends, town-dwelling relatives, and tourists swarm around the houses, into the plaza, and onto the flat rooftops, crowding into every possible vantage point to watch the katsina dance. Along with pickup trucks, cars with license plates from states as faraway as Montana, vans from colleges and tour companies, and even a recreational vehicle from Florida line the dirt road to the mesa-top village.

Although a breeze relieves the searing intensity of the noonday sun, periodic wind gusts also kick up sand, blotting out the details of the landscape below the mesa. The unmistakable profile of the San Francisco Peaks, home of the katsinam and source of life-giving moisture, hovers just above the southwestern horizon like an apparition: still snow-capped in June, at 12,633 feet, Humphreys is Arizona's highest mountain.

The monochromatic expanse of sandstone houses seems to rise out of the mesa top itself. Crawling with spectators, the multistoried buildings are all but obscured: young people sit shoulder to shoulder on flat rooftops; old Hopi ladies in colorful shawls rest on wooden benches and in folding aluminum lawn chairs, three or four rows deep around the edges of the plaza; entire families perch on retaining walls and in the shadows of their houses. On a rooftop on the west side of the plaza, seated in a lawn chair with plastic webbing, a slender Hopi woman in pants keeps time to the drumbeat with her crossed leg;

her Anglo husband hunkers down beside her. A sense of exhilaration and anticipation fills the air.

Spectators strain to see over the shoulders of those in front of them, and tourists of every type seem to outnumber the villagers. A tall, silver-haired man with patrician features stands beside his sparrowlike wife, careful not to block the view of any Hopis. Dressed in a Hawaiian shirt and faded Levis, a large man with a shrublike beard watches from a rooftop, laughing heartily with his Hopi buddy who wears a Chicago Bulls T-shirt. A stringbean of a man, well over 6 feet tall, tries to look inconspicuous by flattening himself against the stone wall of a house.

On the foundations of an unfinished house, students with backpacks and water bottles cluster around their teacher/tour guide, a sturdy, middle-aged man built like an NFL quarterback. Although he projects an air of authority, he replies tersely to their questions in a barely audible voice, trying unsuccessfully to avoid drawing attention to their group. In sharp contrast, on the other side of the plaza, stands a garrulous man in a cowboy hat who has the rugged good looks of the Marlboro cigarette man; his wife, with an unruly thatch of carrot-colored hair, listens patiently to his running commentary delivered in an east Texas drawl. Something her husband says makes her throw back her head in a booming laugh. The elderly, dapper Anglo gentleman standing next to them shoots a disapproving glance at his Hopi companion; the Hopi man simply shrugs, as if to say, "What can you expect? They don't know any better."

After their dance, the katsinam file out of the plaza, only to reappear individually with armloads of food. Each katsina, his sleighbell and turtle-shell rattle jingling and clacking with each step, gestures to a Hopi in the audience to come forward. Meeting the recipient halfway, the katsina distributes fruit, bread, or purchased cinnamon rolls. A Hopi grandmother beams with delight as she staggers under the weight of a watermelon. Clustered on rooftops, children and young adults roar when one of the katsinam tosses a loaf of homemade bread their way. A bent old man shuffles forward to accept a grocery bag of fresh fruit; grinning broadly, he walks away with full arms.

A hush spreads over the audience when the katsinam reenter the plaza; these katsinam have monstrous bulging eyes and woolly black shoulder-length hair. Dressed identically, they represent Esteban, the Moor who ravaged Pueblo women and terrorized villages in the sixteenth century. Their fringed sashes and the foxtails hanging behind them sway as they file back in a long line. A drummer with a brown body and a head with a brown knob on either side and on top and a duck's beak—a mudhead—seated in a chair in the middle of the plaza, begins to drum. At the same instant, the katsinam begin dancing, the rhythm of their hand-held rattles adding to the beat of the turtle shells and sleighbells tied to their calves. The pulse of the music reverberates through everyone's bodies like a pounding heartbeat.

Pulling the edges of her flowered shawl over her head, a Hopi grandmother tucks her skirt around the six-year-old girl beside her to protect her from the blowing sand, but the child is oblivious. Eyes wide with wonder, the little girl stands still, transfixed by the presence of the living katsinam.

Just then, a tall, blond, athletic-looking woman in shorts mutters something in German to the man beside her, and they begin to elbow their way to the front of the crowd, jostling the Hopi grandmother. Undisturbed by the disruption, the old woman lets nothing interrupt her personal connection with the katsinam dancing before her. With her focus as narrow as a shaft of grass, distractions are too insignificant to notice. She keeps her gaze fastened on the katsinam, concentrating her attention through fervent prayers. Setting aside all irrelevant perceptions and idle thoughts, she thinks only of the beneficence of the katsinam.

Nowadays, the Hopi are closing many ceremonies to outsiders because of the insensitivity of visitors. Unaware that they are, in fact, "in church," tourists attend ceremonies in shorts and halters; some blatantly disregard signs prohibiting photography, sketching, and notetaking. The Hopi also object to the trivializing of their ceremonies by "village hopping" —dashing back and forth among mesas to catch a bit of one village's dance and then another village's—practiced by many tourists who consider the dances to be mere entertainment, just another sight to see before returning home. Hopi, in contrast, try to remain for the duration of the entire ceremony in order to honor the katsinam. By doing so, they acknowledge the commitment that the katsinam have made to the village to dance in the baking heat of summer or the icy cold of winter.

The Hopi way of learning differs greatly from the Anglo way. Hopi are taught to use their ears and eyes more than their mouths; everything one needs to know will be revealed in the fullness of time. To the Hopi, the Anglo practice of active questioning indicates their short attention span, if not their bad manners.

Hopi philosophy teaches that each person contributes spiritual energy and that ceremonies are held for the benefit of all people. Everyone must be given the opportunity to pray during the public viewing of the dances because heartfelt prayers can come from anyone; Anglos, as well as Hopi, can represent clouds and contribute to the bringing of rain. But Hopi are not confrontational; as tourists become increasingly offensive and disruptive, the Hopi prefer to close their ceremonies to outsiders rather than to confront the offenders. Thus, today, the Hopi struggle with the spiritual consequences of excluding visitors from their ceremonies.

For the Hopi, probably more than any other Native American group, their past and present blend into a consistent whole. They have lived in the same place for at least a millennium, and although they struggle with the forces of societal change, their culture is remarkably intact. Until the 1850s the Hopi were among the most isolated, and consequently the least known, Indian peoples in the United States. Significantly, the Hopi attribute their ability to withstand external pressure not to geographic isolation, but to spiritual reasons: the power of the katsinam. (*Katsina* [singular] and *katsinam* [plural] refer to the sacred katsina spirits, in contrast to *kachinas*, which are the nonsacred dolls produced for commercial purposes.)

Hopi Basketry

The Hopi, who have probably been making baskets continuously for a longer period than any other Native Americans in the Southwest, continue to be the greatest Puebloan basketmakers (Tanner 1989:49). Hopi women have always woven a variety of baskets for their own use, both for ceremonial and secular purposes, and for trade with members of other tribes and with Hopi from different villages. Since the late 1800s the Hopi have been trading or selling their baskets to collectors. A major factor in the high quality of Hopi basketry has been the annual Hopi Craftsman Show at the Museum of Northern Arizona, in Flagstaff; during the year, the museum staff visits basketmakers in their villages to encourage them in their work.

A bride was required to give her groom a single basket, which was said to sail him into the clouds at his death. Today, on Second Mesa—renowned for its coiled baskets —the bride's family gives the groom's family over a dozen coiled plaques. In return, the groom's uncles weave the bride's wedding robes, which, it is believed, will take her "like a white cloud to the home of Hopi souls" in the Grand Canyon when she dies, for her wedding robes are also her shroud (Page and Page 1982:111). Coiled basketry, one of the oldest forms of Hopi arts, was traditionally made only by women from Second Mesa. Made of yucca and galetta grass, coiled baskets are colored with both natural (plant) and aniline dyes and are woven in a number of forms. Plaques are one of the most popular forms and display a great variety of designs, including katsinam, butterflies, eagles, flowers, stars, and geometric motifs. Coiled baskets also take the form of bowls, jars, trays, miniatures less than 2 inches in diameter, and wastebaskets (for the tourist market).

Using sumac and rabbit brush, only the women of Third Mesa weave wicker baskets. Easily the most colorful baskets in the Southwest because of the wide range of colors of commercial dyes used, wicker baskets are usually woven in the shape of a plaque, which is a flat or nearly flat, round piece with a characteristic "hump" in the center from crossing wefts. Geometric and life-form designs, such as rain clouds and whirlwinds, in three to seven colors adorn these striking baskets. The Hopi also

Annabelle Nequatewa weaving a large coiled basket, 1991. Photograph: Helga Teiwes, courtesy of Arizona State Museum

weave wicker bowls, rectangular trays for wafer-thin *piki* bread, and burden baskets. Men made and used most burden baskets to carry corn or peaches, either strapping the baskets to their backs or loading them onto burros.

The most common baskets are woven of plaited yucca and used as sifters to winnow seeds and grains. Baskets also serve as containers during ceremonial events, when they are placed at altars, filled with meal or bean sprouts, or carried in ceremonial dances; they are the centerpiece of the women's Basket Dance and may also be given as prizes at ceremonial races. To honor their existence, eagles were once buried in special baskets, and when children are born, katsinam personators give them simple woven plaques.

Origins

The place of Hopi origins lies deep below the surface of today's earth. Here Tawa, the Sun Spirit, with the elements of Endless Space, created the First World, inhabited by insectlike creatures. Disappointed when these creatures fought among themselves and misunderstood the meaning of life, Tawa sent Spider Grandmother to guide them upward into the Second World. During the long journey, Tawa transformed them into doglike and bearlike beings with fur and tails who settled into a peaceful existence. When they once more became mired in strife, Tawa sent Spider Grandmother to lead the beings upward into yet another world, the Third World, once more transforming them, this time into human beings.

For many years the people lived in harmony, and despite the chilly climate and dim light, they managed to grow some corn, live in villages, and weave cloth for warmth. Maasaw, Ruler of the Upper World, Caretaker of the Dead, and Owner of Fire, sent Hummingbird to teach the people to make fire, enabling them to cook their food and keep warm. Despite their better life, the people again succumbed to conflict and corruption caused by sorcerers.

A few men of good heart remembered that Tawa was their father; meditating in the kivas, these men discovered a world above them. When they dispatched birds to seek a means of ascent, Catbird reached the *sipapuni* ("hole in the sky"), where he came across Maasaw, from whom he asked permission for the people to take up residence in this, the Fourth World. After Maasaw granted Catbird's request, the Fire People, who had a special relationship with Maasaw, emerged first because they agreed to assume the responsibility for leadership. Later others, who became the Bear Clan, would assume this responsibility. Chipmunk planted a stalk of bamboo in the ground, and the people sang the bamboo into the sky with the force of their songs so that it could serve as the road to the upper world. Spider Grandmother and her young grandsons, Pokanghoya and Polongahoya (the boy warriors) assisted the people.

Upon their arrival, Mockingbird sorted out the people into Hopi, Navajo, Ute, and other groups. Pokanghoya and Polongahoya created the mountains, grass, bluffs, and salt deposits, and with Spider Grandmother's assistance, the people created the sun and moon by the power of their songs. Maasaw and Mockingbird then arranged six ears of corn in a circle, directing the peoples to select an ear of corn, which brought with it a unique way of life and a language. The Navajo chose a yellow ear of corn, which brought with it a short life full of enjoyment and prosperity.

After the others had chosen, the Hopi took the short ear of blue corn, which they knew would last forever. Maasaw and Mockingbird congratulated them because, although their life would be one of hardship, it came with the promise of survival. The Hopi had chosen *Hopivötskwani*, a way of life based on humbleness, patience, and the willingness to endure hardship. Thus, the same virtues that enable the Hopi to successfully grow crops are those that also enable them to fulfill their life plan. Farming is therefore considered to be a spiritual rehearsal and symbolic representation of one's own life.

When Maasaw and Mockingbird instructed the Hopi how to live, they incised rules for the settlement of disputes on two stone tablets, giving one tablet to each of the two brothers who had been chosen as leaders. Younger Brother was to be Hopi, and Older Brother, *pahana*, was to be white.

Maasaw then directed the Hopi to split into bands, which later became the Hopi clans; during their migrations, each band was to gather different knowledge that, when pooled into collective experience, would benefit all Hopi. Thus, each clan has its own history of key events that occurred during its epic journey. For example, when one group of Hopi came upon the body of a dead bear near the Little Colorado River, their leader announced that this important omen meant that from then on they would be known as the Bear Clan.

It was the people of the Bear Clan who arrived first on the Hopi mesas. As each new group (clan) arrived, its people had to persuade the Bear Clan people that they had a special gift to contribute to the well-being of the Hopi people. The people of the Sun Forehead Clan came with warrior status, while the people of the Snake Clan knew how to approach snakes so that these creatures would establish the proper balance for bringing rain.

This version, derived primarily from Courlander (1971), is but one of many variations of the story of Hopi origins. Emory Sekaquaptewa (1999) pointed out that all versions have the same intention, understanding, and use; the Hopi story of creation has the same application as the Christian creation story in the Bible. It is a misconception to think that the Hopi interpret their creation story literally.

Hopi Jewelry

The Hopi did not develop their distinctive style of jewelry—silver overlay—until the 1930s, when Fred Kabotie, the outstanding Hopi artist, and Paul Saufkie, the fine silversmith, incorporated their sense of design into a unique Hopi art form. Although there were Hopi working with silver as early as 1892, the few individuals who practiced silverwork made their pieces in the Navajo and Zuni style with inlaid stones and stamped designs. The Hopi overlay technique did not become popular until after World War II, when the Hopi Silvercraft Guild, established in 1949, used the G.I. Bill to train returning veterans to be silversmiths.

After cutting out two pieces of silver in the same shape, the artist uses a jeweler's

Jack Nequatewa working on silver overlay jewelry, 1991. Photograph: Helga Teiwes, courtesy of Arizona State Museum

saw to cut out the design in one before soldering the two together into one piece. He then puts the piece in acid, which oxides it and turns it black, to emphasize the recessed design, and then he polishes the raised surface to give it a soft sheen. The contrast between the gleaming silver surface and the blackened recessed design creates the unique Hopi style of silverwork.

In 1939–40 Virgil Hubert, working at the Museum of Northern Arizona in Flagstaff, designed the first overlay bracelet, which was executed by Pierce Kywanwytewa. In the 1960s the late Charles Loloma introduced dramatic new styles, using abstract inlay work with katsina faces hidden within its designs and colors. Loloma was famous for his spectacular bracelets and rings, which have inlaid turquoise or lapis inside to signify that the wearer's soul is known only to the wearer. Many other Hopi artists have followed his lead, experimenting with new techniques and materials. Drawing inspiration from crafts such as pottery, woven and embroidered textiles, and kachina carving, as well as from the natural world, Hopi jewelers continue to create pieces in both the silver overlay style and nontraditional, contemporary styles.

Prehistory/Early History

Both archaeologists and the Hopi trace Hopi ancestry to the Ancestral Pueblo people, whom the Hopi call Hisatsinom ("our ancestors"). Archaeologists use the name Hisatsinom to designate the Kayenta Branch Anasazi (Western Anasazi) who occupied northeastern Arizona, as differentiated from the Eastern Anasazi, whose descendants became the Rio Grande Pueblos (Reid and Whittlesey 1997:167).

Based on linguistic, archaeological, and anthropological evidence, anthropologist Fred Plog (Page and Page 1982:149) theorized that long, long ago, the Hopi were Great Basin hunter-gatherers, living in small familial bands, which congregated into large groups once a year. This would explain why the Hopi are the only Puebloan people to speak a language in the Uto-Aztecan language family that is closely related to the Numic languages of the Great Basin. They eventually moved into the Grand Canyon area, where people from the south introduced them to agriculture and the cultivation of corn, which eventually replaced hunting and gathering as their way of life. Called Basketmakers, for the beauty of the baskets they wove, the Hisatsinom of the Basketmaker II period (500 B.C.–A.D. 600) practiced corn agriculture but did not yet make pottery (Reid and Whittlesey 1997:183–86). (There is no Basketmaker I period.)

The Hisatsinom responded to the severe drought of the first twenty-five years of the Pueblo III period (A.D. 1150–1300) by contracting their area of occupation and building smaller settlements. In historic times, the Hopi responded in a similar way: during the drought around 1900, the most land-poor farmers, those of Oraibi, founded farming colonies at Bacabi and Moenkopi. Between 1300 and 1540 (the Pueblo IV period), the Hisatsinom abandoned the Four Corners–San Juan River drainage, and some established separate communities among the Mogollon of the central mountains, while others merged with the Mogollon. In Hopi tradition, this was the beginning of the migrations that took the clans across great distances and eventually to the present-day Hopi mesas (Reid and Whittlesey 1997:199).

At this time (the ancestral Hopi period, known as Pueblo IV), the people suddenly replaced the simple, repetitive designs they had been painting for 500 years with extravagant curvilinear designs in pottery decoration and katsinalike figures in kiva murals. Archaeologists believe that such an abrupt change in style probably reflects a major shift in world view, such as the adoption of the katsina cult. Like maize, the katsina cult is believed to have come from Mesoamerica. By 1500 what is now recognized as Hopi culture had developed, with its elaborate ritual cycle, complex social organization, and finely tuned agricultural system.

Archaeologists and Hopi agree that Homol'ovi is ancestral to the villages of the modern Hopi. Located 60 miles south of the present-day Hopi villages, Homol'ovi (Hopi for "the place of little hills") comprises four separate pueblo ruins located along a 20-mile stretch of the Little Colorado River near what is now Winslow, Arizona. The Hopi consider Homol'ovi I to be the home of the Water and Sand clan people and Homol'ovi II to be home to the Tobacco, Rabbit, Sun, and several other clans (Reid and Whittlesey 1997:200). (Other Hopi clans trace their origins to other places where there are prehistoric ruins: the Badger Clan at Mesa Verde and the Water Clan at Wupatki [Yava 1978:36].) Occupied between 1250 and 1425, the Homol'ovi pueblos included fields of corn, beans, squash, and cotton. The people of Homol'ovi II wove cotton textiles and used cotton as a commodity, enabling them to trade for shells from the Gulf of California, pottery from Awatovi and other Hopi communities, obsidian from Flagstaff, and copper bells and macaws from western and northern Mexico. Around 1400 the inhabitants of Homol'ovi moved to the Hopi mesas, as foretold in the migration plan spelled out in their prophecies. These steep-sided mesas provided protection, while the geology of Black Mesa provided a constant, if not plentiful, source of water.

In the three centuries before European contact, the Hopi not only practiced highly specialized agriculture, but also produced painted pottery and murals, and mined and used coal. The Hopi developed drought-resistant strains of plants, such as maize plants that had roots some 15–20 feet long to reach the aquifer and that grew only slightly higher than the length of their abundant ears. The Hopi also practiced flood-water farming by planting fields in the valleys of major streams that overflowed their banks and by planting crops in the area where water spreads out at the mouth of an arroyo. They also grew their crops in artificial terraces, which they irrigated with ditches or by hand.

In 1300 Hopi pottery blossomed, with brilliant black-on-orange or orange polychromes, followed by black-on-yellow types and the distinctive red-and-black-on-yellow known as Sikyatki Polychrome. These innovative pottery types replaced their undistinguished regional variation of black-on-white Pueblo pottery. Not only did the Hopi develop yellow and polychrome pottery, but they also broke with the geometric tradition of Pueblo pottery designs by decorating their pottery with bird, animal, floral, and human representations in sweeping curvilinear designs. Kiva murals dating from the fifteenth through seventeenth centuries are even more elaborate than the designs on Hopi pottery, and many of these murals could be considered among the finest examples of Native American art. Kiva paintings date back to the eleventh century (Brew 1946:fig. 87); 180 paintings, the largest number known, were found at Awatovi and Kawaika.

Among Native American peoples, only the Hopi used coal in prehistoric times, for cooking, heating, and firing pottery, as pigment, and as a bed for flagstones on their kiva floors. They practiced strip mining and underground mining, removing approximately 450 pounds a day during the 300 years of Hopi coal mining at Awatovi (Hack 1942:18). After the arrival of the Spaniards, the Hopi stopped using coal, possibly because by then the easily mined supply of coal had dwindled and because the friars introduced carts and iron tools as well as draft animals, which made the task of gathering wood much easier.

In 1540 the Hopi saw the first Spaniards when Pedro de Tovar and his horsemen, dispatched by Francisco Coronado from Zuni, arrived in Awatovi. When he was met with hostility, de Tovar retaliated by attacking the village; he then peacefully visited six other Hopi villages. In 1583 Antonio de Espejo entered the area to search for gold, and in 1598 Juan de Oñate made the Hopi submit to the authority of the Spanish king. Franciscan missionaries settled among them in 1629, erecting churches in three Hopi towns; however, in 1633 the Hopi poisoned one of the priests. Twenty-two years later, a missionary inflicted one of the most brutal acts ever committed against a Hopi: the Franciscan beat the Hopi, poured turpentine on him, and set him on fire, for having performed what the priest saw as a highly idolatrous act.

The Hopi had a long tradition of offering asylum to other Indians who wanted to live peacefully. After the Pueblo Revolt of 1680, many Pueblos from Rio Grande villages sought sanctuary with the Hopi; some became absorbed by the Hopi, while others eventually returned to their homeland. Around 1700 a group of Tewa families left the Rio Grande area in New Mexico to establish the village of Hano on First Mesa, where they still have traditional land rights and houses and continue to speak Tewa, a Tanoan language unrelated to Hopi. Today most of these Tewa-speakers are trilingual, speaking Hopi, English, and Tewa. In addition to Hano, other Tewa live with Hopi in Polacca, the government village below First Mesa, which was founded in 1888. According to their oral history, the Hopi-Tewa were invited by the Walpi village chiefs, who knew their reputation as fearless warriors, to move as a single unit to serve as guards of the mesa trail to Walpi, protecting the mesa from Utes and Paiutes (Fewkes 1899:253). The Hopi-Tewa share most, but not all, cultural patterns with the Hopi. (See Dozier's [1966] ethnography of Hano.) As additional protection from raids by Utes, Navajos, Apaches, and Spanish soldiers, the Hopi moved several villages to higher locations on their mesa tops.

One of the most significant events in Hopi history occurred during the winter of 1700–1701, when Hopi hatred of the Spaniards proved to be stronger than their basic belief in nonviolence. Attacking Awatovi, where the people had reverted to Christianity after the Pueblo Revolt, Hopi warriors from other villages killed the men and took women and children captive (Bandelier 1890–92:2:371–72). Neither priests nor military succeeded in their sporadic attempts to bring the Hopis back to Christianity. Throughout the 1740s and early 1750s the Hopi retained their autonomy from the Spaniards, primarily because of their geographic isolation and the difficulties the Spaniards were having with other Indians. Drought and hunger led the Hopi to soften their resistance to the Spanish after 1755, and in 1818 the Hopi requested Spanish protection from Navajo raids, but the Spanish were unable to help.

The isolation of their homeland protected the Hopi for much of their history, enabling them to keep their culture and traditions intact. One of their earliest encounters with Anglo-Americans occurred in 1834, when white trappers raided their gardens and killed about fifteen Hopis. After the war with Mexico ended in 1848, the Southwest came under the control of the Bureau of Indian Affairs (BIA), but the federal government waited nearly forty years to protect Hopi lands, despite a request from the Hopi in 1850 for help in controlling Navajo intrusions on their land. Once the Navajos returned from Bosque Redondo in 1868, they began expanding into Hopi territory as their population rapidly increased. By the 1870s the Mormons had established a large settlement in the Moenkopi area and had begun to expand toward the Hopi villages, taking over more and more Hopi land. As the Santa Fe railroad brought more people to the Southwest, towns quickly sprang up, including Flagstaff, Winslow, and Holbrook, all within 70 miles of the Hopi villages.

Although most of the visitors to the Hopi villages during this period were tourists, some were ethnologists, archaeologists, geologists, and biologists. Among them were Alexander M. Stephen and Jesse Walter Fewkes, who served as informal advisers in dealings with the Anglo world to the village leaders on First and Second mesas who assisted them in their intensive studies. Stephen came to Hopi country around 1881 and lived with the Hopi until his death in 1894, leaving one of the best accounts of Hopi life during this period. Fewkes, who first visited the Hopi in 1890, was a remarkable man who was initiated into the Antelope and Flute religious societies at Walpi. In 1895, when Fewkes began excavating the Sikyatki ruin near Walpi, one of his workmen, a Tewa from Hano named Lesou, took pottery shards home to show his wife, Nampeyo, who became the most famous Hopi potter.

President Chester A. Arthur finally established a Hopi reservation by executive order at the end of 1882. The Hopi had always considered the land occupied by their ancestors to be theirs: bounded by the junction of the San Juan and Colorado rivers in the north, the Arizona–New Mexico state line on the east, the Mogollon and Zuni rim on the south, and the San Francisco Peaks to the west. However, only a small fraction of this area was set aside for them as a formal reservation. When a rectangle of roughly 50 by 75 miles was set aside for the use of the Hopi "and other such Indians as the Secretary of the Interior may see fit to settle thereon," the seeds for today's Hopi-Navajo land dispute (see below) were sown. Overlooking the traditional Hopi government within each autonomous village, the BIA established a system of administration for management of Hopi lands without any agreement with the Hopi people.

In 1887 a government school was built at Keams Canyon. Hopi parents did not understand why their children could not miss school for Hopi ceremonials just as they did on Sundays and other Christian religious holidays. Although village leaders had asked for the school, so many conservative Hopis refused to allow their children to attend that in 1890 troops forcibly rounded up 104 children and hauled them off to school.

The most significant event among the Hopi themselves was the split at Oraibi, the moral center and the largest Hopi village. By the mid-1890s Oraibi was divided between the progressive, pro-Anglo, "friendly" faction and the conservative, anti-Anglo, "hostile" faction. In the 1880s the chief of Oraibi, Lololoma, the leader of the hostiles, went to Washington, D.C., where he was so favorably impressed by the Americans that he completely shifted his position upon his return home. Many of his previous followers then grouped behind Lomahongyoma, a member of the Warrior Society and of the same phratry (a group of related clans) as Lololoma, which made him a legitimate leader. Both factions drew on sacred myths to validate their claims, with the hostile faction refusing to believe that the Anglos were the *pahana* in the Hopi origin story and the progressives blaming misfortune on witchcraft and the underworld.

In 1887 the Dawes Act, designed to divide tribal lands into individual allotments, took effect. When soldiers arrived to survey village lands, the hostiles disrupted the process. By 1891 the split between the hostiles and the friendlies had become irreconcilable, and the hostiles had built their own kiva in Oraibi, since neither side would cooperate with the other in holding ceremonies. The split of religious societies into two was a catastrophe because harmony was essential to the success of the ceremonies.

Lololoma died and a younger sister's son replaced him as the progressive leader about 1901. In 1906 the conservative leader, Lomahongyoma, drew a line in the sand, and it was agreed that the losers of a shoving match would leave the village. When the conservatives lost, they left Oraibi to found the village of Hotevilla. However, the leader of the progressives, Tawaqwaptiwa, no longer supported the Anglos after the BIA forced him to attend the Sherman Institute in California for four years. Feeling understandably betrayed by his forced exile, upon his return he encouraged hostility among the progressives. Christians, who were ordered to leave Oraibi, founded Kykotsmovi (New Oraibi) below the mesa.

Several explanations exist regarding the Oraibi split, which probably resulted from the interaction of many causes. Land was one problem, as pointed out by Laura Thompson (1950) and John Loftin (1991): an expanding arroyo in the Oraibi Valley severely limited the amount of available farmland. Other explanations include a Hopi prophecy of the Oraibi split, the increasing tyranny and religious intolerance of Oraibi religious societies, and a class war worked out in advance by more aristocratic clans and societies to rid the village of lesser people (Page and Page 1982:165).

Toward the end of the nineteenth and the beginning of the twentieth century, representatives of many churches and sects came to Hopi land in addition to the previously mentioned Mormons. Mennonite H. R. Voth had such respect for Hopi religious beliefs that he mastered the complexities of the Hopi language; he also treated the sick and injured with his medical knowledge; finally, he amassed one of the most valuable Hopi collections in existence for the Field Museum in Chicago. However, Voth also revealed information on kiva ceremonies that elders did not want revealed.

Hopi Pottery

Hopi-Tewa potter Dextra Quotskuyva explains that most of her designs "are from the dreams that I had, and from looking at the earth. Everything in the universe—the plants, the rocks—everything in the earth inspires you. Everything seems to have life" (Trimble 1993:119). Another Hopi woman puts it this way: "You go out and get a certain piece of rock. It's not just a rock. It's got energy forces in it, it's a living thing, too" (ibid., 24).

Although women at First Mesa were traditionally the makers of pottery, Hopi pottery design was not a continuous tradition. Perhaps because of its association with the Spanish as a form of tribute, Hopi pottery began a long period of artistic decline in the sixteenth century. Once flowing, bold, and exuberant, Hopi designs became stiff, static, and cramped. In the summer of 1895 archaeologist Jesse Walter Fewkes began excavating the remains of Sikyatki, a Hopi village destroyed by Walpi residents in the fourteenth century in a conflict over land and water rights. Not only were Sikyatki pots elegantly proportioned, they were also decorated with striking, symbolically rich designs in red, brown, and black on a background of light yellow-brown clay.

Karen Abeita and companion, with the large pot she is painting with Sityatki shape and designs (moth motif), 1987. Photograph: Helga Teiwes, courtesy of Arizona State Museum

Even before he began working as a fieldworker for Fewkes, a Hopi named Lesou brought pottery sherds from Sikyatki home to his wife, Nampeyo. Fascinated by their beauty, Nampeyo, a Hopi-Tewa potter from the village of Hano, on First Mesa, began to incorporate Sikyatki designs into her own pottery. Nampeyo became the most famous Hopi potter by developing the Sikyatki revival style, in which she added her own creative interpretation to the prehistoric pottery style. Especially skilled at adapting designs to the specific form of the vessel, Nampeyo was soon making pots that "had a living quality of their own . . . [characterized by] a sense of freedom and a fluid flowing quality of design, together with an appreciation of space as a background for her bold rhythmic forms" (Colton and Colton 1943:44–45).

Nampeyo's descendants, as well as other First Mesa women, such as Garnet Pavatewa, Sadie Adams, and Violet Huma, have been called "outstanding masters of line" (Tanner 1982:92), because they paint fine lines, life forms, and bold curves, and carefully delineate areas with masterful precision. Color and design distinguish Hopi wares from those made by any other Pueblo group: favorite color combinations include black on a base of buff, buff with red-orange, black or black-and-white on a red base. Adapting the design to the specific vessel form and to the space she wishes to use, a Hopi potter uses lines, bands, scrolls, and other geometric elements with stylized bird imagery, such as feathers, beaks, and wings, or with katsinam, clouds, lightning, or rain.

Today, over a century after Nampeyo shaped and decorated her pottery, Dextra and others of her sixth-generation descendants, as well as many other Hopi and Hopi-Tewa women, carry on her tradition of excellence in Hopi pottery-making.

Language and Territory

The Hopi language belongs to the Uto-Aztecan language family and is related to the Numic languages of the Great Basin. (The Hopi-Tewa of Hano on First Mesa speak Tewa, a Tanoan language unrelated to Hopi.) The people of each of the three mesas speak what is essentially a different dialect, but because the three dialects are only differentiated by pronoun and tonal variations, all are mutually understandable.

Pressure to speak English comes from many sources: the English-speaking school system, daily affairs conducted in English, and English-language television, radio, and videos. Yet the Hopi language survives. Hopi linguist and professor Emory Sekaquaptewa cites several reasons for the vitality of the language. First, the Hopi have maintained a geographically and culturally intact speech community from prehistoric times to the present. Embedded in the Hopi language is their spiritual knowledge of the land on which they live:

"The names are derived from historic events, from points on the horizon that mark sunrise and sunset (and determine times for ceremonies and phases of the growing season), from distant natural and cultural phenomena," said Sekaquaptewa (Folb 1986:11). Furthermore, Hopi is the exclusive language for ceremonies, oral literature, and songs. While Hopi songs with historic and religious significance are passed down through the generations, most of the songs in religious and social dances are new songs, composed by contemporary men and women. This enrichment encourages the creative, living nature of the language. Sekaquaptewa calls the songs of the katsinam "the most creative medium in the Hopi language." It is in these songs that "we will find words that dwell on natural forces at work for the benefit of mankind, language filled with the energy of Hopi thought. One katsina song has cloud maidens grinding rain just as a Hopi maiden grinds corn, to prepare it, to bring this life force to the People" (Trimble 1993:109).

When Sekaquaptewa began to create the first dictionary of written Hopi, not only did he have to deal with dialectal differences among the three mesas, but he also had to try to translate the power and style of the Hopi oral tradition into print without losing the true meaning of the words. Working with a team of non-Hopi linguists, Sekaquaptewa developed a standard orthography, which he then checked with Hopi elders for the accuracy of grammar and syntax. He wondered how the switch from oral to written words affects a person's view of the world when "spoken words carry the meaning and power of the Hopi Way . . . in the context of ritual forms, ceremonial formation, architecture (relation of houses to ceremonial places), place names" (Trimble 1993:109). His hope is that the dictionary will inspire younger Hopi to write Hopi literature that will move beyond the oral tradition and "bring the reader the historical, moral realities of life today at Hopi" (ibid., 109–10).

According to the controversial writings of linguist Benjamin Whorf (1950), the Hopi language encourages its speakers to view the world more in terms of events than of things by emphasizing verbs over nouns. Instead of seeing the world as consisting of discrete objects that are separate from other things in the environment, the Hopi, according to Whorf, see the world more as processes, events, and relationships, all in a state of constant flux. The process/event world view of the Hopi, in contrast to the thing/object world view of English speakers, considers the ego to be insubstantial, just one process among many other processes, all changing.

The name Hopi is said to mean "Peaceful People," but this is only one meaning of this word. According to one Hopi leader, "The profound meaning of the word is 'righteous.' We don't use that very much because it sounds too much like 'self-righteous', which I have heard many elders say describes one of our big shortcomings as a people. The closest contemporary explanation is 'virtuous', meaning good, moral, of good behavior. That is my opinion" (Page and Page 1982:21). Today, Hopi is used as a noun (the name of the people and of their homeland), as an adjective, and as both the singular and plural forms.

Part of the Colorado Plateau, Hopi land consists of deserts and broad mesas; juniper

Second Mesa, c. 1990. Photograph: Helga Teiwes, courtesy of Arizona State Museum

and piñon grow at higher elevations on the mesas. Grasslands characterize the valley floors, with desert vegetation—saltbrush, greasewood, and sagebrush—dominating in the lowest elevations. Cottonwoods and willows grow along irregularly flowing streams.

The Hopi villages cluster on or around three mesas. From east to west, a traveler encounters First Mesa, with the village of Walpi at the tip, bordered by Sichomovi, and the Tewa village of Hano; Polacca is located below the mesa. Shungopavi is the westernmost village on Second Mesa, along with Mishongnovi and Shipaulovi. The Hopi Cultural Center is also located on Second Mesa. Third Mesa includes Oraibi, Hotevilla, and Bacabi on top, and Kykotsmovi (New Oraibi) at its base. Moenkopi is located on a detached section of the Hopi Reservation to the west. Each mesa reaches roughly 60 feet above the surrounding plain.

The three Hopi mesas are actually long fingers of land reaching southward from the much larger—roughly 60 miles in length and 30 miles in width—hand of Black Mesa in northeastern Arizona. Black Mesa came into being during the Cretaceous Period, when the region was a vast inland sea. The pressure from sediment draining into this sea compressed the lowest levels into porous layers of sandstone over a layer of impermeable shale. Black Mesa was created when, over millennia, the earth's crust rose and the climate changed. Through time, plants on Black Mesa were compressed into rich coal deposits, and rainwater filtered down through the porous layers of sandstone until it reached the impermeable layer of shale, where it collected underground in aquifers. The southward tilt made the water move toward the southern end of Black Mesa, creating springs that later made life possible for the people who settled there, the Hopi people.

The Tusayan washes, which separate the three southern spurs of Black Mesa, bring sand and silt from Black Mesa to the lower plains, which lead toward the Little Colorado River. Southwest winds carry the sand northward, banking it against the escarpments, a process that gives Hopi country less runoff after rain and more permanent springs than areas of similar climate. Seepages at the ends of the mesas in springs come from the rainwater that has seeped down through the upland sandstone layers to the layer of shale.

Hopi country receives an annual average of 8–10 inches of precipitation, with most of this amount falling in the winter; May and June, when the first plants are maturing, are the driest months. Strong spring winds intensify the dryness of the land. By developing specially adapted strains of plants and planting methods that maximize the moisture content of the soil, the Hopi have been able to survive in an area of sporadic and unpredictable rainfall.

Aboriginal Culture

In the following description, the past tense is used for clarity in the sections on subsistence/material culture, social organization, and political organization, but it is important to keep in mind that many aspects of Hopi culture continue to be practiced today. For this reason the section on religion and world view is written in the present tense.

Subsistence and Material Culture

Agriculture, specifically the growing of corn, has always been so inextricably linked to what it means to be Hopi that the Hopi say, "Corn is life." According to Hopi tradition, corn originated when Maasaw granted the Hopi the privilege of living on the land and caring for it. The Hopi farming year began near the end of February when the Sun Watcher determined the time of planting based on the occurrence of sunrise at a particular horizon spot. After clearing the fields for planting, the men of a matriclan planted and worked the fields together through the harvest, while married men tended their wives' allotted clan land. Using digging sticks, the men planted ten to twenty seeds in holes about a foot deep. By planting their rows of maize far apart, they were able to alternate the location of plants from year to year; thus they did not deplete the soil, and so were able to avoid the necessity of crop rotation.

The Hopi lived in permanent villages year-round. Oraibi, as described by Mischa Titiev in 1944, was laid out in a series of nearly parallel streets with scattered kivas and a plaza between two streets. Made from stone, aboriginal houses had roof beams on the highest level of stones. Men set the stones and beams in place; women plastered the inner walls with mud and then finished the roof with brushwood, grass, and mud. These square, often multistoried houses were entered by means of a ladder from an opening in the roof. Inside, there were fireplaces and bin metates or milling stones for grinding maize, and contiguous rooms for storing food and material goods. The kiva, a ceremonial structure, also had access through an opening in the roof. This semi-subterranean chamber had a firepit, a deflector, and a ventilator shaft to allow the entry of fresh air. The *sipapu* (more properly, *sipapuni*), "the place of emergence," was a hole in the floor near the firepit.

Men wove cotton textiles, often dyeing the fiber black, green, orange, red, or yellow before weaving. Using a vertical loom, they wove women's wedding robes, dresses, and shawls, and men's kilts, shirts, and blankets. Men also used a waist loom to make belts. Women only wove rabbitskin blankets, weaving the strips of fur together on vertical looms. Before the Spanish period, pottery-making was practiced in all the Hopi villages, but the craft died out after the first century of Spanish rule probably because pottery, as the chief item of tribute, was so closely associated with Spanish oppression. (Today women make pottery as well as baskets for the tourist market.)

Hopi: A Matrilineal Society

Hopi has always been a matrilineal, matrilocal society in which matriclans form the basis of social organization. The female members in a matrilineage lived, with their husbands, in adjoining rooms of a large, apartmentlike building; the essential core group in Hopi social structure consisted of one or more older women, their daughters and the daughters' husbands, and their granddaughters and the granddaughters' husbands. These women lived near each other throughout most of their lives. The women of a clan formed the backbone of Hopi society. Among a woman's many roles were being a mother, later a grandmother, a preparer and provider of food, an owner of property, a member of a religious society, and a weaver of baskets or a maker of pottery.

Traditionally, women wore blanket dresses (*manta*) that fastened over the right shoulder, leaving the left shoulder bare; they tied woven belts around their waists and also wore shawls, deerskin leggings, and moccasins. A woman's hairstyle proclaimed her stage in life: before puberty, she wore her hair long; after her puberty ceremony and until she married, she wore it in whorls on either side of her head, with a small piece of hair just in front of her ears trimmed to just below earlength; after marriage, she wore her hair in wrapped braids. Men wore their hair in bangs with short or long hair knotted at the nape of their necks; their clothing included a deerskin or cotton breechclout and a belted cotton kilt, leggings, and moccasins or sandals.

The husband's real home was said to be with his mother's family because he was expected to return there frequently to fulfill his ritual and social responsibilities; if his wife divorced him, he returned to live in his mother's home. When a man married, he went to live with his wife, her sisters, her mother, and possibly her grandmother, and their husbands. At the same time, he remained something of an outsider because his primary responsibilities continued to be in another household, the one in which he was born. Because most property was inherited matrilineally, he did not own the house in which he lived or most of the land he worked for his family. The father provided food and some guidance for his children, although he seldom punished them. Instead, his relationship with them was close and loving; along with his sisters and brothers, he lavished affection and gifts on his children.

A child's behavior was considered to be a reflection on his or her mother's kin group because the mother's brother and other members of the mother's kin group were the main disciplinarians. The uncle—the mother's brother—was the ultimate authority in a family, and children consulted their maternal uncle in making major decisions.

A boy's paternal aunts (his father's sisters) named the boy and teased him as he grew up, building his self-confidence. A mother-in-law referred to her daughter-in-law by a special kinship term and shared a friendly, often affectionate, and cooperative relationship; they were expected to perform specific, mutually supportive services throughout the course of the younger woman's marriage.

The clan has always been the most important group in the Hopi village. Ideally, each clan was divided into a "prime" matrilineage, which controlled the clan house and sacred clan objects, and a "reserve" matrilineage, which could take over if something happened to the "prime" matrilineage. Some fifty nonresidential matriclans once had members living in more than one of the Hopi villages. (In 1999 there were between thirty and forty clans [Sekaquaptewa 1999].) The clan segment in a particular village owned land, with each lineage having use rights over particular parcels, as well as secular and ceremonial responsibilities; not all farmland was clan-controlled. Each matriclan traced its ancestry back to a particular supernatural power, such as Sun, Cloud, or Bear; clan origins went back to the time of Hopi migrations, when each clan arrived on the Hopi mesas with its own contribution to the well-being of all Hopi. The clans considered to be the oldest in a village had the highest status and the greatest responsibilities within the village.

If descent lines proliferated in a village so that there were too many clan members to live together, separate households were formed. In such a case, relationships were amicable, and the family of the Clan Mother (the senior female member of the clan) possessed the recognized clan house as well as the symbol of clan authority—the sacred planting stick. Clan membership not only defined one's primary social relationships but also established an individual's relationships with the supernatural world, for each clan had claim to primary interest in a certain ritual, though it did not have active control over the ritual; the ceremony itself was conducted by others not in the clan (Sekaquaptewa 1999). The clan segment in each village stored its sacred items in a clan house, which was a room adjacent to the dwelling of the Clan Mother, who was responsible for seeing that ritual items were stored and treated with proper respect. The Clan Mother passed down her position to her younger sister or to her daughter, based on the woman's capability and dependability in clan affairs.

Kachina Carving

At the beginning of the twentieth century collectors became interested in *tithu*, the dolls given to Hopi girls. To survive during the Great Depression of the 1930s, Hopis began carving cottonwood kachinas. They sold these in roadside stands along what was then Highway 66 between Gallup, New Mexico, and Williams, Arizona. In time, the market for kachinas had a definite impact on the form they took, for collectors and buyers sought out individual carvers whose styles they liked, encouraging the carvers to refine their techniques and develop styles that appealed to the market. The first known carver to sign his pieces was Jimmy Kewanwytewa in the 1930s (Teiwes 1991: 70). Traders became instrumental in bringing artists and collectors together and also encouraged carvers by entering their finest pieces in juried shows, such as the Annual Indian Intertribal Ceremonial in Gallup, New Mexico, and the Annual Indian Market in Santa Fe. Once a piece won a prize, the artist's career was launched.

Today this tradition continues, but now the Hopi have opened their own stores and enter their own pieces in juried shows. Artists continue to devote weeks or months to creating their finest work, carving exquisite detail into a particular piece. Although women traditionally were recipients of *tithu* rather than carvers, some women have begun carving in recent years, many of them specializing in miniature kachina figures for the commercial market.

The kachinas that are carved today take many forms and styles; while some artists favor realism and action, others prefer to allow the natural curves of the wood to determine the shape of the figure. Still other carvers, such as Manfred Susunkewa, make *tithu* in the old style because of a personal conviction that they should maintain a strong connection to Hopi religion and culture. Carving his figures to resemble the old-style *tihu*—the ancient blocky, unelaborated figures—he uses the old methods, designs, and materials, such as plants, volcanic ash, and other natural pigments for paint. Susunkewa emphasizes, "The kachina doll was never art. They were not rich in style, but rich in spiritual terms" (Wallis 1992:46–49). Unlike many modern kachina carvings, which stand on bases, Susunkewa's *tithu* are to be hung from the wall or held by a string around the figure's neck.

For her study of the development of kachina carving, Helga Teiwes (1991) inter-

Ron Honyouti painting a Katsin Mana kachina, 1987. Photograph: Helga Teiwes, courtesy of Arizona State Museum

viewed twenty-seven male and female modern carvers, including Alvin James Makya, Brian and Ron Honyouti, Dennis Tewa, Wilmer Kaye, and John Fredericks. Best known for his realistic carving of the human body and face, Alvin James Makya (ibid., 81–83) is generally credited with elevating the craftsmanship of kachina carving into an art form. The naturalistic body proportions and lifelike skin and musculature of his figures, such as his Hano clowns who balance on one foot or hold a large watermelon overhead, have brought great acclaim.

The Honyouti family has many kachina carvers, including brothers Brian (Teiwes 1991:85–88) and Ron (ibid., 88–92) and their father. The two brothers are known for carving several motifs now imitated by other carvers, such as pueblo stone houses and a Katsinmana climbing out of a kiva, which they carve into the base of the figure. (A Katsinmana is a Katsina Maiden, or female spirit.) In 1987 Ron won first prize at the Sedona Annual Indian Fair with his carving of a Buffalo Maiden on whose base in the back he carved a small niche in which he placed two almost microscopic Buffalo Dancers.

Striving for realism, Dennis Tewa of Moenkopi creates the effect of wind blowing through clothing: "Hems curl up and capes seem to billow in a gust sweeping through the plaza while the Katsinam dance" (Teiwes 1991:99–102). Tewa's goal in carving such realistic figures is to create a visual record so that future generations of Hopi will know exactly what a katsina looks like; Hopi prophecy holds that when the katsina ceremonies become mere entertainment, the Hopi way will have come to an end.

In contrast to the realistic action style, kachina sculptures—as differentiated from realistic carvings or *tithu*—are popular with many artists and collectors today. These elongated, graceful figures without arms or legs follow the shape of the cottonwood root. Wilmer Kaye (Charles Loloma's nephew), known for his stylized, elongated kachina sculptures, won first prize at the Hopi Arts Exhibition in Flagstaff in 1990 with his Palhikwmana/Sa'lakwmana sculpture which merged two kachinas into one figure (Teiwes 1991:121–22). John Fredericks, who prefers this style because it allows him to retain the natural shape of the wood, thinks that sculptures appeal to non-Hopi both because of their graceful shapes and because collectors can feel their spirituality without knowing the specific symbolism of the kachina (ibid., 123–24).

Most carvers feel that this continuously changing art form is crucial to their existence. Far beyond monetary gain, their carvings embody their spiritual beliefs, the reverence they feel toward life itself. Ramson Lomatewama (1992:24) has said that he continues to carve because "my creations, the kachina dolls that I carve, are manifestations of my attitudes toward life itself. And, if I radiate those positive feelings, somehow or other, my carvings will become the vehicle for those feelings to be carried and further radiated in someone's life."

Political Organization

Traditionally, each Hopi village was an independent entity, comparable to a city-state, and no means existed for uniting the Hopi as a tribe. On each of the three mesas, the villages were laid out in the following order: the "mother" village at the tip of the mesa; then the "colony" or "daughter" village, formed when the mother village became too large; and, farthest from the mother village, the "guard" village, which protected all three villages from intruders.

Recognizing the need for defensive warfare, the Hopi also developed a warrior society. Boys trained rigorously through cold baths, races, and archery for this society, which held a ceremony every year in the fall; society members prayed, made sacred objects, performed ritual smoking, and built an altar.

Hopi government was essentially theocratic, and the chief (*kikmongwi*) of each Hopi village was from the Bear Clan. As the ritual leader and "father" of the people of his village, he was expected to lead his "children" by providing an example of hard work, humility, and good thoughts, and even today the character of a *kikmongwi* is measured against these same criteria (*Qua'Töqti,* 20 October 1983:2). Deriving his influence from his religious position, the *kikmongwi* was responsible for seeing that the many rituals and ceremonial affairs of the village were properly carried out, while other officials acted on his behalf by dealing with political matters. Although most Hopi leaders were men, when the Hopi founded the village of Moenkopi in the mid-1800s, they chose Nashileowi, a woman, for the secular position of political spokesperson because of her economic leadership. (Moenkopi continues to be ceremonially dependent upon Oraibi.)

Gossip and the clowns who perform at katsina ceremonies were, and still are, the primary means of social control. The clowns "acted out" unacceptable behavior by any member of the village, thus bringing attention to their behavior; no one wanted to be the subject of the clowns' pantomimes.

Religion and World View

Life and death, day, and night, summer and winter, the tangible and the intangible: the Hopi still view these not as opposites but rather as complementary pairs that are part of a continuous whole. Instead of duality and opposition, the Hopi have always seen interrelatedness and entirety; as a Hopi, one accepts the existence of evil as the counterpart to good without contaminating oneself with evil. A person strives to become Hopi, an ideal and unachievable state of perfection. The Hopi way of life (*Hopivötskwani*) reflects this process of becoming as well as the hope for the future of the Hopi culture and people. This word can be broken down as *Hopi* ("faith" or "peacefulness"), *pohu* ("path"), *tsiikwa* ("make straight"), and *-ni* (future tense marker); taken together, this word literally means, "Hopi path straight into the future" (Sekaquaptewa 1994).

Life and death are considered to be part of a continuous process, with the spirits of the dead becoming clouds that bring rain to the living. Just as each individual has an earthly life cycle, the sun also has its own daily and yearly cycle. Each morning the sun emerges from its eastern house, and each evening it descends into its western home. "During the night, the sun travels underground from west to east in order to be ready to rise at its accustomed place the next day. Hence day and night are reversed in the upper and lower worlds" (Titiev 1944:173). The Hopi year also reflects this complementarity, for it is divided into two six-month periods: during roughly the first half of the year, the katsinam live among the Hopi; during the second half, they live in their spirit world, atop San Francisco Peaks.

Work as Worship

For the Hopi, work is not a secular activity distinct from their spiritual lives. All activities —farming, hunting, gathering, eating, lovemaking, clowning, praying, and weaving—are

*A Hopi farmer,
c. 1900. Unknown
photographer,
courtesy of
Arizona State
Museum*

forms of worship. The spiritual also permeates the social dimensions of Hopi life—kinship, clanship, residence, and political organization. Emory Sekaquaptewa explains that work symbolizes the Hopi's emergence to humanity; blue corn is the "Hopi law" because, although blue corn requires more work to yield a successful harvest in comparison to other types of corn, it remains the strongest and most durable strain (Loftin 1991:4–5).

The Hopi people, known as the most skilled dry-farmers in the world, consider the endeavor of planting and caring for their crops in the harsh, arid environment of northern Arizona to be an act of faith. Even the planting stick is a sacred object, a physical symbol of the faith and prayer it takes to raise corn and other crops. The Hopi sing to their corn, praying for it and treating it with the same loving care they lavish on their children. George Nasoftie explained, "When one goes [to tend the plants] one can talk humbly to them. One can humbly encourage the plants, saying, 'You will exert yourselves.' One says this to his plants as he reflects on his children and his grandchildren. For them, one sacrifices in his fields" (Evers 1979).

Corn is a metaphor for human life among the Hopi, and many of the words used to refer to the developmental stages of people also refer to the stages the corn plant goes through. The "law of the corn" is the seasonal cycle of corn, which mirrors the cyclical process of human life. Just as humans emerged from a series of previous worlds located below the present world, corn sprouts emerge from their point of origin in the ground. Humans are not considered to be fully alive until their eyes can see; corn plants are only mature when they have developed "eyes," the kernels or the seed grains that ensure the continuation of life. As plants and people age, their bodies can no longer stand upright, and they must rely on support from Mother Earth. The lifeless bodies of both humans and corn plants are said to be without the substance of life; all that remains is only the lifeless corpse and the corn plant harvested of all its ears. Finally, after death and release from the burden of the lifeless body, the breath or soul of both humans and corn plants is said to continue on its journey to become perfected.

Hopi Factions

The issue of the traditionalists versus the progressives is far more complicated than these labels, applied by non-Hopi, might suggest. Traditionally, Hopi villages were autonomous, but in 1937, under the Indian Reorganization Act, the Hopi formed a tribal council with elected officials from each village, their numbers determined by a local census. Initially, because only Christian Hopi or Hopi who supported the BIA turned out to vote—a minority of eligible Hopi voters—the so-called traditionalists claimed that the constitution and the tribal council included in it were not legal.

The late Thomas Banyacya told Suzanne and Jake Page (1982:22–23), who had been asked by Hopi religious elders and the Hopi Tribal Council to write a book about Hopi, that he was the official interpreter for the traditional leaders of the independent Hopi Nation (so named because the Hopi never signed a peace treaty with the United States). The members of the Hopi Tribal Council, according to Banyacya, were persuaded by a Mormon law firm and by the large corporations to sell out their rights to the land in favor of the mineral interests; in the 1970s traditional elders allied themselves with local environmental groups to try to block Peabody Coal Company from strip-mining Black Mesa. When traditional elders asked him to seek help by traveling the world to explain the dire situation, Banyacya went to Stockholm in

1972 to press the Hopi case before the United Nations Conference on the Human Environment.

The Pages found many contradictions in the traditionalists' approach, for, at the time they interviewed him, Banyacya had electricity, appliances, running water, a toilet, and an electric organ and sent his granddaughter to a Mennonite school. In contradiction to Banyacya's claims, the Hopi Tribal Council, instead of being composed of Mormonized Hopi, has some of the most respected Hopi religious leaders as members, while many others fully cooperate with it, and today the Hopi Tribal Council has become an accepted, integral part of Hopi life. Instead of being divided into two rigidly defined, opposing groups, the Hopi exist along a spectrum of opinion; this was true even in the 1980s, when there was a hard-core group of 300–400 traditionalists (out of a population of 10,000). The Pages (1982:34) concluded that "whether a Hopi takes a traditional or progressive stand depends on what subject is being discussed, on which mesa, in which village, and with which clan."

The Katsinam

Following *Hopivötskwani* takes great spiritual strength because it requires a person to adapt to new situations without aggression and to remain faithful to the highest ideals. Helping the Hopi in this difficult way of living are the katsinam, spirit beings who serve as intermediaries to the Hopi deities. Emory Sekaquaptewa called the katsinam "the heart of Hopi life" (Teiwes 1991:6). According to Hopi thought, every entity in the universe, including clouds and rocks, is imbued with spirit and can carry prayers to the deities. The katsinam, who embody the spirits of nature in tangible form, thus act as intermediaries between the Creator and humans; as such, they are not worshiped but rather are respected as powerful spirits that help bring much-needed rain and other blessings to the Hopi. The relationship is reciprocal, for the katsinam want *pahos* (prayer stick offerings) and cornmeal; they also enjoy dancing in the plazas and like to see goodness and sincerity expressed by the Hopi.

The word *katsina* refers to both the incorporeal katsina spirit and the dancer who brings this spirit to life. A Hopi girl receives a katsina doll (called a *tihu*), which is a small, carved wooden representation of a katsina. The katsina spirit is represented as a real being, a symbol of goodness and kindness associated with the spiritual gift of reproduction. Children are taught this at an early age: when fruit or other gifts are received, parents place fruit in the middle of a table and expect the children to go outside with cornmeal to pray for the abundance of what they have received; when the children return, they find even more fruit on the table (Sekaquaptewa 1976:36). Katsinam also admonish: when children misbehave, parents threaten them with the idea that the katsinam will take them away. At a certain time of year, the Soya Katsina tries to take the children, but the parents intervene to protect them, thereby teaching the children not only to understand the importance of good behavior but also to recognize that relatives come to the aid of their children (ibid., 37).

The dancers who embody katsina spirits perform sacred ceremonies during the half of the year when the katsinam are believed to be in the Hopi villages, and when a child reaches spiritual maturity, about the age of puberty, he or she is initiated into the Katsina Society. Sekaquaptewa (1976:38–39) explained that he was not disillusioned when, as a boy, he discovered that katsinam were "personators" with a spiritual essence, because with this knowledge came his entrance into the adult world of his father, uncles, and brothers, whom he held in high regard. He was finally allowed to participate as one of them, which gave him strength for the next phase of his life within his community. Furthermore, a boy achieves great spiritual fulfillment through his ability to project himself into the spiritual world as he performs by losing his personal identity to become the katsina he represents.

The *tihu* (pl. *tithu*) requires respect but not worship. If made and given as a prayer by one of the dancers who embodies a katsina, it establishes a strong bond with the spirit world and represents a blessing to the girl to whom it was given and her family. She treats the *tihu* as her child (*tihu* means "child"), and the *tihu* bestows upon her the power of reproduction. The *tihu* also serves as a vehicle of learning, as children ask their elders about katsina garments, colors, and types, thus helping children to distinguish the different kinds of katsinam who watch over the Hopi. As a girl grows older, she receives other *tithu*; the four forms of *tihu* coincide with four stages of postnatal development: infants, toddlers, girls up to the age of two years, and girls of more than two years (Teiwes 1991:39–40). Boys and girls alike receive the flat figures hung on cradleboards, known as *putsqatihu*, while *putstihu taywa'yta*, dolls with flat bodies and more three-dimensional faces, are given to toddlers. Girls up to the age of two years receive the figures with cylindrical bodies and fully carved heads called *muringputihu*, and when they reach two years of age, a katsina gives them *tithu*, figures with fully carved heads and bodies.

Hopi Ceremonies

According to Hopi belief, when the supreme deity entrusted the Hopi with the responsibility of being "caretakers of Mother Earth . . . the supreme deity and his priests guided the Hopi in the development of a complex and multifaceted religion based on the philosophy that all things, living or not, are melded into a great wholeness," explained Alph Secakuku (1995:2). In order to maintain "the harmony of the world" and to achieve "bountiful harvests and the replenishment of sacred springs, the Hopi secure meditative relationships with supernatural beings through positive concepts and processes" (ibid., 2). The linkage of spirituality, corn, rain, and the act of farming are evident in the words of a contemporary Hopi man who said, "Corn is the center of life, the essence of life. I still have a field. I still plant my corn. Because why should I participate and pray for rain if I don't have any plants for the rains to come and nourish?" (Trimble 1986:38).

The Hopi share ritual responsibilities, which enable everyone to contribute to the maintenance of proper relationships with the supernatural. As mentioned earlier, each clan claims primary interest in certain rituals. The new year begins about the time of the winter solstice when the Soyal Ceremony is held for the purpose of encouraging the sun to begin its journey back to its summer home, bringing needed warmth for the planting of crops. The katsinam, embodied in tangible form by dancers, begin to arrive in the villages at this time. The Powamu season in February "dramatizes the final stages of world creation, and calls upon the katsina spirit beings to invoke substantial growth and maturity for all mankind" (Secakuku 1995:3). Called the Bean Dance, the Powamu is a complex winter ritual. As part of this ceremony, beans are planted and grown in the kivas as prayer offerings. The katsinam appear in the village in greater numbers during this time as well. March brings the katsina night dances, whose most famous variant is the dance of the Horned Water Serpent, with puppets that represent mythical serpents. Day dances follow in April: the katsinam arrive in the plaza of each village at sunrise to dance in place in a line; during intervals between dances, they distribute gifts of food, and different kinds of clowns perform.

The departure of the katsinam in late July coincides with the completion of planting and the harvesting of the first corn crop. The Niman, or Home Dance, celebrates the return of the katsinam to their spirit world, to the life-giving altitudes of San Francisco Peaks, and is a time of the most intense prayer and meditation in Hopi villages. At the Niman, as at the Powamu, the katsinam bring many presents, especially for the children, including *tithu* for the girls, and toy bows and arrows, ball games, and rattles for the boys, which represent the bounty of the harvest. Each woman who was married during the previous year receives a *tihu*, and the bride's mother-in-law presents her to the spirits. Eagles that have been adopted by families and kept on their rooftops are "sent home, bearing prayers and their observations of events in the Hopi world" (Secakuku 1995:5), by being ritually smothered so that they will convey the people's messages to the spirits. (It is legal for Native Americans to take the birds for certain ritual, ceremonial purposes.)

The rest of the ceremonial year is devoted to nonkatsina dances; the timing of these dances varies from village to village, and not all dances are held in every village, for villages are ceremonially, as well as politically, autonomous. Social dances, so called because both men and unmarried women from the villages participate, dancing in pairs of couples, may be held at almost any time during the year. In August the Snake-Antelope Ceremony is held every other year, alternating with the Flute Ceremony; these ceremonies are held to bring the last summer rains, to ensure the maturity of the corn before the harvest, and to prepare the fields for the next planting season. During the last part of August and the first part of September dances that honor other tribes are held as public expressions of gratitude for the abundance of the harvest and for life's blessings in general. In September the girls who have completed their initiation into the Maraw Society dance to consecrate the harvest season. October brings more ceremonies by women's societies, including the Lakon Ceremony (known as Basket Dances) and the O'waqölt Ceremony, both of which focus on healthy impregnation and maternal ideals. Men's societies hold their dances in November.

Shamans

In early times, a now extinct society of Hopi curers used their special abilities to heal others. In the more recent past, some shamans specialized in secular treatment, while others had supernatural abilities. Secular shamans usually passed on their complex body of knowledge—massage, the setting of broken bones, and the use of plants—to their sisters' sons. Their extensive knowledge of the pharmacopoeia of plants around them included which kind of aster could be boiled in water and drunk by women who wished to prolong the period of time after childbirth before conception was possible; bear root as a remedy for a sore throat; and Hopi tea to soothe an upset stomach (Page and Page 1982:108).

Shamans who performed supernatural cures used their powers, usually while in a trance state, to heal those who had been the object of witchcraft. Witches—known as "two hearts" in reference to their own heart and that of the animal whose shape they assumed in order to pursue their evil activities at night—were believed either to voluntarily practice sorcery or to have been unknowingly inducted into a society of witches as a child.

Archaeologists and Hopi Work Together

The collaboration of the Hopi Tribe and archaeologists in contemporary research is enabling the Hopi to protect the remains of their past and archaeologists to better understand their findings. As construction projects and land development continue to destroy many ancestral Hopi sites, Hopi interpretation in the documentation of archaeological sites can help offset some of these losses. The Hopi tribe, which supports this partnership out of respect for its ancestors and a desire to know more about its past, feels that in order to perform a thorough archaeological investigation and interpretation, it is essential to conduct research with the living descendants of the people who left behind these sites. The Hopi do not want to constrain archaeological interpretations unfairly by superimposing their sacred knowledge on the archaeological record, but they do want to be treated as colleagues whose knowledge is regarded with the same respect archaeologists afford each other.

Hopi Leigh Jenkins, the director of the Hopi Tribe's Cultural Preservation Office; Kurt Dongoske, the Hopi tribal archaeologist; and T. J. Ferguson, a director of Southwest programs for the Institute of the North American West in Tucson (Dongoske et al. 1993:24–31), all explored the insights gleaned from the collaboration between the Hopi and archaeologists. When the Hopi emerged into the present world (Fourth World) from the Sipapuni (a limestone cone in the gorge of the Little Colorado River near the Grand Canyon) they encountered Maasaw. They made a spiritual pact with this deity to be stewards of the earth, which included placing their footprints throughout their migrations. Their spiritual journeys led the Hopi through the Southwest and beyond, as they remained in each place for a period of time until their priests received signs that it was time to continue onward, until eventually they arrived at the Hopi Mesas, their rightful place. The placing of Hopi "footprints"—physical evidence such as potsherds—showed that they had vested the area with their stewardship, fulfilling part of their pact with Maasaw. The Hopi tended the earth by establishing ritual springs, sacred trails, shrines, and petroglyphs. They hold that the physical evidence in archaeological sites verifies their clan histories and religious beliefs, and they believe that these sites are not abandoned but are still the resting place of their ancestors, who continue to maintain a spiritual guardianship over these places.

The Hopi oral histories of the clans of Water, Snake, Tobacco, Reed, Greasewood, Sun, Sand, Badger, and Corn hold that these clans once resided in the Tonto Basin of central Arizona. This made an excavation project undertaken by Arizona State University of special significance to the Hopi. The Hopi recognized a rock pile whose features had baffled archaeologists as a Hopi shrine. Hopi elders also explained the esoteric function of ritual artifacts, such as the clan symbols on pottery and rock art identified by a member of the Water Clan.

Jenkins, Dongoske, and Ferguson (Jenkins et al. 1996) explained that reduced access to Hopi ancestral sites and sacred places has become a major threat to the survival of Hopi religion. When the Hopi, in their covenant with Maasaw, took the role of being proper stewards of the earth, they accepted the responsibility of maintaining the irreplaceable life essence of each shrine and sacred place through ceremonies, pilgrimages, and rituals. These rituals must be carried out at specific springs, mountain peaks, and other sacred sites because, unlike Christianity, Hopi religion is place-dependent. However, Hopi access to these sites has become increasingly problematic. In some cases, the Navajo have prevented the Hopi from using identified Hopi sites that are on land awarded to the Navajo but to which the Hopi have access and use through Public Law 93–531. In 1992 at Cliff Spring, Arizona, a group of about forty Navajo confronted a Hopi delegation who were placing *pahos*, prayer feathers, and *piki* (paperlike ceremonial food made from cornmeal) at the spring. Not only did the Navajo remove these sacred articles and throw them down at the feet of the Hopi katsina priest, but they also physically assaulted several Hopi. Similar incidents, as well as vandalism with spray paint, have occurred at sacred locations.

Today the Hopi must choose between releasing information to protect sacred sites and safeguarding their locations with secrecy because non-Hopi have desecrated or vandalized Hopi shrines. The designation of a shrine as important to the maintenance and transmission of Hopi culture under the National Historic Preservation Act is a mixed blessing: although it makes specific sites off-limits to all non-Hopi, it also disseminates this information into the public domain, divulging their locations.

More Recent History

By the 1940s the most serious problems facing the roughly 4,000 Hopi who lived on their reservation were Navajo encroachment on their land base and increasing land erosion caused by a dry climatic phase and overgrazing by Hopi livestock. The Stock Reduction Program of 1944 proved to be beneficial for the Hopi because, in bringing about a shift from sheep to cattle and a reduction in the number of horses on the reservation, it helped preserve more grass, enabling more Hopi to herd for profit. (Cattle, unlike sheep, do not eat plant roots.)

The people of Oraibi experienced the most profound changes because of their tremendous readjustment to the 1906 split. With some clans no longer represented, they were unable to hold a full ceremonial cycle. Men could no longer center their lives on the kiva, and they took on wage work because Oraibi's available farmland was severely limited. When Titiev (1944, 1972) documented the changes in Hopi life at Oraibi between 1932 and 1966, he found that after paved highways linked Black Mesa with cities in Arizona and New Mexico, the Hopi bought automobiles and trucks, so that men could commute either on a daily or weekly basis to cities, returning home on weekends to farm clan lands. Roads not only enabled the Hopi to sell surplus crops and purchase food in cities, but also allowed tourists to flock to the Hopi mesas, especially for the more elaborate ceremonies. The people of Oraibi began to build larger houses, replacing stone and adobe with cinder blocks and cement and filling their new homes with furniture and appliances from the cities. Although clans continued to own the houses, women no longer shared households with their mothers after their Anglo civil or religious weddings; however, brides continued to receive traditional wedding garments.

Contemporary Issues

Tribal administration, the BIA, and construction companies employ many Hopi on the reservation. In 1993 roughly 400 Hopi worked for Peabody Coal Company (Trimble 1993:110), and about $500,000 a year in royalties was coming in from Peabody, money that went into tribal administration of social services and federally funded programs, such as job training. Roughly 1,000 Hopi live off the reservation, generally working in Arizona cities and returning for ceremonies. Some Hopi work as nurses and technicians in the Indian Health Service hospital in Keams Canyon, in two clinics on Second Mesa, or in the hospital in Tuba City. (Both hospitals serve Navajo as well as Hopi.) There is also a Hopi Community Services facility in which Hopi personnel provide special education and care for the mentally and physically handicapped. Indian Health Service doctors often rely on Hopi healers, especially when a case calls for certain kinds of psychosomatic healing in addition to biomedical treatment. As Hopi medicine woman and healer Theodora Sockyma said, "If the doctors can't find anything wrong, it usually has something to do with our culture . . . sickness of the mind, worriness. . . . They need someone to sit down to talk to them. You don't just give them medicine, you have to find out what it's all about" (ibid., 114–15).

Today the Hopi Reservation has six elementary schools, one junior high school, and one high school. Hopi parents campaigned for years for a high school that would allow their children to live at home, and in 1986 Hopi High School opened its doors. Located between Second and Third Mesas, it is a federally funded BIA school with a Hopi school board.

Kykotsmovi is the seat of tribal government. The Tribal Council consists of a chairman, vice chairman, and fifteen council members. The Hopi Reservation is unusual because for many years the superintendent of the reservation was of the same tribe as the people whose affairs he administered: Alph Secakuku, now retired. Hopi Ivan Sidney, who is also retired now, was responsible for the strength of the Hopi police force. During the late 1970s Sidney built up the Hopi police force into a group of well-organized and well-trained men who could fill out reports of arrests in a way that would hold up in court and who used SWAT techniques to scale cliffs at night, necessary skills in the apprehension of pothunters. In 1977 the Hopi police had the best conviction record of any Indian police force in the country (Page and Page 1982:101)—no easy task, for they had to enforce federal, state, county, and Hopi laws. Often seen at Hopi ceremonies, policemen are given time off to attend the ceremonies of their own villages; at such times, they take their orders from the leader of the ceremony that is taking place.

Hopi villages, as well as private individuals, own businesses such as dry goods, convenience, and grocery stores. When the Tribal Council distributed $500,000 to each village, some decided to establish village-owned businesses. The Hopi Cultural Center museum complex, motel, and restaurant, which opened in 1970 at Second Mesa, is owned by the tribe. Some of the individually owned businesses include the Second Mesa store, which sells groceries, hardware, and livestock feed; several gas stations and auto repair shops; and trading posts, including Ferrell Secakuku's and Joseph and Janice Days's Tsakurshovi, both on Second Mesa. Many Hopi have been highly successful in the arts. Generally, they supplement their income with some sort of wage job from waitressing, bussing tables, or handy work and devote their creative energy to jewelry-making, painting, basketry, pottery-making, or the carving of kachina dolls for collectors and tourists.

Black Mesa Coal Mining

In 1969 the Hopi signed an agreement with Peabody Coal Company to strip-mine coal on Black Mesa, and although most Hopi support the mine, some have opposed the contract as a violation of Mother Earth. Prehistorically the Hopi themselves practiced both strip-mining and underground mining. However, because of its association with the domain of the dead, mining was believed to pollute one's spirit and therefore necessitated some form of ritual cleansing before reentering the villages. This association of mining and death took precedence over the utility of the substance being mined. Don Talayesva pointed out that a war chief always went on the salt pilgrimage to protect the group during their journey in the land of the dead; those who dug for sacred clay had to keep their hearts and minds full of good thoughts and intentions to ward off death (Simmons 1942:232–46).

Mining and generating plants have undesired side effects, such as the smog from generating plants, which has begun to hamper accurate observations of the sunrise for ceremonial purposes. Mining has also disturbed some eagle nesting sites—eagles and their feathers play a major role in Hopi ceremonial life—resulting in the abandonment of some sites (Page and Page 1982:192–93). A major Hopi concern is Peabody's use of precious groundwater instead of a railroad to transport coal: to send coal through a 300-mile pipeline, the coal must be mixed into a slurry; this uses 3.9 million gallons of water a day (Trimble 1993:94). The water table at Hopi has already dropped 70 feet as a result of Peabody pumping water from aquifers thousands of feet below the earth's surface, and Hopi farmers believe that Peabody's deep wells are drying up their springs and eliminating runoff from their waters. Former tribal chairman Victor Masayesva summed up the feelings of many Hopi: "It just seems foolish to be using water as a transportation method from a desert climate where you have an average rainfall of 6–7 inches" (ibid., 94–95).

The coal-mining contracts the Hopi have been forced to accept also raise serious questions about Indian sovereignty because the federal government forced the Hopi to accept a contract that generates royalties far below market price (Clemmer n.d. [1970]). When the Hopi tried to enact a severance fee on Black Mesa coal to benefit future generations of Hopi, the assistant secretary of the interior for Indian affairs vetoed the plan (*Qua'Töqti*, 10 February 1983:2; 6 January 1984:2).

Hopi at the Beginning of the Twenty-First Century

Conditions have changed considerably since anthropologist John Loftin (1991:98) recorded that Shongopavi was "the only village that conducts almost all major ceremonies in long form, but even there parts of the Butterfly Dance had to be taught in English for the first time in 1981." Emory Sekaquaptewa (1999) reports that today the kivas are crowded with young people eager to participate:

> The young people are learning the meanings, and, today, they have a better understanding of the message that comes through the symbolism and the words of the songs, especially the admonitions. They're listening to it and understanding it in reference to the life of the Hopi people.
>
> Traditions having to do with historical and cultural values through legends and forms of language are still in place. Cultural institutions related to birth, naming, initiations, and marriages are still actively practiced as well as activities of exchange between families and clans. And the ceremonies for men and women.
>
> But the big difference today is that all of this is being overwhelmed by younger Hopi people. They're listening to the message of the katsina songs in relation to the life of the Hopi people without any thought to politics. Before, they left a lot of the interpretation of the Hopi way of life to outsiders. Now they're figuring it out for themselves. Some of the Traditionalists used to use the words in Hopi teachings in political ways, interpreting them to outsiders to bring attention to themselves. Now that the ones who were known as Traditionalists are dying off, individual Hopis are looking inside themselves for direction instead of being led by other people and giving up their power. It's much healthier.
>
> The other big difference is [that] the Tribal Council's annual budget appropriation includes substantial amounts paid to each village to spend as the villages see fit, so the Tribal Council and the villages are working together. One village used the money to put in drip irrigation in their fields, while other villages have used their payments to restore kivas and historic buildings, and still other villages have developed businesses such as convenience stores. Villages have established business councils to decide how they want to spend the money.

The vitality of Hopi culture and life, evident in the participation of so many young people and in the effective partnership between the Tribal Council and Hopi villages, echoes the description given by the late Abbott Sekaquaptewa, a respected tribal chairman, of the Hopi response to the non-Hopi world: "Throughout the centuries, Hopi have taken on new things and new ways and adjusted them to Hopi society and made them better. This will continue. We want to supplement Hopi life with the white world's new things and ways, but in our own time and in our own way" (Page and Page 1982:37).

The Hopi-Navajo Land Dispute

When the rectangular Hopi Reservation—50 x 75 miles, smaller than Rhode Island—was created by executive order in 1882 inside the far vaster Navajo reservation—nearly the size of New England—the order did not specify that the land was for exclusive Hopi use. A shortage of land, opposing lifestyles (agricultural versus herding), and differing world views made conflict inevitable. As agriculturists, the Hopi lived in settled towns, farmed outlying fields, and maintained shrines in distant areas. Furthermore, the Hopi population increased slowly, while Navajo population soared: since the arrival of Anglo-Americans, the Hopi population has grown from 2,000 to 10,000, while the Navajo population has soared from 12,000 to over 200,000. The Hopi culture and economy are in relative balance with the land, and Hopi land remains remarkably productive. In contrast, uncontrolled overgrazing by the Navajos' sheep has led to such deterioration in the quality of Navajo land that in 1981 the President's Council on Environmental Quality named the Navajo Reservation as one of the three worst examples of desertification in the United States. As pastoralists, the Navajo expanded rapidly, both geographically and in population; they considered any Hopi land that was not permanently occupied to be unused and thus available. Journalist Catherine Feher-Elston compared the Navajo view of land acquisition and settlement to the Anglo view: "If land appears empty, settle on it and wait to see what happens. Hopis view this as aggressive exploitation; Navajos and Americans [Anglos] view it as homesteading" (Trimble 1993:96).

Hopi elders refer to Hopi land as a "shrine" that extends to the Grand Canyon, San Francisco Peaks, the northern reaches of Black Mesa, Zuni Salt Lake, and south of Route 66. In the 1882 executive order, the federal government set aside only about 2.6 million acres, excluding the Hopi village of Moenkopi. In the 1930s 1.8 million acres of the total 2.6 million acres became a Joint Use Area (JUA) to be shared by the Navajo and the Hopi. Even after a 1962 federal court ruling that this area was to be shared, the Navajo continued to control the JUA. A Hopi man expressed an opinion shared by many of his people: "Suppose someone all of a sudden decides to camp in your backyard, and stays there. You try and get him to leave but he won't. Finally you get a judge to deal with the matter, and the judge says that since he was in your backyard for so long he can have half of it to live on" (Page and Page 1982:210).

This complicated legal situation involves many parties, including both the Hopi and Navajo tribal councils, federal mediators, and federal courts. A congressional act in 1975 divided the surface area of the JUA into exclusive Hopi and Navajo areas. (The subsurface rights are to be shared, which means that proceeds from mineral deposits found anywhere in the JUA are to be shared equally by the Navajo and the Hopi.) By 1986 non-Hopi living in the Hopi area were expected to move into the Navajo area and vice versa. Once the particulars had been agreed to by all parties, Congress passed legislation for appropriations to compensate the Navajo who were willing to move, as well as funds for the Navajo tribe to find replacement acreage (public lands purchased by the Navajo Nation). Most Navajos took advantage of the money, using it to purchase homes. However, a small group of Navajos around Big Mountain, an area the courts had designated as Hopi land, were persuaded by militant Anglos to refuse to leave. Trying to protect what they perceive as Indian rights, the Anglos have generated considerable publicity.

Stealing the Sacred

The theft of sacred objects and practices has become a direct threat to the continuation of Hopi religion and in turn to the Hopi themselves, because their survival as a people is so closely linked to the performance of their ceremonies. According to some estimates (Bordewich 1996:188), pothunters have stolen as many as two-thirds of Hopi sacred articles. Since the late 1800s the Hopi have been objecting to the appropriation of their sacred objects and practices by Anglos. Until recently the Smokis, a secret group of Anglo businessmen, performed "Snake Dances" every August in Prescott, Arizona. When Hopi picketed the sacrilegious dances, the Smokis discontinued their annual tradition.

Unfortunately, not all threats to Hopi religious practices are so easily resolved, for many "New Agers" see the Hopi and other Indians as the last hope for "salvaging our natural environment and ennobling our souls" (Bordewich 1996:335). Hopi philosophy is especially appealing, with its timeless prophecies, its "environmental ethos," and its ideals of humility, faith, diligence, and perseverance that will bring about the ultimate triumph of good over evil. The alliance of the late Thomas Banyacya with environmentalists and his international activities further publicized Hopi culture.

The Hopi have been plagued by New Agers, attracted by their spiritual philosophy and way of life. Unfortunately, some of these outsiders have left crystals and other offerings at Hopi shrines. Despite their sincerity, these outsiders fail to understand that their appropriation of these shrines is a desecration that mocks the Hopi religion. When an Anglo woman tried to place a plastic *paho* (prayer stick offering) into a sacred shrine in a Hopi village, the Hopi considered her actions to be a violation that endangered the welfare of Hopi and Anglo alike. They traced her actions to Thomas Mails's book *Secret Native American Pathways* (1988), which includes step-by-step instructions for making imitation *pahos* and other sacred articles. *Pahos* are a form of prayer made visible and are made only by male religious society members. (When Hopi leaders approached Mails about his book, he responded with threats of organizing a boycott against Hopi arts and crafts.)

In response to a Marvel comic book in which criminals put on costumes to look like ogres—there is no such thing as an "ogre katsina" (Sekaquaptewa 1999)—some villages decided to close their dances to outsiders. The Hopi found this intrusion into their culture to be especially offensive because comic books, targeted at children, are bought by many Hopi children. Certain religious practices are not revealed to uninitiated children because knowledge is considered to be a matter of privilege, which comes with age and maturation. Whether intentionally or unintentionally, when outsiders violate these restrictions, the Hopi belief system is held up to ridicule.

One of the most dramatic recent incidents involved the theft of some of the most sacred Hopi religious articles, the *taalawtumsi* which are essential to the performance of the Astotokya, the initiation of young men into adulthood. In 1978 two Anglo pothunters stole the four *taalawtumsi* from a cave, and for the fifteen years while this theft went unsolved, there could essentially be no more new Hopi. When the Hopi finally became desperate enough to consult the FBI and the BIA, they discovered that U.S. law considered the *taalawtumsi* in the same category as a stolen television set. FBI agents soon learned that the Hopi considered the theft to be a homicide: Steve Lund, an FBI agent on the case, said, "I needed to understand (the idols) hurt, they feel, they share human emotions. . . . It was like a kidnapping, or murder" (*Arizona Republic,* 14 March 1993:A-16).

No one was ever prosecuted, because the black market buyer, who paid $1,600 for them, only kept the *taalawtumsi* for a month before he destroyed them. Once he heard about the search, fear that he would be caught led him to chop them into pieces and burn them in a woodstove. Yet the perpetrators suffered for their crime. Hopi Leigh Jenkins said, "Hopi law is simple: Do a wrong against someone, and you will eventually pay for it" (*Arizona Republic,* 14 March 1993:A-17). The Hopi were not surprised when those responsible suffered violent consequences: one man was seriously injured on his motorcycle and was arrested on federal pothunting charges; another said his health began to fail a few months after he stole the *taalawtumsi,* and he had subsequently served three prison terms on drug and burglary charges since the theft; a third man was sentenced to prison three times after the incident for theft, illegal Indian-site excavation, and endangerment, and was killed in a traffic accident; the fourth man suffered a heart attack; and the fifth man died by driving off a road in New Mexico. Although other explanations for these events are possible, the Hopi believe the perpetrators brought illness and violence upon themselves through their crime.

Three of the men traveled to apologize formally to the Hopi of Shungopavi, the village on Second Mesa to which the *taalawtumsi* belonged, thus helping the Hopi "achieve spiritual reconciliation." In November 1992, after much anguished discussion, the Hopi decided to resume the initiations despite the absence of three of the four *taalawtumsi*. (In their flight the thieves had dropped one of the sacred figures, which was then recovered.) The priests recognized that if the ceremony were delayed any longer, knowledge of how to conduct it might be lost forever, because the key priest was already ninety-five years old. Shungopavi village administrator Ronald Wadsworth explained, "In that ceremony you have the whole purpose of being Hopi given to you. . . . It was a very joyous occasion. . . . Women who prepared food for us cried because they were happy for their sons."

References and Further Reading

Volume 9 of the Smithsonian's *Handbook of North American Indians* (1979) contains chapters about various aspects of Hopi culture. An outstanding film is *Hopi Songs of the Fourth World* by Pat Ferrero (1984; New Day Films, 22 Riverview Dr., Wayne, N.J.). Other fine films about Hopi culture include *Hopi: Corn Is Life; Hopi Indian Arts and Crafts; Hopi Prophecy;* and *The Hopi Way. The Chaco Legacy,* about the Hopi's Pueblo ancestors, the Anasazi, makes comparisons to the modern Hopi. Among sources that speak from the Hopi perspective are the newspapers *Hopi Tutuveni, Qua'Töqti: The Eagle's Call,* and *Navajo-Hopi Observer.*

Adair, John. 1944. *The Navajo and Pueblo Silversmiths.* University of Oklahoma Press, Norman.

Bandelier, Adolph. 1890. *The Delight Makers.* Dodd, Mead, New York.

Beaglehole, Ernest, and Pearl Beaglehole. 1935. *Hopi of Second Mesa.* American Anthropological Association Memoir 44.

Bordewich, Fergus. 1996. *Killing the White Man's Indian.* Doubleday, New York.

Brew, John. 1946. *Archaeology of Alkali Ridge, Southeastern Utah, with a Review of the Prehistory of the Mesa Verde Division of the San Juan and Some Observations on Archaeological Systematics.* Papers of the Peabody Museum of American Archaeology and Ethnology, Harvard University, 21. Cambridge, Mass.

Brinkley-Rogers, Paul, and Richard Robertson. 1993. "The Curse of the Taalawtumsi: Stealing the Hopi Soul." *Arizona Republic,* 14 March:A16–17.

Bunzel, Ruth. 1972 [1929]. *The Pueblo Potter.* Dover Publications, New York.

Clemmer, Richard. n.d. [1970]. "Economic Development vs. Aboriginal Land Use: An Attempt to Predict Culture Change on an Indian Reservation in Arizona." Unpublished manuscript.

———. 1978. *Continuities of Hopi Culture Change.* Acoma Books, Ramona, Calif.

———. 1994. "The Hopi Traditionalist Movement." *American Indian Culture and Research Journal* 18, no. 3:125–66.

*———. 1995. *Roads in the Sky: Hopi Culture and History in a Century of Change*. Westview Press, Boulder, Colo. [An anthropologist provides an excellent account of changing Hopi life.]

Colton, Harold. 1959. *Hopi Kachina Dolls*. University of New Mexico Press, Albuquerque.

Colton, Mary Russell. 1938. "The Arts and Crafts of the Hopi Indians." *Museum Notes, Museum of Northern Arizona* 11:3–24.

———. 1939. "Hopi Silversmithing: Its Background and Future." *Plateau* 12, no. 1:1–7.

Courlander, Harold. 1971. *The Fourth World of the Hopi*. University of New Mexico Press, Albuquerque.

Cushing, Frank. 1923. "Origin Myth from Oraibi." *Journal of American Folklore* 36:163–70.

Dobyns, Henry, and Robert Euler. 1971. *The Hopi People*. Indian Tribal Series, Phoenix.

Dockstader, Frederick. 1954. *The Kachina and the White Man: A Study of the Influences of White Culture on the Hopi Kachina Cult*. Cranbrook Institute of Science Bulletin 35. Bloomfield Hills, Mich.

Dongoske, Kurt, Leigh Jenkins, and T. J. Ferguson. 1993. "Understanding the Past through Hopi Oral Tradition." *Native Peoples Magazine* 6, no. 2:24–31.

*Dozier, Edward. 1966. *Hano: A Tewa Indian Community in Arizona*. Holt, Rinehart, and Winston, New York. [A detailed account of Hano culture and history by an anthropologist from Santa Clara Pueblo.]

———. 1970. *The Pueblo Indians of North America*. Holt, Rinehart, and Winston, New York.

Eggan, Fred. 1950. *Social Organization of the Western Pueblos*. University of Chicago Press, Chicago.

Evers, Larry. 1979. *Natwanaiwaia: A Hopi Philosophical Statement*. Videotape. Tucson. [With George Nasoftie.]

Fewkes, Jesse. 1899. "Tusayan Migration Traditions." In *Smithsonian Institution, Bureau of American Ethnology, 19th Annual Report for 1897–98, pt. 2*, pp. 573–633. Government Printing Office, Washington, D.C.

*Folb, Edith, Ed. 1986. *Hopi: Songs of the Fourth World: A Resource Handbook*. Ferrero Films, San Francisco. [Articles that amplify aspects of the film; see headnote, above.]

Forde, C. Daryll. 1931. "Hopi Agriculture and Land Ownership." *Journal of the Royal Anthropological Institute of Great Britain and Ireland* 61:357–405.

———. 1934. *Habitat, Economy and Society: A Geographical Introduction to Ethnology*. Methuen, London.

Forrest, Earle. 1961. *The Snake Dance of the Hopi Indians*. Westernlore Press, Los Angeles.

Geertz, Armin. 1982. "The Sa'lakwmanawyat Sacred Puppet Ceremonial among the Hopi Indians of Arizona: A Preliminary Investigation." *Anthropos* 77:163–90.

Hack, John. 1942. *The Changing Physical Environment of the Hopi Indians of Arizona*. Peabody Museum, Cambridge, Mass.

———. 1942. *Prehistoric Coal Mining in the Jeddito Valley, Arizona.* Peabody Museum, Cambridge, Mass.

Hermenquaftewa, Andrew. 1971. "The Hopi Way of Life Is the Way of Peace." In *Red Power: The American Indians' Fight for Freedom,* pp. 53–63, ed. Alvin Josephy. American Heritage Press, New York.

Hieb, Louis. 1994. "Hopi." In *Native America in the Twentieth Century: An Encyclopedia.* pp. 240–43, ed. Mary Davis. Garland Publishing, New York.

Hodge, Frederick, et al. 1922. "Contributions to Hopi History." *American Anthropologist* 24:253–98.

James, Harry. 1994. *Pages from Hopi History.* University of Arizona Press, Tucson.

Jenkins, Leigh, Kurt Dongoske, and T. J. Ferguson. 1996. "Managing Hopi Sacred Sites to Protect Religious Freedom." *Cultural Survival Quarterly* (winter):36–39.

Kabotie, Fred, and Bill Belknap. 1977. *Fred Kabotie: Hopi Indian Artist.* Museum of Northern Arizona Press, Flagstaff.

Kavena, Juanita. 1980. *Hopi Cookery.* University of Arizona Press, Tucson.

Kealiinohomoku, Joanne. 1980. "The Drama of the Hopi Ogres." In *Southwestern Indian Ritual Drama.* pp. 37–70, ed. C. Frisbie. School of American Research, Santa Fe.

———. 1989. "The Hopi Katsina Dance Event 'Doings'." In *Seasons of the Kachina.* pp. 51–63, ed. L. Bean. Ballena Press Anthropological Papers 34. Ballena Press and California State University, Hayward.

*Laird, David. 1977. *Hopi Bibliography.* University of Arizona Press, Tucson. [Almost 3,000 entries; most comprehensive annotated Hopi bibliography.]

*Loftin, John. 1991. *Religion and Hopi Life.* Indiana University Press, Bloomington. [An account of contemporary Hopi religion, based on field research by a religious scholar.]

*Lomatewama, Ramson. 1992. "I Sing When I Carve." *Native Peoples Magazine* 6, no.1:20–24. [A Hopi kachina maker and public speaker writes eloquently about what the creation of kachinas means to him.]

Malotki, Ekkehart. 1978. *Hopi-tutuwutsi/Hopi Tales.* Sun Tracks, University of Arizona Press, Tucson.

Masayesva, Vernon. 1991. "Epilogue." In *Handbook of American Indian Religious Freedom,* pp. 134–36, ed. Christopher Vecsey. Crossroad, New York.

———. 1994. "The Problem of American Indian Religious Freedom: A Hopi Perspective." *American Indian Religions* 1:93–96.

Nagata, Shuichi. 1970. *Modern Transformations of Moenkopi Pueblo.* University of Illinois Press, Champaign-Urbana.

Nequatewa, Edmund. 1936. *Truth of a Hopi.* Museum of Northern Arizona, Flagstaff.

O'Kane, Walter. 1950. *Sun in the Sky.* University of Oklahoma Press, Norman.

Oswalt, Wendell H., and Sharlotte Neely. 1999. "The Hopi: Farmers of the Desert." In *This Land*

Was Theirs: A Study of Native Americans, pp. 292–328. 6th ed. Mayfield Publishing, Mountain View, Calif.

*Page, Suzanne, and Jake Page. 1982. *Hopi*. Abrams, New York. [This well-written and beautifully photographed book presents contemporary life at Hopi.]

*Qöyawayma, Polingaysi. 1964. *No Turning Back: A True Account of a Hopi Girl's Struggle to Bridge the Gap between the World of Her People and the World of the White Man*. University of New Mexico Press, Albuquerque. [A classic book telling how a Hopi woman adjusts to Anglo and Hopi lifestyles.]

Reid, Jefferson, and Stephanie Whittlesey. 1997. "The Anasazi." In *The Archaeology of Ancient Arizona*, pp. 166–204. University of Arizona Press, Tucson.

Rushforth, Scott, and Steadman Upham. 1992. *A Hopi Social History*. University of Texas Press, Austin.

Schlegel, Alice. 1977. "Male and Female in Hopi Thought and Action." In *Sexual Stratification: A Cultural View*, pp. 245–69, ed. A. Schlegel. Columbia University Press, New York.

Secakuku, Alph. 1995. *Following the Sun and Moon: Hopi Kachina Tradition*. Northland Press, Flagstaff, Ariz.

Secakuku, Ferrell. 1993. "The Hopi View of Wilderness." *Federal Archaeology Report* 6, no. 3:9.

Sekaquaptewa, Emory. 1972. "Preserving the Good Things of Hopi Life." In *Plural Society in the Southwest*. pp. 239–60, ed. E. Spicer and R. Thompson. Weatherhead Foundation, Interbook, New York.

*———. 1976. "Hopi Indian Ceremonies." In *Seeing with a Native Eye*. pp. 35–43, ed. W. Capps. Harper and Row, New York. [A Hopi professor and lawyer writes about Hopi ceremonies, based on his personal experience.]

———. 1979. "One More Smile for a Hopi Clown." *Parabola* 4:6–9.

———. 1980. "The Hopi Tricentennial Year and Era." *Qua'Töqti*, 7 August 1980:1, 3.

———. 1994. Personal communication.

———. 1999. Personal communication.

Sekaquaptewa, Helen. 1969. *Me and Mine: The Life Story of Helen Sekaquaptewa*. University of Arizona Press, Tucson.

*Simmons, Leo W. 1942. *Sun Chief: The Autobiography of a Hopi Indian*. Yale University Press, New Haven, Conn. [A Hopi man tells his life history, spanning the early years of Anglo acculturation.]

Smith, Watson. 1952. *Kiva Mural Decorations at Awatovi and Kawaika-a, with a Survey of Other Wall Paintings in the Pueblo Southwest*. Papers of the Peabody Museum of American Archaeology and Ethnology, Harvard University, 37. Cambridge, Mass.

Stephen, Alexander. 1936. *Hopi Journal*. Columbia University Contributions to Anthropology 23 (2 parts). Columbia University Press, New York.

Talayesva, Don. 1942. *Sun Chief: The Autobiography of a Hopi Indian*. Yale University Press, New Haven, Conn.

Tanner, Clara Lee. 1982. *Southwest Indian Craft Arts*. University of Arizona, Tucson.

———. 1989. *Indian Baskets of the Southwest*. University of Arizona Press, Tucson.

Thompson, Laura. 1950. *Culture in Crisis: A Study of the Hopi Indians*. Harper and Brothers, New York.

Thompson, Laura, and Alice Joseph. 1944. *The Hopi Way*. University of Chicago Press, Chicago.

Teiwes, Helga. 1991. *Kachina Dolls: The Art of Hopi Carvers*. University of Arizona Press, Tucson.

Titiev, Mischa. 1944. *Old Oraibi: A Study of the Hopi Indians of Third Mesa*. Papers of the Peabody Museum of American Archaeology and Ethnology, Harvard University 22, no. 1. Cambridge, Mass.

———. 1972. *The Hopi Indians of Old Oraibi: Change and Continuity*. University of Michigan Press, Ann Arbor.

Trimble, Stephen. 1986. *Our Voices, Our Land*. Northland Press, Flagstaff.

———. 1993. *The People*. School of American Research Press, Santa Fe.

Voth, Henry. 1901. *The Oraibi Powamu Ceremony*. Field Columbian Museum, Chicago.

———. 1905. *Oraibi Natal Customs and Ceremonies*. Field Columbian Museum, Chicago.

Wallis, Tom. 1992. "A Bridge across the Centuries." *Native Peoples Magazine* 5, no. 3:46–49.

Wallis, Wilson. 1936. "Folk Tales from Shumopovi, Second Mesa." *Journal of American Folk-Lore* 49:1–68.

Washburn, Dorothy, Ed. 1980. *Hopi Kachina: Spirit of Life*. California Academy of Science and the University of Washington Press, Seattle.

Whiteley, Peter. 1988. *Bacavi: Journey to Reed Springs*. Northland Press, Flagstaff, Ariz.

———. 1988. *Deliberate Acts: Changing Hopi Culture through the Oraibi Split*. University of Arizona Press, Tucson.

Whiting, Alfred. 1950. *Ethnobotany of the Hopi*. Museum of Northern Arizona Bulletin 15.

Whorf, Benjamin. 1950. "An American Indian Model of the Universe." *International Journal of American Linguistics* 16:67–72.

Wright, Barton. 1973. *Kachinas: A Hopi Artist's Documentary*. Northland Press, Flagstaff, Ariz.

———. 1977. *The Complete Guide to Collecting Kachina Dolls*. Northland Press, Flagstaff, Ariz.

Wright, Margaret. 1972. *The History and Hallmarks of Hopi Silversmithing: Hopi Silver*. Northland Press, Flagstaff, Ariz.

Yava, Albert. 1978. *Big Falling Snow: A Tewa-Hopi Indian's Life and Times and the History and Traditions of His People*. University of New Mexico Press, Albuquerque.

Younger, Erin, and Victor Masayesva, Jr. 1983. *Hopi Photographers/Hopi Images*. Sun Tracks and University of Arizona Press, Tucson.

Our Lady of Guadalupe Mission Church, Zuni Pueblo, 1998. Author photograph

Chapter 4

The Zuni

June 1998   The towering Shalako leans forward on improbably tiny feet, dwarf-
ing his companion. Wrapped in an elaborately embroidered ceremonial robe, the armless
Shalako gazes down through great spherical, protruding eyes, clacking his snoutlike, tu-
bular beak over a ruff of glossy black raven feathers. With his tall crest of black-and-white
eagle feathers, framed by turquoise-colored, buffalo-shaped horns, he reaches an impressive 12 feet in height, creating the dignified appearance appropriate for the great courier of
the Rain Gods. Held near the winter solstice, Shalako is the time when the spirits of all the
Zuni who ever lived are believed to be present in the pueblo. The katsinam (*kokko* sing.) of
the Shalako bear offerings to the ancestors, asking for their help in bringing rain, long life,
and peace to the Zuni people.

As the culmination of the entire year's ritual activities, the Shalako was the perfect
point for Alex Seowtewa to begin painting murals of more than two dozen life-sized Zuni
katsinam on the plaster walls of Our Lady of Guadalupe Church, located in the heart of the
Zuni village. Built in 1629 by colonial missionaries as an anchor of Christianity in the New
World, the church was abandoned in 1820 when priests were recalled from New Mexico.
In 1966 the excavation and renovation of the church began, as a result of the combined
efforts of Zuni religious leaders, Franciscan priest Father Niles Kraft, Zuni tribal officials,
and the National Park Service.

During the years of reconstruction, Father Niles asked Alex to design and carve the confessional of the church. The katsinam that had once adorned the walls of the church were those who admonished the Zunis to attend mass and live according to the teachings of the Church, said Alex's father, Charlie. Alex, realizing that Catholicism had become an integral part of Zuni life in the nearly 500 years since its introduction, suggested to Father Niles that he depict katsinam with more benign and universal appeal, which would embody the similarities between Catholicism and Zuni spirituality, and also highlight Zuni practices, thus preserving Zuni beliefs and history for future generations. Alex and his sons, Ken, Gerald, and Edwin, have been working since 1970 on these murals, which they plan to complete in the year 2000.

Preceding the Shalako is Sayatasha, the Longhorn Katsina, who is the leader of the Council of the Gods and warrior priest of the north and winter. Identified by the horn on the right side of their masks, the men of this group must memorize a six-hour-long prayer that tells the creation story and describes the Zuni place in the universe. Thick crow-feather collars obscure all but the tops of the masks of the Salimopiya, protectors of the six dance groups. Carrying yucca whips, they whip and thus purify people who have suffered bad dreams or bad luck; in the left whip, they carry wild and domestic seeds that are being ritually strengthened for spring planting. Preceding these bodyguards is Huu-tutu, younger brother and deputy to the Longhorn, who balances Longhorn's chant of the northward-turning sun of summer with chants of the southward-turning sun of winter.

Closer to the altar is Shulaawitsi, the diminutive Fire God whose black body—the color of the nadir—is painted with yellow, blue, red, white, and multicolor spots, the colors of the remaining directions. His coloring also symbolizes the blackness of the dark underground cave of origin spotted with glowing embers, corn kernels, and the shimmering, multicolored stars of Orion, the Pleiades, and the Big and Little Dippers. Each year at Shalako, Shulaawitsi kindles fire by friction to light the juniper torch he holds in his left hand. After the torch is lit, together with his ceremonial father, he leads the Council of Gods into the village. Carrying a bundle of prayer sticks, Shulaawitsi's godfather precedes him. In vibrant colors with richly detailed masks and clothing, more katsinam dance toward the altar in the glistening snow of the north wall, completing the winter season.

Life-size katsinam dance across the south wall against a vivid backdrop of fresh spring weather, summer rainstorms, and the clarity of autumn. The sky on this side of the church is painted with such startling realism that it becomes a window instead of a wall: the surface on which it is painted seems to melt away, revealing the actual sky outside. High above the dancers, his body as indistinct and ephemeral as the rain clouds from which he emerges, Kolowisi, the plumed water serpent, spews seeds of life-giving corn from his mouth. A highlight of the south wall is a life-size portrait of a now deceased Zuni religious leader who was greatly respected by his people. During his lifetime, he had declined the honor of being portrayed because he had not wanted to be placed above other

Zunis. Alex Seowtewa's painting is so lifelike that everyone in the village recognizes this man; his realistic likeness is especially important to his family, who had no photographs of their ancestor.

Partially obscured by the southwest corner, and closest to the Christian altar at the front of the church, is a painting of the Galaxy Medicine Society altar against the brilliant clarity of a naturalistic sky. A minute male figure perches atop a wooden beam carved with clouds and stars above brilliant, rainbow-hued prayer sticks planted upright in a kiva floor.

To anyone but a Zuni, the tiny spirit riding the wooden beam in an ordinary blue sky seems surrealistic, an unlikely juxtaposition of the imaginary and the real. But the naturalism of the sky and the presence of the figure convey a fundamental premise of Zuni life: the unseen spiritual world exists side by side with the tangible reality of the everyday. The Galaxy altar completes the murals by condensing their central theme: human beings live every moment of their lives in the presence of the spiritual. The murals of Our Lady of Guadalupe Church also exemplify the many contradictions and ambiguities of Zuni culture. They present a contrast between the revelation of secrets and the preservation of culture, and they also embody the paradox of Zuni ritual symbolism within a Catholic church.

The Zuni aesthetic system is said to be composed of the beautiful (*tso'ya*), which is dynamic, multicolored, and multitextured, and the dangerous (*attanni*), which is old and plain, dark, and untouchable (Tedlock 1993:246–65). The beautiful is apparent in the multilayered, brilliantly decorated dress of most katsinam, while the dangerous is evident in the shaggy, matted hair and murderous cannibalism of disciplinary katsinam. Rather than being mutually exclusive, these two principles are often dynamically combined in figures such as the Knifewing, a magnificent and dangerous mythical bird that seduces young women. The Zuni Olla Maidens, a choral group that performs in secular events such as powwows and tribal fairs, exemplify this blending in their dress, for they wear blouses of brightly patterned fabrics and trimmings—the beautiful—beneath their traditional dark and drab mantas—the dangerous—to intensify the effect of the brilliant colors (Young 1991:169–71).

The fluid, permeable nature of the boundaries between categories gives the Zuni the ability to blend Catholicism and Zuni ritual symbolism in their mission church. Instead of contradicting each other, both traditions add a greater depth of understanding, which intensifies spiritual experience. A good example of this can be seen in the Zuni perception of katsinam who, like saints and angels, are not worshiped but are considered to be intermediaries. This kind of dynamic interaction between the old and the new is characteristic of Zuni life today.

Walking the fine line between revealing time-honored secrets held by esoteric medicine societies and preserving essential religious knowledge is extremely difficult, and some aspects of Zuni religion are simply too sacred to be painted. However, Zunis were deeply saddened when a body of religious knowledge died with the religious elder memorialized on the south wall; motivated by such loss, the Seowtewas are dedicated to creating a permanent record for all of Zuni. This commitment to future generations led members of the powerful Milky Way Galaxy Medicine Society to allow the painting of their altar on the south wall. One of the most powerful groups of curers at Zuni, the Galaxy Society is a highly esoteric and secretive society; only those whose lives have been saved by its rituals may be invited to join, if they are of proper character. It may take years to master the rituals and to gather the articles necessary to complete the initiation.

The murals of Our Lady of Guadalupe Church serve as visual prayers for the continuing vitality of Zuni culture. Just as Shulaawitsi rekindles the fire to light his torch each year at Shalako, it is hoped that the dedication that went into these murals will remind people of the importance of knowing their heritage. Only by understanding the Zuni place in the universe can individuals have the strength to know where they are going. Far more than simply a tribute to the Zuni, these paintings are a breath of life-giving energy meant to inspire future generations of Zuni people to keep their traditions alive by remembering the sacredness of life and the continuing presence of the spirits of the ancestors.

The Repatriation of the Ahayuda (The Zuni War Gods)

Vitally important to the spiritual well-being of the Zuni people, the Twin War Gods not only protect Zuni Pueblo and its way of life but also ensure the prosperity and safety of the whole world. Zuni Charles Hustito, who makes the Younger Brother War God for the Bear Clan, described them as "very sacred religious beings, with great powers. They are 'mischievous,' and unless their powers are controlled through prayers and instructions, they can cause destruction through floods, rains, earthquakes, tornadoes, and other natural means" (1991:2:12). This is why those who make them restrain the War Gods' actions with prayers before turning them over to the Bow Priests who place them in the shrines. At this point, the War Gods become communal property, and any Zuni may approach them to ask for blessings. They are intended to remain at the shrine where they are placed so that they can be allowed to disintegrate through natural exposure.

In 1978 Hustito and other Zuni religious leaders began an effort to recover all the Ahayuda that had been removed from their shrines. Once returned, the War Gods are placed in a special shrine building, open to the sky and protected from theft and designed so that all Zuni can come and pray to them. Many Zuni do this, including athletes and hunters, who say prayers and leave sacred prayer meal (Hustito 1991:2:12).

When Congress passed the Native American Graves Protection and Repatriation Act in 1990, Zuni efforts to recover their stolen War Gods provided an important model for tribes and museums in the successful repatriation of sacred artifacts. The tribe approached the issue with respect for the concerns of museums and collectors, and a genuine interest in documenting the history of the Ahayuda and their role in Zuni culture and society. Drawing upon the professional expertise of the Institute of the North American West and the Zuni Archaeology Program, Zuni leaders persuaded museums and private collectors to return the War Gods for humanitarian reasons. The Museum of New Mexico was also instrumental in arranging the transfer of many War Gods. The Office of the Field Solicitor, Department of the Interior, and the Department of Justice provided the necessary legal assistance so that the Zuni tribe was able to anticipate and fully answer all the questions posed by museums. Working together, the Zuni tribe and these professionals were able to anticipate the repatriation of all sixty-five Ahayuda known to be in the possession of museums and collectors by 1991 (ibid.).

Origins

Before the beginning, only Awonawilona, the Supreme Being, existed in the dark and desolate void of endless space. Pondering this emptiness, Awonawilona projected his thoughts outward through the mists of increase to shape himself into the person and form of the Sun. With his appearance as the Sun, the spaces brightened with light, and the great mist clouds fell and grew to become a system of great, interconnected waters that embraced the entire world. Impregnating the great waters, the Sun Father created Earth Mother and the all-covering Sky Father, which lay close together upon the Great Waters.

In the fourfold womb of the world, the Earth and Sky conceived all the beings of the earth. These unfinished beings crawled like reptiles over one another in the filth and darkness of the first world, the Place of First Formation. Concerned at these appalling conditions, the Sun Father impregnated a bubble capped with foam floating on the surface of the Great Waters. Nurtured by Earth Mother's gentle warmth and soft rain, the cap of foam grew until twin boys were brought forth, the Beloved Twins. Sun Father imparted to them much of his sacred knowledge and devices to assist them in performing their duties, including a cap patterned after the original cap of foam. He armed his sons with great cloud bows and flint-tipped arrows, and to protect them, he gave each a fog-making shield of netting spun from floating clouds and wind-driven spray that would both hide and defend them.

When the Sun Father gave his sons dominion over all humans and creatures, they descended into the sooty netherworld to help these unfortunate beings. A great ladder enabled men and other beings ascend to the second world, the Moss World. Those who did not succeed fell back into the darkness to become demons, who even now escape from the depths when the earth quivers and cracks. Although the Moss World was still as dark as storm-filled night, this world was larger than the previous world, which enabled the beings to increase without crawling upon one another. However, soon they filled up the Moss World until they clamored for more room.

The Beloved Twins again made the Great Ladder grow upward so that the beings could reach the third world, the World of Mud, a cave-world filled with the light of a clear and starry night. But soon even this more expansive land became overcrowded, and once more the Twins had to guide the ever-increasing hordes upward. The fourth and last cave-world, the Wing World, had light as bright as the gray dawn of morning that flares across the sky.

Finally, the Twins led the beings into the great upper world of the Sun, the Daylight World, through a water-filled opening far to the northwest. This opening drained and then quickly refilled itself so that the humans and creatures could emerge. The people and animals resembled each other, for humans had slime-covered bodies with cold and scaly skins and eyes that bulged and blinked constantly like those of the owl, as well as tails that grew longer with age. On webbed hands and feet, they crouched and crawled like lizards and toads. Thus it was not surprising that in this time "when the earth was soft," animals and humans could exchange form.

As it was with human beings, so it was with the world, for it was also young, soft, and unstable, and the people sank into the dank, marshlike earth with silent footsteps. But the world was far from silent and still, for earthquakes shook the ground, and the horrible monsters of the Underworld preyed upon the weak; war and wretchedness were everywhere. The twin children of the Sun led the people eastward, telling them to seek the light under the pathway of the Sun, which would lead them to the middle of the world where all would be stable and they could rest in peace.

The Twins, in counsel with the Sun Father, decided to bake and harden the earth. Hurling their thunderbolts at the land, the Twins made the mountains reel and crack open with a deafening cacophony. With their lightning arrows, they blasted the monsters until the blood gushed forth. After some time, a heavy rain began to fall, quenching fires that had broken out and washing the face of the world. The blood of the monsters hardened, eventually blackening into the dark rocks we see today.

Sheltered beneath the cloud shields of the Twins, the people survived, and after the Twins had hardened the soft new world, the people resumed their journey on an earth now solid and transformed beneath their feet. Their search for the mid-most spot among all the lands, heavens, and oceans of the universe led them through present-day Arizona and New

Mexico, taking them to San Francisco Peaks, the Little Colorado River, and other places that are now honored as sacred shrines where the Zuni continue to leave offerings.

They split into three groups, wandering in separate directions where they encountered a series of adventures as they searched for the Middle Place. One group proceeded to the junction of the Little Colorado River and the Zuni River, where they found the Lake of the Whispering Waters beneath whose waters lay the Village of the Katsinam. They went on to a sandstone canyon, where the Sun Father transformed the Twins from beneficent care-takers of the Zuni into War Gods, the Ahayuda. The Twin War Gods assisted the Zuni at the next place, where they had to overcome the people who already lived there and who at-tacked the Zuni in their quest for the Middle Place. Eventually, this group of Zuni reached Halona: Itwana, the Middle Place.

The southern body of Zunis traveled with the Galaxy Fraternity along the valley of the upper Little Colorado River to the Middle Place by way of Escudilla Peak and El Morro in present-day New Mexico. They endured a long series of adventures with the aid of the Sword Swallower and Big Fire Societies, which helped them fight their way into the Puerco River valley, and they spent time in Chaco Canyon and in the Jemez Mountains, the place of origin for many medicine societies, as well as the prey animals. They then went down

Corn Mountain, Zuni, 1998. Author photograph

the Rio Grande to the Sandia Mountains, Mount Taylor, and the Zuni Mountains, before being reunited with the other Zuni groups.

In their search for the Middle Place, the Zunis were assisted by the Water Spider or Water Skate, who spread his legs out until he reached the four oceans in the cardinal directions, also touching the zenith and nadir. In this position, Water Spider's heart was over the exact center point of the universe, ending the epic migrations of the Zuni people.

However, because the Ashiwi (Zuni people) had not faithfully followed the middle path in their behavior, rain came and the river rose, burying people and houses in mud. Those who had not perished fled in desperation to the top of a nearby mesa, carrying all the corn they could find and naming the mesa Corn Mountain. As the waters continued to rise, the people decided to sacrifice a Rain Priest's most perfect son and daughter, whom they dressed in beautiful clothes and adorned with necklaces of precious stones and shells. Hand in hand, the couple walked into the great flood and disappeared. Kolowisi the Plumed Water Serpent, who had reared his head when the floodwaters were cresting, immediately sank beneath the waters, and the great enveloping sea began to recede. As the flood ebbed, the sacrificed children emerged as pillars of stone standing near Corn Mountain, which was forever stained with a band that showed the crest of the flood.

When the people returned to their valley, they rebuilt their village. Afraid of further misfortune, the people questioned their hearts and performed their ceremonies with dedication to keep the world stable and firm.

(This account comes from several sources, primarily Wright [1994] and Ferguson and Hart [1990].)

Prehistory/Early History

Archaeological culture history and the Zuni origin story share several basic themes, including a shift from foraging to corn agriculture, a migration across the landscape, occasional conflict between groups of people, and the assimilation of different cultural traditions (Ferguson and Hart 1990:25). The earliest evidence for human occupation of the Zuni area dates to the Paleo-Indian period, before 5000 B.C., and the population of the Southwest gradually increased during the Archaic period, from approximately 5000 B.C. to A.D. 1. Living in rock shelters and impermanent semisubterranean and surface houses, Southwestern peoples acquired corn from the peoples of highland Mexico sometime after 1500 B.C., and later bean and squash cultivation (Ford 1981:6–27).

After A.D. 1, greater reliance on agriculture made it possible for the people to live in more permanent villages. In addition to more substantial pit houses, they also constructed large storage pits, indicating that they had begun to grow more than enough food to satisfy their immediate needs. Two hundred years later they were producing pottery, from which archaeologists have been able to distinguish regional cultures on the basis of style. In the northern part of the Zuni area, the Ancestral Pueblo cultural tradition developed, distinguishable by its grayware utility pottery, black-on-white decorated pottery, and circular kivas. In the southern part of the Zuni area, the Mogollon cultural tradition developed, known for its brownware utility pottery, redware decorated pottery, and square kivas. Each cultural tradition was probably composed of separate tribes with different customs, but whose material culture had enough in common to allow archaeologists to date and identify fairly distinct divisions within the two traditions.

Between A.D. 650 and 900 groups in the Anasazi cultural tradition built pit-house villages near present-day Zuni Pueblo. Despite their reliance on hunting and gathering, they produced and stored surpluses, indicated by the aboveground masonry storage bins, granaries, and grinding stones they left behind. Items such as jewelry made from shells from the Pacific Ocean and the Gulf of California provide evidence of a vast regional trade network that extended throughout the Southwest.

Between 900 and 1150 groups within the Anasazi culture began to shift from pit houses to clusters of contiguous-room pueblos closely associated with circular underground kivas. Many villages in the Zuni drainage were organized around a central area consisting of a public building and a large ceremonial chamber, known as a great kiva. These communities were then linked in a trading network centered at Chaco Canyon in the San Juan Basin; one of the outposts of the Chaco Canyon civilization was the Village of the Great Kivas, whose ruins still lie on the Zuni Reservation along the Nutria River.

After the San Juan Basin was abandoned during the twelfth century, the people of the Zuni drainage began to trade more with the people of the Mogollon culture, and between 1250 and 1300, probably for defensive reasons, people began to coalesce into much larger pueblos with 250–1,200 rooms enclosed by high walls. Zuni Pueblo was founded about 1350, and between this date and 1540 people from the Mogollon cultural tradition joined the Zuni (Ferguson and Hart 1990:26).

By the end of the prehistoric period, the population of this region had consolidated at Zuni, Hopi, and Acoma, with the Zuni people living in a core area along the Zuni River and occupying the villages of Hawikku, Kwa'kin'a, Halona:wa, Mats'a:kya, Kyaki:ma, and Kechiba:wa when the Spaniards arrived. Thus, a record of continuous cultural development from small pit-house settlements to large masonry villages of the late prehistoric period connects historic Zuni culture to its prehistoric origins, with architectural features and ceramics that link the Zuni area to the great Chaco Canyon cultural centers to the northeast and to the Upper Gila area to the south.

The Zuni pueblo of Hawikku was the first Southwestern pueblo to be sighted by Europeans in their search for the fabled Seven Cities of Cibola. In 1539 the Franciscan friar Marcos de Niza set out with Esteban, a black Moroccan slave who had survived the ill-fated Panfilo de Narvaez expedition and had spent nearly a decade making his way across Texas toward Mexico. The myth of a magnificent El Dorado had long fascinated Spanish adventurers, exciting the dreams of ambitious peasants and impoverished noblemen who fantasized about a golden land where they could easily make their fortunes and bring honor to their families. Fray Marcos and Esteban exaggerated their experiences around a small kernel of truth, creating a golden city of untold wealth surrounded by herds of enormous animals they called *cibolas* ("buffalo").

Fray Marcos sent flamboyant Esteban ahead with a rattle adorned with rows of colored feathers—his customary harbinger—to the Indians, who were angered by this symbol. One Zuni said he "knew what kind of people they were, and that [they should be told] not to enter the town [because] if they did so, Esteban would be put to death" (Sando 1992:50). When Esteban not only ignored their response but also demanded presents and women, announcing that he was the advance guard of a large armed party, the Zuni kept their promise to execute him. Fray Marcos arrived later, choosing to view Hawikku from a nearby mountain before he claimed it for Spain and retreated to Mexico.

The following year Francisco Vasquez Coronado traveled north with hundreds of soldiers. The 250 Zuni warriors who engaged his troops in battle were overcome by Spanish firepower and withdrew. After this encounter the Zuni were left in peace for the next four decades. Further expeditions followed in 1581 and 1583, and in 1598 Juan de Oñate founded San Gabriel, the first Spanish settlement in New Mexico. He then visited each of the pueblos, obtaining the required Act of Obedience and Vassalage from the Pueblo leaders. With Spanish settlements concentrated along the Rio Grande, the Zuni were protected by geographic isolation, which allowed them to continue their traditional way of life and use of land. Still, their population was decimated by epidemics of smallpox, measles, and other European diseases.

The Zuni continued to live in their six villages along a 15-mile stretch of the Zuni River until they joined all other Pueblos in the 1680 revolt. At this time, all Spanish priests and settlers fled or were killed, including those at the mission at Halona, established in 1643. (In 1632 the Zuni had killed the priest at the Hawikku mission, which had been built in 1629.) Fearing reprisals, the Zuni took refuge on mesa tops, including steep-sided Corn Mountain, where they had built settlements of 5–50-room clusters with sheep corrals; from these mesa tops, they secured water and firewood and harvested and stored their crops only with great hardship (Woodbury 1979:472). When the Spaniards reconquered New Mexico in 1692, the Zuni pledged their allegiance to the Spanish government and consolidated their entire population into Halona, present-day Zuni, an amalgamation of previously independent towns. This consolidation may be responsible for the complexity of modern-day Zuni social and ritual organization (ibid., 472). After killing three overbearing Spaniards who attempted to reestablish the mission at Halona, the Zuni remained free from Spanish settlement until the 1860s, when Spanish-speaking communities were established some 30 miles away.

Early in the eighteenth century the Zuni established peach-orchard farming villages and sheep camps where they could protect their livestock from the Navajo and Apache (Ferguson and Hart 1990:35). During the next century the Zuni intensified their agricultural production to supply corn, wheat, and forage for the U.S. Army at Fort Defiance and Fort Wingate. They did so by constructing additional farming villages at Pescado, Nutria, and Ojo Caliente, villages that had the springs necessary for irrigation. They also built small, isolated farm sites with strong, circular towers where watchmen could warn the people about approaching Navajo and Apache raiders. With the creation of Blackrock Dam, the Zuni founded another farming village, Tekapo, at the end of the irrigation unit.

Even though it was an important trade center, Zuni was only visited at intervals during the Mexican period (1821–46) by miners on their way to the gold fields of California, as well as by Apache and Navajo, who simply took what they needed from Zuni fields and flocks. The first sustained contact that Zunis had with outsiders came when the first anthropological expedition to Zuni arrived in 1879. Led by James Stevenson, the group also included his wife Matilda Coxe Stevenson and Frank Hamilton Cushing.

In 1848 the Treaty of Guadalupe Hidalgo recognized the Zuni land grant made by the Spanish Crown in 1689. Great technological and economic changes followed, for although the introduction of sheep, cattle, and pigs during the Spanish period had paved the way, the shift from a subsistence economy to a cash economy did not occur until Anglo traders replaced itinerant Mexicans in the 1870s. In the last two decades of the 1800s, three Anglo and two Indian traders at Zuni established the value of livestock and introduced the concept of credit buying and pawn; by placing objects of value in the trader's custody, someone who had no sheep could expect the same buying power as a person with sheep (Eggan and Pandey 1979:476). As happened elsewhere in the Southwest, the arrival of the railroad and the advent of cross-country railroad travel brought tourists interested in "Indian curios," which created a new market for Zuni crafts. In addition to more traditional ollas and bowls, Zuni women began to make pottery owls with reddish brown, painted feather details on their white clay bodies.

By the 1890s various Anglo teachers, missionaries, traders, and government officials lived in Zuni. Not only did they increase the dependence of the Zuni on the traders and government, but they were also instrumental in summoning troops from Fort Wingate to halt Zuni witch trials. (With the cessation of warfare, the powerful Bow Priesthood, which acted as the executive arm of the Council of High Priests, turned its energy toward Zuni witches.)

The Bureau of Indian Affairs (BIA) boarding school built in 1907 at Black Rock became a major means by which the government changed the Zuni's traditional agricultural techniques. In earlier times the Zuni had used hand tools and communal labor to cultivate their fields, which they irrigated through ditch and floodwater irrigation techniques. The BIA introduced mechanical tools, draft animals, and individual farming of canal-irrigated fields fed by large reservoirs—techniques that proved disastrous because they could not be sustained. This resulted in the disintegration of the communal labor organization that was the very foundation of Zuni agricultural practices (Ferguson and Seciwa 1994:725). Erosion from overgrazing and clear-cutting of the watershed upstream from Zuni further strained Zuni agriculture in the late 1800s and early 1900s. With the severe erosion of arroyo channels, traditional methods of diverting stream water into fields became inefficient. A series of BIA-constructed reservoirs soon lost their storage capacity due to siltation, resulting in the failure of the agricultural improvements they had supported. This led to the decline of Zuni agriculture from 10,000 cultivated acres in the 1800s to fewer than 1,500 acres today (ibid., 725). The government then promoted the livestock industry as an alternative to agriculture, but overgrazing soon became so serious that stock-reduction programs were instituted in 1938. Impoundment teams rounded up thousands of animals, hauling them to Gallup for sale or slaughtering them and leaving them to rot in pits dug in the railroad right-of-way (Tedlock 1992:25).

The Return of Zuni Salt Lake

Do:k'yana'a (Zuni Salt Lake) plays an important role in Zuni religion and is sacred as the home of Mother Salt, who provides this prized substance for her children. It is sacred, too, because it is a lake; the Zuni consider springs "to be the most precious things on earth" (Ferguson and Hart 1990:51). So sacred is the lake and its vicinity that battles or violence were never contemplated there, and when the Zuni made pilgrimages to the lake, they left offerings in a salt-gathering ceremony (ibid., 89). For centuries this lake has provided the Zuni with salt for trade and for their own consumption. The Zuni did not distinguish between organic and inorganic materials, but considered all things to be living. Zuni Bow Priests kept shrines, where they made offerings to the War Gods at important points along trails and on peaks that marked common boundaries between Zuni and other tribes, including Zuni and Hopi, Zuni and Acoma, Zuni and Navajo to the north, and Zuni and Apache to the south (ibid., 89). The Zuni permitted these tribes to gather salt at the Zuni Salt Lake if they submitted to conditions imposed by the Zuni, such as staying on prescribed trails, camping at recognized campsites, and paying respect to Zuni shrines and religious areas (ibid., 89). Occasionally, the Zuni obtained payment for use of this lake, and in times of war they killed or captured any non-Zuni whom they caught near the lake.

This lake has a long documented history, reaching back to 1598, when Marcos Farfan was sent to explore it by Juan de Oñate (Crampton 1977:25). Farfan found the entire surface, except for the very center, so solidly encrusted with salt that a person could easily walk on the lake without breaking through. He claimed that even the king of Spain did not enjoy salt of such excellent grain, for it was the finest salt in all Christendom. In 1778 Don Bernardo Miera y Pacheco, an officer in the Engineering Corps of the Spanish army, mapped the plains around the Zuni Salt Lake. Jesse Walter Fewkes plotted Zuni trails, as well as an Anglo road, that led to an early Anglo ranch and to the Zuni Salt Lake as they existed in 1890 (Ferguson and Hart 1990:77). Around 1921–23 a film was made of Zunis during a salt-gathering ceremony at the lake. Anthropologist Ruth Bunzel recorded a first-person narrative account in Zuni (with English interlinear and free translation) of a large Zuni-Hopi pilgrimage to Zuni Salt Lake (1935:420–29).

Despite its importance to the Zuni people, Zuni Salt Lake was not included within the boundaries of the 1877 reservation, which made it possible for Mexicans to settle and take up mining at Zuni Salt Lake in 1902. In 1978 Congress passed an act (P.L. 95–280) authorizing the federal government to acquire Zuni Salt Lake in a land exchange with the state of New Mexico. However, although the Zuni have assumed control over the lake, it has taken many years for the title to be transferred because the state claims the mineral rights to the salt in and surrounding the lake (Ferguson and Hart 1990:99).

Language and Territory

The Zuni language remains an unsolved puzzle, for although the Zuni share the same general culture pattern and the same environmental zone as other Puebloan peoples, their language is as distant from other Puebloan languages as English is from Chinese. Such a concentration of three unrelated linguistic groupings—Zuni, Keresan, and Kiowa-Tanoan—within such a small geographic area, among groups that are remarkably similar in cultural traits, challenges both linguists and archaeologists. Of these three language groupings, Zuni is unique because it is spoken only by the inhabitants of what is now a single village. Zuni is a language isolate, which means that it is not related to any other known languages in the world. A relationship to California Penutian has been proposed, but most linguists remain unconvinced that these languages are linked. If such an affiliation exists, it is far too distant to be measured accurately by glottochronology (Newman 1964).

In their own language, the Zuni call themselves the Ashiwi. Today the Zuni live in the principal town, Zuni Pueblo, which is the ancient village of Halona:wa ("Old Halona"), and in outlying farming villages at Ojo Caliente, Pescado, Nutria, and Tekapo, as well as numerous sheep camps or ranches. The farming villages have no civil or religious organization of their own; most people return to Zuni Pueblo itself after the harvest for the great winter ceremonies, but in recent years a few people have chosen to remain year-round in these outposts.

Situated about 40 miles southwest of present-day Gallup, New Mexico, Zuni lies in a fertile valley rimmed by flat-topped mesas, just west of the Zuni Mountains, on the southeastern part of the Colorado Plateau (Young 1988:14). Three miles southeast of the pueblo, the sacred Corn Mountain (Dowa Yalanne) towers 1,000 feet above the plain; in the past, this mountain served as a refuge for all the people of Zuni during times of conflict with outsiders, and it is the location of important Zuni shrines. One of the sharp, clear bands of sandstone that compose this mesa is said to be the high-water line of a flood that occurred at the time of Creation.

The land consists of high, broad valleys and brightly colored sandstone mesas, with forested mountains and sheer-sided canyons to the northeast. West of the pueblo, the land makes an abrupt transition to open, rolling country. The climate in the Zuni area is semi-arid and temperate at an elevation of about 6,400 feet, which means that the winter is not severe although nights may be bitterly cold. Summer may bring a noontime temperature of 110°F with cool, even chilly, nights. Spring winds from the open deserts west of Zuni often blow fine sand and dust across the landscape, causing much discomfort, and May sand storms may be so severe that they destroy the young corn. Although frosts may come as late as May or as early as September, limiting the growing season to a mere 156 days, over the course of centuries the Zuni have developed agricultural methods and strains of crops well suited to the short growing season and arid conditions.

The tiny Zuni River—little more than a trickle in the spring and fall—threads its way through broad, glistening mud flats. From its headwaters near the Continental Divide, the river flows through the pueblo to join the Little Colorado River some miles east of the Arizona border. Although many streams and rivers of the Colorado Plateau on which Zuni is located run only intermittently today, they once carried a continuous water flow. The Continental Divide, just east of the pueblo, separates streams on the eastern side, which flow toward the Rio Grande, from those on the west, which flow toward the Colorado, Salt, and Gila rivers. During the summer season, cloudbursts in the eastern mountains transform the Zuni River into a torrent that overflows its banks and fills arroyos with rushing water. Summer rains begin in early July and last until mid-September; by noon, the morning sky of unclouded, brilliant blue fills with great puffs of white cumulus clouds that steadily increase in density until heavy black clouds form along the southern horizon, and late afternoon brings sudden, violent showers of short duration that move southeast just before sunset. Increasing in frequency, intensity, and duration, rainstorms become most destructive at the end of the season.

Winter precipitation begins with light snowfalls in early December, a time of low temperatures and frequent snow. The temperature moderates after the new year, as snow alternates with a continuous downpour of cold rain, often accompanied by fog. When the snow pack melts on high mountain peaks in and around the Zuni area, runoff provides an important source of surface water and recharges subterranean aquifers. The highest average annual precipitation—26–40 inches—occurs in the pine-clad Zuni Mountains to the northeast, which reach 9,200 feet, while Zuni itself receives only about 12 inches annually. In comparison with the Hopi, the Zuni have a relatively dependable supply of water and fertile, deep soil in their valleys. However, precipitation in the Zuni area is extremely variable: in some years, widespread droughts leave fields parched, but during other periods too much rain falls in the form of violent cloudbursts that wash out fields and roads. In addition to annual fluctuations, this area is also subject to longer term climatic cycles, including severe droughts.

The few springs and permanent streams in the Zuni area have their source in the mountains but yield little water. Thus, it is not surprising that, as agriculturalists, the Zunis venerate springs as shrine areas because they consider them to be gateways to the great water system, which ultimately includes the oceans. The Zuni River is thought to be the pathway that leads the dead during their four-day journey to Katsina Village, located beneath Katsina Lake (Young 1988:16). Zuni Salt Lake, about 43 miles south of the pueblo in Carrizo Valley, is a spring-fed body of water that covers a salt deposit and is known as the home of Old Lady Salt. This lake has great significance to the Zuni people, who continue to make pilgrimages there to gather salt and perform rituals.

Ponderosa pine, Douglas fir, oak, and aspen are common in the higher elevations of the mountains, while piñons and junipers grow in the woodland area. In the valleys the vegetation consists of grasses, small cactus, sagebrush, yucca, greasewood, and other plants adapted to semidesert conditions. At one time deer and bear were plentiful, but today only rabbits, prairie dogs, pack rats, skunks, and coyotes are common.

Aboriginal Culture

Our understanding of Zuni life and thought is much greater than for most other Southwestern groups because of the great minds that have been drawn to study and record this culture. The Zuni, according to their origin stories and the archaeological record, are a composite people, some of whom came from the north while others came from the south. Their cultural inclination toward complexity, coupled with considerable time depth—their language indicates that they existed as a separate people for a very long time—and the settled lifestyle afforded by agriculture enabled the Zuni to put their energy into developing an elaborate culture. The Zuni culture is one of great beauty and sophistication in terms of ceremonialism, myth, and aesthetics, expressed in visual and verbal form in both ritual and secular activities.

Zuni is remarkable for the degree to which its people have kept alive the ancient rituals of their elaborate ceremonial cycle, despite having been exposed to stronger acculturative influences than the Hopi because of Zuni's close proximity to Santa Fe. In June 1998 I saw an illustration of this continuity in the form of katsinam in a crosswalk at Zuni. They stopped the flow of traffic on Highway 53 as they filed across the asphalt to the sound of shell tinklers and turtle rattles, their eagle-feather headdresses fluttering in the late afternoon breeze. One smooth-faced Comanche katsina turned to stare at us inside our vehicle. A long line of cars and pickups stopped to let the entire procession go by, while pedestrians paused on nearby sidewalks to watch with wonder.

Subsistence and Material Culture

The Zuni developed ingenious agricultural techniques, which have enabled them to live in the same location for centuries without depleting these resources. Learned over the course of centuries by precontact Zunis and the Ancestral Pueblo peoples, these techniques enabled them to support their population in a remarkably arid area by meticulously using every available source of water. By planting their fields at the mouths of sandy washes emerging from the hills, Zuni farmers ensured that their crops benefited from the overflow during any rain and from seepage for germination. Their principal crops were six colors of hardy, deep-rooted corn, beans, and squash, to which the Spaniards added wheat, oats, and peaches. (The Zuni obtained most of their cotton from the Hopi.) Men were responsible for most of the agricultural work. In fields that belonged to matrilineal households or to individual males—a man could farm any strip of unused land on the reservation—all the men in a household, along with their relatives, cultivated one field at a time before moving on to the next one. After burning the brush to clear the plot, they built a diversion dam across the arroyo, and then diked the field in harmony with the natural contours of the land to conserve any runoff from rainfall and snowmelt. These floodwater farming methods also prevented gullying, in places where large amounts of runoff occurred, and the loss of topsoil by wind and water, thus controlling erosion. The Zuni also constructed aqueducts out of hollow logs in places where there were permanent sources of water, such as Ojo Caliente.

Zuni women owned and tended "waffle gardens," shallow, square depressions separated by low mud walls that created wafflelike cells; the raised partitions of soil conserved water, regulated temperature, and protected plants from the wind. An adobe wall protected the entire garden plot, which might include chile peppers, onions, squash, melons, pumpkins, tomatoes, or cotton. Women watered these highly productive gardens by hand, carrying water from the river or a well in pottery jars.

The Zuni kept a two-year supply of food on hand (a characteristic that was particularly appealing to Apache and Navajo raiders). Although their diversified agriculture allowed them to develop a rich, sedentary culture, the Zuni also acquired an encyclopedic knowledge of the wild plants and animals, from the Sandia Mountains to the San Francisco Peaks, that provided food, medicines, ceremonial materials, clothing, basketry, soap, clothing, and other articles. Men hunted bison, elk, moose, antelope, mountain sheep, wild pigs, foxes, deer, bears, coyote, bobcats, and mountain lions, as well as small game, such as rabbits, porcupines, badgers, ground squirrels, and beavers (Ferguson and Hart 1990:43). The Zuni also tended extensive flocks of turkeys, whose feathers they used for clothing and rituals, eating the birds only during times of famine. From the Spaniards, they obtained burros, goats, cattle, horses, and sheep, using the latter as negotiable wealth by selling wool in June and lambs in October to provide the cash income needed to buy manufactured items. The Zuni used cattle for meat rather than to supply milk.

Zuni, a compact village intersected by streets or passageways, was composed of two- to five-storied apartment houses, made of stone masonry cemented and plastered with adobe mud. By day these houses were lighted through tiny windows formed of a mosaic of translucent selenite (gypsum) or mica and by night with the light from the family fire. Men laid the stone foundations, built the stone and adobe walls, and put the huge crossbeams in place to support the roof, while women smoothed the mud floor, covered the exterior and interior walls with brown adobe plaster, and whitewashed the interior with burned gypsum.

Sparsely furnished Zuni homes had several built-in features, including a low bench along one wall, small niches in the walls to serve as cupboards, and rafters from which poles were suspended on which to hang clothing. Families stored their carefully wrapped ceremonial dress in a dark inner room. Usually in the living room was a three-compartment "milling box" for the grinding of corn so that three women could grind corn simultaneously. They could bake twenty loaves of bread at the same time in each outdoor beehive, dome-shaped oven; believed to be of Mexican origin, the ovens were made of clay and stone, and plastered for a smooth surface.

Zuni men once wove both wool and cotton garments, while women made baskets of willow, dogwood, and yucca, and well-fired, superbly decorated pottery that featured distinctive designs of deep red and brown-black on a chalky white background. Influenced by Spanish dress, Zuni men replaced their short cotton kilts with loose, white cotton trousers, with slits up the side, and white cotton shirts cinched with cotton belts or concho belts. Their moccasins were well-tanned, reddish brown deerskin with hard rawhide soles. In the 1800s they were still wearing their hair cut square in bangs over the eyes, trimmed at the sides on the level of the mouth, and tied in the back with yarn. They added a headband to keep their hair out of their eyes.

Women of this period wore a *manta*, a knee-length gown of black, diagonally woven cloth, embroidered in dark blue at the top and bottom. Fastened over the right shoulder, it

The beehive ovens of a mother and her daughters, Zuni, 1998. Author photograph

left the left shoulder bare and was belted at the waist with a long woven sash. Women's moccasins were made of white, hard-soled buckskin, above which were wrapped white doeskin leggings that reached to the knee. Knitted wool stockings were worn underneath the moccasins.

The Zuni Socioreligious Organization

Among the Zuni the social, religious, and political systems have always been so closely interconnected with the ceremonial cycle and the kin and clan system that the totality is best referred to as a socioreligious organization, an entire system in itself. The intricate, close-knit nature of their social organization (Eggan and Pandey 1979) with its "marvelous complexity" (Kroeber 1917:183) has been the key to Zuni persistence despite factional disputes. Their elaborate ceremonial life was organized by six esoteric cults, twelve medicine societies, six kiva groups, and twelve priesthoods. Priesthoods, kiva organizations, political groups, families, and clans crosscut each other, uniting the entire pueblo. The six esoteric cults operate independently but synchronically.

The kinship system underlay the religious and political systems. When a Zuni child was born, his or her position was established within the kin-clan group. Children's names, what they would call others, and who they could or could not marry were established. The child's birth order—eldest or youngest—determined how the child would behave and how others would behave toward the child. The child belonged to the mother's clan and household, and this was the household where the greatest responsibilities and loyalties of his or her life would lie. If the child was female, she would spend her entire life in this household. If the child was male, he would return to this household to fulfill his ceremonial and social responsibilities even though he would live with his wife at her mother's home. Zuni kinship terms not only designated consanguineal (blood kin) and affinal (in-laws, or those related through marriage) relatives but also clan kin and ceremonial relatives. Sixteen kin terms were used for blood kin, ten for ceremonial relatives (Ladd 1979:483).

As in all the Western Pueblos, descent was matrilineal, and residence was matrilocal. The women who composed the matrilineage owned the house, and husbands resided in their wives' households. Because his primary responsibility was in his maternal household, the husband was always regarded as something of an outsider in the house where he resided.

The household was the basic economic, social, and religious unit at Zuni, and the fields that belonged to the women of the household were cultivated by the men of the household. The male members of the household also owned fields, usually ones they had recently brought under cultivation; these remained their own even if they severed their connections with the household (Bunzel 1992:477). However, once crops of all fields, whether individually or collectively owned, were harvested, they passed into a storehouse where they were considered to be the collective property of the women in the household. Only women could enter the storehouse from which they drew on these stores for daily food and traded the surplus for other commodities. Each man owned sheep but herded them cooperatively, and from his division of the profits from shearing, he was expected to provide clothing for himself, his wife and children, including any children from previous marriages, and his mother and unmarried sisters if they were not otherwise provided for (ibid., 477).

All matters relating to divorce, death, marriage, and birth were handled within the family. Any property acquired during marriage belonged to the wife, as well as any children. If property had to be divided, it was handled within the families involved, and any disputes were also settled among the involved parties.

The household had no authoritative head who enforced discipline, and the female members usually presented a united front. At Zuni, the household was more important than the clan: in contrast to Hopi clans, Zuni clans had no political function, no clan head, and no clan council. The Zuni clan system was dynamic, with certain clans becoming inactive, and subclans, which were recognized more frequently in the larger clans, providing a mechanism for the "creation" of new clans (Ladd 1979:485). In the early 1800s there were reported to be sixteen active clans (Cushing 1896), and in 1977 there were fourteen matrilineal clans (Ladd 1979:485).

Zuni Religious Organizations

In addition to the all-pervasive Cult of the Ancestors, six esoteric cults existed, each directed to the worship of a particular group of supernaturals, and each having its own priesthood, body of ritual, religious paraphernalia, special places of worship, and calendrical cycle of ceremonies. These six specialized cults included the Cult of the Katsinam, the Cult of the Katsina Priests, the Cult of the Sun, the Cult of the Rain Priests, the Cult of the War Gods, and the Cult of the Beast Gods. The Cult of the Beast Gods was also known as the twelve curing or medicine societies. The religious and ceremonial organizations were the backbone of Zuni ritual life, and membership in these organizations cut across kinship and clan boundaries.

The Cult of the Katsinam had six divisions or groups, with each group having its own kiva. All boys between eight and twelve years of age underwent their final initiation into one of these kiva groups, each of which was associated with one of the six directions. The boy's mother or father chose the kiva when the child was born, but the boy could choose to change his membership to a different kiva later. When a boy joined a kiva group, he acquired a new set of older and younger brothers (his fellow members), as well as fathers (the kiva leaders) and grandfathers (older men). These kinship terms were also used to address the fellow members of any other ceremonial organization the boy could join (Kroeber 1917:186). Membership in a kiva group had no connection with clan affiliation, nor was membership in a particular group binding for life. Each kiva group danced at least three times annually between sometime after the summer solstice and November, when the katsinam were sent home.

The Cult of the Katsinam had its beginning when the Zuni were searching for the Middle Place. A group of women were crossing a stream, and their children were transformed into frogs and water snakes. Frightened, the women dropped them, and they escaped into the water. The bereaved women mourned so for their children that the twin heroes went to search for them. They found the children, who had been transformed into katsinam, "singing and dancing in untroubled joyousness" (Bunzel 1992:516) in a house beneath the surface of Whispering Waters. Upon their return, the twin heroes reported what they had seen, decreeing that from then on the dead would travel to the same place to join the katsinam. Taking pity on the loneliness of their people, the katsinam returned often to dance for them in their plazas, but after each visit they took someone back with them (that is, someone died). Therefore, the katsinam decided that instead of coming in person, the Zuni should copy their costumes and headdresses and imitate their dances so that the katsinam could live with them in spirit. After the katsinam stopped coming in the flesh, they came as rain.

The second cult, the Katsina Priests, bestowed fecundity. Like the katsinam, the katsina priests also lived at Katsina Village. Each priest had a distinctive personality and name. The Koyemsi (Mudheads) showed the results of their incestuous brother-sister parentage in their grotesque appearance and uncouth behavior. These sacred clowns possessed black magic: "in their drums they have the wings of black butterflies that can make girls [sexually] 'crazy'" and "in the knobs of their masks is soil from the footprints of townspeople" (a widely used love charm; Bunzel 1992:521). The chief of the katsina priests was *Pautiwa*, who possessed the three most admired qualities among the Zuni: dignity, beauty, and kindliness. His beautiful, stately appearance was met with hushed reverence.

The Pekwinne—"the most revered and the most holy man at Zuni" (Bunzel 1992:512) —presided over the Cult of the Sun. Believed to derive his power directly from the Sun Father, he was "ultimately held responsible for the welfare of the community" (ibid., 512). Always chosen from the largest clan at Zuni, the Dogwood Clan, the Pekwinne calculated the dates for the solstice ceremonies on the basis of his observations of the position of the sun at sunrise and sunset against a specific geographic point, managed the ceremonial calendar, installed new priests, and officiated over the priests of all the different cults when they functioned jointly.

The Cult of the Rainmakers was directed to the water spirits that lived in the great interconnected water system of the earth. The elaborate worship of the Rainmakers was delegated to twelve priesthoods, each of which had two to six members, who inherited their membership within their matrilineal family group and guarded the fetish of their particular group in that family's house. Membership was open to both men and women, although it was limited by clan affiliation. The Rain Priests had a retreat in the spring and summer to pray for rain.

The Cult of the War Gods honored the Ahayuda, who were born in a waterfall when the Zunis badly needed military leadership as they were traveling to the Middle Place. The Bow Priests—whose membership was limited to those who had taken a scalp in war—and several other groups of priests, who were in charge of the cult, kept a war fetish and scalps, and carved and decorated the figures of the Ahayuda. The Bow Priests joined with the Deer and Bear clans to perform public ceremonies for the Ahayuda (Ladd 1979:488).

The final cult was that of the Beast Gods, the beasts of prey that were the most dangerous and violent gods in the Zuni pantheon. As the priests of long life and the givers of medicine and the power to make this medicine effective, the Beast Gods were the patrons of the curing societies, and the cult consisted of twelve medicine societies, each with its own rituals and curing specialties. If a person was cured by a particular society, such as the Galaxy Medicine Society, he or she then became a member for life.

The Zuni Political Organization

In contrast to Hopi villages, which tended to divide and form new villages (each of which was politically independent from the others) over time, Zuni villages consolidated, unifying themselves into one large pueblo. Zuni's centralized political system was a theocracy that revolved around the Council of High Priests, which acted as a unit, and the Pekwinne who directed the overall ceremonial and religious cycles. Two Bow Priests served as the executive arm of the priesthood, enforcing its decisions regarding the punishment of crimes. Secular officers appointed by the Council of High Priests took care of civil law and relations with the U.S. government.

Witchcraft, the only recognized crime, was thought to be behind any irregularities in these rituals, unusual behavior, or crises such as drought or epidemics. The Council of High Priests—composed of the Rain Priests, officers of the medicine societies, kiva officials, and the Pekwinne—decided who the witches were, and the Bow Priests then executed these "people with two hearts" (Ladd 1979:488). If the relatives of a deceased person accused an individual of having killed their relative through sorcery, the Bow Priests examined the accused and reviewed the evidence. If the accused was found guilty, he was hung by his wrists and tortured until he confessed; if he revealed the source of his power, he might be released or he might be executed. U.S. government authorities stopped the public torture and execution of witches, but convicted witches were killed in secret unless they escaped.

As the religious leaders of the pueblo, the Council of High Priests was supposed to remain "pure in heart" by removing itself from anything connected with violence. Thus, the Bow Priests, who were associated with war, enforced the decisions of the council, including the execution of witches. Although the last public witch trials at Zuni were in 1925 (Smith and Roberts 1954:48), a belief in witchcraft remained "very strong in the 1970s," and the punishment for a witch caught practicing his art against an individual was settled privately between the witch and the person who caught him in the act (Ladd 1979:488).

The Bow Priests also protected the people from outsiders. Probably developed to ensure mutual protection when the Zuni lived in separate towns, the supreme council of Bow Priests had its center of activities in one of the larger Zuni towns. When the Spaniards arrived, no doubt they appointed the head Bow Priest as governor because he was the most obvious leader (Ladd 1979:489). Until around 1692, sometime after the reconquest, the Council of High Priests and Bow Priests controlled both religious and civil affairs.

Before contact, the priestly council appointed and installed various religious officials at the beginning of each year. When the Spaniards introduced a civil government, the religious installation was used to establish the governor and his council at Zuni Pueblo, except that the Spanish governor's cane replaced the feathered staff; later, President Abraham Lincoln gave a cane to each pueblo, which is still used today. A radical change occurred in

1934 when the Zuni people decided to replace the appointment of members of the Tribal Council by the Council of High Priests with open elections by the entire tribe.

Religion and World View

Ceremonialism was so central to the Zuni way of life that anthropologist Ruth Bunzel called ritual "the formal expression of Zuni civilization," saying that "all of Zuni life is oriented about religious observance" (1992:509). Of the complexity of Zuni ceremonialism she wrote, "Nowhere in the New World, except in the ancient civilizations of Mexico . . . has ceremonialism been more highly developed" (ibid., 480).

Cosmology

The Zuni extended the two-dimensional scheme of the four cardinal directions into three-dimensional space by adding the zenith and the nadir to their conceptual model. The order in which the cardinal points were given in ritual observance was important: northeast (yellow), northwest (blue), southwest (red), southeast (white), zenith (all colors), and nadir (black). The Zuni universe was highly structured, with each point of orientation having its own color, animal species, bird species, and rain priests, who, in turn, had their own bow priests and spokesmen. The four underworlds through which the ancestors of the Zuni passed were located toward the nadir. Directionality also played a major role in ritual, and human counterparts took the title of Rain Priests of the Six Directions, who were believed to live along the shores of the ocean and in springs and to take the form of rainstorms, clouds, fog, and dew upon leaving their homes (Bunzel 1932:513). These beings were joined by Bow Priests of the Six Directions, who made lightning and thunder (Stevenson 1904:22); six spokesmen for these priests were the six water-bringing birds: oriole (north), Steller's jay (west), macaw (south), magpie (east), purple martin (zenith), and rough-winged swallow (nadir) (Stevenson 1993:89).

Water imagery was more greatly elaborated among the Zuni than among any other Southwestern people, for the Zuni considered every body of water—oceans, rivers, streams, and lakes—to be part of a great interconnected system linked by underground passages. All the seeps, springs, ponds, and caves on the earth were gateways to this system and were regarded as sacred (Bunzel 1992:487), and springs and underground waters were home to Kolowisi, the horned water serpent. The Rain Makers, or Rain Priests, were water spirits who lived in the great water system of the world. Cumulus clouds were their houses, and the mist was their breath; their children were the singing frogs that filled puddles after the drenching summer rains, and their footprints were the ripple marks along the edge of ditches washed out by heavy rains (ibid., 513). Their six bow priests (warriors) made lightning and thunder (Stevenson 1904:22), and their six spokesmen (*pekwinne*, sing.) were six water-bringing birds (Stevenson 1993:89). The rain priests came to Zuni on winds from the southwest or southeast, while their winter counterparts, the snow priests, came from the northeast and northwest (Stevenson 1904:21).

While some katsinam came from Sipapulima in the east, most katsinam lived in the west at Katsina Village, at the bottom of the lake the Zuni encountered on their journey to the Middle Place. The katsinam sang and prayed for rain and the growth of crops at this lake, which is two days' walk from Zuni. The Sun Father had several sons: the Ahayuda twins, who were active primarily in winter, and Payatamu, who belonged to the summer. These supernaturals were warriors, hunters, athletes, gamblers, and diviners, and they guarded the Zuni people from their six hilltop shrines within a 10-mile radius of Zuni. Living even closer to Zuni were other supernaturals, including the corn plants; Navajo priests, which were actually enemy scalps transformed into bringers of water and seeds; and sacred bundles whose contents constituted a microcosm of the Zuni universe. At the center of the bundles was a stone inside of which beat the heart of the world.

World View

The Zuni continue to hold that everything has a spiritual essence because all things belong to one great system of interrelated life. Constituting this great totality are the sun, stars, clouds, mountains, plants, animals, human beings, and even items of human manufacture, such as houses and pottery. Although all of these things are living beings with their own personalities, only people possess human faculties. The conviction that all life is sacred and interrelated shapes the great complexity of the Zuni cosmological system: Sun Father, Earth Mother, and others who reside in their realms are relatives of the Zuni people. Although the supernatural is a single great divine essence, it may take individual forms, such as Sun Father, which still remain part of a much larger collective force (Bunzel 1992:480).

Inhabiting the world are two categories of living beings: the raw people, and the cooked or daylight people. Daylight people live off cooked food, while raw people eat raw food or food that has been sacrificed to them by the daylight people. Because raw people are supernaturals, such as Mother Earth, Father Sun, Moonlight-Giving Mother, and White Shell Woman, but may take human form, humans—daylight people—should treat everyone with respect.

Each human being has a spiritual essence or soul, which is associated with the head, the heart, and the breath (Bunzel 1992:481). While skill and intelligence come from the head, emotions and profound thought originate in the heart. "I shall take it to my heart" means that I am moved deeply by something, I am thinking about it at great length, and I will remember it for a long time (ibid., 481). During mourning ceremonies, women say, "We all cry. It is so beautiful that our hearts hurt" (ibid., 509). The word for life translates literally as "daylight," which is why humans are "daylight people," and the breath is so symbolic of life that inhaling is an act of ritual blessing. A person derives the power of a holy object by breathing in its sacred presence; by holding a folded hand in front of one's nostrils, one can also inhale the sacred essence of prayer. Feathers symbolize the breath.

The Zuni name for their pueblo, the Middle Place, embodies their belief that their village is situated in the center of the universe. Also encoded in this name is the Zuni ethos: to follow the path of the Middle Place, a middle path that is achieved by living life in measured harmony without great intensity. This philosophy, which prizes peaceful moderation over violent extremes, rejects intense individual emotional experiences, so that the most desired personality traits are a "pleasing address, a yielding disposition, and a generous heart" (Bunzel 1992:480). The following characterization conveys the highest form of praise: "Yes, [he] is a nice polite man. No one ever hears anything from him. He never gets into trouble. He's Badger Clan and Muhekwe kiva, and he always dances in the summer dances" (ibid., 480). Not only does this individual consistently maintain his ceremonial responsibilities, but his demeanor also conforms to Zuni ideals of discipline, even temperament, placid disposition, and restraint.

The Cult of the Ancestors

Because the dead bestowed all blessings in life, the worship of the ancestors was central to all Zuni ritual, and every Zuni participated in the Cult of the Ancestors, regardless of age, sex, or other ceremonial affiliations. Even in ceremonies focused on the worship of other beings, the ancestors were included through prayers and offerings of food, which was especially evident at Grandmothers' Day (Catholic All Souls Day) when great quantities of food were sacrificed in the fire and the river. Also offered were prayer meal, smoke, and a special prayerstick that was painted black and decorated with feathers from the backs of turkeys. The Cult of the Ancestors was fundamental to Zuni religion, and other classes of beings, such as the katsinam, merged their identity with the ancestors.

The ancestors were considered to be beneficent protectors of the living who guided and nourished them. Identified with the greatest blessings of all, clouds and rain, the ancestors also bestowed health, fecundity, and well-being. Pointing to the great cumulus clouds that pile up on the southern horizon on summer afternoons, Zuni mothers told their children, "Look, there the grandfathers are coming!" (Bunzel 1992:510). All individuals had direct access to the ancestors without the mediation of priests, and no fetishes or other paraphernalia were used in their worship; there were no special places where their worship was held. People did not pray to their own specific ancestors but rather to all the ancestors collectively.

Even though the dead were essentially benevolent, the recently deceased might yearn for the dear ones they had left behind, appearing in dreams until the living person died of grief and joined them. This was why the dead were implored through offerings of cornmeal and prayersticks not to trouble the living. The first witch introduced death among the daylight people, and witchcraft is still believed to be one of the major causes of death

(Tedlock 1972:258–61). Death also had other causes: the dead might appear in dreams and take the living with them, or death could come if a katsina dance continued for too many days (Bunzel 1932:634). The length of every person's life was predetermined (Benedict 1935:2:51, 65). People were warned of their deaths in dreams; landslides or out-of-season thunderstorms forecast the death of a Rain Priest (Bunzel 1933:54).

Although the body was buried the day after death occurred, the person's spirit remained in his or her home for four days, after which it departed for Katsina Village (Bunzel 1992:482). Geographically, Katsina Village lay at the bottom of a small lake known as the Lake of Whispering Waters, so named because "the water made a noise that sounded like the quiet whispering of unseen people" (Wright 1994:137). The lake had within it a six-chambered house that was the mystic home of the divinities of the six directions and the dead who were finished with their mortal lives (Stevenson 1904:32). When a Rain Priest died, he joined other Rain Priests at the four oceans of the world (Bunzel 1992:482), while a Bow Priest became a lightning maker (Stevenson 1904:20, 110). Those who belonged to the Societies of the Completed Path went to join their raw counterparts at the home of the Priests of the Completed Path (Bunzel 1932:517).

Those who had died were no longer mentioned by name, although they were addressed in a group as ancestors in general, katsinam, or the dead of a smaller society (Stevenson 1904:570). Only the Rain Priests did not lose their separate identity because their successors invoked them by name (Bunzel 1992:656). The dead formed the nearest and most intimate part of the great spiritual essence of the universe. They were so closely identified with rain that if rain fell after a death, that person was considered to have bestowed it upon the Zuni.

Ritual Practice and Belief

Rituals—a set of practices through which participants relate to the sacred—among the Zuni ranged from acts performed by individuals to highly structured, elaborate ceremonies conducted by the large esoteric cults, which were held privately or publicly. Nearly all Zuni ceremonies were calendrical, that is, cyclical and recurrent. The best known ceremony was probably the Zuni Shalako celebrated in December and described at the beginning of this chapter.

The predominant theme of Zuni religion was the request for increase and prosperity (Young 1988:113, 145, 172)—specifically, the desire for rain, which lies at the heart of Zuni ritual practice (Young 1991:164) and is evident in the wide range of rain and water imagery. Individual rituals could be directed to any part of nature. In picking red-willow shoots for prayersticks, one had to apologize to the willow next to the one that was cut by offering a bit of jeweled cornmeal and prayer (Tedlock 1992:106). If a deer was to be persuaded to lay down its life for humans, it had to be stalked ritualistically, enchanted by sacred songs, killed in a prescribed manner, and then received as an honored guest so that it would "tell others of his tribe that he was well treated in his father's house" (Bunzel 1992:488–89). Anthropologist Barbara Tedlock described how a Zuni friend knelt beside a deer he had just killed to say softly in Zuni, "May you visit us often. Be happy" (1992:118–21). Then "he lit a hand-rolled cigarette, took a deep drag, and blew strong wild-tobacco smoke into her hair . . . [and then] gently sucked the remaining breath from her nostrils." By breathing the final breath from a dying game animal, a hunter improves his relationship with all animals; this ritual bestows success in hunting as well as the knowledge of which animals to kill and which ones to let go (ibid., 121).

Like the Ancestral Pueblo people, the Zuni made small stone animals for use in ritual. Known as fetishes, these tiny animal carvings had small bundles of magical objects—beads, arrowheads, feathers, and other objects—tied to them to enhance their power. Although the best known fetishes were those of the six Beast Gods, fetishes could be of other forms. For example, the *mili,* which represented the Breath of Life given by Awonawilona, the Supreme Being of the Zuni, was a perfect ear of corn wrapped in buckskin, covered with the feathers of various birds, and set in a basketry base (Bahti in Cushing 1988:5). One of the most sacred objects—because of its power to bring life-giving rain—was a short section of cane with some water and a tiny live frog inside.

Long ago when the earth was still soft and inhabited by monsters, the Twin War Gods, to make the world safe for humans, hurled thunderbolts at the predatory Beast Gods, shriveling them into small stone remnants. Since these small stone fetishes incorporated the power of the Beast Gods, they were used in any context that invoked the Beast Gods, especially in the rituals of the curing societies. The hearts of the great animals of prey were known to be infused with a spirit or medicine of magical influence over the hearts of the animals upon which they prey (game animals). The predatory animals never failed to overcome their prey by breathing upon them even at a great distance, for their breath pierced the heart of the game animals, causing their limbs to stiffen and the animals to lose their strength. Mountain Lion, the chief of the Beast Gods, possessed additional powers in the senses of sight and smell, which, because they were derived from his heart, were preserved in his fetish since his heart still lived, even though his person had been changed to stone.

Poshaiank'ia, the Father of the Medicine Societies, once appeared in human form to bring agriculture, the use of prayersticks, and to organize the medicine societies. He then left for his home in Sipapulima, where he vanished beneath the world but still heard the prayers of his earthly children. In ancient times, he was guarded on all sides by his six warriors—bow priests—which are the sacred animals of prey: Mountain Lion (north), Bear (west), Badger (south), Wolf (east), Eagle (zenith), and Mole (nadir) (Cushing 1988: 16). Knifewing was sometimes assigned to the zenith instead of Eagle, while Gopher sometimes took the place of Mole (Bunzel 1992:528).

Each of these figures was carved with its own distinguishing characteristics. The long, lean Mountain Lion, called Long Tail, had a very long tail laid lengthwise on his back from the rump nearly to the shoulders; his rounded ears were not prominent. Bear, called Clumsy Foot, had a jutting tail and ears somewhat larger than those of Mountain Lion on his rounded body. Badger, called Black Mark Face, was either naturalistically carved or crudely rendered. Wolf, or Hang Tail, was characterized by his erect ears and hanging tail. Eagle, or White Cap, tended to be a crude bird form with naturalistic or conventional wings, while Mole, because he was considered to be the least powerful, was usually a rude carving without definite form.

Just as the animal fetishes derived their power from the animals they represented, so too, images and living beings associated with water and rain were endowed with rain-bringing power. To encourage bountiful rain, the Zuni painted images of frogs, toads, tadpoles, and water serpents on pottery containers and on kiva walls (Young 1991:164). The Zuni explained that their ancestors had painted and carved turtles, toads, frogs, and insects that lived in or near bodies of water on rocks surrounding the pueblo to bring rain to the area (ibid., 164). Such associational power was not limited to images, for some katsina dancers carried living turtles in their hands as they performed the summer rain dances (Young 1988:125–27).

The Zuni Aesthetic System

Aesthetics—what a given culture considers to be beautiful—breaks down the boundaries between different arenas of human experience; thus, the ritual attire of the katsina dancers, the decoration of a house, and even the choice of food served to guests at the Shalako feast all express the Zuni aesthetic.

Many scholars have commented on the sophistication and richness of the Zuni aesthetic system. The Zuni aesthetic of the beautiful is captured in the word *tso'ya,* which cannot be precisely translated into English but combines a sense of the "dynamic, multicolored, chromatic (in the musical sense), varied, new, exciting, clear and beautiful" (Tedlock 1993:48–63). (The presence of such a multilayered word in the Zuni language shows that the Zuni have given the idea of beauty considerable thought.) In nature, the Zuni use *tso'ya* to describe the structural iridescence of a rainbow, as well as the final stages of a sunset when mackerel clouds layered with many shades of red, yellow, blue, and purple blaze against a sky tinged with palest green. Butterflies, mammals, birds, and reptiles are also *tso'ya* because they have variegated coloration and dynamic behavior. The Rocky Mountain swallowtail butterfly exemplifies this word in the rainbowlike play of colors on its hind wing, where a series of yellow spots are heavily outlined in black paralleled by black-bordered zones of opalescent blue and a large, round, red shimmery spot. Both its variegated coloration and its erratic flight course with many instant changes of direction qualify this butterfly as *tso'ya* (ibid., 48–63).

The same aesthetic ideal of layered colors and textures combined with dynamic movement makes a line of katsina dancers *tso'ya*. They wear cotton and woolen textiles, silk, hanks of multicolored yarn, paper butterflies, plastic flowers, popcorn, chiles, feathers, branches of evergreen, hides and furs of various animals, sticks of cottonwood and sagebrush, shell-encrusted bandoliers, and silver and turquoise jewelry. The dance line as a whole is *tso'ya* not only because of their multitextured, multicolored dress but also because of their asymmetrical placement, for instead of bunching together or evenly spacing the individualist dancers—who stand out from the other dancers because of their masks—the dance leader places them asymmetrically, for example, in the fifth, twelfth, and fourteenth positions in line (Tedlock 1993:57).

The dress and behavior of Knifewing also express *tso'ya*. This handsome but dangerous mythical bird has obsidian knives as wings and wears an elaborate opalescent bandolier of abalone and mother-of-pearl rainbow. In Zuni lapidary and wall paintings, his legs, wings, and tail are posed in perfect symmetry, while his head is turned, adding an asymmetrical element. But majestic elegance would not be sufficient alone to make Knifewing *tso'ya*; his behavior in fireside tales together with his appearance are what give him this quicksilver quality. Knifewing is known for his soaring flights, as high as that of an eagle, punctuated by sudden turns and swoops to earth to seduce young women (Tedlock 1993:57).

Not limited to the visual realm, *tso'ya* also applies auditorily. The Zuni musical repertory includes distinct ceremonial genres: softly sung corn-grinding songs, medicine-society songs with simple texts and diatonic melodies, and katsina songs with complex allegorical texts. Anthropologist Barbara Tedlock explained that a newly composed katsina song was *tso'ya* because "two diatonic melodies, stretching to nearly an octave, each with its own tonality, set of tones and tonal relations, are united through a subtly embroidered refrain of chromatic riffs. Further, these melodies and riffs should produce a single complex stepped-diagonal construction that begins low and ends high" (1993:58–59). The performance of such a song is beautiful when its loud and clearly enunciated delivery does justice to the two-octave range.

Song texts are beautiful when they consist of literal and allegorical levels of meaning that appear simultaneously, a quality exemplified in a song that appeared during the summer of 1972 entitled "They Went to the Moon Mother." The song's performer-composer explained to Tedlock (1993:59) that his song was "simultaneously about two stars . . . and two American astronauts each wearing two stars on their helmets, who [he believed] may or may not have been lying about their ride to the Moon Mother on a . . . rocketship," which is referred to as "the dragonfly." By means of their "sacred rainmaking bundle" (which is Houston Control), they report that the moon will bless them by providing silt deposits of the kind thought by scientists to be on the moon. These deposits are a blessing because these same silt deposits occur after every heavy rain in the Southwest, implying that rain will come. In one line, the word *stretching* is reiterated to convey three metaphorical meanings: the rocketship reaching the moon, corn plants reaching out for the rain, and people reaching old age: "rainmakers soaking the earth with rain making lightning, thundering, coming, coming, stretching, stretching, stretching." Tedlock reported that this song was repeated more than twenty times by request of the Mudhead (Koyemshi) clowns, which was high praise, for the Koyemshi are the ultimate judges and critics of all katsina performances.

In contrast to the beautiful is the dangerous, *attanni*. Embodied in bears and ravens, this word refers to things that are dark and untouchable, shaggy and old, powerful and dangerous. Both animals contribute their skins and feathers to the esoteric medicine societies and to katsinam because they are so powerful. Bears are *attanni* because they have such a keen sense of smell, can run so fast, hunt from ambush, and surprise their victims by swatting them. Ravens circle for hours riding the wind currents until they suddenly somersault and drop from an altitude of 500 feet to grab part of a fawn for their supper; they are *attanni* because of their aggressive behavior, including their raucous call, and their sleek black appearance highlighted by a sharp roman beak.

The muddy masks and bodies and ragged dress of the Koyemshi, the ambiguous figures modeled of clay and carved of stone, and the shaggy hair and costumes of cannibalistic ogres, when coupled with their terrifying behavior, make these beings *attanni*. As anthropologist Jane Young pointed out, these beings derive their power from their ambiguity (and thus unpredictability), for they have fluid, permeable boundaries (1991:166–67). In the Zuni origin story, this indeterminate quality is what made the first beings, which were neither completely human nor animal, so repulsive, and the soft, unstable earth, with its unpredictable earthquakes and fierce creatures, so horrifying.

Yet it is the interplay between these two qualities that is the essence of the Zuni aesthetic. Long ago, when the earth was still soft, the people had to choose between two speckled green eggs and two dull white eggs. The Zuni chose the dappled green eggs, which contained chicks with downy pinfeathers of yellow and blue, red and green; however, when they molted, their adult plumage was black, for they were ravens, while the birds inside the plain eggs were brilliant, multicolored macaws. Barbara Tedlock summed up the story's meaning: "The beautiful eggs contained multicolored chicks that molted and matured into dangerous black ravens: for Zunis ever since, the beautiful has had the dangerous somewhere near or even bursting into the midst of it" (1993:62–63).

The Zuni sense of the beautiful as multicolored, luminous, and complex is evident in their jewelry with its jet, coral, opalescent abalone, mother-of-pearl, spiny oyster shell, and exquisite cluster settings of turquoise. The Zuni are famous around the world for their jewelry, and it is estimated that over 80 percent of the families at Zuni make jewelry. Until the Navajo introduced them to silver-working in the 1870s, the Zuni made only shell, stone, and turquoise disc beads and tab pendants, and turquoise and shell overlay mosaic on objects of shell, bone, and wood, as did the Ancestral Pueblo peoples. The Zuni prize abalone for its light-catching and reflective properties. In recent times, the Zuni have used the lapidary skill they cultivated in the making of animal fetishes to make necklaces of very small animal and bird forms strung on lengths of shell disc beads. Although made by other Indians as well, animal bead necklaces of Zuni manufacture exhibit such attention to detail that each small creature has a unique individuality rather than an assembly-line appearance. In the 1930s the Zuni made necklaces of large pieces of turquoise cut in leaf shapes, which they set in large silver bezels and hung from strings of massive coral beads. Leekya Desyee was known for his high level of skill and craftsmanship in making these necklaces; his work is characterized by the degree to which he allowed the veins of the matrix of the turquoise to become a strong feature of the whole design.

In 1872 one of the first Navajo silversmiths, Atsidi Chon, came to Zuni to make silver jewelry for sale (Adair 1944:121–28).In return for the hospitality of a Zuni named Lanyade, Atsidi taught him how to make silver ornaments. When Atsidi returned to Navajo country after a year, Lanyade was the only silversmith at Zuni. After Lanyade taught several other Zunis to make silver jewelry, the craft began to spread through the village. In time the Zuni developed a distinctive style of lapidary work, which emphasizes the turquoise rather than the silver by using many small settings of precisely cut, well-matched stones. Trader C. G. Wallace, who learned to speak Zuni, kept the Zuni supplied with turquoise and silver, and encouraged them in their production of jewelry and other art forms, exerting a strong

Leonard Martza,
Zuni silversmith,
Zuni Pueblo, 1998.
Author photograph

influence in the 1920s. By that time the Zuni were making a considerable amount of jewelry in the cluster setting style.

Sometime in the late 1940s the Zuni began to further develop their preference for a multiplicity of small settings, creating a style known as needlepoint. Rows of tiny, sliverlike turquoise stones are set so closely in miniature bezels that the turquoise stones seem to lose their separate identity to become a semitransparent blue veil that lies over a silver surface. The light and feathery effect gives this type of jewelry a sense of insubstantiality, in strong contrast to the massive pieces of turquoise characteristic of Navajo jewelry. The Zuni also make an even finer style, known as petit point, which features tiny circular settings of turquoise.

At the same time they were developing the needlepoint style, the Zuni also began to use another method for setting stones, known as cloisonné or channel work. Channel jewelry is made by soldering narrow strips of sheet silver to a backplate and then filling the small chambers with carefully cut and polished stones or shell. The Zuni aesthetic is evident in their figures of Sun Father, Rainbow, and Knifewing supernaturals, for they combine the sheen of silver with the deep rich colors of jet and turquoise, with iridescent abalone or mother-of-pearl.

Pottery-making is another art at which the Zuni excel. In the late 1800s and on into the first half of the 1900s, Zuni women were making well-fired and superbly decorated pottery in three major styles: rounded water ollas, dough bowls with interior and exterior decoration, and ceremonial pots with stepped sides. For carrying water, women made large, rounded ollas painted with distinctive deer and medallion designs. The most characteristic feature of Zuni pottery is a white-tailed deer with a lifeline—or "breathline"—running from his nose to a quite visible heart as he poses in profile within the swallowtail butterfly's house that arches over him. Another favorite motif is the large sunflower medallion.

Zuni pottery fits their aesthetic ideal when the design elements are divided into vertical areas that alternate between two different fields. They express the same sense of order and regularity evident in their jewelry design in their pottery design by freezing sequential narrative time within simultaneous visual space, so that visual images that roughly correspond to narrative events are portrayed on the surface of a single pot. In contrast to the Hopi conception of beauty, which favors painted designs that complement the shape of the pot, the Zuni ideal features images that dominate the shape of the pot. Zuni potters paint a double line, broken in one place—the spirit break—at the junction of the neck and the body of the pot. They decorate the neck band with large, complex motifs—usually a central diamond flanked by trumpetlike scrolls of black and red elements—and on the body of the pot, in the middle of three horizontal bands, they often paint a series of stylized birds with long flowing tails.

Zuni potters once made large dough bowls for mixing their cornmeal dough, which they decorated inside and out. These much flatter bowls had out-flaring rims decorated with designs similar to those on the ollas and again divided into a band just below the lip of the pot and the central bowl area by a line with a spirit break. They decorated both areas with diamond and trumpet-scroll motifs and painted stylized red birds in the bottom of the pot's interior, while exterior designs tended to be nonrepresentational, featuring triangles with antecedents in prehistoric pottery.

The Zuni are known for the large number of ceremonial bowls they made, which are quite different from their everyday pottery in both shape and decoration. These distinctive bowls have four terraced extensions of the rim spaced at equal intervals around the circumference, each bearing a figure. Water imagery is prevalent in their sacred pottery, including such motifs as dragonflies, frogs, tadpoles, and Kolowisi, the horned water serpent. They also introduce an element of the dangerous by tying or tacking onto the edges and inside bottoms crudely naturalistic figures of snakes, toads, frogs, tadpoles, and dragonflies (Tedlock 1993:61), which embody *attanni* because of the power they invoke and the unpredictability of their behavior.

A:Shiwi A:Wan Museum and Heritage Center

For nearly thirty years the Zuni considered various concepts for a tribal museum until they finally settled on an eco-museum, an approach that is most compatible with their cultural and environmental values. The majority of the collections are either part of the series of 4,000 historic and contemporary photographs taken at Zuni or the Tribal Archives, established in 1990, that serve as a repository for Zuni historical records. One of the unique aspects of A:shiwi A:wan Museum and Heritage Center is the central role played by the community, for the Tribal Archives are accessible to all Zuni individuals, and the community is involved in exhibitions, outdoor workshops, and school programs. Museum staff collaborate with local community members and national museums to mount exhibitions. Elders share traditions with Zuni children, working in the traditional Zuni "waffle garden," cooking area, and an adobe workshop, and school programs provide activities and resources for all grades of public and parochial schools in Zuni.

More Recent History

World War II was an important turning point for the Zuni, as it was for all Native American peoples, because returning veterans—over 200 Zuni served their country—became a catalyst for social and political change. Despite a concerted effort to reintegrate them into ceremonial activity, these veterans had great difficulty adjusting to the restrictions of Zuni life and only began to exert their full influence in the 1950s (Adair and Vogt 1949). In the postwar period major changes occurred, beginning with the shift of political power from the priests to the politicians and the growth of factions into political "parties"; the tribal council gained more control over reservation resources and activities, such as craft enterprises, and tried to attract industry to the reservation while also expanding the educational system (Eggan and Pandey 1979:479). Extending its jurisdiction in the 1950s, the tribal council used federal funds to introduce electricity and domestic water and sewer lines, and to construct over 800 single-family dwelling in suburban subdivisions. Today these subdivisions, located away from the old village, include grassy lawns, sidewalks, streetlights, paved streets, and central heat, gas, and electricity. The tribal council also established a water board, police department, housing authority, and utility authority, as well as committees for education, legal aid, economic development, recreation, fire fighting, and agriculture (ibid., 479).

The Zuni have become increasingly dependent upon the modern industrial cash economy for their needs, and every household has a pickup truck or car for easy access to Gallup, Grants, and Albuquerque to buy appliances, furniture, and groceries. Today the Zuni suffer from unemployment, underemployment, substandard living conditions, and lack of adequate education, and per-capita income remains far below the national average. The major source of income is wage labor, which includes federal, tribal, and local industries and off-reservation employment, followed by arts and crafts (Ladd 1979:494). Livestock and agriculture provide some income, and nearly every household at Zuni has someone involved in lapidary and silverwork. Most Zuni sell their work through traders in Gallup, Albuquerque, and Santa Fe, New Mexico or Flagstaff, Arizona, but in the 1960s the tribe established the Zuni Craftsmen's Cooperative Association to provide marketing and merchandising services and a ready outlet for craftsmen at competitive prices. Zuni Arts and Crafts has stores in Zuni Pueblo and San Francisco, California, to market their jewelry and crafts.

Contemporary Issues

Tribal Government

In the 1890s, when federal officials jailed the Bow Priests, preventing them from exercising their traditional authority on behalf of the Council of High Priests, the U.S. government undermined the traditional Zuni political system. The Council of High Priests was then forced to involve itself directly in secular affairs, which led to severe political turmoil and factionalism. By 1934, no longer able to install a governor and tribal council by traditional means, the Zuni accepted the provisions of the Indian Reorganization Act (the Wheeler-Howard Act), which provided for the election of a tribal council, although the transition from theocratic to democratic government took several decades. In 1970 the Zuni ratified the tribal constitution, structuring the tribal government to include a legislative branch (governor, lieutenant governor, and six tribal councilmen with four-year terms), an executive branch (overseen by the governor, lieutenant governor, and tribal secretary), and a judicial branch (Ferguson and Seciwa 1994:723).

The tribal council is elected by popular vote and installed by the Council of High Priests. Ironically, in this matrilineal society, women did not receive the right to vote until 1965, the same year in which secret balloting was instituted. As in other New Mexico pueblos, the insignia of office are canes: today only those presented by Abraham Lincoln in 1863 are used. (The original set from the Spanish Crown is no longer used.)

Zuni Land Claims

When the Zuni Reservation was established in 1877, its boundaries did not include the Zunis' farming village of Nutria, whose springs supply a major portion of the Zuni River. Frank Hamilton Cushing, learning of this upon his arrival at Zuni in 1879, enlisted the aid of Eastern writers and news reporters. Although his actions eventually led to his removal from Zuni, Cushing and his friends brought enough pressure through their national campaign against the "land grab attempt" by ranchers that the government slightly enlarged the reservation to include the springs and village at Nutria (Ferguson and Hart 1990:93).

Recognizing that their land base was not large enough to support their population, in 1917, 1935, and 1949 Zuni leaders petitioned the federal government for more land. Although the boundaries of the reservation were increased, its size still remains inadequate, and successive Zuni tribal councils continue to initiate litigation of land claims. Having failed to file a land claim under the Indian Claims Commission, the Zuni had to obtain special legislation to enable them to sue the federal government for compensation for lands taken without payment. In 1978 Congress passed this legislation in an act (P.L. 95–280) that also provided for the return of Zuni Salt Lake.

For over a century Zuni leaders have tried to protect their ownership and use rights to Kolhu/wala:Wa, located in eastern Arizona, at the confluence of the Zuni and Little Colorado rivers. Beneath this lake, which is fed by waters from a sacred spring, lies the village of Kokko ("Katsinam") where Zunis return after death to live. On one of the nearby mountains is an opening into the underworld, where Zuni religious leaders enter subterranean chambers in order to communicate with their ancestors and the Kokko, and on another mountain is the location where the Koyemshi (Mudheads) were created. Every four years —and more frequently in times of drought—between forty and sixty Zunis undertake a religious pilgrimage that lasts four days and covers over 110 miles to Kolhu/wala:Wa. Along the way, they leave offerings, say prayers, and gather sacred paint pigments; after reaching Kolhu/wala:Wa, they conduct rituals to bring peace and prosperity to the world. Most of the private owners of land supported the Zunis' right to cross their land, and Apache County officials made every effort to protect the Zunis during their pilgrimages, including setting up roadblocks on Highway 666 under the direction of Zuni religious leaders. However, Earl Platt, a wealthy attorney who owns a large ranch along the pilgrimage route, has tried to have Zuni religious leaders arrested for trespassing on his land. Lengthy court battles ensued until in 1990, after more than a century of work, the Zunis were finally guaranteed easement and use rights of Kolhu/wala:Wa (Ferguson and Seciwa 1994:726).

At the present time, the Zuni Reservation consists of four tracts of federal trust land in New Mexico and Arizona. In addition to the main reservation, Zuni lands also include the Salt Lake and two tracts on and near Kolhu/wala:Wa. The Zunis filed a claim for lands taken without payment in the Court of Claims (Docket 161–79L), and when this case was litigated in 1981, the Zuni filed a land claim for damages to their lands—erosion, takings of water, coal, salt, and other property, and damage to archaeological sites—caused by the acts and omissions of the U.S. government (Ferguson and Seciwa 1994:726). The Zuni tribe initiated litigation to adjudicate the water rights within the Zuni River basin in the 1980s, but this case was dismissed by the New Mexico courts and is awaiting reinstatement. The Court of Claims decided in 1987 that all Zuni claims for land taken without payment were valid, and in 1990 the Zuni tribe was awarded $25 million in compensation. Congress also passed the Zuni Land Conservation Act (P.L. 101–486) the same year, authorizing payment of an additional $25 million and establishing a permanent trust fund to be used for the rehabilitation of degraded lands and the initiation of sustainable development (ibid., 726). The Zuni are working on a plan for sustainable development to restore their landscape, improve their living conditions, enhance educational opportunities, and increase individual income.

References and Further Reading

Volume 9 of the Smithsonian's *Handbook of North American Indians* (1979) contains chapters about various aspects of Zuni culture.

Adair, John. 1944. *The Navajo and Pueblo Silversmiths.* University of Oklahoma Press, Norman.

Adair, John, and Evon Vogt. 1949. "Navaho and Zuni Veterans: A Study of Contrasting Modes of Culture Change." *American Anthropologist* 51, no. 4:547–61.

Bandelier, Adolph. 1892. *An Outline of the Documentary History of the Zuni Tribe. Journal of American Ethnology and Archaeology* 3. Houghton, Mifflin, Boston.

Bedinger, Margery. 1973. *Indian Silver: Navajo and Pueblo Jewelers.* University of New Mexico Press, Albuquerque.

Bell, Barbara, and Ed Bell. 1975–77. *Zuni: The Art and the People.* 3 vols. Squaw Bell Traders, Grants, N.Mex.

Benedict, Ruth. 1934. *Patterns of Culture*. Mentor Books, New York.

———. 1935 *Zuni Mythology*. 2 vols. Columbia University Contributions to Anthropology 21. Columbia University Press, New York.

Bohrer, V. L. 1960. "Zuni Agriculture." *El Palacio* 67, no. 6:181–82.

Bunzel, Ruth. 1932. "Zuni Katchinas." In *Forty-Seventh Annual Report of the Bureau of American Ethnology*, pp. 837–1086. U.S. Government Printing Office, Washington, D.C.

———. 1933. *Zuni Texts*. Publications of the American Ethnological Society 15. Ed. Franz Boas. Stechert, New York.

———. 1935. *Zuni*. Columbia University Press, New York.

———. 1972 [1929]. *The Pueblo Potter: A Study of Creative Imagination in Primitive Art*. Dover Publications, New York.

*———. 1992. *Zuni Ceremonialism*. University of New Mexico Press, Albuquerque. [This volume contains three studies published in 1932 by the Smithsonian Institution: *Introduction to Zuni Ceremonialism, Zuni Origin Myths, Zuni Ritual Poetry*. This classic work by an early anthropologist contains a wealth of detailed information.]

Bureau of Indian Affairs (BIA). 1973. *The Zuni Reservation: Its Resources and Development Potential*. Report 207. U.S. Dept. of the Interior, Billings, Mont.

Camazine, Scott M. 1980. "Traditional and Western Health Care among the Zuni Indians of New Mexico." *Social Science and Medicine* 148:73–80.

Camazine, Scott M., and Robert Bye. 1980. "A Study of the Medical Ethnobotany of the Zuni Indians of New Mexico." *Journal of Ethnopharmacology* 2:365–68.

Canfield, Anne Sutton. 1980. "Ahayu:da—Art or Icon?" *Native Arts West* 1, no. 1:24–26.

Caywood, Louis. 1972. *The Restored Mission of Nuestra Senora de Guadalupe de Zuni*. St. Michaels Press, St. Michaels, Ariz.

Crampton, C. Gregory. 1977. *The Zunis of Cibola*. University of Utah Press, Salt Lake City.

Cushing, Frank Hamilton. 1882–83. *My Adventures in Zuni*. Peripatetic Press, Santa Fe.

———. 1892. "A Zuni Folktale of the Underworld." *Journal of American Folklore* 5, no. 2:49–56.

———. 1896. *Outlines of Zuni Creation Myths*. Thirteenth Annual Report of the Bureau of American Ethnology 1891–92. Washington, D.C.

———. 1920. *Zuni Breadstuff*. Museum of the American Indian, Heye Foundation, Indian Notes and Monographs 8. New York.

*———. 1931. *Zuni Folk Tales*. Alfred Knopf, New York. [Written by the first participant-observer at Zuni, this is Cushing's best known work.]

———. 1988 [1883]. *Zuni Fetishes*. KC Publications, Las Vegas, Nev.

Dutton, Bertha. 1963. *Friendly People: The Zuni Indians*. Museum of New Mexico Press, Santa Fe.

Eggan, Fred, and T. N. Pandey. 1979. "Zuni History, 1850–1970." In *Handbook of North American Indians*, vol. 9: *The Southwest*, pp. 474–81.

Eriacho, Wilfred. 1979. Coauthored with T. J. Ferguson. "The Zuni War Gods: Art, Artifact, or

Religious Beings: A Conflict in Values, Beliefs, and Use." Paper presented at the New Directions in Native American Art History Symposium, Albuquerque.

Ferguson, T. J., and Wilfred Eriacho. 1990. "*Ahayu:da* Zuni War Gods: Cooperation and Repatriation." *Native Peoples* 4, no. 1:6–12.

*Ferguson, T. J., and Richard Hart. 1990 [1985]. *A Zuni Atlas.* University of Oklahoma Press, Norman. [Although written by non-Zunis, this well-researched atlas contains archaeological, historical, and ethnohistorical material approved by Zuni political and religious leaders.]

Ferguson, T. J., and Barbara Mills. 1982. *Archaeological Investigations at Zuni Pueblo, New Mexico, 1977–1980.* Zuni Archaeology Program Report 183. Pueblo of Zuni, Zuni, N.Mex.

Ferguson, T. J., and Cal Seciwa. 1994. "Zuni." In *Native America in the Twentieth Century: An Encyclopedia,* pp. 723–27. Ed. Mary B. Davis. Garland Publishing, New York.

Fewkes, Jesse W. 1890. "On the Use of the Phonograph among the Zuni Indians." *American Naturalist* 24:687–91.

———. 1891. "A Few Summer Ceremonials at Zuni Pueblo." *Journal of American Ethnology and Archaeology* 1:1–61.

Ford, Richard I. 1981. "Gardening and Farming before A.D. 1000: Patterns of Prehistoric Cultivation North of Mexico." *Journal of Ethnobiology* 1:6–27.

Green, Jesse. 1979. *Zuni: Selected Writings of Frank Hamilton Cushing.* University of Nebraska Press, Lincoln.

———. 1990. *Cushing at Zuni: The Correspondence and Journals of Frank Hamilton Cushing, 1879–1884.* University of New Mexico Press, Albuquerque.

Handey, Edward. 1918. "Zuni Tales." *Journal of American Folk-Lore* 31:451–71.

Hardin, Margaret Ann. 1983. *Gifts of Mother Earth: Ceramics in the Zuni Tradition.* Heard Museum, Phoenix, Ariz.

Hart, E. Richard. 1973. *The Zunis: Experiences and Descriptions.* Pueblo of Zuni, Zuni, N.Mex.

———. 1983. "Zuni Relations with the United States and the Zuni Land Claim." In *Zuni History,* pp. 29–32. Institute of the American West, Sun Valley, Idaho.

Hill, G. Richard. 1983. "The Zuni Land Claim Litigation." In *Zuni History,* p. 36. Institute of the American West, Sun Valley, Idaho.

Hodge, Frederick. 1910. "Zuni." In *Handbook of American Indians North of Mexico,* 2:1015–1020. Bureau of American Ethnology Bulletin 30. Washington, D.C.

Hustito, Charles. 1991. "Why Zuni War Gods Need to Be Returned." In *Zuni History: Victories in the 1990s.* Published by the Zuni Tribe, available at A:shiwi A:wan Museum and Heritage Center.

Kroeber, Alfred. 1916. "Thoughts on Zuni Religion." In *Holmes Anniversary Volume,* pp. 269–77, ed. F. W. Hodge. James William Bryan Press, Washington, D.C.

———. 1917. "Zuni Kin and Clan." *Anthropological Papers of the American Museum of Natural History* 18, no. 2:39–204.

*Ladd, Edmund. 1979. "Zuni Social and Political Organization." In *Handbook of North American Indians,* vol. 9: *The Southwest,* pp.482–91. [A scholar from Zuni presents a concise account of Zuni socioreligious and political systems.]

———. 1979. "Zuni Economy." In *Handbook of North American Indians,* vol. 9: *The Southwest,* pp. 492–98.

———. 1983. "Zuni Religion and Philosophy." *Exploration: Annual Bulletin of the School of American Research (Zuni and El Morro* issue):26–31.

Leighton, Dorothea, and John Adair. 1966. *People of the Middle Place: A Study of the Zuni Indians.* Behavior Science Monographs. Human Relations Area Files Press, New Haven, Conn.

Levy, Gordon. 1980. *Who's Who in Zuni Jewelry.* Western Arts Publishing, Denver.

Li, An-che. 1937. "Zuni: Some Observations and Queries." *American Anthropologist* 39:62–76.

Long, T. P. 1978. "The Prevalence of Clinically Treated Diabetes among Zuni Reservation Residents." *American Journal of Public Health* 68:901.

Newman, Stanley. 1958. *Zuni Dictionary.* Indiana University Research Center in Anthropology, Folklore and Linguistics Publication 6. Indiana University Press, Bloomington.

———. 1964. "A Comparison of Zuni and California Penutian." *International Journal of American Linguistics* 30, no. 1:1–13.

———. 1965. *Zuni Grammar.* University of New Mexico Publications in Anthropology 14. University of New Mexico Press, Albuquerque.

———. 1982. "Vocabulary Levels: Zuni Sacred and Slang Usage." *Southwestern Journal of Anthropology* 11:345–54.

Nusbaum, Aileen. 1926. *Seven Cities of Cibola: Zuni Indian Tales.* G. P. Putnam's Sons, New York.

Parsons, Elsie C. 1916. "The Zuni A'Doshle and Suuke." *American Anthropologist* 18:338–47.

———. 1917. "Notes on Zuni." *Memoirs of the American Anthropological Association* 4:151–327. Lancaster, Pa.

———. 1919. "Increase by Magic: A Zuni Pattern." *American Anthropologist* 21:279–86.

———. 1922. "Winter and Summer Dance Series in Zuni in 1918." *University of California Publications in American Archaeology and Ethnology* 17:171–216.

———. 1924. "The Scalp Ceremonial of Zuni." *Memoirs of the American Anthropological Association* 31:1–42.

———. 1933. *Hopi and Zuni Ceremonialism.* Memoirs of the American Anthropological Association 39. Menasha, Wis.

———. 1939. *Pueblo Indian Religion.* 2 vols. University of Chicago Press, Chicago.

Rodee, Marian, and James Ostler. 1986. *Zuni Pottery.* Schiffer Publishing, West Chester, Pa.

———. 1990. *The Fetish Carvers of Zuni.* Maxwell Museum of Anthropology, Albuquerque.

Roscoe, Will. 1991. *The Zuni Man-Woman.* University of New Mexico Press, Albuquerque.

Sando, Joe S. 1992. *Pueblo Nations: Eight Centuries of Pueblo Indian History.* Clear Light Publishers, Santa Fe.

Schneider, David, and John M. Roberts. 1965. *Zuni Kin Terms.* Human Area Relations File, New Haven, Conn.

*Seowtewa, Ken. 1992. "Adding a Breath to Zuni Life." *Native Peoples* 5, no. 2:10–19. [A Zuni artist writes about what creating the murals in Our Lady of Guadalupe Church means to his family and the people at Zuni.]

Simmons, Marc. 1974. *Witchcraft in the Southwest.* Northland Press, Flagstaff, Ariz.

Smith, Watson, and John Roberts. 1954. *Zuni Law: A Field of Values.* Papers of the Peabody Museum of American Archaeology and Ethnology 43. Peabody Museum, Cambridge, Mass.

Stevenson, James. 1883. "Illustrated Catalogue of the Collections Obtained from the Indians of New Mexico and Arizona in 1879." In *Second Annual Report of the Bureau of American Ethnology for the Years 1880–1881,* pp. 307–422. Washington, D.C.

Stevenson, Matilda Coxe. 1887. "The Religious Life of the Zuni Child." In *Fifth Annual Report of the Bureau of American Ethnology for the Years 1883–1884,* pp. 533–55. Washington, D.C.

*———. 1904. "The Zuni Indians: Their Mythology, Esoteric Fraternities, and Ceremonies." In *Twenty-third Annual Report of the Bureau of American Ethnology for the Years 1901–1902,* pp. 3–634. Washington, D.C. [A classic work written by one of the best known early anthropologists at Zuni.]

———. 1993 [1915]. *The Zuni Indians and Their Uses of Plants.* Dover, Mineola, N.Y.

Stoffle, Richard W. 1975. "Reservation-based Industry: A Case from Zuni, New Mexico." *Human Organization* 34, no. 3:217–25.

Tedlock, Barbara. 1961. *Music of the Pueblos, Apache, and Navaho.* Taylor Museum, Colorado Springs Fine Arts Center R 611317. [Recording.]

———. 1970. *Zuni.* Canyon Records ARP 6060. [Recording.]

———. 1971. *Summer Songs from Zuni.* Canyon Records 6077. [Recording.]

———. 1980. "Songs of the Zuni Kachina Society: Composition, Rehearsal and Performance." In *Southwestern Indian Ritual Drama,* pp. 7–35, ed. Charlotte Frisbie. University of New Mexico Press, Albuquerque.

———. 1986. "Zuni." In *The New Grove Dictionary of American Music,* 4:597–98, ed. H. Wiley Hitchcock. Macmillan, London.

———. 1990. *Music from Zuni Pueblo: Featuring Chester Mahooty and Family.* Tribal Music International, Rainbow Cassette Studio. [Recording.]

*———. 1992. *The Beautiful and the Dangerous: Encounters with the Zuni Indians.* Viking, New York. [An eminent scholar of Zuni culture writes eloquently about her experiences at Zuni by fusing anthropological data with life-story narratives, legends, and myths.]

———. 1993 [1984]. "The Beautiful and the Dangerous: Zuni Ritual and Cosmology as an Aesthetic System." In *Arts of Africa, Oceania, and the Americas,* pp. 48–63, ed. Janet Berlo and Lee Ann Wilson. Prentice Hall, Englewood Cliffs, N.J.

Tedlock, Dennis, trans. 1972. *Finding the Center: Narrative Poetry of the Zuni Indians, by Andrew Peynetsa and Walter Sanchez.* Dial Press, New York.

Wilson, Edmund. 1979 [1956]. "The Zuni Shalako Ceremony." In *Reader in Comparative Religion*, pp. 288–96, ed. William Lessa and Evon Vogt. 4th ed. Harper and Row, New York.

Woodbury, Richard. 1979. "Prehistory: Introduction." In *Handbook of North American Indians*, vol. 9: *The Southwest*, pp. 22–30.

Wright, Barton. 1985. *Kachinas of the Zuni.* Northland Press, Flagstaff, Ariz.

*———. 1994 [1988]. *The Mythic World of the Zuni.* University of New Mexico Press, Albuquerque. [Museum curator and scholar Wright has edited and illustrated Cushing's classic work in a style that makes these stories come alive.]

Young, M. Jane. 1981. "Ethnoastronomy: The Zuni Case." In *Archaeoastronomy in the Americas*, pp. 183–91, ed. Ray Williamson. Ballena Press and Center for Archaeoastronomy, Los Altos, Calif.

———. 1982. "We Were Going to Have a Barbeque, But the Cow Ran Away: Production, Form, and Function of the Zuni Tribal Fair." *Southwest Folklore* 5:42–48.

*———. 1988. *Signs from the Ancestors: Zuni Cultural Symbolism and Perceptions of Rock Art.* University of New Mexico Press, Albuquerque. [A professor and well-known scholar of Zuni culture interprets Zuni rock art as perceived by the Zuni people, with great sensitivity.]

———. 1991. "Permeable Boundaries: Ambiguity and Metaphor in Zuni Ceremonialism and Daily Life." *Southern Folklore* 48:159–89.

———. 1992. "Morning Star, Evening Star: Zuni Traditional Stories." In *Earth and Sky: Visions of the Cosmos in Native American Folklore*, pp. 75–100, ed. Ray Williamson and Claire Farrer. University of New Mexico Press, Albuquerque.

Zuni Pueblo. 1966–73. *Zuni Tribal Newsletter*, mimeograph.

———. 1969. *Zuni Comprehensive Development Plan for a Better Zuni by '75: Presented by the Pueblo of Zuni with the Cooperation of Local, State, and Federal Agencies.* Pueblo of Zuni.

———. 1972. *The Zunis: Self-Portrayals*, trans. Alvina Quam. University of New Mexico Press, Albuquerque.

———. 1983. *Zuni History.* Institute of the American West, Sun Valley, Idaho.

Part 2   Rancheria Farming

Wave clouds over Baboquivari, Tohono O'odham Reservation, 1966. Photograph: Keith Pierce

Chapter 5 The O'odham

June 1995

The range of mountains shimmers in the 114° heat; faded with distance, the mountains are all but indistinguishable from the pale sky with its scattered, ineffectual clouds. The memory of monsoon floods lies locked far beneath the bone-dry wash, its sandy surface marred by the faint tracks of a speckle-tailed lizard.

Our Tohono O'odham guide, Alex, steers his pickup off the paved highway and onto a bumpy, overgrown dirt road through the desert. My heart soars at the sight of red-tailed hawks circling in the direction of Baboquivari, the majestic peak that can be seen from nearly every village on the reservation.

Alex directs our attention: "Look! See that roadrunner in the wash? There's a hawk's nest in that saguaro over there. My people told the time of year by the ripening of all the different plants because they bloom at different times. The yellow palo verde blossoms are dropping off when the purple ironwood blooms. Now the ironwood is about at the end of its season and the saguaro fruit is ripening. In some places, though, the saguaro flowers are still blooming. It's late this year."

When we arrive at the saguaro camp, two Tohono O'odham women are sitting on a bench under the shade of a ramada made of mesquite posts and plywood. Two vans are unloading their passengers, naturalists who have come to watch the saguaro harvest. People of all ages are emerging from the vehicles, laden with water bottles and cameras.

Soon Vivian, the younger O'odham woman, is leading us across the desert as she wipes her face with a red bandanna. Though she is less than 5 feet tall, she easily hefts the 12-foot pole, guiding it gently to the top of the saguaro. Surrounded by sprawling ocotillo, cholla, prickly pear, and barrel cactus, the naturalists look on intently. Soon the sun's fiery intensity will melt their initial enthusiasm; perspiration already trickles down my back, plastering my hair to my neck.

I hear a loud wail from the six-year old boy next to me and look down to see him pulling away from a teddy-bear cholla, whose thorns have just penetrated the thin fabric of his shorts. On the other side of him, his wilted mother observes wryly, "It looked so picturesque in those old issues of *Arizona Highways*—harvesting the saguaro fruit just as a red sun sinks behind purple mountains." Her husband, sweat streaming down his face, struggles to breathe under the load of his camcorder and pleads, "C'mon, hon, just a little bit longer. Just think about being able to show this to your mom in Michigan."

Overhearing the conversation, Vivian laughs a deep, throaty laugh. "No, we O'odham don't run away from the desert when it's at its hottest. We run to the heart of the desert's heat. That's why we're the Desert People." Everyone joins in a weak laugh, too wilted from the heat to see much humor.

In her long-sleeved flannel shirt, black jeans, sunglasses, and baseball cap, Vivian is the only one covered against the sun's searing intensity. Noticing how unprotected several scantily dressed guests are, she observes, "We'd better get moving so we can head back to camp soon." A few people have already begun to take on the rosy glow of freshly cooked lobsters.

A rangy pre-teenager with a devilish glint in his eye decides to take advantage of the momentary diversion. Covering his mouth with his hand, he whispers to his little brother, "Betcha I could hit that with my slingshot. A rock'd get that fruit real easy."

Vivian wheels to face him, raising her voice for the first time that day. "No! The saguaros, they are people, too! See how he stands up, just like us? See his arms? You hit his head with a rock and you might kill him. You wouldn't throw a rock at your little brother there, would you? Or cut his skin? It's the same with that saguaro, you stab his skin and he dries up and dies, too."

The boy steps back, chastened by the unexpected outburst. His father glares down at him. "You know better than that!"

Moving to a nearby saguaro, Vivian aims the pole at a watermelon-pink fruit at the top of one arm. "See, this is what we're looking for," she explains, as a tender bud falls to the ground. "The deep red ones that have already split open are too ripe. And it's important to leave the solid green ones to ripen."

Skillfully maneuvering the pole to avoid the hard green buds, she brings it down to rest on the ground. "Who wants to try it?" Most of her audience is sweltering in the heat, but a few hardy souls volunteer.

Once everyone who so desired has tried their hand at harvesting, Vivian reaches into the bucket, splits open a few harvested buds and distributes them. "That's right, go ahead, it's good," she encourages a man who stands near her.

Charles, a tall man with the lean frame of a runner, raises a piece to his lips. He utters an expression of pure delight as the sweet crimson fruit melts in his mouth. "It's . . . it's . . . it's like . . . ," Charles searches for a comparison, "like kiwi fruit!" Vivian turns to the rest, instructing us, "Go ahead and scoop it out. Eat the pulp with the seeds. When you finish, put it on the ground so it's open to the sky." Bending down, she carefully places the rind, split like the petals of a flower, on the desert floor beside her. "That tells the Creator we need rain and we'd be grateful for it. That's the way the old ones used to do it."

Everyone samples the fruit while Vivian replenishes the bucket from nearby saguaros. She leads her grateful guests back to the welcome shade of the ramada, where we eagerly slake our thirst from water bottles. The older Tohono O'odham woman in her broad-brimmed straw hat stands in the sun, tending the contents of a kettle over an open fire; an old-fashioned bibbed apron protects her faded cotton print dress. She stirs the brew with a saguaro-rib rod before joining us under the ramada.

Vivian proudly introduces the woman: "This is my mom." People gather around the card table where the older woman has begun to peel the just-gathered fruit with a knife. In response to a chorus of friendly greetings, she looks up shyly, her leathery face breaking into a wide grin, displaying a gold tooth.

In a soft, low voice, breathing between the syllables in the lilting accents of the O'od-ham language, the older woman describes the syrup-making process. Vivian translates for us. "First, we scoop out the fruit, like she's doing now. . . . That's the hard part. . . . Then we strain it through a screen to get rid of the seeds. . . . And then we add water and sugar and boil it down over the fire."

Uttering a quiet cry of surprise, her mother turns abruptly and walks quickly toward the kettle. She grabs the saguaro rod and stirs the bubbling syrup mixture just on the verge of burning. "See, it's important to keep an eye on it all the time," Vivian chuckles. "After it boils for a while, we strain it some more through a cloth so you get out the rest of the seeds."

When the older woman returns, she says something in O'odham with a big grin as she opens a small jar of saguaro syrup for people to sample. Vivian explains, "My mother said to tell you we had a bigger jar yesterday but the dogs broke it last night. Those dogs are smart: they knew what was inside!"

"What all do you use this for?" asks a spry grandmother in a soft, southern accent.

"Oh, we make a lot of things, like jelly and the syrup and saguaro wine," replies Vivian.

"Wine?" booms a big man with a florid face. Mopping his brow with a towel, he edges forward. "You make wine with this stuff? We'll have to look for it in the store," he says, turning to his wife.

Vivian chuckles and says something in O'odham to her mother, who giggles. "You won't find it in the store. It's ritual wine. We ferment the pulp to make it into wine for the drinking to bring down the rain."

A tall, thin man in a photographer's vest inquires, "Is it a ceremony like those dances up on the Hopi mesas?"

Vivian smiles. "No, it's nothing like that; it's just for us O'odham, the time when they sing down the rain. They drink the wine after the medicine man has blessed it. All that drinking, it brings the clouds that bring the rain. That's why our new year begins when the saguaro fruit ripens."

Of all Southwestern native peoples, the O'odham lived the most precarious existence in a desert where drought and starvation were ever present realities. Here the moderation that comes of continuous availability was unknown. Their view of life is predicated upon the extremes of the desert: feast and famine, deprivation and excess. Moderation is not an option here, for the environment shifts radically from scarcity to abundance when the intense heat that lasts for months is suddenly broken by the crack of thunder: lightning rips open an afternoon sky as black as night, and rain transforms washes of dry sand into rushing torrents within minutes.

When the world simmers as temperatures soar, rain must come if life is to go on. Using their bodies to plead for rain, the Tohono O'odham drink themselves into a ritual stupor. The highly perishable saguaro wine has such a low alcoholic content that great quantities must be ingested before there is any intoxication; these amounts make the drinker vomit, a recognized feature that brings "instant relief and a sense of well-being . . . allowing a person to experience reality in another way" (Weil 1970:10–12). For the Tohono O'odham, vomiting is a ritual of renewal, and they say with pleasure, "Look, he is throwing up the clouds" (Underhill 1946:67), the clouds that bring the life-giving rain.

The Tohono O'odham, the Akimel O'odham (Pima), and the Hia C-eḍ O'odham lived in the western two-thirds of southern Arizona and northern Sonora, Mexico, land covered by the Sonoran Desert. Depending upon the relative availability of water in their particular territory, these groups developed their own ways of adapting to the desert, taking their names from their particular environmental niches.

The Tohono O'odham (Desert People) sing many songs for rain, reflecting the vital importance of moisture in their lives, for they lived in an area without a permanent source of water. The Spaniards called them Papago—from the O'odham name for them, Papahvi-o-otam, meaning "Bean People"—because of their reliance on the tepary and mesquite beans, a major source of protein. In 1986 they chose to become officially known as the Tohono O'odham Nation (Juan 1994:637).

Of the three O'odham groups, the Akimel O'odham (River People) were the only ones able to live in permanent villages; they lived along the Gila River and its tributaries, which supplied year-round drinking water as well as water for their crops. When the Spaniards asked them who they were, they responded, "Pi ma:c" ("I don't know what you are saying") (Zepeda 1999). To the Spaniards, their answer sounded like "Pima," which became their official tribal designation.

"We are from the sand, and known as Sand Indians, to find our way of life on the sand of the earth. That is why we go all over to seek our food to live well," the late Miguel Velasco told his relative Fillman Bell (Bell, Anderson, and Stewart 1980). He was describing the traditional life of his people, the Hia C-ed O'odham (Sand People).

Despite variations in lifestyle among the three groups, they are all O'odham—"We, the People." Today, all three groups are united by a resurgence of the O'odham *Himdag*, "the People's way of life." Essentially a shared world view, *Himdag* involves all things, all people, and all actions. It also encompasses European-derived concepts of religion, history, tradition, language, and belief. According to Alex, our Tohono O'odham guide, "*Himdag* is a way of being in the world," based on values of family, community, generosity, and respect for the earth.

The Tohono O'odham and Kitt Peak National Observatory

Astronomy, an activity that does not deplete natural resources or pollute the air, can benefit both scientists and Native Americans, who own some of the last undeveloped land in the United States. Over forty years ago the National Science Foundation (NSF) created a national optical observatory. After two years of looking for the best location in the western United States, Kitt Peak in Arizona was selected out of 150 potential sites, and the observatory was built on 200 acres leased from the Tohono O'odham.

Over the years, however, a climate of mistrust has developed between the observatory and the Schuk Toak District in which it is located. Employment opportunities vary greatly among districts, from the most prosperous, the San Xavier District, where the Desert Diamond Casino is located, to the poorer districts such as Schuk Toak, whose members consider the observatory to be a potential source of income. Before the U.S. government imposed a centralized tribal government in 1937, each village attended to its own needs, which is why communication has never flowed smoothly from tribal to district and village levels of government. Although the observatory is located on district land, its lease is with the Tohono O'odham Nation, which prevents the observatory from giving preferential treatment to district members; notification of employment and educational opportunities must be directed to the

Tohono O'odham artist Ron Miguel with the marble plaque he made of I'itoi, the Creator, holding up the world of the O'odham, 1999. The surface of the world is cracked to represent the cultural loss being experienced by tribal peoples. Baboquivari, home of I'itoi, can be seen in the background. Ron dedicated this plaque to his grandfather, Jose Miguel, who was present when the Tohono O'odham Tribal Council signed the lease with Kitt Peak National Observatory in 1958. Ron himself has worked at Kitt Peak for over five years. Author photograph

tribal government at Sells, but such information does not always filter down to members of the district, who believe the observatory should be giving them more benefits.

The observatory, which has always employed Tohono O'odham and has sold their baskets and other crafts in the observatory visitors' center, has expanded its educational opportunities for tribal members over the last ten years despite severe staff cutbacks because of NSF budget cuts. Scientists have been working with students and teachers at reservation schools to improve math and science skills as well as interest in related careers. Working with the Tohono O'odham Career Center at Sells, the observatory has also provided paid internships for tribal members, which exposes them to a wide range of work experience, including administrative and clerical duties; these internships have led to the employment of several individuals at Kitt Peak. In 1999 the education office at Kitt Peak submitted to the NSF a grant proposal for funds to place trained volunteers in three levels of tribal schools: at the elementary level, students would participate in activities based on solar and lunar observations; in middle schools, students would use their observations to improve math skills; and at the high-school level job skills and higher education would be emphasized, as well as tribal entrepreneurial enterprises. This program would also involve native storytellers and would enhance community involvement by using astronomy as a catalyst for learning native culture, language, and science.

Origins and Early History

Earth-maker created the world, but in time the people forgot their spirituality and their relationship to the animals and the plants, killing them without regard for their well-being (Underhill 1946:8–12). After a flood from which the supernaturals escaped, I'itoi (Elder Brother) created the O'odham and their neighbors, teaching them various ceremonials and arts (Russell 1975 [1908]:206–30).

Hohokam, derived from the O'odham word *he hu kam* ("the old ones") refers to the prehistoric people who once lived in the same territory as the present-day O'odham. Most O'odham consider themselves to be the descendants of the Hohokam, the ancient civilization that built Casa Grande, the three-story adobe complex from which an Arizona city takes its name. Only the Hohokam, as they are known to archaeologists, called the Sonoran Desert, and it alone, home. Today, nearly all that remains of the Hohokam lies buried and silent, yet they once densely settled the entire area that is today Phoenix and Tucson, farming the fertile valleys of the Gila, Salt, and Santa Cruz Rivers with an elaborate system of canal irrigation. More than any other part of their culture, their extensive networks of irrigation canals distinguish them from other prehistoric peoples who lived in Arizona. Using digging sticks and stone tools, they dug canals by hand and cleaned and maintained the canals and gates. The effort involved in building and maintaining these irrigation networks meant that they had to develop an elaborate social organization in order to direct labor and make decisions about whose fields received how much water and at what times (Reid and Whittlesey 1997:76–77). By conceptualizing the Hohokam more as a cultural system than as a distinct people, we can consider the degree to which peoples who might not have been ethnically Hohokam participated in the Hohokam culture. Some peoples may have adopted such cultural features as the ball courts and associated rituals, while others may have borrowed only their pottery designs; still others may have participated in their social organization but not their religious system.

During the late 1300s and early 1400s, widespread changes swept through the Southwest: not only did the Hohokam abandon the Arizona deserts, but also the Ancestral Pueblo of the Colorado Plateau coalesced into the present-day pueblos of Hopi and Zuni. Drought or the eventual salinization of their fields, after centuries of irrigation with mineral-laden desert water, might have led them to abandon the desert; such crises in their subsistence patterns could have led to conflict within villages, which might have resulted in the collapse of their society. Or perhaps the Hohokam simply adopted a simpler style of life because their culture was collapsing; the modern O'odham might indeed be the descendants of the Hohokam.

When Father Eusebio Kino and his Jesuits arrived in 1687, they found one group of people speaking the same language—the Piman language, in the Uto-Aztecan language family—but practicing three different kinds of adaptation, depending upon the special demands of the particular region in which they lived. The Tohono O'odham, who lived in the central section with 5–10 inches of annual rainfall, had developed a two-village mode of adaptation, dividing their year between summer "field" villages and winter "well" villages. To the north and east along the Gila, Salt, and Santa Cruz Rivers, where some 10–15 inches of rain falls each year, the Akimel O'odham had developed a one-village, or single, permanent village, adaptation. And in the extremely dry western section, with 0–5 inches of rainfall per year, the Hia C-ed O'odham had developed a nomadic, no-village mode of adaptation.

Tohono O'odham

The homeland of the Tohono O'odham had higher mountain ranges and intermontane valleys, with greater populations of the same animals and plants that lived farther west. Their mode of adaptation is referred to as two-village because they spent winters near permanent springs in the mountain foothills ("well" villages) where they hunted deer, and the rest of the year in the intermontane plains, which they farmed at the mouths of washes after summer rains had watered their fields ("field" villages).

They erected temporary rock dams in the upper drainageways and used brush to make spreader dams that channeled runoff from summer rains. Before the summer rains, men climbed the mountainsides to construct these rock dams, which channeled the runoff from rainfall into a single major arroyo where it entered the valley. When the summer monsoons brought flash floods down the arroyos, they erected spreader dams across the mouths of the arroyos in order to distribute the water across their fields.

In July or August, as soon as the fields were wet, the Tohono O'odham planted seeds of drought-resistant varieties of corn, beans, squash, cowpeas, and melons. After they harvested their crops in October and November, and when the water was gone from the reservoirs, they left for their winter villages. In the spring and summer they collected wild plants, such as prickly pear fruits and pads, mesquite, agave, amaranth greens, acorns, cholla buds, and saguaro fruit. The saguaro fruit was so essential to their culture that its harvest marked the beginning of the Tohono O'odham year.

The Akimel O'odham

The Akimel O'odham lived beside constantly flowing rivers—the Gila, Salt, and Santa Cruz—which made possible year-round residence in a single village, a one-village mode of adaptation. Here they farmed the rich alluvial farmlands, fished for freshwater fish, and collected abundant flora and fauna. Their rancheria settlements included domiciles that were separated from one another by hundreds of yards, with each brush house set in the

Traditional O'od-ham round house, with ramada to the right, Gila Indian Center, 1999. Author photograph

midst of fields. Their villages contained no more than 2,000 inhabitants in 5–10 locations (Kino 1948:196).

Spanish accounts do not mention Akimel O'odham irrigation (Hackenberg 1983:165). The abundant, above-normal rainfall of the seventeenth century created slow-moving rivers, swamps, and runoff spread over floodplains with islands in the Gila River, whose water table was so near the surface that the land was ideal for planting (ibid., 165). The Akimel O'odham thus probably did not need to make use of irrigation at that time. Relying primarily on the corn, cotton, squash, tobacco, and gourds they raised, the Akimel O'odham also traded their surpluses for Tohono O'odham hides, mescal, and chiltipiquines, a spicy pepper. The Akimel O'odham supplemented their harvests with wild plants and, to a lesser degree, rabbits, mountain sheep, deer, and fish.

Hia C-ed O'odham

El Gran Desierto, the vast desert along the eastern side of the Lower Colorado River Valley that spans the international border, was home to the Hia C-ed O'odham. Temperatures there soar to 120°F, and what little rain the region receives comes in two seasons, July–August and December–January. The highly localized downpours of the summer monsoons with their spectacular lightning displays begin when masses of warm, moist, and unstable air from the Gulf of Mexico collide with the hot, dry air rising above the mountain ranges. The winter storms, which cover the whole sky, move in from the Pacific Ocean and the Gulf of California. However, very little of this precipitation is effective because of the terrain, which consists of steep upper mountain slopes and short bajadas (the outwash slopes between the upper slopes and the floodplains). The 60–70°F rain quickly evaporates upon hitting the sun-heated basaltic rocks, which already measure 150–60°F. Plants do not grow well in the resulting landlocked basins, which become deposits of soluble salts. A few microenvironments on or near the bajadas support edible plants, such as mesquite, types of palo verde, ironwood, cat's claw, various types of cacti, and perennials. Scarce animal life includes desert bighorn sheep, foxes, bats, deer, antelope, coyote, hares, bobcats, skunks, rodents, ringtails, snakes, lizards, and many species of birds.

The scarce supply of water and food caused the Hia C-ed O'odham to lead a nomadic existence, traveling by foot over great expanses of desert in search of water, wild plants, and game. They ranged from the Gulf of California to the Tinajas Altas Mountains in Arizona (southeast of present-day Yuma). In hard times, they harvested shellfish in the Gulf of California and traded salt, seashells, and ceremonies for the pottery and agricultural products of the River Yumans of the Colorado Delta. Living in the most extreme reaches of the desert, they depended upon natural stone tanks in the mountains that stored water from infrequent summer cloudbursts; they knew every rock tank that might hold a few gallons of moisture after a rare thunderstorm. Without any permanent settlements, they followed a no-village mode of adaptation.

Two O'odham scholars, Fillman Bell and Ofelia Zepeda, have collected oral histories of Hia C-ed O'odham elders, some of which have been published (Bell, Anderson, and Stewart 1980). In these interviews, the elders mention, as foods they relished, twenty-one wild plant species, nine cultivated plant species, and at least twenty-three animal species, which represent thirty-two families of flora and fauna. In one of these oral histories, the late Miguel Velasco observed, "We drank the desert fruit juices in harvest time. The desert food is meant for the Indians to eat." Another elder, Alonso Puffer, said that "sand food" itself might be changing for the worse: "The Sand Indians dug a sweet potatolike plant with long roots that grows in the sand, and [they] ate it raw. Now these same plants are very bitter. They don't taste the same" (Nabhan 1993:58). Puffer was referring to dune root (*Pholisma sonorae*; *hia tadk,* or "dune root"), which has a taste similar to sweet potato (ibid., 52).

Before the arrival of the Spaniards, the Tohono O'odham relied on wild plants and animals for some 75 percent of their subsistence, with agricultural products supplying the rest of their nutritional needs (Castetter and Bell 1942:57). In contrast, the Akimel O'odham relied upon agriculture for 60 percent of their annual food intake, with 40 percent from wild food sources (ibid., 57). Even the Hia C-ed O'odham practiced minimal agriculture. Living in different environments gave the groups access to different foods: the Tohono O'odham and Hia C-ed O'odham traded the wild foods they collected for the cultivated crops of the

Akimel O'odham. In times of drought, when the Tohono O'odham had little to exchange, they worked for the Akimel O'odham, earning a share of the crop for their labor.

The Spanish and Mexican Periods

Although the O'odham were able to solve their subsistence needs with diversification, they were facing a new threat to their existence when the Spanish arrived. Groups of Apaches were sweeping down from the east, and by the end of the 1760s they had forced one group of O'odham, the Sobaipuris, who lived in the San Pedro Valley beyond the eastern edge of the Sonoran Desert, to relinquish control of their territory. The Spaniards eagerly enlisted the O'odham as allies against the Apaches. Despite reports that describe Jesuit contact as peaceful, the O'odham obviously objected to their presence, for they revolted against the Spanish in 1695 and again in 1751, and sporadically throughout the entire period of Spanish and Mexican domination, which lasted until 1853 (Fontana 1983: 137). A silver strike in 1736 near the present Arizona-Sonora border brought a flood of Spanish prospectors, and after the 1751 O'odham revolt, Spanish soldiers built two more presidios in the region; the inevitable influx of ranchers and farmers followed the troops. By the time the king of Spain had expelled the Jesuits from the New World in 1767, they had established over twenty-four missions and *visitas* (mission-visiting stations) in O'odham territory; Franciscan friars continued their work. In 1775 one of the two presidios was moved to Tucson, a Tohono O'odham village on the Santa Cruz River and a mission *visita* of San Xavier del Bac.

Spanish contact provided the Tohono O'odham with European crops and animals, as well as mining and cattle ranching, which brought them into the cash and barter economy. O'odham soldiers were paid in cash and absorbed European ideas of warfare and military organization (Fontana 1983:138). Once Mexico gained independence from Spain in 1821, Mexican ranchers, farmers, and miners moved into O'odham territory near Caborca in Sonora, taking so much land that the Sonoran Tohono O'odham began a small-scale war in 1840 that ended with their defeat in 1843 (Fontana 1981:57, 60). Many O'odham moved north at this time, for although the 1853 Gadsden Purchase split their territory, half in Arizona and half in Sonora, Tohono O'odham could still pass freely over the international border. Using the border to facilitate horse-stealing operations, both Mexicans and Tohono O'odham stole horses in Sonora, selling them to Tohono O'odham who lived in Arizona, who resold them to Akimel O'odham living on the Gila River (Fontana 1983:140). Many Tohono O'odham intermarried with Mexican peasants as well.

When 1898 brought further conflict over land and cattle (Fontana 1983:140), more Tohono O'odham came north, bringing with them strong mission traditions, which may have intensified belief in St. Francis (Spicer 1981:139). San Xavier, the mission near

Tucson, was already an important influence among the Arizona Tohono O'odham, and the annual pilgrimage to Magdalena, Sonora, drew Indians from a wide area through the 1800s. Probably begun in the two decades after the 1821 Mexican Revolution (Nabhan 1991:29), this event combines the image of St. Francis Xavier, the great Jesuit saint, with the October 4 feast day of St. Francis of Assisi, the patron saint of the Franciscan order. In the early nineteenth century, when Catholic priests withdrew from the outlying areas because of the intensification of Apache raiding, the Tohono O'odham continued to carry out Christian rituals. Without pressure to conform to the strictures of Catholicism, the Tohono O'odham, unlike the Pueblos of the Rio Grande area, had no need to compartmentalize the two religious systems. Instead of integrating their traditional beliefs and practices with the newly introduced religion, as did the Yaqui, the Tohono O'odham simply added aspects of Catholicism to their own religion. Anthropologist Edward Spicer (1981:514) referred to this process as "simple addition" because a powerful saint and the associated ritual—candles, rosaries, and hymns in Spanish—were added to traditional beliefs and practices. Tohono O'odham Catholicism, known as Sonoran Catholicism, consisted almost entirely of the veneration of St. Francis Xavier, the founder of the Jesuits, interpreting him as a source of supernatural healing power similar to existing Tohono O'odham mythological figures (ibid., 513). By 1900 many villages had small wattle-and-daub chapels surmounted by crosses and adorned with pictures of St. Francis. Aided by fellow villagers, the family who owned the pictures of St. Francis conducted weekly services consisting of Catholic prayers and hymns in the Spanish language, all in praise of the saint. Individuals continued to take part in the traditional religion, and the village chapel to St. Francis coexisted with the village round house where the saguaro wine was prepared.

In contrast to the Tohono O'odham, the Akimel O'odham never experienced sustained interaction through the establishment of a Spanish or Mexican community on the Gila River. Instead, they visited Hispanic communities, had contact with Spanish and Mexican expeditions along the Gila River, and were influenced by Sonoran O'odham who came to live among them (Ezell 1983:153). Wheat had the greatest impact of all Spanish items, because its introduction set up a chain reaction that affected virtually every aspect of Akimel O'odham culture. Their traditional crops were summer crops, but wheat, planted in the fall and harvested in the spring, introduced year-round agriculture. Wheat became so significant to the Akimel O'odham that May began to replace June (The Saguaro-Harvest Moon) with May (The Wheat-Harvest Moon) as the beginning of the their year.

Wheat proved to be extremely profitable, for the Euro-Americans, who were colonizing Sonora, preferred it to maize; the growing market they created also led to an increased demand for Akimel O'odham baskets, blankets, and captives (Escudero, in Ezell 1983:153). For much of their history, Akimel O'odham women had been weaving large jars and coiled basket granaries in which to store food surpluses. They had also become known for their aesthetically pleasing and technically excellent baskets and cotton blankets; their blankets were valued trade items a century or more before Navajo blankets came on the market. (Today the name Pima cotton, after the tribe, designates cotton of especially high quality.)

Thus the Akimel O'odham were drawn into the marketplace, and surplus production for profit and commerce replaced redistribution and reciprocity, the mechanisms that had governed the exchange of goods in their society. Until this time, material goods usually had united the people; eventually, profit motive and dependence upon the market would lead to the near destruction of their society. The changes begun by the introduction of wheat continued to spread throughout all layers of their culture. To accommodate the growing market, they had to cultivate more land and had to rely more on irrigation agriculture. This demanded greater cooperation and thus a more formalized, institutionalized social structure with new occupational specialties and a more sharply defined division of labor; women had to devote more time to the production of trade items, while men were forced to assume greater agricultural responsibility (Ezell 1983:154). At the same time, partly because of the greater surplus of grain in Akimel O'odham towns, Apaches intensified their raids. The

Maricopa-Akimel O'odham Mollie Juana, 1880. The Maricopa are a River Yuman tribe who moved east to live with the Akimel O'odham in the 1800s. Courtesy of Arizona Historical Society, No. 15792

O'odham responded by marshaling their men—sentinel duty and arms drill were required for all men—and by shifting the purpose of their raids on the Apaches from vengeance to planned war campaigns modeled on those of the Spaniards (Russell 1908:38–39, 55). The Akimel O'odham began to place a higher value on courage and skill in war; from this heightened preoccupation with war came increasing ritual and technological developments related to warfare.

To protect their villages, the Akimel O'odham contracted their territory at the eastern and western edges. Year-round agriculture enabled them to increase the density of their settlements, which in turn led them to formalize their political organization by establishing a formally recognized, hereditary paramount chief. By the time the Americans assumed control over present-day Arizona, the Akimel O'odham were considered to be a formidable power bloc in the Southwest, both for their thriving commercial enterprises and for their military prowess in holding the Apaches at bay (Ezell 1983:155). It is not surprising that the Spaniards, Mexicans, and later the Anglo-Americans all accorded the Akimel O'odham the designation of "nation" (Emory 1848:111).

The Pilgrimage to Magdalena

In the early nineteenth century, as Apache raiding intensified, the priests who had introduced Catholicism to the region chose to withdraw from outlying areas, leaving the Tohono O'odham to continue practicing Catholicism on their own. Today the pilgrims come, often on foot, from as far away as the Gila River, some 200 miles away, to celebrate St. Francis of Assisi's feast day, October 4, in the town of Magdalena, where Father Kino is buried and where the image of St. Francis Xavier resides.

While many pilgrims continue to go to Magdalena, others attend the festival at alternative locations that have grown up in response to political events and demographic change. When the pilgrimage began in the two decades after Mexico's independence in 1821, most of the pilgrims were O'odham, but in the last half of the 1800s they were joined by Yaqui refugees from southern Sonora and by Hispanics and Anglo-Americans. When the anticlerical movement that followed the Mexican Revolution of the 1910s shut down the church at Magdalena, the O'odham pleaded with the Mexican government, which failed to respond. The venerated statue of St. Francis then vanished, only to reappear in Cuwi Gesk, a small Mexican O'odham village some 100 miles northwest of Magdalena. Over the last half-century, Cuwi Gesk —which has been renamed San Francisquito—has replaced Magdalena as a pilgrimage site for many O'odham.

In recent decades it has become increasingly difficult for American O'odham to cross the border, something many O'odham families used to do every year. They have responded by establishing their own fiesta sites in Arizona, both in the San Xavier District at the mission and in different districts of the larger Tohono O'odham reservation. Community members of the sponsoring district donate up to four cattle, and twenty to thirty key community members spend almost a week cutting firewood, decorating the plaza and booths, and preparing food. A free feast-day meal, Yaqui dancing, and an alcohol-free social dance follow the public mass at the chapel (Nabhan 1991:34).

Author and ethnobotanist Gary Paul Nabhan (1991:32–33) described the event in San Francisquito, Sonora, which included dancing on the night of October 3 to *waila* music provided by the Alex Gomez Band from the U.S. Tohono O'odham reservation. The O'odham controlled the two-day, two-night ceremony that followed: older women hosted a rosary in the chapel; a *maestro* (the prayer leader who organizes the participants of the Wi:gida, the ancient rain ceremony still held each summer at Quitovac, Sonora) led the procession of the reclining saint around the plaza to the accompaniment of songs and prayers; and then each night women served everyone who entered the adobe feast house traditional O'odham fiesta foods: pinto beans, large wheat tortillas, yeast bread buns, *carne con chile colorado*, and canned fruit.

The resilience of the Tohono O'odham people is evident in their response to the changing circumstances that threatened their celebration of St. Francis. They have overcome political crises by finding new fiesta sites, demonstrating that it is not the place as much as their relationship to the saint that is essential to their culture.

The Anglo-American Period

By the 1850s the Tohono O'odham were feeling the pressure of an ever increasing flow of white settlers, ranchers, and miners into their territory. Mining had begun to take place on a larger scale, focusing on Ajo's rich copper deposits and gold and silver in the Baboquivari, Comobabi, and Quijotoa Mountains. Mines and ranches did provide jobs for Tohono O'odham, and also wells (dug for mining centers) where they could water the livestock they were raising for the market. These wells also enabled the Tohono O'odham to establish permanent villages, such as Fresnal and Cababi, which they could inhabit year-round (Ezell 1983:167), instead of dividing their year between summer field villages and winter well villages.

O'odham territory came under American control with the 1853 Gadsden Purchase. After the Civil War, the U.S. military turned its energies to controlling the Apache, and by the early 1870s troops had managed to subdue all Apaches but the Chiricahuas. The return to relatively peaceful conditions enabled the Tohono O'odham to disperse their villages and to broaden the area they used for their summer fields. When pervasive drought conditions returned in 1870, the Tohono O'odham responded by developing a livestock industry that became the keystone of their modern village economy. (In Father Kino's time, winter wheat was not important to the Tohono O'odham because their valleys were deficient in winter rainfall.) Much of their homeland, which had been abandoned during the Apache wars, was now covered by heavy grass, making it ideal for cattle. In the beginning, cattle were family property, although families herded their cattle together and kept them in a common corral used by the entire village (Underhill, in Hackenberg 1983:167). The behavior of the former hunting chief served as the model for the village official who presided over cattle operations, for herding, like hunting, required the manpower of the entire village. As a communal enterprise with a need for joint economic decision making, the cattle industry strengthened the political organization of the village, providing important functions for village chiefs and councils of family heads (Hackenberg 1983:167).

At the same time that the Tohono O'odham were establishing their cattle industry, white cattlemen were appropriating O'odham grazing land and water holes. The Tohono O'odham, who had never fought against the United States, had no treaty to protect their land. Until this time, Anglo–Tohono O'odham relations had been peaceful as they joined forces against their common enemy, the Apaches. With their land under siege from white encroachment, the Tohono O'odham, whose population also included Sonoran O'odham who had moved north, were finally able to get the government to begin setting aside land for them. Three reservations were established by executive order: in 1874, the San Xavier Reservation southwest of Tucson, with more than 71,000 acres; in 1882, Gila Bend Reservation with 10,235 acres; and in 1916, the main Tohono O'odham Reservation at Sells, west of Tucson, with 2,774,370 acres.

The cycle of erosion, arroyo-cutting, and extreme drought that began in the 1870s destroyed any chance for self-sufficiency based on agricultural development (Hackenberg 1983:167), and as early as 1881 wells drilled for mines, ranches, and the growing city of Tucson began to drain the aquifer under Indian land. To compensate for damage to the channel of the Santa Cruz River caused by severe erosion during the 1890s, after 1912 the Bureau of Indian Affairs drilled wells and provided pumps for the San Xavier Reservation. Two years later, the BIA began to drill for artesian wells at eleven villages on the large Tohono O'odham reservation, but the lowering of the water table since then has seriously endangered the supply of well water.

A period of excessive rainfall between 1905 and 1920 brought prosperity to Tohono O'odham crops and livestock, and with the accumulation of wealth, families began to separate their herds from those of the village, forming individual ranches (Hackenberg 1983:172). Those families who lived in areas where rainfall and permanent grass were most abundant became more prosperous, and the resulting social differentiation gave rise to rivalries over water and grazing rights. The cattle that Tohono O'odham families had accumulated during the prosperous years of the 1920s left the range overstocked; with the drought of the 1930s, these rivalries intensified (ibid.). To settle the conflicts and promote effective management, the tribe divided the reservation into nine fenced grazing districts. In the nineteenth century, when Apache raiding was at its peak, the Tohono O'odham had clustered into several defensive centers, which formed the basis for these districts. The division into districts, upon which their tribal government was later based, meant that Tohono O'odham government was less centralized and more locally autonomous.

In contrast to the Tohono O'odham, the Akimel O'odham experienced great prosperity during the first decade of American rule because they provided supplies for some 60,000 prospectors who passed through their villages between 1848 and 1854 en route to California (Bancroft, in Hackenberg 1983:170). The Overland Mail Company, which established a route through their villages in 1858, contracted for the entire Akimel O'odham wheat crop to ship to California settlements. Before and during the Civil War, the U.S. government relied on the Akimel O'odham and Maricopas not only to supplement their military forces against the Apaches, but also to supply provisions. (The Maricopas are a River Yuman tribe who moved east to live near their Akimel O'odham allies.) Both the construction of a wagon road linking El Paso and Fort Yuma and the opening of the San Antonio–San Diego stage line in 1857 required food and shelter for men and animals; by 1859 Americans had erected several trading posts and mills.

A fundamental change began to occur in Akimel O'odham society as they became enmeshed in the cash economy and as the notion of private property began to supplant ideals of reciprocity and sharing. In addition to their growing dependence upon the cash economy, the Akimel O'odham found themselves in the midst of changing conditions. When the construction of Fort McDowell and Fort Grant in 1865 released manpower for farming from the Pima military establishment by removing the need for a defense perimeter, the Akimel O'odham expanded the range of their settlements. No longer so constrained by the Apache threat and no longer united against a common enemy, the Akimel O'odham did not need the spartan militarism and strict discipline that had held their society together. Experiencing the impact of a prosperous cash economy, in the 1862–69 period they began to shift from a spirit of cooperation to one of competition, as individual villages attempted to move upstream, securing more advantageous irrigation locations (Hackenberg 1983:170). In 1870, at the peak of their prosperity, they produced 3 million pounds of wheat (St. John 1859; Fontana 1976:51).

However, when 1870 ushered in the driest conditions in 600 years in the Gila watershed, the Akimel O'odham had to cut back their farmland to less than 20 percent of the area they had farmed in 1859 (ARCIA 1976–77 [1870]:338). Overly dependent upon a cash economy based on wheat, their society experienced conflict over the allocation of water: in 1879–80 warfare between the O'odham villages of Santan and Blackwater erupted over this precious resource; twenty-four murders occurred between 1878 and 1898; and eighteen "witches" were killed between 1860 and 1887, according to Akimel O'odham calendar sticks (Russell 1908). In addition to these rapidly changing conditions, white settlers flooded into the land above Akimel O'odham territory, diverting the life-giving water. Encouraged by a brief respite of abundant rainfall between 1881 and 1884, the Florence Canal Company constructed a diversion dam that would have appropriated the entire flow of the Gila River for non-Indian settlers by 1887, had the company not gone bankrupt. Nevertheless, after the Civil War, settlers and cattle ranchers moved into the area in unprecedented numbers, diverting the waters of the Gila. Ranchers also accelerated the overgrazing begun by the Spaniards, triggering erosion and floods, such as one in 1868 which wiped out three villages.

After centuries of economic stability, the Akimel O'odham were plunged into a disastrous depression, and by 1895 the government had to issue rations to the Indians. The vitality of their culture withered when the flowing river that had given them their name (River People) became an empty riverbed. Cut off from mainstream society, the Akimel O'odham began to look inward in apathy and despair. After their water was withdrawn, they became a "peasant" society, like those characterized by George Foster (1962:44–47), with absolute limits on their resources and impotence in their relations with the outside world. During the forty "years of famine," as many Akimel O'odham referred to this period, alcoholism and violence within families and communities increased at an alarming rate. Akimel O'odham George Webb (1994 [1959]:124–25) chronicled the loss:

> The green of those Pima [Akimel O'odham] fields spread along the river for many
> miles in the old days when there was plenty of water. Now the river is an empty bed
> of sand. . . . Now you can look out across the valley and see the green alfalfa and
> cotton spreading for miles on the farms of white people who irrigate their land
> with hundreds of pumps running night and day. Some of those farms take their
> water from big ditches dug hundreds of years ago by Pimas.

In 1859 the federal government had created the Gila River Reservation for the Akimel O'odham and Maricopas, and in 1879 the Salt River Reservation was created for the Akimel O'odham and Maricopas who moved north of Phoenix; however, in the absence of protected water rights, their fields remained dry. Forced to shift to wage labor to support themselves, the Akimel O'odham struggled for water and survival. In 1930 the federal government constructed Coolidge Dam at San Carlos in an effort to restore their water; however, the Coolidge Dam reservoir was never filled to more than two-thirds of its capacity (Hackenberg 1983:175).

In the 1870s, after much Apache raiding had ceased and the Southern Pacific Railroad had been built, the Tohono O'odham made their Akiciñ summer field camp into a year-round village so that they could work on the railroad and in Akimel O'odham fields. In 1912 the government established the Ak-Chin Reservation to protect the village's farmlands for the Tohono O'odham and the Akimel O'odham who migrated there after the decline of Akimel O'odham agriculture along the Gila River.

The Restoration of San Xavier Del Bac

Soon after 1775 the Franciscan missionaries who replaced the Jesuits began an ambitious construction program that included San Xavier del Bac. Tohono O'odham from the village of Wa:k (Bac) were paid to lay the stone foundations, mold and fire the bricks, burn and slake the lime, raise the walls, and construct the arches and the vaulted and domed roof (Fontana 1995:31). In 1692, when they were introduced to Catholicism by the Jesuits (who were expelled by the Spanish Crown in 1767), the people of this village added the name of St. Francis Xavier to their village, and today the boundaries of the parish and the boundaries of the San Xavier District of the Tohono O'odham Nation are the same. The Catholic population of the Wa:k community is still baptized, confirmed, married, and buried under the auspices of the mission, while many of the children attend the mission's elementary school instead of public, off-reservation schools.

The professionally decorated plaster interior of the mission church began to fall from the walls in 1989, the first sign that water had been penetrating the thick brick-and-stone walls. The Patronato San Xavier, a nonprofit corporation devoted to the preservation of the church, came to the rescue. The group's board members include Tohono O'odham from San Xavier, the Franciscan Father Guardian of the mission, and the bishop of Tucson, who reminded the corporation that despite its designation as a historic landmark, the church is a pilgrimage destination, place of prayer, and an active parish church.

When the restoration was under way Tohono O'odham Gregory Gomez, one of the workers employed by the Morales Construction Company, said, "I feel I'm a part of history working here. And if I ever leave, then I will be a part of history" (ibid., 34).

In 1992, after the exterior had been sufficiently waterproofed, work began on the painted and sculptural art inside. Local Tohono O'odham worked side by side with Italian conservators so that local parishioners would become qualified caretakers of their own church, able to carry out a scheduled maintenance routine. By the end of April 1995 four Tohono O'odham apprentices, Timothy Lewis, Gabriel Wilson, Donald Preston, and Mark Lopez, had helped the international conservation team to repair, stabilize, clean, and integrate the decorations in over half the church's interior.

Working on the restoration of San Xavier changed Timothy Lewis's life, for at the end of his third year Lewis, who had been born and raised at Wa:k and had had no previous artistic experience, demonstrated such determination that the chief conservator offered him a position working with the European restoration crew in Austria and Italy during a six-month break in work at the mission. The trip not only brought him valuable work experience but also a wife, Matilde Rubio, a Spanish conservator whom he met his first day in Salzburg and married in his village three months after he returned to Arizona. Lewis believes, "All of this happened to me for a reason. I'm supposed to be here, doing this. And the mission, it changed my life. It helped me find a job, a purpose, a wife. I guess God had a plan for me" (Somers 1997:2B).

Aboriginal Life

Material Culture

As a rancheria people, O'odham built sprawling settlements with a "camplike" settlement pattern that resembled those of migratory peoples rather than those constructed by "deeply rooted town dwellers" (Bahr 1983a:178). They interspersed unclaimed patches of desert into both their permanent and temporary settlements, and constructed both public and private structures in their villages. The single public structure was the meeting area, where men held their nightly council meeting. Located within shouting distance of the farthest family's house and near the compound of the local group headman, who was in charge of its upkeep, the meeting area included a round, dwelling-type house in which no one lived. East of the round house was a ramada near which was a fireplace for the nightly meetings. The people also cleared an area immediately east of the council house to serve as a central plaza; much farther away from the council house were open spaces set aside for rituals.

Private structures consisted of each family's household compounds, comprising individual houses for each couple or unmarried adult in which to sleep and to store possessions, including pottery and basketry. Family members shared a ramada, a cooking enclosure, food storage houses, a corral, and a brush hut for the seclusion of menstruating women (Bahr 1983a:180). Thus, O'odham villages consisted of a central community house with plaza and sacred grounds and rancherias, or household compounds, for each family.

O'odham Social and Political Organization

O'odham kinship was patrilineal, with five patrilineal clan names that were grouped into patrilineal moieties, the Buzzard and the Coyote moieties. Neither clan nor moiety was related to marriage; clan membership only determined the kin term used to address one's father (Bahr 1983a:187). After marriage, couples tended to settle in the household of the husband's father (patrilocality), and the basic unit of social structure was the patrilineal extended family: a couple, married sons, and unmarried daughters (Russell 1908:197; Ezell 1983:151).

At the same time, Piman social organization emphasized the maintenance of multiple and far-flung contacts, with considerable flexibility in the inheritance of fields and post-marital residence. Families generally changed their permanent place of residence only once or twice in a lifetime, but they constantly moved for short periods between the households of relatives and friends in different local groups. Each economically and politically self-sufficient settlement or local group was composed of several households; the more sedentary O'odham had larger villages. The regional band encompassed several villages or local groups; socially, these bands were nearly insignificant, but the local groups within these bands attended one another's ceremonies. Certain ceremonies, including the summer wine feast, required the attendance of several different local groups; representatives from different local groups had to take appropriate cardinal positions for the proper performance of these ceremonies, which were performed on a directional scheme (Bahr 1983a:186–87).

Each local group had a headman and a shaman. The headman was at the center of public life. He attained his position through his generosity and the respect in which others held him, but he exercised little control or actual authority; he determined the agenda of village meetings and was entitled to speak first and last on issues. On important issues, such as whether to go to war or whether sorcery was being practiced, he could only voice his opinion, for decisions were made through consensus.

Additional offices were associated with the position of headman, such as Wise Speaker, Fire Maker, Keeper of the Smoke, Keeper of the Meeting, Keeper of the Plaited Basket, The One Above, The One Ahead, The One Made Big (Underhill 1939:72). The title Wise Speaker refers to the long poetic orations given at each ritual of the ceremonial cycle; this responsibility was usually divided among a group of ceremonial officials, but as group ceremonial life became more complex, the oratorical repertory grew, and the number of individuals who were entitled to perform was increased. Ritual oratory figured in almost every kind of public ceremony. Fire Maker, Keeper of the Smoke, and Keeper of the Meeting were titles referring to the second duty—organizer and main speaker—associated with the position of headman; this duty was not divided among individuals. The position of Keeper of the Plaited Basket also was not shared; this role involved building the fire and keeping the group's sacred bundle. Because greatness could not be monopolized, the fourth aspect of headman—his political status—was shared among several men. The One Above, The One Ahead, The One Made Big are some of the titles that such individuals could take when they served in these positions associated with the "great man" aspect of headmanship (Bahr 1983a:185–86).

O'odham Religion

The underlying theme of O'odham ceremonialism was the attainment of the power needed to sustain human society. Individual men embarked on journeys to gather this crucial power, embodied in scalps (another reason for warfare), rain, feathers, and seeds, which they brought home to ensure the well-being of all people. Each ceremony had songs, oratory, and drama, which told the stories of these great spiritual journeys. The O'odham acquired power through a dream vision, which usually occurred during a sleeping state when an animal spirit appeared to teach the person songs and other knowledge (Bahr et al. 1974:308). In some cases, the supernatural visitor might take the dreamer on a journey to the mountains or to the ocean (Underhill 1939:169). The quest for power took men away from their villages as they contacted powerful supernatural forces by killing an eagle, slaying an enemy, or undertaking the salt pilgrimage (see below); upon their return, they had to undergo purification rituals and afterward were often visited by a supernatural in animal form, which became the source of power (Underhill 1946:192–252).

Shamans and Curing

In contrast to the village headman, the shaman existed outside the spotlight of leadership, remaining in the background as an intellectual and philosopher. While the headmen ran the ceremonial cycle, shamans foretold the future and worked magic by summoning spirit helpers with songs and using the powers they derived from their breath and heart. They provided spells to bewitch the enemy before battle, divined the position of rain clouds, reduced the strength of athletic teams from other villages, and foretold where the enemy could be located. Not only did shamans develop a theory of sickness, but they also were the principal heroic type celebrated in popular song and poetry (Bahr 1983b:193). Although performed and passed on by laymen, ritual oratory celebrated the experience of shamanic journeys from the earth to the sky or underworld and back again. Laymen also performed the ceremonial songs and drama that celebrated shamanism. The only aspect of shamanism that was not public was curing; after Anglo influence took over, this was the sole aspect of shamanism still practiced. The most powerful form of diagnosis was an all-night session in which the shaman summoned his spirit helpers by singing songs given him by spirits; the shaman called out his lifelong collection of spirits by singing his entire repertoire of songs (ibid., 194–95).

The O'odham theory of illness includes over forty kinds of "dangerous objects"—animals, birds, insects, rodents, and natural phenomena—that can cause "staying sickness." The dangerous objects were endowed with dignity and rights called "ways" (contracts) at the time of creation (Bahr et al. 1974), and if a human trespasses upon its "way," causal agents called "strengths" enter the person's body to create symptoms of "staying sickness." A "strength" may remain latent for years, so that an adult may suffer from "wind sickness" because he ran through a whirlwind when he was a child. Rather than the particular animal causing the illness, the cause is an impersonal, abstract "power" or "strength" associated with the animal.

Such long-ago incidents may have been forgotten, so a shaman is needed to trace the disease to a "way" with the assistance of his spirit helpers. In both the shorter, daytime form of diagnosis and the longer form, which takes an entire night, the shaman blows on the patient and sucks out "strengths" from his body. The central practice in both diagnosis and curing is blowing, which the shaman may augment by using tobacco. The shaman blows tobacco smoke over the patient's body, while fanning him with eagle feathers and using quartz crystals to "illuminate" the "strengths" (Bahr et al. 1974). At the same time, he sings songs taught him by his tutelary spirits to please the spirits, which leads them to communicate the nature of the illness to him (ibid., 182). After diagnosis, a ritual curer treats the disease by establishing a prayerful relationship with the spiritual representatives of the "way" of the dangerous object through singing to them and asking them to help on behalf of the patient. By blowing tobacco smoke on the patient and applying appropriate fetishes to the patient's body, the ritual curer introduces the curative strength of his breath and the fetishes into the patient's body (ibid.). The spirits, pleased to hear the songs, cause the "strengths" to diminish.

A medicine person rather than a shaman performs the curing ceremony; instead of sucking, the curer sings ritual songs and employs his breath to persuade the spirits to stop causing the illness. Each sickness has its own specific fetishes, which are portions or products from animals' bodies, images of animals or plants, or actions such as wiping an animal's mouth and then wiping the mouth of the patient (Bahr et al. 1974:284–98). The curer also presses fetishes to the patient's body to introduce the fetish's curative power (ibid).

Sandpaintings are one kind of fetish that ritual curers apply to the patient's body. Made by the Tohono O'odham (and probably other O'odham) to treat diseases caused by owls, horned toads, and wind, sandpaintings and their rituals not only remove sickness from the patient but also strengthen the patient by putting something into his body. Using a stick, the curer incises the outlines of the design on the sand background or on the bare ground and directs his assistants to fill in the outlines. The colors have directional symbolism: white for east, green or blue for south, black for west, red for north. The pigments come from ashes (white); dried, ground creosote leaves and green sand (green); purchased laundry bluing (blue); mesquite charcoal (black); and rhyolite (red). These paintings, which are roughly 3–4 feet in diameter, are made outdoors, usually in the daytime, so that others can come and benefit; thus, they occupy a position in between private curing rituals and public religious festivals. It is especially important that the painting for the curing of wind sickness be done outside so that the wind will destroy it. Private rites are not conducted outside at night because of ghosts. Depending upon the number of songs and their repetition, a ceremony may last six to eight hours or even all night; daytime rites are generally shorter. The ritual curers sing, touch, press, hit, or whip the patient (and the curers) with objects, which are then placed on the painting. The curers transfer the spiritual substance of the painting to the patient's body by touching the image and then the patient's body (Bahr, in Wyman 1980:235).

Waila

Waila (also known as "chicken scratch") is a style of O'odham social dancing that goes back at least a hundred years. The word is derived from *baile* (Spanish for a social dance), and waila's main dance styles are of European origin: the polka, the schottische (called *choti* by the O'odham), and the mazurka. Some waila bands favor instrumentation that includes electric and bass guitars, drum kit, alto saxophone, and button accordion, while other bands, such as the Gila River Old Time Fiddlers, prefer the strings of fiddles and guitars and the beat of a single drumhead.

James S. Griffith, director of the Southwest Folklore Center at the University of Arizona, said that the O'odham at San Xavier Mission probably learned how to play guitars, violins, and European drums when the European-descended peoples traveled through southern Arizona on the way to California in the 1850s and 1860s. At this time, they were also introduced to waltzes, two-steps, mazurkas, and quadrilles (Means 1995:36). The saxophone may have been introduced by the marching bands the O'odham encountered in government boarding schools in the twentieth century. The Tohono O'odham, whose traditional territory straddles the international border, may have brought Mexican *norteño* music with its polkas and accordions as part of the legacy from German railroad workers. The two styles, *norteño* and waila, are distinct because of the latter's more relaxed tempo and faintly dissonant guitar chords. Still used for social occasions, such as weddings, birthdays, and church feasts, waila can last from dusk till dawn as the band plays in a shelter near a dance area decorated with ribbon streamers. But in other ways—amplification, a wider range of instrumentation, and today's more relaxed dance step—waila has changed since the 1950s. Also changing is the setting in which waila is performed, for today it is popular in bars and dance halls near O'odham country. Waila is even gaining national recognition at such venues as the Smithsonian's Festival of American Folklife in Washington, D.C., where the Alex Gomez Band performed; the National Folk Festival in Johnstown, Pennsylvania, where the Southern Scratch Band played; and even Carnegie Hall in New York City, where the Joaquin Brothers performed. Angelo Joaquin Jr. organizes the annual Waila Festival held each April near the Arizona Historical Society in Tucson. Waila is best described as a living tradition that continues to change because of younger players who incorporate influences from rock, country, and reggae. Manuel Osequeda Jr., a keyboardist and manager of Simon and Friends, a band from the northwest corner of the Tohono O'odham Reservation, writes songs in the Tohono O'odham language. Osequeda told freelance writer Andrew Means, "I'm trying to do it in Tex Mex style but in our own language . . . I want to do a song about the environment, survival . . . about our environment and our Mother Earth. We have fruits that we eat in the desert and that's how we survive. . . . There's a lot of respect for traditions. I think Native Americans are trying to educate the outside world and share our culture with them" (ibid., 40).

Ceremonies

Like the Pueblos, the O'odham had a set of communal rituals to celebrate the life cycle of corn and to bring rain. Curing, once only part of a much larger ritual system, eventually became the center of O'odham ritual as nearly all the communal rituals disappeared. The O'odham traditionally celebrated both public and private rituals. Each Tohono O'odham village kept a fetish bundle wrapped in eagle down in a basket in the hills. Instead of a priestly hierarchy, ordinary men performed the songs and speeches that composed the ceremonies.

Communal ceremonies included those held in the central plaza, such as the summer cactus wine feast and a "naming ceremony" by which local groups honored each other, and those held on the sacred grounds peripheral to the village, such as the *ma'amaga* (the corn harvest and deer-hunting ritual held in September), the *wi:gida* (a harvest and "prayerstick" ritual), and three purification rites for eagle killing, warfare, and the salt pilgrimage (Bahr 1983a:180). In autumn they also held intervillage athletic contests of racing and kickball, and a Deer Dance. Private rituals (girls' puberty dances, childbirth purification ceremonies, and ritual cures for sickness) were held for individuals in private homes (ibid.).

Medicine men fermented some of the syrup made from the saguaro cactus fruit into ceremonial wine for the four-day saguaro wine feast, which is still practiced in a few villages today (Lopez, in Moreillon 1997:1). During the two nights it took for the syrup to ferment in the village communal round house, men, women, and children danced in a large circle outside the Rain House around a fire in the middle of the ceremonial grounds (central plaza). After the wine had been tasted, several men ran to neighboring villages to invite them to the feast by delivering a ritual oration called the "running speech." The men who lived in those villages responded with another oration known as the "return running."

Both orations began with a description of the desolation of the land without rain and explained that the world would burn unless rain fell. When the guests arrive, the orators in the host village greeted them with a seating speech before the sit-and-drink ceremony. In addition to drinking, this complex ceremony included sermons and ritual orations. The Mockingbird Speech, named for the great imitator of songs and actions, concluded this ceremony, which clearly links wine drinking, ritual drunkenness, and life-giving rain. Summoned by Mockingbird's joyous drunkenness from the "medicine man's liquid, rainmaker's liquid," Wind brings dust storms, lightning, and rain (Sheridan 1996:120).

The lying earth was beautifully wet and finished
On top of that came out various seeded things, *opon, su'uwat, da:pk* [types of wild
    greens], and every kind of cactus, well did they ripen.
It was this that was our last wish and it had happened
As you will see
(From the Mockingbird Speech, in Underhill et al. 1979:35)

Another major ceremony, the Wi:gida, has been interpreted as a harvest celebration, a blessing of newly sown crops, a prayerstick ritual, and a community identity renewal ceremony (Nabhan 1993:77) (*wi:gĭ* refers to the downy feathers of eagles or other birds.) Every four years, in autumn, several villages cooperated to stage this major ceremony of grand renewal and purification. Ruth Underhill, who devoted her career to recording Tohono O'odham life and ceremonies, stated that the purpose of the Wi:gida was to "keep the world in order and prevent a flood. Keeping the world in order was a function of the Pueblo solstice ceremonies, and, indeed, the respective dates of the prayerstick festival come as near to summer and winter solstices as they do to harvest" (1946:154). The Wi:gida, with its many Puebloan traits, shows how important agriculture was to the Tohono O'odham, for it includes prayersticks, masked dancers, and prayers intended to keep the world in order. Men from the participating five villages took ten days to compose songs and to prepare prayersticks made from turkey down, which symbolizes rain and renewal (Lamphere 1983:761).

The ocean wind from far off overtakes me.
It bends down the tassels of the corn.
The ocean water hurts my heart.
Beautiful clouds bring rain upon our fields
(From a Salt Pilgrimage song [Underhill 1993 [1938]:131–32])

Tohono O'odham men undertook a dangerous eight-day pilgrimage to the Gulf of California to seek the ocean wind that brings the rain. They honored the ocean with gifts by throwing cornmeal on the waves and casting prayersticks into the sea, hoping that the monsoon moisture would accompany them northward as they returned home. If they were successful, great dust storms and dramatic displays of lightning would herald life-giving downpours that soaked the earth. So arduous was this almost waterless, four-day journey that the Tohono O'odham name for "south" means "the direction of suffering" (Underhill 1993 [1938]:111). The degree of suffering and the sight of the miraculous ocean brought men into contact with the supernatural. Individuals undertook the journey for the sake of their people, giving offerings to the ocean and bringing back "corn"—the white kernels of salt the ocean deposits on its shore. The great miracle was rain, for if the journey was undertaken properly, the ocean wind would blow, bringing life-giving rain.

Protected by special rituals and ceremonies, the men had to speak a special language for the duration of their journey, because they traveled too near the heart of power to use familiar terms for such powerful beings as the sun, which they referred to as the "shining traveler" (Underhill 1993 [1938]:112). All young men volunteered for the journey once they were old enough. They had to undertake the trip in four successive years in order to tame the magic; each year they had to make new equipment lest pregnant or menstruating women contaminate their sandals, nets for salt-carrying, bridles, and gourd water bottles (ibid., 112–13). Originally undertaken on foot, the journey was later made on horseback. Each night the men would camp in specific locations, lying with their heads in the direction of the sea, "so that 'its power can draw them on'" (ibid., 113). To people who had never seen such an unbounded body of water, the supreme act of courage came when they entered the "outspread waters"; braving the breakers, they had to step into "the appalling element and bring out a blessing" (ibid., 121). A man prayed that the sea would accept his offering of cornmeal that he threw onto the waves and would bless him with a vision: "A flight of white gulls may beckon him into the ocean depths, where he will learn wonders, or perhaps a strange sea coyote will come walking on the water and speak to him" (ibid., 129).

Although other groups, such as the Zuni, also undertook salt pilgrimages, those journeys were not as elaborate as those of the Tohono O'odham. Fraught with danger, this epic journey was a test of endurance and included tests of strength, such as running along the beach and advancing into the ocean, which they considered to be the very edge of the world. Other ritual elements, such as the prayersticks, cornmeal, and speeches and songs with their rain and cloud imagery, were prayers for agricultural munificence. Thus, in their salt pilgrimage, the Tohono O'odham fused the quest for individual power with the securing of blessings for community well-being and agricultural prosperity. (See Lamphere 1983:761–62.)

More Recent History

When the Tohono O'odham (then Papago) tribe organized under a council in 1937, their constitution provided for a chairman, vice chairman, secretary, and treasurer elected by the whole tribe. Each district had its own council—another element that added to their autonomy—as well as representation on the Tohono O'odham Tribal Council in the form of two council members elected by district members. In addition to the nine districts of the large reservation, San Xavier and Gila Bend each had a district, bringing the total number of councilmen to twenty-two. By the 1930s the Tohono O'odham were firmly entrenched in the non-Indian cash economy for their livelihood: they had been selling their labor to mines and ranches, and their wood, farm produce, pottery, and baskets to non-Indians as early as the 1880s (Fontana 1983:145). From about 1920 until the 1960s, when cotton farming became mechanized, the Tohono O'odham provided most of the labor on off-reservation farms for long-staple cotton, one of southern Arizona's major industries (ibid., 145).

Today, less than one-third of the Tohono O'odham are able to live on the reservation year-round because reservation unemployment has been as high as 60 percent. While many work in Tucson and other nearby towns, others find seasonal agricultural jobs. Those who live on the reservation are employed by tribal and governmental agencies or make their income by cattle raising and limited farming.

It took World War II to enlarge the Akimel O'odham world. Ira Hayes, probably the best known O'odham veteran, helped raise the American flag atop Mount Suribachi on Iwo Jima and was featured in one of the most popular photographs of World War II, which served as the basis for a bronze statue. (Ira Hayes Memorial Day is celebrated in Sacaton, Arizona, at a park named after Hayes, a Marine veteran, on the third Saturday of every February.) However, when Indians returned from the war, they were faced with the same level of discrimination and economic hardship they had hoped to leave behind. Many, including Ira Hayes, faced a postwar life of such despair that they succumbed to alcoholism. Other Akimel O'odham decided to take control over their own destiny. When veterans returned, they elected a fellow O'odham veteran as council chairman and council members who shared his progressive ideas, such as renegotiating leases, drilling wells, and developing economic enterprises to increase tribal income. Time brought further tribal development, such as the construction of a tribal cultural center near the interstate highway.

Today the Akimel O'odham seek a balance between the economic development that will provide jobs, income, and education for their youth, and the destruction of their desert homeland as Phoenix continues to creep closer. Income from their Ak-Chin Casino near Phoenix has enabled them to begin meeting critical housing needs.

The Contemporary World of the O'odham

"The O'odham are a contemporary people, which is difficult for some people to accept," says Tohono O'odham linguist and professor Ofelia Zepeda (1999). Most accounts of the O'odham deal with their past instead of their present and future, failing to mention the success of their educational programs and tribal programs for economic development, and the strength of their language. At the same time they continue many of the old traditions, such as the saguaro wine festival. Each summer, the Tohono O'odham in Quitovac, Sonora, continue to celebrate the Wi:gida, their ancient rain ceremony, and many Tohono O'odham in Arizona either make the pilgrimage to Magdalena or celebrate the Feast Day of St. Francis each year. Sonoran Catholicism is still practiced in villages on the reservation. As Zepeda describes it, "There are little churches in tiny villages—and no priests. Maybe just a saint's table and a candle. The villagers go in and say rosary together" (Trimble 1993:359).

The desert itself is another constant presence in the lives of the O'odham. Zepeda (1995:2–3) speaks lovingly of "the odor of wet dirt" that "precedes the rain . . . an aroma so strong for some that it wakes them from sleep." This cherished smell is that of "the fine dust that must settle on all the needles and spines of saguaro and all manner of cactus, the dust that settles on the fine leaves of ocotillo and other leafed plants." When rain comes, the smell of this dust mixes with the scent of these desert plants that "give off an aroma only when mixed with rain." Then everyone inhales deeply, remarking "about the *si s-wa'us u:wǐ* (it smells like wetness)." Zepeda says, "To the women, my mother, my grandmother, there was beauty in all these events, the events of a summer rain, the things that preceded the rain and the events afterward. They laughed with joy at all of it."

Today the O'odham have six reservations, two of which they share with the Maricopa. (See chapter 7.) Akimel O'odham and Maricopa live in the Salt River Pima-Maricopa Community, which borders the affluent non-Indian community of Scottsdale, Arizona. Their Hoo-hoogam Ki Museum features exhibits on the traditional lifestyles and history of both cultures; other tourist facilities include the Red Mountain Trap and Skeet range; the Cypress Golf Course, which has two nine-hole courses and a driving range; and Native Hands Arts and Crafts, which also has a restaurant.

Akimel O'odham and Maricopa also share the Gila River Indian Community, which is located on both sides of Interstate 10, north and south of the Gila River. Today, the reservation's economy is based on agriculture, including wheat, barley, cotton, citrus, and vegetables; the Gila River Casino at Firebird and the Gila River Casino at Lone Butte Industrial Park; and the leasing of land. The tribal government formed a corporation that has established several popular enterprises, including Firebird International Raceway; Compton Terrace, which has a large amphitheater for concerts; and Firebird Lake, used for professional drag boat racing.

Despite their ancestry, the O'odham of the Ak-Chin Indian Community consider themselves to be neither Tohono O'odham nor Akimel O'odham, but rather Ak-Chin O'odham. (Older maps sometimes mistakenly label this reservation the Maricopa Ak-Chin Indian Reservation, because the nearest settlement to the reservation is the non-Indian community of Maricopa.) In addition to Harrah's Phoenix Ak-Chin Casino, most of the economy is based on Ak-Chin Farms, Inc., a large-scale agricultural enterprise run by the tribe. They also have the Ak-Chin Him-Dak, which is a unique community museum and culture center where local families create and maintain the exhibits for themselves and for visitors.

The Tohono O'odham Nation includes the main reservation west of Tucson, Arizona, and noncontiguous reservations at San Xavier and Gila Bend. Visitors are drawn to the Desert Diamond Casino, the Tohono O'odham Swap Meet, and the historic Mission San Xavier del Bac, which also has a gift shop and museum.

In 1997 the Bureau of Land Management turned over a tiny piece of land south of Ajo to the Hia C-ed O'odham. This area—one of their historic burial grounds—is only a small fraction of their homeland, which lies south of Interstate 8 between Gila Bend and Yuma, Arizona, within Organ Pipe Cactus National Monument, Cabeza Prieta Game Range, and Barry Goldwater Air Force Range, and extending into Mexico. Not until the mid-1980s did about 1,200 Hia C-ed O'odham receive recognition from the Tohono O'odham Nation, giving them equal access to social services, education, and health benefits. Some Hia C-ed O'odham have married Tohono O'odham and now live in their villages, but most live in such towns as Ajo, Gila Bend, Stanfield, and Caborca.

Education and Language

The inspiring film *Power and the Pride to Win* shows how the students and administrators of Baboquivari High School worked with the community to revive their school, which had fallen to the lowest academic standing in Arizona. Drawing upon their traditions and their community, students, parents, administrators, and tribal leaders developed a plan to involve everyone in improving their school. The tradition of consensus building became the basis for their approach, as they met and provided a forum for everyone to voice their concerns, so that they could develop what became a sixty-five-point action plan to enhance student achievement at Baboquivari High School. They developed more meaningful classes by focusing on skills that would help students prepare for college and for careers, while at the same time integrating cultural traditions, such as language, dancing, and arts, into the curriculum. The science department incorporated traditional cultural beliefs to provide a cultural view of science; tribal elders came to share their knowledge, and students also took field trips around the reservation to see how technology had affected their local environment, including plant and animal communities.

In addition to curriculum development, the improvement effort focused on building morale by involving everyone in a cleanup project and by encouraging parents to come and be a part of their children's education. They also instituted a no-pass, no-play program in which students were required to pass all their classes before being allowed to play on the school's athletic teams. The result was students who were proud of their degrees and who looked forward to their future: in 1985 only half the students had graduated, but by 1989 more than three-quarters (84 percent) were completing their education.

Baboquivari High School,
Sells, Arizona, 1999. Author
photograph

The encouraging changes at Baboquivari High School were part of an overall Tohono O'odham education plan approved in 1987, which was supervised by Bernard Siquieros and Rosilda Lopez-Manuel. As depicted in the film, traditionally matters were decided through the process of consensus that involved going to a person with whom you had a difference of opinion, discussing the pros and cons of the issues for yourself and the other person, and then settling on a workable solution. Unlike the concept of "majority rules," in a decision reached through consensus no one can discount the solution by saying that they did not vote for that particular choice; instead everyone has reached a mutually satisfying decision and thus has a stake in the result as well as in the strategy used to reach it. In developing the tribal education plan, the Tohono O'odham were careful to include the viewpoints of elders, young people, and professionals. As Lopez-Manuel said, "As a people, we've known we had to pull together to be strong; you can't be successful unless you do" (Trimble 1993:371).

Seal of the Tohono O'odham Nation, painted by the class of 1986, Baboquivari High School, Sells, Arizona, 1999. Author photograph

Also shown in the film was the use of the O'odham language. Students actively used their language, and portions of the film, depicting traditional ways of meeting to discuss decisions, used English subtitles to translate the O'odham language. At the beginning of the twentieth century most Native Americans in the United States spoke their own languages. However, today so few children are learning their languages that Victor Golla of Humboldt State University (1994:311) predicts that, of the 150 Indian languages still spoken today, only about 20 will survive. Fortunately, O'odham is among those that continue to be actively used and taught to children, both in homes and in schools.

One of the people dedicated to maintaining and preserving Native American languages is Ofelia Zepeda, a professor of linguistics and American Indian studies at the University of Arizona, where she teaches O'odham, her native language. In 1999 the MacArthur Foundation named her as one of its fellows, describing her as "a unique force on behalf of the continued life of endangered languages" through "her singular work in advancing the field of Native language scholarship." Soon after its founding, she became codirector of the American Indian Language Development Institute (AILDI), a summer institute that offers college-credit courses in linguistics and bilingual and bicultural education. Students come from all over the United States to attend AILDI, which emphasizes the needs of Native American communities and offers courses on a variety of Southwestern indigenous languages. AILDI has experimented with traditional applications to teach math and science, such as teaching concepts of probability with Tohono O'odham stick games and writing computer programs to produce the "man in the maze" symbol (Trimble 1993:371). In addition to strengthening O'odham language skills, the program has reinforced the concept of community—an important tradition, for as Tohono O'odham educator Juana Jose has said, "Indian peoples have historically banded together because they needed each other's support. Cooperation, not competition, is crucial in classes" (ibid.).

The late tribal chairman Josiah Moore knew the value of education. Raised in Santa Rosa, Moore worked as a painter, counselor, and social services coordinator while attending Arizona State University, where he received his education degree in 1964. After working for the Tohono O'odham Nation, he returned to Arizona State to study school administration and ten years later was named state director of Indian education. Moore wanted his fellow O'odham "to believe that they can function in the white man's world without compromising their heritage. . . . We know our culture and have our own standards, values, and traditions. We need to bring this to the forefront" (Duarte 1986b:D2).

State-funded, locally controlled charter schools help preserve tribal cultures, enabling children to "get a solid sense of themselves before going off the reservation to other schools," explained S. Jo Lewis, principal of Blackwater Community School at the Gila River Indian Community (Creno 1997:A1). At the school, community volunteers fluent in the O'odham language teach students, and science classes include traditional methods for growing corn, beans, and squash; during recess, children play *thaka,* a traditional Akimel O'odham game that resembles hockey. No longer are children forced to choose between their own cultures and academics, as they were in the 1950s when they were still punished for speaking their languages. In 1997 Arizona had ten reservation charter schools that included schools for Navajo, Hopi, O'odham, and Maricopa children (ibid., A11); these schools not only have increased educational opportunities for students but also have renewed Indian communities by involving elders and family members.

Economic Development

Today most employed Tohono O'odham who live on the reservation work either for the tribal government or in civil service jobs with federal agencies; over half the tribe now lives off-reservation (Trimble 1993:372). Homes on the reservation range from traditional mud-and-saguaro-rib homes to makeshift shacks with plywood walls. Although fortunate families live in brick houses or mobile homes, it is not uncommon for rural O'odham villages to lack indoor plumbing. "The first year they put electricity in my village was 1968," said Eddie Manuel, of the Gu Vo District about 100 miles west of Tucson. "Later running water started going to the houses," he said. "But about 25 percent still rely on outhouses. And some people still haul water in the back of pickup trucks" (Volante 1993:2). Overcrowding remains a serious problem, according to Noreen Pablo, assistant director of the Tohono

O'odham Housing Authority, with "two or three families living in a three-room house, or even a one-room house" (ibid., 2). Tohono O'odham Sharmain Garcia, who worked with the tribe's health department in the early 1970s (1999), believes that very little of the income from the Tohono O'odham Desert Diamond Casino filters down to those who need it the most, but many others see gaming as the logical solution to the lack of reservation jobs.

Recently, however, the Tohono O'odham have used income from their gaming enterprises to build and staff their own college, which opens its doors in 2000. They also constructed a new nursing home so that tribal elders can be cared for in more familiar surroundings. In 1995 tribal lawmakers created a tribal scholarship fund with casino profits, and these scholarships now enable many students to pursue higher education. "To me, it's just so exciting, because here's the chance to improve our lives," said Rosilda Manuel, director of the Tohono O'odham Education Department (Volante 1995:1A, 13A). To ensure that students not only educate themselves but also use the skills and knowledge they gain to benefit the whole tribe, scholarship recipients are required to sign a contract agreeing to return to work for the tribe on the reservation after they finish school. Scholarship recipients must seek employment with the tribe for a period equal to half the time they have spent in school. This can include working for the Indian Health Service in Tucson.

Two students whose lives have been changed by the scholarship are Nicole Chavez and Reanetta Martinez. Chavez, who was salutatorian of her Baboquivari High School class, originally planned to get a bachelor of arts degree and leave the reservation for greater job opportunities. She struggled financially while finishing her freshman year at the University of Arizona and was unable to pay her room and board during her sophomore year, until she was awarded the scholarship, which enabled her to continue her education. Now she looks forward to working on the reservation and helping her people move forward. Chavez said, "A lot of it has to start with tribal leaders. They need to be open to changes and new ideas—and that's what I think the students coming in can offer" (ibid., A13).

Martinez said, "I think it's a really good idea. It's a small payback we have to make" (ibid., A13). The scholarship helped her quit her job as a Girl Scouts registrar and enroll in business administration courses at Pima Community College before pursuing a University of Arizona degree in the management of information systems.

In 1995, 235 tribal members shared $1,018,762 in tribal scholarships, which surpasses the $710,000 provided the previous year from federally funded scholarships, and each student can receive as much as $17,500 per year (ibid., A1). One of the benefits of a tribal scholarship fund is that the tribe itself sets the eligibility criteria, alleviating some of the problems that Indian students face when they compete for funding. Glenn Johnson, director of the University of Arizona American Indian Graduate Center, explained, "If you went to a (non-Indian) college prep school, you're going to have greater consideration than if you went to Baboquivari High School or Tohono O'odham High School. It's very difficult for any reservation-based tribe to compete for mainstream scholarships" (ibid., A13).

O'odham Program Steers Children Away from Drugs

In April 1999 in Washington, D.C., a Tohono O'odham program was among eight exemplary programs in the country honored by drug-abuse-prevention officials for successfully steering children away from substance abuse. Retired general Barry McCaffrey, director of the Office of National Drug Control Policy, told the award winners, "You were selected not just for the hard work and skills you have contributed, but frankly as models. We want to be able to go to others and say, Here are examples of ordinary Americans who came together and made a difference" (Specht 1999:1C).

In 1994 Regina Siquieros created an innovative plan called Cultural Enhancement through Storytelling, which uses Tohono O'odham tribal storytellers to persuade reservation children to stay in school and away from drugs and alcohol. This storytelling curriculum has been instrumental in helping some 400 seventh-graders at Baboquivari Middle School, who had previously been the most disaffected part of the community, find greater respect for their tribal roots and themselves. Discipline complaints at the school dropped by half in the first four years after the program was introduced. Siquieros described the dramatic changes: "When we started, the students were very somber, they never smiled, and they seemed to wear black clothes all the time. When we walked around the school, we sometimes had to physically pull kids apart who started fighting right in front of us. Now, they are smiling and happy, the incidents of drugs and fighting have gone way down, and you see colors all over" (Specht 1999:10C).

All seventh-graders receive classroom-based curriculum focusing on health studies, social-science courses, and language arts. The health-studies component emphasizes "problem-solving skills and natural highs," such as exercise, singing, and dancing, as opposed to the debilitating effects of drugs and alcohol, which are explained in detail (Specht 1999:10C). Students participate in social-science courses that emphasize pride in their ancient culture as they interact with Tohono O'odham role models. They learn the value of possessing multicultural skills as they develop their abilities in language arts by using storytelling to build their identity as American Indians.

Three clubs—Winter Storytelling Nights, the Heritage Club, and the Running Club—reach beyond the classroom. In 1998 the school's basketball team won the state small-school championship thanks to their running training, but even more important are the spiritual values that come through the physical focus of running, a long tradition among the Tohono O'odham people because of the vastness of their desert homelands. Andrew Ramon, the counselor for the Running Club, explained, "We are not training for speed, this is for the spiritual state you can reach when you are running long distances" (Specht 1999:10C). Eventually Ramon wants to lead a spirit run tracing the annual 100-mile salt pilgrimage the Tohono O'odham once made to the Gulf of California in Mexico.

Today community-based Compass Health Care, Inc., of Tucson operates the program, which is funded by a $150,000 annual grant from the Community Partnership of Southern Arizona and the regional behavioral health authority. Bernard Siquieros, Regina's husband, explained the transformation in Tohono O'odham education: "When I grew up, we went to (Bureau of Indian Affairs) schools where they tried to stamp out the language and culture; they wanted us all to assimilate, to make that transition to white culture. Now, the kids are shown we can celebrate our uniqueness, that different cultures are important to America" (Specht 1999:10C).

Health

The late Miguel Velasco said, "The reason so many Indians die young is because they don't eat their desert food. I worry about what will happen to this new generation of Indians who have become accustomed to present food they buy at markets" (Bell, Anderson, and Stewart 1980). The O'odham have the highest documented rate of diabetes in the world. Scientists theorize that over time the O'odham adapted to their feast-or-famine lifestyle by developing a "thrifty" genotype that enabled them to store calories during times of abundance, which they could use in times of starvation (Wendorf and Goldfine 1991). This metabolism was suited to the high levels of soluble fiber in traditional foods, such as tepary and mesquite beans and cactus fruit, which made them slow to release carbohydrates during digestion. However, the dietary intake of fat has gone from 15 percent in the 1890s to 40 percent in the 1990s (NIH 1995:19). A steady diet of highly processed foods, such as white flour, lard, sugar, and junk food, combined with a sedentary lifestyle, has brought about extremely high diabetes rates.

Tribal leaders are recognizing the need to combat this disease at a national level, for diabetes is now the fourth-leading cause of death among Native American people (Roubideaux 1999:55). The Indian Health Service Diabetes Program includes a national office in Albuquerque and consultants in each Indian Health service area, and special services in many Indian centers throughout the country; recently, Congress authorized $30 million each year until 2002 for diabetes prevention and treatment services for Native Americans (ibid., 57). In 1990 the Native American Research and Training Center at the University of Arizona, in cooperation with six Arizona tribes, launched a camp for Indian children with diabetes that provides diabetes education as well as extensive physical activity (ibid.).

In addition to exercise, management of diet is essential in combating this debilitating disease. Many wild and cultivated plants native to the Southwest are unusually rich in the kind of complex carbohydrates that can help control diabetes. Before they can be used, however, they must be preserved and cultivated. In the 1980s many Tohono O'odham farmers realized that some of the crops they had known as children could no longer be found.

Responding to this need, Dr. Barney Burns, Dr. Gary Paul Nabhan, Mahina Drees, and Karen Reichhardt founded Native Seeds/SEARCH, a nonprofit seed-conservation organization. Since 1983 this Tucson-based organization has been reintroducing these crops to O'odham gardeners. Today, Native Seeds/SEARCH is a major regional seed bank with over 1,800 collections (many of them rare or endangered); 90 percent of the crops are not being systematically preserved elsewhere. For over fifteen years, this organization has been preserving the wide variety of wild plants and crops grown and harvested not only by the O'odham but also by other native Southwestern farmers. (SEARCH stands for Southwestern Endangered Arid-land Resource Clearing House.) This includes Hopi varieties of corn, especially the blue corn; Havasupai field and tree crops, especially their renowned peaches; the many crop varieties of the New Mexico Pueblos, such as hot and mild chiles, squash, and melons. Other seeds come from the plants of Western Apache, Navajo, and River Yumans, who have been farming the floodplains of the Gila and lower Colorado Rivers since A.D. 800. The Tohono O'odham and Akimel O'odham have developed some of the most drought-resistant, heat-tolerant, and alkali-adapted crops in the world. Traditionally, they raised sixty-day corn, tepary beans, and striped cushaw squash, crops that would produce during the brief, torrential summer rains.

In addition to mitigating the severity of diabetes, these varieties of plants also serve as the primary resource for breeding programs to increase the commercial crops' resistance to insects, diseases, and droughts and freezes. The sunflowers grown by the Havasupais were recently discovered to be the only kind of sunflowers that are 100 percent resistant to a rust strain that is devastating all sunflower hybrids in the United States and Canada. Such native crop diversity strengthens all major food crops, ensuring future stability in the global food supply.

O'odham Basketry

Traditionally, O'odham women made both pottery (for cooking and storing water) and baskets (for carrying loads, parching, and storage). Basketry took many forms; one of the most useful was trays, which served in the preparation of all kinds of food, including the winnowing of wheat and the catching of fine flour after it was ground on a stone metate with a stone mano. Ideal for mixing foods and collecting mesquite beans, trays were also used to parch wheat with live coals. In 1916 Mary Kissell (1972 [1916]:193) noted that the tray was used "only on ceremonial occasions . . . as an eating dish, when the small

water-tight tray of the Papago medicineman is called into service, both as a drinking cup and a pinole dish, when on expeditions to the sea for sacred salt, and when curing the sick." Bowls, many of which were water-tight, were useful for carrying cactus fruits and seeds, and even for watering horses; deep bowls were used for wine-making and drinking. Women also made large storage jars for storing grain.

Today only a small amount of pottery is made, but both the Tohono O'odham and the Akimel O'odham continue to weave baskets. The Akimel O'odham once made large numbers of durable willow baskets, many of them in a whirlwind pattern called *sivalik*. Once feared to be dying out, Akimel O'odham basketry has been experiencing a revival since the

Some Akimel O'od-ham granary baskets were so large that weavers had to complete these baskets sitting inside them, c. 1910. Courtesy of Arizona Historical Society, No. 26,024

beginning of the 1980s (Tanner 1989 [1983]:155). Perhaps because they lived by rivers and for many years had a more prosperous existence, the Akimel O'odham did not market their basketry as aggressively as did the Tohono O'odham, who have created a major market for their work. Akimel O'odham women have a reputation as master weavers; their designs combine complicated line patterns with fine craftsmanship. In comparison with the basketry of the Tohono O'odham, their willow coiled baskets are thinner walled and more flexible, and their designs are more dynamic and imaginative (ibid., 173).

Today Tohono O'odham weavers not only make more coiled baskets than any other Southwestern tribe, but also produce the greatest variety of forms (Tanner 1989 [1983]:120, 123). Living in the desert away from rivers, they needed the income from the tourist market and produced many forms to appeal to the Anglo market, including bowls with lids and handles, jars in a variety of sizes and shapes, plaques, wastebaskets, life-form baskets, and miniature baskets made of horsehair. Women use a variety of desert plants as material, but today they rely primarily on green beargrass, unbleached (green) yucca, bleached (white) yucca, and black devil's claw to accentuate design elements. They also make plaited baskets, such as those used by medicine men for the storage of their ritual equipment. They are known for the great versatility of their stitch combinations in coiled basketry, creating a lacy and delicate effect.

The *kiaha* or burden basket is no longer made but has a long history with all O'odham groups. Women used the ribs of the saguaro for the three rigid supports, agave as fibers for cordage for the basket itself, and cat's claw for the ring around the top. It was used to transport firewood, water ollas, and other burdens on the back. Made by the Pimas until the turn of the century and until about 1940 by the Tohono O'odham, the *kiaha* was once said to be alive and to move about on its own three spindly saguaro-rib legs (Tanner 1989 [1983]:151). Then one day, as a line of *kiaha* were helping the people of a Tohono O'odham village move from their summer field village back up to their winter well village, Coyote, the trickster, teased them, mocking their spindly spider legs. Offended, the *kiaha* said, "Oh! Oh! . . . If that is the case, we will cease to carry burdens on our own! We won't walk again. The women must carry us on their backs from now on" (Underhill 1982 [1951]:17). From that time on, the *kiaha* have never carried their burdens alone.

The "man in the maze," a popular symbol used in Tohono O'odham basketry, depicts a man who goes through many changes and turns in the maze of life. According to one interpretation, the man goes deeper into the pattern over the course of his life, becoming stronger and gaining more understanding. The dark center of the design represents death, which the man realizes is coming. Not yet ready to face death, he is able to prolong his life for a while by retreating to a small corner of the design. After a period of cleansing and reflection, and the passing on of his knowledge for future generations, the man is restored to a state of harmony and accepts death peacefully.

References and Further Reading

The Handbook of North American Indians, vol. 10 (1983), contains chapters by Kenneth Stewart, Martha Kendall, Sally Giff Pablo, Timothy Dunnigan, and others on various aspects of O'odham culture. See also Bernard L. Fontana, *Guide to Contemporary Southwest Indians* (Southwest Parks and Monuments Association, Tucson, 1999). *The Runner* is the newspaper of the Tohono O'odham.

Allen, T. D. 1974. *Arrows Four: Prose and Poetry by Young American Indians*. Washington Square Press, New York. (This includes some prose and poetry written by Tohono O'odham students.)

ARCIA. 1976–77 [1870]. *Annual Reports to the Secretary of the Interior*. AMS Press, New York.

*Bahr, Donald. 1975. *Pima and Papago Ritual Oratory: A Study of Three Texts*. Indian Historian Press, San Francisco. [A professor at Arizona State University, Bahr has worked extensively with various Tohono O'odham experts to document aspects of ritual orations and practice.]

———. 1983a. "Pima and Papago Social Organization." In *Handbook of North American Indians*, vol. 10: *The Southwest*, pp. 178–92.

———. 1983b. "Pima and Papago Medicine and Philosophy." In *Handbook of North American Indians*, vol. 10: *The Southwest*, pp. 193–200.

Bahr, Donald, Juan Gregorio, David Lopez, and Albert Alvarez. 1974. *Piman Shamanism and Staying Sickness*. University of Arizona Press, Tucson.

Bahr, Donald, Joseph Giff, and Manuel Havier. 1979. "Piman Songs on Hunting." *Ethnomusicology* 23, no. 2:245–96.

Bahr, Donald, and Richard Haefer. 1978. "Song in Piman Curing." *Ethnomusicology* 23, no. 1:89–122.

Bell, Fillman, Keith Anderson, and Yvonne Stewart. 1980. *The Quitobaquito Cemetery and Its History*. Western Archaeological and Conservation Center, Tucson.

Bennett, P. H., T. A. Burch, and M. Miller. 1971. "Diabetes Mellitus in American (Pima) Indians." *Lancet* 2, no. 7716 (17 July):125–28.

Brown-Kampden, Catherine. 1978. "The Maze of Life Design of the Pima-Papago." *Masterkey* 52, no.2:67–70.

Bureau of Ethnic Research. 1971. *Political Organization and Business Management in the Gila River Indian Community*. Research Report Series. University of Arizona Press, Tucson.

Castetter, Edward, and Willis Bell. 1942. *Pima and Papago Agriculture*. University of New Mexico Press, Albuquerque.

Creno, Cathryn. 1997. "New Traditions from Old: Charter Schools Seek to Preserve Tribal Cultures." *Arizona Republic*, 18 May, pp. A1, A11.

Crosswhite, Frank. 1980. "The Annual Saguaro Harvest and Crop Cycle of the Papago, with Reference to Ecology and Symbolism." *Desert Plants* 2, no. 1:1–62.

Densmore, Frances. 1929. *Papago Music*. Bureau of American Ethnology Bulletin 90. Washington, D.C.

DeWald, Terry. 1979. *The Papago Indians and Their Basketry*. Tucson.

Dobyns, Henry. 1951. *Papagos in the Cotton Fields, 1950*. Privately printed, Tucson.

———. 1962. *The Papago People*. Indian Tribal Series.

Doelle, William. 1977. "Desert Resources and Hohokam Subsistence: The Conoco-Florence Project." *Arizona State Museum Archaeological Series* 103:70–77, 94–99. (Describes the ecology of the Tohono O'odham saguaro harvesting.)

Duarte, Carmen. 1986a. "O'odham Constitution Unites Old and New." *Arizona Daily Star*, 9 March, p. D1.

———. 1986b. "Tohono O'odham Leader Carries a Legal Pad in Hand and Legends in Head." *Arizona Daily Star*, 9 March, p. D2.

Emory, William. 1848. *Notes of a Military Reconnoissance, from Fort Leavenworth. In Missouri, to San Diego, in California, Including Parts of Arkansas, Del Norte, and Gila Rivers. Made in 1846–1847.* U.S. Congress, Senate. 31st Cong., 1st sess. Senate Executive Document 7 (serial no. 505). Washington, D.C.

*Evers, Larry, ed. 1981. *The South Corner of Time: Hopi, Navajo, Papago, Yaqui Tribal Literature.* University of Arizona Press, Tucson. [This collection provides a glimpse of the eloquence of O'odham oratory and poetry.]

Ezell, Paul. 1961. *The Hispanic Acculturation of the Gila River Pimas*. American Anthropological Association Memoir 90. Menasha, Wis.

———. 1983. "History of the Pima." In *Handbook of North American Indians*, vol. 10: *The Southwest*, pp. 149–60.

Fan, Mary. 1998. "Tohono O'odham Want Lease Revised." *Arizona Daily Star*, 27 September, pp. A1, 6.

Fontana, Bernard. 1976. "The Faces and Forces of Pimería Alta." In *Voices from the Southwest*, pp. 45–54, ed. D. C. Dickinson, D. Laird, and M. Maxwell. Northland Press, Flagstaff.

*———. 1981. *Of Earth and Little Rain*. University of Arizona Press, Tucson. [For over thirty years Fontana, an ethnologist and field historian at the University of Arizona, has lived near the edge of the San Xavier Tohono O'odham Reservation. He is a respected scholar and key source on Tohono O'odham culture and life and was actively involved in the restoration of San Xavier Mission.]

———. 1983. "History of the Papago." In *Handbook of North American Indians*, vol. 10: *The Southwest*, pp. 137–48.

———. 1995. "Restoring San Xavier del Bac 'Our Church': Tohono O'odham Work to Restore the 200-Year-Old Church Built by Their Ancestors." *Native Peoples* 8, no. 4:28–35.

Forbes, Robert H. 1948. Three-page memorandum on geology and history of I'itoi Ki. 26 July. Arizona Historical Society archives, Tucson. (Forbes is believed to have been the first white man to climb Baboquivari Peak.)

Foster, George. 1962. *Traditional Cultures and the Impact of Technological Change.* Harper, New York.

Gaillard, D. D. 1894. "The Papago of Arizona and Sonora." *American Anthropologist* 7:293.

———. 1896. "The Perils and Wonders of a True Desert." *Cosmopolitan* 21:592–605.

Garcia, Sharmain. 1999. Interview at Kitt Peak National Observatory, 6 February.

Golla, Victor. 1994. "Languages." In *Native America in the Twentieth Century,* pp. 310–12. Garland Publishing, New York.

Hackenberg, Robert. 1983. "Pima and Papago Ecological Adaptations." In *Handbook of North American Indians,* vol. 10: *The Southwest,* pp. 161–77.

Hayden, Julian. 1987. "The Vikita Ceremony of the Papago." *Journal of the Southwest* 29:273–324.

Howard, E. A. 1887. "Report of Agents in Arizona: Pima Agency, 1887." In *Annual Report of the Commissioner for Indian Affairs to the Secretary of the Interior.* U.S. Government Printing Office, Washington, D.C.

Innis, Gilbert C. 1994. "Pima." In *Native America in the Twentieth Century,* pp. 452–54. Garland Publishing, New York.

Juan, Vivian. 1994. "Tohono O'odham." In *Native Americans in the Twentieth Century,* pp. 637–39. Garland Publishing, New York.

Kino, Eusebio. 1948. *Kino's Historical Memoir of Pimeria Alta: A Contemporary Account of the Beginnings of California, Sonora, and Arizona . . .* Edited and translated by Herbert Bolton. 2 vols. in 1. University of California Press, Berkeley.

Kissell, Mary. 1972 [1916]. *Basketry of the Papago and Pima.* Rio Grande Press, Glorietta, N.Mex.

Knowler, William, Peter Bennett, Richard Hamman, and Max Miller. 1978. "Diabetes Incidence and Prevalence in Pima Indians: A 19-Fold Greater Incidence Than in Rochester, Minnesota." *American Journal of Epidemiology* 108, no. 6:497–505.

Kroeber, Clifton, and Bernard Fontana. 1986. *Massacre on the Gila: An Account of the Last Major Battle between American Indians, with Reflections on the Origin of War.* University of Arizona Press, Tucson.

Lamphere, Louise. 1983. "Southwestern Ceremonialism." In *Handbook of North American Indians,* vol. 10: *The Southwest,* pp. 743–63.

MacArthur (John D. and Catherine T.) Foundation. 1999. Announcement of 32 New MacArthur Fellows: Ofelia Zepeda Named MacArthur Fellow. Press release.

Means, Andrew. 1995. "The Waila Music of the O'odham Peoples of Arizona." *Native Peoples* 8, no. 2 (winter):34–40.

Meister, Cary Walter. 1989. *Historical Demography of the Pima and Maricopa Indians of Arizona, 1846–1974.* Garland Publishing, New York.

Moreillon, Judith Lynn. 1997. *Sing Down the Rain.* Kiva Publishing, Santa Fe. (Illustrated by Michael Chiago, a Tohono O'odham artist who has been depicting the everyday and ceremonial life of his people for nearly thirty years.)

Nabhan, Gary Paul. 1978. "Chiltepines: Wild Spice of the American Southwest." *El Palacio* 84, no. 2:1–5.

*————. 1982. *The Desert Smells Like Rain: A Naturalist in Papago Indian Country.* North Point Press, Farrar, Straus and Giroux, New York. [A curator at Tucson's Arizona-Sonora Desert Museum, Nabhan has won awards for his nature writing; his work provides insight into the lives of today's O'odham, especially with regard to farming and nutrition.]

————. 1986a. "Papago Indian Desert Agriculture and Water Control in the Sonoran Desert, 1697–1934." *Applied Geography* 6:43–59.

————. 1986b. "Ak-cin 'Arroyo Mouth' and the Environmental Setting of the Papago Indian Fields in the Sonoran Desert." *Applied Geography* 6:61–75.

————. 1991. "The Moveable O'odham Feast of San Francisco." *Native Peoples* 4, no. 2:28–34.

————. 1993 [1985]. *Gathering the Desert.* University of Arizona Press, Tucson.

Nabhan, Gary, James Berry, Cynthia Anson, and Charles Weber. 1981. "Papago Indian Floodwater Fields and Tepary Bean Protein Yields." *Ecology of Food and Nutrition.* 10, no. 1: 71–78.

National Institutes of Health (NIH). 1995. *The Pima Indians: Pathfinders for Health.* National Institute of Diabetes and Digestive and Kidney Disease. National Institutes of Health Publication 95–3821.

Papago Dance Songs. 1973. Canyon Records. Canyon C-6098. [Recording.]

Rea, Amadeo. 1983. *Once a River: Bird Life and Habitat Changes on the Middle Gila.* University of Arizona Press, Tucson.

Reid, Jeff, and Stephanie Whittlesey. 1997. *The Archaeology of Ancient Arizona.* University of Arizona, Tucson.

Roubideaux, Yvette. 1999. "Diabetes in Indian Country." *Native Peoples* 12, no. 4:54–58.

Russell, Frank. 1975 [1908]. *The Pima Indians.* University of Arizona Press, Tucson.

St. John, Silas. 1859. Letter, Pima Villages, New Mexico, 16 September 1859, to A. B. Greenwood, commissioner of Indian affairs, Washington, D.C. Manuscript. In Letters Received—Pima Agency, 1859–61, Record Group 75, National Archives, Washington, D.C.

Saxton, Dean, and Lucille Saxton. 1973. *O'othham Hoho'ok A'agitha—Legends and Lore of the Papago and Pima Indians.* University of Arizona Press, Tucson.

Shaw, Anna Moore. 1968. *Pima Indian Legends.* University of Arizona Press, Tucson.

————. 1974. *A Pima Past.* University of Arizona Press, Tucson.

Sheridan, Thomas. 1988. "Kino's Unforeseen Legacy: The Material Consequences of Missionization among the Northern Piman Indians of Arizona and Sonora." *Smoke Signal* 49–50. Tucson Corral of Westerners, Tucson.

————. 1996. "The O'odham (Pimas and Papagos): The World Would Burn without Rain." In *Paths of Life*, pp. 115–40, ed. Thomas Sheridan and Nancy Parezo. University of Arizona Press, Tucson.

Somers, Cindy. 1997. "Mission in Life: While Working on the Restoration of San Xavier

Mission, Timothy Lewis Finds Himself, a Purpose and a Wife." *Tucson Citizen*, 8 March, pp. B1–2.

Specht, Jim. 1999. "O'odham Anti-Drug Effort Hailed as Model." *Tucson Citizen*, 9 April, pp. C1, C10.

Spicer, Edward H. 1981 [1962]. *Cycles of Conquest: The Impact of Spain, Mexico, and the United States on the Indians of the Southwest.* University of Arizona Press, Tucson.

Spitz, Jill Jorden. 1998. "$2,000 Check Leaves Some O'odham Poorer." *Arizona Daily Star*, 15 February, pp. A1, A13.

Tanner, Clara Lee. 1989 [1983]. *Indian Baskets of the Southwest.* University of Arizona Press, Tucson.

Tohono O'odham Tribe. 1984. *Tohono O'odham: Lives of the Desert People.*

Tohono O'odham Tribe. 1985. *Tohono O'odham: History of the Desert People.*

Traditional Papago Music, Vol. 1. 1972. Canyon Records. Canyon C-6084. [Recording.]

Trimble, Stephen. 1993. *The People.* School of American Research Press, Santa Fe.

Underhill, Ruth. 1938. *A Papago Calendar Record.* Anthropological Series 2(5), University of New Mexico Bulletin 322. Albuquerque.

———. 1939. *Social Organization of the Papago Indians.* Columbia University Contributions to Anthropology 30. New York.

———. 1940. *The Papago Indians of Arizona and Their Relatives the Pima.* Indian Life and Customs Pamphlet 3. U.S. Bureau of Indian Affairs, Branch of Education, Lawrence, Kans.

———. 1946. *Papago Indian Religion.* Columbia University Contributions to Anthropology 33. New York.

———. 1982 [1951]. *People of the Crimson Evening.* Filter Press, Palmer Lake, Colo.

*———. 1985 [1979]. *Papago Woman.* Waveland Press, Prospect Heights, Ill. [A classic work, an account of the life of Chona, who was an old woman in 1931, when Underhill began recording this material. All of Underhill's work is a key source for Tohono O'odham culture and life.]

———. 1993 [1938]. *Singing for Power: The Song Magic of the Papago Indians of Southern Arizona.* University of Arizona Press, Tucson.

Underhill, Ruth, Donald Bahr, Baptisto Lopez, Jose Pancho, David Lopez. 1979. *Rainhouse and Ocean: Speeches for the Papago Year.* Museum of Northern Arizona, Flagstaff.

Vanderpool, Tim. 1998. "Unrest on the Reservation." *Tucson Weekly*, 19–25 February, pp. 16–18.

Volante, Enric. 1993. "Tribes Point to Poverty, Look to Gaming." *Arizona Daily Star*, 11 April, pp. B1–2.

———. 1995. "Casino Jackpot for Scholars: Beneficiaries Must Return Tribe's Favor." *Arizona Daily Star*, 8 October, pp. A1, A13.

Webb, George. 1994 [1959]. *A Pima Remembers.* University of Arizona Press, Tucson.

Weil, Andrew. 1970. "Throwing Up in Mexico." In *The Marriage of the Sun and Moon, A Quest for Unity in Consciousness*, chap. 2. Houghton Mifflin, Boston.

Wendorf, Michael, and Ira Goldfine. 1991. "Archaeology of NIDDM: Excavation of the 'Thrifty' Genotype." *Diabetes* 40:161–65.

Whited, S. 1894. "Pima Agency." In *Report on Indians Taxed and Indians Not Taxed in the United States (Except Alaska) at the Eleventh Census, 1890*, pp. 137–46. U.S. Government Printing Office, Washington, D.C.

Wing, Cyndee, and David Wing. 1990. *Power and the Pride to Win*. Film. Presidio Film Group, Tucson.

Wright, Harold Bell. 1929. *Long Ago Told: Legends of the Papago Indians*. D. Appleton, New York.

Wyman, Leland. 1980. *Southwest Indian Drypainting*. School of American Research, Santa Fe, and University of New Mexico Press, Albuquerque.

*Zepeda, Ofelia. 1995. *Ocean Power: Songs from the Desert*. University of Arizona Press, Tucson. [A professor at the University of Arizona, Zepeda is the foremost scholar of her people's language and culture.]

———. 1999. Personal communication.

Zepeda, Ofelia, ed. 1982. *When It Rains: Papago and Pima Poetry*. University of Arizona Press, Tucson.

Zepeda, Ofelia, and Jane H. Hill. 1991. "The Condition of Native American Languages in the United States." In *Endangered Languages*, pp. 135–55, ed. R. H. Robbins and E. M. Uhlenbeck. Berg, Oxford, England.

The sea ania (the Yaqui flower world), home of little brother deer. Mural by Danny Leon, Old Pascua, 1993. Photograph: Helga Teiwes, courtesy of Arizona State Museum

Chapter 6 The Yaqui

April 1995 The attention of everyone in the darkened auditorium is riveted on the young Deer Dancer making his entrance with a brisk shake of the gourd rattles in his hands and the deer-hoof rattles around his waist. The cocoon rattles wound around his lower legs crackle like tiny pebbles in a paper bag, and his deer's head quivers with all the uncertainty of a real deer poised for flight as the red ribbons on the antlers flutter gracefully.

A group of older men at the back of the stage sing deer songs, accompanying themselves on a water drum and rasps. Already on stage are two young *pahkolam* (Pascolas, "the old men of the fiesta") who have been dancing, accompanied by drum and flute music. The *pahkolam* accent the rhythm of their steps with the tambourinelike jangle of the wooden *sonasum* in their right hands; with each step, their cocoon rattles rustle and the bells around their waists jingle like sleigh bells. Their distinctive wooden masks with flowing white beards are worn to one side, exposing their faces.

Despite his naturalistic head, the Deer Dancer would be mute and lifeless without the music of the deer singers: their water drum provides his heartbeat, their rasps his breathing, and their words his voice. Dancing to the beat of the music in his bare feet, he brings the wilderness world alive as he dips his head forward to drink from a gently flowing stream. Suddenly he jerks his head upward, alert to a noise only he can hear, and the muscles in his chest and arms tense with fear as he listens intently. His entire body quivers with a throbbing pulse.

Escaping, he enters an imaginary forest, surrounded by other creatures that are just becoming active in the early morning. Birds begin to sing as the first light of the sun pushes back the darkness of the night. The deer looks toward the east where the sun is rising over the mountains; he so loves the dawn wind that he rubs his antlers against the wind as he enjoys the peaceful quiet of the new day. Dew sparkles on the blades of grass and on the leaves of many different plants. Gliding with the flowing freedom of a wild creature, the Deer Dancer brings alive his home, *sea ania,* the enchanted, ethereal flower world.

Felipe Molina, a Yaqui teacher and writer, explains, "Good deer dancers . . . dance the meaning of the song, and . . . are greatly respected because they help the Yaqui people to see the close connection all living things have in common on earth. . . . We believe that our ancestors the Surem could actually talk with the animals that lived in the wilderness . . . the Surem spoke to our brother the deer, because they needed him to survive in this world . . . [they asked] the deer's forgiveness for having to kill him" (Evers 1981:193).

The sharp intake of breath from the Australian Aboriginal man seated next to me tells me that he recognizes this in the boy's dance. Astonished at the young boy's ability to imitate the movements of a deer, he whispers to his friends in Koori. The Dancers of the Dreaming, an Aboriginal dance group from Australia's Northern Territory, are in Tucson as part of a cultural exchange. Earlier, they shared stories and traditional food with Yaqui children here at Richey Elementary School; after the Deer Dance, the Dancers of the Dreaming will perform. But now it is the children's turn to entertain their guests.

Although the inhabitants and landscape of their worlds differ, the beliefs and experiences of the Yaquis and the Aborigines have remarkable similarities. Throughout their history, elders in both cultures maintained schools for young men in which oral texts were taught, especially those regarding the sacredness of specific places. Both believe in the reality of other, unseen worlds, which the Creator has given them a spiritual responsibility to dance and sing into existence. They believe that they have been entrusted with maintaining the well-being of the earth, including its animals, plants, and landscape. The Aborigines imitate the movements of the kangaroo in a dance honoring this important food source, just as the Yaqui celebrate their special relationship with their little brother, *saila maso,* the deer.

Both peoples have survived efforts to destroy them and their cultures. The Yaqui, the only group discussed in this book whose traditional homeland lies outside the American Southwest, fled to the United States after the Mexican government initiated a program of genocide against them. The Yaqui diaspora made them the most widely dispersed Indians in North America. Today's cultural exchange between these two groups is a tribute to the resilience and strength of both peoples against great odds.

Origins

In the beginning, the Creator, Itom Achai, gave the Surem, the ancestors of the
Yaqui, the land along the Rio Yaqui in Sonora, Mexico. The Surem, a peaceful little people,
were never sick and never died. They lived in the Yoania, which was both a world and a way
of being, "a religion of the woods and a place of supernatural beings and forces" (Trujillo
1995:4).

One day, the people discovered a big, ash-colored palo verde tree, which, through
strange vibrations, emanated a message. After the village elders tried unsuccessfully to understand the talking tree's message, they sought out a Sea Hamut (a "flower woman") who
lived deep in the forest. They took the wise woman to the vibrating tree, where she began to
interpret its prophecies. She told of seeds that would be planted and cultivated as food, of
death, and of a conflict between good and evil forces, and of strange white men from far
away who would profess to understand this conflict.

The Surem, confused by the tree's message, divided into two groups, those who refused
to accept these changes and those who chose to remain. Those who feared or spurned the
prophecies left to create various creature kingdoms, said by some to be underground and
by others to be beneath the sea. Those Surem who remained grew tall and strong in anticipation of the prophecy, becoming the Yoemem, the Yaqui people.

The Evil Forces of the Lenten-Easter Season

Yaqui educator Octaviana V. Trujillo explains, "The Yaqui dramatization of evil is
earnestly thought to be for the eventual glory of Jesus," and members of the Fariseo
Society "are often apprehensive lest their assumed role of evil be confused with their
deep devotion to Jesus and to the ritual of the Catholic Church" (1995:6–7). The Fariseos ("Soldiers of Rome," or "Pharisees") represent the people who persecuted and executed Christ, and their ritual function is the enactment of the pursuit, capture, and
crucifixion of Jesus; their members include a captain, drummer, flutist, sergeant,
Pontius Pilates, and standard flag bearers. The Caballeros (Horsemen) ally themselves with the Forces of Evil during the early part of Holy Week as "guards of Christ"
and try to keep the Chapayekas (temporary workers of evil deeds) from going too far
in their taunting antics. The captain of the Caballeros carries a wooden sword, and the
corporals bear lances.

The Chapayekas, in their helmet masks with long thin noses—*chapa* means "sharp" and *yeka* means "nose" in Yaqui—and large ears, are probably the most distinctive figures in the Yaqui Easter celebration. Garbed in overcoats, raincoats, or blankets, Chapayekas also wear "rattle belts" with deer or pig hooves and leather sandals, and carry wooden swords and daggers.

On the first Friday of Lent, a few Chapayekas begin the search for Jesus, but by Holy Week, their numbers increase to as many as twenty. At first timid and hesitant, they slowly develop into sinister aggressors over the course of the forty days of the Easter season. With rosaries hidden beneath their masks to protect them from the evil they represent, the Chapayekas march around the village, following religious processions and making fun of the devotions by rattling their swords and daggers, yet quaking in fear when they hear the name of sacred individuals, such as Christ or the Blessed Virgin.

Holy Thursday brings the Pursuit of the Old Man, a preview of Christ's sufferings on the Way of the Cross. His capture occurs that night in the cottonwood bower that represents the Garden of Gethsemane, constructed earlier by the Chapayekas. On Good Friday, Pontius Pilate, lance in hand and wearing a black cape, supervises the Chapayekas' construction of the cross. Flowers are laid on the cross to bless it when it is laid on the ground; as it is raised, these flowers fall to the ground. After Christ is crucified, the Chapayekas dance jubilantly around the village in a backward manner to indicate their evil nature. In their glee, they pantomime everything from Anglo golfers to Indians on bicycles to figures in popular culture, such as Bart Simpson. Meanwhile, the body of Christ is laid on a sacred bier, which is placed in the plaza, where the people of the village venerate it throughout the afternoon. About midnight, a procession of men and women takes place, which symbolizes the Resurrection.

Infuriated that Christ's body has disappeared, the Chapayekas prepare to do battle the next day. Before the battle begins, they lead a figure of their chief, Judas, on a donkey around the Stations of the Cross. As their evil army rushes the church three times, villagers, including the Pascolas, Deer Dancer, and children who represent the Little Angels, pelt the Fariseos with flowers to weaken them. After they are defeated, the Chapayekas burn their masks and the Judas figure, to take their place once more in the world of men.

Yaqui Contact History

Yaqui culture, remarkable for its fusion of European and indigenous traditions, evolved from their unique history, resulting in a new, emergent cultural system. Edward Spicer, the foremost non-Yaqui authority on Yaqui life (1961), divided Yaqui contact history into four phases, each characterized by a particular type of cultural change. In the *rancheria period*, the Yaquis maintained their traditional type of rancheria communities. The arrival of the Jesuits in 1617 introduced the *mission period*, which was characterized by the acceptance of Spanish innovation. The first Yaqui Revolt, in 1740, inaugurated the *autonomous period*, a 150-year period of freedom from Spanish or Mexican domination that allowed the Yaquis to experience a time of cultural fusion and resynthesis. The reestablishment of Mexican control marked the beginning of the *relocation period*, when the Yaquis dispersed throughout Mexico and the southwestern United States, going through a period of cultural revival and assimilation.

The Rancheria Period (1533–1617)

The northernmost and most populous of the Cahitan speakers (Cahitan is in the Uto-Aztecan language family), the Yaqui lived along the lower 60 miles of the Rio Yaqui, a 6,000-square-mile area that included some of the most fertile regions of Mexico. According to Pérez de Ribas, the first missionary to enter Yaqui territory, in the early 1600s, 30,000 Yaquis were living in 80 rancherias (1645:2:62), with each rancheria averaging about 300–400 people (Spicer 1961:13). In response to recurrent flooding, they moved their villages, which consisted of dome-shaped houses and ramadas for shade in food preparation and sleeping. In addition to practicing nonirrigation agriculture, they also dug ditches into the floodplain from the edge of the river to irrigate by using the reliable annual floods of the Rio Yaqui; amaranth, beans, corn, squash, and cotton were among their pre-contact crops. Each rancheria was autonomous and held its own religious ceremonies, including Deer and Coyote Dances to thank Itom Achai for sustaining the people. Although acculturation destroyed nearly all traces of pre-Spanish culture, it is believed that the Yaqui reckoned kinship bilaterally, practiced rancheria exogamy, and had no rules regarding postmarital residence (Beals 1943:47–52).

In 1533, when the Spaniards arrived, they mistakenly called the people Yaqui, a name that has been used by non-Yaquis for the Yoemem since this time. The Yaqui were prepared to meet the armored foreigners because of the prophecies of the Talking Tree; Yaqui elders offered to share their land with the Spaniards, but the Europeans had come to conquer. Fierce warriors who organized tribally under a single captain during military campaigns—through their system of military associations with ranked offices, the Yaqui could muster a fighting force of 5,000–7,000 warriors (Spicer 1961:14–19)—the Yaquis defeated the Spanish soldiers. Later, in 1610, the Yaquis invited the Jesuit missionaries to return by themselves.

The Good People of the Lenten-Easter Season

Combating the Evil Forces are members of other ceremonial societies: the church organization, the Matachini dance society and the *fiesteros*. They are led by the Maestro, his assistants, and the Cantoras, women who sing the Latin and Spanish hymns that accompany his prayers. Children, Angelitos and Angelitas (Little Angels), wearing light-colored long dresses, scarves, and crowns, guard the holy figures and the altar

Yaqui Deer Dancers, Pascolas, and Matachinis at the Feast of San Ignacio, Pascua, 1955. Courtesy of Arizona Historical Society, No. 22607

with switches made of mesquite. The Matachinis, male dancers under vow to the Blessed Virgin, wear cane crowns with brightly colored streamers as they dance to violin and guitar music. Malinches are young boys who act as a special guard to the Virgin and dress like her in embroidered blouses and long skirts (Trujillo 1995:9).

The Pascolas (old men of the fiesta), Deer Dancer, and musicians also perform at certain fiestas and lead some of the ceremonial processions with the Matachinis. Wearing a blanket wrapped around his hips like a pair of pants, the Pascola dances a shuffling dance in time to the drum and the flute or the harp and violin. The deer dancer, in a shawl wrapped as a skirt over rolled-up pants, dances to songs that tell of the deer hunt, part of hunting rituals that predate the Spanish arrival. Musicians accompany them on native instruments: two men scrape rasps over half-gourds, while another beats a drum made of a half-gourd floating in a pan of water.

The Passion Play begins on the first Friday of Lent and continues every Friday until Palm Sunday eve with processions around the Way of the Cross. Stopping at each of the fourteen stations, the Maestro leads the devout in Catholic orations, while being taunted by the Chapayekas. On Palm Sunday, the Matachinis, Pascolas, and deer dancer lead a procession bearing the image of Christ to represent his entry into Jerusalem. After the Maestro leads Catholic orations, the procession stops in front of the church, where a service is conducted, and then the crosses are revisited. On Wednesday evening of Holy Week, the Maestros chant the Psalms in the church, which the Fariseos and Caballeros have decorated with cottonwood branches, symbolizing the wild country through which Jesus wandered. The Chapayekas boldly enter the church, symbolizing "the penetration of evil ones to the very sanctuary of Christ" (Trujillo 1995:15). Pushing back their masks, the Chapayekas howl to represent the "terror of the wild animals and birds during the increasing darkness" (ibid.). The Fariseos enter the church and begin the traditional whipping in which all ceremonial groups participate to symbolize the lashing Jesus received and to bless and forgive family members and friends. On Holy Thursday, in the cottonwood bower that represents the Garden of Gethsemane, the Chapayekas capture the figure of Christ. On Friday, after a man has carried a large cross in a procession, the Chapayekas destroy the stations, symbolizing the crucifixion, and guard the decorated bier in the church all night, only to discover near dawn that Christ's body has vanished. On Holy Saturday, led by a straw Judas, the Evil Forces attempt three times to capture the church, but each time, Good triumphs, defeating Evil with flowers, music, and prayer. Afterward, the Chapayekas strip off their coats, blankets, and masks, flinging them at the foot of the effigy of Judas, which is set on fire, scourging the forces of evil. Their godparents rush the Chapayekas to the church to be rebaptized as the Matachinis, Pascolas, and Deer Dancer dance in triumph; at sunset, the Matachinis dance their beautifully colorful Maypole dance.

The Mission Period (1617–1767)

The arrival of the Jesuits created a situation of culture contact almost unique in Native American history, because it was one of few cases in which an indigenous people invited outsiders to live among them. This initiated an intensive program of directed culture change that had three major aspects: the introduction of Christianity, the consolidation of the Yaqui population, and the addition of agricultural items and techniques. During the mission period (1617–1767) the Jesuits, who had learned the Yaqui language thoroughly, came to be respected by the people because they did not forcibly impose their religion on the Yaquis but instead discussed native ceremonies, suggesting Christian interpretations. In many ways, Christianity was compatible with Yaqui religion, including the belief in a Universal God and the symbol of a cross, which was similar to the Yaqui sun symbol, representing the place where "Our Father" lives (Molina et al., n.d.). As an unconquered people free from the pressure of Spanish settlers, forced tribute, or forced labor, the Yaqui accepted the Jesuit presence in an atmosphere of trust and cooperation, integrating the new religion with native beliefs and practices.

In addition to introducing Christianity, which they taught by means of pageants, the Jesuits also consolidated the Yaqui rancherias even further for administrative purposes. It is said by some Yoemem that four Yaqui leaders, accompanied by a band of angels, walked the boundaries of each town, sanctifying it with their singing; they marked the town's boundaries with wooden crosses and began the tradition of honoring its saint or supernatural patron in an annual festival. After renewing the sacredness of the Yaqui lands, the Yaqui named the villages, beginning in the east and moving westward. According to some accounts (Molina et al., n.d.), the Yaqui had been living in seven villages, each dedicated to one star in the Big Dipper, since the time when the Surem divided, but they did not name their villages until after the arrival of the Jesuits. The seven church-centered towns, located at intervals of 6–8 miles from near the mouth of the Rio Yaqui to 50 miles upstream, included Cocorit (Cocoim), Bacum (Bahcom), Torim, Vicam, Potam, Rahum, and Huirivis (Huivism); Belem, the eighth town, was created as a "guardian" village to look after the others. Instead of the 300–400 inhabitants in their traditional rancherias, the new Yaqui communities consisted of 3,000–4,000 inhabitants; the common government system and the realignment of family groups made it easier to hold religious ceremonies and strengthened their culture.

With never more than ten missionaries in Yaqui territory, the Jesuits relied on trained Yaqui assistants to administer the new towns, which led the Yaquis to develop their own leadership and administrative skills "under the guidance of a benign . . . but rather coercive missionary policy" and "created a psychological environment for the acceptance of change on the part of the Yaquis" (Trujillo 1998:69). Religious instruction and church ritual thus diffused outward from the missionaries through the recently trained Yaqui associates to the Yaqui townspeople, a process that facilitated the blending of ritual forms with traditional Yaqui ones, giving the forms meanings the Jesuits had not intended. Although some Christian and Yaqui beliefs were complementary, some Christian ideas were not easy to reconcile with Yaqui concepts: the division of an afterworld into good and bad regions, and a supernatural world where men and animals were separated and where power was concentrated in the Trinity. Church and government were closely linked in the Jesuit system: although Yaqui governors were elected, they had to be approved by church dignitaries; in major decisions, the governors and church officials deliberated together.

Finally, the third area of directed culture change centered on agriculture. Agricultural techniques introduced by the Jesuits resulted in increased production, which led to a considerable surplus. Already farmers, the Yaquis saw the benefit of better tools, crops—the Jesuits introduced such crops as wheat, pomegranates, peaches, and figs—and work animals, including sheep, cattle, and horses.

Yaqui towns continued as thriving agricultural communities despite the discovery in 1684 of a silver mine roughly 30 miles from one of their towns. But by the 1730s an increase of mining brought an influx of Spanish settlers who resented what they perceived to be missionary control of so much valuable land. Hostility worsened as the Spanish continued to expand their settlements in Yaqui territory and sought to gain greater control over the Yaqui towns. Finally, in 1740, the Yaquis joined their Mayo neighbors to revolt against the Spanish. Sparing only the Jesuits, they killed or drove out all Spaniards from the river towns and nearby territory.

The Autonomous Period (1740–1887)

The Yaqui-Mayo Revolt of 1740 ushered in the autonomous period (which overlaps with the final years of the mission period). Toward the end of 1740, 5,000 Yaquis were killed at the Hill of Bones, crushing their resistance, and the Spanish built a presidio at the eastern edge of Yaqui country. Shortly afterward, however, Spanish soldiers were withdrawn to fight the Seri Indians, and in 1767 the Jesuits were expelled from the New World by the Spanish church. These events left the Yaquis in a state of relative autonomy for roughly 150 years, during which time they modified the Jesuit institutions to fit their own needs. During the remainder of the Spanish period, the Yaquis lived in a state of constant defensive preparedness to protect their local autonomy and communal control of the land.

In 1771, when the missions were secularized because the settlers wanted Indian land, the government tried to institute taxation through tribute and land allotment, but strong Yaqui resistance kept local officials from carrying out this program. By the early 1800s Spanish organization on the northwestern frontier was clearly disintegrating, and from 1810 to the early 1820s the Yaquis remained aloof while Spaniards fought each other in the War for Independence. Many Yaquis, however, had chosen to move out of Yaqui country when Jesuit agricultural enterprises stopped operating, seeking wages on haciendas or in the mines. In response to relocation, Yaquis adapted by maintaining their identity through a strong awareness of their homeland and by continuing to practice their socioreligious institutions in new locations (Trujillo 1998:71). This ability to maintain their cultural identity despite dislocation became crucial when warfare increased from the 1820s onward, causing a decline in agricultural activity and an increased need to seek work outside Yaqui territory.

After Mexico became independent, both the Mexican government and the Sonoran state government tried to impose political and economic control. In response, the Yaquis, united with the Mayos, Pimas, and Opatas, sought to establish an independent indigenous nation. When the Mexican government tried to enforce taxation in 1825, Juan Banderas, who was said to have had a vision of the Virgin of Guadalupe, led a force of 2,000 Indians that drove all non-Yaquis from the territory. Although the Mexicans executed Banderas in 1833, the political disorganization of the state of Sonora meant that, for the most part, Yaqui towns were left to themselves for about the next forty years. In the 1850s, to enforce the Laws of Reform that opened Yaqui land to settlement, Mexican troops confiscated cattle and food, laid waste to farmlands, shot captured leaders, and imprisoned women and children; the 1868 massacre of 120 Yaquis in the church at Bacum became a symbol of Mexican cruelty to Yaquis. These brutal methods brought a short peace to southern Sonora but also intensified Yaqui resistance to the Mexican program. Between 1885 and 1886 Cajeme led Yaquis and Mayos in a brilliant campaign. Although guerrilla fighting continued, Cajeme's execution in 1887 ended organized military operations by the Yaquis.

Relocation Period (1887–1906)

Since genocide, military occupation, and colonization had not ended Yaqui resistance, government officials hoped that dispersing the Yaqui population would hasten the assimilation process, so they initiated a policy of deportation of Yaquis to other parts of Mexico outside Sonora. They sold thousands of Yaqui men and women to the owners of henequen plantations in the Yucatán and sugar cane plantations in Oaxaca, thousands of miles from the Yaqui homelands. Many Yaquis hid themselves, merging with the Mexican population of Sonora, while hundreds of others fled across the border to the United States to settlements that had grown up in southern Arizona or to other states. Walking 400 miles or more, they arrived with few possessions and lived in fear of being deported for execution. Men found work on the railroad, on outlying ranches, or on farms, where they became known for their conscientious work. Cotton farmers, who separated workers into ethnic groups, "claimed that they could identify rows picked by the Yaquis at a glance by the neat and thorough method of their work" (Trujillo 1998:71).

The Yaquis sought political asylum in the United States, which they officially received in

1906; in 1978 they finally received tribal recognition and reservation land. During that time, they began to practice the religious ceremonies they had had to observe underground in Sonora, where as recently as the 1920s whole communities were massacred by Mexican soldiers during ceremonies (Molina et al., n.d.). Many Yaquis have names that reflect their tribal history: Refugio Savala, whose name means "refugee" in Spanish, escaped with his parents from their home in Sonora, Mexico, in 1904, during the most intense period of Yaqui deportation and persecution by the Mexican government.

In 1939 the president of Mexico, Lázaro Cárdenas, who had beaten the Yaquis in 1917, spoke of the "Yaqui Tribe" and issued a presidential decree that set aside the north bank of the Rio Yaqui, a small portion of the south bank, and the Bacatete Mountain area, giving this area the legal status of an "indigenous community." At this time the Mexican government also initiated a program of agricultural development that included the Yaqui area. Many Yaquis returned to this area, which covers roughly one-third of their traditional territory, but many others remained in their newly formed communities in Arizona. Seeking to re-create their age-old homeland in the new country, they renamed the Arizona mountains with Yaqui names and named their streets after the original Yaqui towns (Molina et al., n.d.). Yaqui people in Arizona, however, still feel a close tie to their homeland, and they continue to maintain close contact with their relatives in Sonora.

Changes in Yaqui Settlement Patterns

Over the last four centuries the Yaquis have reorganized their settlements in response to three major events: the arrival of the Jesuits in 1617, Mexican military occupation in 1887, and their departure from their homeland. The Jesuits consolidated the Yaqui population into towns, each with its own central plaza that surrounded an adobe-walled church; grouped around the plaza were buildings to house the civil, military, and ceremonial organizations introduced by the Jesuits. Although they did not accept the Spanish grid plan of town layout, the Yaqui did adopt the new style of rectangular, wattle-and-daub houses, surrounding them with fenced household compounds. From the 1620s until the 1880s, three major features characterized Yaqui towns: their larger size (3,000–4,000 persons), the town plan of public buildings surrounding the centrally located church, and a sharper rural-urban contrast between these concentrated population centers and the traditional scattered houses of the rancheria settlements (Spicer 1983:252). The Yaqui maintained this settlement pattern from the 1620s until the 1880s.

In 1887, when Mexican troops began military occupation of Yaqui towns, they introduced the grid plan of settlement into the larger Yaqui towns. A dual pattern began to develop, with Mexican troops and some assimilated Yaquis living in contiguous, Mexican-style houses along streets in one area of the town, while most Yaquis continued to reside in irregularly scattered fenced compounds on all sides of the central grid. This combined pattern of the Spanish-Mexican grid plan surrounded by scattered Yaqui houses became fixed in the twentieth century.

After the Yaquis left their homeland, they established church-centered urban communities—which they referred to as barrios—in Tucson, near Phoenix, and in Mexican cities. Whenever possible, Yaqui families settled around the small open-front churches, suited to their distinctive ceremonial needs, which became the focus of community life. Of the twenty-one Yaqui communities that existed during the 1970s, eighteen maintained their own churches, making them self-sufficient centers of traditional life. These communities included nine towns along the Rio Yaqui, five barrios in Sonoran cities, and four communities in Arizona: Old Pascua and New Pascua (also known as Pascua Pueblo or Yaqui Reservation) in Tucson, Barrio Libre in South Tucson, and Guadalupe near Tempe. The other Yaqui settlements in southern Arizona are Eskatel (Penjamo) near Scottsdale, Chandler High Town southeast of Phoenix, Yoem Pueblo in Marana, and Somerton near Yuma. In 1992, 5,928 Yaquis were living in the eight Arizona communities, with a grand total of 10,000–11,000 Yaquis living in seven western states (U.S. Census and special tribal study in R. Spicer 1994:709).

Our Lady of Guadalupe

When Juan Banderas led his people against the Mexican government in 1824, the Yaquis adopted Our Lady of Guadalupe as the symbol of Indian independence, just as had the original rebels against Spain. Over 450 years ago, the Blessed Mother—as Our Lady of Guadalupe—was said to have appeared to Juan Diego to bring a message to the Indians of Mexico and to all the people of the Americas (Trujillo 1998:72). Today, her image appears on votive candles that are left at shrines on her day of celebration in December, and she remains a treasured being to Yaqui and Mexicans alike.

Each aspect of her depiction is rich in symbolism, beginning with her downcast eyes, which convey humility and reveal that she is not a deity, in contrast to Indian gods who always looked straight ahead. Her dark skin and black hair are those of an Indian, and her hands, instead of being held with palms together in the traditional European style of prayer, clasp each other to indicate that she is bringing a gift. The maternity band she wears around her waist shows that she is about to give birth, signifying that someone is yet to come, and the stars on her mantle, symbolic of the shower of stars that were believed to accompany the ending of an era, symbolize that a new era is beginning. The sun, which played a major role in indigenous religions of the Americas, shines behind her, symbolizing that she is greater than the sun, which she hides but does not extinguish. She stands on the moon to show that she is also greater than the god of night, the moon god. Finally, the angel beneath her, by representing an intermediary god, also indicates the ending of the old era and the beginning of a new era, ushered in by Our Lady of Guadalupe.

In 1904, when a Franciscan friar, Father Lucius, arrived in a small Yaqui community at the eastern foot of South Mountain, near Phoenix, he brought the symbolic *santa* of the Virgin of Guadalupe. By 1910 he had acquired 40 acres for the Yaquis to build a permanent settlement on high ground west of the Highline Canal. Unable to secure the land beside the Western Canal where the Yaquis had been living, because of its value as potential farmland, Father Lucius was able to get a U.S. government patent, signed by Woodrow Wilson, for the 40 acres because the site was so high in elevation that it could not be irrigated and was thus worthless as farmland. The previous camp, which continued to serve as a burial site, was referred to as Old Guadalupe and the new settlement became simply Guadalupe (Trujillo 1998:75–76).

The Yaqui Town

Although the fusion of native and European practices is most evident in their religion, the Yaquis also organized their towns in a way that reflects this unique synthesis. Evident in their selective acceptance of Spanish-Mexican concepts of town layout, Yaqui values made their towns more Native American than Mexican. By the 1880s the Yaquis had forged their own unique form of community, quite different from the peasant community the Mexican nation-state was pressuring them to create. Their refusal to take the politically and economically inferior position of peasants was indicative of their determination to remain autonomous; they rejected authority focused in one individual and remained guided by their own distinctive value system. (As landless agricultural laborers or farmers on small landholdings, peasants must pay taxes to the state in the form of money, produce, or labor.)

By the nineteenth century the town was the fundamental unit of Yaqui life and the embodiment of egalitarian Yaqui values: "Every man was a soldier expected to serve when necessary as a fighting man, and every man was also regarded as assuming an equal part in the government of the town as person, as governor, and as elder participating in reaching the agreements in the general assemblies. Yet every man was at the same time a farmer" (Spicer 1980:221). The Yaqui system of government was based on the unity of civil, military, and religious organization; unanimous agreement as a basis for action; the recognition of seniority in participation; the total community's review of executive and judicial activity; and the interdependence of the five governmental domains discussed below (ibid., 178).

Underlying these principles was the concept of the town as a single, sacred entity, related to the sacredness of the original Eight Towns (*wohnaiki pweplum*) established under Jesuit leadership; wherever the Yaquis later settled, they maintained a certain degree of devotion to the Eight Towns. The Yaqui distinguish between the natural world of the *huya ania* and the urban world of the *pweplum* (from Spanish *pueblo*). These words convey not only a place but also the inhabitants of that place; even though individuals may be identified in each realm, an important meaning is that of an undifferentiated totality. Thus, at one level, all the residents of a town are considered to be an enveloping whole with each specialized part of its government organized in such a way that together, they work for the good of the whole.

Each of the Eight Towns duplicated the same political and ceremonial system, which fused European and Yaqui features of local government. In the twentieth century Sonoran Yaqui communities revived the entire framework of nineteenth-century town government; in Arizona Yaqui communities, only the church and the customs authority exist, suggesting that these are the essential features of community for the maintenance of Yaqui cultural continuity (Spicer 1980:179–80).

The town was governed by five domains of responsibility or authorities—the church, the governors, the military, the customs authority (*kohtumbre*), and the *pahkome* (Spanish *fiesteros*, or "fiesta makers"). Each of these authorities had its own clearly marked jurisdictions, but they were also capable of functioning together in matters that affected the entire town. ("Authority" is the closest translation of the Yaqui word *ya'ura*, which refers to the exercise of a particular kind of authority.) All five authorities were equal in power, with real authority vested in the elders of the community who had served in town offices and acted as spokesmen, deferred to by all other speakers in a public meeting.

The *church authority* cared for statues and directed prayers, singing, and sacred dance; more highly differentiated than the other authorities, it was subdivided into four organizations. The five *governors* and their assistants transmitted decisions to the people and served as spokesmen for the town with outsiders; they settled family disputes and decided land assignments. The *military society* guarded the governors, administered punishment, and, historically, directed warfare; the close association between the governors and the military is indicative of the fact that late nineteenth-century Yaqui towns were under constant attack. The customs authority maintained the sacred Yaqui Law and nominated civil authorities; it was in charge from Ash Wednesday (in January or February) to the Day of Finding the Holy Cross (in May). The *pahkome* were responsible for the annual celebration of the town's patron saint and played vital roles in affirming the sacred relationship with the land; they governed the summer-autumn ceremonial season.

The Yaqui Social World

Based on this sense of the town as a sacred community, the ideals of Yaqui social life were cooperation and shared responsibility rather than individual power. A strong sense of solidarity was expressed through a shared dedication to the church, the general assembly, and the *pahko*. The primary cultural orientation in society was toward serving God through the church and its associated sodalities; individuals could participate either by taking an individual vow or by being elected by acclamation in a general assembly. In meetings of the town council, the five specialized authorities worked together to create a sense of solidarity. The annual town fiesta, called the *pahko*, created a sense of solidarity among the town's households, which were basic and important units within the structure of the town. The *pahko* linked the church and the households by organizing the latter into two competing segments that were brought into unified action for a common purpose: the enactment of the triumph of the Christians over the Moors and the honoring of the town's patron saint.

Three types of social groups played important roles in Yaqui life: kindreds (relatives), *compadrazgo* (fictive kin), and *cofradias* (brotherhoods). As described earlier, at the time of contact, the Yaqui probably reckoned kinship affiliation bilaterally and had no unilineal descent groups or fixed residence pattern. After 1890 Yaqui household composition was greatly influenced by deportation and their dispersal to southern Arizona and various parts of Mexico. Thus, a household could consist of any number of nuclear families related in a variety of ways, including ritual kinship. In the 1600s, as part of their religious conversion program, the Spaniards introduced a social institution, godparents and godparental cooperating groups, which took on great significance in Yaqui social structure. The Yaquis transformed this ritual kinship system into a formal set of rights and obligations for rites of passage, such as baptism, confirmation, and marriage, and for illnesses, care of the dead, and induction into ceremonial societies. The complex system of coparenthood (*compadrazgo*) meant that an individual might have as many as a dozen, or even more, pairs of godparents, each of whom was obligated not only to the godchild and the godchild's parents, but also to all the other godparents (Spicer 1940:91–116). Thus, the institution of *compadrazgo* enabled the Yaquis to reconstitute an extended-family type of household when actual extended families were disrupted after the Yaquis fled their homeland.

Also introduced by the Jesuits was the *cofradia*—an organization of laymen dedicated to the service of a Christian saint or other supernatural being. This the Yaquis fused with their ceremonial sodalities after the Jesuits were expelled in 1767. Three of the most important male sodalities were the Matachinis, dedicated to the Virgin Mary; the Caballeros (Horsemen), which served the Infant Jesus; and the Fariseos ("Soldiers of Rome," or "Pharisees"), which were dedicated to the Christ crucified. During Lent and Holy Week, the latter two *cofradias* dramatized the last days of Jesus in a unique Passion Play. Behaving as ceremonial clowns, the Chapayekas, a segment of the Fariseo sodality, donned helmet masks and played the role of evil beings; the Caballeros managed the Chapayekas.

The Yaqui Spiritual World

The Relationship of Pre- and Post-Christian Worlds

Yaqui Felipe Molina explained that the Yaqui conceive of several supernatural worlds (*aniam*), in the sense of realms or domains; these worlds "are visible only in the private eye of dream and vision, and they are made public only when they are put into words in stories individuals tell of their own experiences and those of others" (Evers and Molina 1987:45). There is the *yoania* (enchanted world), which is paired with the *tuka aniya*, or "night world," and the *sea ania* (flower world), which is linked to the *huya ania*, or "wilderness world," which governs the ground and vegetation (Refugio Savala, in Painter 1986: 27). Although Yaquis do not agree on the character of each world or its precise relation to other worlds, they use the term *batnaataka* for the timeless period before history, the time when the earth was still inhabited by the Surem, the legendary precursors of the Yaquis.

The Yoania. The *yoania*, which lies within the *huya ania*, is the primordial, most ancient of worlds, a mythic, enchanted place apart from time and space and yet accessible in the present; the *yo hoaram* (enchanted homes) inhabited by enormous snakes and monsters are the source of Yaqui deer songs, according to Yaqui Don Jesus (in Evers and Molina 1987:62–64). The *yoania*, the Yaqui homeland and pre-Christian way of life, was home to the Surem, the ancestors of the Yaquis. These little people, who never died, were instead renewed each month by the new moon. God was believed to have been present but unknown during Surem times; Yaquis have compartmentalized the concepts of the *yoania* and God, using different vocabularies for each concept.

The *yoania*, still present today, can appear in visions in isolated desert places, in secret mountain caves, and in dreams because humans and nature shared a common psychic life, communicating by means of *seataka*, a special power some people are still born with today. Such people feel a special affinity for the natural world: "when he is in the forest he lives among things that are alive, and knows them, such as the lakes and springs and trees. . . . He will notice much about the coming up of plants and flowers and new leaves on trees and also, with his hearing, he will notice any chirp of a bird from a distance," explained a Yaqui (Painter 1986:14–15). Yaqui Refugio Savala added that "even today a man with *seataka* has a tendency to watch the movements of the heavenly bodies, the stars, the winds, which way the wind and the clouds go . . . that is his *seataka*, his way of doing things" (ibid., 27). Bestowed in the womb, this supernatural power cannot be inherited or acquired; a person who possesses it is much more alert as well as considerate, kindhearted, and strong-willed. Someone with *seataka* also has the ability to learn and to master everything and to do it well.

The Huya Ania. Literally meaning "tree world" or "forest world," *huya ania*, as the physical and spiritual domain of untamed wilderness, is usually translated as "wilderness world." The *huya ania* embraced the Rio Yaqui as it flowed out of the Sierra Madre toward the Gulf of California, the green rustling canebrakes, groves of cottonwood trees, wooded areas of mesquite. Before the coming of the Jesuits, the *huya ania* also included the Yaquis' scattered rancheria settlements surrounded by brush, trees, and cactus (Spicer 1980:64).

The *huya ania* also has an aura of enchantment, for the *yoania* may manifest itself there. Thus, the *huya ania* was not limited to its physical dimensions, for this world—"the ancient and honorable realm" of respected powers (Spicer 1980:64)—was a spiritual world where great beings had once lived and perhaps still resided. This all-pervasive spiritual domain was a place in which the source of power came unsolicited through dreams and visions; someone who received such a visitation had the obligation to follow its dictates in order to help other people. Magical creatures—supernatural fawns, mountain sheep, or water serpents—possessed special forms of power from this world, which they could make available to humans, transforming a person's life.

The Sea Ania. The *sea ania*, "flower world," is the *huya ania* in bloom, thus symbolizing the most beneficent aspects of the wilderness world. Refugio Savala explained that the *sea ania* contains "all the celestial bodies, the stars, sun, moon, the heavenly world, the natural world. It makes the winds, and the winds bring the clouds from the sea, and the wind carries them to where the *huya ania* is. It was the force of good before they knew God" (Painter 1986:28). Often described as "a legendary country to the east under the sunrise . . . connected with the good," it is often mentioned in Yaqui deer songs, for this is the domain of *sailo maiso,* "our little brother, the deer" (ibid., 19). Because the Deer Dancer brings the *sea ania* into physical manifestation, providing a tangible connection to this world, he has become a symbol of Yaqui identity.

Essential to an understanding of Yaqui spiritual beliefs, the native concept of flowers (*sewam*) embraces both native and Catholic symbolism and was probably used by the Jesuits as a vehicle to explain the Catholic faith to the Yaquis. Yaquis associate flowers with the Blessed Virgin, and it is believed that the blood of Jesus as it fell from the cross mingled with the earth and was miraculously transformed into flowers that filled heaven and earth (Trujillo 1995:5). Flowers symbolize heavenly glory (*gloria*) and divine grace, and heaven is conceived to be full of flowers (ibid.). Yaqui educator Octaviana V. Trujillo (ibid.) explains, "Flowers (spiritual blessings) are the reward for the loss of sleep, fatigue, self-sacrifice, and harsh penance endured during the Yaqui Easter Ceremony." The most dramatic ritual use of flowers occurs on Holy Saturday morning when they are used to ritually kill the Fariseos. Although anyone who has seen the desert bloom seemingly overnight after a rainstorm can easily comprehend the concept of flowers as miraculous, the flower concept has its basis in Uto-Aztecan symbolism.

The Huya Ania and Pweplum Dichotomy

According to Yaqui belief, the land within the boundaries of the Eight Towns (*wohnaiki pweplum*) was bestowed by God on the Yaqui people, sanctifying Yaqui ties to their homeland (Molina et al., n.d.:7). After the Jesuits introduced town organization, the Yaqui conception of the universe began to change: instead of composing the totality of the universe, the *huya ania* (wilderness world) became a specialized part of the whole, the world that surrounded the town, the *pweplum* (from the Spanish *pueblo*). In contrast to the incorporeal *huya ania,* which could not be controlled, the *pweplum* was characterized by its structured order, organized religious activity, and emphasis on the tangible products of economic effort. Despite its spiritual component as the place where people fulfilled the religious devotion demanded by Christian supernaturals, the *pweplum* nevertheless had a definite material character.

The Yaqui Synthesis

The religion practiced by the Yaquis today combines native beliefs and practices, Catholic doctrine and liturgy, and medieval liturgical drama introduced by the Jesuits. While some native concepts have been integrated into Catholic traditions, others have been completely reconceptualized. Still others, such as the Deer Dancer, have remained untouched by Christianity.

How did the Yaquis come to expand their conception of the universe, blending their own beliefs and practices with those of Catholicism to form a new religion? Although the Jesuits discussed native ceremonies, suggesting Christian interpretations, they certainly never anticipated the fusion of the two (Spicer 1961:7). Thinking of themselves as soldiers in the "militia of Jesus," the Jesuits believed that they were bringing religious truth to a people who had no religion, and they foresaw a time when the Indians would reject their traditional beliefs and accept all the tenets of Catholicism.

Using a traditional technique for teaching fundamental Christian concepts, the Jesuits, Franciscans, and other missionary orders in New Spain directed native peoples in the dramatization of the key events of Jesus' life to make his life, death, and resurrection tangible and vivid. They introduced three religious dramas: the Conquest of the Moors by the Christians; the Conversion of Malinche, the first Indian to become Catholic; and the Passion and Resurrection of Christ. By the twentieth century, the Passion of Christ had become the major Yaqui ceremony; except for military defense, this ceremonial was "the most inclusive cooperative enterprise in which the Yaquis engaged as Yaquis" (Spicer 1980:71). The culmination of the Yaqui ceremonial year, this elaborate morality play dramatizes the triumph of Yaqui institutions over evil and is "the major artistic as well as religious expression of Yaqui life" (ibid., 71).

Why did this religious drama have such a profound effect on Yaqui culture? Unencumbered by the usual bureaucratic missionary structure, the Jesuits arrived excited to save so many eager souls who were anticipating all that they were bringing. The Jesuits' enthusiasm and the Yaquis' receptivity created a unique situation of culture contact, characterized by an atmosphere of mutual trust, which led the Yaquis to consolidate their population as the Jesuits proposed. This voluntary acceptance heralded decades of revolutionary changes, steadily transforming the Yaquis' conception of their universe. The earth, which had always provided for all the needs of the people, became even more bountiful under the direction of the Jesuits, who introduced new agricultural techniques, animals, and crops. The new settlement pattern gathered together as many as 4,000 persons in each community, working together for a common goal. In the dramatization of Christ's Passion, the supernaturals introduced by the Jesuits came alive because of the concerted efforts of the *cofradias*. The dramatic results of the coordinated efforts of every member of the community had a profound and lasting impact.

The dual division of the Yaqui ceremonial year into winter-spring and summer-autumn exemplifies the synthesis of European and Yaqui beliefs and practices. Although their ritual events celebrate those of the Roman Catholic calendar, such as Ash Wednesday and Easter, the Yaquis' seasonal dichotomy has more in common with the Pueblo year than with the European year. The Zuni and the Hopi divide their year into halves, with a winter-spring season dominated by katsinam and a summer-autumn season that focuses on the bounty of nature; the Tewas take this a step further with their double chieftainship through which the heads of the summer and winter moiety associations each rule the pueblo for half a year.

In Yaqui towns, the winter-spring season—from Ash Wednesday until the Day of Finding the Holy Cross (that is, from January or February to early May)—is a time of solemnity, sadness, and restrictive taboos; the customs authority takes charge during this period (Spicer 1983:255). Sinister Chapayekas in the company of men dressed as soldiers march around the town, creating a growing sense of dread and evil intent, which culminates in the chaotic disruption and eventual restoration to order during Holy Week. In marked contrast, the summer-autumn season is a time of relaxed pleasure and festive abundance as everyone enjoys the blessings conferred by the Virgin, who symbolizes Mother Earth and the bounty of nature (ibid.). The Matachinis, in their bright ribbons and tall headdresses with colorful streamers, dance to light-hearted, lively violin and guitar music, and a sense of well-being permeates the town. The *pahkome* lead the town through this joyous period.

Another aspect of the fusion of Christian innovation and aboriginal beliefs and practices is the attribution of Yaqui interpretations to the physical manifestation of Christian symbols. The Virgin Mary was identified with a female deity called Our Mother, who was associated with trees, flowers, and the earth; at least one form of the cross was dressed and ornamented as a woman at the spring festival of the Day of Finding the Holy Cross (Spicer 1983:260). The synthesis of beliefs and practices is especially apparent during the Easter ceremony, in the symbolic triumph of good over evil when the Good People defeat the Evil Forces in a ritual battle held in front of the church.

Other participants in the Easter celebration, who also appear at other times of year, are unrelated to Christian symbolism. The Pascolas—hosts of most ceremonies—draw on an extensive oral literature, to which they contribute as well; they also pantomime dramas with the Deer Dancer, portraying themselves as the foolish protagonists of absurd narratives. The Deer Dancer performs the only surviving animal dance, to songs about the beautiful and sacred flower world that is home to the deer and lies beneath the dawn to the east.

A Yaqui Approach to Cultural and Linguistic Survival

In her 1991 doctoral dissertation, Octaviana V. Trujillo explored how the perceptions of tribal members shape their responses to language acquisition, educational attainment, and Yaqui cultural development. Through her research, Trujillo realized that if her tribe's language development needs were to be met, progress would have to come through a "whole community" approach—specifically, a family-centered milieu. When she was elected vice chair of the Pascua Yaqui Tribal Council, she established a tribal education department, whose personnel in 1993 undertook a comprehensive community survey that included such data as living patterns, language abilities, employment, and level of education. They surveyed two-thirds of the entire reservation community: 957 adults and 922 children. The results showed that over 80 percent of both adults and children spoke English, while over 75 percent of adults and less than 50 percent of the children spoke Spanish, and less than 25 percent of adults and 10 percent of the children spoke Yaqui (Trujillo 1997:19).

To increase adult training and employment opportunities by raising the literacy levels of parents and older siblings, as well as to raise learning outcomes for Yaqui children, the education department undertook Project Kaateme, the Pascua Yaqui Even Start Family Literacy Program. Emphasizing the strengths of the Yaqui family, Project Kaateme incorporated parents as tutors by fostering their participation in school settings, while out-of-school youth who were increasing their literacy skills served as role models for younger children. Yaqui culture, traditions, and language served as the subject, context, and medium for learning experiences; using Yaqui cultural knowledge as the primary vehicle for activities not only ensured the continuing vitality of Yaqui culture but also increased the self-confidence of parents and the sense of self-worth among children and young adults. At the same time, the framework of a home environment that nurtured learning also supported linguistic competence in English, addressing the concerns of parents that their children might not acquire the standard American academic form of English necessary for access to a good education and employment.

Today, Project Kaateme staff members teach adult classes in Yaqui-as-a-second-language through the auspices of Pima Community College in Tucson, as well as offering similar instruction to preschoolers. Thanks to revenues generated through the tribe's gaming operation, which opened in 1994, educational opportunities have increased significantly. With casino revenues, the tribe is constructing a new learning center that will bring together the early childhood learning programs—Head Start and Project Kaateme—as well as future projects integrating language and culture (Trujillo 1997:20). During their early years in the United States, the Yaqui isolated themselves, outwardly suppressing their identity, language, and religious practices as protection against the perceived threat of deportation to Sonora. Historically, they adapted culturally and linguistically to ensure their survival, but today, as Trujillo points out, their focus has shifted "to reflect the awareness that in a democratic multicultural society it is the right of every culture, as it is with every individual, to thrive" (ibid., 20).

The Pascua Yaqui Tribe

The image of the Yaqui Deer Dancer is featured on the official seal of the Mexican state of Sonora; a larger-than-life bronze Deer Dancer stands at the edge of Ciudad Obregon. The Mexican equivalent of the Plains warrior on horseback who has come to embody the American West, the Yaqui Deer Dancer is used for political and economic reasons (Evers and Molina 1987:7). At the same time, not only the Deer Dancer but Catholic supernaturals and ceremonies as well have become the primary expression of Yaqui ethnic identity, enabling the Yaquis to survive their diaspora and to re-create a vital social and spiritual life in the refugee communities of southern Arizona.

The Yaquis became so widely dispersed during the seventy years after Cajeme's defeat that by the 1950s they could be found in most Mexican states and in at least six states in the United States. In addition to their six permanent settlements in Sonora and Arizona, they lived and worked as far away as Los Angeles, California, and Tlaxcala in central Mexico. They had begun to cross the border into the United States as early as 1887 (Spicer 1940: 20); by 1910 at least 1,000 Yaquis had entered the United States. New campaigns of military repression in 1916–17 and 1926–27 (Spicer 1954:34–35) brought fresh waves of refugees. By the 1950s approximately 4,000 Yaquis lived in Arizona (Spicer 1961:75). Fear of deportation kept them from reinstituting the Easter ceremony until 1906.

The Yaquis first found work on the railroads, and then in the cotton fields when the cotton boom began during World War I. Until the mechanization of the cotton harvest in 1948, many Yaquis worked at weeding and thinning the growing plants and harvesting ripe cotton, dividing their year between the work season, which they spent on cotton farms, and the ceremonial season, when they returned to their villages. Unemployment, which may reach 50 percent in some communities, continues to be a problem, despite job training programs initiated in the 1960s. Some Yaquis work as teachers, secretaries, health care professionals, administrators, and construction workers. Bingo and high-stakes gaming have brought in revenues for the tribe.

The Pascua Yaqui Association, formed by a group of Yaquis committed to combating poor housing and poverty, was able to persuade Congress (through Rep. Morris Udall) to grant them 202 acres of land southwest of Tucson in 1964; with grants from the federal government and the Ford Foundation, augmented by donations from individuals, they were able to build New Pascua Pueblo. Many people who had lived on the cramped 40 acres of Old Pascua moved there, as well as those who had lost their homes at Barrio Libre because of freeway construction. In 1978 the people of New Pascua won federal recognition as the Pascua Yaqui Tribe. That action gave them access to the same health and social-service programs as other Indian tribes. Four years later they were able to increase their reservation by 892 acres. All Yaquis in the United States, regardless of residence, may enroll in the Yaqui tribe. In 1988 the Yaquis ratified a BIA-approved constitution providing for legislative, judicial, and executive branches of government, and elected a tribal council. In the early 1980s the Tucson City Council provided Housing and Community Development Block Grant funds to rebuild over fifty decrepit homes at Old Pascua; the religious plaza has also received an office, new kitchens, and an activity center (R. Spicer 1994:708–9). Guadalupe and Yoem Pueblo also received funds to repair housing.

Language

While most Native Americans had to adapt bilingually and biculturally to the Anglo-American presence, the Yaqui also had to adapt to a third cultural variable, the Hispanic presence, and this made them trilingual and tricultural. However, as Octaviana Trujillo (1997:11), former Pascua Yaqui chairwoman and director of the Center for Indian Education at Arizona State University, points out, it is often overlooked that indigenous peoples were bilingual and bicultural long before contact with Europeans because of their familiarity with neighboring indigenous groups. Contact with Europeans "has occupied a relatively short period in the Native American social experience." What is unique about European contact in Native American history is its far-reaching impact, which has led to "the profound cultural and linguistic diversity that characterizes the contemporary social landscape" (ibid.).

The Yaqui language reflects their adaptation during the early intercultural period. Rather than translate Spanish words into Yaqui or coin new Yaqui terminology, they incorporated Spanish words, as well as grammatical structure, to accommodate the new items and concepts introduced by Jesuit missionaries. Although they lacked formal schooling, most Yaqui were literate, and many spoke several languages (Spicer 1980). Yaqui leaders wrote in Yaqui to their literate Yaqui friends who had moved to other parts of Sonora, and to their Mexican contemporaries in Spanish (Trujillo 1997:11); church ceremonies were written in both Spanish and Yaqui (Barber 1973). The Yaquis considered themselves to be more civilized than Mexicans and other indigenous groups and, with the exception of technical skills, equal to European Americans (Trujillo 1997:11).

Yaqui oral history tells of their presence in what is now Arizona from time immemorial (U.S. Congress, Senate, 1994), but the major migration came between 1900 and 1910, when the Mexican government tried to deport them to the Yucatán. As political refugees, the Yaquis lived in cultural enclaves at the edges of cities or in work camps, without assimilating into the dominant society because they lacked legal status (Spicer 1961). Fearing deportation, they minimized their contact with government officials and other non-Yaquis. In the United States, Yaquis were relegated to third-class status, for Mexican Americans had already taken the second-class status the Yaquis had had in Mexico.

The dynamics of living for nearly a hundred years in proximity to Spanish- and English-speaking communities has left a legacy of trilingualism in contemporary Yaqui communities (Trujillo 1997:12). Although this pattern enabled them to survive, it has also kept them from becoming competent in the standard forms of Spanish and English required for educational achievement (ibid., 10). In its educational initiatives, the Pascua Yaqui Tribe has focused on reviving the use of the Yaqui language and on enhancing English and Spanish skills. In 1984 the tribal council adopted the Pascua Yaqui Tribe Language Policy, based on a policy declaration that begins, "The Yaqui language is a gift from *Itom Achai*, the Creator, to our people, and, therefore, shall be treated with respect. Our ancient language is the foundation of our cultural and spiritual heritage without which we could not exist in the manner that our Creator intended" (Pascua Yaqui Tribe 1984). Reflecting the interrelationship of language and culture, the policy statement establishes the tribe's authority over not only language-related issues but also the requirement of tribal approval for all external research and studies.

The Yaqui Deer Dancer

The Yaquis are the most recent of all the tribal peoples discussed in this book to have received federal recognition as Indians. In 1977, at the hearing before the Senate Select Committee on Indian Affairs, Yaqui leader Anselmo Valencia argued the status of his people as U.S. Indians, beginning with their residence in the Southwest, including

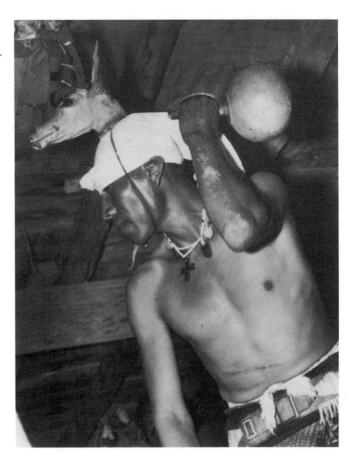

Yaqui Deer Dancer at the Feast of San Ignacio, Pascua, 1955. Courtesy of Arizona Historical Society, No. 22611

present-day Arizona, long before the region came under U.S. jurisdiction. Most Pascua Yaqui were born in the United States, and many have served in the U.S. armed forces. But, Valencia contended, it is the continuation of the Yaqui Deer Dance and deer singing that "makes the Yaquis Indians in every sense of the word" (ibid., 6). He explained, "In the deer dance, we sing to honor the great mountains, the springs, the lakes. We sing of our father the Sun, and of creatures living and dead. We sing of trees and leaves and twigs. We sing of the birds in the sky and of the fish in the ocean. . . . All the songs played are . . . ancient Yaqui Indian stories" (1977:6). Anselmo Valencia was saying that the Deer Dancer and his songs lie at the heart of Yaqui ethnic identity, intimately entwined with Yaqui memories of their tribal history and survival. Deer songs, the one cultural domain in which the Spanish language has had little effect, remain an essential expression of Yaqui-ness; these songs and the dancer who performs them provide the key to Yaqui resilience and endurance as a people.

Perhaps their struggle for survival has made the Yaqui people treasure their culture and fight for its survival even more than those who have had an easier time. Against all odds, the Yaqui have preserved their ceremonial life, infusing it with vitality as they pass on their traditions to their children. One such child is Glafiro Perez, who describes his life as a blending of two worlds. He attends school, where "I learn about math, science, history, English, and computers. I like football and wrestling because they are rough sports, and I enjoy playing Nintendo games, the clarinet, guitar, and writing poetry. I am also a Deer Dancer. . . . My great-great-great-grandfather was a Deer Dancer" (1993:46). When he was fourteen years old, after he had been a deer dancer for four years, he began passing on to the next generation the knowledge that had come to him from previous generations by teaching his nephew, Roman, the sacred ways and steps to the songs. At this time, he explained, "the Deer Dance makes me feel respect, responsibility, and love toward God. To me, the dance signifies a cleansing of the world. It makes me grateful for our elders that taught us the way they were taught. Being part of it makes me very proud to be a Yaqui. The Deer Dance stands for all the good in the world. The deer . . . is our brother" (ibid., 49).

References and Further Reading

The Yaqui Bulletin is an occasional publication of the Pascua Yaqui Tribe, printed at New Pascua Village, 4730 W. Calle Tetakusin, Tucson, AZ 85710.

Barber, Carroll G. 1973. "Trilingualism in an Arizona Yaqui Village." In *Bilingualism in the Southwest*, pp. 295–318, ed. Raul Turner. University of Arizona Press, Tucson.

Beals, Ralph L. 1943. *The Aboriginal Culture of the Cahita Indians*. Ibero-Americana 19. Berkeley, Calif.

*Evers, Larry, and Felipe Molina. 1987. *Yaqui Deer Songs Maso Bwikam: A Native American Poetry*. Sun Tracks and University of Arizona Press, Tucson. [The Deer Song tradition lies at the heart of Yaqui culture. Evers, an English professor at the University of Arizona, and Molina, a Yaqui deer singer who has been governor of Yoem Pueblo, write eloquently about Yaqui culture as revealed in these songs.]

———. 1992. "The Holy Dividing Line: Inscription and Resistance in Yaqui Culture." *Journal of the Southwest* 34:3–46.

Giddings, Ruth. 1959. *Yaqui Myths and Legends*. University of Arizona, Tucson.

Griffith, James, and Felipe S. Molina. 1980. *Old Men of the Fiesta: An Introduction to the Pascola Arts*. Heard Museum, Phoenix.

Hu-DeHart, Evelyn. 1984. *Yaqui Resistance and Survival: The Struggle for Land and Autonomy, 1821–1910*. University of Wisconsin Press, Madison.

*Kaczkurkin, Mini Valenzuela. 1977. *Yoeme: Lore of the Arizona Yaqui People*. Sun Tracks and University of Arizona Press, Tucson. [A Yaqui scholar and educator provides insights into the stories and culture of her people.]

Kelley, Jane Holden. 1978. *Yaqui Women: Contemporary Life Histories*. University of Nebraska Press, Lincoln.

McGuire, Thomas R. 1986. *Politics and Ethnicity on the Rio Yaqui: Potam Revisited*. University of Arizona Press, Tucson.

Moises, Rosalio, Jane Holden Kelley, and William Curry Holden. 1971. *The Tall Candle: A Personal Chronicle of a Yaqui Indian*. University of Nebraska Press, Lincoln.

Molina, Felipe S., Octaviana Salazar, and Mini V. Kaczkurkin. n.d. *The Yaqui: A People and Their Place*. Exhibit guide. Pueblo Grande Museum, Phoenix.

Painter, Muriel Thayer. 1971. *A Yaqui Easter*. University of Arizona Press, Tucson.

———. 1986. *With Good Heart: Yaqui Beliefs and Ceremonies in Pascua Village*. University of Arizona Press, Tucson.

Pascua Yaqui Tribe. 1984. *Yaqui Language Policy for the Pascua Yaqui Tribe*. Tribal Council Resolution. Tucson, 15 September.

Pérez de Ribas, Andres. 1645. *Historia de los triumphos de nuestra Santa Fee entre gentes las mas barbaras y dieras del Nuevo Orbe*. A. de Paredes, Madrid.

Perez, Glafiro, and Emily Vance. "Glafiro: A Young Yoeme Deer Dancer." *Native Peoples Magazine* 6, no. 2:46–50.

Savala, Refugio. 1980. *Autobiography of a Yaqui Poet*. Ed. Kathleen M. Sands. University of Arizona Press, Tucson.

Seyewailo: The Flower World: Yaqui Deer Songs. Division of Media and Instructional Services, University of Arizona, Tucson. [Videotape narrated by Felipe Molina.]

*Spicer, Edward H. 1940. *Pascua: A Yaqui Village in Arizona*. University of Chicago Press, Chicago. [Spicer's work provides a thorough introduction to Yaqui studies; he was the best known non-Yaqui scholar of Yaqui culture and history.]

———. 1947. "Yaqui Villages Past and Present." *Kiva* 13, no.1:1–12.

———. 1954. "Potam: A Yaqui Village in Sonora." Memoirs of the American Anthropological Association 77. Menasha, Wis.

———. 1961. *Perspectives in American Indian Culture Change*. University of Chicago Press, Chicago.

———. 1968. "Development Change and Cultural Integration." In *Perspectives in Developmental Change*, pp. 172–200, ed. Art Gallaher Jr. University of Kentucky Press, Lexington.

———. 1980. *The Yaquis: A Cultural History*. University of Arizona Press, Tucson.

———. 1981 [1962]. *Cycles of Conquest: The Impact of Spain, Mexico, and the United States on the Indians of the Southwest, 1533–1960*. University of Arizona Press, Tucson.

———. 1983. "The Yaqui." In *Handbook of North American Indians*, vol. 10: *The Southwest*, pp. 250–63.

———. 1988. *The People of Pascua*. University of Arizona Press, Tucson.

Spicer, Rosamond B. 1994. "Yaqui." In *Native America in the Twentieth Century: An Encyclopedia*, pp. 708–10, ed. Mary B. Davis. Garland Publishing, New York.

*Trujillo, Octaviana Valenzuela. 1991. "Yaqui Views on Language and Literacy." Ph.D. diss., Arizona State University, Tempe. [A former chair of the Pascua Yaqui Tribe of Arizona, Trujillo is the director of the Center for Indian Education at Arizona State University. She is one of the foremost Yaqui scholars, especially in linguistic studies.]

———. 1992. "Guadalupe: Conflict and Civil Rights in a Tricultural Setting." In *Martin Luther King, Living the Dream in Arizona,* pp. 77–79, ed. Gretchen Bataille. Arizona State University, Tempe.

———. 1995. *Hiapsi Wami Seewan: Flowers of Life.* Atlatl, Phoenix. [A curriculum guide on Yaqui culture and art.]

———. 1997. "A Tribal Approach to Language and Literacy Development in a Trilingual Setting." In *Teaching Indigenous Languages,* pp. 10–21, ed. J. Reyhner. Northern Arizona University, Flagstaff.

———. 1998. "The Yaqui of Guadalupe, Arizona: A Century of Cultural Survival through Trilingualism." *American Indian Culture and Research Journal* 22, no. 1:67–88.

U.S. Congress, Senate, Committee on Indian Affairs. 1994. "Pascua Yaqui Tribe Extension of Benefits: Hearing before the Committee on Indian Affairs." 103d Cong., 2d sess., 27 January, p. 11.

Valencia, Anselmo. 1977. *Trust Status for the Pascua Yaqui Indians of Arizona.* Hearing before the U.S. Select Committee on Indian Affairs, 27 September. Government Printing Office, Washington D.C.

Yaqui Music of the Pascola and Deer Dance. 1973. Canyon Records C-6099. [Recording.]

Yaqui Ritual and Festive Music. 1976. Canyon Records C-6140. [Recording.]

Quechan woman wearing a beaded collar necklace made with characteristic Quechan designs, c. 1890. This wide ring of netted beadwork that covers the whole upper body was appropriate summer attire for Quechan women of the late 1800s. Courtesy of Arizona Historical Society, No. 69,925

Chapter 7 The River Yumans

September 1998   The rocks are beginning to cool from the sun's fiery heat as I climb a hill to get a better view of Spirit Mountain. Following a diagonal path up the rocky incline, I make my way around cholla and yucca interspersed with pungent, olive green creosote. The air glows with suspended dust particles in this hour before sunset. Far below, a once-white jeep bounces along the washboard road, raising a plume of flourlike dust. Quiet is soon restored, and a peaceful stillness begins to settle on the canyon and on the mountain that dominates it.

Spirit Mountain, in the Newberry Mountains of southern Nevada, is visible for many miles in three states. To the south, the land slants sharply, like a huge plate tilted toward the great Colorado River, which divides California from Arizona. Gazing at the majestic peak capped by white granite bluffs, I wish I could cast myself back through time to observe the events that this mountain has witnessed. For Spirit Mountain, more than any other landmark in the Southwest, lies along a crucial artery, the mighty Colorado River. Throughout history this river has been a conduit for vast, sweeping change and the almost constant movement of peoples. From its vantage point Spirit Mountain has seen fierce battles won and lost, the dispersion of many peoples, their decimation by disease, the expansion of an empire, the dismemberment of homelands, and the transformation of the river itself.

Spirit Mountain is, first of all, a place of beginnings: according to Yuman belief, all the peoples of the world spread out upon the earth from this starting point, each group choosing its own place. Yet long before these groups separated, the pottery-making Patayan ancestors of all the Yuman peoples lived in the linear oasis on either side of the river and in the desert and plateau as far east as present-day Flagstaff. They recorded their myths in images still visible today on the desert floor, on canyon walls, and on the base of Spirit Mountain itself. Spirit Mountain remains unchanged, rooted in the rock of the earth's crust. At first, when I turn to see the casinos and bright lights of Laughlin just across the river, where the business of the day is just beginning, this embodiment of the fast-paced, glittering world stretching nearly to the foot of such a sacred landmark saddens me. But then, on an evening thermal, a raven wheels by, making circles in the sky overhead. I look back at Spirit Mountain, memorizing the details of its massive, unmoving form. The mountain remains the same even as light, shadow, and colors continue to change as the sun's last rays filter through the atmosphere. So, too, the mountain has remained unchanged through time, standing firmly planted in the midst of swirling and at times devastating change. Its reassuring presence envelops me as I realize that Spirit Mountain embodies a much more enduring reality than the fleeting world spread out beyond it. Taking a deep breath, I inhale the sanctity of this place, knowing that, just as it has throughout the ages, Spirit Mountain will outlast us all.

In much the same way as their mountain has endured, so too have the River Yumans, a people of dreams and visions. Today Avi kwa'ami (Spirit Mountain) may gaze across the river at the bright lights and casinos of Laughlin, but it also looks southward toward Avi Casino in California and Spirit Mountain Casino in Arizona, both owned by the Fort Mojave Tribe. Farther south, the Chemehuevis ferry tourists across the river to London Bridge at Lake Havasu City. Still farther downstream are other Mojave, joined by the Chemehuevi, Hopi, and Navajo to create the Colorado River Indian Tribes—the CRIT Indians. These people live in relative prosperity because of the water that makes possible their agricultural enterprises. The Quechan and the Cocopah also remain on the river near its mouth, while to the east the Maricopa live with the Akimel O'odham (Pima). Time has brought vast change, but the Yuman peoples have endured, demonstrating the determination and resilience of their spirit.

Origins

Matavilya the Creator was born from the union of Earth and Sky. After he had built a sacred house, the Great Dark House, where Mojave dreamers would later receive their power, he offended his daughter, Frog Woman, who bewitched him, causing his death. Matavilya was cremated and the Great Dark House was burned, establishing the precedent for Mojave funerals as a communal ritual featuring songs, speeches, a mock battle, and the burning of images representing the dead.

Mastamho, Matavilya's brother, had to finish Matavilya's work by giving shape and form to the land. Plunging a willow stick into the earth, he drew out the waters that became the Colorado River; with the river came fish and ducks. Mastamho used the mud of its banks to make the mountains on both sides of the river and planted seeds of melon, corn, pumpkin, and beans in the fertile floodplains so that the people would have food to eat. He taught them about the foods they grew and showed them how to make pottery vessels in which they could cook and store the food. He showed the people how to build fire when they were cold and a ramada for shade when they were hot. He taught them how to know day from night and how to count. Mastamho conferred upon unborn souls the powers of which they would later dream, giving them direction in life.

Then he built a winter house of logs and dirt to serve as the model for their dispersal over the earth: inviting the Mojave into the house, he divided them, creating the Quechan and Kamias; he instructed the others to sit outside the house, the Chemehuevi to the west, the Hualapai to the northeast, and the Yavapai to the southeast. According to the Mojave version of Creation, Mastamho then showed them how to make war clubs, instructing, "I want you to rush and seize and kill and fight and take slaves" (Chooksa Homar, in Kroeber 1948:61), before he told them to practice on a non-Mojave man standing outside the house.

Finally, he dispersed the tribes, telling them to go in these directions, "You can go, you Hualapai, and scatter in the mountains there. . . . You Chemehuevi can do the same, and you Yavapai too. But I will do differently for the Mohave. They will have everything along the river: whatever grows there will be theirs" (Chooksa Homar, in Kroeber 1948:56). With his work completed, Mastamho transformed himself into a fish eagle and flew south to the sea. (This narrative is a composite drawn from Kroeber [1925, 1948], Stewart [1983:65–66], and a publication by the Fort Mojave Indian Tribe [n.d.].)

Prehistory and Early History

The Patayan ancestors of the River, Delta, and Upland Yuman peoples lived in a lowland region bordering the lower Colorado River and the surrounding desert (home of the River and Delta Yumans) and in an upland region consisting of the canyons and plateaus of the upper Colorado River (home to the Upland Yumans). Of all the prehistoric peoples of the Southwest, they are the least known because the flooding of the river, which brought fertile alluvial soil to the farmlands of the River Yumans, also destroyed their riverine sites. The barren desert that characterizes most of their territory has made archaeology extremely difficult as well. Another obstacle has been the ephemeral nature of Patayan sites. In contrast to those of the Hohokam, Patayan remains are confined to the surface. Their lifestyle was one of considerable movement across vast areas on an annual basis, which necessitated the use of nets, baskets, and brush shelters—all of which tended to be perishable (Reid and Whittlesey 1997:116, 129). Furthermore, the desert—and the evidence it contains—is easily damaged by human, animal, and vehicular travel.

The Patayan and their Yuman descendants were great travelers who journeyed across the desert to trade as well as to procure food and resources. In historic times, the Mojave traveled westward to the Chumash of California to trade for shells and acorns, and eastward to the Hopi to acquire Hopi cotton cloth and blankets (Forbes 1965:148, 158). In exchange for the wild game, animal skins, and mineral pigments of the Hualapai and Havasupai, the Mojave traded mesquite, corn, pottery, and shell. Juan Bautista de Anza reported in 1774 that the Halchidhomas traveled "as far as the coast tribes of California, but also that they make this journey in four days," averaging 50 miles per day (ibid., 62). Criss-crossed by an enormous network of trails, the western desert, with its shrines, cairns, and campsites, provides evidence that the Yumans and their ancestors were avid travelers.

Archaeologists divide Patayan (which overlaps with the Hakataya) culture history into three periods: Patayan I (A.D. 700–1000), characterized by red-ware pottery and a distinctive type of shoulder on jars; Patayan II (A.D. 1000–1500), marked by new vessel forms with a unique "stucco" type of finish that gave pots a rough-textured surface; and Patayan III (1500–c. 1600), which shows refinement in ceramics (Reid and Whittlesey 1997:121–23). Patayan pottery, found along trails at Hohokam sites, points toward a history of fighting and trading between Patayan and Hohokam groups (Reid and Whittlesey 1997:123). At the beginning of Patayan III, Lake Cahuilla had disappeared for good. Previously, this freshwater lake had periodically filled and dried up as the level of the Colorado River changed; now the people who lived on its shores were forced to move into the deserts and uplands. The bands of Patayan people who had lived on its eastern shores moved to the lower Colorado River valley, while those on the western shores dispersed into the foothills and mountains of western and Baja California (ibid., 123).

The Patayan left behind intaglios to mark their system of interconnecting trails, by digging into the desert pavement—a layer of pebbles coated with a dark deposit of microbial origin—immense figures of humans, animals, stars, and geometric shapes. Preserved by the extremely arid conditions, these 200-foot-long figures may be related to a pilgrimage to the sacred Spirit Mountain, which celebrates the events of creation, or may represent symbolic or real journeys to other sacred places. Although we will never know with certainty the meaning of these images, we can see similarities in the cultural traditions of their descendants, the River Yuman peoples, who sing ritual song cycles recording ancestral wanderings and journeys to sacred mountain places to acquire power.

In time, some Yumans moved to the mountains and plateaus of northwest and central Arizona to become the Upland Yumans—the Hualapai, Havasupai, and Yavapai. The River Yumans spread out along the lower Colorado and Gila Rivers, separating into various groups. Intertribal warfare, so interwoven into the fabric of River Yuman culture that the Mojave version of creation includes instructions on the use of the war club, led to numerous shifts and amalgamations of the population. Groups belonged to one of the two opposing military alliances: the Quechan league, which included the Mojave, Yavapai, Kamia, Chemehuevi, Hia C-ed O'odham, and western Tohono O'odham; or the Maricopa league, which included the Cocopah, Halchidhoma, Hualapai, Havasupai, Kavelchadom, Akimel O'odham, and eastern Tohono O'odham (Dobyns, Ezell, and Ezell 1963). By the mid-nineteenth century, only the Mojave, Quechan, and Cocopah lived on the Colorado River. First identified by the Spanish as the Cocomaricopa, the Maricopa, as they are known today, had moved eastward to settle along the middle Gila near the Pima. The remnants of other River and Delta Yuman tribes—the Halyikwamai, Kahwan, Halchidhoma, and the Kavelchadom—had joined the Maricopa by 1840.

After the Halchidhoma had been expelled, the victorious Mojave invited, or at least tolerated, the arrival of the Chemehuevi, a group who had broken away from the Las Vegas Southern Paiutes. By the early 1850s the Chemehuevis had claimed the rich Chemehuevi and Colorado river valleys. (See chapter 11.)

These groups continued to live in the lush, linear oasis of the river valley until the United States turned its attention westward, driven by the dream of Manifest Destiny. Anglo-Americans soon realized the strategic importance of the Colorado River. From the mid-1800s until construction of the railroad in 1877, they relied on the river as a major transportation route, using a fleet of steamboats to supply troops stationed at Fort Yuma and Fort Mojave and miners in the gold fields of California and Arizona. Spaniards had come earlier, searching for silver, followed by American "mountain men" seeking beaver skins, but not until their land came under American control did the superior arms and numbers of white soldiers force the Indians to surrender their land. Already weakened from European diseases, for which they had no natural immunity, they accepted reservations that were but a fraction of their former territories. The character of the river remained essentially the same until the 1930s, when dams tamed it by removing the threat of flooding and using the power to generate electricity. Only then did the land become desirable to Anglo settlers, who took up residence on both sides of the river.

Language

The languages of the Yuman subfamily of the Hokan language family are more closely related than are those in other North American language families. The Yuman subfamily has four branches: River, Pai, Delta-California, and Kiliwa. The River branch consists of Mojave, Quechan, and Maricopa, along with the extinct dialects Halchidhoma and Kavelchadom. The Pai subgroup includes the Upland Yumans (treated in chapter 8). The Cocopah speak a language in the Delta-California branch of this subfamily, as did the Hayikwamai and Kahwan. The Kiliwa of Baja California speak the language that bears their name.

The Chemehuevi are the only non-Yuman-speaking group who reside along the Colorado River. Their language belongs to the Southern Numic branch of the Uto-Aztecan linguistic family.

Aboriginal River Yuman Culture

The cultures of the River and Delta Yumans are so similar that they are grouped together here. In addition to occupying different environments from the Upland Yumans, the River and Delta Yumans are also set apart by their patrilineal descent patterns, inherited chiefdomship, and rancheria settlements along the river banks.

Although the river brought rich nutrients in its annual floods that enabled River Yuman peoples to live a life of relative abundance, as a major transportation artery the Colorado also provided a direct route for epidemic disease. During the sixteenth century Spaniards transmitted numerous pathogens, including smallpox, measles, plague, typhus, influenza, and cholera; each of these caused very high mortality among Native Americans. These pathogens were passed on not only from direct contact with Spaniards but also by Native American traders and travelers. As Richard Stoffle and others have pointed out, this was an on-going process: the trans-Atlantic direct transmission of infectious diseases to Native American populations continued into the final quarter of the nineteenth century (1995:181–203). Much of what is known of the River Yumans (as well as other Southwestern peoples) comes from ethnographic research conducted *after* their original populations had been decimated by disease, and thus is set in a specific time frame.

River Yuman Subsistence

The River Yumans lived along the lower Colorado and Gila Rivers in rancheria settlements, with each house separated from its nearest neighbor by 100 yards or more. Each sprawling settlement was separated from the next by 4–5 miles. In warm weather a ramada was all that was necessary for shade and sleeping; foodstuffs could be conveniently stored on the roof. In winter, the people lived in low rectangular houses with a cottonwood frame layered with mud several inches thick; usually they placed their houses on a low rise of ground near a river bank or pond. The Cocopah also built round or oval, brush-covered frame houses for summer. After the Maricopa moved eastward on the Gila River, they adopted the round houses of their Piman neighbors.

Spirit Mountain casts its gaze across the river, the lifeblood of this land. Each spring, swollen with the melting snows of the Rocky Mountains, its place of origin, the Colorado River overflowed its banks, spreading silt-laden floodwater over the bottomlands for distances as great as 2 miles from the river. When the river was calmer, the Mojave swam and ferried across it, using rafts for long trips. The beneficence of the river, with its annual spring floods, enabled them to grow abundant crops in the lush oases of the river valleys, despite occasional crop failures. Even late floods that destroyed some sown fields (Forbes 1965:189) were not widely destructive, for the water spread gently over the bottomlands. It was the river that made life possible for the River Yuman peoples, for otherwise the terrain

The emergence place of Yuman peoples: Spirit Mountain (at right), Nevada, 1998. Author photograph

—arid mesas, flanked by jagged, barren mountains, which rise up from the river—with its oppressively hot summers and extremely low precipitation would never have supported their dense populations. The fertile river valley forms a green oasis in a hot desert where only 4.5 inches of rain falls each year, and the long summer season has maximum daily temperatures that soar to 125°F. Much of the floodplain is covered with brush and trees, such as cottonwoods, willows, arrowweed, cane, and rushes, while mesquite and screwbean trees grow on land that is not flooded every year.

By the end of June the river would recede, leaving behind such rich silt deposits that crop rotation and fertilization were unnecessary. Raising crops was a relatively low-risk enterprise with high potential yield (Bee 1983:86): the Cocopah raised 30 percent of their food, while the Mojave relied on agriculture for fully 50 percent of their food (Castetter and Bell 1951:238). A man could use any piece of land not already being cultivated; this plot became his private property, which he marked by piling ridges of dirt along its boundaries. The farmer cleared his land and then, with every step, he punched a hole in the moist soil about 4–6 inches deep, using a planting stick with a wedge-shaped point. His wife followed behind him, dropping about six seeds into each hole and then burying them with soil she pressed down by hand. The Mojave farmer planted most of his field in maize, which, along with tepary beans, ripened rapidly in the intense summer heat and was ready for the women to harvest in late September and October.

After the spring floods had receded, women collected a variety of wild seeds and wild plants in the fertile bottomland as well as on the adjacent desert mesas. The mesquite tree was so important to the Mojave that they called it "our tree of life" (Trimble 1993:396). From its roots they carved cradles and tools, while its sap provided glue, and its bark, clothing and shoes. Women ground its beanlike pods into pith that their families ate as mush or cakes; fresh mesquite beans provided a nutritious juice. After mesquite beans became dry enough to rattle in their pods, they were as sweet as candy. Women fired their pots in fires of mesquite wood. Mesquite also fueled the fires in which individuals were cremated along with their belongings.

The Mojaves relied on squaw fish, hump-backed suckers, mullet, and bony tail for their principal flesh food, for game was scarce along their section of the river and they seldom went far afield to hunt. In the river, as well as in adjoining muddy sloughs and ponds, they used dip nets, with seines or drag nets, traps and weirs, and large, canoe-shaped basketry scoops (Stewart 1983:59). Farther south along the river, on the delta, the Cocopah enjoyed a plentiful supply of deer and javelinas. The Cocopah men would undergo ritual purification before setting out on a hunt. Individuals stalked game with bow and arrow or joined their tribesmen in communal rabbit drives, using fire and trapping animals in snares or nets (Williams 1983:104). They also ate raccoons, wood rats, beavers, insects, wild geese, and ducks (Drucker 1941:98–99; Kelly 1977:24).

The Cocopah constructed tule balsa, cottonwood dugouts, and log rafts that they guided with poles across the river. To ferry small children or to transport small items, River Yuman peoples used large pottery ollas or baskets, which they pushed as they swam alongside (Drucker 1941:124).

River Yuman Social and Political Organization

The River Yuman tribes are unique in the Southwest for their sense of tribal unity. Although each tribe was divided into bands for purposes of attack or defense, these bands did not weaken tribal cohesion or their sense of national consciousness. The Mojave had at least three bands—northern, central, and southern divisions—which were further subdivided into settlements or local groups. Families moved freely from one area to another within their tribal territory, so that residence locality was relatively unimportant; what mattered was their identity as Mojave or Quechan or Cocopah. Only the Maricopa were not originally a tribe; by 1857, the time of the decisive battle between the Mojaves and Quechans against the Maricopas and Pimas, the Maricopas were a Yuman-speaking amalgam of other peoples forced from their aboriginal homelands on the lower Colorado River beginning in the eighteenth century.

River Yuman political and social organization was characterized by informality: no individual or group had significant authority over others. With no organized tribal council, each settlement had its own prominent men, who had attained their power by dreaming and who led because others respected them rather than because they wielded any real authority. A group of elderly men reached a decision on the qualifications of a candidate for leadership status on the basis of how he related his dreams; the power of a man's dreams had to be continually manifested in his successful negotiation of practical matters. Public support based on the competence a man demonstrated determined how long he held his status as leader.

Each Mojave band had at least one subchief: the northern and southern divisions each had one, while the central division, which was the most populous, had five (Stewart 1983: 62). The concept of an overall head chief for the Mojave tribe may have developed after white contact.

All River Yuman tribes had nonlocalized, exogamous patrilineal clans, whose functions in the precontact period have been lost, although by contact times all women in the clan were known by the clan name rather than by their personal names (Stewart 1983:2). Each of the fifty Cocopah clans was identified with a specific totem—an animal, plant, or natural phenomenon whose name was believed to have been provided by the Creator at the beginning of time (Williams 1983:109). The Quechans also had patrilineal clans with "namesakes," or totemic associations (Forde 1931), as did the Mojave.

After a couple married, their choice of residence was flexible, although there was a patrilocal bias. The basic unit for economic and social cooperation was the nuclear family, while the core of each settlement was an extended family. Friends and relatives came to gossip and to share meals in an almost continuous stream during the day.

River Yuman Warfare

The River Yuman tribes waged war against each other for at least three centuries. Originally directed at conquest and the seizure of territory, intertribal wars took on a new character after 1830, when several communities had been forced to relinquish their land. As early as the sixteenth century many small tribes, such as the Halyikwamai and Halchidhoma, were losing their struggles for independence and were being forced off the Colorado River because their farmlands were under attack from both upriver and downriver enemies (Kroeber and Fontana 1992 [1986]:104–5). Some anthropologists theorize that River Yuman tribes resorted to warfare for economic reasons, instead of intensifying their agricultural production (Stone 1981:183–97; Graham 1975:451–62), but others point out that the Mojaves, Quechans, and Halchidhomas cultivated wheat in historic times, which would have given them an additional crop (Kroeber and Fontana 1992:124–25). Other motives included vengeance for the loss of kinsmen, the strong sense of tribal nationalism, and the conviction held by each tribe that they were the chosen people.

The reasons for warfare probably changed over time, especially after horses became available in Mexico. The best known explanations center on concepts of diffusion and acculturation after the Mexican market opened: River Yuman tribes raided for plunder in the form of horses, food, and captives who could be sold to Mexicans for slaves, while the desire to acquire horses reinforced the sense of ethnic superiority and nationalism held by each tribe (Dobyns et al. 1957:46–71). Whether for some of these reasons or for a related but separate reason, in 1857 Mojave and Quechan warriors traveled by foot more than 160 miles across the Sonoran Desert to attack the Gila River Pimas and the amalgam of peoples that had coalesced to become the Maricopas. In this decisive and bloody battle, the Quechan were almost annihilated and the Mojave experienced their first major defeat.

Men who had experienced "great dreams" (those that conferred power in battle) were the primary ones who carried on warfare, although men who had not had proper war dreams might join a major expedition. Mastamho, the culture hero, instituted warfare by decreeing that some men would always be given "great dreams," which men were eager to validate by demonstrating their prowess in battle.

Ten or twelve of these men might undertake a raid at will, but entire tribes took part in major expeditions. Scouts, who had also dreamed their special powers, reconnoitered the route to locate water holes and the enemy's position. The war party attacked settlements at dawn in a battle array, in which challengers from opposing sides met in single combat before the general melee. A single war chief led Mojave warriors in three different ranks designated by the weapons they wielded: archers, clubbers, and stick-men. They scalped fallen enemies and later celebrated a successful battle with a Scalp Dance. Those who had killed enemies had to purify themselves by repeated bathing and by abstention from salt and meat for several days.

Although different tribes preferred different weapons and varied the number of warriors carrying each kind of weapon, both Upland and River Yuman warriors carried identical weapons, most notably, the short, heavy mesquite or ironwood club shaped like a mallet or potato masher. Designed for hand-to-hand combat, these clubs could be shorter than 1 foot but were never longer than 2 feet. They also used tapering staves or truncheons, which were 2–4 feet long and made of mesquite, for slashing and beating. Willow, cottonwood, and even mesquite bows were used, and the Yavapai used rattlesnake venom, spiders, centipedes, a variety of long-winged bee, and walnut leaves to poison their arrows (Kroeber and Fontana 1992 [1986]:73). Nearly all warriors carried knives and daggers.

River Yuman Religion and World View

Dreaming. Dreaming guided all River Yuman peoples to special abilities, permeating almost every phase of their thought and endeavor, including warfare, gambling, lovemaking, and curing (Stewart 1983:65). All talents, skills, and achievements in life were believed to derive from dreams dreamed in the mother's womb, which projected the dreamer back in time so that Mastamho could confer power upon the unborn soul. Although prenatal dreams were forgotten after birth, they repeated themselves with the onset of adolescence; for this reason, recurring dreams were believed to indicate the bestowal of special powers, which were validated by success in the waking world, whether in battle, healing, or other endeavors (ibid.). Shamans had the most elaborate dreams, and the portion of the creation myth they dreamed indicated their curing specialty, such as rattlesnake bites or witchcraft.

Although "great dreams" bestowed power upon relatively few people, who became village headmen, shamans, war leaders, singers, and funeral orators, all dreams were believed to have meaning. Without the requisite dreams, learned information and skills were thought to be ineffectual. Dreamers recited their dream experiences in song cycles, each of which consisted of 50–200 songs, which formed the basis of River Yuman ceremonialism (Stewart 1983:65).

Shamanism. A shaman was a specialist who had dreamed the power to cure one or several forms of illness. The shaman acquired power through a dream "journey" by traveling outside the social world to meet the supernatural (Lamphere 1983:746). Depending upon which portion of the creation myth he had dreamed and which powers Mastamho had conferred upon him, he could cure rattlesnake bites, sickness caused by ghosts, soul loss, or sickness due to contact with enemies. Shamans directed their curing rituals toward the removal of a foreign object or spirit from the patient's body, which had been sent by an animal or mountain spirit. To accomplish an effective cure, the shaman brought the supernatural into the social world by allowing the spirit helper to enter his body. The spirit helper then enabled the shaman to remove the source of illness (ibid.).

A shaman led a precarious existence because his powers were also believed to cause disease, especially as he aged and wished to keep those to whom he had a special attachment in a special place where he could then visit them in dreams (Stewart 1983:66). Shamans were killed if they were suspected of witchcraft or if they lost too many patients. The Mojave distinguished between "fast witching," which caused instant death as the witch shot power into a person, and "slow witching," where the witch used a person's dreams as the vehicle for causing the victim to sicken and die over a long period of time (ibid.).

The Mourning Ceremony. The most powerful and moving of River Yuman rituals was the cremation ceremony. The cremation of Matavilya at the time of creation established the prototype for the mourning ceremony. Singing and wailing preceded an imminent death. Mourners sang some 30 song cycles with 200 songs in each, and funeral orators made ceremonial speeches extolling the virtues of the deceased (Stewart 1983:66). Immediately after death, in order to transmit them to the land of the dead, the body and the possessions of the deceased—including the house and granary—were set on fire. Once the funeral pyre had been lit, mourners cast their personal offerings on the fire as men and women danced in line, arm in arm, moving back and forth to the accompaniment of song. The funeral orator addressed the dead, encouraging him to end his ties with his loved ones on earth, and wailing intensified as the dancing continued around the funeral pyre. After the funeral of a prominent warrior or chief, the people held a commemorative mourning ceremony featuring a ritual reenactment of warfare in his honor (ibid., 67).

During the four days after the funeral, relatives ate no meat, salt, or fish, and drank no cold water, purifying themselves by bathing in a preparation of arrowweed roots steeped in water and fumigating themselves from the pungent smoke of burning arrowweed. The orators and those who had tended the corpse also had to undergo fumigation. Female mourners cropped their hair to ear level, while men cut theirs to shoulder length.

The River Yumans believed that the soul spent the first four days after cremation revisiting significant places in the individual's life; deceased relatives then welcomed the soul into the land of the dead, a place of abundance that was located downstream and was closed to those who had not been tattooed. Eventually, the soul died again and other ghosts cremated it (Stewart 1983:67).

The Ward Valley Nuclear Waste Dump Site

One of the biggest issues facing all River Yuman people today is the proposed nuclear waste dump at Ward Valley, California, only 20 miles from the Colorado River. This remote corner of California's East Mojave Desert is sacred aboriginal territory for the five lower Colorado River Indian tribes, and leaders from the Fort Mojave, Chemehuevi, Cocopah, Quechan, and Colorado River Indian Tribes have asserted their religious and sovereignty rights at federal hearings, at meetings with government officials, and in the courts. In 1998, after they brought their case before the Environmental Protection Agency's (EPA) National Environmental Justice Advisory Council, the council recommended that the agency stop the dump project; however, the EPA failed to do so (Klasky 1999:58). All four of the nuclear waste dumps built by U.S. Ecology, the company chosen to build the Ward Valley facility, are now leaking radioactive material into the surrounding groundwater and land (ibid., 57).

For the last decade Native Americans and a coalition of environmental and social-justice activists have fought against plans initiated by nuclear utilities, one of America's most powerful industries. The Ward Valley area is critical habitat for the threatened desert tortoise, and environmental groups and Indian tribes used the Endangered Species Act to block an attempt to transfer public land for the site (Klasky 1999:58). Placing their jobs in jeopardy, scientists with the U.S. Geological Survey issued a report warning that nuclear wastes would eventually make their way to the Colorado River. Singer Bonnie Raitt, singer Jackson Browne, actress Tracy Nelson, and poet John Trudell held concerts and readings to increase public awareness and to raise money for the cause. Fort Mojave tribal leader Steve Lopez explained the sacredness of Ward Valley to the Mojave: "There is no church or cathedral out here. The entire valley is sacred to us. Ward Valley, we call it Silyaye Ahease, is our history, our culture and our future" (ibid., 58). At the start of the twenty-first century, the long battle to save Ward Valley continues, merging social justice, cultural preservation, and Native American sovereignty rights.

River Yuman History and Contemporary Issues

While River Yuman tribes shared similar cultural traditions, their particular histories varied, depending upon the timing of their encounters with European-Americans. This section provides a brief history and present-day account of each reservation, proceeding from north to south along the Colorado River. The account is drawn from Bee (1983, 1994), Butler (1994), Flores (1994), Fontana (1999), Stewart (1983), Trimble (1993), and Williams (1983, 1994).

The Fort Mojave Reservation

The Mojave (Ahamakav, "the people who live along the river") are the largest group in the Yuman language family. Only the people of the Fort Mojave Reservation, located near Needles, California, still live in the shadow of Spirit Mountain, which is visible in the Arizona, Nevada, and California portions of their reservation. Established by War Department General Order 19 in 1870 and by executive order in 1911, the Fort Mojave Reservation is governed by council members who must not only plan and administer tribal regulations but also consider the regulations of federal, state, and county governments of the three states in which their reservation is located.

Historically, their territory once encompassed a vast area that straddled the Colorado River and extended from some 15 miles north of the present Davis Dam, south for nearly 170 miles, and north nearly to modern Blythe, California. Although they first encountered a European, Don Juan de Oñate, governor of New Mexico, in 1604 at the confluence of the Colorado and Bill Williams Rivers, they did not experience significant change until white trappers and fur traders began to travel through their country in the 1820s. The Mojave, who had always been great travelers—they sometimes covered 100 miles a day in a loping run—served as guides through rough mountain terrain and across the desert along the Mojave Trail to the Pacific coast. By the late 1840s Anglo-American visitors ventured more frequently into their territory: prospectors en route to the California gold rush, explorers seeking a route for a transcontinental railroad, and steamboat captains attempting to determine the navigability of the Colorado.

Intertribal warfare kept Mojave warriors involved in ousting other tribes, such as the

Halchidhoma (whose remaining members joined the Maricopa), instead of focusing their attention on Anglo-Americans. In 1857 the warriors of the powerful Quechan-Mojave alliance were defeated by the Pima and Maricopa. The following year, still reeling from this unprecedented defeat and apprehensive about the increasing numbers of Anglo-Americans traveling through their territory, Mojaves attacked a wagon train; this event led the U.S. military to construct Fort Mojave in the Mojave Valley. Mojave resistance ended in 1859 when their warriors were mowed down by rifle fire during a battle.

After the fort was built, Mojave leader Irrateba (also spelled Irataba, Arateba, and Yara Tav) and his followers decided to move to the Colorado River Valley, where the Colorado River Indian Reservation was established in 1865. Almost three-quarters of the Mojave chose to remain behind in Mohave Valley with Chief Homose Kohote. The Mojave enjoyed traditional rule until the death of their last chief, Pete Lambert (Sukulyi Hi-ar) in 1947. Today they have a constitution, and elect seven council members and a tribal chairman. The tribe maintains its own police force and trial and appellate court, which has jurisdiction over civil and some criminal cases.

After the Fort Mojave Indians formed a tribal council in 1956, they began to push agricultural leases from five-year to ninety-nine-year leases, which attracted more stable investors. In 1976 they were able to begin improving their housing. Their two casinos, Spirit Mountain Casino on the Arizona side of the river and the much newer Avi Casino and Hotel on the California side, have brought in much needed revenues for the people of Fort Mojave. Agriculture remains a major tribal business and source of income. However,

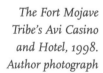

The Fort Mojave Tribe's Avi Casino and Hotel, 1998. Author photograph

Fort Mojave, checkerboarded with private land, is difficult to irrigate successfully, so the tribe leases some 15,000 acres, or 41 percent of its land; unemployment is roughly 46 percent (Trimble 1993:403). Other tribal enterprises include housing developments, a car wash, smoke shop, gas station, and an auto racetrack, as well as water, sewer, gas, telecommunications, and electricity projects (Butler 1994:357). Their most ambitious development enterprise is a 3,998-acre planned community, Aha Macav, in Nevada, which will include recreational, commercial, residential, and casino facilities; the tribe has issued revenue bonds for a water and sewer project in connection with this enterprise (ibid., 357).

The Chemehuevi Reservation

September 1998

The midday air shimmers, reflecting the heat of the desert. With Spirit Mountain at our backs, we leave the lush oasis of the Colorado River and head south on Highway 95. To the west, the land seemingly stretches endlessly across half of California, a sere and desolate desert, broken only by stark mountain ranges and a series of dry lakes.

We reach the turn-off to the Chemehuevi Indian Reservation, 30,000 acres of dry mountains and forbidding desert dotted with creosote and ocotillo. The 15-mile, dead-end road winds down bajadas where plants cluster along small washes, forming dusty green lines in an otherwise tan landscape.

Then, much to our surprise, the bleak landscape suddenly gives way to Havasu Landing, a flourishing resort at the end of the road. A convenience store, delicatessen, and gas station in a strip mall sit at the top of the rise that slopes down to the harbor, where there is a marina with a club-boathouse, restaurant and bar, casino, and dock with about twenty small pleasure craft moored. At the end of the dock, the two-story, Chemehuevi-owned ferry is loading. I smile when I see the name painted on its bow, *Dream-Catcher,* thinking that the Ojibwa Indians who live in the upper Plains and Midwest probably had no idea that their dream-catchers would become such a widely distributed item of popular culture.

A sun-bleached young man in a tropical shirt welcomes us on board while Jimmy Buffett music sets a Caribbean mood. The engines start and we are soon under way, pulling out of the harbor and past the jetty, across broad Lake Havasu rimmed by distant desert mountains. Sunlight glints off the surface of the lake, while jet skiers shoot across its surface. In less than half an hour, we reach the Arizona side. Set back in the harbor is London Bridge; brought from England by a Lake Havasu City developer, this bridge is said to be the second-largest tourist attraction in the state. Rising beside the bridge on one side of the harbor is a small English village with Tudor architecture; across the inlet, facing the village, stands a row of sleek, modern condominiums. This confusion of cultures creates a surreal, theme-park quality that makes me glad when we are once more on the lake headed back to the Chemehuevi side. But as we glide across the waters of this manmade lake, as unnatural

The Colorado River near Lake Havasu, 1998. Author photograph

as London Bridge in the Arizona desert, I can't help but remember the Chemehuevi homes, graves, and farmland that lie beneath the waters. When Parker Dam closed its head gates in 1939, Lake Havasu flooded most of the Chemehuevi Valley. As Chemehuevi basketmaker Mary Lou Brown says, "I have to throw flowers on the water here if I want to honor my people, because that's where they are—underneath" (Trimble 1993:407).

By the early 1850s the Chemehuevi had moved into the rich Chemehuevi and Colorado River valleys near the Mojave, who tolerated their presence. Once part of the Las Vegas band of Southern Paiute, the Chemehuevi numbered about a few hundred people. These desert people retained their language, in the Southern Numic branch of the Uto-Aztecan language family, but adopted many aspects of Mojave culture, becoming floodplain farmers, adopting the powers of dreaming, and developing a sense of tribal unity based on warfare. By 1904 the Chemehuevi were considered to be the most successful Indian farmers on the river (Trimble 1993:407).

The railroad reached Parker, Arizona, in 1905, and irrigation was successfully introduced on the Colorado River Indian Tribes (CRIT) Reservation, making this reservation more attractive to many Chemehuevis, who moved there. In 1907 the Chemehuevi Reservation was established to protect their land in the Chemehuevi Valley. However, after Parker Dam created Lake Havasu, the Chemehuevis who had farmed in the inundated valleys were left homeless. Most Chemehuevis joined the Mojave on CRIT land, and others had to seek wage labor off the reservation. After the tribe adopted a new constitution in 1970 and began to remodel a resort that caters to boaters on Lake Havasu, many tribal members began to return to the Chemehuevi Reservation, although most Chemehuevis remained at CRIT.

Water is a major issue, for the Chemehuevis as well as for other tribes who live along the Colorado River. The Chemehuevi Reservation is nearly impossible to farm. Struggling financially after having lost their farmland to Lake Havasu, the Chemehuevis have developed a plan to bring in about $1 million a year to use for tribal development programs. This controversial plan, which the Chemehuevis submitted for federal approval in fall 1998, would lease part of their Colorado River water allocation to a private company, which would then resell the water to southern California cities. The Bureau of Indian Affairs has been collecting public comments, and Interior Secretary Bruce Babbitt is currently deciding this issue (Kelley 1998:A7).

Edward Smith, Chemehuevi vice chairman, explains his tribe's position: "We knew we had the water, and year after year it just keeps going down there [to southern California]. . . . Right now, we're giving it away. Why let it go down and let someone else use it for free when we can lease it? We're a poor tribe" (Kelley 1998:A7).

Water officials in Arizona and California are afraid that this is the first skirmish in a new legal battle over water in the desert Southwest. While a Chemehuevi victory would involve only a small amount of water—5,000 acre-feet a year, which is just a small fraction of the 4.4 million acre-feet of Colorado River water in California's entitlement—such a legal victory could inspire four other tribes along the lower Colorado to sell parts of their river allocations (Kelley 1998:A7). The Colorado River Indian Tribes are the biggest players in water rights because they have rights to about 700,000 acre-feet of water, nearly all of which goes to Arizona, providing about 22 percent of Arizona's total water allotment (ibid.). While the Colorado River Indian Tribes use all of their allocation to grow alfalfa, cotton, and vegetables on their 75,000 acres, they are considering selling their water because it would be much more lucrative to do so. The total amount of tribal river allocations adds up to about 900,000 acre-feet, which is about 12 percent of the 7.5 million acre-feet allocated to all of California, Arizona, and Nevada. Water officials fear that if water rights can be sold or traded so that water becomes a market-driven resource, some states could become dry. At present, the use of Colorado River water is governed by the doctrine of prior appropriation, which means that if those first in line to use the water do not do so, the water automatically goes for free to those with lower-priority claims. At present, Indians have some of the highest priority water rights, but if they fail to use that water, in a sense, they are giving it away.

The Colorado River Indian Tribes (CRIT) Reservation

September 1998

Continuing south on Highway 95, we reach Vidal Junction and turn east to Parker, Arizona, an Anglo enclave community at the northern edge of the Colorado Indian River Tribes Reservation. Parker is an incorporated community located on and surrounded by reservation lands; Poston, also on the reservation, is 20 miles farther south. Intermarriage among the four tribes has created a unique ethnic blend. Although the Mojaves—who have the ancient ties to the land—still dominate in numbers and political power, most people who live at the CRIT Reservation are descended from all four tribes.

The Colorado River Indian Tribes Administrative Center is located on the outskirts of Parker. This modern complex, surrounded by carefully landscaped lawns, includes a tribal public library, archives, and a museum, as well as office buildings for tribal government. The Colorado River Indian Tribes Museum and Library has an active program that includes conducting oral history interviews, offering classes in language and culture, engaging in artifact and document collection and preservation, and conducting archaeological site recording. Tribal elders share their knowledge about cultural and spiritual traditions, and discuss current issues, such as legal cases, in regularly scheduled meetings. The meetings have been videotaped since 1984 to preserve the elders' knowledge for future generations.

While each of the four groups has its own seal to symbolize its culture, the Colorado River Indian Tribes wanted to create a tribal seal that would represent their people as a unified group. In 1966 they held a contest to create a tribal seal that would represent the reservation's resources, economy, and people. John Scott's winning design features a sunburst design around the edges, with fifty-two points to represent a full fifty-two weeks of sunshine. Riverside Mountain, flanked by its range, stands on the horizon, with the Colorado River flowing diagonally from the mountains behind the checkerboard of farmed parcels on the reservation. A shaft of wheat and a branch of cotton represent the major agricultural products, grain and cotton, and the four feathers, two on each side of the

Tribal seals of the Colorado River Indian Tribes (clockwise from upper left): Mojave, Chemehuevi, Hopi, Navajo, Colorado River Indian Tribes (center), 1999. Author photograph

mountains, represent the four tribes of the reservation: Mojave, Chemehuevi, Hopi, and Navajo.

The Colorado River Indian Tribes Reservation runs north to south along 90 miles of shoreline, stretching from just north of Parker, Arizona, nearly to Blythe, California, with acreage in both Arizona and California. Established in 1865 for the "Indians of the said river and its tributaries," this reservation was originally intended for the Mojave. Later, the Mojaves, who settled on the north end of the reservation near Parker, were joined by about 200 Chemehuevis who took up residence farther south.

Under the provisions of the Indian Reorganization Act (IRA), in 1937 the members of the Colorado River Tribes adopted a constitution, electing Mojave Jay Gould as their first tribal chairman. During World War II President Franklin Roosevelt signed an executive order establishing internment camps for Japanese-Americans. The Poston Relocation Center, one of ten wartime camps established to house 20,000 internees, was located on Colorado River Indian lands between 1942 and 1945. By not opposing this plan, the Tribal Council avoided losing this land permanently to the War Department; in compensation, they received improvements to the land and the development of irrigation facilities (Flores 1994:125).

In 1945 the BIA opened the land to Hopi and Navajo immigrants suffering the impact of the Depression and federal stock-reduction programs. The new arrivals moved into the empty barracks once occupied by the Japanese Americans. Concerned that they would be overwhelmed by these immigrants, the Mojave and Chemehuevi stopped the flood of new-comers in 1952. Today the Colorado River Indian Tribes, recognized by other tribes across the nation as particularly progressive, have taken the initiative to develop resources, especially by granting long-term development leases. Their primary economic base is agriculture, which approaches the maximum area possible with available water rights—over 130,000 acres of irrigated land (including the 11,000-acre tribal cooperative). This has helped reduce unemployment to 10 percent (Trimble 1993:403). Cotton, wheat, alfalfa, feed grains, lettuce, and melons are the primary crops.

Another tribal enterprise is Aha Quin Park, a resort on the California side of the river in Riverside County. In addition to agricultural leases, the tribes also grant commercial, recreational, small business, and residential leases that provide income for tribal operations employing over 300 people, the largest payroll in LaPaz County (Flores 1994:125). The twenty-eight departments of tribal government are headed by a council composed of a chairman, vice chairman, secretary, and treasurer; a system of committees assists the council. Tribal courts and police work with local, county, and state governments in matters of jurisdiction.

Having an Anglo enclave inside reservation lands has created a unique jurisdictional situation. Congress removed 900 acres from the reservation in 1908, when the Southern Pacific Railroad was building a new line to Los Angeles, to provide a town site at the river crossing (Hilpert, in Sheridan and Parezo 1996:234). The tribes received the proceeds when building lots were auctioned, as well as unsold lots; thus, the town itself lay within the reservation, and the tribes also owned lands within the town. A dispute arose in the 1980s when the tribes decided to develop some of the lots they owned in Parker, and city officials insisted on their right to regulate building activities. When Parker officials cut off electricity and water service to tribal buildings in town, the tribes filed a federal lawsuit claiming jurisdiction. In 1989 Judge Roger Strand ruled that the town of Parker "does not have the authority to impose or enforce any building or zoning ordinances with respect to this tribal property" (Helliker 1988:35–39).

The tribes continue to develop new tribal enterprises, such as a 10-acre recycling plant, opened in 1992, which cleans approximately 3.5 million pounds of activated carbon per year; the same year, the tribes signed an agreement with McDonald's Corp. to begin building a $750,000 McDonald's restaurant near the Moovalya Plaza Shopping Center on the reservation (Flores 1994:127). The tribes also receive income from hunting and fishing licenses; recreational facilities at Lake Moovalya, one of the finest lakes in the Southwest for water skiing; and the Blue Water Casino in Parker (Fontana 1999:16).

The Fort Yuma Reservation

"The Colorado River was a lifeline, a wonderful thing. Today it's a small brook. And something's got to happen to keep the river from getting too salty to use." These are the words that Harold Chaipos, the late Quechan elder, used to describe the river that made possible the life of his people (Trimble 1993:410). The Quechan (Yuma), who lived along the Colorado River at its confluence with the Gila River, controlled one of the few Colorado River crossings in the east-west routes, a strategic position that made them important in precontact trade and later in trade and travel conducted by the Spaniards, Mexicans, and Anglos.

The Spaniards, in their effort to secure the Colorado River crossing, began by entertaining four Quechans in Mexico City in 1776–77 (Forbes 1965:201–8). To consolidate Spanish interests, they established two settlements nearby, which the Quechan destroyed in 1781, as the Spaniards grew increasingly arrogant and took Quechan support for granted. Not until 1852 were outsiders able to establish a foothold, when the U.S. Army built Fort Yuma to protect American interests by assuring the growth of steamship and railroad travel in the area, as well as the town of Yuma, Arizona.

During the California gold rush, the Quechan ferried prospectors across the river, but when Anglo competitors put them out of business, they became pilots and woodcutters instead. After 1877, when the completion of the railroad ended the steamship industry, some men found employment as laborers, while women worked as domestic help in Anglo homes.

In 1884 the federal government established a reservation for the Quechan on the west side of the Colorado, but over the next ten years, Anglo settlers became so envious of Quechan farmlands that they persuaded the Quechan to signed a fraudulent "agreement" with the federal government, which promised the Indians irrigation water in return for the cession of land that remained after individual allotments were issued in a local application of the Dawes Severalty Act of 1887 (Bee 1994: 524). This document, on which the signatures of tribal members had either been coerced or forged, resulted in the loss of their most fertile land along the river (ibid., 524).

The proximity of Yuma, Arizona, undermined Quechan traditions, for Anglos appointed Quechan leaders and took their children to boarding school in town, breaking down clan affiliations. Anglo farmers began to encroach on Quechan farmland, shrinking reservation boundaries. By 1910 the best reservation land had been sold, and Quechan farmers had to pay for their irrigation water. Most of the land was leased to non-Indians, and the tribe lived in poverty.

Not until the 1960s, with President Lyndon Johnson's War on Poverty, did money begin to flow into the Quechan community, providing new housing and contributing to economic development. The settlement of a 1965 land claim pro-

Quechan runners, mid-1800s. Courtesy of Arizona Historical Society, No. 9640

vided funding for a tribal council, so that members could work for tribal government full time. The tribal government consists of a seven-member council, with a president and vice president who serve four-year terms, and five members who are elected biennially.

Other successful land-claims settlements followed: in 1978, 25,000 acres were returned to the tribe, and in 1983, 80 percent of a $15 million settlement was distributed among tribal members (Trimble 1993:413–14). In the 1990s tribal enterprises included an irrigation project and a sand-and-gravel operation. The tribe also established the Quechan Paradise Casino and modern recreational vehicle parks for the large numbers of winter visitors who come to the Yuma region from colder climates. For those wanting to learn more about their culture, they built the Fort Yuma Quechan Museum. Hunting is a popular activity, but most of the land on the reservation is allotted to individual families, from whom permission must be granted before visitors may hunt in those areas (Fontana 1999:15).

Quechan tradition lives on in their Memorial Day gathering that honors the dead, as well as in shorter versions of the tribal mourning ceremony, which bereaved families sponsor during the year. At these events, male orators still make speeches and sing sacred song cycles in the native language, and women dance in their brightly colored long dresses and beaded shawls. Eloquent speakers of Quechan are still honored today, for this ability is considered to be a manifestation of their personal dream power.

The Cocopah Reservation

Cocopah Hope Miller refers to the Cocopah homeland as "this land which goes on," saying, "I am here and own this land with my heart" (Trimble 1993:419). The Cocopah have lived in their homeland, the lower Colorado River and its delta, for many centuries. Farthest south on the river, they were probably among the first Native Americans in the Southwest to encounter Europeans. In 1540 Spanish explorer Hernando de Alarcón wrote of seeing 1,000 men at one point and 5,000–6,000 farther on, which indicates how heavily populated the delta must have been at that time (Williams 1975:19–29). The Treaty of Guadalupe Hidalgo in 1848 and the Gadsden Purchase in 1853 divided the Cocopah homeland, leaving some Cocopah families in the United States and others in Mexico.

In 1905 the creation of the Salton Sea destroyed most of the Cocopah Indians' traditional floodwater farming. Anglo farmers had attempted to irrigate the Imperial Valley with a series of canals, but floods in the Colorado River in 1905–7 broke the irrigation levees, inundating the Salton Sink, a salt-covered depression, and forming the Salton Sea, a body of salt water that covered about 450 square miles. Colorado River engineers eventually stopped water from flowing into the Salton Sea, but their dams, canal building, channel construction, and the increasing salinity of the remaining water made impossible the resumption of traditional floodwater agriculture.

Today the Cocopah are split into American and Mexican groups; until U.S. immigration officials stopped their seasonal movement across the border in the 1930s, they had remained in close contact. One band of Cocopah live in Sonora, another in Baja California, while the two American bands live in Somerton, Arizona, where in 1917 Frank Tehanna, a Cocopah leader, pressured the government to establish a reservation.

In 1964 the Arizona Cocopah formed a tribal council and began to build adequate housing, with indoor plumbing and electricity. From a low of 58 people just after World War II, their population has now risen to about 1,000, and in 1985 a land-claims settlement returned 4,000 acres of leasable land (Trimble 1993:417).

The Arizona Cocopah own and operate the Cocopah Casino, the Cocopah Bend RV and Golf Resort, and a tribal museum (Fontana 1999:14). Part of the 22-mile round trip traveled by the Yuma Valley Railway excursion train runs through the Cocopah Reservation; along the route, which follows the Colorado River, visitors can view the desert, wildlife, and produce being grown near the river (ibid.).

One of their traditional plants has drawn the interest of international researchers. Each May the Cocopah rafted to the mouth of the river to collect a halophyte, a wild wheat that thrives on seawater. Today researchers in Australia, Namibia, and Morocco are hybridizing and growing this plant experimentally to see if it could be an important future food source (Williams 1994:121).

Until recently, the Cocopah burned all of a person's belongings when he or she died so that they would accompany the person to the spirit world. They also held a commemorative ceremony the following year to be sure that the dead person would not return to look for anyone or anything. Today funeral and commemorative ceremonies continue to be major events in the Cocopah year, and traditional male singers come great distances to pay their respects and to perform ancient rituals. They still sing the long, "dreamed" cycles of song that recount Cocopah origin stories about the emergence of twin supernatural beings and how the ancestral Cocopah lineages came from totemic creatures, plants, and objects.

The Maricopa: The Gila River and Salt River Reservations

The Maricopa—the Pee-Posh (Piipaash, "the people"), as they call themselves—are an amalgam of River Yuman peoples who began to migrate eastward from the Colorado River before the arrival of Europeans, perhaps in the late thirteenth or early fourteenth century (Harwell and Kelly 1983:74). The first migrants were probably the Cocomaricopa or the Kavelchadom. The Halchidhoma came to the Gila Valley by 1840, joining other Yumans from the Gila Bend area. Between 1820 and 1840 Kahwan families, along with Halchidhoma families, moved into the Gila Valley area near Sacate–Maricopa Wells.

Today, most Maricopas live near Laveen on the Gila River Indian Reservation; these are descendants of the Kavelchadom, Kahwan, and Halyikwamai. The next largest concentration of Maricopa—descendants of the Halchidhoma—live at Lehi on the Salt River Reservation. While sharing their reservations with the Akimel O'odham, with whom they have close relations, both groups of Maricopa have their own unique heritage.

By the mid-nineteenth century, the Maricopa had established a powerful confederacy with the Pima, providing protection from Apache raiders to the U.S. Army, pioneers, ranchers, and prospectors on their way to California; they also supplied them with food-stuffs. In 1863, to ensure the cooperation of the Maricopa and Akimel O'odham, the federal government established the Gila River Indian Reservation. When settlers in Florence, Arizona, upstream from the reservation, diverted the Gila River, many Maricopa moved to present-day Laveen, at the confluence of the Gila and Salt Rivers. At the same time the Maricopa-Halchidhoma moved to modern-day Lehi (near Mesa, Arizona, on the Salt River

Reservation). The Maricopa in these new locations were able to continue farming, while their O'odham neighbors died of thirst and starvation. President Hayes enlarged the Gila River Indian Reservation and established the Salt River Reservation in 1879.

In 1934, under John Collier's Indian Reorganization Act (IRA), the Akimel O'odham and Maricopa established a constitution-based tribal government and seven districts linked by a council. The Maricopa near Laveen and the Maricopa-Halchidhoma at Lehi are represented as districts in tribal councils. (See chapter 5 for more information about the Gila and Salt River Reservations.)

References and Further Reading

The Handbook of North American Indians, vol. 10 (1983), contains chapters about various aspects of Yuman culture.

See also chapter 11 for more sources on the Chemehuevi specifically.

Bean, Lowell, and Sylvia Vane. 1994. "Chemehuevi." In *Native America in the Twentieth Century: An Encyclopedia*, pp. 94–95, ed. Mary Davis. Garland Publishing, New York.

*Bee, Robert. 1963. "Changes in Yuma Social Organization." *Ethnology* 2, no. 2:207–27. [Bee's work provides the best introduction to the Quechan.]

———. 1981. *Crosscurrents along the Colorado: The Impact of Government Policy on the Quechan Indians*. University of Arizona Press, Tucson.

———. 1983. "Quechan." In *Handbook of North American Indians*, vol. 10: *The Southwest*, pp. 86–98.

———. 1994. "Quechan." In *Native America in the Twentieth Century: An Encyclopedia*, pp. 524–25, ed. Mary Davis. Garland Publishing, New York.

Booth, Peter, and Ralph Cameron. 1994. "Pee-posh." In *Native America in the Twentieth Century: An Encyclopedia*, pp. 439–41, ed. Mary Davis. Garland Publishing, New York.

Butler, Elda. 1994. "The Mojave." In *Native America in the Twentieth Century: An Encyclopedia*, pp. 355–57, ed. Mary Davis. Garland Publishing, New York.

Castetter, Edward, and Willis Bell. 1951. *Yuman Indian Agriculture*. University of New Mexico Press, Albuquerque.

Crawford, James M. 1989. *Cocopah Dictionary*. University of California Press, Berkeley.

Daniel, Roger, Sandra Taylor, and Harry Kitano. 1986. *Japanese Americans from Relocation to Redress*. University of Utah Press, Salt Lake City.

Densmore, Frances. 1932. *Yuman and Yaqui Music*. Bureau of American Ethnology Bulletin 110. U.S. Government Printing Office, Washington, D.C.

Dobyns, Henry. 1989. *The Pima-Maricopa*. Chelsea House Publishing, New York.

Dobyns, Henry, Paul Ezell, and Greta Ezell. 1963. "Death of a Society: The Halchidhoma." *Ethnohistory* 10, no. 2:105–61.

Dobyns, Henry, Paul Ezell, Alden Jones, and Greta Ezell. 1957. "Thematic Changes in Yuman Warfare: Cultural Stability and Cultural Change." In *Proceedings of the American Ethnological Society*, pp. 46–71. Seattle.

Drucker, Philip. 1941. "Yuman-Piman." *Anthropological Records* 6, no. 3:19–230. Culture Element Distributions 17. University of California Press, Berkeley.

Ezell, Paul. 1961. *The Maricopas: An Identification from Documentation*. University of Arizona Anthropological Papers 6. University of Arizona Press, Tucson.

Fathauer, George. 1954. "The Structure and Causation of Mohave Warfare." *Southwestern Journal of Anthropology* 10, no. 1:97–118.

Flores, Amelia. 1994. "Colorado River Indian Tribes." In *Native America in the Twentieth Century: An Encyclopedia*, pp. 124–27, ed. Mary Davis. Garland Publishing, New York.

Fontana, Bernard. 1958. "History of the Colorado River Reservation." In *Social and Economic Studies: Colorado River Reservation*, Report No. 2., pp. 1–66. Bureau of Ethnic Research, Dept. of Anthropology, University of Arizona, Tucson.

———. 1963. "The Hopi-Navajo Colony on the Lower Colorado River." *Ethnohistory* 10:163–82.

———. 1999. *A Guide to Contemporary Southwest Indians*. Southwest Parks and Monuments Association, Tucson.

Forbes, Jack. 1965. *Warriors of the Colorado: The Yumas of the Quechan Nation and Their Neighbors*. University of Oklahoma, Norman.

———. 1973. "Nationalism, Tribalism, and Self-Determination: Yuman-Mexican Relations, 1821–1848." *Indian Historian* 6, no. 2:18–22.

*Forde, Daryll. 1931. "Ethnography of the Yuma Indians." *University of California Publications in American Archaeology and Ethnology* 28, no 4:83–278. [A pivotal reference on the Quechan (Yuma).]

Fort Mojave Indian Tribe. n.d. Publication, n.p.

Fradkin, Philip. 1981. *A River No More: The Colorado River and the West*. Alfred A. Knopf, New York.

Gifford, Edward. 1926. "Yuma Dreams and Omens." *Journal of American Folk-lore* 39, no. 151:58–69.

———. 1933. "The Cocopa." *University of California Publications in American Archaeology and Ethnology* 31, no. 5:257–334.

Graham, Edward. 1975. "Yuman Warfare: An Analysis of Ecological Factors from Ethnohistorical Sources." In *War, Its Causes and Correlates*, pp. 451–62, ed. Martin Nettleship et al. Mouton Publishers, The Hague.

Hackenburg, Robert, and Bernard Fontana. 1974. *Aboriginal Land Use and Occupancy of the Pima-Maricopa Indians*. 2 vols. Garland Publishing, New York.

Harrington, John. 1908. "A Yuma Account of Origins." *Journal of American Folk-lore* 21, no. 82:324–48.

———. 1929. "The Mojave." *El Palacio* 27, nos. 1–7:16–19.

Harwell, Henry, and Marsha Kelly. 1983. "Maricopa." In *Handbook of North American Indians*, vol. 10: *The Southwest*, pp. 71–85.

Helliker, Kevin. 1988. "Showdown in Parker." *Arizona Trend* 2, no. 6:35–39.

*Hinton, Leanne, and Lucille Watahomigie, eds. 1984. *Spirit Mountain: An Anthology of Yuman Story and Song*. Sun Tracks and University of Arizona Press, Tucson. [This collection of stories and songs in Yuman languages with English translations provides a rich introduction to Yuman oral literature and culture.]

Kelley, Matt. 1998. "Tribal Plan to Sell Water Threatens Arizona." *Arizona Daily Star*, 18 October, pp. A1, A7.

Kelly, Isabel, and Catherine Fowler. 1986. "Southern Paiute." In *Handbook of North American Indians*, vol. 11: *The Great Basin*, pp. 368–97.

Kelly, William. 1949. "Cocopa Attitudes and Practices with Respect to Death and Mourning." *Southwestern Journal of Anthropology* 5, no. 2: 151–64.

———. 1977. *Cocopa Ethnography*. Anthropological Papers of the University of Arizona 29. University of Arizona Press, Tucson.

Key, Harold. 1970. "A Mohave Cremation." *Kiva* 36, no. 1:23–38.

Klasky, Philip M. 1999. "A Victory in the Making," *Winds of Change* 14, no. 3:56–58.

Kroeber, Alfred. 1902. "Preliminary Sketch of the Mohave Indians." *American Anthropologist* 4, no. 2:276–85.

———. 1925. *Handbook of the Indians of California*. Bureau of American Ethnology, Bulletin 78. Washington, D.C.

———. 1948. "Seven Mohave Myths." *University of California Anthropological Records* 11:1–70.

Kroeber, Clifton, and Bernard Fontana. 1973. *A Mohave War Reminiscence, 1854–1880*. University of California Press, Berkeley.

*———. 1992 [1986]. *Massacre on the Gila: An Account of the Last Major Battle between American Indians, with Reflections on the Origin of War*. University of Arizona Press, Tucson. [This examination of the decisive 1857 battle between the Maricopas and Pimas (Akimel O'odham) against the Quechans and Mojaves is rich with details about these tribes in war and peace.]

LaCourse, Richard. 1980. "A Preliminary History of the Colorado River Peoples." *Manataba Messenger* 26 (September):6.

*Laird, Carobeth. 1976. *The Chemehuevis*. Malki Museum Press, Banning, Calif. [The key ethnography for the tribe.]

———. 1984. *Mirror and Pattern: George Laird's World of Chemehuevi Mythology*. Malki Museum Press, Morongo Indian Reservation, Banning, Calif.

Lamphere, Louise. 1983. "Southwestern Ceremonialism." In *Handbook of North American Indians*, vol. 10: *The Southwest*, pp. 743–63.

Martin, Douglas. 1954. *Yuma Crossing*. University of New Mexico Press, Albuquerque.

*McNichols, Charles. 1944. *Crazy Weather*. Macmillan, New York. [Set at the beginning of the twentieth century, this novel is a fine evocation of Mojave life on the river.]

Reid, Jefferson, and Stephanie Whittlesey. 1997. "The Patayan." In *The Archaeology of Ancient Arizona,* pp. 111–30. University of Arizona Press, Tucson.

Roth, George. 1976. "Incorporation and Changes in Ethnic Structure: The Chemehuevi Indians." Ph.D. diss., Northwestern University.

Sheridan, Thomas E., and Nancy J. Parezo. 1996. *Paths of Life: American Indians of the Southwest and Northern Mexico.* University of Arizona Press, Tucson.

Smith, Gerald A. 1977. *The Mojave Indians.* San Bernardino County Museum Association, Bloomington, Calif.

Spier, Leslie. 1933. *Yuman Tribes of the Gila River.* University of Chicago Press, Chicago.

———. 1936. *Cultural Relations of the Gila River and Lower Colorado Tribes.* Yale University Press, New Haven.

Stewart, Kenneth. 1947. "An Account of the Mohave Mourning Ceremony." *American Anthropologist* 49, no. 1:146–48.

———. 1966. "Mohave Indian Agriculture." *Masterkey* 40, no. 1:4–15.

———. 1983. "Yumans: Introduction" and "Mohave." In *Handbook of North American Indians,* vol. 10: *The Southwest,* pp. 1–3, 55–70.

Stoffle, Richard, Kristine Jones, and Henry Dobyns. 1995. "Direct European Immigrant Transmission of Old World Pathogens to Numic Indians during the Nineteenth Century." *American Indian Quarterly* 19, no. 2:181–203.

Stone, Connie. 1981. "Economy and Warfare along the Lower Colorado River." *Anthropological Research Papers* 24:183–97.

Taylor, Edith, and William Wallace. 1947. "Mohave Tattooing and Face-Painting." *Masterkey* 21, no. 6:183–91.

Trimble, Stephen. 1993. *The People.* School of American Research Press, Santa Fe.

Williams, Anita Alvarez De. 1983. "Cocopa." In *Handbook of North American Indians,* vol. 10: *The Southwest,* pp. 99–112.

*———. 1994. "Cocopah." In *Native America in the Twentieth Century: An Encyclopedia,* pp. 120–22, ed. Mary Davis. Garland Publishing, New York. [Williams's work provides the best background available on Cocopah culture and life.]

Part 3   Foraging and Farming

Havasu Falls, Havasupai Reservation, 1998. Author photograph

Chapter 8 The Upland Yumans

A sense of belonging to the land on which they live, land given them by the Creator, has sustained the Pai (Hualapai [Walapai] and Havasupai) and Yavapai through time. Their presence in the Southwest is indeed ancient—their Patayan ancestors lived on and near the Colorado River far back into prehistoric times—and for many centuries these groups, known collectively as the Upland Yumans, have occupied nearly one-third of present-day Arizona. Their original territory was vast, covering the northwestern portion of the state from the Colorado River on the north and west, south to the Gila River, and as far east as San Francisco Peaks. The Upland Yumans held one of the largest and most ecologically diversified territories in the Southwest at the time of contact. Bands traveled from mountain slopes covered with pine forests through plateau lands of sage and juniper down to simmering deserts.

The Upland Yumans carried on the trading traditions of their Patayan ancestors and were a vital link in a far-reaching network that connected the Indians of the Pacific Coast to the Eastern Pueblos. Cherum, a Hualapai headman of the 1850s and 1860s, traded Pai buckskins for Hopi and Zuni textiles, which he exchanged for horses from the Mojaves. Next he traded the horses for guns and ammunition from the Southern Paiutes, who had obtained these firearms from Utah Mormons (Dobyns and Euler 1970:23). The Hualapai also bartered deer and mountain sheep skins for crops grown by their Havasupai relatives (Kroeber 1935:64–66). They traded meat for corn, pumpkins, and beans raised by the

Mojave, when they were at peace with them. Hualapai basketry, dried mescal, and especially the rich red ochre pigment they gathered from a cave in Diamond Creek Canyon in Middle Mountain band territory (Kristine Jones in McGuire 1983:33) were highly valued commodities. Hualapai women wove many forms of basketry, including large burden or firewood baskets, water bottles smeared with red paint and piñon pitch, conical seed-gathering baskets, trays for winnowing and parching seeds, and stone-boiling containers (Kroeber 1935:79–86). The Yavapai traded dried mescal and meat for corn with the Akimel O'odham, and baskets, buckskin, and mescal to the Tohono O'odham; some also traded buckskin, baskets, and ram's horns with the Hopi. All groups traded with the Navajo for their fine blankets.

The Upland Yuman tribes share what is essentially the same culture. The differences among these groups seem to be the result of adaptation to different ecological zones and differential culture contacts. The Hualapai traded with the Mojave, and the Southeastern Yavapai shared matrilineal kinship and basket styles with the Western Apache. The Havasupai have long been friends, allies, and trading partners with the Hopi, whose annual salt pilgrimage to the Grand Canyon brought them to Havasupai territory. During times of drought, Hopi families came to live with the Havasupai, and during the winter months, some Havasupai families went to live with the Hopis of Third Mesa. To bring rain and ensure the fertility of their crops, the Havasupai performed katsinalike dances until about 1900, when they were confined year round to their reservation in Cataract Canyon (Schwartz 1983:19).

Although the Havasupai and Hualapai are politically separate groups today—the result of U.S. government policy—they are ethnically one people, the Pai, or Pa'a, who continue to intermarry and to speak variants of the same language. Until the Pai were confined to reservations, their people belonged to one of three subtribes, and the Havasupai (the Havasooa Pa'a, or "Blue-Green Water People") were a band in one of these subtribes. After the Mexican War, Anglos generally approached Pai country from Mojave territory along the Colorado River. Entering through the westernmost reaches of Pai territory, the first band they encountered was the Hualapai Mountain Band, the Pine-Clad Mountain People (Wala Pa'a), which led them to extend this name, Hualapai, to other Pai groups. Despite their shared ancestry, the Pai and the Yavapai were traditional enemies. The Yavapai, who lived south of the Pai in central and west-central Arizona, had a territorial range of approximately 10 million acres, which included desert basin and range, central mountains, and portions of the Colorado Plateau.

The Upland Yumans speak the Pai or Upland Yuman language, one of the four subgroups of the Yuman language family. The languages spoken by the Havasupai and the Hualapai are so alike that they have only minor differences, and Yavapai can be understood quite easily by speakers of both Havasupai and Hualapai.

The Havasupai

July 1998

Echoing off the red cliffs of the steep-sided canyon, the whinny of a horse breaks the stillness of the morning. Sunlight creeps down the western wall, illuminating the tops of sacred Wii'gleva, the twin towers of stone that watch over the Havasupai people. A faint breeze stirs the leaves of a cottonwood tree whose soothing green foliage contrasts sharply with the terra-cotta canyon walls. Birds sing and chatter as the village of Supai begins to come alive.

I open my door at Havasupai Lodge to discover three horses grazing a few feet away. Someone left the gate open last night, allowing them access to the grassy quadrangle. An enterprising young mare overturns a trash can, nosing through the refuse, delighted with the variety she finds. The other two are systematically munching the grassy lawn, seasoning their feast periodically with a rose from the bush the gardener was tending so lovingly yesterday. I talk softly to the nearest one, who begins to nuzzle my hand, hoping for a handout. He has a kind of tough, cocky attitude that is hard to resist.

In the distance, the bark of a dog reverberates off the canyon walls, and a horse chimes in, neighing in response to the whinnying of a nearby mustang. I hear the stamping of hooves and see a cloud of dust rise as several horses run through the town snorting and whickering. A donkey brays sharply in loud nasal tones, his harsh, breathy cry echoing in the still air.

Wii'gleva, stone pillars that are the caretakers of the Havasupai, Supai, 1998. Author photograph

The aroma of frying sausage fills the air, and a young man shuffles to the door officiously to turn the sign on the door of the cafe, unlocking the door. From a house on the other side of the grassy helipad come the muted strains of an electric guitar. Across from the cafe, a young man with waist-length hair, a Walkman clipped to his belt, and headphones in his ears, looks over a "packers needed" notice posted on the door of the general store, while an old man sits down on the bench in front of the store. Soon his friends will join him to exchange news and to watch the parade of weary hikers begin to drift into town, drawn on by the sweet reward of Havasu Falls' turquoise waters.

Navajo Falls, Havasu Falls, and Mooney Falls are strung out along the creek beyond the village. The tribe takes its name from this water: *ha* (water), *vasu* (blue-green), and *pai* (people). Its color comes from a high concentration of lime, which also creates travertine terraces in pools below the falls, and the mist and spray from the plummeting water also deposit lime on the cliff walls in flaring aprons of travertine.

Gazing up at the canyon walls, still untouched by the direct rays of the sun, I find it hard to believe that the outside world exists. Yet less than twenty-four hours ago, we were on the canyon rim, checking in with officials and waiting in the shade of the tribal trailer to descend the trail with our horse packer. Delayed by the tardy tourists who were riding his horses out, our Havasupai horse packer arrived around noon, and we set off under a blazing sun. His mustangs, Toy and Little Mary, easily meandered down the initial 1.25 miles of steep switchbacks. We trusted their surefootedness, rationalizing that they did not want to plummet over the side of the Grand Canyon any more than we did. Fortunately, this proved to be true.

After the switchbacks, we reached the red-rock inner gorge, where we trotted along a sandy wash for most of the remaining 6.75 miles. Debris on the trail told its own story: an abandoned ore cart and a rusted wheelbarrow spoke of past mining efforts, while a plastic Gatorade bottle and a thick wool sock bespoke more recent events. We came upon a British family resting against boulders, beneath a shady ledge. Around the next bend, three sun-burned teenagers in tank tops and shorts staggered beneath the weight of their packs.

The first sign that we were nearing our destination was the crystalline blue-green water of Havasu Creek, where we stopped to water our horses. Less than a mile later, we passed the rodeo grounds on the outskirts of town: Hualapai Trail had become Main Street, a dusty tree-lined lane. Soon we were riding through the town square, where elders sat on a bench in front of the general store beneath a single shady cottonwood. There they exchanged news while they watched young men ride into town, tying up horse and mule trains at the hitching post in front of the store to unload supplies.

Horses are the lifeblood of the Havasupai: they bring tourists and their gear, haul supplies, and transport the U.S. mail, which leaves the village postmarked, "The Mule Train Mail Havasupai Indian Reservation." Nearly every family is involved with horses and tourism. Men lead pack trains or maintain the horse and hiking trails that are periodically washed out by summertime flash floods, while women work in the cafe, the twenty-four-room lodge, or the tourism office. Supai has no paved streets or parking lots, nor does it need any, for the only motorized vehicles are the tribe's tractor, backhoe, fire truck, and a few three-wheelers used by community health workers. Nearly every house has several horses grazing in its front yard, and children ride bareback with ease at an early age.

U.S. Post Office sign, Supai, 1998. Author photograph

The tourist boom began with an *Arizona Highways* article in 1963, and by 1975 tourism had reached 10,000 annually (Trimble 1993:218). Today, about 25,000 visitors descend each year (Kammer 1998:T-1). Guests must make advance reservations by phone or mail with the Tourist Office or lodge before embarking and pay a $15 entry fee per person.

Although life in Supai may seem serenely sublime to outsiders, the reality is considerably less idyllic. Agriculture, once the main occupation of the tribe, today only supplements the income derived from tourism and some leasing of grazing land. Tourists bring in hundreds of thousands of dollars in income for Supai, but families involved in packing must also pack in feed, hay, and salt for their horses. And tourism provides only seasonal employment, for once the tourist season ends, most households become single-income families forced to rely on a salary derived from a job at the school or in federal and tribal administration. Nearly everyone lives in the canyon year-round.

Supai is a study in contrasts: reggae music booms through an open bedroom window, while in the town center the Guardians of the Grand Canyon are practicing their dance steps for the forthcoming Peach Festival. Some Havasupais never leave the canyon; others keep a car at the parking lot at Hualapai Hilltop and make their grocery runs to Kingman, a two-hour drive away. Most leave every few months to shop, see doctors and dentists, and visit friends and family. Younger people may go out every couple of weeks. Several families have satellite dishes, and most households have VCRs. One piece of equipment from the outside remains controversial—the camera. Most people do not like having their picture taken, especially when the photographer does not bother to ask them. A Havasupai in a Bob Marley yarn beret told me that recently a woman sold T-shirts with silkscreened photos of children whose pictures she had taken without permission. James Uqualla Jr., former Havasupai chairman, explained, "We become hosts for the people who . . . are coming into our living room. . . . You have to make it clear that you are not an attraction but the caretakers of this gorgeous place in the canyon" (Trimble 1993:220).

Despite the enchantment of its turquoise waters and red cliffs, Supai, as a year-round home, became a prison, especially to a people accustomed to leading a dual life as farmers *and* plateau people. Although today identified with Havasu Canyon, the Havasupai lived in winter homes on the plateau until 1882, when government officials restricted them to the canyon year-round. The canyon that summer visitors consider "a landlocked Polynesia" becomes a wintry prison when the lack of sunlight stops all agriculture from November to March, and the canyon is transformed "from a lush oasis to a barren place of confinement" (Hirst 1985:10).

In winter the canyon is a far different place from the sunny oasis tourists come to enjoy. Then the sun does not clear the canyon walls until 10:00 or 10:30 and disappears by 3:00 or 3:30. The humidity makes the cold penetrate one's body, and the creek, which stays at a constant 70°, steams in the bitingly cold morning. The birds whose songs fill the summer mornings are gone; only the ravens remain to perch on fence posts and on the bare branches that scratch the sky. Snow, which covers the plateau, becomes a mere drizzle by the time it reaches the warmer air in the bottom of the canyon; the colder air also traps the smoke of cottonwood fires, making it level out at 50 feet and spread over the canyon floor. Originally the canyon floor was covered only sparsely with mesquite, desert ironwood, and willow, but once they were no longer allowed to live in their winter homes on the plateau, the people had to plant and tend cottonwood like a crop for fence posts and firewood (Hirst 1985:11–12). In the early 1970s harsh winters and inadequate generator capacity often left families in darkness and cold for hours, even days at a time; in 1973 Supai was isolated for over a month, during which time food and the fuel for the village generators ran out (ibid., 13–14).

Origins

Havasupai tradition tells of Yuman migrations from Moon Mountain, near present-day Blythe, California, on the Colorado River, to Matwidita Canyon northwest of Peach Springs, where a dispute sent groups in different directions (Hirst 1985:29–30). The people who continued to walk toward the sunrise came to Havsuwa (Havasu Creek), where they remained for many generations together with another people until the resources of the canyon could no longer support their growing numbers. When a large group, led by Huug Mata (a Pueblo mudhead), left, one couple did not want to leave and looked back as they climbed. Turning to stone, they became Wii'gleva. There they stand today as pillars of stone that look down at their beloved canyon as caretakers of the Havasupai.

One of the most sacred places to the Havasupai is Red Buttes, about 15 miles south of Grand Canyon Village. Very long ago, at the time when the great flood covered the earth, the people put a small girl in a cottonwood log and blocked the ends with pitch to save her. They also placed food, water, birds, and animals inside the log with the girl and instructed her to look for San Francisco Peaks so that she could find her way. After the water drowned all the people, the girl emerged from the log at Red Buttes, the place "where our heart is," the place where the Havasupai were born as a people (Purtesoy 1998).

Havasupai Aboriginal Culture

Until their year-round confinement in the canyon, the Havasupai roamed across the vast Coconino Plateau along the Grand Canyon's southern rim as far south as present-day Flagstaff and Williams, covering an area some 90 miles wide by 75 miles long (Spier 1928:91). The Havasupai ranged through a wider elevation span than any other Southwestern group, for they spent summer on the well-watered farmland of Havasu

Creek, some 5,300 feet below the rim of the Grand Canyon, and in the fall they hunted at 12,000 feet on the upper slopes of San Francisco Peaks, the Havasupai "Center of the World."

Subsistence and Material Culture

As passionately as the Havasupai loved their canyon, "the tang of autumn in the air turned their thoughts to a winter home on the mesa, and started them packing their possessions with a happy abandon. All summer they had planned for this—harvesting, preserving their food, and setting aside a portion to take with them" to the plateau, where they would have "the full sweep of the vaulted sky above, with endless miles in which to wander," wrote an observer in 1900 whom Flora Iliff quoted in her ethnography of the Havasupai (1954:200–201).

So important was their autumn return to the open expanses of the plateau that the Havasupai marked this time as the beginning of their year. Mid-October found families returning to their semi-permanent camps scattered over the surrounding plateau. Each family had customary locations where they wintered, and often several families settled within a short distance of each other. From these camps of conical huts covered with brush and earth, individuals or groups of men from several households went off to hunt deer, antelope, and rabbit.

In the fall families gathered the piñon crop, which in favorable years played an important role in the Havasupai economy. They also gathered the nuts of the yellow pine, wild walnuts, and juniper berries. In the spring, women collected greens, such as amaranth, thistles, desert plume, wild rhubarb, watercress, and desert trumpet (Whiting 1985:52–53). Families lived on the wild plant foods and crops they had preserved for winter use. When food ran low, they returned to their fields and storehouses, which were small walled granaries in the rock cliffs of the canyon.

During the fall and winter, some families traveled east to spend a month or so with the Hopi, helping them harvest their crops and visiting with other Pueblos. The Hopi held the Havasupai in special esteem, calling them Co'onin and including a Co'onin (Supai) Katsina in their pantheon, who bears a stylized resemblance to the Havasupai in traditional ceremonial dress. Specific Havasupai and Hopi families maintained close relationships year after year but seldom intermarried because of their different patterns of postmarital residence. Although a newly married Havasupai couple initially stayed with the wife's people, they eventually settled among the husband's family following Yuman custom, while among the Hopi a couple lived with the wife's parents. If a Havasupai and a Hopi married, one spouse would have to give up his or her tradition in the choice of where to live (Hirst 1985:34–35). The Zuni also had cordial relations with the Havasupai, though not so close as those of the Hopi; Cushing (1965 [1882]:362–74) reported that the Zuni called the Havasupai Kuhni (Little Brothers). Other families wandered west to winter with the Hualapai, where they sometimes met Paiute from the north and Mojave from the Lower Colorado. Their relationships with these two groups were often hostile, except when sponsored by the Hualapai (Whiting 1985:11).

The relative contribution of agricultural products varied from family to family and from year to year, and when both agricultural produce and wild food supplies were in short supply, some families went to live with Hopi or Hualapai families. When there was an abundance of easily harvested wild seeds and game, the Havasupai neglected or stored agricultural produce; Whiting observed that they considered farming to be a supplement to their foraging way of life (1985:27, 34).

In early spring families moved back into the canyon to repair their summer homes and prepare their fields for planting. In April or May they irrigated by flooding one section after another, planting corn two days after the flooding (Spier 1928). In historic times peaches, apricots, figs, and sunflowers were added to their traditional crops of corn, beans, and squash. By June families began to harvest the corn they had planted in mid-April, and by fall they had harvested and preserved by drying the rest of their crops and many kinds of wild plant foods. This included mesquite that was found near the village, and mescal, which grew along the rim of the canyon.

The Havasupai needed dry, light foods that could be stored in a small space and transported long distances because they had to pack most of it out to the plateau. So much effort was involved in the preparation of mescal in the spring that entire families would move into the upper branches of Cataract Canyon, where century plants (*Agave utahensis*) were abundant. Alfred F. Whiting (1985:48–50) gave the following account of how the Havasupai processed mescal. First, men gathered firewood and prepared the roasting pit in sandy soil (gravel allowed too much steam to escape). The women collected mescal heads by inserting chisel-pointed sticks, 2–3 feet long, at the base of the plant. Pounding the stick with a rock loosened the head, which they then trimmed of its leaves, freeing the head, which they brought back to the fire-pit area. The pit, some 4–6 feet across and 4 feet deep, was filled with brush and wood to about 4 feet above the ground. After layering stones over the pile, they lit the fire and let it burn down for about an hour or two; men then tamped down the hot rocks with poles, and women covered the rocks with grass. Each family placed the mescal heads they had collected in their pie-shaped section of the pit. After covering the pile with more grass, and a layer of dirt 6 inches deep, the mescal was allowed to cook for 12–48 hours. Once it had been cooked, the mescal was piled outside the pit. Women sliced the core of the freshly baked heads and dried it in the sun. They also mashed the cooked heads with stones and spread the mescal out on drying racks to make mescal mats, which they folded into convenient widths for storage and transportation while they were still pliable. None of the other foods demanded as much processing as mescal.

Women also dried and stored such wild foods as prickly pear fruit, old-world figs, the ripe fruits of the broad-leaved yucca, and mesquite, and such cultivated food plants as melons, squash, peach, and corn (ibid., 48).

Havasupai women were known for the fine baskets they wove in both twined and twilled techniques. Tourists in the Grand Canyon appreciated the quality of Havasupai basketry, and in the 1930s some thirty weavers were creating some of their most beautiful work. Only a few women continue this craft today.

Havasupai Social and Political Organization

With only 200 members in their village in 1858 (Ives 1861), the Havasupai had little need for rigid political organization. Leadership took the form of advice and persuasion, without any true authority or power. The primary qualities valued in a leader were bravery in war, wisdom, dignity, and good temper. Instead of formal status positions, individual achievement was the basis of ranking for the head chief and leaders considered to be of lesser prestige. Men discussed and decided most issues informally inside the sweatlodge rather than by holding any kind of formal council meeting.

In contrast to other Upland Yumans, the Havasupai, because of their greater reliance on agriculture, had a slightly more structured system of inheritance to determine the ownership of land. They still traced kinship bilaterally, but the title to farmland usually belonged to men, with all sons sharing in the inheritance. If a family failed to cultivate a plot for a few years, the rights to the land reverted to the community and another household could then lay claim to the land (Schwartz 1983:17). Women held no property.

The Havasupai were the largest Pai band. Each nuclear or extended family worked and lived together as a unit; over time, the composition of this unit changed. Most newly married couples lived with the wife's parents (matrilocality) for a brief period before settling with the husband's parents (patrilocality).

Havasupai Religion

Religious activities were in the hands of different types of shamans who controlled the weather, ensured hunting success, and treated illness. Before extended hunting expeditions, a game shaman sang special songs designed to quiet deer and to prevent them from running when hunters approached; such songs told the deer that the hunters were sorry for killing them but needed them to assuage their hunger.

For the Upland Yumans, as for the River Yumans, dreaming was essential to the process of becoming a practitioner, for the shaman learned the songs he needed from his dreams. Each curing shaman possessed a spirit that had come to him in a dream; it was this spirit that the shaman dispatched to discover the cause of the patient's illness so that he could treat it. In addition to the general curing shaman, there were those who specialized in treating wounds or fractures, and one type of shaman specialized in curing the bites of snakes, scorpions, and black widow spiders.

Sorcery, ghosts, spirits, harmful dreams, and ill-intentioned shamans could cause illness. To treat illness, the shaman sang all night over the patient, while he sent his spirit into the patient to seek out the cause of illness. After he had diagnosed the cause, the shaman often made a cut with an obsidian or flint blade and sucked the afflicted area. Another form of treatment involved exhorting the malevolent spirit to leave the patient in peace.

The people held a round dance each fall at harvest time to bring rain and prosperity. Their major ceremony, the harvest festival, was as much a social gathering as a religious activity, for the Havasupai invited Hopis, Hualapais, and Navajos to visit, feast, and barter during the two to three days of the event

In the Yuman tradition, elders exhorted the crowd on the right way to live, and fiery orators continue to address their people today. "It's breathtaking to listen to a traditional orator speak. You hear that oratory every occasion that there's a public meeting," said former tribal chairman James Uqualla (Trimble 1993:223).

Each person is believed to possess a soul in his heart; this soul leaves the body during dreams and at death, when it journeys to the land of the dead in the sky (Schwartz 1983:19; Spier 1928). Like their River Yuman relatives, the Havasupai traditionally cremated their dead and destroyed the personal property of the deceased.

Havasupai History: The Anglo-American Period

Unlike the other Upland Yumans, the Havasupai were not forced to flee or fight for their land. Protected in their isolated area deep in the Grand Canyon, they were not defeated but did lose most of their land—including their fields at Moenkopi near Tuba City—to Mormons and Navajos. In the early 1880s government officials, who did not understand the importance of their winter hunting-and-gathering territory, restricted the Havasupai to a 518-acre parcel of land in Cataract Canyon.

The Havasupai agreed to this small area after hearing Hualapai accounts of their forced removal to La Paz and living in dread of a similar exile being forced upon them. Many families, however, continued to winter in their old homes on the plateau, although hunting became increasingly difficult because of the presence of herds of cattle and flocks of sheep, as well as the influx of prospectors, settlers, and tourists. Once railroad land was released for homestead and mineral rights on odd-numbered sections, in the late 1880s, the Havasupai "found themselves adrift in a sea of hatred and rejection from their own land" (Hirst 1985:54).

Malnutrition from the loss of game and wild plants made the Havasupai even more susceptible to disease. With very little natural immunity to European diseases, many Havasupai died from a wave of smallpox, measles, and influenza that swept through their population in the 1880s. By 1890 the Havasupai and the Hualapai believed that their gods had deserted them. In this time of despair, the message of Wovoka, the Paiute prophet, reached Pai country. Wovoka's message held that by performing the Ghost Dance, Indian people could contact their dead loved ones, bringing them back to life, wiping out the whites, and restoring the earth to its natural balance. By 1889 Indian people from nearly all areas of the West were sending emissaries to bring back Wovoka's message. The following year, alarmed by false reports of a new "Indian uprising," U.S. troops massacred several hundred Sioux encamped at Wounded Knee Creek because of their participation in this movement. In the spring of 1889 the Hualapai held their first Ghost Dance, and in early 1891 the Havasupai held a four-day Ghost Dance in Cataract Canyon, which was witnessed by several Hopi traders (Hirst 1985:56). Although the Hualapai lost interest in the movement, the Havasupai continued the Ghost Dance practice into the early years of the twentieth century.

Some Havasupai continued to winter in their old homes on the plateau until finally, in the 1920s, Grand Canyon park rangers broke up nearly all the winter camps. When the Grand Canyon National Park was established, much of the Havasupai traditional land was lost, including the area known as Indian Gardens. In 1975 they were given back 185,000 acres of their homeland, as well as exclusive use rights to 95,300 acres in Grand Canyon National Park. However, the federal government has placed significant restrictions on how they may use the 185,000 acres, restricting the use of this land primarily to grazing, which can bring in no more than $100,000 a year. They are not allowed to develop any tourist enterprises on the plateau. Significantly, the government did not place similar restrictions on the uranium mining company that has been allowed to develop an operation upstream from the Havasupai.

The general public became aware of the poverty of the Havasupai when tourism brought large numbers of people to the canyon in the 1960s. During this decade, the tribe finally received power lines, a water system, new housing, a new store, the tribal cafe, and tribal offices.

In 1939 the Havasupai adopted a tribal constitution. The seven-member Havasupai Tribal Council is elected for two years, and the council selects the chair and vice chair from their numbers. Supai has a Head Start program and an elementary school with a bilingual program. Once students are ready to attend high school, they must leave the reservation, often to attend government boarding schools as far away as Oregon and California. However, their land and their language bring most Havasupai home again. In 1997 the population numbered 658, with an unemployment rate of 10.7 percent (Arizona Department of Commerce).

Contemporary Issues

Reggae

July 1998

The sun has just gone down, streaking the sky with red clouds and staining the cliffs with crimson. Sitting on the deck of the Havasupai Lodge, I am savoring the stillness and enjoying the sounds of the village winding down for the day: muted laughter inside houses, horses whinnying to each other from front yards, birds chattering as they go to nest. Suddenly, ripping through the peaceful quiet comes the boom of a CD player reverberating off the walls of the canyon. I immediately think, "Oh no! This is just what I came down here to escape. Not here, too!"

But after a few minutes, curiosity overcomes me, and I decide to investigate. All I can hear is the bass vibrating through my body, and I want to know exactly what the music might be. It seems to be emanating from a nearby house, so I simply follow the sound along the embankment of a wash where a trio of little girls are pulling at the branches of a mesquite tree. An eight-year-old turns to flash me a shy smile.

The full sound is now clearly audible, and I can identify the unmistakable, rousing rhythm of the reggae beat. Of course, it would be reggae, the Jamaican music first popularized by the late Bob Marley and his Wailers, the music of choice among so many young Southwestern Indians, Hopis, Hualapais, Tohono O'odham, and Havasupais.

Havasupai homes, Supai, 1998. Author photograph

The joyous beat makes me think of "Reggae Inna Hopiland." In that chapter of his book *Light of the Feather,* educator Mick Fedullo explained that reggae appeals to Native Americans because its lyrics "constantly assert the themes of standing up for one's rights even under oppression; of holding fast to the ideals of love, hope, and peace; of stoutly defending one's religious point of view; and of steadfastly refusing to abandon true cultural roots" (1992:83). It is easy to see why such music not only resonates so deeply with Native Americans but also transcends cultural boundaries, connecting to the musical fiber that is in us all.

By now I am caught up in the irresistible rhythm: my body is humming with the booming beat that cruises through my bloodstream. Once she sees my smile, the little girl lets her grin widen until it reaches from ear to ear. She hands me a mesquite pod like the one she pops into her mouth. When I ask about the music, she glances toward the frame house, where music and curtains are flowing out through an open bedroom window. Her brother, a bare-chested teenager, his long hair held back in a ponytail, has to turn down the volume before he can hear me. He leans out to tell me we're listening to Israel Vibrations performing "Free to Move." I give him a thumbs-up and tell him what good music it is, which makes him smile. Turning to go, I think to myself, how appropriate! These words not only offer hope for the present, but also speak to the time before the Havasupai were imprisoned year-round in the canyon, the old days when they also were free, to roam the surrounding plateau.

Uranium Mining

Just after breakfast the next morning, I meet with Matthew Purtesoy, who runs the tribal museum and is working to keep Havasupai culture alive. When I ask him what he considers to be the biggest issue facing the Havasupai today, he immediately responds, "Uranium mining. A mining company is ready to begin mining uranium up top as soon as the price of uranium goes up again." The tribe fears contamination from a spill of radioactive waste, which could easily be swept down into Havasu Creek with a flash flood of sufficient magnitude. "All it takes is for it to drain into the water and it'll seep out in the canyon. What we need is for people to write to their congressmen to stop the mining from happening," he adds.

"The place where they're planning to mine is especially sacred to us. We call Red Butte 'where our heart is' because in our creation story, that's where the little girl in the cottonwood log came out after the flood." Matthew goes on to discuss the spiritual practices of his people.

We believe it's all inside each person to carry their own spirit. It's handed down from parents to their children. Each person prays in their own way in the canyon.

In the old days, people used to carry offerings up into the rocks, like a spear or an arrowhead or a gourd. Maybe a piece of cloth or some corn. There's a rebirth of Havasupai tradition going on now, more interest from the young people. We have several sweat lodges near the creek; the sweat lodge is the root of our spirituality. That is where we sing special sweat house songs, mostly for healing.

After I leave Purtesoy, I go into the cafe to study the mural with text that he helped compose. Depicted are day and night, with a Havasupai basket, Havasu Falls, and Wii'gleva. The accompanying text reads:

The circle is a sacred symbol to our civilization. In this mural the circle is depicted as a woven basket. The basket is the most prevalent art form of the Havasupai. The circular basket invites us to focus on the waterfall within its center. The waterfall represents life and is shown here housing the spirit of our ancient ones. It is through the waters and the rocks that the ancestral sprits speak to us. The rocks of *Wii'gleva* are regarded with respect and are the guardians over our village.

The night to day transition represents transitions in life. We begin in a stage of innocence and ignorance. We go through the stages of introspection, illumination, and wisdom. If our focus is on giving as the waters freely give, we will gain clear vision as the eagle.

The previous afternoon I had found Purtesoy in his studio with several other men, painting wooden pieces for use in their performance in the August Peach Festival. I asked him about the Havasupai dance group he directs, the Guardians of the Grand Canyon. He replied:

In 1994 we only had eight members, but now we're up to twenty-five. We're bringing back the Supai Katsina who is very important to our culture. Prophecy says Supai will come back to the village when the world is being overcome by floods, fires, and earthquakes. He'll help save all people, the animals, plants, and water, too. So we dance to satisfy nature and to make her feel good and happy. To let the Creator know we're breathing air and living and to give thanks for all that. That's why we named our dance group the Guardians of the Grand Canyon. To protect the canyon from things like uranium mining. It's up to all of us to take care of the canyon. It's in our hands.

The Peach Festival

Celebrated today in August so that the children can be reminded of the old ways before they leave for boarding school, the Peach Festival has long been the highlight of the Havasupai year. In 1998 the Havasupai sent invitations to some twenty-one tribes for the four-day festival, which includes a powwow, a volleyball tournament, jackpot roping, country western dancing, reggae, an all-night traditional circle dance, Supai dances, sweat lodges, and a cultural exchange. One of the annual highlights is the Miss Havasupai contest among eighteen- to twenty-one-year-old girls, who are judged on their ability to perform traditional activities, such as weaving baskets, grinding corn, and dancing and singing in the Havasupai tradition. Another important event is the memorial wake during which Mojave wake songs are sung all night, and then, between 5:00 and 6:00 the following morning, a ramada piled high with gifts and blankets is set on fire, in the Yuman tradition, to honor those who have died.

Water

For the Havasupai water is a force to be reckoned with. The flood of February 1993 caused their creek, which is normally about 30 feet wide and 1 foot deep, to swell to 800 feet wide and 20 feet deep. Rushing through their village with a velocity of 15 feet per second, the water caused extensive damage not only to their utility lines but also to their 500-year-old irrigation system, two pedestrian/equestrian bridges, and the horse/foot trails, the only land access to Supai. The tribe contacted Water Wright Engineers, Inc., from Denver to work with them to rehabilitate the damaged facilities.

Supai's isolation presented unique problems because all materials and equipment had to be packed in by horse or flown in by helicopter. For many items, the cost of transportation was much greater than the cost of the materials themselves. Heavy equipment was not used (to keep costs to a minimum and because of its limited availability), which meant batching concrete by hand and delivering it in a concrete mixing truck. Havasupai workers and their assistants moved boulders weighing as much as 2,000 pounds without heavy equipment.

The Havasupai vice chairwoman, Bernadine Jones, does not hesitate when I ask her to identify the biggest problem facing the tribe today. "Water. Water is critical to our future." Having just hiked up from the three thundering waterfalls, along the steadily flowing stream, I hesitate and ask her to explain. She continues, "They're planning to expand the facilities in the Tusayan area, building more lodges for the Grand Canyon. That will require drilling wells. It's not on tribal land, so we can't do anything about it except to protest. The government hasn't done any impact studies to show how the drilling of wells on the plateau will affect the water down here in Supai. But it's obviously got to have some effect. Who knows, eventually, the Havasupai may have no creek!"

In the version of the Canyon Forest Village Development preferred by the U.S. Forest Service, 48 million gallons of drinking water would be used every year, with almost all of this coming out of Valle, a community about 30 miles south of Grand Canyon National Park that shares an aquifer with the canyon (Bodfield 1998). Although a developer-funded hydrological report maintains that the project would have little impact, other researchers disagree. David Kreamer, a hydrologist at the University of Nevada who has studied the area for fifteen years, says, "I think there's rather compelling evidence that the small springs of the Grand Canyon are connected to the aquifer and have a potential to be seriously impacted by ground-water pumping in the Coconino Plateau" (ibid.). The situation is even more grave than elsewhere in the state because northern Arizona lacks the strict regulations found in Phoenix and Tucson; this means that as soon as developers buy the land, there are no prohibitions to keep them from drilling wells.

Havasupai chairman Lincoln Manakaja, who wants to limit the number of visitors to the Grand Canyon, has pledged to fight attempts to drain more groundwater from the canyon aquifers. "Our Mother's veins are the fractures and faults of the Coconino Plateau, these are the pathways for the water, the lifeblood, to flow for all creatures and plants to survive" (Bodfield 1998:B1).

The Hualapai

July 1998

Billowing, steel-gray storm clouds are beginning to gather over Aubrey Cliffs by the time we reach Peach Springs. The sky had been completely clear earlier that morning when we headed out of Supai. As we rode past the corral full of rodeo cattle herded down into Supai for the Peach Festival, our packer predicted, "It's hotter this morning; it's going to rain."

The ride up and out was much pleasanter than our ride down into the canyon. Our packer traded horses with me, letting me ride his mount, Little John, whose trotting gait—the preferred pace for packers who make the 16-mile round trip from Supai to Hualapai Hilltop and back on a daily basis—was infinitely more comfortable.

Reaching the switchbacks, we slowed our pace and chatted amiably the rest of the way. We asked how many horses he had and were told fifteen. "It's hard to feed them all, so I brand them and turn them loose each fall, recapture them in the spring. Each one goes into a different canyon. There's a canyon with spotted walls, just like the pattern on one of my horses." He shot us a look to see if we were buying what he said, then continued, "There's a stallion who's spotted who lives in that canyon. That's why the mare had a spotted foal after we brought her back in the spring."

Soon we saw Hualapai Hilltop just over the rim, where a couple of tourists stood at the edge of the pavement, pointing their cameras at the string of pack-laden horses meandering along the trail just in front of us. How strange to know that we will be in someone's scrapbook as part of a picturesque vacation to the Grand Canyon.

As beautiful as the canyon was, it was good to see the horizon widen again, and I began to understand some of the exhilaration the Havasupai must have felt each autumn

Hualapai girl, Hualapai Reservation, c. 1985. The caption says, "I am a Hualapai, the northern boundary of my land is in the middle of the Colorado River." Courtesy of Lucille Watahomigie

Nya Hwalbay yivch yu

Haka'a꞉ma yiḟaḏa nya nyimaḏch hamv'okyu

when they left their narrow canyon for the freedom of the plateau. After handclasps and goodbyes, we set off across the rolling sweep of the plateau. Soon we were sailing over the undulating road across a limitless expanse of pale blue-green sage dotted by low juniper and piñon groves.

Turning right onto Route 66, we quickly arrive in Peach Springs, Hualapai tribal capital, where the recently opened Hualapai Lodge provides a delicious lunch of Hualapai tacos. After the meal, I find a pay phone and call Lucille Watahomigie to let her know of our arrival.

I can't help but notice that Peach Springs School is set in a stand of the pine trees that give their name to the Hualapai people. The doors are locked because it is summer vacation, but I spot a janitor mopping the hall floor. As soon as I ask where I can find Lucille Watahomigie, he beams with pride and recognition: ah, yet another educator coming to check out our nationally known program. Although the school seems deserted, it is easy to imagine the halls filled with the laughter of children, for banners in the Hualapai language and children's artwork decorate the walls of the well-kept school.

Following the janitor's directions, we turn into a large room filled with computers, tables, and books. The first person I see is a young woman seated at a long table proofing the pages of a Hualapai dictionary. Hidden behind a bank of computers to her left are two women wearing T-shirts emblazoned with the tribal seal and sitting in front of monitors filled with Hualapai words. Having heard so much about her two decades of inspired and aggressive leadership and the many publications her bilingual/bicultural program has produced, I expect to find a woman well past middle age. The federal government singled out her program as one of the top bilingual curricula in the United States, and Hualapai publications serve as models at numerous reservation schools.

I am surprised to find that one of the youthful women at a computer is Lucille Watahomigie herself. In 1976, after earning her master's degree in education from the University of Arizona and working in teacher training there, she agreed to come home to direct the Bilingual/Bicultural Program for her tribe. With colleagues Philbert Watahomigie and Malinda Powskey, she built a program whose success has drawn native people from as far away as Canada to gather ideas for their own programs. By using modern technology—computers, VCRs, a video studio, CD-ROMs—to record and make available to students their traditional culture, the program is not only preserving but also keeping alive the vitality of Hualapai culture.

From meager beginnings when, according to Philbert, the only Hualapais at the school were "the janitors and the kids" (Trimble 1993:209) and only elementary grades were taught, the school has expanded to include kindergarten through twelfth grade, with over half the staff from Peach Springs. Community involvement is the heart of the program, for individuals share photographs, documents, and personal knowledge to produce curriculum guides and come into the classroom to talk to the students. Elders such as Bertha Russell and Elnora Mapatis share their knowledge through oral traditions and through field trips during which the students gather plants and make traditional foods.

Along with Malinda Powskey, Jorigine Bender, Josie Uqualla, and Philbert Watahomigie Sr., Lucille Watahomigie wrote a 562-page manual, *Hualapai Cultural and Environmental Curriculum Guide,* to provide the teaching staff with culturally based study units designed specifically for Hualapai children. Intended to guide teachers as they plan their individual classroom programs, the manual uses both the Hualapai and English languages to develop skills through activities relevant to Hualapai children. Intended to encourage fluency and literacy in both the English and Hualapai languages, so that children can participate fully in either world, the program's success is evident in the greater number of Hualapais who graduate from high school and go on to college.

Using federal Title VII funds, Lucille and her colleagues have produced at least two to three books each year for use in the school. Among them are *Ethnobotany of the Hualapai* (1982), *H'dE* ("Prickly Pear," 1983), *Waksi: Wich Hualapai Cattle Ranching* (1983), *Ko—Pinyon* (1983), *Historic Landsites of the Hualapai Tribe* (1984), *Hualapai Gwadi Hualapai Spudi* ("The Hualapai Cradleboard," 1982), and *Wildlife on the Hualapai Reservation* (1986).

Both the River and Upland Yumans have a long tradition as great orators, but unfortunately, once written and translated into English, Hualapai oration loses much of its power, beauty, and richness. This is why bringing the elders and the children together plays such a key role in the curriculum, and to ensure that the elders' knowledge and presence will not be lost, educators are taping them with video cameras as they tell traditional stories. As a native speaker and trained linguist, Lucille Watahomigie has collected, transcribed, and translated numerous stories and texts. The oral tradition transmits not only the language and history, but also the basic values and philosophy of a culture. She expresses this eloquently in *Spirit Mountain:* "Oral tradition is the conveyor of memories, passed on from generation to generation, memories of the land once occupied by the Hualapai, contacts with other tribes, their history; it tells the people who they are today on the basis of who they were yesterday" (Hinton and Watahomigie 1984:11).

Origins

The following account of Hualapai creation comes from Paul Talieje's narration in *Spirit Mountain* (Hinton and Watahomigie 1984:15–41).

In the beginning, it rained and rained until a great flood surged over the whole earth, sweeping away everyone and everything in its path. Only one old man was saved, and he was placed on Wikahme' (Spirit Mountain), the only land that was not swallowed by the waters. In his loneliness, the old man looked up into the sky toward the east. He saw something coming, small and dark. It was Dove, bringing instructions from the Creator and Giver of Life:

A mountain sheep's horn, you obtain it, you do that,
A nice, sharp and pointed one,
With that good one dig a hole in the middle of the ground, you do this,
If you do that, water will drain into, into the hole; it will dash in and drain through the
  hole, and so it will be.
(Hinton and Watahomigie 1984:17)

The old man did as Dove instructed and indeed, the water drained and the ground dried and the grass began to grow again. Dove brought back green grass in his beak to show the man, and the man was happy.

In time, the old man passed away, and eventually, the Creator and Giver of Life created the twins, Ma✱vil (Older Earth-Brother) and Judaba:h (Younger Earth-Brother), whom he placed on Spirit Mountain. (The ✱ in Ma✱vil is an interdental—that is, the sound it represents is in between the *d* and *th* sounds in the English language.) Night after night, Ma✱vil dreamed the same dream. In this dream, he was told he "would be given a gift to think about, to contemplate, to make sense out of, in his heart" (Hinton and Watahomigie 1984: 21).

One morning when he rose, Ma✱vil told his younger brother,
Last night I dreamed a dream,
I was told that I do this,
That we do this, it has been said, it has been told.
(Hinton and Watahomigie 1984:21)

Following the instructions in the dream, the brothers began to gather canes cut from along the Colorado River below Spirit Mountain. They piled them up, scraped them, and cleaned them, placing them on the ground with the tops toward the east. "Just before dawn, those ones there will come alive," Ma✱vil said (Hinton and Watahomigie 1984:21).

The brothers retired for the night, taking care to sleep without wiggling or shaking and staying very quiet, lest they disturb the creation process. As midnight approached, the canes began to make noises.

Thus it happened; then, before the sun rose from the horizon,
When the land was just becoming pretty,
"All right, the people have arrived, it seems," he said.
(Hinton and Watahomigie 1984:23)

The twins gathered the newly created people together, instructing each group on how to live a proper life and giving each all that they needed to begin their existence. Ma✱vil gave laws first to the Navajos and Hopis, sending them on their way with sheep and goats for their food and clothing.

Then he said to the Mojave, "Somewhere to the south find a land . . . plant crops . . . those plants you will eat and live there, this is to be so" (Hinton and Watahomigie 1984: 36). Ma✱vil gave them seeds and told them to live on fish and to make clothing of the leaves of the water willow. And the Mojave moved south and settled in what became Fort Mojave, near present-day Bullhead City. After Ma✱vil had named all the people, he said to one group,

"You Hualapai, you, Hualapai,
This is what your name is going to be,
Nowhere, no far away lands,
Different lands, some strange lands belonging to others,

You are not to go or be anywhere;
Here, the water that lies here
The land here, the land along this river,
Here, you roam here,
Be around here,
You are to be here, it is destined."
(Hinton and Watahomigie 1984:37–38)

Aboriginal Hualapai Culture

Subsistence and Material Culture

In the spring and summer, while the Havasupai were farming in the canyon, their Hualapai relatives pursued an annual round—a fairly regular pattern of movement —to follow the sequence of ripening wild plants and to avoid overexploiting plants in any particular locale. They also returned frequently to their villages to tend small plots of ground, which they farmed. In addition to their diversion dams along rivers and tributaries to irrigate gardens of squash, beans, watermelons, wheat, and maize, the Hualapai also channeled springs in cliff faces to flood adjacent fields and used natural runoff from mountain springs (Dobyns and Euler 1976:10–12).

In small, semi-nomadic bands, the Hualapai left their winter villages to gather agave or wild mescal in foothills and canyons. They baked mescal stalks in earth ovens for several days so that they could eat the delicious inner core. The women then crushed the outer layers into a pulp, formed them into slabs, and dried them in the sun, so that they could then be boiled for food, mixed with water to drink, or stored for future use (Kroeber 1935:52–53). Families or camps of families then moved down to the valleys to gather stick-leaf (*Mentzelia albicaulis*), whose pods are a rich source of protein and carbohydrates (Smith 1973).

The Hualapai returned to the foothills and canyons in midsummer to harvest the ripened fruits and seeds of several species of cactus—saguaro, barrel cactus, tuna and prickly pear, and yucca—which they made into beverages or stored for future use (McGuire 1983:32). In late summer and early autumn, they collected ripened piñon cones and juniper and sumac berries. They made the piñon nuts into a paste or soup by baking and drying them; by crushing and soaking the berries of sumac and juniper, they prepared a beverage. Hualapai elder Annie Querta spoke with nostalgia of these traditional foods, comparing pounded piñon nuts to peanut butter, ground mesquite to popcorn balls, and crushed squawbush berries mixed with water to Kool-Aid: "I miss that food. I always tell this young grandchildren that we do that. But when they don't see it, they don't believe it!" (Trimble 1993:201).

During the winter the Hualapai encamped in larger, more sedentary groups. Men and boys hunted rabbits and rodents communally, either by a drive involving several men or by individual stalking; men also hunted bighorn sheep, pronghorn antelope, and mule deer (Kroeber 1935:70–76). In camps of about twenty-five, there were usually four men who were seasoned hunters. The groups were big enough to drive and ambush bighorn sheep and deer and surround rabbits, but not so big that they would put too much pressure on local resources (McGuire 1983:32). The meat was supplemented with the nutritious vegetables and fruit the women had stored.

At each camp, the people built dome-shaped huts constructed of poles and branches on a four-pole foundation, which they covered with juniper bark or thatch, and occasionally mud; in summer, shade was all they needed, while in winter, sturdier mud-plastered huts kept out the cold. Sweat lodges played an important role in Pai culture: in addition to undergoing ceremonial sweats, which they used for purification, men also took part in social sweats. When they had finished their work, men relaxed in the sweat lodge, catching up on the local news and exchanging gossip, even gambling. Women entered sweat lodges primarily for healing.

Rabbit-skin robes were especially prized as both clothing and bedding to protect against the biting winter cold. A child's blanket took about forty rabbit skins, while an adult man's robe could take a hundred. Buckskin and juniper bark provided the material for the double apron and dress worn by women, and the breechclout, hide shirt, and leggings worn by men; both sexes wore moccasins. From the Mojave and Quechan, the Hualapai obtained shell ornaments, which they wore as pendants. They also tattooed their faces or limbs (Kroeber 1935:110) and used red hematite for temporary facial decoration.

Hualapai Social and Political Organization

For most of the year, several families lived together in camps, where these twenty or so individuals cooperated economically and socially. Bilateral descent and nuclear-family households gave people the flexibility to leave one band and join another where they had relatives in case of disputes or changing availability of resources. Reckoning descent through both paternal and maternal lines gives individuals a larger pool of relatives upon whom they can call in time of need.

Several Pai bands were grouped into one of three subtribes, each of which had its own territory. The Middle Mountain People organized themselves into two bands in the northwest area, closest to Spirit Mountain; the Yavapai Fighters, composed of four bands, lived farthest south; the Plateau People had seven bands and lived to the east. (The Havasupai were one band of the Plateau People subtribe.)

When resources were abundant, all the camps in an Upland Yuman band resided together. Each band, which included 85–250 people, ranged over an area between 350 and 1,500 square miles. Camp headmen, chosen for their prowess in warfare, wisdom, and oratorical abilities—decided how subsistence activities should be coordinated but wielded little authority to enforce their decisions; their position was often inherited. Band head-men, chosen from the pool of local camp headmen, had more power, and still more influential were the subtribe chiefs who led their people in war.

Hualapai Shamanism

With power and songs derived from dreams, shamans controlled the weather, fixed fractures or snake bites, and cured the sick, using technique that were essentially the same as those of their Havasupai relatives. Always, they called on Spirit Mountain to help them, a mountain so powerful "that a doctor does not dare approach it directly. He must get his spirit to do it for him," said Hualapai elders George Walker and Old Mike (Trimble 1993:199).

Hualapai History: The Anglo-American Period

Continuous contact with Anglo-Americans began in the 1860s, after immigrants began to take an 1857 wagon road that led through the center of Pai territory. Known to Congress as the "35th Parallel Route" (Trimble 1993:202), this trail from the Rio Grande to California eventually became Route 66; later, parts of it became Interstate 40. In 1859, in response to Mojave raiding, U.S. troops built Fort Mojave on the western edge of Pai country. After a brief respite when the military withdrew during the early years of the Civil War, the Pai were inundated with Anglo-Americans who for the first time came to stay in the central mountains. Prospectors flooded the area when gold was discovered in 1863 and the Prescott mines opened. In 1863, soon after Union troops were able to wrest control from the Confederates, Arizona Territory was created from the western New Mexico Territory. To supply the territory's new capital, men blazed hundreds of miles of mule trails and wagon roads to bring goods from steamboat ports at La Paz, Fort Mojave, and Hardyville on the Colorado River over land to Fort Whipple and Prescott (the first and second capitals of Arizona Territory, respectively).

Ranchers followed prospectors and soldiers, their herds trampling, devouring, and displacing the wild plants and game that had sustained the Upland Yumans. When Pais killed horses, mules, and oxen for food, settlers demanded their removal. In 1865 the Hualapai War erupted when drunken Anglos murdered a Pai leader. The Pais retaliated by killing miners, which led to the U.S. cavalry setting fire to Pai rancherias. Tenacious fighters led by brilliant leaders, the Hualapai fought so fiercely that "officers from Prescott say they would prefer fighting five Apaches to one Hualapai" (Dobyns and Euler 1971:46). However, the army burned camp after camp with its scorched-earth tactics, killing nearly one-quarter of the Hualapai by the end of 1868.

Further weakened by an epidemic of whooping cough, the Pai surrendered and were herded to La Paz, near present-day Ehrenburg on the Colorado River. Many died from epidemic disease, spoiled rations, and starvation, because the people soon weakened in the heat and humidity to which, as lifelong mountain and plateau dwellers, they were unaccustomed. In the spring of 1875 the Hualapai left for home, trudging for days over plains of sagebrush until they reached the pine-covered hills of their homeland. Those who remembered the long walk said they "began to run, laughing and shouting, as they neared their old homesites" (Hirst 1985:46).

After their leader promised the territorial governor that they would stay at peace, they were allowed to remain in their homeland, which by then was held by Anglo settlers and miners. Their traditional means of subsistence gone, the Hualapai were forced to become a pool of cheap laborers for mines and ranches. In 1881 railroad crews diverted the spring water that had made farming possible for the Peach Springs band, forcing them to give up their canyon fields below; the Peach Springs depot site grew into the central Hualapai village (Trimble 1993:205).

The Pai managed to survive through wage work as washerwomen, servants, nannies, or army scouts who tracked Chiricahua Apaches. Concerned for the welfare of their scouts, the army recommended a Hualapai reservation, which President Chester Arthur established in 1883, south of the Grand Canyon on roughly one-tenth of their original territory.

The Hualapai, who also sent people to become disciples of Wovoka, held their first Ghost Dance at Grass Springs in the spring of 1889 (Hirst 1985:56). When the Ghost Dance failed to revive a man who had just died, they began to lose faith in this practice; they held their final Ghost Dance in 1895 (Dobyns and Euler 1967).

After the passage of the Indian Reorganization Act of 1934, the Hualapai designated the Peach Springs site as their tribal capital, and created an elected, nine-member council, along with a constitution and bylaws. Today, their tribal council includes a chair, vice chair, and seven other council members.

Contemporary Issues

The Peach Springs Bilingual/Bicultural Program

As described earlier, supporters of the preservation of indigenous languages in the United States face serious obstacles, and since the late 1960s hundreds of indigenous-language maintenance programs have been undertaken. The Peach Springs Bilingual-Bicultural Program is a nationally recognized model that has inspired many others. As a community-based endeavor, this program uses curriculum, from kindergarten through eighth grade, that has as its goal the development of understanding of the Hualapai students' own community and environment. When the students work on botany, they start their study with the plants that surround them; as they broaden their learning, they compare botanical information from other parts of the country with the botanical resources in

Hualapai girls,
Peach Springs
School, c, 1985.
Courtesy of Lucille
Watahomigie

their own community. Designed to build dignity and self-esteem, the curriculum reinforces cultural values, showing children what it is to be Hualapai through such activities as harvesting and roasting agave hearts, visiting the old sites important in their religion, running the Colorado River, and learning how to make baskets. In addition to learning about their own community and natural environment, students also learn about how diverse cultures have contributed to the history of the United States.

Lucille Watahomigie, director of the Peach Springs program, identifies several crucial components of the program's success in addition to community involvement. The tribal council supports and endorses the program, the administration pays close attention to staff training and professional development, and cooperative arrangements exist with linguists and researchers (Watahomigie and Yamamoto 1983). Unusual even for reservation schools, the program has a largely Hualapai staff, including the director, which encourages full community involvement; at the beginning, the staff invited their own kin to participate as resource people for language and culture. One of the first administrators of the Peach Springs Elementary School went on to an important career in Hualapai tribal politics, and many relatives of staff members, as well as the staff themselves, are active in tribal politics. These connections have established supportive relationships between the tribe and the school's bilingual/bicultural program. Although most of the certified teaching staff at Peach Springs is non-Hualapai, the director is a native speaker of Hualapai, and the Hualapai staff who serve as uncertified teacher aides are encouraged to earn undergraduate degrees, which many of them have done. Nearly all the teaching staff have attended the American Indian Language Development Institute (co-founded by the program's director) to earn college-credit courses in linguistics and bilingual/bicultural education. Finally, the geologists, botanists, medical researchers, and computer and media technicians who come to learn about the Hualapai tribe and its environment are required to leave copies of data and publications with the school, while linguists provide linguistic training to Hualapai speakers; such cooperation between highly trained researchers and the school has led to broader curricula, including workshops led by writers who instruct the children in creative writing about all that they are learning.

Grand Canyon West

Opened in 1988, Grand Canyon West, on the western part of the Hualapai reservation, features spectacular Grand Canyon views. Over 3,000 tourists come during the summer months to enjoy this recently opened 108-mile stretch of the canyon, an enterprise that is governed by the Hualapai Enterprise Board, a committee of independent tribal members and nonmembers. Hualapai River Runners, established in 1973, is the only Indian-owned and -operated river rafting concern in the Grand Canyon.

The recently constructed Hualapai Lodge in Peach Springs was built to accommodate visitors to Grand Canyon West and the wildlife conservation area in the high desert of northern Arizona. This conservation area consists of over 1 million acres of land bordered by the Grand Canyon, in an area that is home to herds of elk, desert bighorn sheep, mountain lions, and turkeys, as well as deer and other animals. Diamond Creek Road, the only road into the Grand Canyon, is maintained by the Hualapai Tribe, which allows conditional access by car or truck and issues sightseeing permits.

Most jobs on the reservation are related to government services and to the Peach Springs School. In 1994 the population was 1,979, with an unemployment rate of 40.3 percent (Arizona Department of Commerce). The main revenue for the tribe comes from forestry, cattle ranching, wildlife, and Colorado River raft operations. With land that ranges from 2,000 feet to nearly 7,000 feet above sea level and encompasses high mountains, vast plains, and deep gorges, Hualapai country has much to offer hikers, fishermen, hunters, and river runners.

The Great Seal of the Hualapai Tribe

"The hills and the mountain has a life in it. The ground which we stand on has a life in it . . . we must try and worship the land and the ground and the stars and the skies, for they are the mighty spirits, which guide and direct us, which help us survive," said Weldon Mahone, son of a Hualapai tribal leader (Trimble 1993:199–200). These values are reflected in the Great Seal of the Hualapai Tribe. Encircled by a band of the pine trees that give the tribe its name, the seal features the bowed heads of a man and a woman framed by the sun rising over canyons. Hualapai Tribal River Running interprets the tribal seal as follows:

> The Great Spirit created Man and Woman in his own image. In doing so, both were created as equals. Both depending on each other in order to survive. Great respect was shown for each other; in doing so happiness and contentment was achieved then, as it should be now.
>
> The connecting of the Hair makes them one person, for happiness or contentment can not be achieved without each other.
>
> The Canyons are represented by the purples in the middle ground, where the people were created. These canyons are Sacred, and should be so treated at all times.
>
> The Reservation is pictured to represent the land that is ours, treat it well.
>
> The Reservation is our heritage and the heritage of our children yet unborn. Be good to our land and it will continue to be good to us.
>
> The Sun is the symbol of life, without it nothing is possible—the plants don't grow—there will be no life—nothing. The Sun also represents the dawn of the Hualapai people. Through hard work, determination and education, everything is possible and we are assured bigger and brighter days ahead.
>
> The Tracks in the middle represent the coyote and other animals which were here before us.
>
> The Green around the symbol are pine trees, representing our name Hualapai—
> PEOPLE OF THE TALL PINES.

The Yavapai

July 1998

Early the next morning we drive east from Seligman, headed for the territory of the Yavapai, the People of the Sun. Yesterday's threatening storm broke soon after we left Peach Springs with a drenching, driving rain that pelted the earth with hailstones and flooded the streets of Seligman. Puddles still dot the damp highway.

Visible for many miles in all directions, San Francisco Peaks stand alone on the horizon, rising high above the surrounding plateau. The highest point in Arizona, at 12,633 feet, Mount Humphreys is but one of several discrete summits spaced around the rim of an exploded volcano. Usually regarded as a single mountain, San Francisco Peaks appear to float in the sky from the Hopi mesas 80 miles away.

Unlike many other mountains, San Francisco Peaks stand in splendid isolation, surrounded by the sky. The sheer physical presence leaves a profound impression, and it is easy to understand why these mountains play such a major role in the spiritual beliefs of

all the native peoples who lived in this area. Home to Hopi katsinam, San Francisco Peaks, according to Navajo belief, were a supernatural being with a power and an intelligence imbued by an inner form implanted at the time of Emergence. Medicine men from many tribes gathered medicinal herbs from the slopes.

Emergence place of the Yavapai, Montezuma Well, 1998. Author photograph

Today I am seeing San Francisco Peaks and the surrounding land from the perspective of the Yavapai, as the marker of the northeastern boundary of their territory. We turn south from Flagstaff, into the Sedona Red Rock country and the middle Verde Valley, the homeland of the Wipukpaya, the subtribe known as the Northeastern Yavapai. As we descend through Oak Creek Canyon with its woodlands of oak and juniper, I think of how abundant this land was for the Yavapai, for whom it supplied a steady and varied food supply: acorns, walnuts, and manzanita berries in the autumn; fresh greens, such as wild spinach and amaranth, in the spring; and agave throughout the year. When coupled with game and the crops they planted, this country was a land of plenty for the Yavapai, who knew precisely where to find edible plants and animals. Each plant, root, and animal had its place, its proper season when it was ripe or most plentiful. With their intimate knowledge of the local area, they knew hundreds of species of seeds, grasses, roots, and similar plants. Even though the Yavapai spent most of their lives following the sequence of ripening plant foods, they were still able to spend months at a time in places where resources were most abundant.

Our first stop is Montezuma's Well, the limestone sink where the Yavapai people entered the present world. Fed by continuous springs, the limestone sink was formed long ago by the collapse of an immense underground cavern. Both the Hohokam (around A.D. 1100) and Sinaguan (between A.D. 1125 and 1400) peoples used its waters, and the remains of their irrigation ditches, thickly coated with lime, are still visible, along with their dwellings.

Clouds are beginning to build in anticipation of afternoon thunderstorms, and distant flashes of lightning illuminate the horizon. A friendly ranger in his eighties leans out of his small office to ask if I have any questions. When I tell him I have come to see the Yavapai emergence place, he says, "A delegation of Yavapai elders were here earlier this year. They come every year on their Exodus Day pilgrimage to climb down the trail to the water so they can collect some for their ceremonies. That water is very sacred to them."

I thought of the words Yavapai elder John Williams wrote with Mike Harrison, "North of Camp Verde there is Montezuma Well. We call it *Ahagaskiaywa*. This lake has no bottom and underneath the water spreads out wide. That's where the people come out first" (Trimble 1993:229).

Origins

Long ago, when there was no water in Ahagaskiaywa (Montezuma Well), the people lived there inside the earth with their gods. But their chief was a bad person who mistreated his daughter until, in her anger, she made him very sick. Then she caused a flood and tried to kill everyone else. The chief, knowing he was dying, told the people to burn his body when he died and to protect his heart from coyote. He told them that if they covered his heart with dirt something would grow from it. After his death, the people did as he had directed, and corn grew from the place where the dirt covered his heart. The corn grew and grew until it reached the side of the well.

When the flood came, all the people and animals climbed up the roots of the corn plant. The floodwaters rose until they reached the level of the earth that surrounds Montezuma Well. All of those who climbed out of the well spoke the Yavapai language.

In time, the people lost their way and gave in to corruption. Their evil behavior brought about another flood from which only two beings were saved: a girl and a woodpecker. As the rain increased and the water rose, the people put this girl in a hollow cottonwood log with enough food to sustain her. The woodpecker made a hole in the log so she could breathe. The girl stayed in the log for forty days and nights, finally emerging in the place that is today known as Sedona. Her name was Komwidapakwia, "Old Lady White Stone," in honor of the white stone she had brought with her for protection, and she was First Woman, from whom all the Yavapai people are descended.

Impregnated when she opened her body to Sun and then, later, to purified spring water dripping inside a cave, she gave birth to a daughter, who had a son in the same manner. His name was Lofty Wanderer, and when he was still a boy, a monster eagle killed his mother. Raised by his grandmother, Old Lady White Stone, Lofty Wanderer learned from a quail who had killed his mother. Already having killed many of the monsters who inhabited the world, using his great supernatural powers, Lofty Wanderer drew on all of his powers to kill the monster eagle in his home, the high cliffs now known as Bell Rock. Today, all that remains of the monsters slain by Lofty Wanderer are the mountains that surround Sedona, which are stained red with the blood of the monsters (Ruland-Thorne 1993:1–6). Before Lofty Wanderer left this world, he called all the beings together in a cave in the Red Rock Mountains of Sedona to teach them the right way to live and then sent each group of humans to their special place in the world. Only the Yavapai remained at the Center of the World, the place of beginning (Gifford 1932:243; Harrison and Williams 1977:42; Williams and Khera 1975:94).

Aboriginal Yavapai Culture

Subsistence and Material Culture

The Yavapai practiced an annual round, similar to that of the Hualapai, except that it extended over an area roughly twice as large. Moving across the land in rhythm with the sequence of ripening plants, the Yavapai covered a 10 million-acre territory in central and western Arizona. Although individual bands did not range over this entire area, most bands had access to three environmental zones: the Sonoran desert, the central mountains, and the transition zone located between 6,500 feet and 8,000 feet. This ensured them a steady and reliable food supply of many different plants and animals. They also practiced horticulture by planting corn, beans, and squash in washes or streams and near springs. Returning intermittently in between hunting-and-gathering trips, they checked on the progress of their crops.

The time of greatest abundance, autumn, was when the nuts (acorns, piñon, and walnuts), berries (mulberry, manzanita, lemon berries, juniper, hackberry, and cedar), and seeds (sunflower, wild grasses, and golden-eye) of the higher elevations were ripening, as well as the fruits of the banana yucca. The Yavapai also harvested the corn, beans, and squash they had planted months before. Women gathered and processed the summer fruits, seeds, and berries, while, in the areas vulnerable to attack, men stood guard. Grinding the seeds and nuts on bedrock mortars and grinding stones, the women then stored them in pots and baskets sealed with plant gum. They kept these containers in caches and caves to use in winter when fresh plant foods were scarce. Agave, with its year-round availability, was a staple of the Yavapai diet. Local Yavapai bands gathered at large stands of agave to spend as long as three to four months in one area harvesting, roasting, and drying the agave hearts, and then caching them in strategic areas. This is what Yavapai elder Mike Burns called "the essential food" (Trimble 1993:232).

While men and older boys drove deer into blinds, individual hunters wearing deer-head masks stalked them at close range; men, women, and children participated together in animal drives for antelope and rabbits. The Yavapai used a variety of weapons: bows and arrows to hunt birds and larger game; throwing sticks for smaller animals; and traps and snares for foxes, coyotes, and wildcats. Everyone looked forward to spring, when fresh leafy greens—wild spinach, thistle, chenopod, and amaranth—provided a welcome change from their diet of dried food and meat. In midsummer bands traveled to the desert area of their territory to collect the ripening fruits and seeds of saguaro and prickly pear cactus, palo verde, and mesquite.

Houses were simple structures built on a dome-shaped framework of poles, covered with mud, and thatched with willow. Ramadas provided shade in the summer, and caves, which held heat well, were ideal for winter. Yavapai women, especially those of the Southeastern subtribe (which was close to the Western Apache, from whom they learned basketry), wove fine coiled baskets. Highly prized today by collectors, Yavapai baskets are made of willow. Some of these flat baskets have intricate designs, while others are simple and elegant; the Yavapai-Prescott tribe has taken one of their baskets as their tribal emblem.

Yavapai Social and Political Organization

Yavapai social organization was well adapted to a nomadic lifestyle, for bilateral kinship provided the flexibility for individuals and families to leave a local group when they had a disagreement and to join another group in which they had relatives. A newly married couple lived first with the bride's group, followed by a stay with the groom's local group. After this initial period, the couple decided where they wanted to live.

Ideally suited to a fluctuating resource base, Yavapai political organization was also flexible. When resources could be gathered, hunted, and grown efficiently by a local group, several extended families camped together; at other times, a few families moved off to harvest areas on their own. In areas of plentiful food resources as many as ten families might camp and travel together (Gifford 1936:254, 297), and during the 1850s and 1860s up to a hundred households of the Southeastern Yavapai subtribe gathered each winter (Gifford 1932:189).

Several families composed a camp or local group led by an older man, often a former war chief. Each morning he delivered an oration from the roof of a hut, instructing the people on the right way to live and advising them on where and when to hunt and gather food. Leadership was informal, and people followed a particular man because his personality won their confidence. Some men in a local group were leaders only in wartime; such men had distinguished themselves with their outstanding fortitude and skill in battle. Local groups joined for war expeditions, each group under its own war chief.

While younger people link themselves to their specific Yavapai reservation community, elders still identify themselves as descendants of one of four subtribes: the Western, Central, Northeastern, and Southeastern. The Tolkapaya (Western Yavapai) held the largest area, ranging from the Colorado River almost to Prescott and almost as far south as the Gila River. The Yavepe (Central Yavapai) lived in the area around present-day Prescott and Jerome. The Wipukpaya (Northeastern Yavapai) ranged as far north as present-day Flagstaff, the middle Verde Valley, the Bradshaw Mountains, and present-day Sedona. The Kewevkapaya (Southeastern Yavapai) lived in the southern part of the Verde Valley, the Bradshaw Mountains, the Tonto Basin, and the Superstition and Pinal Mountains around present-day Globe. After 1700 Apache people began moving into Yavapai country, and the two groups intermarried and influenced each other's cultures. The Southeastern Yavapai had the closest ties with the Apache; they developed matrilineal clans, probably as a result of their contact with the San Carlos and Tonto Apaches, who were known to have matrilineal clans.

Yavapai History: The Anglo-American Period

Once the Yavapai found their food-collecting rounds disrupted by miners and ranchers, they began raiding settlers for food. Conflict inevitably followed: the Yavapai Wars, "a ten-year Vietnam War," in the words of Camp Verde chairman Ted Smith (Trimble 1993:233). This decade-long war left central Arizona with a legacy of morbid place names, such as Bloody Basin and Skull Valley. Indian families were the casualties at these places, for unlike the well-armed Apaches, the Yavapai had only their hunting weapons to use in battle. Their weaponry was no match for the sophisticated guns and ammunition of the U.S. Army. During a single encounter in Skeleton Cave above the Salt River Canyon, soldiers killed seventy-six Yavapais. Defeat finally came when the army systematically destroyed the winter food supplies of the Yavapai.

Most of the Yavapais surrendered in 1873, to be incarcerated on a reservation in the Verde Valley, where disease soon reduced their population by one-third. After the government promised them an irrigation canal, the Yavapai and Tonto Apache (who were also imprisoned there) excavated an irrigation ditch with wooden sticks, broken shovels, and rusty spoons. Their successful harvests alarmed government contractors in Tucson, who made huge profits by selling low-quality rations to dependent tribes. The Tucson contractors forced the government to abolish the Verde Reservation and to relocate the Indians to the San Carlos Apache Reservation near Globe, Arizona, in 1874. The Yavapai were forced to walk roughly 180 miles over rugged terrain in midwinter, while sustaining themselves only on the wild foods they found. The forced march not only demoralized their spirit, but also brought death to many: 1,500 Yavapai began the journey, but only 200 remained alive to return to their homeland in the 1880s and 1890s.

When the Prescott-Yavapai returned, they tried to settle at the abandoned military post at Fort McDowell, but most of the arable land was occupied by Anglo and Mexican squatters. Living near locations where they could obtain wage labor, they worked resolutely to obtain reservation status for their communities. In 1903 Theodore Roosevelt established the Fort McDowell Reservation by executive order. The Yavapai-Prescott community is contained within the city limits of Prescott, Arizona. The Camp Verde Reservation, established in 1910, had several noncontiguous parcels added throughout the next sixty years, including Middle Verde, Clarkdale, and Rimrock. Each of the three major Yavapai reservations has developed separately and today considers itself to be a separate tribe with its own government.

Contemporary Issues

Fort McDowell Yavapai Tribe

The development of the Yavapai community at Fort McDowell has been shaped by two key variables: the growth of the Phoenix metropolitan area, which is only 26 miles away, and the fight for their water resources, for their reservation is bisected by the Verde River (Mariella and Mitchell-Enos 1994:710–11). In 1906, only three years after the reservation was established, the BIA recommended that no funds be spent on the irrigation system, which Yavapai farmers had labored to develop and maintain in the face of periodic flooding of the Verde River. Instead, the BIA planned to relocate the residents of the Fort McDowell Reservation to the Salt River Pima-Maricopa Reservation, where they would live without water rights on the lands of their traditional enemies.

Fortunately, the Yavapai had Dr. Carlos Montezuma, who was able to mobilize national leaders and to keep the Yavapai on their land. A Yavapai who had been taken from his family in the late 1860s and raised by non-Indians, Montezuma grew up in Chicago and was one of the first American Indians to earn a medical degree (1889). He spoke out in Congress and in the national press for Yavapai land and water rights, and was a prominent Indian activist in the first two decades of the twentieth century.

Two Yavapai leaders kept Montezuma's legacy alive when they secured the right to vote in federal and state elections for Arizona Indians who live on reservations. Frank Harrison, a World War II veteran, and Harry Austin, a Fort McDowell leader, filed a lawsuit that finally secured these voting rights in 1948. (In this same year, New Mexico finally extended voting rights to Indians living on reservations; Utah kept reservation-dwelling Indians from voting until 1957.)

After 1948 Orme Dam and reservoir were the major issue facing the Fort McDowell community. Planned to provide flood control and to create a storage basin for the Colorado River water that the Central Arizona Project was to bring into the Salt River valley, this dam would result in the flooding of nearly 65 percent of the reservation. This acreage included the best land, the fertile river bottomlands the Yavapai used for farming, cattle grazing, wood cutting, housing, and recreation; all that was left were higher desert areas unsuited for agriculture. Finally, in 1983, after years of concerted effort from the tribe, along with environmental, taxpayer, and religious groups and concerned citizens, the Bureau of Reclamation withdrew its proposal for Orme Dam.

The impending construction of Orme Dam kept the Fort McDowell community from obtaining government funding during the 1970s, the period of significant federal funding for Indian tribes. In the 1980s the tribe took matters into their own hands by opening the first Indian gaming operation in Arizona. This has provided a substantial source of income, which the tribe has used wisely. They put 60 percent of the revenue into tribal operations, such as health, housing, and economic development projects, and 6 percent into the support of charitable off-reservation causes, and distributed the remaining 34 percent among all adult tribal members. Until tribal members reach the age of twenty-one, their money is kept for them in a savings account; if they wish to gain access to this money before then, they must graduate from high school or obtain a GED (Bahti and Bahti 1997: 139).

In the late 1980s the Fort McDowell community initiated major community development activities, including several housing and community infrastructure development programs, the reclamation of farmland along the alluvial floodplain of the Verde River, the expansion of the tribal farm to 3,000 acres, and several commercial enterprises (Mariella and Mitchell-Enos 1994:711). The Fort McDowell Indian Community Water Rights Settlement Act of 1990 established their rights to 36,350 acre-feet of water and approximately $25 million of compensatory funds for the tribe to use in community and economic development. State Route 87, which leads from Phoenix through the southern end of their reservation, is being widened, which will provide a commercial corridor for development (ibid., 711).

Fort McDowell is the largest Yavapai reservation, both in acreage and in population, with 24,967 acres and 765 people; the Prescott Reservation has 1,399 acres with 159 people; and the Camp Verde Reservation has 1,092 acres on which 618 people reside (1990 Census; Mariella and Mitchell-Enos 1994:712). In addition to the Fort McDowell Gaming Center, the tribe also offers horseback riding on the reservation through Fort McDowell Adventures (Fontana 1999:32). Out of Africa Wildlife Park is located on leased reservation land, although it is not a tribal enterprise (ibid.).

Yavapai Prescott Indian Tribe

July 1998

On our way north to the Grand Canyon, we head through Prescott, nestled in the mountains of central Arizona about 90 miles northwest of Phoenix. The impressive Prescott Resort and Conference Center looms over the highway from a bluff at the junction of Highways 69 and 89, and shuttle buses emblazoned with the words "Bucky's Casino" trundle up the steep hillside to the casino of the same name. Only a small sign identifies the Yavapai Gaming Center offices in a small strip mall next to the Yavapai Casino. Many Prescott residents prefer the comfortable intimacy of the older, smaller Yavapai Casino to Bucky's, which attracts more tourists.

We drive up the hill to the grand resort with its full parking lot. Several cars trail coke cans, with the words "Just Married" painted across their back windows. A blossom-laden gazebo stands on a grassy overlook with a sweeping view of the surrounding mountains; yellow roses line a trellis and white fence along the walkway to the gazebo, where many weddings are held.

In the lobby of the resort is a life-size sculpture of Viola Jimulla, who served as chief of her people from 1940 to 1966. Unlike many tribes, the Yavapai-Prescott people rejected the Indian Reorganization Act and continued to rely on a hereditary chief. Initially, Chief Sam Jimulla led the tribe; upon his death, his wife Viola and later their two daughters, Grace Mitchell and Lucy Miller, and then their granddaughter Patricia McGee (from 1972 to 1988), continued to lead their people. A 1988 election brought a change in leadership, and then Patricia McGee returned as tribal president in 1990.

Just outside the series of conference rooms is a scale model of the tribe's plans for a Yavapai-Prescott Indian Cultural Heritage Center, which will include a museum, a "living village," and powwow grounds on land adjacent to the resort. Owned and operated by the Yavapai-Prescott tribe, Bucky's Casino and the Yavapai Casino have helped transform the economic status of the tribe. On their land, they have built both industrial and commercial properties, which include Sundog Industrial Park, Frontier Village Shopping Center, and the Prescott Resort and Conference Center, along with the two casinos. The relationship between the tribe and the city of Prescott is unusual, for it is based on working cooperation. The present-day Prescott city limits surround the Yavapai-Prescott tribal land base; as the tribe increases its economic development, the resulting job opportunities benefit Prescott residents as well as tribal members.

Camp Verde: The Yavapai-Apache Nation

The Great Seal of the Yavapai-Apache Nation explains their unique ethnic heritage, so different from that of the other two major Yavapai reservations:

Great Seal of the Yavapai-Apache Nation, 1998. Author photograph

Feathers—In our beginning we were two distinct Tribes, warring against the people coming into our valley. Inter-marriages made our togetherness very close in relations. As shown in the seal, being together to the very end, our forefathers were all herded to San Carlos.

Crown [worn by Apache Crown Dancers]—This symbolizes the Apache in our people. It is the pride of being what you are.

Bell Rock [in Oak Creek Canyon]—This symbolizes the Yavapai in our people. It is they who have their roots to the canyon and the surrounding area since [the beginning of] time. Their legends tie into the land around all of us.

Circle—In our culture, the circle symbolizes the cycle of life. One must face the world as going out from one's home, and when life has been completed, returning back to the land.

Rainbow—This symbolizes our religion. We are taught to believe in something and walk in this beauty of life; not to deviate from what we believe in.

As symbolized in their seal, the Apaches and Yavapai formed close ties during their internment at San Carlos. Many of those who returned settled near the abandoned army post at Fort Verde, and today their descendants live at Camp Verde, where the Apache ethnic

Bell Rock, near Sedona, Arizona, 1998. Author photograph

heritage predominates (Mariella and Mitchell-Enos 1994:712). The limited size of their land base has meant that most tribal members had to work for wage labor in the copper mines and smelters of the Verde Valley. When the mines closed in the 1930s and 1940s, they returned to farm their small reservation parcels (ibid.).

Their economic resources include proximity to three prehistoric ruins: Montezuma Castle, Montezuma Well, and Tuzigoot National Monument. The Yavapai-Apache recently opened the Cliff Castle Casino and Best Western Lodge at the Montezuma Castle exit on Interstate 17, which the tribe hopes will generate enough income to build new community facilities, such as a hospital and school. Blazing Trails Stable, next to the lodge and casino, is licensed by the U.S. Forest Service and conducts its rides in the Coconino and Prescott National Forests (Fontana 1999:23).

References and Further Reading

The Smithsonian's *Handbook of North American Indians*, vol. 10 (1983), contains chapters about various aspects of Yuman culture. For the Hualapai, the extensive list of Hualapai Bilingual Materials Publications is given in *Hualapai Cultural and Environmental Curriculum Guide* (Peach Springs, Ariz.: Hualapai Bilingual Program, 1984).

Bahti, Tom, and Mark Bahti. 1997. *Southwestern Indians.* KC Publications, Las Vegas.

Barnett, Franklin. 1968. *Viola Jimulla: Indian Chieftess.* Southwest Printers, Yuma, Ariz.

Bodfield, Rhonda. 1998. "Water 'Veins' Could Be Cut, Critics Fear." *Arizona Daily Star,* 4 October.

Bourke, John G. 1971 [1891]. *On the Border with Crook.* University of Nebraska Press, Lincoln.

Coffeen, William R. 1972. "The Effects of the Central Arizona Project on the Fort McDowell Indian Community." *Ethnohistory* 19:345–77.

Corbusier, William T. 1969. *Verde to San Carlos: Recollections of a Famous Army Surgeon and His Observant Family on the Western Frontier, 1869–1886.* Dale Stuart King, Tucson.

Cushing, Frank Hamilton. 1965 [1882]. *The Nation of Willows.* Northland Press, Flagstaff.

Dobyns, Henry F., and Robert Euler. 1967. *The Ghost Dance of 1889 among the Pai Indians of Northwestern Arizona.* Prescott College Studies in Anthropology 1. Prescott, Ariz.

*———. 1970. *Wauba Yuma's People: The Comparative Socio-Political Structure of the Pai Indians of Arizona.* Prescott College Press, Prescott, Ariz. [Provides excellent ethnographic background.]

———. 1971. *The Havasupai People.* Indian Tribal Series, Phoenix.

———. 1976. *The Walapai People.* Indian Tribal Series, Phoenix.

Fedullo, Mick. 1992. *Light of the Feather.* William Morrow, New York.

Fontana, Bernard L. 1999. *A Guide to Contemporary Southwest Indians.* Southwest Parks and Monuments Association, Tucson.

*Gifford, Edward W. 1932. "The Southeastern Yavapai." *University of California Publications in American Archaeology and Ethnology* 29, no. 3:177–252. [Gifford's works are classic ethnographies of the Yavapai.]

———. 1936. "Northeastern and Western Yavapai." *University of California Publications in American Archaeology and Ethnology* 34, no. 4:247–354.

Harrison, Mike, and John Williams. 1977. "How Everything Began and How We Learned to Live Right." In *The Yavapai of Fort McDowell: An Outline of Their History and Culture,* pp. 40–46, ed. Sigrid Khera. Fort McDowell Mohave-Apache Indian Community, Fort McDowell, Ariz.

Hinton, Leanne. 1984. *Havasupai Songs: A Linguistic Perspective.* Gunter Narr Verlag, Tübingen.

*Hinton, Leanne, and Lucille J. Watahomigie, eds. 1984. *Spirit Mountain: An Anthology of Yuman Story and Song.* Sun Tracks and University of Arizona Press, Tucson. [This collection of stories and songs in Yuman languages with English translations provides a rich introduction to Yuman oral literature and culture.]

*Hirst, Stephen. 1985. *Havsuw 'Baaja: People of the Blue Green Water.* Havasupai Tribe, Supai, Ariz. [This moving account of the fight for the expansion of the reservation includes accounts by Havasupai storytellers; this book is recommended by the Havasupai tourist office.]

Iliff, Flora Greg. 1954. *People of the Blue Water.* Harper and Brothers, New York.

Iverson, Peter. 1982. *Carlos Montezuma and the Changing World of American Indians.* University of New Mexico Press, Albuquerque.

Ives, Joseph C. (U.S. Army Corps of Topographical Engineers.) 1861. "Report upon the Colorado River of the West Explored in 1857 and 1858 by Lieutenant Joseph C. Ives." U.S. Cong., Senate. 36th Cong., 1st sess. Senate Exec. Doc. 90. U.S. Government Printing Office, Washington, D.C.

Kammer, Jerry. 1998. "Visitors Find Magic in Land of Havasupai." *Arizona Republic,* 17 May, pp. T-1, T-12.

*Khera, Sigrid. 1979. *The Yavapai of Fort McDowell.* Fort McDowell Indian Community, Fort McDowell, Ariz. [Anthropologist Khera's deep commitment to the Yavapai people is evident in these classic works.]

Khera, Sigrid, and Patricia Mariella. 1982. "Long-Term Resistance to Relocation in an American Indian Community." In *Involuntary Resettlement and Migration,* pp. 159–78, ed. Art Hansen and Anthony Oliver-Smith. Westview Press, Denver.

———. 1983. "Yavapai." In *Handbook of North American Indians,* vol. 10: *The Southwest,* pp. 38–54.

Kroeber, Alfred, ed. 1935. *Walapai Ethnography.* By Fred Kniffen, Gordon MacGregor, Robert McKennan, Scudder Mekeel, and Maurice Mook. Memoirs of the American Anthropological Association 42. American Anthropological Association, Menasha, Wis.

Manners, Robert A. 1974. *An Ethnological Report on the Hualapai (Walapai) Indians of Arizona.* Garland Publishing, New York.

Mariella, Patricia, and Violet Mitchell-Enos. 1994. "The Yavapai." In *Native America in the Twentieth Century: An Encyclopedia,* pp. 710–12, ed. Mary Davis. Garland Publishing, New York.

Martin, John C. 1985. "The Havasupai Land Claims Case." In *Irredeemable America: The Indians' Estate and Land Claims,* pp. 271–300, ed. Imre Sutton. University of New Mexico Press, Albuquerque.

———. 1986. "The Havasupai." *Plateau* 56, no. 4:3–32.

———. 1994. "Havasupai." In *Native America in the Twentieth Century: An Encyclopedia,* pp. 231–33, ed. Mary Davis. Garland Publishing, New York.

McGuire, Thomas R. 1983. "Walapai." In *Handbook of North American Indians.* vol. 10: *The Southwest,* pp. 25–37.

McKee, Barbara, and McKee, Edwin. 1974. *Havasupai Baskets and Their Makers.* Northland Press, Flagstaff.

Morris, Clyde P. 1971. "A Brief Economic History of the Camp and Middle Verde Reservations." *Plateau Magazine* 44 (fall):43–51.

Purtesoy, Matthew. 1998. Personal communication.

Ruland-Thorne, Kate. 1993. *Yavapai: The People of the Red Rocks, The People of the Sun*. Thorne Enterprises Publications, Sedona.

Schroeder, Albert H. 1953. "A Brief History of the Havasupai." *Plateau* 25, no. 2:45–52.

———. 1974. *A Study of Yavapai History*. Garland Publishing, New York.

Schwartz, Douglas. 1983. "Havasupai." In *Handbook of North American Indians,* vol. 10: *The Southwest*, pp. 13–24.

Smith, Charline G. 1973. "Sele, A Major Vegetal Component of the Aboriginal Hualapai Diet." *Plateau* 45, no. 3:102–10.

Smithson, Carma Lee. 1959. *The Havasupai Woman*. University of Utah Anthropological Papers 38. Salt Lake City.

Smithson, Carma Lee, and Robert Euler. 1994. *Havasupai Legends: Religion and Mythology of the Havasupai Indians of the Grand Canyon*. University of Utah Press, Salt Lake City.

Spier, Leslie. 1928. "Havasupai Ethnography." *Anthropological Papers of the American Museum of Natural History* 29, no. 3:81–392.

Thrapp, Dan L. 1964. *Al Sieber: Chief of Scouts*. University of Oklahoma Press, Norman.

Trimble, Stephen. 1993. *The People*. School of American Research Press, Santa Fe.

U.S. Congress, Senate. 1936. *Walapai Papers*. 74th Cong., 2d sess. Sen. Doc. 273.

U.S. Indian Claims Commission. 1950. *The Hualapai and Yavapai Indians*. Report by Henry F. Dobyns et al. Garland Publishing, New York.

Watahomigie, Lucille. 1994. "Hualapai." In *Native America in the Twentieth Century: An Encyclopedia*, pp. 246–47, ed. Mary Davis. Garland Publishing New York.

Watahomigie, Lucille, Jorigine Bender, and Akira Yamamoto. 1982. *Hualapai Reference Grammar*. American Indian Studies Center, University of California, Los Angeles.

Watahomigie, Lucille, and Akira Y. Yamamoto. 1983. "Action Linguistics with the Hualapai Bilingual/Bicultural Program." Manuscript. Peach Springs Bilingual Program.

———. 1987. "Linguists in Action: The Hualapai Bilingual/Bicultural Education Program." In *Collaborative Research and Social Change: Applied Anthropology in Action*, pp. 77–98, ed. Donald Stull and Jean Schensul. Westview Press, Boulder, Colo.

Whiting, A. F. 1985. *Havasupai Habitat: A. F. Whiting's Ethnography of a Traditional Indian Culture*, ed. Steven A. Weber and P. David Seaman. University of Arizona Press, Tucson.

Williams, John, and Sigrid Khera. 1975. "Ethnohistory of the Yavapai." Manuscript.

Roy Yazzie carving green Utah alabaster, 1987. Photograph: Helga Teiwes, courtesy of Arizona State Museum

Chapter 9 The Navajo

September 1996

Covered in camouflage, the hogan is unique. Perhaps the men who constructed it for today's Enemyway ceremony used Army-surplus camouflage because of its military association, for the patient is, after all, a Desert Storm veteran suffering from recurrent nightmares. Outside the north wall of the hogan, a man in sunglasses mounted on a palomino stallion keeps the curious away so that the evil unleashed by the ceremony will have a direct path to return northward, the direction of evil and power. Surveying the crowd, he can hear muffled singing inside the hogan led by an Enemyway singer with a reputation for successful ceremonies, enhanced by the fact that he is an ex-Marine who barely escaped death in Vietnam.

At the other end of the dance area stands the ramada where the patient's relatives serve guests, many of whom have traveled great distances. Constructed specifically for this Enemyway, the entire structure, made of piñon posts and roof beams covered with juniper boughs, measures some 17 yards in length and is about 6 yards wide. A canvas partition divides the structure into halves, so that the patient's family and his wife's family each have their own area to receive guests. In the cool, dark interior, friends sit at picnic tables or recline on the earthen floor as they gossip about local events. Women serve bowls of steaming mutton stew and plates heaped high with hot frybread, while outside girls spear frybread with long forks, turning it in pans of sizzling grease, and the aroma of roasting mutton mingles with the cedar smoke of cooking fires.

Under a much smaller ramada just outside the large structure, several elderly men reminisce about their own Enemyway ceremonies, held to purify them after their return from World War II. All wear broad-brimmed hats with high crowns encircled by thin silver bands, and jewelry with large pieces of turquoise on their wrists and around their necks. From behind the main shelter comes the laughter of men and women playing cards on a blanket spread between pickup trucks. Nearby, children play with plastic action figures, while their older brothers and sisters, oblivious to their surroundings, listen to heavy-metal music on headphones.

Pickup trucks are parked in solid banks several rows deep on either side of the dance area, where the social dance will be held each night from somewhere around 9:00 P.M. until perhaps 2:00 A.M. This part of the Enemyway is commonly called a Squaw Dance, because girls select their partners—who can either join them or pay them money—and in years past mothers often chose husbands for their daughters at this event. Since the public social dancing held outside in the dance area occurs simultaneously with some of the private, all-night Enemyway singing held inside the ceremonial hogan, the entire three-day ceremony has earned the misnomer Squaw Dance among Navajos as well as non-Indians.

From the bed of a pickup truck, a heavyset woman is selling turquoise-colored snow cones to eager customers who crave something wet and cool. She grimaces at potential competition when a woman and her sisters park their red pickup, heaped with fresh watermelons and cantaloupes, on the other side of the dance area. The woman's bright-eyed, five-year-old girl crawls into the truck bed to grab a melon, which she hands eagerly to her mother, who slices through the rind to the ripe red fruit. Grabbing the slice and shoving it into her mouth in one smooth motion, the little girl grins as the sweet juice dribbles down her chin. Customers flock to the pickup for samples, beginning with a plump woman with an enormous turquoise brooch pinned to her olive velveteen blouse. Two teenage girls wander by, giggling about the boy who just lost his wallet down the outhouse. A bent grandmother, her full skirts swaying, crosses the plaza to buy several cantaloupes, followed by a lean older man in a vivid orange-and-turquoise patterned shirt, his chin framed by a long, wispy beard. As he ambles away bearing a watermelon, one sister points to him with her lips, Navajo-style, whispering that he is a renowned Nightway singer.

A middle-aged man in sunglasses walks over to the truck and turns over several melons. Unable to decide, he leaves, only to return with his sharp-featured wife who selects three melons, which she piles into her husband's arms as she peels a $10 bill from her wallet. As soon as the couple are out of hearing range, one sister comments, "You can sure tell who holds the purse strings in that family!" Two elderly men who are leaning against the truck laugh heartily.

The patient's wife, a slender woman in her fifties, walks across the plaza to enter the hogan. Despite the 90° heat, she carefully keeps the royal blue Pendleton blanket over her

Lorraine Sammons and her daughter Samantha selling melons from their pickup truck, Navajo Reservation, 1996. Author photograph

head and shoulders as tradition decrees; later relatives will pour gifts over her head, literally showering her with their appreciation in a show of wealth.

Judging from outer appearances, one could easily conclude that the old ways are rapidly disappearing from Navajo culture. But in much the same way as camouflage covers the hogan within which a centuries-old ceremony is going on, Navajo culture and identity continue to flourish beneath a misleading exterior.

Two clues to the roots of Navajo resilience lie in the nuances of their language and in the identity of Changing Woman, the Holy Person who created them. The structure of the Navajo language clearly emphasizes movement and change, for no state is considered to be permanent when the universe is perceived as being in constant flux. The Navajo say, "We were created from Changing Woman," because according to Navajo belief Changing Woman created the first four clans of Navajo people from her own skin. Changing Woman's very name embodies ephemerality and resilience. Identified with the powers of the earth to rejuvenate and re-create itself, Changing Woman is a young girl in spring, a woman in summer, a mature woman in autumn, and an old lady in winter. Each spring she renews herself, beginning the cycle of life once more.

The Navajos' ability to adapt served them well on their migration southward from their Athapaskan homeland in Canada through varied terrains and climates. The Navajo have become known for their ability to incorporate technologies and beliefs from many other cultures into their own, remaking these borrowed items into distinctly Navajo products without any loss of cultural identity.

Weaving Past into Present through Navajo Textiles

Navajo weaving embodies not only the multiethnic nature of the Southwest but also the dynamic creativity of Navajo culture. Spanish sheep, Pueblo looms, English baize (Spanish *bayeta*), Anglo-American tastes, Mexican serapes, Germantown yarns, and, above all, Navajo creativity are woven into the history of Navajo textiles. Weaver D. Y. Begay stressed that Navajo weaving has historically been a "form of communication between tribes," because long before trading posts emerged, Navajo women had created a market for their blankets far beyond the borders of the Southwest (1994:81).

Navajo women probably learned weaving from the Pueblos, for the loom they use today is structurally identical with the prehistoric Pueblo loom of the tenth century, and their earliest blankets had the same broad stripes characteristic of Pueblo blankets (Amsden 1974:31). Among the oldest products of Navajo weaving is the woman's dress, which uses two identically shaped and woven blankets to make a straight, sleeveless dress belted at the waist. Unable to obtain a red color from vegetable dyes, Navajo women prized *bayeta* (baize), which they unraveled and rewove in their own blankets. Through trade with Pueblo middlemen, and directly from Europeans during times of peace, the Navajo acquired this red flannel cloth, which was manufactured in England and transported to the Southwest by way of Spain and then Mexico.

In the early 1800s Navajo women began to weave chief's blankets, which were so widely traded that they were worn by Indians from the northern Great Plains to the Mexican border. Although not a badge of chieftainship, these blankets did symbolize power and affluence. Three phases of increasing complexity in design share an underlying structure based on broad black and white stripes, interspersed with bands of indigo blue, plain bars of *bayeta* red, or geometric figures, usually a serrated diamond.

Navajo women continued to express their ingenuity by creating blankets using the same basic design elements in new patterns, such as all-over or zoned geometric patterns with or without subtly striped backgrounds achieved by using two dark colors. In the mid-1800s, when Navajo women were captured by Mexicans, they learned to use Spanish dyes and designs, such as the large central diamond motif, to create "slave blankets." Sometimes called a Mexican Saltillo serape design, these stepped and wedge-edged geometric designs later combined with brilliant aniline dyes to create "eye dazzler" rugs.

After the Navajos returned from Bosque Redondo, traders encouraged women to weave heavier, larger, and thicker textiles suitable for use as rugs in Eastern drawing rooms. Already prized by the Ute, Apache, Pueblos, Mexicans, and Southwestern Anglos, Navajo blankets soon became a precious commodity in the Eastern market.

Trader Lorenzo Hubbell of Ganado, Arizona, pioneered the sales of Navajo rugs on the East Coast with the Ganado Red style, which is still made today. Known for its deep, rich red color, attractively set off by the natural colors of the wool—white, black, and gray—the Ganado Red features a large central motif surrounded by lesser geometric elements on either side. From the early 1870s on, Navajo weavers felt the influence of new design ideas and new materials, especially aniline dyes and ready-spun and pre-dyed Germantown yarns. No longer isolated, the Navajo people were suddenly connected to the outside world by the transcontinental railroad, and after 1900 entrepreneur Fred Harvey, Santa Fe Railroad concessionary, began to feature Navajo women weaving rugs so that travelers could see firsthand the work that went into this craft. New ideas flooded the reservation through an influx of catalogues, rugs from the East, and tourist interest, inspiring Navajo women to create exuberant designs of large diamonds and zigzags, broad complex bands, and, after 1880, pictorial rugs that recorded their graphic impressions of novel sights and stirring events. Flags, cows, men, horses, eagles, and square-wheeled railroad cars became common motifs.

However, dirty and poorly spun yarn, poor weaving techniques, and the traders' practice of selling rugs by the pound eventually led to a decline in Navajo weaving that traders began to combat by actively working to improve the quality of weaving. From their efforts a variety of regionally based designs emerged; although still known by their regional designations, these designs are no longer limited to the weavers from each particular area. The Crystal rug began under the guidance of trader J. B. Moore between 1897 and 1911–12 (Amsden 1974:194). Beginning with technical improvements, Moore sent wool to the East to be scoured and carded, then later supervised its dyeing. He also introduced non-Navajo motifs, such as simple geometric features inspired by Plains beadwork and oriental hooked elements around a large central motif that was roughly diamond-shaped. Well-established by 1925, the Two Gray Hills style features the black, white, and gray of native wool arranged in a layout similar to the Crystal with a large central diamond and a hooked triangle in each corner. Today, woven of finely carded and spun materials with a thread count as high as 110 wefts to the inch and so light in weight that it qualifies as a blanket, the Two Gray Hills has become the finest example of Navajo weaving (Tanner 1982:76). In the 1930s Mary Cabot Wheelwright and trader L. H. (Cozy) McSparron of Chinle, Arizona, encouraged local weavers to use the softer colors of old vegetable-dyed rugs in striped patterns, and the Lippencotts of Wide Ruins improved the natural dyes, giving Wide Ruin rugs greater clarity.

Contemporary weaver D. Y. Begay explained that, although Navajo women today no longer weave as a career, most of them practice it because "knowing how to weave is intimately bound up with being Navajo" (1994:84). Navajo weaving is undergoing revitalization with the help of Navajo weavers, museum personnel, and anthropologists. Women like D. Y. Begay are not only experimenting with techniques, material, designs, and colors by weaving brilliantly colored textiles, but also passing on their skill to many young Navajo weavers. In 1996 Begay, along with Navajo weavers Kalley Keams and Wesley Thomas, collaborated with the staff of the National Museum of the American Indian, Washington, D.C., on two exhibitions, "Woven by the Grandmothers: Nineteenth-Century Navajo Textiles from the National Museum of the American Indian" and "Contemporary Navajo Weaving: The Gloria F. Ross Collection of the Denver Art Museum." The previous year Navajo weavers helped staff at the Museum of Northern Arizona, Flagstaff, select, curate, and develop the exhibition, "*Hanoolchaadí*: Historic Textiles Selected by Four Navajo Weavers." Davina R. Two Bears explained, "Knowledge gained from the teachings of *Ná'ashjé'ii Asdzáán*, Spider Woman, is being shared by her pupils, *Diné* weavers, to the public in its purest form —directly from the weavers' words. Their strength, humor, wisdom, and sincerity are conveyed to the audience" (1995:64).

Wesley Thomas shared his memories of his mother's weaving at the Navajo Weaving Symposium, part of the eighth annual Navajo Studies Conference, held in March 1995 at San Juan College in Farmington, New Mexico. Some of the weavers whose work had been in the Museum of Northern Arizona exhibition also attended, as did Dr. Ann Lane Hedlund, the anthropologist who organized both that exhibition and the weaving symposium. Thomas recalled hearing the thumping sounds of his mother's weaving fork, which she called "the heartbeat of the loom." A weaver's rug was her child, and when she sold a rug, she was finding a good home for her child. All of the weaver's thoughts became a part of the finished product, from her inspiration to gathering the materials and stringing her loom. She would sing prayers to bless each step of the process, sanctifying her weaving space with prayers and keeping her tools together so that her thoughts would not be scattered. In the Navajo way, the rug already existed upon her loom, and the energy in the weaving fork projected the design into the weaver, who then brought it into manifestation so that it could be seen by others. Thus, the rug's physical beauty was but the outer manifestation of the inner, spiritual beauty the weaver brought to the process of creation.

Origins

The story of Diné (as the Navajo call themselves) creation is one of emergence through a series of worlds, each of a different color and filled with its own beings. The First, or Black, World was "a floating island in a sea of water mist," inhabited by Mist Beings (Yazzie 1971:9). Lit by neither sun nor moon, the Black World was illuminated only by dim, colored columns of cloud in each of the four directions. When disagreement and fighting developed, the entire population decided to climb upward through a hole in the sky into the Blue World, where four cloud columns provided more light than had those of the previous world. Harmony prevailed at first in the Blue World, but eventually bitter quarreling took over, and yet again the Beings climbed upward in the hope of finding a better life. The Yellow World in which they found themselves was more orderly and better lit, but after a time, when Coyote, the great trickster, kidnapped Water Monster's baby, the monster retaliated by sending a flood. Crowding into a hollow reed, the people climbed upward into the Fourth World (the Fifth World, according to some versions). Meanwhile, the surging floodwaters continued to rise, nearly swallowing Turkey, the last animal to come through the reed, staining his tail feathers with the white foam of the surging waters.

Once on the surface of the Fourth World, the present world, First Man and First Woman formed the four sacred mountains from soil they had brought from mountains in the Third World. They planted the mountains, dressed them, and imbued the mountains —Blanca Peak to the east, Mount Taylor to the south, San Francisco Peaks to the west, and Hesperus Peak to the north—with life by placing Inner Forms (Holy People) within them. Each mountain had its own direction, color, jewel, and special properties. Along with other Holy People, they placed stars in the sky and created the seasons and day and night. They also filled the world with all its natural beauty by "dressing the earth" with vegetation, animals, plants, and other mountains. Special prayers and chants accompanied the creation of each aspect of the sky and earth, prayers and chants that even today "keep the sky and the earth and the day and the night beautiful" (medicine man Sandoval in O'Bryan 1993:24). Once created, everything in the universe existed in the state of spiritual symmetry and perfect balance known as hózh . Each of the four directions had its own sacred mountain, fastened to the earth with a rainbow and given life through the placement of its own Holy Person. In turn, the mountains connected the earth and sky.

One morning, just as the sun was rising, a dark cloud covered Gobernador Knob. Drawn by the sound of a baby crying, First Man and First Woman found a baby girl born of dawn and darkness. The baby became Changing Woman, one of the most beloved Navajo Holy People, and when she reached puberty, a Kinaaldá was held for her, just as it is held today to usher Navajo girls into womanhood. In time, Changing Woman fell in love with the Sun, a being so handsome that few women could resist him. She gave birth to twin boys, Monster Slayer and Born-for-Water, and later created the first four clans of the Navajo people from the skin on her own body. The Navajo landscape is rich with myth, for each event of creation is linked to a specific location on their land.

Archaeologists have a different view of Navajo origins, and place the arrival of the Apacheans—Navajos and Apaches—in the Southwest between A.D. 1000 and 1500, although a recent theory proposes that the Navajo migrated into the Southwest before A.D. 1100 and intermarried with the Anasazi (Kelley and Francis 1994:210–20). The Apacheans migrated southward from the Mackenzie Basin of Canada, where the nucleus of Athapaskan speakers is located, possibly searching for more plentiful resources for their growing population. Just as earlier people had unknowingly crossed the temporary land bridge across the Bering Straits into North America, the Apacheans steadily expanded into new territory. The Rocky Mountains were ecologically similar to the land they had left behind. For this reason, many archaeologists believe that the Apacheans followed the mountain chains of the Rockies (Huscher and Huscher 1942), while others consider it more likely that they took a High Plains route (D. A. Gunnerson 1956) or a Great Basin route (Steward 1936:62).

Navajo Peacemaker Court

Navajo Peacemaker Court is founded on a hallmark of Native American justice, the principle of fair compensation rather than retribution. Approved by the tribal council in 1982 and implemented in 1990, Navajo Peacemaker Court is based on the recognition that nothing can undo a wrong, which means that the parties involved need to acknowledge the pain inflicted and reach a mutually acceptable resolution based on fair compensation for that suffering. In 1995, 300 peacemakers operated in 7 court divisions across the reservation in cases involving vehicular, property, marriage, and land disputes; domestic violence; failure to file a death certificate; bigamy; and substance abuse. Some criminal cases are also handled in Peacemaker Court; after the parties have agreed to stop physical violence, the convicted person works out a solution with the victim, thus avoiding prison time.

Peacemaker Court has proven to be economically sound, saving thousands of dollars in legal fees as well as years of court battles. It also replaces the confrontational approach of District Court with Navajo practices and values, making Peacemaker Court a more comfortable place for elders less accustomed to the modern world. The peacemaker guides and mediates by incorporating traditional values into the modern legal process: when children are involved, the peacemaker reminds parents about their traditional roles in childrearing; elders often contribute their wisdom. A blessing prayer opens each session by asking for spiritual assistance and acknowledging that all parties are acting with "good heart," which means that everyone present is open to all viewpoints and is willing to work out a mutually satisfactory agreement. The session then proceeds in a spirit of goodwill and "right thinking."

Everyone has the opportunity to be heard, while others listen in respectful silence. Young people, who might not be allowed to speak in District Court, have a voice in

Peacemaker Court; in one case, children recounted how deeply their parents' alcoholic behavior frightened and hurt them. Another case involved a nineteen-year-old substance abuser, whose mother spoke of the emotional pain he inflicted on her. Rather than simply seeking answers to the immediate problems, Peacemaker Court addresses the nature of the underlying relationships. Thus, it does not polarize the parties involved, but instead unites them as they join in seeking a mutually acceptable solution.

Hózhǫ́ (the essence of harmonious relations among the human, holy, and natural worlds) and *nitséskees* (right thinking) are the foundation upon which the court is founded. *Nitséskees* recognizes the creative power of intention, the spirit in which an endeavor is undertaken that is inseparable from the outcome. Thus harmonious results come only from mutual respect and a shared desire to achieve a fair and just outcome. In giving people a voice, sometimes for the first time in their lives; in allowing them to see and hear the impact their behavior has had on their loved ones; and in empowering everyone involved to reach their own solution: in all these ways Peacemaker Court is a powerful tool for the restoration of *hózhǫ́*.

Language

The Navajo language is of the Na-Dené phylum and the Athapaskan (also spelled Athabascan) family. Except for the Eskimo (Inupiat and Yup'ik), the Na-Dené probably represent the final migration of peoples into the Americas from northeast Asia. Other Athapaskan speakers live in Oregon, northern California, Canada, and Alaska. Because the Navajo and various Apache groups—together, the Navajo and the Apaches are known as Apacheans—are the only Athapaskan speakers in the Southwest, they are also referred to as the Southern Athapaskans.

The Navajo language presents clues to the Navajo past: Dinétah, as they call their homeland in the Four Corners region of the Southwest, is almost identical to Denedeh, the word of the same meaning in languages of the Northern Dené phylum. The Navajo modified some words to fit their new surroundings. For example, the gliding motion of an owl's wing reminded early Navajos of the movement of a canoe's paddle in a lake, so they extended the meaning of the Athapaskan word for "paddle a canoe" to "the gliding flight of an owl" (Underhill 1956:5). Other words, such as the term for corn (meaning "food of the strangers"), suggest that they were among the last Indians to enter the Southwest.

Today the Navajo language continues to live and grow, for modern technology has enriched what Navajo poet Luci Tapahonso (1993:109) called "the verbal dexterity" of colloquial Navajo. Tapahonso cited the example of *béésh nitséskees* (thinking metal) for "computer" to show the Navajo language's capability of expressing unfamiliar terminology. (*Béésh* itself originally meant "stone knife"; its meaning later expanded to become "metal knife.") Unlike some Indian languages, which have not grown to express concepts lying outside their cultures, the Navajo language has long been known for the incorporation of new elements and concepts. Renowned linguist Robert Young (1972:228–32) cited many examples of the language's expanding lexicon from the beginning of Navajo contact with other cultures. For example, loan words include the borrowing of similar forms—*beeso* ("money," from Spanish *peso*) and *kaaboleita* (from English *carburetor*)—and words to express new cultural concepts that describe function, use, or appearance: *ch'osh doo yit'iini* ("invisible bug," that is, "microbe") and *gháá'ask'idii* ("the one with a hump-back," that is, "camel"). Navajo humor is evident in terms related to politics: *politics* is *na'adlo* (deceived by trickery), while *politician* is *bina'adlo'ii* (one who deceives).

Territory

Standing well above the lower basins of southern Arizona and the Rio Grande Valley of northern New Mexico, the Colorado Plateau on which Navajo land is located ranges in elevation from 2,760 feet to 10,388 feet above sea level. The Navajos' present-day reservation spans parts of three states—Arizona, New Mexico, and Utah—and overlaps the Four Corners region, where those three states and Colorado come together. A land of great ecological diversity, its considerable range in elevation determines temperature, rainfall, vegetation patterns, and the length of the growing season. Monthly temperatures range from an average low of 29°F in winter to an average high of 97°F in July and early August.

Three climatic zones exist: in addition to the cold, subhumid climate of the mountainous areas, there is a steppe climate in the middle elevations and an arid desert climate. Topographically, there are alluvial valleys, rolling upland plains, rugged tablelands, and mountains; the predominant pattern is one of long north-south valleys with washes, with mesas rising abruptly from the valley floor. The mountains of Navajo country include, from east to west, the Jemez Mountains, which rise just west of the Rio Grande; the San Mateo Mountains, which run northeast from Mount Taylor; Mesa de los Lobos, northeast of Gallup, New Mexico; the Chuska and Lukachukai Mountains, which follow the state line between Arizona and New Mexico; the Carrizo Mountains, north of the Chuskas; Black Mesa; and Navajo Mountain. High-country forests of pine, oak, spruce, fir, and aspen cover most of the mountains. Although the mountains receive 22 inches of annual rainfall, elevation limits the growing season to ninety days a year at best; frosts have been recorded during every month of the year.

Below the mountains are plateau and mesa regions where piñon, juniper, and sagebrush grow on the mesa tops, while cottonwoods, elms, and willows flourish where there is water. From east to west, these are the Chaco, Manuelito, Defiance, Shonto, Rainbow, and Kaibito Plateaus. Deep canyons cut through these plateaus, providing water for crops and protection from enemies. Chaco Canyon, in Chaco Mesa, and Canyon de Chelly and

Canyon del Muerto, in the Defiance Plateau, are among the best known canyons of Navajo country. These tablelands and plains account for nearly half the reservation and receive about 12 inches of rainfall each year. The lowest elevations, which receive some 8 inches of annual rainfall, are covered with sagebrush, greasewood, yucca, and grass. Only two areas—Monument Valley and the Painted Desert—are true deserts, so dry that few plants grow and most of the animals are small. Large mammals include mule deer, pronghorn, bighorn sheep, elk, coyote, gray wolf, mountain lion, bobcat, grizzly bear, and black bear, while blacktailed jackrabbit, porcupine, and Gunnison's prairie dog are among the smaller mammals (Jett and Spencer 1981:3).

The Complementarity of Science and Traditional Knowledge

In universities from Harvard to Berkeley, Native American students struggle with reconciling the concepts and facts presented in university classrooms with the teachings of their peoples. How can evolution be true without negating their own creation stories? How can they embrace the scientific enterprise without rejecting their own cultural and spiritual identity? Scientific methodology favors specialization and a quantitative approach, while traditional Indian world views are based on the symbiotic relationship of all things and a more qualitative approach. Yet science provides the knowledge and technology that can solve many of the serious problems facing reservations today, such as unprotected landfills, drought, vegetation depletion, and poor development of livestock.

When Carl Etsitty graduated from the University of Arizona in May 1997, he spoke of this moral dilemma: "I am Navajo. The Earth is our Mother. All of her creatures are our relatives. The Elders' teachings revere the frog as one that brings the rain to Navajo lands, but science teachers encouraged us to dissect the frog" (Windham 1997:39). This assignment involved a conflict between two belief systems and also between the resulting choice of strategies: should he step back to see the holistic overview of symbiotic relationships, or should he focus on the precise measurement of each part of the frog's anatomy? After earning his degree, Carl had decided to leave science until he heard about Significant Opportunities in Atmospheric Research and Science (SOARS), sponsored by the National Science Foundation at the University Corporation for Atmospheric Research (UCAR) and the National Center for Atmospheric Research (NCAR), both in Boulder, Colorado. "I completed the application because it represented an opportunity to continue the path of scientific research as guardian of Mother Earth" (ibid., 39).

With a mixture of excitement and skepticism, Carl drove to Boulder, where university students from across the country were participating in research projects under the direction of scientists at NCAR. The mentor/scientist requested by Carl was Lee Klinger, whose research centered on acid fertilization of moss in forest decline. Realizing that Carl was discouraged by the university science approach based on reductionist models instead of a holistic world view, Klinger introduced Carl to complexity theory, succession theory, and geophysiological approaches to knowledge. Carl has now

> been able to embrace strategies that allow me to study science with my
> heart and with my mind. I can travel within the wheel as a scientist while continuing to learn and practice traditional Indian knowledge. It is still my wish
> to live and work with my relatives on Indian lands and with the traditional scientific community to bring all people closer to the vision of a good tomorrow.
> (Windham 1997:39)

Returning to the University of Arizona to earn a graduate degree in the department of soil, water, and environmental science, Carl continued working with Klinger to research the hypothesis that treating forest soils with lime can help offset the indirect effects of air pollution that accelerate natural forest succession. Today Carl works for the Environmental Protection Agency in Washington, D.C.

Scientists Helmut Hirsch and Helen Ghiradella, professors of biology at the State University of New York at Albany, are also drawing inspiration from the Indian perspective on knowledge. After speaking with Navajo park ranger Lupita Litson in Canyon de Chelly, Arizona, they decided to develop a program that reintroduces values and reverence into the Western educational setting (Hirsch and Ghiradella 1994). While American Indian communities emphasize a *sustainable society*, measuring success by the ability to live in harmony with the rest of the world by making the most of available resources, the scientific community tends to measure success by the grant money scientists bring in and the sophistication of the technology it buys. These factors, as well as the increasing focus on reductionism—taking everything apart into its components without looking carefully at the properties of the intact "system"—have alienated Indian and non-Indian students alike.

After his return to Albany, Hirsch integrated some of Litson's ideas into his dedication talk for a new science dormitory, a residential program intended to introduce students in the biomedical sciences to Native American viewpoints on knowledge as well as to attract interested Native American students. "As our resources diminish— as they must, if our population keeps growing—we must use our current position of strength to plan for that future . . . [by] encouraging *sustainable scientific achievement*" (Hirsch and Ghiradella 1994:41 [emphasis in original]).

Hirsch went on to emphasize that technology should be considered an extension of creative thinking instead of an end in itself and that we must change the present scientific climate so that it allows for a diversity of approaches, including those that are not highly dependent upon the growth of technology. These ideas echo the wisdom of Litson's grandfather, who had told her that "Western society would attempt to replace all stories of other people with its own," which would be the end of life because "when all peoples have the same story, then humans will cease to exist" (Hirsch and Ghiradella 1994:39). This had led her to ask, "As scientists and as citizens desperately concerned with the future, how can we be sure that *all* our stories will be cherished and heard, not only those produced by the research and scholarship fashions of the moment?" (ibid., 40 [emphasis in original]).

Hirsch ended his address by stressing that educators and students alike have the responsibility to see "that our stories, and those of others, survive, lest humans cease to exist" (Hirsch and Ghiradella 1994:42).

Prehistory and Early History

The Apacheans left Canada as hunter-gatherers adapted to a cold climate: the men hunted big game with bows and arrows, and fished in rivers and lakes, while the women gathered berries, processed hides, and made buckskin clothing decorated with porcupine quillwork, and wove baskets (rather than making pottery). They used a sinew-backed bow, and not the simpler staff bow that the Pueblos used. The Apacheans also introduced hard-soled moccasins into the Southwest, replacing Pueblo sandals. Their forked-pole, bark- or skin-covered dwellings were the precursors of the hogans and wickiups they would build when they reached the Southwest. They brought with them shamanistic practices; the Athapaskan emphasis on curing would shape the direction of Navajo healing ceremonies. They respected and feared the dead and considered it vital to celebrate a girl's passage into womanhood (Opler 1983:372–80). Organized into family groups and loosely knit bands, they had informal leaders who had limited and temporary authority. Proto-Athapaskan kinship was probably unilineal or double unilineal (Dyen and Aberle 1974:124).

By 1400 the Apacheans arrived in the Southwest in small bands of undifferentiated migratory peoples (Opler 1983:382). Resilient and resourceful, these Southern Athapaskans had had to adapt to many ecological niches on their southward journey. Once they reached the Southwest, change continued to be a vital process that exposed them to different cultures and ways of life, providing important stimulus for their own way of life. They learned quickly from their new neighbors, taking on many borrowed traits from their Plains and Pueblo neighbors. Most Apaches remained more influenced by the peoples of the Great Plains, especially the Kiowa-Apache who joined the Plains-dwelling Kiowa. The

Apacheans eventually divided themselves into seven groups, each with its own territory and lifestyle: the Kiowa-Apache, Lipan, Mescalero, Jicarilla, Chiricahua, Western Apache, and Navajo. Through time, the Navajo (and to a lesser extent the Western Apache) borrowed many Pueblo traits, which they reworked into what became distinctly Navajo culture, while other, more eastern Apache groups took on more Plains traits (ibid., 380–81).

Moving into the relatively unoccupied spaces of the region, the Navajo spread into the Four Corners area until they were encircled on three sides by Puebloan peoples; only to the north lay other peoples, the Utes and Southern Paiutes. As smaller hunting and gathering groups, the Navajo were able to live off country that could not support the agricultural towns of the Pueblos. Adapting to their new surroundings, Navajo men whose ancestors had once hunted caribou used their skills to hunt deer, antelope, and rabbits, and women expanded their subsistence base to include cactus fruits, piñon nuts, and new varieties of greens, seeds, roots, and berries. Impressed by the more lavish cultural inventory of the Pueblo, made possible by agriculture, the Navajo began to transform their nomadic foraging existence into a more agriculturally based way of life by cultivating family plots of corn, pumpkins, squash, tobacco, chile peppers, and beans. No other Athapaskan group took so readily to farming: their very name derives from *nava hu* ("place of large cultivated fields") in the language of the Tewa-speaking Pueblos (Brugge 1983:496).

After the Pueblo Revolt of 1680, Puebloan people sought refuge with the Navajo, intensifying the diffusion of Pueblo ideas. By this time the Navajo had settled into what they called Dinétah (the Land of the People)—what is now the Gobernador–Largo Canyon–Navajo Reservoir district of northern New Mexico. There the Navajo remained free from direct Spanish and Mexican interference; this situation enabled them to maintain independence from ecclesiastical, military, and political domination, while selecting certain items from Spanish culture, such as sheep, goats, and methods of animal husbandry. The Navajo experienced considerable Spanish influence indirectly when Pueblo refugees, fleeing from Spanish reprisals, sought shelter with the Navajo in the canyons of present-day northwestern New Mexico.

This region became the site of intense cultural growth as Pueblo peoples brought with them all the wealth of their culture, such as techniques for weaving, decorated pottery, masonry homes, inheritance through female clans, and their religious practices and beliefs, including katsina dances. Even more Pueblo refugees flooded into the Dinétah when news of Vargas's reconquest came in 1693. The Pueblos watched the Spaniards sweep through the Rio Grande Valley, defeating each minor Pueblo alliance with their superior weaponry. In 1696, when the Jemez tried unsuccessfully to resist Vargas, many Jemez, Keresans and Tewas poured into the canyon country in the San Juan Valley above present-day Farmington, New Mexico; the next forty years were a time of peaceful coexistence and cultural sharing between the Navajo and the Pueblo. Even today, the mesas of Gobernador and Largo Canyons are filled with the remains of hogans and small pueblos, and defensive towns atop ridges attest to the need for protection against their mutual enemy, the Utes. Intermarriage between the Navajo and Puebloans increased, and new Navajo clans were created, such as the Zuni, Hopi, and Jemez clans. The great influx of Pueblo peoples has led some anthropologists (Luckert 1975:14) to speculate that by 1700 up to 25 percent of the population were Pueblo refugees.

During this period, the Gobernador was what David Brugge calls "the center of a cultural development that has no equal in Apachean history" because the influx of Pueblo refugees joined "the two major ancestral roots of traditional Navajo culture, Athapaskan-Apachean and Anasazi-Puebloan" (1983:493). The Puebloan refugees shared their complex of ceremonial practices and beliefs, which led the Navajo to adopt the use of altars, corn pollen, ceremonial wands, masked dancers, prayersticks, and sandpaintings. Rich in rock art, the canyons of the Gobernador reflect a shared concern with religion: petroglyphs and pictographs depict katsinam, Kokopeli (the hunchback flute player), animals with heart lines, sun shields with macaw feathers, and figures reminiscent of prehistoric kiva murals, imagery associated with Pueblo beliefs (Schaasfsma 1963). The borrowing was mutual, for although the Navajos were probably inspired by the Pueblo tradition of portraying sacred subjects in graphic form (on walls and altars and in sandpaintings), there was a noticeable absence of Pueblo-style kivas in the Gobernador region, signifying that a predominantly Navajo religious pattern probably prevailed at this time (Schaasfsma 1966: 9–10). Archaeologists have also found Pueblo and Navajo ritual paraphernalia together in excavated caches.

Around 1700, when the Navajo acquired Spanish livestock, they easily adapted their old social organization, which had served them well as hunters and gatherers, to the new activity of livestock raising. At this time, Ute raiders from the north pressured the Navajo to begin moving southward and westward. By about 1750 drought and the intensification of Ute hostility exacerbated the fundamental differences between Pueblo and Athapaskan values. The Navajo responded with a revitalization movement that took the form of retaining only those introduced beliefs and practices that were compatible with their values, and after twenty transitional years, they had integrated Pueblo traditions into their own culture by reworking items that fit with Athapaskan values. They rejected kivas, stone houses, decorated pottery, and traits that tended to structure society too rigidly, such as the use of whipping for social control and some religious practices (Brugge 1983:495). They retained other culture traits, such as livestock husbandry and weaving, but weaving, a male activity among the Hopi, became a female occupation among the Navajo.

The Navajo also borrowed certain ceremonial patterns that fit in with their own belief system. Instead of borrowing the Pueblo emphasis on rainmaking or fertility, the Navajo incorporated the Puebloan items that would aid in healing, an Athapaskan ceremonial focus. Corn pollen, used by the Pueblos to promote fertility, became an essential Navajo sacrament as the Navajo extended its use to bless the patient with the state of harmony and well-being known as *hózhǫ́*. Influenced by the Pueblo priesthood, the Navajo developed a ceremonial specialist called a singer, who painstakingly learned a body of religious knowledge, to gain prestige over the shaman, who was relegated to diagnosing illness. The masks, prayersticks, and sandpainting altars that Navajo singers used were of Pueblo origin, but were reworked into distinctly Navajo forms; Navajo Yeibichai—the dancers who embody Navajo Holy People—resemble Pueblo katsinam. Navajo residence groups are quite dispersed in comparison to the densely settled Pueblo towns with their permanent religious structures (kivas), so the Navajo singer must travel to his or her patient. Thus, the Navajo borrowed the most transportable aspects of Puebloan ceremonialism. For example, they reworked the concept of permanent altars inside kivas, basic to Pueblo practices, into one of temporary altars, which they created inside their hogans. They did this by expanding and elaborating just one element of the Pueblo altar, the ephemeral sandpainting, into the entire altar.

The acquisition of the horse increased Navajo mobility, enlarging the range and frequency of contact with non-Navajos, but it also altered the character of social relations within the tribe. It was now possible to visit more frequently and to attend ceremonial events from much greater distances. Thus, the audiences at ceremonials became larger, and this may have led to an elaboration of the ceremonies themselves.

Farming made the Navajo especially vulnerable to raiding. By 1754 Ute and Comanche raids forced the Navajo to abandon the Gobernador region for areas farther west toward Canyon de Chelly and south near Taylor (Schroeder 1965:59), and an area north and south of present-day Gallup, New Mexico (Young 1972:170). From the Pueblos, they had learned sheep and goat herding; the tortuous canyons and lofty mesas of northwestern New Mexico were unsuited to pastoral activities (Haskell 1975:178), but their new territory proved to be much better terrain, especially for their flocks of sheep. In 1774 the Navajo successfully drove encroaching Spanish settlers from the eastern portion of their territory (Reeve 1959:39–40). However, when Mexican independence in 1821 opened trade with Anglo-Americans, the New Mexicans received better supplies of firearms, and the Navajo became the target of slavers from Mexico, New Mexico, and other Indian tribes. Decades of raids, retaliation, and ineffective peace treaties followed, and escalating warfare with aggressive New Mexicans forged the Navajo into a nation, though they had no central government and each Navajo band remained loyal to its own headman.

Although the Navajo farmed more than any other Apachean group, by the late 1700s and early 1800s they began to shift their economic dependence to herding, and their herds increased dramatically during the first half of the nineteenth century (Bailey and Bailey 1986:19). They did, however, supplement herding with intensive farming, hunting, gathering, and raiding. When herding sheep, they sometimes planted corn, melons, beans, and squash in the spring and left them untended until the fall harvest. Goats remained a dietary mainstay, although sheep, despite their lower subsistence value, were more economically important because they provided wool for domestic and trade textiles, including women's dresses. Horses, mules, and burros were a source of transportation and food, as well as a source of prestige, and cattle, which required far less care than sheep and goats, were raised for trade (ibid., 36–37).

Herding became the backbone of Navajo subsistence for many reasons, but the most significant reason can be found in their cultural values. Once acquired, sheep and goats quickly became a measure of status and wealth as well as a marker of cultural identity. Both literally and metaphorically, sheep are life to the Navajo. The Navajo emphasis on movement and change, as previously mentioned, is the foundation of their world view. Navajo mythic heroes travel restlessly in their search for sacred knowledge; Navajos consider life itself to be a journey; and the structure of the language stresses detailed movement. Pastoralism—with its daily demands of herding the flock from place to place and its seasonal requirements for fresh pasturage—is in keeping with the cultural values of a nomadic heritage.

As they shifted their economic orientation during this period toward herding, the Navajo dramatically changed their settlement patterns. Instead of remaining throughout the year in a single, more or less permanent camp near their fields, they began to divide the year between summer and winter residences owned by individual family units. Practicing transhumance—the seasonal movement of flocks from summer to winter pastures —instead of true nomadism, the Navajo shifted their herds from higher elevations in the summer to lower ground in the winter, where forage and water were available for the animals.

The period between 1800 and 1850 was one of intensified raiding for livestock as their economy shifted toward pastoralism. Between 1821, when Mexico took over the territory from Spain, and 1848, when the United States assumed control, the Navajo and "Mexican" populations waged almost constant warfare (McNitt 1972:59–91). By the mid-1800s, herding and raiding had become inextricably linked, for the Navajos' increased reliance on sheep and goats led them to intensify their raiding of herds owned by European American settlers, which in turn increased the settlers' hostility and brought retaliation. Another reason for Navajo raids was retaliation on the Spanish, and later Mexicans, and the Pueblos, who routinely captured Navajos as slaves. It is estimated that between 1846 and 1850, 20,000 horses and mules and 800,000 sheep and cattle were stolen in northwestern New Mexico (Spicer 1981:216). New Mexicans became so enraged at the Navajo that they seized more Navajo women and children as slaves, and by 1860 it was reported that as many as 5,000–6,000 Navajo slaves—over half the Navajo population at this time—were living with families in New Mexican villages (ibid., 217).

When the United States acquired much of the Southwest from Mexico in 1848, government officials promised settlers protection from marauding Navajo and Apache, who had become a serious threat in the Rio Grande Valley. The Navajo continued to raid Anglo settlers who had invaded their land despite the construction of forts and attempts at negotiating treaties (which were useless since the Navajo had no centralized authority, and the Anglos never understood the autonomous nature of Navajo bands). A driving force behind many Navajo raids was simply the recovery of their own people, for the Navajo had lost thousands to slavery. Slave traders wanted the hostilities to continue because they viewed war as an opportunity to capture more Navajos. When the Civil War drew the troops east, any military control over New Mexican slave raiders ceased, exacerbating the situation (McNitt 1972:379).

Things became so chaotic that in 1862, the newly appointed military commander for New Mexico, General James Carleton, developed a plan for the forced relocation of Mescalero Apaches and Navajos to Fort Sumner in east-central New Mexico. Although a military board had recommended another location because of poor water, an inadequate supply of wood, and threat of floods at Fort Sumner, Carleton insisted on the location. Fort Sumner, also known as Bosque Redondo, was to be the new home for the Mescalero and the Navajo —who were traditional enemies.

General Carleton appointed Kit Carson, a reluctant campaigner who believed the Indians would eventually agree to terms without the need for war. Nevertheless, Carson led his troops against the Mescalero, subduing them in five months. In 1863 Carson led more than 700 New Mexico militiamen against the Navajo. Using the scorched-earth strategy later employed by General William T. Sherman in his March to the Sea across Georgia, Carson's troops destroyed any hogans, cornfields, peach trees, water holes, animals, and people in their path. The Utes, Pueblos, and Mexicans, longtime enemies of the Navajo, increased the frequency and ferocity of their raids by taking Navajo sheep and horses, and capturing women and children for slaves. A brutal winter, combined with the destruction of their resources, brought defeat to the Navajo; by the end of 1864 about 8,000 Navajos had surrendered. The Long Walk, a death march for hundreds, followed when soldiers forced the Navajo to walk 250 miles from Fort Defiance to Fort Sumner along the Pecos River in east-central New Mexico. Soldiers shot stragglers and slavers stole children; without wagons, nearly everyone had to walk.

Confined to Bosque Redondo, which was basically a concentration camp, the Navajo died in great numbers. Carleton had vastly underestimated the number of Navajos and was able to provide food, blankets, and shelter for only half their numbers. Droughts, poor agricultural land, epidemics, and raids by other tribes led to the death of many Navajos, and within months over 2,000 had died of disease brought on by crowded conditions, bad water, and insufficient food (the result of inadequate rations and continued crop failure). Government officials, realizing the economic difficulty of continued detention, decided to make a treaty with the Navajo that would allow them to return to a fraction of their former territory on both sides of the Arizona–New Mexico territory line. The government provided farming equipment, seeds, cattle, sheep, and goats.

Their years in exile had a lasting impact on the Navajo: not only did they cease large-scale raiding, but they also developed a sense of political unity, thinking of themselves as one people for the first time in their history. Today the Long Walk continues to be a powerful component of Navajo identity. Returning to their homeland, including the Four Sacred Mountains, further reinforced their ties to the land, forging another element in their identity as a people.

As Edward Spicer pointed out, in the Southwest the processes of Hispanicization, Mexicanization, and Anglicization were incomplete and occurred at different rates among different groups, depending upon such factors as the kinds of conditions established by the conquerors, the kinds of organizations permitted by the invaders, and the political institutions through which they maintained dominance (1981:567–76). These assimilation programs were products of the dominant group's traditions and values: the Spaniards focused on religious conversion, the Mexicans emphasized political values, and the Anglo-Americans were primarily guided by economics. While other Southwestern groups experienced the forced impact of all three groups, the Navajo experienced governing only by the last group. The resilience of Navajo culture was nurtured by the kinds of cultural contact they experienced (which had been under their control, for the most part, until their defeat by U.S. military forces), a reservation that retained much of their traditional territory, the relatively unstructured nature of their cultural institutions, and their cultural response to outside influences which enabled them to rework and incorporate useful traits. After their return to their homeland, their economic self-sufficiency meant that the U.S. government had less leverage in controlling their assimilation, as noted by Indian agent William Parsons in 1886: "Their very independence and industry makes them less susceptible than other tribes to civilizing influences. Other tribes which receive supplies of food and clothing, can be induced to cut their hair and wear the garb of the white men" (RBIA LR GR).

Another significant difference in the Navajos' experience was the issue of allotment. In 1887 the passage of the Dawes Severalty Act led to the division of communal Indian land among individuals (with any remaining land sold to white settlers). Fortunately, the federal government kept the Navajo reservation from being allotted, and Indian Service officials worked to expand it in the late nineteenth and early twentieth centuries. The retention of a land base within their traditional territorial range promoted the continuity of tribal identity (Spicer 1981:577) as well as a greater degree of cultural autonomy.

The fact that cultural transmission occurred through the resident extended family was also beneficial in the maintenance of Navajo culture (Bailey and Bailey 1986:297). This basic core institution—a multigenerational and self-sufficient unit providing for traditions to be passed on from the oldest and most conservative members to the youngest—was a major factor in the continuity of Navajo culture.

The highly complex Navajo ceremonial system survived because of its flexible structure: in comparison with the rituals of other Native American groups, the Navajo have no ritual calendar, no clan-controlled ceremonies, and no rigidly organized priesthood. Therefore, the disappearance of a clan did not mean the extinction of a ceremonial. Furthermore, because most Navajo ceremonials focus on the healing of individuals rather than on the welfare of the community, the loss or change of particular ceremonials through time has not endangered cultural survival.

The Navajos' incorporative response to outside influences also encouraged cultural resilience, for instead of being threatened by traditions foreign to their own, the Navajo willingly accept innovation. They possess a distinctive cultural ability to borrow only that which is useful and appropriate and to rework the borrowed trait into a form that is distinctly Navajo, without any loss of cultural integrity.

Other factors, however, have tended to undermine Navajo cultural autonomy. One of these was their treatment as wards of the government during the crucial sixty or seventy years after their return from Bosque Redondo. They thus missed the formative period of reservation government, because reservations were then viewed as permanent institutions, rather than as transitional communities that would eventually be functioning units in the Anglo-American political system (Spicer 1981:574–76). At the same time that the Navajo were losing an opportunity to gain valuable experience of self-government, which could have integrated their government into the national system, their traditional institutions were being weakened and lost as a result of increasing dependency. The Navajo were being administered by a system that was responsible to the bureaucracy and not to the Indians themselves, and the passage of time only increased the complexity of the web of bureaucracy that bound them. Recovery was slow because of drought, corrupt Indian agents, and raiding by other groups, but eventually harvests improved, and the herds grew larger, giving the Navajo a degree of economic independence. The Navajo population also increased, leading the government to expand reservation holdings three times in the late 1800s.

Once Navajos began to trade their surplus wool in 1875, trading posts began to develop into an essential economic institution; until this time, the level of trade was so low that it could not sustain licensed traders (Bailey and Bailey 1986:59). The wool trade continued to develop along with the growth of Navajo herds, which brought about an increase in trading posts as traders found other marketable items, such as piñon nuts, goat skins, and sheep pelts. When the railroad reached western New Mexico in 1881, trading posts sprang up along its route. In addition to exchanging goods through bartering, traders extended credit if Indians could provide an item left as security; pawn could be recovered later, with products to pay back the extended credit (Iverson 1990:53). When Navajos pawned jewelry and blankets, traders soon recognized the appeal of these beautiful objects to non-Indians. Soon the traders began to encourage women to weave rugs and men to become master silversmiths. As well as increasing commerce between the eastern and western United States, the railroad also brought an influx of tourists eager for a glimpse of this once isolated region.

With the development of trading posts and the expansion of herds beyond the subsistence level, farming decreased as a means of subsistence, although families continued to plant small fields. Trade networks—trading posts and intertribal and Mexican American networks—supplied foodstuffs, manufactured goods, and items of Indian manufacture, and subsistence-oriented herding gave way to commercial herding, while weaving and silversmithing became even more market-oriented. As Navajos were integrated into the national economy, the trading post became increasingly important to Navajo life by providing the items they could no longer provide for themselves.

Material Culture

The hogan (*hooghan*, literally, "place home") was the basic Navajo dwelling, and in the early 1800s conical, forked-pole hogans ("male hogans") still dominated, although by the end of the century they would be replaced by the roomier, hexagonal or octagonal, cribwork hogans ("female hogans"). Piñon or ponderosa pine logs serve as the larger timbers for the framework, with juniper often taking a minor role in the construction. Once made, the

Norma Irvin standing in front of her mother's hogan with her daughters, Malynda, Michelle, and Natalie, New Mexico, 1994. Author photograph

framework is chinked with material such as tree limbs, brush, or stones, and finally with tamped damp earth (Jett and Spencer 1981:15–17).

The doorway faces east—specifically, the direction of the first appearance of the rising sun at the time of construction—to catch the blessing of the first rays (Newcomb 1940:18, 23) and to accommodate the importance of east in ritual activities (Franciscan Fathers 1910:56). More practically, such an orientation offers greater protection against prevailing southwesterly winds and accompanying storms, as well as against the cold north wind of winter (Jett and Spencer 1981:17). Originally, the entry was covered with hides or a woven mat of material such as yucca or juniper bark, but once Navajo women became proficient weavers, they began using old handwoven blankets hung from pegs inside or outside the hogan.

Each hogan has a smoke hole at or near the center of the roof, allowing light to enter from above (Haile 1937:2). The hearth is located directly underneath the smoke hole. The hogan interior, though never physically subdivided, is divided functionally. North is the woman's side of the hogan, where the loom is erected and the kitchen supplies and utensils are kept, and south is the man's side (Correll 1965:31). Opposite the doorway, to the rear of the hogan (the west side), is the part reserved for the eldest female or male as the place of honor. Such an honorific, gender-based subdivision of interior living space is a northern Athapaskan, not a Puebloan trait (Morice 1909:593). Other structures might include a sweat lodge, a small storage hogan, and a ramada. While the family moved with the herd, they might build a temporary lean-to brush shelter.

When women began to weave, they replaced their buckskin clothing with Pueblo-like dresses made of two identical black blankets with red borders. By 1900 most women were wearing the full calico skirts and velveteen blouses now associated with the Navajo (Kluckhohn et al. 1971:242–46). Men wore shirts, short trousers, breechclouts, and, after the advent of weaving, blankets. Silver jewelry became popular in addition to the turquoise bead necklaces and earrings the Navajo had long worn, which they acquired through trade with the Pueblos. (Atsidi Sani, who is believed to have been the first Navajo silversmith, learned the rudiments of silverworking from an itinerant Mexican craftsman in the early 1850s [Bahti 1997:14].) By 1795 the weaving produced by Navajo women was described by one writer of that time as "finer than that of the Spaniards" (Underhill 1953:110). New Mexicans paid for these highly prized blankets with livestock and material items; however, they also captured Navajo women, forcing them to weave what became known as "slave blankets" as part of their duties.

Social Organization

Although the following description is written in the past tense, many of these practices are still followed today.

Loretta Denny Bahe and her son Fernando inside her parents' hogan, Arizona, 1999. Author photograph

Navajo society was matrilineal and matrilocal, with descent traced through the mother, and a married couple usually (but not always) built their hogan near the dwelling of the wife's mother. Thus, children grew up in close association with their matrilineal relatives. Navajo kinship terminology reflected this matrilineal and matrilocal orientation. Each of the mother's sisters was called *shimá yaazhi* (little mother), and her children were called by the same terms as biological brothers and sisters. Although the father's brother was called "father," his children were not called by sibling terms.

The bond between a mother and her children was the strongest and most enduring tie in Navajo culture and was expressed as affection, care, and sustenance (Aberle 1961:166; Witherspoon 1970:59). Although the father-child bond was secondary, the father's role was complementary to the mother's role, for he provided strength and leadership, and made possible conception, reproduction, and subsistence. The complementarity between parental roles was evident in Navajo clanship, for children were "born of" the mother's clan and took the mother's clan as their own; at the same time, children were "born for" the father's clan and had their secondary clan affiliation through the father.

The position of women in Navajo society was a very strong and influential one, for women have always played important roles not only in social and economic life, but also in political and religious activities. The woman owned the hogan and controlled a large share of the property, which was usually inherited by her descendants, thus keeping it in the matrilineal family line. She was responsible for cooking, cleaning the hogan, weaving, washing clothes, and caring for the children. Later in the nineteenth century, when Navajo textiles began to bring good prices, a woman had a ready source of income through weaving. Women have always become ceremonial practitioners, both singers (priests) and diagnosticians (shamans). (Women generally did not become singers until after menopause.) And, as noted above, women continue to select their dance partners in the so-called Squaw Dance.

Matrilocal residence took a man away from his family of origin, thus dividing his loyalties and responsibilities between his new household and his birth household. A man was responsible for the building and repair of the hogan, the hauling of water and wood, and the chopping of firewood; at the same time he continued to play an important role in his mother's family by attending ceremonies at his old home and sharing in the expenses incurred. He visited his mother frequently at her hogan and retained close ties with his family of origin, including economic ties. Adults who acted irresponsibly brought shame to their entire family, and the worst thing that could be said of someone was that "he acts as if he didn't have any relatives" (Kluckhohn and Leighton 1962:100).

Kinship terminology reflected expected behavior in each set of relationships and indicated from whom a person might seek aid and how much help the individual could expect from that person, the degree of authority one person exercised over another, and whether two people could joke about sexual matters. David Aberle (1961) summed up Navajo kin behavior by saying that there were relatives with whom one was bashful and those with whom one was easy. This meant that some people had to be treated with formality and deference, and some even had to be approached through intermediaries, while at the other end of the spectrum were relatives with whom one could joke, even obscenely. Among the most distant and respectful relationships was the one between a man and his wife's mother: the mother-in-law taboo forbade direct contact between them as a sign of mutual respect. At the other extreme was the joking relationship a young man had with his mother's brother; nearly all topics were permitted, including sexual conquests and the size of genitals (ibid.). Unlike many matrilineal societies in which the mother's brother was important, in Navajo society he was less important unless the father was not present.

The primacy of age was particularly important, and old men and women were considered to be repositories of wisdom. Their opinions were valued when communitywide decisions were being made, but an elder, even one who was poor, with many descendants had a more secure position than one who, even if wealthy, had few children and grandchildren. This stemmed in part from the days when a man could count on the armed support of his sons, grandsons, and daughters' husbands (Downs 1972:26). The relationship between grandparents and their grandchildren was warm and affectionate, and grandparents were known as great storytellers, especially during the long nights of winter when it was proper to speak of sacred things because much of nature was sleeping. It was then that grandmothers taught their grandchildren to make string games as they recounted the stories behind them, and grandfathers spoke of how things came to be in the world. Such stories, part entertainment and part moral teaching, were an essential aspect of Navajo life, and they were the special responsibility of grandparents to pass on to their grandchildren.

Among siblings, age determined authority throughout their lives. If many years separated the oldest child from siblings, the firstborn exercised authority that approached that of a parent. Advice and guidance from an older brother or sister was expected to be followed, or at least received respectfully. Conversely, it was difficult for an older brother to deny requests for money or assistance in farming or herding from a younger sister because he was expected to provide for her as would a parent. In general, consanguineal (blood) kin could speak directly to each other, while among affinal kin (relations through marriage rather than blood), a man was expected to go through intermediaries, and a woman communicated directly only to her female affines (Aberle 1961:162).

In the first half of the 1800s the Navajo did not live in towns, but rather in isolated family groups. The Navajo ideal was a matrilineal, matrilocal society structured in terms of (1) the nuclear family; (2) the residence group, which was a matrilocal extended family; (3) a group or network of relatives who lived nearby and cooperated for certain purposes (sometimes referred to as an "outfit"); and (4) the matrilineal clan (Spencer and Jennings 1977: 303). The nuclear family was the smallest unit, with each nuclear family occupying its own hogan, while the basic economic and social unit was the (matrilocal) resident extended family. The residence group, a self-sufficient group living in close proximity, provided for cultural transmission from the oldest and most conservative members to the youngest. Each residence group was organized around a head mother, a sheep herd, a traditional land-use area, and sometimes agricultural fields (Witherspoon 1983:525), but it did not own property collectively, for livestock was individually owned and jointly managed, and fields were jointly used. Children or adults of either sex had the responsibility for herding because, mounted on horseback, one person could tend a flock as large as two hundred animals. Lambing and shearing were shared by the entire residence group.

The next largest cooperative unit consisted of a group of relatives who occupied neighboring territories and who helped each other economically and with physical labor on a regular basis, such as pooling resources to arrange an expensive healing ceremony or sharing supplies during times of need (Aberle 1963:1–7). While the members of an extended family lived within shouting distance of each other, the related families who worked together on larger tasks (the "outfit") could be dispersed over many square miles.

After the nuclear family, the residence group, and the cooperative kin group, the largest kin group of all was the matrilineal clan. Today, the four clan affiliations are one's own clan, one's father's clan, one's mother's father's clan (*shichei*), and one's father's father's clan (*shinálí*). In contrast to the nuclear family, the residence group, and the cooperative kin group, which were spatially distinct, clans were scattered throughout Navajo territory. Most of the sixty Navajo clans were named for localities—Water Flowing Together, Bitter

Water—suggesting that clans may once have been localized; today, despite their wide geographic spread, clans tend to be concentrated in certain sections. Although there was no clan government or law—unlike Hopi clans, Navajo clans were not corporate entities—people could not marry into their mother's or father's clans or into any member of related clans. Such related clans were grouped into phratries composed of two to six clans, usually with one large clan and several minor ones; about nine phratries existed, with eight unassigned clans (Aberle 1961:183).

When a Navajo met another Navajo within or outside of their homeland, one of the first things they exchanged was the names of their respective clans. This information let each of them know if they were related, in which case they could not date each other. If they were in fact related, clan information further told them the nature of their relationship—for example, a "grandfather" was expected to give his "grandchild" loving advice. These relationships had nothing to do with relative age; in clan relationships, a "grandfather" might be the same age as his "grandchild."

The fluid, unstructured nature of Navajo social organization—the very quality that made it so adaptable to changing needs—has also made it difficult to describe, and the wider network of cooperating relatives (the "outfit") is a concept that scholars have described in many different ways (Aberle 1961; Adams 1963; Collier 1951; Kluckhohn and Leighton 1962; Levy 1962; Ross 1955; Shepardson and Hammond 1970; Witherspoon 1975). The considerable variation in residence-group composition at different points in a family's development led Louise Lamphere (1977:77–78) to apply a model based on Fortes's (1963) developmental cycle of domestic groups, involving the terms *set* and *network*. She defined the set as "those adults within one or two genealogical links of any particular ego" (ibid., 127), and the network as the "unbounded system of relationships between pairs of people making up a field of activity" (ibid., 94). A person's set changed throughout the course of his or her lifetime because as individuals were born and matured and died, the composition of the domestic group changed. In the first phase of the cycle, the newly married couple lived with the wife's relatives (usually), and the young couple might at first share the same hogan as the parents, but soon they constructed their own dwelling. The second phase began when the young couple became economically self-sufficient and was able to establish their own camp, usually near the parent camp. This might also be about the time that one or both of the parents were reaching the end of their lives. In the third phase, the children of the once young couple married and formed their own new households; fission again occurred. A person's network was equally dynamic. Lamphere stressed the overlapping nature of the groups to which each individual belonged, from the residence group to the nearby clan segment. Thus, a network of social ties existed, giving each individual alternative groups of people to call upon for economic and physical aid.

In the late twentieth century increasing population on a limited land base made the normal fissions in residence groups impossible. Contributing factors were the decline in pastoral and agricultural activities and greater access to distant neighbors. Lamphere's study, set in the 1960s, demonstrated the flexibility of Navajo social structure based on cooperative activities, for she documented that when an individual recruited aid for ceremonial cooperation or simply transportation, he or she turned to people on the basis of proximity and kinship. Primary kin were asked before secondary kin, and coresidents and kin were recruited before nonlocal kin. An individual asked for help in this order: residential members (the most easily recruited); primary and secondary kin outside the residence group, with those who lived in the same neighborhood being the most likely to help; neighbors with whom the individual had clan ties; and finally, in the case of funerals or large ceremonies, distant clan relatives (Lamphere 1977:178).

Artist Conrad House

Conrad House, a contemporary multimedia (printmaking, ceramics, beadwork, and glass) artist from the Window Rock area, told his story in *All Roads Are Good: Native Voices on Life and Culture* (1994:90–101). His father is Navajo/Oneida and his mother is Navajo. House honors the strength of the women in his family in his black drawings and collage work by using black and cochineal red in reference to the traditional *biił* woven dresses. Yet he reaches beyond cultural boundaries to draw from other cultures as well as his own, including Haida and Tlingit designs, Anasazi pottery, contemporary Southwestern pottery, Seminole patchwork, and Crow color and designs.

Many modern Native Americans, said House, "must go through the library to find out about themselves. . . . How is a Navajo raised in New York City going to find out about the wonderful smell of sage or cliffrose?" (House 1994:95).

He acknowledges the need "to preserve our past in museums, as a way for people to know and understand our existence. Such preservation is a way for the coming generations to see who we were and who we are" (House 1994:92). Yet he feels that sacred objects, such as medicine bags and masks, should be returned to the earth and the people to whom they originally belonged because of their power. "You have to be cautious and careful and need to know the songs and knowledge before you open a *jish*, or medicine bag. . . . The masks have got to breathe because there's energy in them—in the Navajo way, they're alive" (ibid., 95). This is why elders "are protective of that knowledge . . . a lot of our younger Indian people have misused the imagery and the meaning behind these sacred objects" (ibid.).

The survival and existence of a culture, says House, depends upon learning about the sacredness and significance of the land by spending time with your relatives and people. It is important to seek out knowledgeable people familiar with traditions. House brings contemporary relevance to the Navajo creation story by pointing out that most versions mention the emergence of the people from four previous underworlds into the fifth world, where they are today. The fifth world—the glittering world—is all around, in shiny glass, metal, and plastics. House explains that, despite warnings and signs to be careful, the people did not listen and brought a state of chaos and misfortune upon themselves. But, he says, there will always be a group that will respect the old ways and continue the cycles and bring order out of disruption. The need to maintain harmony with the natural world sustains the people, as it has throughout the centuries. Even in the taking of sumac or yucca for making a basket, a woman showed her reverence for the plant by asking for permission and giving thanks. House concludes,

> What you strive for in this world is *hózhǫ́* (beauty, balance, harmony).
> How you live, how you treat one another, the way you cook, how you arrange
> your home, how you live in your surroundings—in the *Diné* (Navajo)—way
> this would be art and religion . . . your home and environment are your
> church, your place of prayers. . . . Life is still going on; our culture is not dead.
> It lives in us . . . ours is an ongoing, living culture. (House 1994:101)

Political Organization

As pastoralists, the Navajo were scattered over a wide area. Their largest political divisions were loosely defined local groups organized around charismatic headmen (*naat'aanii*, "one who orates"). The local group was mobilized only as a means to deal with outsiders—whether Anglo, Mexican, other Indian tribes, or other Navajo groups—for offensive and defensive warfare and for negotiations with outsiders. Each headman was chosen informally on the basis of such factors as his exemplary character, oratorical ability, age, experience, wealth, family, and ceremonial knowledge. He led by persuasion rather than by coercive authority and had no influence beyond the group he directed.

In the 1850s Navajo raiding became so severe that government officials sought out Navajo leaders to sign treaties. Many headmen, who owned large herds themselves, supported the abandonment of raiding and even signed treaties agreeing to the cessation of raiding, but younger men continued raiding to build their herds. Officials of the U.S. government attributed far wider authority to Navajo headmen than they in fact possessed, considering them to be tribal chiefs. Anglo-Americans had a difficult time understanding that there was no single headman with the authority to speak for all Navajo, while, on the Navajo side, lack of a centralized governing body with coercive authority closed potential avenues to peace. Authority, in Navajo thinking, was constantly changing, so that in his lifetime a headman wielded more power at one time and far less at another. New leaders and new factions constantly emerged to challenge the old organization, and only a few headmen had influence beyond their local group.

Religion and World View

Although many Navajos belong to Christian churches and the Native American Church, many also continue to practice traditional ceremonialism today. (Of course, these are not exclusive categories of participation.) Thus, even though the following section describes beliefs and practices of the 1700s and 1800s, it is written in the present tense.

World View

The essence of Navajo philosophy lies within the phrase *sąʼa nághái bikʼe hózhǫ́*. The subject of countless interpretations, this phrase has been described as "universal beauty, harmony, and happiness" into which a person becomes incorporated at the time of death (Witherspoon 1977:53) or as the goal of living to old age by following the path of *hózhǫ́* ("journeying into old age by way of spiritual beauty" [Gold 1994:4]) and then, upon death, being reincorporated into the life force that will animate future generations of living beings. *Hózhǫ́*, often used as an abbreviation for the whole, is much more than a central religious concept—indeed, it is the Navajo way of living, for this word embodies the sacredness of all life and lies at the core of the Navajo world view. Spirituality, health, harmony, and beauty, ideals celebrated in the girls' puberty ceremony, are completely intertwined.

The basic premise of the Navajo world view is that all things are interrelated and interdependent, so that to exploit or destroy any aspect of creation is also to harm oneself. All aspects of the natural world are imbued with sacredness and life: every mesa, mountain, animal, and direction is alive and has its own name and personal history. Each must be approached in the proper way to maintain balanced relationships in the universe. Reciprocity plays a key role in maintaining that balance, which means that humans have a responsibility to stay in proper relationship to the beings of the natural and supernatural worlds. Because all things are interrelated, giving and receiving—just like the inflow and outflow of breath—are complementary processes in life that cannot exist independently; in order to receive something of value, a person must give something of value. Whether sprinkling a yucca plant with corn pollen before digging its roots for ritual shampoo or offering a piece of turquoise to the Holy People while saying a prayer, reciprocity is a direct measure of how much one appreciates the Holy People.

Reflecting the emphasis on movement in their language, the Navajo view the world as a place of motion, process, and flux. No state of being is permanently fixed: to ensure that the universe continually reanimates itself, humans have a daily responsibility to renew the

Spider Rock, Canyon de Chelly,
Arizona, 1994. Author photograph

proper balance of the universe through songs, prayers, offerings, and proper thought and actions (Griffin-Pierce, in press).

The Kinaaldá, the major rite of passage for girls, embodies and affirms the woman's role in maintaining the balance of the universe. Held at the time of her first menses, this four-day ceremony identifies the girl with Changing Woman, for whom the first puberty rite was performed, and equips the girl "with the physical, moral, and intellectual strength she will need to carry out the duties of a Navajo woman" (S. M. Begay 1983:7). She demonstrates her powers of endurance by running at dawn and her willingness to work industriously by grinding cornmeal and preparing a corncake 3–4 feet in diameter for many guests. An "ideal" woman—one who possesses "physical strength, perfect health, beauty, energy, and ambition," as well as a good character—molds the girl's body; the ideal woman is believed "to possess the power to reshape the girl and to remake her in her own image" (Frisbie 1967:359).

The Diyin Diné'e

Most commonly translated as "Holy People," the Diyin Diné'e are a class of beings that possess supernatural powers. They include such well-known Navajo deities as the Sun, Changing Woman, the Hero Twins (Monster Slayer and Born-for-Water), First Man, and First Woman. Each Navajo ceremonial is related to a particular group of Holy People who are capable of assuming human form; the source of the ceremonial is a myth that relates how the ancestors of the Navajo acquired the ritual procedures from the Holy People (Spencer 1957).

Navajo Ceremonials or Chantways

The Navajo world view finds expression in a system of chantway myths (stories that explain the origin of various ceremonials used primarily for healing) and in their story of the creation of the universe and the emergence of the people from a series of previous worlds. This rich and complex body of oral literature describes the origin, the procedures, and the efficacy of each ceremonial or chantway. A ceremonial, or chant (also known as a sing), may last two nights, five nights, or nine nights. Occasionally, a one-day ceremonial may be conducted. Each ceremonial combines several discrete rites, such as the consecration of the hogan, setting out of prayersticks, and sandpainting. As part of the ceremonial, patients purify themselves by consuming emetics and purgatives, bathing in yucca suds, taking sweat baths, and practicing sexual abstinence (during and for four days after the ceremonial).

The Navajo cosmos is systematic and structured, with each direction having its own color, precious stones, type of corn, bird, and sacred mountain with an "inner form" or Holy Person. The setting of the ceremonial reflects this model of the cosmos, for the hogan is circular like the horizon, and ritual actions using symbolic objects reflect the color and directional symbolism (Lamphere 1983:752–53).

Ceremonial Practitioners

Navajo ceremonialism has roots in Northern Athapaskan shamanism—the ceremonial emphasis on bodily health and the curing of illness is purely Athapaskan—and Pueblo priestcraft. By incorporating and elaborating only those elements of Pueblo priestcraft that were compatible with their Athapaskan values, the Navajo developed a highly complex ceremonial system. The men and women who diagnose illness, prescribe the proper ceremony, or locate missing objects are in the shamanistic tradition, for they acquire their powers through individual vision experiences. The most common kind of Navajo diagnosticians are handtremblers who spread corn pollen along their hands and arms, say prayers, and then enter a trancelike state in which their hands tremble, indicating the cause of the problem and the appropriate ceremony. Other diviners are stargazers, crystalgazers, and listeners. The singer (chanter), a highly trained practitioner who conducts the ceremony, is much more of a priest than a shaman, for he or she has learned the appropriate songs, medicines, and ritual actions necessary for curing through a long apprenticeship to a singer who knows the specific ceremonial. Power derives from careful adherence to the precisely replicated details of the ceremonial.

Cause and Treatment of Illness

Because thoughts and actions are creative, individuals reap their results through illness or health, misfortune or well-being. One experiences illness or misfortune by committing violations—disregarding proper relations with the Holy People, animals, the ghosts of Navajos or non-Navajos, or witches. "We have to relate our lives to the stars and the sun, the animals, and to all of nature or else we will go crazy, or get sick," explained a Navajo father (Toelken 1979:96).

The healing of one or more individuals, the focus of most Navajo ceremonials, is accomplished by restoring the patients to a state of *hózhǫ́*. Because healing is a by-product of the restoration to harmony, the root cause, rather than the recurring symptoms of an illness, is treated. Although humans try to keep their lives in order by following the path of *hózhǫ́*, many things happen in life. The Navajo view of life is that the world can be dangerous, fraught with the ever-present possibility of illness or injury. Power may be used for positive effects (healing) or negative ones (witchcraft). In addition to witches (living people who manipulated the supernatural to harm or kill the living), lightning, bears, coyotes, snakes, and ghosts may also cause illness.

To cure the patient, the practitioner must invoke the cause of illness and bring it under control, thereby transforming evil into good. The power to heal comes from the precise replication of ceremonial procedures that restore the patient to a state of orderliness and health. Harmony is restored simultaneously in the physical, spiritual, mental, and social domains of the patient's life. The honoring and maintaining of proper relations through reciprocity is evident throughout the ceremonial. The Navajo protagonist is a mythic figure who gives offerings to the Holy People in exchange for power. In similar fashion, the patient offers ritual prestations to the singer/priest who is conducting the ceremonial. The singer gives offerings to the Holy People, who then heal the patient. Anthropologist

David Aberle (1967:27) explained this process: "an unbroken chain of reciprocity binds the supernatural figure [the Holy Person], the hero, the singer and the patient together."

Sandpaintings

Sandpaintings are but one rite in a ceremonial. From the distinct set of paintings that belong to a specific chant, the chanter selects those that will best heal the patient, never using the entire repertoire of paintings on a single occasion. In the two-night form of a chant, one sandpainting is made, while the last four days of a nine-night ceremonial would have sandpaintings. After its sanctification, the patient sits on the painting while the chanter performs a ritual to enhance the absorption of its healing power. Immediately afterward, the remains of the painting are taken outside to an area north of the hogan, where they are returned to the earth.

According to Navajo belief, a sandpainting heals because the ritual image attracts and exalts the Holy People; serves as a pathway for the mutual exchange of illness and the healing power of the Holy People; identifies the patient with the Holy People it depicts; and creates a ritual reality in which the patient and the supernatural dramatically interact, reestablishing the patient's correct relationship with the world of the Holy People (Griffin-Pierce 1992:43). For the Navajo, the sandpainting is a dynamic, living, sacred entity that enables the patient to transform his or her mental and physical state by focusing on the powerful mythic symbols that re-create the chantway odyssey of the story's protagonist, causing those events to live again in the present. The performative power of sandpainting creation and ritual use reestablish the proper, orderly placement of the forces of life, thus restoring correct relations between the patient and those forces upon which the patient's spiritual and physical health depend. The sandpainting works its healing power by reestablishing the patient's sense of connectedness to all of life (Griffin-Pierce 1991:66).

More Recent History

In 1923, when the Navajo Tribal Council was established, its primary purpose was to deal with mineral companies interested in drilling on Navajo land, as well as to administer timber resources and develop the underground water supply for stock purposes. Modeled after Anglo-American institutions (Kelly 1968:48–75), rather than on Navajo institutions, the tribal council was the Navajos' first centralized political organization.

The size of the reservation made the council ill equipped to deal with issues specific to local areas, and in 1927 the reservation was divided into smaller administrative units, known as chapters, that dealt with more localized problems. The people in each chapter elected officers, who met to discuss specific issues; in many ways, the chapter organization merely formalized the existing tradition of local groups. Eventually nearly a hundred chapters existed, which not only dealt with local issues but also helped keep the tribal council in touch with concerns around the reservation (Iverson 1990:60). However, the 1923 *Regulations Related to the Navajo Tribe of Indians*, which provided for a tribal council, contained no plan for the establishment of a governing body as an instrument for tribal self-determination, making it clear that the federal government intended to maintain tight control over reservation affairs (Young 1972:188).

By the time of the Depression in 1929, the Navajo population had outgrown its resource base, and severe overgrazing had destroyed groundcover, leading to wind and water erosion. In November 1933 the tribal council was asked to sanction and implement stock reduction, which had been recommended earlier that year by the commissioner of Indian affairs, John Collier. Anthropologist Richard White, looking through government records, concluded that Boulder Dam (later renamed Hoover Dam for the man who had secured its authorization) was the catalyst for drastic stock reduction because of the misperception that Navajo overgrazing was allowing too much silt into the Colorado River, which would pile up behind the dam, destroying its usefulness (1983:212–314). The national climate of economic-growth-at-all-costs embodied in the New Deal lent urgency to Boulder Dam, for the dam was supposed to protect the Imperial Valley from flood while making possible an improved irrigation system for the valley and guaranteeing water to Los Angeles and southern California. Efforts at stock reduction did not result from the recognition of overgrazing alone, for the U.S. Geological Survey identified "the Navajo Reservation as Public Enemy No. 1 in causing the Colorado Silt problem" (NA RG 75 BIA CCF:51–52).

Until this time, most Navajos had simply ignored the existence of the tribal council, because they had remained largely untouched by its actions. Suddenly, this was no longer possible, and people began to view the tribal council with apprehension because of its endorsement of this government program (Young 1972:196). For the Navajo, who considered their animals to be gifts from the Holy People, the thinning of their herds was traumatic in itself, and the methods used created great bitterness, for goats and sheep were shot and left to rot or captured and left to starve in their holding pens (Downs 1964:92–93). Primarily because the old tribal council was associated with stock reduction, the federal government urged the formation of a new tribal governing body with a constitution. Although this would give greater power to the tribe, it still meant that any actions would continue to be subject to the secretary of the interior (Young 1972:202–3).

As White pointed out, the Navajo, whose herds had enabled them to retain relative economic independence, did not become dependent until the 1930s, when "they were stripped of their stock and made largely dependent on wages and various public programs for their living" (1983:320). Stock reduction brought about the collapse of the commercialized herding industry, which meant that more of the Navajo work force had to turn to wage labor to supplement farming, herding, and crafts. The status of women deteriorated as the economy shifted to wage and welfare, making women dependent financially on their husbands and sons. With most men's jobs located off the reservation and so distant that men could only return home on weekends, men had greater financial importance but less influence on daily family life (Lamphere 1989:431, 453). Aberle regarded stock reduction as the impetus behind the spread of the Native American Church, for peyotism had been known to Navajos north of the San Juan from their Ute neighbors but did not spread south of the San Juan until 1936 (1983:564). Over the course of the next four years, it gained many adherents in Navajo communities (Aberle and Stewart 1957), and between the 1930s and the 1950s Navajo peyotists grew from a handful to become the largest single tribal element in the Native American Church.

When World War II began, the Navajo had just begun to recover from the Depression and the realignment of their economy after stock reduction. Of the 3,600 Navajos who enlisted, a select few became the famed Navajo Codetalkers, who developed and used a code derived from the Navajo language, playing a crucial role in winning the war in the Pacific. Many veterans had the Enemyway ceremony, used for returning warriors, performed for them to cleanse and purify themselves after contact with enemy dead and to realign themselves with their people. During World War II, when thousands of Navajo left the reservation to work, large-scale exposure to Anglo-American society had a profound effect on Navajo society. Off-reservation employment became more desirable, spurring the demand for American-style schooling that would enable the Navajo to obtain better paying, skilled and professional positions. Many returning members of the armed forces attended college through the G.I. Bill, while others sought wage work. Many commuted great distances so that they could maintain homes on the reservation, while others moved to nearby towns, such as Flagstaff, Arizona, and Albuquerque, New Mexico. In the 1950s, through a federal relocation program, the government provided one-way bus or train tickets from the reservations to cities such as Los Angeles, Denver, and Dallas, where officials helped relocated families get settled and find jobs; while some Native Americans succeeded, others became trapped in a cycle of poverty.

The fifteen years that spanned stock reduction and World War II were critical to the development of the Navajo Nation and ushered in such profound changes that ethnohistorians Garrick and Roberta Bailey (1986:230) described the impact of these years as greater than that of the Bosque Redondo experience.

Contemporary Issues

Three reservation areas in New Mexico are detached from the main reservation but participate in Navajo tribal government. In 1990 the Ramah Reservation near Zuni Pueblo had a population of 1,114; the Alamo (Puertocito) Reservation, 80 miles southwest of Albuquerque, had 1,228; and the Cañoncito Reservation, 40 miles southwest of Albuquerque, had 1,181 people (Navajo Nation, Division of Community Development 1995).

The reservation boundaries in New Mexico include what is known as the "checkerboard" portion of the reservation: blocks of land ranging from one square mile (a section) to much larger units may be private lands, railroad lands, state lands, or public lands, the latter managed primarily by the federal Bureau of Land Management (BLM). The Navajo land base is divided into five agencies: Western Navajo, Chinle, Fort Defiance, Shiprock, and Eastern Navajo. The 21 land management districts and the 110 chapters that constitute them do not completely coincide, for some council members represent two or even three chapters in the tribal legislature.

In 1990 the office of president replaced the office of tribal chairman. The three branches of tribal government include an eighty-eight-member legislature, the Navajo Nation Council, whose members are elected from local chapters; an executive branch represented by the president; and a judicial branch with district courts and a Supreme Court. The delegates to the legislature are elected to four-year terms by secret ballot and popular vote. Women have long been involved in tribal politics, serving on the tribal council, taking an active role in chapter politics, and serving as chapter officers or as paid administrators for chapters. Annie Wauneka, daughter of the leader Chee Dodge, served on the tribal council from 1951 to 1978, and Irene Stewart has been another prominent council member. Council meetings are held in the Navajo language inside the octagonal hogan-shaped Council House in Window Rock, Arizona. The advisory committee, comparable to the cabinet in the federal government, selects the trained and uniformed Navajo police force. The

Canyon de Chelly, Arizona, 1999. Author photograph

court system, separate from the police force, is headed by seven judges appointed for life by the tribal council. Council members probably have the most difficult job balancing past and future. Navajo scholar Marshall Tome (1983:680) imagined what thoughts might go through the mind of a reflective council member: "Once in a while we try to work against each other because we are afraid that we might lose our jobs or make someone who has more influence than we do mad at us. . . . There aren't many jobs here that pay money and we all need money if we are going to live."

Today, the Navajo Nation consists of 25,351 square miles, making it not only the largest reservation in the United States but also larger than ten states (it is closest in size to West Virginia). In 1995, of the 259,556 Navajos in the United States, 159,481 resided in the Navajo Nation (Navajo Nation, Division of Community Development 1995:5). The Navajo are the largest reservation-based tribe in the United States. Navajo medical anthropologist and educator Jennie Joe reflected, "I see a Navajo Nation, not a tribe. I see Navajo students getting into Harvard Medical School. We have a full-time lobbyist for the Navajo Nation in Washington, D.C. I meet Navajos at Heathrow Airport in London and walking down the streets of Paris" (Trimble 1993:126). She explained the Navajo ability to travel far from home and to incorporate new things into their lives without any loss of cultural identity: "We wouldn't be called 'Children of Changing Woman' if we were not [able to do this]" (ibid., 130). In facing the future, the Navajo people will have to call upon the same courage, intelligence, and resilience they have shown throughout their history.

Their ability to incorporate useful traits from other societies has seen them through many new beginnings and changes from their arrival in the Southwest, when they gave up nomadism for a more settled agricultural life based on the raising of corn, to their acquisition of sheep and horses and the adoption of pastoralism. Further, according to Navajo Charlie Mitchell, after the return from Bosque Redondo, "Every bit of our old behavior was wiped from us," for the Navajo had to relinquish raiding for a subsistence based on farming and sheep raising (Underhill 1956:182). Since their return from Bosque Redondo, and especially since the stock reduction programs of the 1930s, the Navajo economy (and thus all other aspects of Navajo culture) has become increasingly intertwined with the U.S. national economy.

Much of what has taken place in the larger society is visible in its extreme form on the reservation, including dealing with unemployment and underemployment, balancing the mining of irreplaceable resources against economic gain, developing renewable resources and alternative sources of energy, having to accomplish more with less because of budgetary cutbacks, building or repairing the infrastructure (including highways, bridges, buildings, telephone and electric lines), and facing social problems, such as domestic violence, substance abuse, and urban gangs. Cultural differences exacerbate these conditions and also add other problems, such as self-determination and sovereignty, religious freedom, and the appropriation of intellectual and sacred property by outsiders. With a population that has doubled since 1960, most of the challenges the Navajo face today stem from over-population of their land base.

Education

When Navajo veterans returned from World War II, they were alarmed by the lack of educational facilities for their children. Once considered to be an intrusive element that attacked the foundations of Navajo culture, educational institutions were regarded by the returning servicemen as necessary to the survival of the Navajo people. Previously children had gone without schooling because their roles as sheepherders took priority over American-style schooling, but after World War II the Navajo demanded more local schools to replace the boarding schools and the few scattered BIA schools on the reservation. In the 1950s, when the bureau, the states, and the tribe collaborated to fund schools for Navajo children, thousands of Navajo children were able, for the first time, to attend school and return to their families at night (Iverson 1990:85).

Between 1950 and 1960 enrollment more than doubled, and the tribal council established a $10 million scholarship fund to finance the college and university education of an increasing number of young Navajos (Young 1972:225). Today Navajos send their children to mission schools, BIA boarding and day schools, public schools, or community-controlled contract schools. Locally elected school boards hire employees to run contract schools, so named because contracts with the BIA supply at least partial funding. The existence of day schools means that only children in the most remote areas must attend boarding schools; the Navajo Nation's Head Start program offers early childhood education.

The Navajo Nation was among the first Native American tribes to develop innovative programs that integrated Navajo culture with Anglo-American education and job-skills training, such as those at Rough Rock and Rock Point Demonstration Schools in 1966. In 1968 the Navajos opened Navajo Community College (now known as Diné College), the first locally controlled Indian college of its kind. Postsecondary education is available at Navajo Community Col-

Harry Walters, head of Diné studies, Diné College, Tsaile, Arizona, 1999. Author photograph

Hogan with Ned Hatathli Cultural Center, Diné College, Tsaile, Arizona, 1999. Author photograph

lege, with main campuses in Tsaile, Arizona, and Shiprock, New Mexico; Crownpoint Institute of Technology in New Mexico offers vocational and technical training. The college, guided by the Diné philosophy of learning, has a curriculum based on Navajo principles of honoring and maintaining balance in the universe. Navajo culture, including history, language, and medical knowledge and practice is formally taught. Funding is federal, tribal, and private. Wilson Aronilth Jr., a professor in the Navajo studies program (1990:iii) at Diné College, explained the importance of Navajo education: "The heart of Diné education lies within ourselves, in our language, in our native culture, in our own values, in our own beliefs, in our history, in our arts and crafts, in nature and in the Holy People. When we understand our own education, then we will have self understanding: where we came from, whom we came from, who we are, what we are, why we are here and where we are going. We will then walk in beauty and everything will finish in beauty."

In spite of such innovative programs, in 1990 only 41.2 percent of the Navajo Nation, in comparison to 75.2 percent of the general U.S. population, had graduated from high school, while only 2.9 percent of Navajos on the reservation, versus 20.3 percent of the general population, had earned bachelor's degrees (Navajo Nation, Division of Community Development 1995:5).

Today, the challenge is not to enroll Navajo students in school but to encourage them to graduate. In 1990 there were 37,808 Navajos under ten years old on the reservation, making them by far the largest percentage of the population.

Economy and Health

In 1990 the per-capita income of Navajos on the reservation was only $4,106, in comparison to $14,420 for the general U.S. population; 57.4 percent of Navajo Nation families lived below the poverty level, in comparison to only 10 percent of U.S. families (Navajo Nation, Division of Community Development 1995). Over half of all homes on the reservation lack complete plumbing, and nearly half of all Navajo homes still rely on wood as their primary heating fuel; only one-fourth of Navajo homes have telephones (Navajo Nation, Division of Community Development 1995:3).

President Lyndon Johnson's War on Poverty in the 1960s created the Office of Economic Opportunity (OEO), which funded the Office of Navajo Economic Opportunity (ONEO), from which came the grass-roots legal-aid organization called Dinébeiina Nahiilna Be Agaditake ("Attorneys Who Contribute to the Economic Revitalization of the People," or DNA). After surviving early years marked by politics and controversial issues, DNA began to thrive because it helped so many people, including those whose cases dealt with grazing rights disputes, landlord-tenant problems, and workmen's compensation claims (Iverson 1990:92–93). The solid foundation Navajo leaders built during the 1950s and the 1960s led the tribal council to pass a resolution in 1969 officially designating the Navajos as the Navajo Nation (ibid., 86). The 1970s marked the beginning of leaner times because of government cutbacks. In 1989 anthropologist Stephen Kunitz (1989:182) described the reservation economy as follows: "unemployment and underemployment on the reservation is around 50 percent and of the people who are employed, two-thirds work in the service sector." Most current reservation jobs exist through the federal government (for example, BIA schools and Indian Health Service clinics) or tribal government. Of employed persons sixteen years old and over, 19 percent are in educational services, 14 percent in retail trade, 10 percent in public administration, 9 percent in construction, 7 percent in health services, and 5 percent in mining (Navajo Nation, Division of Community Development 1995:4). With the federal government's pressure to downsize and to contain costs, the future looks uncertain for the reservation economy, which depends heavily on federal support of human and social services.

The Navajo Nation has merged the Division of Economic Development with the Division of Community Development to lower the operating costs of tribal government. To attract the interest of companies, the Navajo Nation Division of Community Development sends information packets emphasizing the benefits of doing business within the Navajo Nation. Advantages include cheaper costs of labor, electric power, and natural gas than those available at nearby off-reservation cities, and a work force whose skills are enhanced through programs sponsored by the Navajo Department of Employment and Training. Although there are business taxes, there are no taxes in the areas of franchise, income, personal property, or unemployment. The Navajo Nation is also one of the few tribes in the

United States to have a full spectrum of established policies and codes to regulate business. To develop new employment opportunities, the Navajo Nation created industrial parks in Chinle, Fort Defiance, Leupp, and Sanders, Arizona, and in Church Rock, Shush Be Toh, Shiprock, Tooh Dineh, and Farmington, New Mexico (Navajo Nation, Project Development Department, n.d.). A business roster of on-reservation manufacturing plants includes General Dynamics, Tooh Dineh Industries of Packard Electronic Company, Chih To Industries, Inc., and Navajo Forest Products Industry. In addition to tourism, the Overall Economic Development Plan for the Navajo Nation for 1996 and 1997 included several major economic development projects, including the Ganado Shopping Center, the Antelope Point Resort, and the Kayenta Shopping Center.

In 1962 Congress passed the Navajo Indian Irrigation Project Bill, which resulted in one of the most promising tribal enterprises, Navajo Agricultural Products Industries (NAPI), a huge, corporate tribal farm that employs 300 full-time and 1,500 seasonal personnel and has annual sales of $32 million. Located south of Farmington, New Mexico, NAPI develops, operates, and manages the agribusiness functions of the Navajo Indian Irrigation Project, and nearly two-thirds of the planned 110,630 acres are now under cultivation, with storage and processing facilities for alfalfa, beans, corn, onions, barley, wheat, and potatoes. Campbell Soup buys beans; Frito-Lay and Eagle Snack Foods buy potatoes; and NAPI packages its own products under the Navajo Pride label. An important part of NAPI is a state-of-the-art research and testing lab in which scientists analyze soil chemistry and groundwater to formulate optimum plant-feeding programs.

The Navajo people are working to improve their economy without destroying their traditional way of life, a challenge that has faced Navajos since the beginning of Anglo contact. In 1994 Navajo voters rejected casino gambling on the reservation, in contrast to many other Native American tribes. Today only a minority of Navajos continue to live off the land with herds of sheep, for most families live in modern houses, many with hogans nearby for ceremonies and, in some cases, for older family members. Members of the extended family often live and work in off-reservation towns but return for weekends and share their income with those who tend the sheep, goats, and cattle.

The resilience and creativity with which Navajo families solve their economic dilemmas are especially apparent in the film *Weave of Time*, which focuses on the persistence of Navajo identity in the remarkable Burnside family. Filmmaker Suzanne Fanshel (1981) recorded anthropologist John Adair's relationship with this family, using Adair's film footage spanning fifty years. The legendary weaver Mabel Burnside Myers reflects on her mother's weaving, while Mabel's daughter Isabell uses her talent in this field when she and her husband live in Washington, D.C., while he attends law school. Isolated from the rest of their family, they run out of money, but Isabell generates income with her weaving demonstrations at the Smithsonian Institution; in her husband's words, she "wove us out of that predicament."

The stagnant reservation economy is closely related to Navajo health problems, both in the nature of those problems and in the nature of health care itself. Because income comes from a wide range of fluctuating sources, a large segment of the population relies on traditional forms of social organization—a large extended family—to ensure continuing resources; since large families are valued, contraception is not widely practiced, especially among the poorest part of the population (Kunitz 1989:179). Until a generation ago, epidemic diseases were the most significant causes of death, but today accidents of all types, particularly from motor vehicles, are far more prevalent among the Navajo than among the general population: in 1992 the rate was 143 deaths per 100,000 Navajos in comparison to only 29 deaths per 100,000 in the general U.S. population (Indian Health Service 1996: 53). Men in their twenties and thirties have the highest death rate, leading anthropologists to theorize that this is due in part to the marginal position of young men in their wives' kin groups; a higher rate of domestic conflict also supports this (Kunitz 1989:109). In many families, husbands are the primary breadwinners but have little say in family matters because of the demands of their off-reservation wage jobs; when they are at home, husbands must deal with their wives' decisions based on a matrilineal/matrilocal tradition.

Although alcoholism is generally considered the most significant health problem facing the Navajo, anthropologists Jerrold Levy and Stephen Kunitz (1974) pointed out that much drinking behavior is not alcoholism. The mortality rate from alcoholic cirrhosis among the Navajo is not significantly different from the national average (Kunitz and Levy 1974). One reason for the most common form of drinking is peer-group solidarity; many Navajo men go for long periods of time without drinking, and the pattern of drinking for most Navajo men who have been known as heavy drinkers is to either give up their drinking entirely or to become much more moderate (ibid.). Relatively well-educated Navajos follow the drinking styles found in the larger American society, with an occasional drink at home after work and on weekends.

Most Navajos experience no conflict between modern medicine and traditional healing ceremonies, which focused on curing rather than symptomatic relief. One prominent Navajo ceremonialist differentiates among diseases that only ceremonialists can cure, those that only Anglo physicians can cure, and those that both can cure (Adair and Deuschle 1970:33). This does not mean that the traditional system has expanded to include "white diseases," but rather that the Navajo have accepted the proven effectiveness of such treatments as antibiotics. While the core values of Navajo religion remain intact, there has been a shift away from the longer and more expensive ceremonials because of the expense of training practitioners and the absence of potential apprentices due to off-reservation wage work. Shorter versions of the ceremonials, peyotism (the Native American Church), and Christianity have begun to replace the more elaborate ceremonials.

The first hospitals on the reservation were alien and forbidding, often a last resort. In the old days a hogan in which someone had died had to be abandoned or destroyed; when a person died in a hospital, the hogan remained uncontaminated. The Navajo, known for their avoidance of the dead, once called hospitals "houses of death." Today the Indian Health Service is working with the Navajo Nation to incorporate Navajo values into its programs. With the shift in disease patterns away from epidemic diseases, the Navajo Area Indian Health Service, in cooperation with the Navajo Nation and local communities, has set new goals regarding parenting, fitness, comprehensive school health education, interpersonal violence, elder involvement, and community self-sufficiency (Navajo Area Director's Health Promotion Status Report 1996). As part of the program, they have related each of these areas of concern to the values represented by the four directions. East, which represents the beginning of life and the process of thinking, is associated with successful parenting. South, the direction of the planning process and the development of physical abilities, stands for fitness and physical activity, and comprehensive school health education. West, which represents life, the development of social competence, and the importance of relationships, is associated with reducing and preventing interpersonal violence. Finally, north, the direction of hope, so that people have strength and healing in the winter times of their lives to complete the cycle of life in harmony and balance, stands for the involvement of elders in community health programs.

Energy Resources

After World War II renewed interest in the natural resources of the Navajo reservation led companies to discover large oil and gas fields in the Four Corners area. Millions of dollars in oil royalties poured into the tribal treasury, which tribal leaders used to expand tribal government, renovate the police and court system, establish a tribal school program, build new chapter houses, and found the Navajo Forest Products Industry (NFPI) and an electrical distribution system (Navajo Tribal Utilities Authority) (Iverson 1990:87). Oil companies were the first to begin operations on Navajo land, and forty years later, in the 1960s, coal, vanadium, helium, and uranium companies followed. However, although the fees from leases have enriched the tribal treasury, these fees have constituted a relatively small return for the depletion of this finite resource. Mining has also devastated the landscape. After the removal of coal in the strip-mining process, a vast, open pit remained; only in recent years has the federal government required the restoration of the land. Widespread air pollution resulted from the coal-burning plants, and the water table has dropped dramatically from the diversion of water because of its use as a means of transporting the coal to the plants.

An even more serious health problem came from exposure to uranium mining in the 1970s, when companies paid little attention to the safety of their workers, and when many men and women received high levels of radiation, which resulted in death or debilitating illness (Spieldoch 1999). Radioactive materials were so widespread in some areas that unknowingly many families built and lived in homes made of uranium-irradiated materials (Aberle 1983:650).

Although the extraction of energy resources is the biggest business in Navajo country, most of the profits from the extraction and processing go to U.S. corporations rather than to the Navajo. Tribal income from these resources operates government and supplies welfare but does not develop the Navajo economy. Aberle (1969:249–50) likened the reservation to a colony, because the reservation provides raw materials as well as a market for manufactured goods for the dominant society; only the corporations that exploit the reservation profit, while the Navajo people continue to deplete their nonrenewable resources.

The Navajo-Hopi Land Dispute

The Navajo-Hopi land dispute dates back to President Chester Arthur's executive order of 1882 that established the Hopi Reservation. In the 1930s, 1.8 million acres of the total 2.6 million acres were designated as a Joint Use Area (JUA). By the 1950s the Navajos in the JUA far outnumbered the Hopis. In 1975, when Congress passed the Navajo-Hopi Land Settlement Act dividing the JUA into Navajo and Hopi areas, the Hopis on the Navajo side were ordered to move to Hopi land, just as the Navajos on the Hopi side were to move to Navajo land by 1986. Congressional appropriations compensated the Navajos who were willing to move and also provided funds for the Navajo Nation to find replacement acreage—public lands it could purchase. Unfortunately, many of the Navajos who were living on the Hopi side were among the most traditional, least acculturated Navajos. Many moved to other parts of the already overcrowded reservation, creating hardship for both those who relocated and their hosts, while the relocation commission moved many others into tract housing in Gallup, New Mexico, or Winslow or Flagstaff, Arizona. In general, the commission moved individual households, ignoring the rich network of social ties that makes up Navajo society. Older people, uprooted from a lifetime of herding sheep on familiar land, were disoriented and lost in an urban existence; at the mercy of unscrupulous real estate agents, without wage work, and unable to pay property taxes, many lost their homes. One study described relocation as a clash between Hopi property rights and Navajo human rights (Kammer 1980).

Climbing Shiprock

Native Americans are sharing the outrage of indigenous peoples all over the world at climbers who desecrate their sacred mountains. In 1995 the National Park Service (NPS) drafted a climbing management plan to accommodate native views of Devil's

Tower, Wyoming, which plays a cultural role for over twenty tribes. Meeting with tribal representatives, the Access Fund (an organization that works to preserve access for climbing while at the same time promoting and preserving natural resources), and two local climbing clubs, the NPS worked out a compromise between the Indians' preference that no one climb the peak and the desire of climbers to have continuous access—a voluntary ban for the month of June. Most of the few climbers who violated the ban were foreigners, but one local guide, Andy Petefish, was outraged and claimed that the closure "violates the free exercise rights of Americans claiming their spiritual pathway to be 'climbing'" (Roberts 1998:91).

For over three decades, prohibitions against climbing certain rock formations have been in effect on the Navajo Reservation, but such restrictions only seem to tempt climbers to make outlaw ascents. Just after Navajos had completed a three-year ritual of removing the curse caused by the 1955 ascent of Spider Rock in Canyon de Chelly, Arizona, two climbers made a second ascent in 1960, which necessitated another three-year cleansing ritual (Roberts 1998:90). Because Spider Woman intercedes to link the living and the dead, to climb Spider Rock is to disrupt the delicate balance between the human and the supernatural worlds. In 1997 a climber, who had tried unsuccessfully to get permission, climbed Shiprock anyway, only to find later that the locks of his car had been jimmied and $6,000 worth of climbing, camping, and photographic gear stolen (ibid., 93). As part of the Enemyway ceremony, warriors once left offerings of precious stones atop Shiprock to re-create the actions of Monster Slayer, who made the world safe from his enemies, and Born-for-Water, who performed protection rites at home, but after a Sierra Club climbing party profaned it in 1939, "Shiprock could never be used this way again" (McPherson 1992:35).

Totem Pole Rock in Monument Valley, said by some to be a line of prayersticks and by others to be a frozen Ye'ii held up by lightning, has also been climbed. The violation is believed to have offended the spirit, which curtailed the amount of rain that falls in Monument Valley (Roberts 1998:29). The Anasazi, whom Navajos believe used magical climbing techniques to get up steep rock faces to their cliff dwellings, so offended their gods through their greed, competition, and uncontrolled pride that their gods destroyed them. Navajo elders consider present-day rock climbing to be symptomatic of the same kind of dangerous cultural arrogance, which will eventually destroy Anglos just as it destroyed the Anasazi so long ago.

Facing the Future

The strength of Navajo identity derives, in large part, from the powerful bond all Navajos feel toward their homeland. Today this relationship is as sustaining and real as it was in 1868 when Navajo leader Barboncito told General Sherman why the Navajo must return to their land from Bosque Redondo: "When the Navajos were first created, four mountains and four rivers were appointed for us, inside of which we should live, that was to be our country, and was given us by the first woman [Changing Woman] of the Navajo" (Correll 1979:130–32). During a 1988 Navajo Community College trip to Dinétah, I saw this same sense of absolute certainty and the immediacy with which past events live in the landscape of the present. Standing atop a mesa, a young Navajo woman pointed out landmarks on the horizon, her voice ringing with enthusiasm and conviction when she recognized each familiar peak. When she spotted Gobernador Knob, her voice lifted joyously: "Oh! There's where First Man and First Woman found Changing Woman when she was a baby!" Her words conveyed an overwhelming sense of delight and awe.

A major resource is the Navajo world view that embraces continuous growth and renewal. Instead of expecting good conditions to be permanent and lasting, Navajos know that change and disruption are a natural part of life and that humans are responsible for bringing order out of chaos. The story of Navajo emergence is the story of overcoming imbalance and excess with continual evolution and renewal. Navajo artist Conrad House (1994:96–101) likened Navajo growth to cycles that

always continue on and on, forever like the seasons. There will always be a time of disruption and chaos, and out of that comes order. [The Navajo ceremonial basket] holds our world view. It has the opening to the east and the rainbow band encircling. Designs of clouds, mountain, red evening sunset, night sky, white dawn, and the seasons are indicated on that band. It suggests the ups and downs of life spiraling around—cycles.

Although economic and educational necessity may make it difficult to live on the reservation, Navajos cope by returning home whenever possible. A hidden strength of Navajo kinship is its ability to span great distances through its network of clanship. Since clans are nonlocalized, clan bonds expand to unify people who live at opposite ends of the vast reservation and also provide a means of relating even in an impersonal setting, such as a large eastern university.

In October 1996, after I delivered a presentation, the staff of the Center for World Religions at Harvard hosted a dinner that included three Navajo students and two Anglo staff members. The three students were majoring in unrelated fields whose departments were located on different sides of the enormous campus, yet the students knew each other because they were related through clanship. After a biochemical engineering student left to take a mathematics exam, the young man with a long ponytail and a metal feather dangling from his ear said, "He's my grandson." He glanced at Donald, the Anglo administrator seated beside him, waiting for his response.

Frowning, clearly baffled, Donald asked, "What do you mean?"

With a sly smile, the Navajo nodded at the female student sitting next to me, "And she's my niece." Donald looked completely bewildered because it was clear that not more than a few years separated the three.

After a carefully timed pause, giving the non-Navajos at the table a chance to absorb the impossibility of his claims (in Anglo reckoning, at least), he continued,

It's all in our clan system. I'm Kinya'áanii [Towering House Clan], one of the first four clans. Changing Woman made us out of the skin on her breast. And she [his "niece"] is Azeetsoh din'é [Big Medicine People Clan]. Our clans go way back together. It's the way the clans are related to each other. It's the same with him [the "grandson," who had left]. You take into account the clan you belong to—I take my mother's clan—and the clan I was born for—that's my dad's clan. And then there's my grandpa's clan on my mother's side and my grandpa's clan on my father's side and her clan for all those same relatives. That's how we know we're related.

Donald, still puzzled, asked, "But what does that mean?"

The Navajo student looked at him with amazement because he had just explained the meaning, according to Navajo thinking. I interjected, "For example, you don't date someone in your clan, because you're related to them." The Navajo student chuckled because this was so self-evident: "It would be like dating your sister." Pausing, he then went on, "We act the way we're related. A grandfather passes on his stories to his grandchildren. An uncle is there to be counted on. That's how these two are to me."

The female student broke in to explain the magnitude of the clan's importance. "Your clan is your place in the universe. I know my clan, the clan I was born for, my *nálí's* [maternal grandfather] clan and my grandpa-on-my-dad's-side's clan, so I'm fixed in space and time. I know who I am then." She spread her hands like a plant capable of withstanding the strongest of winds because of its deep-reaching roots anchored in every direction. Her relationships were transportable, for in encountering any Navajos, all she had to do was to hear their clans and their key relatives' clans, and she had ready-made relationships that informed her of how to treat these individuals and what she could expect from them.

Kinship connects each Navajo to the movement and flow of generations, creating a vital connection as real today as it was in the past. The flexibility and resilience of the Navajo clan system embodies the living nature of Navajo culture and its ability to bring order out of chaos, enabling its people to meet demands they could never have imagined a century ago. Navajo culture is carried within the soul of each individual, assuring each person of his or her place in the universe.

References and Further Reading

The Smithsonian's *Handbook of North American Indians*, vol. 10 (1983), contains chapters about various aspects of Navajo culture. To keep up with current affairs, the weekly tribal newspaper, *The Navajo Times*, is excellent.

Aberle, David F. 1961. "The Navajo." In *Matrilineal Kinship,* pp. 96–201, ed. D. Schneider and K. Gough. University of California Press, Berkeley.

———. 1963. "Some Sources of Flexibility in Navaho Social Organization." *Southwestern Journal of Anthropology* 19, no. 1:1–8.

*———. 1966. *The Peyote Religion among the Navajo.* Aldine Press, Chicago. [Aberle, a respected anthropologist in Navajo studies, presents this key study of the Native American Church.]

———. 1967. "The Navajo Singer's Fee: Payment or Presentation." In *Studies in Southwestern Ethnolinguistics,* pp. 15–32, ed. D. H. Hymes and W. E. Bittle. Mouton, The Hague.

———. 1969. "A Plan for Navajo Economic Development." In volume 1 of *Toward Economic Development for Native American Communities,* A Compendium of Papers Submitted to the Subcommittee on Economy in Government of the Joint Economic Committee. 91st Cong., 1st sess., Joint Committee Print, pp. 223–76. U.S. Government Printing Office, Washington, D.C.

———. 1983. "Peyote Religion among the Navajo." In *Handbook of North American Indians,* vol. 10: *The Southwest,* pp. 558–69.

Aberle, David F., and Omer C. Stewart. 1957. *Navaho and Ute Peyotism: A Chronological and Distributional Study.* University of Colorado Studies, Series in Anthropology 6. Boulder, Colo.

Acrey, Bill P. 1978. *Navajo History: The Land and the People.* Shiprock Consolidated School District No. 22, Dept. of Curriculum Materials Development, Shiprock, N.Mex.

Adair, John. 1944. *The Navajo and Pueblo Silversmiths.* University of Oklahoma Press, Norman.

Adair, J., and K. W. Deuschle. 1970. *The People's Health.* Appleton-Century-Crofts, New York.

Adams, William Y. 1963. *Shonto: A Study of the Role of the Trader in a Modern Navaho Community.* Bureau of American Ethnology Bulletin 188. U.S. Government Printing Office, Washington, D.C.

*Alvord, Lori Arviso, M.D., and Elizabeth Cohen Van Pelt. 1999. *The Scalpel and the Silver Bear.* Bantam Books, New York. [This moving firsthand account of the first Navajo female surgeon details her struggle to blend biomedical practice and Navajo philosophy based on a balanced and harmonious life.]

*Amsden, Charles A. 1974 [1934]. *Navaho Weaving: Its Technic and History.* Rio Grande Press, Glorieta, N.Mex. [A classic work on the history of Navajo weaving.]

Aronilth, Wilson. 1990. "Foundation of Navajo Culture." Unpublished manuscript on file at Navajo Community College Library, Tsaile, Ariz.

*Bailey, Garrick, and Roberta Bailey. 1986. *A History of the Navajos: The Reservation Years.* School of American Research Press, Santa Fe, N.Mex. [An excellent history, this book is a study of the interacting forces that make the Navajo unique.]

Bedinger, Margery. 1973. *Indian Silver: Navajo and Pueblo Jewelers.* University of New Mexico Press, Albuquerque.

*Begay, D. Y. 1994. "A Weaver's Point of View." In *All Roads Are Good: Native Voices on Life and*

Culture, pp. 80–89, ed. Tom Hill and Richard W. Hill Sr. Smithsonian Books, Washington, D.C. [The Navajo perspective on weaving and life comes across clearly in this book presenting the views of many native artists.]

Begay, Shirley M. 1983. *Kinaalda: A Navajo Puberty Ceremony*. Navajo Curriculum Center, Rough Rock Demonstration School, Rough Rock, Ariz.

Benally, Clyde. 1982. *Dinéjí Nákéé' Nááhane': A Utah Navajo History*. San Juan School District, Monticello, Utah.

Between Sacred Mountains: Navajo Stories and Lessons from the Land. 1982. Sun Tracks and the University of Arizona Press, Tucson. [This beautifully written book with its many stories, recollections, and poetry was created by Navajo elders and young people from Rock Point, Ariz.]

Brugge, David M. 1983. "Navajo Prehistory and History to 1850." In *Handbook of North American Indians*, vol. 10: *The Southwest*, pp. 489–501.

———. 1994. *The Navajo-Hopi Land Dispute*. University of New Mexico Press, Albuquerque.

Brugge, Doug. 1997. *Memories Come to Us in the Rain and the Wind: Oral Histories and Photographs of Navajo Uranium Miners and Their Families*. Red Sun Press, Jamaica Plain, Mass.

Collier, Malcolm C. 1951. "Local Organization among the Navaho." Ph.D. diss., University of Chicago.

Correll, J. Lee. 1965. "The Navajo Hogan. *Navajo Times* 6, no. 24:29–31.

———. 1979. *Through White Man's Eyes: A Contribution to Navajo History: A Chronological Record of the Navajo People from Earliest Times to the Treaty of June 1, 1868*. 6 vols. Navajo Heritage Center, Window Rock, Ariz.

Dawson, Susan E. 1992. "Navajo Uranium Workers and the Effects of Occupational Illness: A Case Study." *Human Organization* 51, no. 4:389–98.

*Discovery Channel. 1993. "A Clash of Cultures." Part 1 of *How the West Was Lost*. Discovery Communications, Bethesda, Md. [Videotape. This compelling documentary tells the story of the Long Walk in the 1860s, when the Navajos were exiled to Bosque Redondo, N.Mex. The story is told from the Navajo perspective, in interviews with descendants of those who went through this ordeal.]

Dobyns, Henry F., and Robert C. Euler. 1972. *The Navajo Indians*. Indian Tribal Series, Phoenix.

Downs, James. F. 1964. *Animal Husbandry in Navajo Society and Culture*. University of California Publications in Anthropology 1. Berkeley, Calif.

———. 1972. *The Navajo*. Holt, Rinehart, and Winston (Waveland Press), New York.

Dyen, Isidore, and David F. Aberle. 1974. *Lexical Reconstruction: The Case of the Proto-Athapaskan Kinship System*. Cambridge University Press, New York.

*Fanshel, Suzanne. 1981. *A Weave of Time: The Story of a Navajo Family 1938–1986*. Direct Cinema, Los Angeles. [This outstanding film, based on the work of John Adair, provides a moving and accurate portrayal of Navajo life from just before World War II to modern times.]

Fortes, Meyer. 1963. "Time and Social Structure: An Ashanti Case Study." In *Social Structure:*

Studies Presented to A. R. Radcliffe-Brown, pp. 54–84, ed. M. Fortes. Russell and Russell, New York.

Franciscan Fathers. 1910. *An Ethnological Dictionary of the Navajo Language*. St. Michael's Press, St. Michael's, Ariz.

*Frisbie, Charlotte J. 1967. *Kinaaldá: A Study of the Navaho Girl's Puberty Ceremony*. Wesleyan University Press, Middletown, Conn. [A respected anthropologist, Frisbie has written exhaustive studies that provide an in-depth look at Navajo culture and beliefs.]

———. 1987. *Navajo Medicine Bundles or Jish: Acquisition, Transmission, and Disposition in the Past and Present*. University of New Mexico Press, Albuquerque.

Frisbie, Charlotte J., and David P. McAllester, eds. 1978. *Navajo Blessingway Singer: The Autobiography of Frank Mitchell*. University of Arizona Press, Tucson.

*Gilpin, Laura. 1968. *The Enduring Navaho*. University of Texas Press, Austin. [Gilpin's classic photographs and texts present an excellent introduction to Navajo life.]

Gold, Peter. 1994. *Navajo and Tibetan Sacred Wisdom: The Circle of the Spirit*. Inner Traditions International, Rochester, Vt.

Goodman, James. 1982. *The Navajo Atlas: Environments, Resources, People, and History of the Diné Bikéyah*. University of Oklahoma Press, Norman.

Griffin-Pierce, Trudy. 1991. "Navajo Ceremonial Sandpaintings: Sacred, Living Entities." *American Indian Art* (winter):58–67, 88.

*———. 1992. *Earth Is My Mother, Sky Is My Father: Space, Time, and Astronomy in Navajo Sandpainting*. University of New Mexico Press, Albuquerque. [This book explores the spiritual world of the Navajo, which is based on a belief in the interconnectedness of all living beings, and relates this belief system to ceremonial practices.]

———. In press. "Navajo Religion: The Continuous Renewal of Sacred Relations." In *Treatise of Anthropology of the Sacred, Vol. 6: Native Religions and cultures of North America*, ed. L. Sullivan. Jaca Book, Milan.

Gunnerson, Dolores A. 1956. "The Southern Athabascans: Their Arrival in the Southwest." *El Palacio* 63, nos. 11–12:346–65.

Gunnerson, James H. 1956. "Plains-Promontory Relationships." *American Antiquity* 22, no. 1:69–72.

*Haile, Father Berard. 1937. *Some Cultural Aspects of the Navajo Hogan*. Mimeo. Fort Wingate Summer School, Fort Wingate, Ariz. [Father Haile, an early ethnographer of Navajo culture, wrote extensively on Navajo ceremonialism.]

Hartman, Russell, Jan Musial, and Stephen Trimble. 1987. *Navajo Pottery: Traditions and Innovations*. Northland Press, Flagstaff, Ariz.

Haskell, John L. 1975. "The Navajo in the Eighteenth Century: An Investigation involving Anthropological Archaeology in the San Juan Basin, Northwestern New Mexico." Ph.D. diss., Washington State University.

Helm, June. 1965. "Bilaterality in the Socio-territorial Organization of the Arctic Drainage Dene." *Ethnology* 4, no. 4:361–85.

Henderson, Eric. 1989. "Navajo Livestock Wealth and the Effects of the Stock Reduction Program of the 1930s." *Journal of Anthropological Research* 45:379–403.

Hirsch, Helmut V. B., and Helen Ghiradella. 1994. "From Canyon de Chelly to the Science Longhouse in Albany, Educators Look at Contemporary Science Teaching." *Winds of Change* 8, no. 2:38–42.

House, Conrad. 1994. "The Art of Balance." In *All Roads Are Good: Native Voices on Life and Culture,* pp.90–101, ed. Tom Hill and Richard W. Hill Sr. Smithsonian Books, Washington, D.C.

Huscher, Betty H., and Harold A. Huscher 1942. "Athapaskan Migration via the Intermontane Region." *American Antiquity* 8, no. 1:80–88.

Indian Health Service. 1996. *Regional Differences in Indian Health.* U.S. Dept. of Health and Human Services, Washington, D.C.

*Iverson, Peter. 1983. *The Navajo Nation.* University of New Mexico Press, Albuquerque. [A good introduction to recent Navajo history, by a respected scholar.]

———. 1990. *The Navajos.* Chelsea House Publishers, New York.

*Jett, Stephen, and Virginia Spencer. 1981. *Navajo Architecture: Forms, History, Distributions.* University of Arizona Press, Tucson. [This classic work presents extensive documentation of the Navajo hogan and other architectural forms.]

Johnson, Broderick, and Ruth Roessel. 1974. *Navajo Livestock Reduction: A National Disgrace.* Navajo Community College Press, Tsaile, Ariz.

Kammer, Jerry. 1980. *The Second Long Walk: The Navajo-Hopi Land Dispute.* University of New Mexico Press, Albuquerque.

Kelley, Klara B., and Harris Francis. 1994. *Navajo Sacred Places.* Indiana University Press, Bloomington.

Kelly, Lawrence C. 1968. *The Navajo Indians and Federal Indian Policy, 1900–1935.* University of Arizona Press, Tucson.

Kluckhohn, Clyde. 1944. *Navaho Witchcraft.* Papers of the Peabody Museum of Archaeology and Ethnology 22. Cambridge, Mass.

Kluckhohn, Clyde, W. W. Hill, and Lucy Wales Kluckhohn. 1971. *Navaho Material Culture.* Harvard University Press, Cambridge.

*Kluckhohn, Clyde, and Dorothea Leighton. 1962. *The Navaho.* Anchor Books, Doubleday, Garden City, N.Y. [This classic book was recommended to me by the Navajo educator who arranged my first visit to my Navajo family; Kluckhohn was probably the best known anthropologist of Navajo culture.]

Kunitz, Stephen. 1989. *Disease Change and the Role of Medicine: The Navajo Experience.* University of California Press, Berkeley.

Kunitz, Stephen, and Jerrold Levy. 1974. "Changing Ideas of Alcohol Use among Navajo Indians." *Quarterly Journal of Studies on Alcohol* 35:243–59.

*Lamphere, Louise. 1977. *To Run after Them: Cultural and Social Bases of Cooperation in a Navajo Community.* University of Arizona Press, Tucson. [This scholarly study of Navajo social networks was written by one of the most respected anthropologists in Navajo studies.]

———. 1983. "Southwestern Ceremonialism." In *Handbook of North American Indians*, vol. 10: *The Southwest*, pp. 743–63.

———. 1989. "Historical and Regional Variability in Navajo Women's Roles." *Journal of Anthropological Research* 45:431–56.

Leighton, Dorothea. 1947. *Children of the People.* Harvard University Press, Cambridge, Mass.

Levy, Jerrold. 1962. "Community Organization of the Western Navajo." *American Anthropologist* 64:781–801.

Levy, Jerrold E., and Stephen J. Kunitz. 1974. *Indian Drinking: Navajo Practices and Anglo-American Theories.* Wiley-Interscience, New York.

Levy, Jerrold E., Raymond Neutra, and Dennis Parker. *Hand Trembling, Frenzy Witchcraft, and Moth Madness: A Study of Navajo Seizure Disorders.* University of Arizona Press, Tucson.

*Luckert, Carl W. 1975. *The Navajo Hunter Tradition.* University of Arizona Press, Tucson. [Luckert carries on the tradition of Leland Wyman in studies of Navajo ceremonialism.]

Mayes, Vernon, and Barbara Bayless Lacy. 1989. *Nanisé: A Navajo Herbal: One Hundred Plants from the Navajo Reservation.* Navajo Community College Press, Tsaile, Ariz.

*McAllester, David. P. "Shootingway, An Epic Drama of the Navajos." In *Southwestern Indian Ritual Drama*, pp. 199–237, ed. C. J. Frisbie. School of American Research, University of New Mexico Press, Albuquerque. [McAllester is the most respected ethnomusicologist in Navajo studies.]

McNitt, Frank. 1972. *Navajo Wars, Military Campaigns, Slave Raids and Reprisals.* University of New Mexico Press, Albuquerque.

McPherson, Robert S. 1992. *Sacred Land, Sacred View: Navajo Perceptions of the Four Corners Region.* Brigham Young University, Salt Lake City, Utah.

*Mitchell, Emerson Blackhorse, and T. D. Allen. 1967. *Miracle Hill: The Story of a Navaho Boy.* University of Oklahoma Press, Norman. [A heartwarming account of growing up in two cultures, this book reveals the exhilarating and exhausting challenges in vivid images.]

Morice, A. G. 1909. "The Great Dené Race." *Anthropos* 4:582–606.

NA, RG 75, BIA, CCF. National Archives, Record Group 75, Bureau of Indian Affairs, Central Classified Files 52368–1937–021, Navajo, Annual Report of the Navajo District, 1937, pp. 51–52.

Natay, Ed Lee. 1968. *Memories of Navajoland.* Recorded and edited by Raymond Boley. Canyon Records ARP 6057. {Recording.]

Navajo Area Director's Health Promotion Status Report 1996. Draft. Navajo Area Indian Health Service, Window Rock, Ariz.

Navajo Nation, Division of Community Development. 1995. *Navajo Nation Profile*. Shiprock, N.Mex.

———. 1993. *1990 Census: Population and Housing Characteristics of the Navajo Nation*. Printing Co., Scottsdale, Ariz.

Navajo Nation, Office of Economic Development. 1992–93. Brochure. Window Rock, Ariz.

Navajo Nation, Project Development Department. n.d. Business packet. Window Rock, Ariz.

Newcomb, Franc J. 1940. *Navajo Omens and Taboos*. Rydal Press, Santa Fe, N.Mex.

———. 1964. *Hosteen Klah: Navaho Medicine Man and Sand Painter*. University of Oklahoma Press, Norman.

*O'Bryan, Aileen. 1993. *Navaho Indian Myths*. Dover Publications, New York. [Retitled republication of *The Dine: Origin Myths of the Navaho Indians*. Smithsonian Bureau of American Ethnology Bulletin 163. U.S. Government Printing Office, Washington, D.C., 1956.]

Opler, Morris. 1983. "The Apachean Culture Pattern and Its Origins." In *Handbook of North American Indians*, vol. 10: *The Southwest*, pp. 368–92.

Parezo, Nancy. 1983. *Navajo Sandpainting: From Religious Act to Commercial Art*. University of Arizona Press, Tucson.

RBIA LR GR. Records of the Bureau of Indian Affairs, Letters Received, General Records. Williams Parsons to Atkins, 26 April 1886.

Reichard, Gladys A. 1934. *Spider Woman: A Story of Navajo Weavers and Chanters*. Macmillan, New York.

*———. 1950. *Navajo Religion: A Study of Symbolism*. Bollingen Series 18. Princeton University Press, Princeton, N.J. [This classic work was written by an anthropologist who devoted her life to Navajo studies.]

Roberts, David. 1998. "When Cultures Collide: The Climbers versus Native Americans Conundrum." *Climbing* 181:88–95, 163.

Roessel, Faith. 1997. "Guest Essay." *Native Peoples* 10, no. 2:5.

Roessel, Ruth. 1973. *Navajo Stories of the Long Walk Period*. Navajo Community College Press, Tsaile, Ariz.

———. 1981. *Women in Navajo Society*. Navajo Resource Center, Rough Rock Demonstration School, Rough Rock, Ariz.

Ross, William T. 1955. "Navajo Kinship and Social Organization: With Special Reference to a Transitional Community." Ph.D. diss., University of Chicago.

Schaasfsma, Polly. 1963. *Rock Art in the Navajo Reservoir District*. Museum of New Mexico Papers in Anthropology 7. Santa Fe, N.Mex.

———. 1966. *Early Navaho Rock Paintings and Carvings*. Museum of Navajo Ceremonial Art, Santa Fe, N.Mex.

Schroeder, Albert H. 1965. "A Brief History of the Southern Utes." *Southwestern Lore* 30, no. 4:53–78.

Schwarz, Maureen Trudelle. 1997. *Molded in the Image of Changing Woman: Navajo Views on the Human Body and Personhood*. University of Arizona Press, Tucson.

Shepardson, Mary, and Blodwen Hammond. 1970. *The Navajo Mountain Community: Social Organization and Kinship Terminology.* University of California Press, Berkeley.

Spencer, Katherine H. 1957. *Mythology and Values: An Analysis of Navaho Chantway Myths.* Memoirs of the American Folklore Society 48. Philadelphia.

Spencer, Robert, and Jesse Jennings. 1977. *The Native Americans.* 2nd ed. Harper and Row, New York.

Spicer, Edward H. 1981. *Cycles of Conquest: The Impact of Spain, Mexico, and the United States on the Indians of the Southwest, 1533–1960.* University of Arizona Press, Tucson.

Spieldoch, Rachel. 1999. "Uranium Is in My Body." In *Contemporary Native American Cultural Issues,* pp. 307–16, ed. Duane Champagne. Alta Mira Press, Walnut Creek, Calif.

Steward, Julian H. 1936. *Pueblo Material Culture in Western Utah.* Anthropological Series 1(3), University of New Mexico Bulletin 287. Albuquerque.

Tanner, Clara Lee. 1982. *Southwest Indian Craft Arts.* University of Arizona Press, Tucson.

*Tapahonso, Luci. 1993. "The Kaw River Rushes Westward." In *A Circle of Nations: Voices and Visions of American Indians,* pp. 106–17, ed. John Gattuso. Beyond Words Publishing, Hillsboro, Ore. [One of the foremost Navajo poets, Tapahonso creates work that is powerful and moving.]

Toelken, Barre. 1979. *The Dynamics of Folklore.* Houghton Mifflin, Boston.

Tome, Marshall. 1983. "The Navajo Nation Today." In *Handbook of North American Indians,* vol. 10: *The Southwest,* pp. 679–83.

Trimble, Stephen. 1993. *The People: Indians of the American Southwest.* School of American Research Press, Santa Fe, N.Mex.

Two Bears, Davina. 1995. "Hanoolchaadí: Historic Textiles Selected by Four Navajo Weavers." *Native Peoples* 8, no. 3:62–68.

Underhill, Ruth. 1953. *Here Come the Navajo!* U.S. Bureau of Indian Affairs, Branch of Education, Washington, D.C.

*———. 1956. *The Navajos.* University of Oklahoma Press, Norman. [This book, by an anthropologist who spent many years with the Navajos, is a good starting point for learning about traditional culture.]

Vogt, Evon Z. 1961. "Navaho." In *Perspectives in American Indian Culture Change,* pp. 278–336, ed. E. H. Spicer. University of Chicago Press, Chicago.

White, Richard. 1983. *The Roots of Dependency: Subsistence, Environment, and Social Change among the Choctaws, Pawnees, and Navajos.* University of Nebraska Press, Lincoln.

Windham, Thomas L. 1997. "Bridging Two Worlds: Native American Students Bring Traditional Knowledge to the Study of Atmospheric Sciences." *Winds of Change* 12, no. 1:38–42.

Witherspoon, Gary. J. 1970. "A New Look at Navajo Social Organization." *American Anthropologist* 72, no. 1:55–65.

———. 1975. *Navajo Kinship and Marriage.* University of Chicago Press, Chicago.

*———. 1977. *Language and Art in the Navajo Universe*. University of Michigan Press, Ann Arbor. [This classic book is an excellent study of Navajo language as it relates to world view.]

———. 1983. "Navajo Social Organization." In *Handbook of North American Indians*, vol. 10: *The Southwest*, pp. 524–35.

*Wyman, Leland. 1970. *Blessingway*. University of Arizona Press, Tucson. [Wyman was the foremost scholar of Navajo sacred sandpaintings and devoted his life to documenting the sandpainting images of various chantways.]

———. 1983. *Southwest Indian Drypainting*. School of American Research Southwest Indian Arts Series, Santa Fe, and the University of New Mexico Press, Albuquerque.

*Yazzie, Ethelou. 1971. *Navajo History*. Navajo Community College Press, Many Farms, Ariz. [Yazzie's work, as well as other publications from Navajo Community College Press, presents Navajo perspectives on history and culture.]

*Young, Robert. W. 1972. "The Rise of the Navajo Tribe." In *Plural Society in the Southwest*, pp. 167–237, ed. Edward Spicer and Raymond Thompson. Interbook, New York. [Young is renowned for his work on Navajo language.]

Young, Robert, and William Morgan. 1980. *The Navajo Language: A Grammar and Colloquial Dictionary*. University of New Mexico Press, Albuquerque.

Apache woman, early 1900s. Courtesy of Arizona Historical Society, No. 58629

Chapter 10 The Apaches

October 1998

Looking out into the sea of Chiricahua and Anglo faces in the darkened auditorium, I begin my presentation on the drawings and paintings done by Native American prisoners of war. Today is "'*Ikéké Jagał,* Cultural Continuance in a Traditional Chiricahua Community," an all-day seminar being held at the University of Arizona in collaboration with the Chiricahua Apache Prisoners of War Descendants and sponsored by the Arizona State Museum and the university. The great-great-great-grandson of Cochise and his family are in the audience. Others are direct descendants of the warriors who rode with Geronimo and Naiche, Cochise's son. After their surrender in 1886, roughly 512 Chiricahuas, almost the entire population of all their bands, were shuffled from prison sites in Florida to Alabama to Oklahoma as prisoners of war for twenty-seven years. In 1912 they were finally allowed to settle on the Mescalero Apache Reservation in New Mexico but did not arrive until the following year. Today descendants of the two-thirds of the POWs who accepted this offer still reside there.

To put the work of Naiche and other Chiricahua artists in a broader perspective, I am describing artwork done by Plains Indian prisoners of war. Although I am speaking of Zotom, a Kiowa warrior, the same spirit of fierce resistance and remarkable resourcefulness also burned in the hearts of the Chiricahua. The drawing projected on the screen behind me depicts Kiowa, Cheyenne, Arapaho, and Comanche prisoners gazing out to sea, flanked by two military guards with a cannon pointed at them. Entitled *On the Parapet of Fort Marion Next Day after Arrival,* at first glance it appears to be a scene of submission and surrender, which in the Anglo perspective portrayed the inevitable outcome of the confrontation between Anglo progress and Native American resistance. However, Zotom, the Kiowa artist, was a man of great strength and character, accustomed to hardship.

Naiche, son of Cochise, at Fort Pickens, Florida, 1887. Courtesy of Arizona Historical Society, No. 22355

Throughout his three years of imprisonment, he arrogantly resisted the imposition of white practices and, upon his return home, he reverted to traditional Kiowa spirituality. Thus, Zotom probably saw the fortress as a high place, a man-made mountain similar to the hills of the southern Plains where men sought sacred visions. For him, the experience of imprisonment was probably a warrior's journey into a dangerous land, which, if a man faced it and learned from it, would surrender secret and powerful knowledge (Wade and Rand 1996:47–48).

The Plains prisoners such as Zotom, as well as the Chiricahua, must have had moments of emotional desolation and catastrophic feelings of despair, for in addition to being separated from their wives and children, these young, vigorous warriors were on the other side of the continent from their homeland, exiled to an alien land with a hot, humid climate, which caused their moccasins and clothing to mold. The oppressive landscape, with its thick stands of moss-hung pines that obscured any view of the sky, only exacerbated their sense of spiritual imprisonment. There is a word in Athapaskan that means "sadness for a way of life that is gone forever"; accustomed to roaming freely across the great expanses of their homeland, the Chiricahua knew that their way of life was gone forever.

Not only were the Chiricahua imprisoned in a mountainless land far from home, but they were also far removed from the boundaries of the land intended for them by the Giver of Life. The land itself served as a cultural text, with specific geographic features acting as mnemonic devices for moral stories that helped the Chiricahua to live in a way that kept their lives in order and allowed them to prosper. Being separated from the sacred mountains and places of their homeland meant isolation from a vital source of spiritual strength. Thus, the imprisonment of the Chiricahua, a people whose beliefs were based upon maintaining orderly and balanced relations, was particularly horrifying because their continued presence in such a land violated the natural and moral order of their universe. The sense of spiritual dislocation must have been profound and unrelenting.

While engaged in the creative process, Naiche could remove himself from the emotional and spiritual desolation of his present surroundings. It is common for artists to experience a sense of flow, in which time seems suspended and the conditions of the present cease to exist as the artist becomes immersed in the world he or she is depicting. The periods of time that Naiche could devote to his art must have been the few moments of hope and remembered joy in what was otherwise a time of unrelenting darkness. Whether consciously or unconsciously, during the process of painting, Naiche was immersing himself in the happiness of the past, which no doubt comforted him in the despair of the present.

Instead of depicting scenes of war exploits or his present surroundings, Naiche chose to paint the Chiricahua Girls' Puberty Ceremony, the ceremony that has the greatest overall importance for his people. Not only does this ceremony bring together all members of the community to celebrate gift-giving and generosity of spirit, but even more important, it summons the vital forces of life, most notably White-Painted Woman, the embodiment of procreation. In depicting this ceremony, Naiche was calling upon White-Painted Woman, with her life-giving powers of regeneration and renewal, to see his people through their darkest period and to ensure their continuation.

That Naiche was drawn to this subject repeatedly shows how close it was to his heart. His repetition of subject matter indicates that he derived a certain degree of comfort and fulfillment from painting this ceremony, which affirms traditional Chiricahua values. The spirit of White-Painted Woman, with all her powers of renewal and rebirth, infuses the pubescent girl during the ceremony, ensuring the continuation of the Chiricahua people.

The Chiricahua were known to use sandpaintings to create sacred images. Naiche would have shared a belief in the power of sacred imagery to re-create a mythic reality, opening the way to sacred time and space. Even though the content of his paintings was not esoteric, he must have been aware of the power of imagery to create a desired outcome. Instead of selecting as his subject matter warfare, which was a more popular artistic theme among Native American prisoners of war, he chose a particular ceremony that focuses on procreation and life. In this way, Naiche's hide paintings became visual prayers for the rebirth of his people.

It is clear from the presence of the many Chiricahua in the audience that Naiche's prayers were answered; in the face of extreme pressure to assimilate, they are keeping alive their traditions, their language, and their identity as Chiricahua.

Another speaker in the seminar is a man whose grandfather, the youngest warrior with Geronimo's band, survived the twenty-seven-year imprisonment to settle in the Whitetail district on the Mescalero Apache Reservation in 1913. He speaks of the leadership role the Chiricahuas have taken on the Mescalero Apache Reservation. Most of the people there are mixed descendants of Chiricahua, Mescalero, and Lipan Apache, but are especially proud of their Chiricahua heritage. A dignified gentleman in jeans, plaid cowboy shirt, and glasses, with his white hair cut short, he served on the Mescalero Apache Tribal Council for over two decades. "We call ourselves Mescalero Chiricahuas. We're different from the other Chiricahuas, the ones who stayed in Oklahoma. We still practice our traditional ceremonies and we've always placed a high value on the oral history traditions and culture of our people." He describes his people as "a humble but very proud people" who "take an active part in activities that add to our own traditional teachings."

During the break I meet Jordan Torres, who is a descendant of Cochise and Naiche, and whose sculpture is on display in the lobby. A modest man in his thirties, Torres makes only a brief allusion to his success, in a comment about the difficulty of keeping orders for his work filled while continuing his job at the Inn of the Mountain Gods. He introduces his young daughter, a smiling four-year-old with beaded barrettes in her long hair and wearing a modified Apache camp dress. "She'll be having her own ceremony someday," he says.

Only later, when I read a newspaper clipping, do I realize how many awards across the

United States he has won for his alabaster and limestone sculptures. Each stone sculpture of a buffalo or Chiricahua warrior or maiden takes from forty to seventy hours of work. His work, which ranges from highly representational to more expressionistic pieces, speaks to many people with its powerful spirit. Although many galleries are eager to show his work, he would rather display his pieces where he "can meet the people and discuss what a piece means."

Together, the Chiricahua, Lipan, and Mescalero have created a new Apache community on the Mescalero Reservation. But it was not always this way. Five hundred Mescalero were imprisoned with over nine thousand Navajo under the miserable conditions of Bosque Redondo, New Mexico, in the mid-1860s (Opler 1983b:422). Although the Mescalero eventually slipped away from the Bosque to return to their homeland, they did not receive a reservation until 1873 (ibid., 422–23). The reservation was created by executive order, and they did not receive clear title to the land until 1922. Conditions on the reservation were bleak: outbreaks of disease, the loss of stock and possessions to bands of white outlaws and hostile settlers, and other hardships kept the Mescalero in a state of turmoil.

In 1903 thirty-seven Lipans who had been driven from Texas into Mexico were brought to Mescalero to live; another group arrived in 1905. After full freedom was restored to the Chiricahua in 1912, they were given the choice of remaining in Oklahoma or returning to the mountainous country of the Southwest to live with the Mescalero. (The citizens of southern Arizona raised such an outcry at the thought of their return that any request to live in their homeland was out of the question.) Of the 271 remaining Chiricahuas, 187 moved to Mescalero (Opler 1983b:409), and by 1959 78 percent of the 1,300 Apaches at Mescalero were of mixed Chiricahua ancestry (Boyer 1962:32, 33). (Tribal affiliation is taken from one's mother, regardless of the father's affiliation.) Despite the intertribal synthesis that characterizes the population of the Mescalero Reservation, those who claim Chiricahua descent proudly emphasize this part of their heritage.

I conclude my presentation with slides of the Girls' Puberty Ceremony to show how the values of longevity, an even temperament, endurance, and prosperity are embodied in specific symbols. I intersperse slides taken by a friend at Mescalero with ones taken at San Carlos and White Mountain, where the Western Apache live. When I ask for questions, a young Chiricahua woman raises her hand. "Some of those pictures were from the Western Apache," she says in a soft but confident voice. "We have our own way of doing it. I just want people to understand that there's not just one Apache way. The Chiricahuas have our own way to do the ceremony." I thank her for her comment, and after my talk is finished, I sit down beside her in the audience to discuss the differences. Her pride in being Chiricahua is evident as she gestures to the young girl beside her, "I want her to know the right way because she'll be having her feast soon." (Both the Chiricahua and Mescalero refer to this ceremony as a feast in English.)

Today it is clear that the Chiricahua are not only surviving but also keeping their traditions alive and that, despite extreme pressures, their culture is strong and vital. The young woman's comments about the Chiricahua Girls' Puberty Ceremony, the presence of the Chiricahua Prisoner of War Descendants themselves, and the title of the tribal leader's talk, "Contributions of the Chiricahua Prisoners of War: Tribal Strength through Diversity" speak to the survival of their identity as Chiricahua.

Language and Migration

The Chiricahua are one of seven Apachean tribes whose prehistoric origins are discussed in chapter 9; others include the Kiowa-Apache, Jicarilla, Lipan, Mescalero, Western Apache, and Navajo. (The use of the term *Apachean* rather than *Apache* means that the Navajo are included.) Scholars agree that the Apacheans came from the Mackenzie Basin of Canada, where the nucleus of Athapaskan speakers is located (Sapir 1936). The various dialects spoken by the Apacheans belong to the Athapaskan language family, which is divided into three geographic divisions, the Pacific Coast, Northern, and Southern. Thus, the languages spoken by Southern Athapaskans (the Apacheans) are related to languages spoken by Athapaskans in Alaska, Canada, and northern California. Until A.D. 1300 the Apacheans were a single group or several closely related groups (Hoijer 1956; Hymes 1957); they arrived in the Southwest at least by A.D. 1400.

Linguists are able to determine the relative times at which each group split away from the main group of Apacheans. Kiowa-Apache is so different from the other Apachean dialects that Harry Hoijer considers it to be a second Apachean language from southwestern Apachean, under which the other six dialects are subsumed (1971). Kiowa-Apache divided from Lipan and Jicarilla around A.D. 1500; at this time, the Kiowa-Apache moved eastward onto the southern Plains, while the Western Apache, and then the Navajo, moved westward and southward (Opler 1983a:385). By 1600 the Lipan and Jicarilla no longer had contact with the Western Apache and the Navajo, and during the next century the Lipan and Jicarilla divided linguistically and culturally, with the Lipan moving into central and south Texas and the Jicarilla establishing themselves in northern New Mexico and southern Colorado (ibid., 385). The Chiricahua and Mescalero, probably the last to split from each other, established themselves in a central position, remaining in contact with most other Apacheans except for the Kiowa-Apache; eventually, the Chiricahua moved into southwestern New Mexico, southeastern Arizona, and northern Mexico, while the Mescalero established themselves farther east, reaching into part of Texas (ibid.). As the Spaniards penetrated new areas, they found evidence that the Apacheans were already well established in all the areas they occupied in historic times. The Apacheans called themselves *tinneh, dine, tinde, ⁿdé*, or *inde*, meaning "people" or "man"; most believe that the word *Apache* is derived from a Zuni word meaning "enemy."

Apache Culture

After they separated from each other, each group moved into what became its own territories and adapted to the local conditions of climate, terrain, and available food sources. Their contact with nearby non-Apacheans—Puebloan and Plains peoples—provided an array of cultural traits from which they selected specific traits that they adapted to their own cultural beliefs and practices.

Social and Political Organization

All Apaches lived in extended family groups with matrilocal residence. The separate dwellings of nuclear families were clustered nearby so that families related by blood and marriage could work together. When a man married, he took on lifelong responsibilities to provide military, moral, and economic assistance to his wife's extended family, especially her parents. In the company of his affines (in-laws), a husband was expected to demonstrate respect in speech and action by using indirect forms of speech and practicing avoidance, especially toward his mother-in-law. After an appropriate mourning period following the death of his spouse, a man often married his wife's sister (sororate) and a woman, her dead husband's brother (levirate); these traditions helped both to heal the emotional loss of death and to provide for surviving mates and children. Before marriage, the boy's relatives gave gifts to the girl's kin (progeny price).

Grandparents, especially maternal grandparents, played a major role in instruction and discipline, and the importance of their role was reflected in kinship terminology; maternal and paternal grandparents are called by different terms. Same-sex siblings were very close, while those of the opposite sex had to restrain their speech and behavior toward each other. Parallel cousins (children of the father's brother or mother's sister) were considered to be siblings, while cross-cousins (children of the father's sister or mother's brother) were addressed by separate kin terms. All cousins of the opposite sex were treated with restraint and even avoidance. Most Apaches reckoned kinship bilaterally, but the Western Apache (and Navajo) developed strong matrilineal clans and linked clans (phratries), possibly because of Western Pueblo contact.

Extended families who lived near each other exploited the resources of their area together, forming a local group that could support economic, martial, and ceremonial enterprises beyond the resources of a single extended family. Because the local group brought unrelated families into a larger encampment, marriage often occurred between members. The most dynamic family headman led each local group; as he aged and his influence waned, another leading man emerged from the local group to take his place. Although he exercised influence, he had no coercive power, and those who disagreed with his policies were free to move elsewhere. The Chiricahua leader Cochise exemplified the qualities of a respected leader through his wisdom, history of success, and the deep sensitivity he showed to the needs of his people, including the less fortunate members of his group. After their territory had been invaded by Anglos, one Chiricahua characterized the demands of leadership among his people: "Ability in war and wisdom make the leader. It's easier to get to the front if you are a good fighter. . . . The leader is not chosen, he is just recognized" (Sweeney 1991:91).

Even more ambitious enterprises and emergencies called for the next level of political organization, the band, which comprised several local groups. Band consciousness was especially strong among the Chiricahua and the Western Apache. (Possibly because of the need for pasturage, the Navajos had no bands.) Only the Western Apache were organized at a level that was intermediate between the band and the tribe; these subtribal groups—the Cibicue, White Mountain, San Carlos, and Southern and Northern Tonto—were divided into bands.

Subsistence and Material Culture

In early days Apaches roamed the mountains as semi-nomadic hunters and gatherers, relying totally upon wild plant and animal foods. With differential culture contacts and adaptation to different environmental conditions, they began to practice agriculture in varying degrees. Some groups practiced casual agriculture by planting some crops, which they left to ripen on their own while they went on their seasonal round, and then returning to harvest them. The Apaches who lived in closest proximity to the Pueblos—the Western Apache and Jicarilla (and Navajo)—gave more attention to agriculture than did other Apache tribes (Opler 1983a:380). The Lipan practiced some agriculture; the Chiricahua and Mescalero farmed very little (two of the three Chiricahua bands practiced no agriculture at all), and the Kiowa-Apache not at all (ibid., 370). Accompanying their degree of reliance on agriculture was a system of associated ritual traits, such as prayersticks, the ritual use of cornmeal, and rain ceremonies (ibid.). Families moved frequently within the territory of their local group to take advantage of plants that grew at different elevations and matured in different seasons. The most important plant was the agave, or century plant, whose shoot they roasted and whose crown they baked and then dried in the sun for storage. (See chapter 8 for a detailed description of this process.) Women also gathered mesquite beans, sumac berries, juniper berries, piñon nuts, and many wild greens. House construction—the wickiup in the highlands and the tipi on the plains—was the women's task.

Men hunted deer and antelope in addition to raiding, which became increasingly important as a subsistence activity as white encroachment cut off their access to traditional food-gathering locations. Raiding involved five to fifteen men, who rode to their nearest neighbor to take food and horses; this was called in Western Apache "to search out enemy property" (Basso 1983a:476). In contrast, warfare ("to take death from an enemy") was led by the relative of a slain individual to avenge his death (ibid.).

Religion and World View

Origins

The Giver of Life created the universe. Another important holy being is White-Painted Woman (Changing Woman, White Shell Woman), whose sons, Child Born of Water and Killer of Enemies, triumphed over the evils of the world personified as monsters, making the world safe for humans (Basso 1983a:477; Opler 1983b:433). The Mountain Spirits ensure the well-being of the people by protecting them from epidemic diseases and enemies (Opler 1983b:416). "In the beginning" evil animals and beneficent animals played a hidden-ball game to determine whether there should be light or perpetual darkness. The trickster and opportunist, Coyote, shifted his loyalties during the game, depending upon which side was winning at that moment (Opler 1983a:368–69). Specific events that occurred during the game determined the characteristics of many animals and birds.

The Western Apache, Jicarilla, and Lipan (and Navajo) share an origin story based on emergence from the underworld. These same tribes share an account of the origin of agriculture when a man traveled down a waterway in a hollow log, aided by his pet turkey (Opler 1983a:368–69).

Shared Beliefs and Practices

Among the vestiges of the Apaches' northern origin in their ceremonies and world view are the concept of power granted by nonhuman helpers, a fear of ghosts of the recently dead, and the Girls' Puberty Ceremony. Such shared traits are referred to as Proto-Apachean, meaning the common base from which the historic Apache evolved. Athapaskan-speaking tribes of northwest Canada and Alaska also conceptualize a nonpersonalized, immanent power in the universe that could be acquired, experience a much greater fear of ghosts of the recently dead than do the Canadian Algonquians, and celebrate a Girls' Puberty Ceremony, which includes the drinking tube and scratching stick (Honigmann 1981:718–19, 726–27). Another shared belief is that disease is caused by contact with certain animals, such as the bear, and with lightning (Vogt 1961:289).

Proto-Apachean religion was centered on a shaman who performed curing ceremonies and derived his power from such supernatural manifestations as visions (Vogt 1961:289). After their arrival in the Southwest, the Apaches' rituals began to combine priestcraft and shamanism. Priestly (standardized) rituals, important among all Apaches, are exemplified by the Girls' Puberty Ceremony and by curing chants, both of which involve extensive

Apache Creation Story: The Things Legends Are Made Of, *by Duke Wassaja Sine, pen and ink and water-colors, 1988. Photograph by Helga Teiwes, courtesy of Arizona State Museum*

memorization taught by active practitioners to their apprentices. Other rituals that required learning by rote included the Jicarilla "long-life ceremonies" and the Kiowa-Apache sacred-bundle ceremonies (Opler 1983a:373). Among the Western Apache, a shaman primarily used his personal experiences with supernatural power to acquire knowledge that could embellish established rites (Goodwin 1938:28–30). The Western Apache distinguished between those who possess a power and those who do not; the former included not only singers, who manipulate their power on behalf of others to diagnose and cure sickness, but also individuals who predict future events, locate lost objects, and increase the chances of success in hunting (Basso 1970a:38).

Power

The supernatural power that pervades the universe can be acquired by those who respect it. Such power, eager to be of service, could approach a man or a woman through objects and beings, such as stars, animals, and plants, which serve as channels to direct the individual in performing specific rites. Power itself, rather than its vehicle, is sacred and is acquired either through a dream or through a visionary experience. A Chiricahua or Mescalero shaman is guided on a journey to a special place, such as a cave in the mountains (Opler 1969:24), and the supernatural power that resides there takes on human form to teach the shaman its sacred songs and procedures. When the shaman leaves with ritual objects, he is assured that the supernatural power will provide assistance when it is properly summoned through the appropriate songs and prayers (ibid., 24). The Western Apache distinguish between power that selects an individual to be its owner and power that an individual actively seeks by learning the appropriate chants and songs (Basso 1970a:40–42).

Although both Apache and Yuman shamans acquire power through a dream-journey, the Apache relationship with the supernatural is different from that of the Yuman shaman, whose body is entered by a spirit. The Western Apache medicine man, who has a more indirect relationship with a power, is able to diagnose and cure effectively because of his ability to "sing" to his power in the right way through the body of chants and prayers that belong to that particular power. One Western Apache told anthropologist Keith Basso, "Our songs come from those things (the power) and go back to them when we sing them. . . . When a power hears its songs then it will want to listen. If you don't sing songs, a power won't know where to find you, and it won't work for you" (Basso 1970a:42–43). Although the entire body of ceremonials is not as complex as that of the Navajo, Western Apache chants are also extremely intricate and lengthy, and must be performed flawlessly, word for word and line for line (ibid.:43).

Apache religion thus combines shamanism and priestcraft. Among the Chiricahua and Mescalero, a solitary shamanistic vision is the means to the acquisition of power, but the rites bestowed by the power may be taught to others with the permission of the power source (Opler 1983a:372).

Eschatology

Apacheans believed that when a person died, a dead kinsman appeared to the dying to lead him or her on a four-day journey to the north where the afterworld was located. Properly performed funerary practices helped to ensure a peaceful departure, but a ghost could return after reaching the afterworld to avenge a past injury or because of loneliness, so extraordinary precautions were necessary regarding death and burial (Opler 1983a:377–78). Neither scalping nor the collection of an enemy's body parts were part of the Apachean culture pattern because of the Athapaskan fear of contamination from the dead, and when they did adopt this practice after arriving in the Southwest, they accompanied it with purification rituals (ibid., 380). Death released a person's ghost, which, unless it was dispatched to the afterworld and remained there, could inflict great injury to the living. A ghost experience was believed to predict death; because ghosts were thought to return

Western Apache Girls' Puberty Ceremony (Sunrise Dance): Linette Anderson (left), dressed to represent White-Painted Woman (Changing Woman), at the beginning of her ceremony. She holds the decorated cane she will keep for use in old age and stands with a friend in front of singers and the medicine man (far left), 1981. Photograph: Helga Teiwes, courtesy of Arizona State Museum

when they had been involved in inharmonious relations, it was important to remain on good terms with everyone. Both ghosts (the spirit of a dead person) and witches (humans who abused power for their own ends) were capable of persecuting others (ibid., 378).

The Girls' Puberty Ceremony

Also known as the Sunrise Dance or Feast, the Girls' Puberty Ceremony is learned rather than acquired through a vision experience (making it more priestly than shamanistic). Each Apache tribe has its own version of this major Apachean ceremony: for example, the Chiricahua do not use the cane, which is central to the Western Apache form of the ceremony.

One of the best documented versions is that of the Western Apache, thanks to the work of Keith Basso (1966, 1970a). This rite reaffirms traditional values for everyone present and infuses the girl with White-Painted Woman's powers of renewal and rebirth. The ceremony emphasizes four crucial life objectives, beginning with the attainment of a healthy

Linette runs around the cane in each of the four directions, symbolizing that the entire expanse of the universe is now within her reach, 1981. Photograph: Helga Teiwes, courtesy of Arizona State Museum

Linette's "sponsor," a woman of exemplary character who belongs to a different matrilineal clan, prepares Linette by tying a piece of abalone shell in her hair, identifying Linette with White Shell Woman (Changing Woman), 1981. Photograph: Helga Teiwes, Arizona State Museum

old age, which implies that a person has stayed on good terms with the supernatural forces of life. The girl becomes Changing Woman, known as the giver of "many years." The special cane held by the Western Apache girl was made for her to symbolize her old age; by running around the cane when it is placed to represent each of the four stages of her life, she "owns" those stages and will therefore be imbued with the power to attain them. She is thus assured of longevity.

Second, the girl needs a good, even disposition to maintain friendly relationships with others. A highly esteemed person in Western Apache society is one who does not display hostile feelings that might anger a relative or upset someone who might decide to seek revenge by employing witchcraft. She must be friendly, generous, and adroit enough to avoid situations that might lead to conflict. The feathers of the oriole decorate the girl's cane because this bird is considered to be a living model of good conduct.

All Apache women had to possess stamina and endurance for the many food-gathering and household tasks they had to perform each day. The third life objective, endurance and physical strength, is symbolized both by the morning runs the girl must undertake as part of the ceremony and by the molding of her body by her godmother. The godmother massages the girl's legs, back, and shoulders, kneading strength and other desirable qualities of womanhood into the girl's body. The godmother serves as a role model and molds the girl's character at the same time she massages her body. Thus, it is essential that the godmother be of exemplary character because she kneads her own character traits into the girl's body, shaping the girl's personality and path in life. Unrelated to the girl by blood or marriage, the godmother, by taking this honored role, creates a lifelong bond of mutual support, as binding as the ties of actual kinship would be between her family and the girl's family if they were related by blood.

Several things symbolize prosperity and freedom from hunger, the fourth life objective. The buckskin on which the girl dances ensures a plentiful supply of meat. The girl is protected from famine when corn, candy, and fruit are cascaded over her head. And because the wealth of a woman is measured in blankets (while that of a man is counted in horses), by throwing a blanket into each of the cardinal directions, the girl ensures that she will always have an abundance of all she needs in life.

Although it is not an annual, cyclical event, the ceremony is usually held once a year. For all Apache tribes, the event, which brings distant clan relatives together—Apache clans are not localized—is the most festive and social occasion of the entire year, a time of excitement and activity, gossip and courting, bartering and joking, with an abundance of food and drink for everyone. Most of all, there is a powerful sense of connection and community. The most important values are reaffirmed in the ceremony itself, while, as it is performed today, there is also a powerful sense of belonging and an affirmation of tribal identity. It takes many people working together to make the ceremony successful, demonstrating what the community can do when its members cooperate to achieve a shared goal. The ceremony is a tangible marker of how much support everyone can count on from others, which makes the world feel stable and comprehensible. And because the ceremony invests the girl with the power of White-Painted Woman, the entire community is protected against sickness, drought, famine, and poverty, bringing the good things within reach of everyone.

In the Mescalero version, singers recount tribal history from the beginnings to the present, imbuing the past with energy and life so that it actually lives again in the present (see Farrer 1980, 1991). They re-create the world, assuring its continuity, harmony, and balance, and consider this ceremony to be "*the* crucial factor in their ethnicity and their success in coping with the rigors of survival as a people in a pluralistic society not of their making" (Farrer 1980:126 [emphasis in original]).

Ceremonialism

While most ceremonials conducted by the Chiricahua and other Apaches centered on curing or protection against illness, rites were also conducted to diagnose illness, to locate and confound the enemy, to find lost persons and objects, and to improve luck in hunting, games of chance, and lovemaking (Opler 1983b:416). Today, many older ceremonials are no longer performed because they are so expensive and because fewer Apaches are acquiring power (Basso 1970a:47). Western Apache curing ceremonials began at sundown and ended either at dawn of the following day or just before midnight; both types had one-, two-, four-, and eight-night forms (Basso 1983a:479). Shorter rituals were conducted to determine which power was causing the illness and to prescribe treatment, while longer ceremonials neutralized the power and eliminated the illness (ibid., 479).

All Apache peoples shared three themes in their ceremonialism: the identification of the patient with the supernatural, the attraction of supernatural power through reciprocity (prestation), and the removal of evil influences from a patient's body (Lamphere 1983:746–49). Identification with the supernatural is exemplified in the Girls' Puberty Ceremony, for the girl becomes White-Painted Woman/White Shell Woman during her ceremony, symbolized by the abalone shell she wears on her forehead in the Western Apache version or the necklace of abalone shell she wears among the Eastern Apache in this ceremony. She also dances on her knees, her hands raised to the sun as she assumes the posture in which White Shell Woman was impregnated by Sun, father to Slayer of Monsters (Killer of Enemies) (Basso 1970a:65).

The Crown Dancers also "become" the spirits of the Mountain Gods in the same way that the Hopis who dance specific katsinam become those katsina spirits. (Opler [1983a: 373] holds that this "strongly suggests Pueblo influence and considerable Apachean time-depth in the Southwest.") The Crown Dancers (known as the *gaan* among the Western Apache and *gaa'hé* among the Eastern Apache) embody the Mountain Spirits and perform at night, bringing the spiritual world into physical manifestation. Their heads crowned with wooden slat headdresses, four Mountain Spirit Dancers and a clown wield their wooden swords as they dance around the fire. The bull-roarer, which is whirled on a length of string to produce a distinctive, resonating sound, drums, and singing accompany their dancing among the Western Apache. The bull-roarer is not used among the Eastern Apache.

The Apache singer attracts supernatural power through the proper songs, prayers, and offerings. A typical Chiricahua ceremony begins with the patient's formal request to a singer and the presentation to him of four ritual objects required by the "power" to ensure its participation, because the singer is the intermediary through whom the power works (Opler 1983b:416). When the singer then summons it, the power hears its songs and comes to heal the patient, linking the patient, the power, and the singer in a system of reciprocity. In addition to prayer, singing, and ritual smoking, other rites in the ceremony include marking the patient with pollen, white clay, red or yellow ocher, charcoal, or iron ore; brushing with feathers; administering special foods or herbs; and sucking at the afflicted spot with a tube to remove the influences that caused the illness (ibid., 416).

Sandpainting rituals exemplify both the identification of the patient with the supernatural, as the patient sits on the surface of the painting, and the attraction of supernaturals through prestation. Sandpainting is frequently used, especially among the Western Apache and Jicarilla (and Navajo) (Opler 1983a:373). The practice of sandpainting has also been documented for the Chiricahua, Mescalero, and Lipan Apache (Wyman 1983:191). Apache and Navajo sandpainting rituals share some procedures, including making a trail of footprints, which the patient follows to enter the painting before sitting upon it; surrounding the painting with objects planted upright in the sand; applying dry pigments to the patient's body; applying parts of the singer's body to corresponding parts of the patient; blessing the painting with cattail or corn pollen and meal; singing over the patient; preserving portions of the pigments for use as medicine; brushing sickness from the patient; and performing a shock rite in connection with certain paintings (Wyman 1983:191). (In a shock rite, the impersonator of a deity frightens the patient, causing him or her to faint. When the impersonator revives the patient, he or she can count on that deity for protection.)

The Holiness Rite, the most elaborate single Jicarilla Apache ceremonial, cures diseases caused by improper contact with either bears or snakes and includes the creation of dry paintings on four consecutive days, the first day of which includes a shock rite with a man who impersonates a bear. This is nearly identical, both in intention and practice, to the Navajo shock rite; further, the Navajo have two ceremonies that treat bear sickness (Mountainway) and snake disease (Beautyway). These resemblances led Morris Opler (1943:81, 94) to conclude that the three ceremonies belong to a "Navajo-Jicarilla ritual complex."

The Jicarilla also make sandpaintings for their ceremonial relay race, which is held in mid-September (Opler 1944; 1946:116–34). Based on the mythological concepts of racing for the sun and moon, this ceremony was given by the supernaturals to the Jicarilla to ensure a balanced and abundant supply of food (Tiller 1992 [1983]:446). The Llañero band represents the moon and the plants, while the Ollero band, which races against the Llañeros, stands for the sun and the animals (Opler 1946:118). The sandpaintings made for each band always include the sun and the moon, as well as two birds believed to be especially fast, such as hummingbirds or cliff swallows; after dancing in place, the runners march out to their race, stepping on each figure of the painting as they go (Opler 1944: 80–91).

The Chiricahua Apache made "ground drawings" to protect against epidemics and to prevent the enemy from following: a Chiricahua told Opler, "Something happens to the enemy always. They give up before they get to the place of the ground drawing, or they cannot pass it" (1996 [1941]:265). Chiricahua medicine men also made "steps of pollen just like those made at the girl's puberty rite and have the patient walk through. Anyone else who wants to can walk through after the patient finishes. They call it "the trail of long life" (ibid.).

A Mescalero Apache medicine man made a sandpainting of four figures that symbolized long life—such as the bison, bear, snake, mountain lion, or moccasin print—and prayed to each figure, asking it to keep evil away, on each night of a four-night ceremony to cure those whose illness had been caused by "witches," according to Opler (Wyman 1983: 195–96). The Mescalero also used pollen painting on several occasions during the Girls' Puberty Ceremony (e.g., Farrer 1991:174). The singer traced a ground drawing of many animals on the floor of the Lipan Apache girl's tipi for her puberty rite (ibid.). The Cibicue, White Mountain, and San Carlos subtribes of the Western Apache made some of the most elaborate sandpaintings among the Apaches; called medicine circles, medicine disks, or sun disks, these paintings were as complex in design as those of the Navajo, measuring some 16 feet in diameter and containing figures of supernaturals in human form (Goodwin 1938:33). The Western Apaches also painted buckskins with the same figures they drew in sandpaintings, for use in curing and battle (ibid.; Bourke 1892).

Finally, the theme of removal of evil influences is evident when a singer removes the cause of the illness, using such techniques as sucking and blowing, brushing, pulling, and gesticulating to frighten the influences (Lamphere 1983:747). Sickness and misfortune are believed to come from witchcraft—the malicious use of this power—as well as through natural or supernatural forces that have been offended or angered. It is thought that witches shoot foreign substances—bits of bone and hair of the dead—into the victim; thus, the witch's "arrow" must be extracted by sucking or other means.

Basketball at Fort Apache

Basketball is a popular sport on most Indian reservations, and the Fort Apache Reservation is no exception. In 1998 the Falcons, the boys' team at Alchesay High School at Whiteriver, Arizona, took second place in the state finals of their division. Basketball great Kareem Abdul-Jabbar—who had first come to the Fort Apache Reservation in 1995 to research a book on the Buffalo Soldiers, the all-black cavalry regiment that was stationed at Fort Apache after the Civil War—volunteered as co–head coach of the Falcons in October 1998. Abdul-Jabbar explained, "I come from a tough area myself—I was born in Harlem, and I know what the kids here are going through. . . . The negative aspects of life on the reservation are well documented, but that fate can be overcome. I want these kids to go as far as I did. I want to teach them the value of education, and what it can mean to their lives" (Lambert and Benet 1998:197).

The presence of the basketball star has provided a great morale boost to the Falcons, who plan to continue trying for the championship.

Influences from Non-Apacheans

After they entered the Southwest, the Apacheans separated into smaller groups, each moving into a different area and adapting to its distinctive ecological conditions. Through contact primarily with Plains and Puebloan peoples, and further elaboration of their own culture and language, they developed the characteristics that have distinguished them in the recent past. Such cultural borrowing was not one-sided, for many Pueblo traits and concepts appear to be of Apachean origin (Parsons 1939:2:1039–64). Apache people were highly selective about the traits they borrowed, choosing only those that fit with the basic Apachean culture pattern and, in every case, reworking the content and concepts to harmonize with their culture pattern.

To clarify these influences, the six Apache tribes can be grouped into three major divisions. (The Apaches never grouped themselves into such divisions.) Experiencing the greatest contact and influence from Plains peoples, the Kiowa-Apache, the Lipan, and the eastern band of the Jicarilla developed the most nomadic, equestrian cultures. (As Plains cultures, the Kiowa-Apache and the Lipan will be discussed here only briefly.) The Western Apache (and the Navajo) had the closest contact with the Puebloans, which probably led to their greater reliance on farming (and herding for the Navajo), the development of a semi-sedentary lifestyle, and the adoption of matrilineal kinship. The Chiricahua, the Mescalero, and the western band of the Jicarilla were the least influenced by Plains or Puebloan cultures.

The Kiowa-Apache, who lived on the southern Plains, took many traits from their neighbors, such as depending upon the bison for subsistence and using the horse travois and tipis (including the inheritance of heraldic tipis). They occasionally practiced scaffold burial and mutilated their bodies in mourning. They also formed shield groups, counted coup in battle (touching an enemy to demonstrate courage because of the close contact), and had dance societies for men, women, and children. Present at the Kiowa Sun Dance and assigned a place in the Kiowa camp circle, the Kiowa-Apache, like the Kiowa, used treasured tribal medicine bundles (Opler 1983a:380).

The Lipan Apache of Texas and northern Mexico showed slightly less Plains influence, for they lacked shield groups, tribal medicine bundles, and heraldic tipis. However, they depended upon hide receptacles rather than on baskets and pots, used tipis more than other Apaches (except for the Kiowa-Apache), and valued being the person to have delivered the first strike to a fallen foe. The Lipan also had many non-Plains traits, such as concern about contamination from the dead, an emergence story, some agriculture, supernatural impersonators, and an elaborate Girls' Puberty Ceremony.

Although the Jicarilla Apache of northern New Mexico hunted bison on the Plains, they also had katsinalike dancers and enjoyed close relations with the people of Taos, Picuris, and San Juan pueblos. They were the only Apachean group whose bands took on the characteristics of moieties similar to those of the northern Rio Grande Pueblos. Their two bands, the Llañero and Ollero, joined together at certain ceremonial functions and competed in the annual relay race, described earlier, which is similar to those held at Taos, San Juan, and Isleta (Opler 1946:1–2, 116–34). The people of the eastern band/moiety, the Llañero, who lived nearer the Plains, used tipis more consistently than did the members of the western moiety, the Ollero. The Jicarilla also wove baskets, made pottery, and celebrated a Girls' Puberty Ceremony. Their concern about enemy ghosts led them to develop extensive restrictions surrounding the taking of enemy scalps.

The Western Apache also had considerable interaction with the Pueblos, which was reflected in their reliance (greatest of all the Apache tribes) on agriculture, complex version of the katsinalike dancers, and frequent use of sandpaintings in ceremonies.

The Jicarilla Apache

In the beginning, Black Sky and Earth Woman bore Black *Hạ·ščín*, the Supreme Supernatural who created the first man and woman, animals, and birds. The Jicarilla people emerged from the underworld on ladders of sunbeams to follow the newly created Sun and Moon, their source of light. The Wind Deity rolled back the water that covered the earth, Monster Slayer killed the monsters that inhabited the earth, and the Supernaturals eliminated the other obstacles that made the earth unsafe. When the world was safe and dry, the Supreme Deity made four sacred rivers to delineate the boundaries of their homeland: the Arkansas, Canadian, Rio Grande, and Pecos (Tiller 1992 [1983]:1–3).

The Jicarilla developed a dual-band system to adapt to the two diverse geographic areas of their sacred lands—high plains country, which rises westward into plateaus, and mesas with intermontane basins. The Llañeros (plainsmen) followed the bison out onto the plains but returned to trade and winter near Taos, Pecos, and Picuris. The Olleros (potters) became semi-settled agriculturists who lived in the western region, where the southern Rockies extend into north-central New Mexico.

By 1848 Anglo control had been established over Jicarilla territory, and the influx of white settlers made it impossible for the Jicarilla to pursue their old way of life. Already occupied by Hispanic peoples, the land could not support all three groups of people. The long history of conflict that colored the prevailing attitude of New Mexicans toward the Indians led the army to build a series of forts in the heart of Jicarilla country: Fort Massachusetts in southern Colorado, Fort Union near Las Vegas, New Mexico, and Cantonment Burgwin near Taos, New Mexico (Utley 1967:85–87). In 1851 the tribe signed a treaty with the government agreeing to remain within certain territorial boundaries and to cease hostilities. Although part of the tribe attempted to live up to its terms for the next two years, when drought hit, Jicarilla farmers were forced to raid for meat. After a long period of raiding, retaliation, and misunderstanding, complicated by gold strikes in the Cimarron area, the people were exiled to the Mescalero Reservation.

After a long struggle and much negotiating, tribal leaders won the support of the governor of New Mexico, whose coalition of influential individuals persuaded the president to sign an executive order creating the Jicarilla Apache Reservation in 1887. Jicarilla historian Veronica Tiller calls the successful effort of Jicarilla leaders to regain their land "the most important act of self-determination" in the tribe's history (1992 [1983]:228). Outside the Jicarilla sacred lands, its boundaries gerrymandered to appease mining interests, the original reservation included 416,000 acres but was increased in 1907 to 742,315 acres in an effort to increase self-sufficiency through livestock raising (Cole 1994:46).

Until 1920, however, the future of the Jicarilla was bleak because the people suffered from malnutrition, poverty, substandard housing, and disease—some 90 percent of them had tuberculosis by 1914—and their population dropped to fewer than 600 people (Trimble 1993:289). Despite their requests for education, the government did not build a school on the reservation until 1903, but when schools were constructed, they contributed to the spread of the tuberculosis bacterium.

The Jicarilla slowly began to emerge from "the twilight years," as Tiller calls the reservation period from 1887 to 1934 (1992 [1983]:118). Through legislation such as the Dawes Act, the government had tried to make the Jicarillas into self-supporting farmers on land unsuited to agriculture, while neglecting their health, education, housing, and sanitation needs. Under the Indian Reorganization Act of 1934 the tribe adopted a constitution, by-laws, and a corporate charter that enabled the Jicarilla to relinquish allotments, purchase a trading post, acquire livestock, and adopt conservation programs (ibid., 159). Once they finally had livestock, a feasible means of economic support, individually and collectively the Jicarilla were able to move forward, transforming themselves through their own efforts from "a dying, poverty-stricken race to a prosperous people with a thriving livestock economy" (ibid.).

Between 1950 and 1970 the tribe developed significant oil and natural gas deposits on their land, leading to an increase in tribal royalties of over $1 million annually. The new income was used to develop the Stone Lake Lodge recreation complex and a tribal education fund. Health services and new housing became available during the 1960s. As the income and level of concern of tribal members increased, and as the federal government sponsored programs in schools, a tribal linguistic and cultural renaissance took place (Cole 1994:47). Today the Jicarilla keep their culture alive through the Girls' Puberty Ceremony;

the four-night Bear Dance, which brings spiritual blessings and long life for the community; and the annual relay race between the Olleros and Llañeros (ibid.). Today the relay race is the only time when people separate into rival groups, for Jicarilla identity and allegiance now lie at the tribal level. In 1964 the tribal council established the Jicarilla Arts and Crafts Industry to foster the preservation of traditional leatherwork, basketry, and beadwork skills; Jicarilla women demonstrate their crafts at the Jicarilla Arts and Crafts Museum in Dulce, New Mexico (Fontana 1999:84). The tribe also operates the Apache Nugget gaming casino near the Jicarilla Inn in Dulce (ibid.).

The Chiricahua Apache

The largest of the four bands of Chiricahuas was the Eastern Chiricahua, who called themselves the Chihennes, or Red Paint People. Mexicans and Americans referred to various sections of this band as the Mimbres, Mimbreños, Mogollons, Warm Springs, and

Coppermine Apaches, names that described specific locations they inhabited (Opler 1983b: 401). They occupied most of the Chiricahua territory in New Mexico west of the Rio Grande in the Cuchillo, Black, Mimbres, Mogollon, Pinos Altos, Victoria, and Florida mountain ranges (Opler 1965:1–2). Mangas Coloradas, Delgadito, Victorio, Nana, Loco, Mano Mocha, Fuerte, Itan, and Chuchillo Negro led the Chihennes from the 1820s through the 1870s (Sweeney 1991:4).

The Chokenens or Central Chiricahua, whose most prominent leader was Cochise, lived in the southeast corner of Arizona and a small area in northern Mexico that included the Dragoon, Dos Cabezas, and Chiricahua Mountains. They also ranged east into southwestern New Mexico, south into the Sierra Madre, and north to the Gila River. Their leaders from the 1820s through the 1870s included Relles, Matias, Tapila, Yrigollen, Miguel Narbona, Pisago Cabezon, Posito Moraga, Esquinaline, and Cochise, who had become the leading chief of his band by the mid-1850s (ibid., 5).

Located primarily in Mexico but also including small sections of southwestern New Mexico and southeastern Arizona, the Southern Chiricahua band called themselves Nednhis or Enemy People, in reference to their fearsomeness (Opler 1941:1–2). Mexicans and Americans knew them as the Janeros, Carrizaleños, and Pinery Apaches, in reference to places where they lived (Sweeney 1991:4). Their homeland was the mountains along what is now the international border with Mexico, but they roamed deep into the Sierra Madre in the Mexican states of Chihuahua and Sonora (Opler 1941:1–2). The section of the band known as Janeros took their name from a town in northwestern Chihuahua, where they had friendly relations, and from 1820 through the 1870s their leaders were Juan Diego Compa, Juan Jose Compa, Coleto Amarillo, Arvizu, Laceris, Galindo, Natiza, and Juh (Sweeney 1991:4). The Carrizaleños, who took their name from another Chihuahuan town, were led by Jasquedega and Cristobal in the 1830s; by Francisquillo, Francisco, and Cigarrito in the 1840s; and by Cojinillin and Felipe in the 1850s (ibid., 4). Mexican campaigns hit both groups hard during this time period, virtually wiping out the Carrizaleños.

The smallest Chiricahua band, the Bedonkohes, was assimilated into one of the other bands during the 1860s, with most of them choosing to follow Cochise after the death of Mangas Coloradas (Sweeney 1991:5). They lived northeast of the Central Chiricahuas in the Mogollon Mountains and Gila River area. Geronimo was born into this band.

Although the band was the political unit with which people identified, all the bands recognized themselves as Chiricahua, considering themselves to be related and visiting frequently, especially to share puberty ceremonies, marriages, and social dances. Most of the time they enjoyed peaceful relations with each other. In contrast to the band, a stable political unit, the local groups that made up each band were flexible. Each family that belonged to local group could join another local group whenever they chose, depending upon the availability of resources, the death of a leader, epidemics, or conflict within the group. Cochise was remarkable because the members of all local groups in the Central

Chiricahua band recognized him as their overall leader, while other Chiricahua bands had several local group leaders, a much more common occurrence (Sweeney 1991:5–6).

Although Fray Marcos de Niza, who in 1539 headed the first Spanish expedition into southeastern Arizona, does not mention the Chiricahua, this is probably because the Chiricahua intentionally remained undetected in their mountain strongholds (Goodwin 1969 [1942]:66–67). Despite numerous attempts throughout the eighteenth century, the Spanish were unable to dislodge the Chiricahuas, and after Mexico took control in 1821, political instability resulted in a cessation of military campaigns against the Indians.

Once the United States obtained the land south of the Gila River through the 1853 Gadsden Purchase, the Chiricahuas found their hunting and gathering territories increasingly endangered by prospectors eager to exploit California's mineral wealth, surveyors trying to establish roads, and settlers and veterans seeking land. The Chiricahua, who had at first been conciliatory toward Anglos, became more aggressive after 1852 when gold was discovered at Pinos Altos, New Mexico, and Anglo depredations against Indians increased (Bartlett 1854, 1:308–40). Furthermore, the United States, which was now responsible for Chiricahua raiding into Mexico, had a vested interest in curtailing their movements.

In 1863 Eastern Chiricahua leader Mangas Coloradas (then in his seventies), realizing that he could not defeat the Americans and eager for peace, went to Pinos Altos, where under a flag of truce he was tortured and shot. As historian Dan Thrapp (1974:83) explained, "The greatest tragedy of the affair was less the death of the aging chieftain than the lasting distrust generated on the part of Apaches toward white Americans and soldiers." Losing Mangas Coloradas, his father-in-law, in such an inhumane way proved once more to Cochise that Americans could not be trusted, and war became a way of life for him for the rest of the 1860s. Thomas Jeffords's friendship with Cochise, romanticized in Elliot Arnold's *Blood Brothers* and the motion picture and television show *Broken Arrow*, probably began in the fall of 1870 when Cochise visited the Canada Alamosa Reservation (Sweeney 1991:296). In contrast to the legend perpetuated in the novel, which has Jeffords bravely seeking out Cochise in his stronghold in the Dragoon Mountains to sign an agreement to allow safe passage of Jeffords's mail riders, Apaches said that Jeffords's visit was hardly voluntary and resulted from his capture (Ball 1988 [1980]:27–28), while Opler thought they became acquainted when Jeffords was a trader (Sweeney 1991:296). However their legendary friendship began, Jeffords did become one of the few men Cochise trusted, and it was with Jeffords's assistance that Gen. O. O. Howard helped establish a Chiricahua Reservation in the southeastern corner of Arizona Territory (Howard 1907:184–225; Sladen, n.d.).

Despite the sincere commitment of all three men to the reservation, a series of events soon destroyed the chances for a peaceful way of life there. After a great influx of Apaches from other reservations, where conditions were less favorable, depleted the rations, the Chiricahua were accused of raiding in Mexico. Then violence erupted after a trader sold whiskey to the Indians. In 1876, after Cochise's death ended a period of remarkably unified leadership, the reservation was abolished (Opler 1983b:405). The army then consolidated all disparate groups of Apaches in Arizona on the San Carlos Reservation, where all suffered from insufficient rations and conflict among Anglo administrators as well as among the various Apache groups. About 300 Chiricahua bolted in 1877, though some returned a year later. Victorio led his followers into Mexico, where he was killed by Mexican soldiers in 1880.

In 1885 Geronimo, hearing that he was to be arrested, escaped to Mexico with forty-two men, women, and children (ibid., 407). After two major campaigns against them, they surrendered in 1888. Along with those Chiricahua who had served as scouts and those who had not fled the reservation, they were sent into exile in Florida prisons. Promised that they would be housed with their wives and children, Cochise's son Naiche, Geronimo, and fifteen other men were sent to Fort Pickens, Florida, on the other side of the state from Fort Marion in St. Augustine, where their families were incarcerated (Opler 1983b). Over 20 percent of the Chiricahuas sent to Florida died before the end of 1889 (ibid., 408). When General Crook, outraged by the suffering of his former Chiricahua Indian scouts (President Grover Cleveland had overridden Crook's terms of surrender), and the Indian Rights Association protested the treatment and location of the Chiricahua, the government decided to transfer them to Mount Vernon Barracks, near Mobile, Alabama, in 1887 and 1888. Hardly any healthier, conditions in Alabama led to even more sickness and death. In 1894 the government freed the Chiricahuas of their prisoner-of-war status and moved them to Fort Sill, Oklahoma, where the Chiricahua organized themselves into settlements based on their old local groups and began to raise crops and cattle.

The Chiricahua are one of the few Southwestern tribes whose reservation was not established on a portion of their homeland; even after the turn of the century, Arizona settlers were still so fearful of the Chiricahuas that they raised a public outcry against a reservation in southern Arizona. In 1912 the government finally restored full freedom to the 271 surviving Chiricahuas, giving them the choice of taking allotments of land in Oklahoma or moving to the Mescalero Reservation in New Mexico. The Fort Sill Apache are those who chose to stay in Oklahoma, while in 1913, 187 joined the Mescalero, settling in their own section of the reservation, known as Whitetail. By the 1970s most of the nearly 2,000 Apaches at Mescalero had moved to a single large community near the agency center, which had better access to off-reservation roads, schools, hospital, traders' stores, and post office (ibid., 409).

Everyone at Mescalero lost a great leader when half-Chiricahua, half-Mescalero Wendell Chino died at age seventy-four in November 1998. (Chino identified himself as Chiricahua because his mother was Chiricahua.) Serving as president of his tribe for thirty-four years, he demanded that the federal government honor its treaties regarding the land and its resources. Roy Bernal, chairman of the All-Indian Pueblo Council and a member of Taos Pueblo, described Chino as a "modern warrior," whose stances affected Indians all over the country: "In the scheme of the twentieth century, it has been said that Wendell Chino was a Martin Luther King or a Malcolm X of Indian Country" (LeDuff 1998:A24). In the mid-1960s it was Chino who created lumber and cattle companies controlled by the tribe instead of renewing contracts with non-Indian companies. Under his guidance, the tribe built the Inn of the Mountain Gods resort, Casino Apache, a timber mill, and a metal fabrication plant, as well as schools, a hospital, and a health center. However, in the early 1990s Chino caused a split at Mescalero when he invited nuclear power companies to bury their radioactive waste on tribal land to increase tribal revenues, and the tribe rejected his proposal. Despite the controversy he stirred—Chino was sometimes described as a benevolent dictator—he made a tremendous difference not only among his people but also as a nationally and internationally known spokesman for Indian issues and as the president of the National Congress of American Indians.

The Mescalero Apache

The mescal, or agave, plant, which gives its name to the Mescalero, was a staple of their diet and especially plentiful in their territory. They ate it fresh, sun-dried it to store in parfleches (leather storage containers that fold nearly flat) for later use, or placed it in sealed caves for emergencies or times of scarcity. Each spring, men helped the women dig the large roasting pit in which they baked the heavy crowns that lay at the base of the new stalk growths. They prepared sotol in a similar manner, roasted stalks of beargrass and amole, and harvested other edible plants (Opler 1983b:432). Men hunted bison, deer, elk, bighorn sheep, and at least a few families practiced some agriculture (ibid., 431).

The Mescalero lived in an area of valleys and flats separated by mountain ranges as high as 12,022 feet. Changes in elevation provided a range of game animals and wild plants. Bounded on the west by the Rio Grande, their extensive territory reached southward into the Mexican states of Chihuahua and Coahuila, east into Texas, and northward into Colorado. They concentrated their settlements west of the Pecos River but traveled farther east to hunt bison and antelope, seek enemies, and acquire horses.

Today the Mescalero live on a portion of their sacred lands, almost half a million acres near the sacred Sierra Blanca Mountain in south-central New Mexico. However, theirs has been a long struggle to keep their culture and their land. After a large percentage of their land came under American control through the Treaty of Guadalupe Hidalgo in 1848 and the Gadsden Purchase of 1853, prospectors and settlers streamed into their land, steadily depleting the game and plants upon which the Mescalero depended. From Fort Conrad, Fort Craig, Fort Fillmore, Fort McRae, Fort Stanton, and Fort Thorn, all established between 1851 and 1855, U.S. troops launched military campaigns against the Mescalero (Opler 1983b:422). During the American Civil War, once Union forces gained control of the area, Gen. James Carleton began his efforts to concentrate the Mescalero at Bosque Redondo, the 40-mile area on the Pecos River at Fort Sumner where the Navajos were also to be imprisoned. Eventually 500 Mescaleros were imprisoned with their enemies, the Navajo (of whom there were over 9,000), in confined conditions where crops failed repeatedly, the water was too alkaline to drink, rations were inedible, and firewood was insufficient (Opler 1983b:422). In 1865 hunger and discontent drove all but nine Mescaleros back to their homelands; by 1868 the Bosque was acknowledged to be a failure, and all prisoners were allowed to return home.

After years of hardship and negotiation, the Mescalero Reservation, which consists primarily of the eastern slopes of the White and Sacramento Mountains, was established in 1873 by executive order. Outbreaks of disease resulted from exposure to European diseases to which the Indians had no immunity, such as the smallpox epidemic of 1877. The Desert Land Act of 1877 opened up more lands to settlement, increasing settlers' desire for Indian land. The following year, the Lincoln County War between two rival groups of cattlemen kept the Indians in a state of turmoil (Opler and Opler 1950:27).

When the Chiricahua were ordered to move from their homeland just west of the Mescalero, to join the Western Apache at San Carlos, Victorio and some of his Warm Springs band fled rather than comply. The army accused the Mescalero of giving Victorio sanctuary and forced the tribe to move to Fort Stanton, where they were disarmed and forced into a manure-laden corral; fourteen Mescalero who resisted were killed, and others who had not complied were hunted down (Opler 1983b:423).

The Mescalero did not receive clear title to their reservation until 1922, an uncertainty that kept them from protesting having to share this small area with other Apache tribes. In 1883 they were forced to share their land with the Jicarilla, with whom they had enough linguistic and cultural differences to breed mistrust on both sides; by 1887 all the Jicarilla had returned north to their former territory (Opler 1983b:423). In 1903 the Mescalero were joined by thirty-seven Lipans who had been driven into Mexico from Texas, and ten years later they received over half of the surviving Chiricahuas (ibid., 424).

With their land largely unsuited to agriculture, the Mescalero-Chiricahua-Lipans have developed cattle and timber industries, and most recently tourism. The natural beauty of their land provides the ideal setting for their luxury resort hotel, the Inn of the Mountain Gods, with its artificial lake and golf course. They have also developed a tourist complex with a ski run and another with a motel, restaurant, and gift shop, as well as a fish hatchery from which to restock reservation streams. In 1973 the tribe built a museum to display photographs and selected Apache artifacts (Fontana 1999:63). Unfortunately, isolated from any urban areas, and with enterprises that employ few people, the Mescalero suffer from high rates of unemployment and underemployment, which together often surpass 70 percent (Opler 1983b:427).

The Western Apache

By at least 1850 the Western Apache had divided into five major groups or subtribes that lived in the mountainous area of east-central Arizona: farthest east were the White Mountain Apache; the San Carlos lived to the southwest; the Northern and Southern Tonto Apache were located to the northwest; and the Cibicue resided between the Tonto and the White Mountain subtribes (Basso 1983a:463). (The Western Apache did not divide the Tonto group; Goodwin [1969 (1942):41] made this distinction on the basis of geographical and dialectal criteria.) The Western Apache are the only Apache tribe with subtribal divisions; today, the White Mountain, San Carlos, and Tonto Apache have tribal status. Their contiguous territories reached from nearly the eastern edge of present-day Arizona (held by the White Mountain Apache), to south of Tucson along the San Pedro River (San Carlos Apache territory), nearly as far west as Prescott, and beyond Flagstaff to the north. The Tonto Apache, who occupied the region north of the Salt River and west of the Cibicue Apache, became distinct from other Western Apache subtribes. Today the Tonto have intermarried with the Yavapai and share several small reservation fragments with them; collectively, they are known as the Camp Verde Yavapai-Apache.

After the Gadsden Purchase opened all of Arizona to Anglo settlers and prospectors who intruded into Western Apache territory, open hostility erupted into an almost forty-year war that ended with the assignment of the Western Apache onto reservations. Caught up in a military and civilian war on all Apaches and the discovery of gold in 1863 in Northern Tonto territory, the Western Apache retaliated by massacring whites. The White Mountain and Cibicue Apache, whose geographic isolation had kept them comparatively free from conflict with the military, watched the construction of Camp Goodwin, on the Gila River (territory of the White Mountain Apache), in 1864 (ibid., 480). Aware of the inevitable devastation experienced by other Apaches, they accepted offers of peace and did not resist the establishment of Camp Ord (later Fort Apache) in 1868; some served as scouts for Gen. George Crook in his campaigns against the Chiricahua and Tonto Apaches.

In 1871 a mob of Tucson citizens and Tohono O'odham Indians slaughtered over seventy-five San Carlos Apache women and children in the Arivaipa Valley. Known as the Camp Grant Massacre, after the nearby army camp under whose protection the Apaches had had supposed sanctuary, this brutal slaughter finally pushed President Grant to initiate a peace policy that called for the consignment of Indians to reservations where they would be given protection and encouraged to become self-supporting through stock raising and agriculture. Four reservations were established: Fort Apache for the Cibicue and northern White Mountain bands; Camp Verde for the Tonto Apaches and the Yavapai; Camp Grant for the San Carlos and southern White Mountain bands; and a Chiricahua Reservation in western New Mexico (ibid., 480). Corrupt and incompetent agents and epidemics caused by poor housing and food characterized conditions on the reservations. When the government decided to consolidate the reservations in 1874, with all Arizona Apaches—many of whom had had no previous contact—at San Carlos and all New Mexico Apaches at Mescalero, renewed fighting broke out and continued until 1884. The final large-scale outbreak came in 1886, when Geronimo and his followers escaped to Mexico for sixteen months before being exiled to Florida.

The U.S. government then focused on three objectives: economic development resulting in self-sufficiency, the conversion of all Apaches to Christianity, and assimilation through the education of Apache children (ibid., 482). Cattle raising succeeded at both Fort Apache and San Carlos, while the lumber industry, which began in the 1920s, became a thriving industry. In 1954 the White Mountain Apache began developing recreational facilities by constructing artificial lakes and dams and constructing hunting, camping, fishing, and ski facilities. Fort Apache firefighters are widely recognized in the U.S. Forest Service and travel to many locations during the fire season. However, despite these advances, the unemployment rate at Fort Apache in 1969 was about twice the national average, and 80 percent of housing was substandard (Century Geophysical Corporation 1970), with most homes lacking butane heat and indoor plumbing and only about half having electricity.

Missionaries arrived at San Carlos and Fort Apache in 1900, but few Apaches were receptive to their message at that time. In the face of deprivation and trauma, several cults founded by influential shamans flourished. Between 1903 and 1907 Big John led a movement known as *daagodigha* ("spiritual movement starts," which means "they will be raised upward"), which held that eventually all followers would temporarily ascend into the sky while the destruction of evil forces on earth occurred; afterward the followers would return to their former homes, where they would live in a state of abundance (Basso 1983a:486). In 1921, after receiving a vision from Yusn (the Giver of Life), Silas John Edwards (Silas John, as he was known) founded a religion stressing moral behavior, including abstinence from drinking, fighting, and witchcraft, and use of new ceremonial forms to replace many traditional curing rituals. The Silas John movement spread to Mescalero and to non-Apachean peoples and eventually became institutionalized as part of reservation religious life (ibid., 486–87). Despite these two nativistic movements, Anglo missionaries converted increasing numbers of Apaches. The high cost of ceremonials has tended to decrease the number and complexity of rituals, but traditional curing ceremonials as well as the Girls' Puberty Ceremony continue today.

In the government and mission schools constructed at Fort Apache and San Carlos between 1895 and 1922, children were subjected to brutal punishment, such as whipping, solitary confinement, and shackling to a ball and chain (Spicer 1981), treatment that led to a profound mistrust and hatred of the Anglo educational system (ibid., 485). Although

Plaque at entrance of Hon-Dah Resort and Casino, near Pinetop, Arizona, 1999. Author photograph

these harsh measures were discontinued, the school system has continued to suffer from serious problems, such as substandard education, which fails to prepare Apache students for higher education (ibid., 486).

The White Mountain Apache Tribe owns and operates Hon-Dah Casino and Resort south of Pinetop, Arizona; located in the scenic White Mountains of Arizona, the reservation offers many opportunities for fishing and boating. The tribe also runs the White Mountain Apache Culture Center in Fort Apache and the Fort Apache Historical Park; the latter is a 288-acre historic site with buildings that date back to the Apache Wars and a replica of a traditional Apache village (Fontana 1999:28). Fishing, hunting, and rafting on the Salt River on the San Carlos Apache Reservation are also popular outdoor activities. Many visitors come to the Apache Gold Casino Resort as well; in 1995 the tribe opened the San Carlos Apache Cultural Center (ibid., 30). The Tonto Apache Tribe also owns and operates a casino and restaurant, the Mazatzal Casino, located at the south edge of Payson, Arizona, a popular summertime retreat for those who live in the southern Arizona desert (ibid., 24).

Western Apache Oral Literature

Native Americans have transmitted their traditions and histories through a wide range of speech genres, which not only convey traditional values but also show people how to cope with the moral challenges of the present by reminding them that these values are still applicable in today's world. Oral traditions have been highly developed into a verbal art that transmits history, literature, spiritual beliefs, and ways of life. Nowhere is the richness of Native American oral literature more evident than in the work of anthropologist Keith Basso, who has opened a door to the inner world of the Western Apache people, illuminating their cultural values through the use of language. Traditions of narrative art, such as metaphor, humor, and place-making (cultural geography), exist among nearly all (if not all) Native American cultures. Basso's writings afford the best glimpse of the richness of these oral traditions as used by the Western Apache, allowing us to imagine the depth that exists in other Southwestern cultures and languages.

Wise Words

"Only the really good talkers can make them up like that. They are the ones who *really* speak Apache. They are the ones who make up 'wise words' and don't have to use someone else's," a Western Apache consultant explained to Basso (1976:118 [emphasis in original]). The consultant was praising the creative skill of a certain group of Western Apache men and women who form a kind of intellectual elite by virtue of a reputation for extensive cultural knowledge, balanced thinking, and critical acumen. Their advanced age exempts them from participation in the full round of daily activities that occupies most of the population, leaving them with an abundance of time for *baiyan diidała'at'ee* ("old people talking together"), the conversational setting in which "wise words" are most frequently created and used.

"Wise words" are a distinctive speech genre that uses metaphor to express mild personal criticism. In an extremely subtle process, the person's identity can only be inferred from contextual information. Certain behavioral attributes that indicate undesirable qualities are applied to the larger semantic category to which the individual belongs. The following example, "Dogs are children," is explained by the fact that "both of them, children and dogs, are always hungry . . . when they don't get food they come to a place where someone is cooking. . . . Both of them get into everything and don't leave anything alone. So you have to shoo them away. If you don't, they might break something" (ibid., 100).

The full power of "wise words" becomes evident in an example given by a Western Apache consultant, who told how her grandmother used "wise words." Her mother had gone to the hospital in Whiteriver, and the consultant's older sister was supposed to look after the children and cook for them. When the sister went out partying with two female cousins and did not return until quite late, the consultant's grandmother had to come take care of the children. "I guess she knew my sister had been running around. When my sister came in my grandmother didn't say anything at first. Then she said to my older brother, 'Butterflies are girls and one of them just flew in'" (ibid., 106–7). The sister understood that the grandmother was drawing a parallel between butterflies and those young girls who act mindlessly by having a good time when they should be helping out at home. "That's how they use 'wise words', these old people—when they want to say something bad about someone" (ibid., 106–7). Creating and interpreting these metaphorical statements means being able to assign nonliteral meanings to spoken messages—a task that requires considerable creative skill and linguistic competence.

Place-Making as Cultural Geography

"We gave her clear pictures with place-names. So her mind went to those places, standing in front of them as our ancestors did long ago. That way she could see what happened there long ago. She could hear stories in her mind, perhaps hear our ancestors speaking. She could recall the knowledge of our ancestors," Lola Machuse told Basso (1996:86). "Certain localities" have the capacity to evoke "entire worlds of meaning," explained Basso (ibid., 5). Lola Machuse was interpreting a subtle conversational exchange she had had with two other women two days before, known as "speaking with names," in which the local landscape is mentioned in a way that produces "a beneficial form of heightened self-awareness" (ibid., 83), while also commenting indirectly on the moral conduct of individuals who are absent.

In this exchange, the woman named Louise begins speaking about her younger brother, "My younger brother . . ." (Basso 1996:79).

Lola says, "It happened at Line Of White Rocks Extends Up And Out, at this very place!"

Emily adds, "Yes. It happened at Whiteness Spreads Out Descending To Water, at this very place!"

Lola continues, "Truly. It happened at Trail Extends Across A Red Ridge With Alder Trees, at this very place!"

After Louise laughs softly, Robert Machuse says, "Pleasantness and goodness will be forthcoming." Lola repeats her husband's words.

Finally, Louise asks Clifford, the Machuses' ancient yellow dog, "My younger brother is foolish, isn't he, dog?"

Lola explained that Emily and she could see that Louise was overly worried about her younger brother's apparent lack of common sense when he stepped on a snakeskin near a roundup camp. Instead of immediately going to a ritual specialist, as another member of the roundup crew suggested, he said that no harm would befall him. The night before the conversation took place, Louise's brother was taken to the hospital at Whiteriver after suffering from cramps, spreading numbness in his legs, and vomiting.

Instead of criticizing Louise's brother, Lola and Emily mention particular places that evoke narratives to make Louise feel better. In this emotionally charged context, "speaking with names" is a recommendation that Louise recall the ancestral stories connected with those places and allow ancestral voices to speak directly to her. Her friends are advising her to "travel in your mind . . . to view the place whose name has just been spoken" and there, "in the tracks of your ancestors . . . recall stories of events that occurred at that place long ago" and "appreciate, as if the ancestors were speaking to you directly, the knowledge the stories contain. Bring this knowledge to bear on your own disturbing situation. Allow the past to inform your understanding of the present. You will feel better if you do" (Basso 1996:91).

When Louise laughed softly after remembering the story of humorous events that had occurred at Trail Extends Across A Red Ridge With Alder Trees, everyone could tell that her spirits had briefly improved as the ancestral knowledge encapsulated in the story provided comfort and hope. Robert then formalized the success of the encounter by saying, "Pleasantness and goodness will be forthcoming!" Louise's comment to the dog was a way of politely (indirectly) thanking her companions for their concern and politeness in refraining from voicing the truth about her brother's foolishness.

The evocative power of Apache place-names reveals a major difference between Anglo-American and Native American historical accounts: while Anglo-American accounts tend to be temporally based, Native American accounts are based on the features of the earth. The Anglo-American variety of history strikes Apaches and other Indians as detached, distant, and unfamiliar because it hardly "speaks the past into existence" in the manner of Apache accounts. Geographically adrift, an Anglo-American account fails to engage the reader or to provoke a sense of wonder, for, as Western Apache Charles Henry said, "It's pretty mainly quiet. It stays far away from all our many places" (Basso 1996:34).

References and Further Reading

The Smithsonian's *Handbook of North American Indians*, vol. 10 (1983), contains chapters about various aspects of Apache culture.

Adams, Alexander. 1976. *The Camp Grant Massacre.* Simon and Schuster, New York.

Ball, Eve. 1970. *In the Days of Victorio: Recollections of a Warm Springs Apache.* University of Arizona Press, Tucson.

*———. 1988 [1980]. *Indeh: An Apache Odyssey.* University of Oklahoma Press, Norman. [This remarkable book tells the story of Chiricahua warriors from Cochise to men at Mescalero, through the words of Kadlugie and Eugene Chihuahua.]

Bartlett, John R. 1854. *Personal Narrative of Explorations and Incidents in Texas, New Mexico, California, Sonora, and Chihuahua Connected with the United States and Mexico Boundary Commission, During the Years 1850, '51, '52, '53.* 2 vols. D. Appleton, New York.

Basehart, Harry W. 1967. "The Resource Holding Corporation among the Mescalero Apache." *Southwestern Journal of Anthropology* 23:277–91.

———. 1970. "Mescalero Apache Band Organization and Leadership." *Southwestern Journal of Anthropology* 26:87–106.

*Basso, Keith H. 1966. *The Gift of Changing Woman.* Bureau of American Ethnology Bulletin 196. Smithsonian Institution, Washington, D.C. [The most respected contemporary anthropologist of Western Apache culture, Basso writes books that speak eloquently of the complexities of language, word play, and world view.]

———. 1968. "The Western Apache Classificatory Verb System: A Semantic Analysis." *Southwestern Journal of Anthropology* 24, no. 3:252–66.

———. 1969. *Western Apache Witchcraft.* Anthropological Papers of the University of Arizona 15. University of Arizona Press, Tucson.

———. 1970a. *The Cibicue Apache.* Holt, Rinehart, and Winston, New York.

———. 1970b. "To Give Up on Words: Silence in the Western Apache Culture." *Southwestern Journal of Anthropology* 26:213–30.

———. 1976. "'Wise Words' of the Western Apache: Metaphor and Semantic Theory." In *Meaning in Anthropology*, pp. 93–121, ed. K. Basso and H. Selby. School of American Research Book. University of New Mexico Press, Albuquerque.

———. 1983a. "Western Apache." In *Handbook of North American Indians*, vol. 10: *The Southwest*, pp. 462–88.

———. 1983b. "Western Apache Placename Hierarchies." In *Naming Systems: 1981 Proceedings of the American Ethnological Society*, pp. 37–46, ed. E. Tooker. American Ethnological Society, Washington, D.C.

———. 1988. "'Speaking with Names': Language and Landscape among the Western Apache." *Cultural Anthropology* 3, no. 2:99–130.

———. 1990a. "Strong Songs: Excerpts from an Ethnographer's Journal." In *Our Private Lives: Journals, Notebooks and Diaries*, pp. 26–37, ed. Daniel Halpern. Vintage Books, New York.

———. 1990b. *Western Apache Language and Culture: Essays in Linguistic Anthropology.* University of Arizona Press, Tucson.

———. 1994 [1979]. *Portraits of the "Whiteman": Linguistic Play and Cultural Symbols among the Western Apache.* Cambridge University Press, Cambridge, England.

———. 1996. *Wisdom Sits in Places: Landscape and Language among the Western Apache.* University of New Mexico Press, Albuquerque.

Basso, Keith H., ed. 1971. *Western Apache Raiding and Warfare: From the Notes of Grenville Goodwin.* University of Arizona Press, Tucson.

Basso, Keith H., and Ned Anderson. 1973. "A Western Apache Writing System: The Symbols of Silas John." *Science* 180, no. 4090: 1013–22.

Basso, Keith H., and Morris Opler. 1971. *Apachean Culture History and Ethnology.* University of Arizona Press, Tucson.

Bellah, Robert. 1942. *Apache Kinship Systems.* Harvard University Press, Cambridge, Mass.

Bourke, J. G. 1892. "The Medicine Men of the Apache." *Annual Report of the Bureau of American Ethnology* 9:451–595.

———. 1971. *On the Border with Crook.* University of Nebraska Press, Lincoln. [Originally published in 1891 by Charles Scribner's Sons, New York.]

Boyer, Ruth McDonald. 1962. "Social Structure and Socialization among the Apaches of the Mescalero Reservation." Ph.D. diss., University of California, Berkeley.

Breuninger, Evelyn, Elbys Hugar, and Ellen Ann Lathan. 1982. *Mescalero Apache Dictionary*. Mescalero Apache Tribe, Mescalero, N.Mex.

Castetter, Edward, and Morris Opler. 1936. *The Ethnobotany of the Chiricahua and Mescalero Apaches*. University of New Mexico Press, Albuquerque.

Century Geophysical Corporation. 1970. "Interim Planning Report No. 7004 on Analysis of Existing Conditions, Fort Apache Indian Reservation." Mimeo.

Cole, D. C. 1988. *The Chiricahua Apache, 1846–1876: From War to Reservation*. University of New Mexico Press, Albuquerque.

——. 1994. "Apache." In *Native America in the Twentieth Century: An Encyclopedia*, pp. 44–48, ed. Mary Davis. Garland Publishing, New York.

Debo, Angie. 1976. *Geronimo: The Man, His Time, His Place*. University of Oklahoma Press, Norman.

Deloria, Vine, Jr. 1969. *Custer Died for Your Sins: An Indian Manifesto*. Macmillan Company, Collier-Macmillan Ltd., London.

Dobyns, Henry F. 1971. *The Apache People*. Indian Tribal Series, Phoenix.

——. 1973. *The Mescalero Apache People*. Indian Tribal Series, Phoenix.

Farrer, Claire R. 1973. "The Performance of Mescalero Apache Clowns." *Folklore Annual* 4 and 5:135–51.

——. 1978. "Mescalero Ritual Dance: A Four Part Fugue." *Discovery* 1978:1–13.

——. 1980. "Singing for Life: The Mescalero Apache Girls' Puberty Ceremony." In *Southwestern Indian Ritual Drama*, pp. 125–59, ed. C. Frisbie. Advanced Seminar Series. University of New Mexico Press, Albuquerque, and School of American Research, Santa Fe.

——. 1990. *Play and Interethnic Communication: A Practical Ethnography of the Mescalero Apache*. Garland Publishing, New York.

——. 1991. *Living Life's Circle: Mescalero Apache Cosmovision*. University of New Mexico Press, Albuquerque.

Farrer, Claire R., and Bernard Second. 1981. "Living the Sky: Aspects of Mescalero Apache Ethnoastronomy." In *Archaeoastronomy in the Americas*, pp. 137–50, ed. Ray Williamson. Ballena Press Anthropological Papers 22. Ballena Press and the Center for Archaeoastronomy, Los Altos, Calif., and College Park, Md.

Ferg, Alan, ed. 1988 [1987]. *Western Apache Material Culture: The Goodwin and Guenther Collections*. University of Arizona Press, Tucson.

Flannery, Regina. 1932. "The Position of Women among the Mescalero Apache." *Primitive Man* 5, no. 1:26–32.

Fontana, Bernard L. 1999. *A Guide to Contemporary Southwest Indians*. Southwest Parks and Monuments Association, Tucson.

Getty, Harry T. 1964. "Changes in Land Use among the Western Apaches." In *Indian and*

Spanish American Adjustments to Arid and Semiarid Environments, pp. 27–33, ed. C. Knowlton. Committee on Desert and Arid Zone Research, Contribution No. 7. Lubbock, Tex.

Gifford, Edward W. 1940. "Culture Element Distribution: XII—Apache-Pueblo." *University of California Publications in Anthropological Records* 4:1–208.

Goddard, Pliny Earle. 1911. *Jicarilla Apache Texts*. Anthropological Papers of the American Museum of Natural History 8, no. 1. New York.

———. 1918. *San Carlos Apache Texts*. Anthropological Papers of the American Museum of Natural History 24, no. 3, New York.

———. 1919. *Myths and Tales from the White Mountain Apache*. Anthropological Publications of the American Museum of Natural History 24, no. 2. New York.

———. 1920. *White Mountain Apache Texts*. Anthropological Publications of the American Museum of Natural History 24, no. 4. New York.

*Goodwin, Grenville. 1935. "The Social Divisions and Economic Life of the Western Apache." *American Anthropologist* 37, no. 1:55–64. [With Opler, Goodwin laid the bedrock of Apache ethnography.]

———. 1937. "The Characteristics and Function of Clan in a Southern Athapaskan Culture." *American Anthropologist* 39:394–407.

———. 1938. "White Mountain Apache Religion." *American Anthropologist* 40, no. 1:24–37.

———. 1939. *Myths and Tales of the White Mountain Apache*. Memoirs of the American Folklore Society 33, New York.

———. 1969 [1942]. *The Social Organization of the Western Apache*. University of Arizona Press, Tucson.

Goodwin, Grenville, and Charles Kaut. 1954. "A Native Religious Movement among the White Mountain and Cibicue Apache." *Southwestern Journal of Anthropology* 10:385–404.

Goodwin, Grenville, and Clyde Kluckhohn. 1945. "A Comparison of Navaho and White Mountain Ceremonial Forms and Categories." *Southwestern Journal of Anthropology* 1:498–506.

Gunnerson, Dolores A. 1974. *The Jicarilla Apaches: A Study in Survival*. Northern Illinois University Press, Dekalb.

Haley, J. 1991. *Apaches: A History and Culture Portrait*. Doubleday, New York.

Hoijer, Harry. 1938. *Chiricahua and Mescalero Texts*. University of Chicago Press, Chicago.

———. 1956. "The Chronology of the Athapaskan Languages." *International Journal of American Linguistics* 22, no. 4:219–32.

———. 1971. "The Position of the Apachean Languages in the Athapaskan Stock." In *Apachean Culture, History, and Ethnology*, pp. 3–6, ed. Keith H. Basso and Morris E. Opler. Anthropological Papers of the University of Arizona 21, Tucson.

Honigmann, John J. 1981. "Expressive Aspects of Subarctic Indian Culture." In *Handbook of North American Indians*, vol. 6: *The Subarctic*, pp. 718–38.

Howard, Oliver O. 1907. *My Life and Experiences among Our Hostile Indians: A Record of Personal*

Observations, Adventures, and Campaigns among the Indians of the Great West with Some Account of Their Life, Habits, Traits, Religion, Ceremonies, Dress, Savage Instincts, and Customs in Peace and War. A. D. Worthington, Hartford, Conn.

Hymes, Dell H. 1957. "A Note on Athapaskan Glottochronology." *International Journal of American Linguistics* 23, no. 4:291–97.

Kaut, Charles R. 1957. *The Western Apache Clan System: Its Origins and Development.* University of New Mexico Publications in Anthropology 9. University of New Mexico Press, Albuquerque.

Lambert, Pam, and Lorenzo Benet. 1998. "Walking Tall." *People* 50, no. 19:197–99.

Lamphere, Louise. 1983. "Southwestern Ceremonialism." In *Handbook of North American Indians,* vol. 10: *The Southwest,* 743–63.

LeDuff, Charlie. 1998. *New York Times,* 9 November:A24.

Mails, Thomas. 1974. *The People Called Apache.* Prentice-Hall, New York.

Mauldin, Barbara. 1984. *Traditions in Transition: Contemporary Basket Weavers of Southwestern Indians.* Museum of New Mexico Press, Albuquerque.

*Opler, Morris E. 1936. "A Summary of Jicarilla Apache Culture." *American Anthropologist* 38:202–23. [The best known and most respected scholar of Apache culture, Opler laid the foundation for Apache studies.]

———. 1938a. *Dirty Boy: A Jicarilla Tale of Raid and War.* Memoirs of the American Anthropological Association 52.

———. 1938b. *Myths and Tales of the Jicarilla Apache Indians.* Memoirs of the American Folklore Society 31.

———. 1938c. "The Sacred Clowns of the Chiricahua and Mescalero Indians." *El Palacio* 44:75–79.

———. 1941. *An Apache Life-Way: The Economic, Social, and Religious Institutions of the Chiricahua Indians.* University of Chicago Press. [Reprinted in 1965 by Cooper Square Publishers, New York, and in 1996 by University of Nebraska Press, Lincoln.]

———. 1942. "Adolescence Rite of the Jicarilla." *El Palacio* 49:25–38.

———. 1943. *The Character and Derivation of the Jicarilla Holinesss Rite.* University of New Mexico Bulletin, Anthropological Series 4, no. 3.

———. 1944. "The Jicarilla Apache Ceremonial Relay Race." *American Anthropologist* 46:75–79.

———. 1946. *Childhood and Youth in Jicarilla Apache Society.* Publications of the Frederick Webb Hodge Anniversary Publication Fund 5. Southwest Museum, Los Angeles.

———. 1969. *Apache Odyssey: A Journey between Two Worlds.* Holt, Rinehart, and Winston, New York.

———. 1983a. "The Apachean Culture Pattern and Its Origins." In *Handbook of North American Indians,* vol. 10: *The Southwest,* pp. 368–92.

———. 1983b. "Chiricahua Apache" and "Mescalero Apache." In *Handbook of North American Indians,* vol. 10: *The Southwest,* pp. 401–18, 419–39.

Opler, Morris E., and Catherine H. Opler. 1950. "Mescalero Apache History in the Southwest." *New Mexico Review* 25, no. 1:1–36.

Parmee, Edward A. 1968. *Formal Education and Cultural Change: A Modern Apache Indian Community and Government Education Programs*. University of Arizona Press, Tucson.

Parsons, Elsie Clews. 1939. *Pueblo Indian Religion*. 2 vols. University of Chicago Press, Chicago.

Perlman, Barbara H. 1987. *Allan Houser (Ha-O-Zous)*. David R. Godine, New York.

Perry, Edgar, Canyon Z. Quintero Sr., Catherine D. Davenport, and Corrine B. Perry. 1972. *Western Apache Dictionary*. White Mountain Apache Tribe, Fort Apache, Ariz.

Reagan, Albert. 1930. *Notes on the Indians of the Fort Apache Region*. Anthropological Publications of the American Museum of Natural History 31. American Museum of Natural History, New York.

Sapir, Edward. 1936. "Internal Linguistic Evidence Suggestive of the Northern Origin of the Navaho." *American Anthropologist* 38, no. 2:224–35.

Skinner, Woodward B. 1987. *The Apache Rock Crumbles: The Captivity of Geronimo's People*. Skinner Publications, Pensacola, Fla.

Sladen, J. A. n.d. "Making Peace with Cochise, Chief of the Chiricaua [*sic*] Indians, 1872." Manuscript (82 pp.), compiled from penciled notes made in the 1880s. Frant Phillips Collection, Bizzell Memorial Library, University of Oklahoma, Norman.

Sonnichsen, C. L. 1979 [1958]. *The Mescalero Apaches*. University of Oklahoma Press, Norman.

Spicer, Edward. 1981 [1962]. *Cycles of Conquest*. University of Arizona Press, Tucson.

Stanley, F. 1967. *The Jicarilla Apaches of New Mexico, 1598–1967*. Pampa Print Shop, Pampa, Tex.

Stockel, H. Henrietta. 1991. *Women of the Apache Nation: Voices of Truth*. University of Nevada Press, Reno.

Sweeney, Edwin. 1991. *Cochise: Chiricahua Apache Chief*. University of Oklahoma Press, Norman.

Tanner, Clara Lee. 1982. *Apache Indian Baskets*. University of Arizona Press, Tucson.

Taylor, Benjamin J., and Dennis J. O'Connor. 1969. "Indian Manpower Resources in the Southwest: A Pilot Study." Bureau of Business and Economic Research, Arizona State University, Tempe.

Thrapp, Dan L. 1967. *The Conquest of Apacheria*. University of Oklahoma Press, Norman.

———. 1974. *Victorio and the Mimbres Apaches*. University of Oklahoma Press, Norman.

Tiller, Veronica E. Velarde. 1992 [1983]. *The Jicarilla Apache Tribe: A History*. University of Nebraska Press, Lincoln.

Trimble, Stephen. 1993. *The People*. School of American Research Press, Santa Fe.

Utley, Robert M. 1967. *Frontiersmen in Blue: The United States and the Indian, 1848–1865*. Macmillan, New York.

———. 1977. *A Clash of Cultures: Fort Bowie and the Chiricahua Apaches*. National Park Service, Washington, D.C.

Van Orden, Jay. 1994 [1991]. *Geronimo's Surrender: The 1886 C. S. Fly Photographs*. Arizona Historical Society Museum Monograph 8. Arizona Historical Society, Tucson.

Van Rockel, Gertrude. 1971. *Jicarilla Apaches*. Naylor, San Antonio, Tex.

Vogt, Evon Z. 1961. "Navaho." In *Perspectives in American Indian Culture Change*, pp. 278–336, ed. Edward H. Spicer. University of Chicago Press, Chicago.

Wade, Edwin L., and Jacki Thompson Rand. 1996. "The Subtle Art of Resistance: Encounter and Accommodation in the Art of Fort Marion." In *Plains Indian Drawings 1865–1935: Pages from a Visual History*, pp. 45–49, ed. Janet Catherine Berlo. Harry N. Abrams, New York.

Worcester, D. 1979. *The Apaches: Eagles of the Southwest*. University of Oklahoma Press, Norman.

Wyman, Leland. 1983. *Southwest Indian Drypainting*. School of American Research, Santa Fe, and University of New Mexico Press, Albuquerque.

Bryce Canyon, Utah, called by the Paiutes "Red Rocks Standing Like Men in a Bowl-Shaped Recess," 1999. Author photograph

Chapter 11 The Southern Paiutes

June 1999

Standing at the edge of Bryce Canyon, I can see why the Paiutes called Bryce Canyon "Red Rocks Standing Like Men in a Bowl-Shaped Recess." The pillars of rock do stand upright like the inhabitants of a village that trickster Coyote turned to stone. The western edge of Bryce Canyon is a watershed: precipitation that falls behind me flows north toward the Great Basin, while the rain and snow that fall in front of me flow southward to eventually reach the Colorado River.

The land of the Southern Paiute is time made visible, for ancient Cretaceous layers lie exposed beside younger Tertiary layers. In Paleozoic times Arizona and Utah were part of a great shelf that periodically flexed downward, allowing the sea to flood its margins. Over the course of some 60 million years, as the land was alternately elevated and submerged, the sea deposited horizontal layers of sediments, and millions of years later rivers and streams brought new layers, including the red, iron-rich sediments that became the Pink Cliffs at Bryce. When the earth pulled apart about 10 million years ago, thus exposing layers of sediment deposited over the course of 144 million years, it tilted great blocks so that layers on the Table Cliffs now tower 2,000 feet above the same layers on the adjacent Paunsaugunt Plateau. Water eventually eroded the land exposed by the uplift to form the cliffs known as the Grand Staircase, a vast series of steps that descend from roughly 9,000 feet at Bryce to the 5,000-foot-high valley where the Kaibab Paiute Reservation is located, before rising again in a steep curve to reach about 8,000 feet at the North Rim of the Grand Canyon. The Pink Cliffs of Bryce Canyon, on the eastern edge of the Paunsaugunt Plateau, are the uppermost step in the Grand Staircase, which descends successively to the Gray, White, Vermilion, and, finally, Chocolate Cliffs of the Kaibab Plateau before bottoming out and then ascending once again.

Southern Paiute territory is also a land of limitless space, for nowhere else in the Southwest are such vast distances visible: looking southward, I can see Navajo Mountain; to the northeast, the Black Mountains. On the clearest days the view extends up to 200 miles over vast reaches of the Southwest, including northern Arizona and even New Mexico.

After lunch at the picnic area, as we drive south toward Kanab, Utah, I try to identify what makes the Mormon presence so evident. Besides the obvious markers like Adopt-a-Highway signs for groups such as "Glendale Ward Young Men and Women," and a teenager wearing a Brigham Young Cougars T-shirt, the communities could be from the 1950s, with their neatly mown lawns and carefully tended rose bushes. (Mormons divide areas geographically into wards.) Teenagers have short hair and no body-piercing, and there is not a single gang symbol spray-painted on any dumpsters. Just before we rejoin Highway 89, I spot another Adopt-a-Highway sign, one that speaks eloquently of the Mormon impact on the Paiute people: "Panguitch First Ward Girl Scout Troop." Panguitch, Utah, is a Mormon town that took its name from the group of Southern Paiute who lived in that region.

Once we enter the Kaibab-Paiute Reservation, the impact of the Mormons on Paiute life becomes even more evident. When the 12-by–18-mile reservation was set aside over the course of several years for the use of the Kaibab Paiute people, they had to share it with two non-Indian enclaves: Moccasin, a Mormon town, and Pipe Spring National Monument, the site of a ranch built by the Mormons for a church tithing herd (cattle contributed by Mormon families as a tenth of their income). Pipe Spring was a free-flowing spring that drew prehistoric Basketmaker and Pueblo Indians and Paiutes who camped there during their yearly migrations. Throughout Paiute country, Mormons displaced Paiutes by constructing forts and villages around springs, forcing the Indians to become dependent upon the Mormons for water.

Earlier on our trip, we toured Glen Canyon Dam, which has also had a major impact on Southern Paiute culture, especially in terms of water releases on Southern Paiute cultural resources. The Grand Canyon and more than 600 downstream miles of the Colorado River—from above the Kaiparowits Plateau to Blyth, California—are located within Puxant Tuvip, the sacred land where the Southern Paiute people were created. Aboriginally, Southern Paiutes occupied nearly 60 percent—317 of 540 miles—of the river bank of the Colorado River Corridor. This corridor extends 255 miles downstream from the dam to the end of the free-flowing river at Separation Canyon within Grand Canyon National Park. Water releases from Glen Canyon Dam change the Colorado River's rate of flow, sediment-carrying capacity, rate of rise and fall, and water temperature; all of these factors, in turn,

have a direct impact on natural and cultural resources, including plants, animals, minerals, and archaeological sites.

As stewards of the Grand Canyon—the spiritual center of their traditional territory—the Southern Paiutes are working today in partnership with federal and state entities that manage the Colorado River Corridor. The Southern Paiutes have a monitoring project to assess the effects of the Glen Canyon Dam on the cultural resources of the canyon. In the face of encroaching factors—changes in the river itself and an increase in tourist traffic—the Southern Paiutes are keeping track of the changing condition of their cultural resources. Individuals known for their traditional knowledge identify cultural resources with both physical and spiritual dimensions; these resources are generally subsumed under four major categories: plants, animals, rock art, and archaeology. Examples of cultural resources include natural landscapes, plant communities, and archaeological sites.

Grand Canyon, spiritual center of the Southern Paiutes, 1999. Author photograph

Origins

In the beginning, all was water. Wolf, known as the "people's father" because he had made heaven and earth, told his younger brother, Coyote, to make the earth. When

Coyote could not accomplish this, Wolf dove down to the bottom of the water to bring up clay from which he created the land and animals. According to others, Water Woman, Ocean Woman's daughter, created the earth, and then Coyote made animals of mud before he created people. Coyote then carried the people to their homelands in the basket in which they had been placed by Ocean Woman. Handing the narrow-necked water jar with its precious contents to Coyote, Ocean Woman admonished Coyote to take them to a distant land where they could hunt and gather all the food they needed. He was not to open the jar under any circumstances until he had reached the perfect place. Coyote, who had been absent from home for quite some time, was eager to see his brother Wolf, so he agreed to take on this task.

Bearing the heavy basket on his back, Coyote began to walk. Soon the sounds coming from the jar aroused his curiosity, tempting him to peek inside. When he could resist no longer, Coyote opened it, only to have people tumble out in every direction. As they came out and scrambled away in different directions, Coyote gave them names: the Havasupais, the Hualapais, the Mojaves, the Quechan, the Pimas, and others, even the Europeans. Overcoming his amazement at last, Coyote closed the jar, leaving only a few people, the Ningwi (the Southern Paiutes), whom he took to Wolf. After scolding his foolish younger brother for his disobedience, Wolf helped Coyote mold and name the Ningwi as special people. Together they carried the people to a place where the deer and mountain sheep are abundant and much agave grows, a special place at the edge of the Grand Canyon shaped by the majestic Colorado River, where they remain today. (This version is derived from Fowler and Parezo 1996; Kelly 1976; and Laird 1976).

Territory and Language

As told in their origin story, the Colorado River is the heart of Southern Paiute territory. Their traditional territory followed a huge arc of land around the north and west sides of the river; only the San Juan Paiutes live east of the Colorado River. This area, which stretches some 350 miles east and west, ranges from the high Colorado Plateaus, through canyon country, through basin and range, and into the Mojave Desert (Fowler 1966:15–16). The plateaus above 7,000 feet are covered with dense forests of spruce and fir, with pine at the lower elevations of the coniferous belt, while the middle elevations of 5,000–7,000 feet feature piñon, juniper, and sage, with desert uplands of creosote and mesquite. The Hurricane Fault ledge and the Grand Wash cliffs divide the plateau country to the east from the lower basin country with its alternating valleys and ranges of mountains that seldom reach above 7,000 feet.

Sixteen identifiable groups of Southern Paiute once lived in this broad L-shaped swath of territory that spans southern Utah, northern Arizona, southern Nevada, and the adjacent area of California (Kelly and Fowler 1986:368). (This includes the Arizona Strip, which is the northwestern area of Arizona separated from the rest of the state by the Colorado River/Grand Canyon.) Those who lived farthest north and east took on Plains traits, while those in the southwestern part of this territory, such as the Chemehuevi, adopted many characteristics of River Yuman culture. In fact, the Antarianunts, who lived in the extreme northeastern part of Southern Paiute territory, were considered by some anthropologists to be Ute (Kelly 1934) and by others (Stewart 1942:237) to be Southern Paiute. The Southern Paiute, as well as the adjacent Ute, belong to the Southern Numic branch of the Uto-Aztecan linguistic family.

Prehistory and Early History

Based on their prehistoric brownware pottery, language, and myths, Numic-speaking peoples probably came from southern California and the Pacific coast, spreading into the Great Basin and the Southwest. Sometime after A.D. 1000, bands of Southern Paiute moved from the Death Valley region into the area north of the Colorado River. The Southern Paiute people view themselves as related to the people archaeologists call the Virgin River Anasazi (SPC 1995:11). The remains of dwellings and artifacts reflect their long history along the Colorado River, where they farmed, gathered plants, hunted, traded with other Indian peoples, and conducted ceremonies (ibid., 11). By the mid-nineteenth century Southern Paiute territory covered a contiguous area from Death Valley northeast to Utah's West Desert and south to Monument Valley and the Painted Desert, embracing the northwestern corner of the Southwest and the southeastern area of the Great Basin.

Living in such a cultural frontier, the Southern Paiute found their homeland to be a crossroads where Great Basin peoples of the high arid deserts of Nevada and Utah met with the River Yumans of the Colorado River, the Upland Yumans of the Arizona plateaus, the Navajos, and the Hopis. The Utes brought the Southern Paiutes the travois (a two-pole drag harnessed onto dogs and horses for transporting goods and sometimes people), the tipi, and the Bear Dance, while the Mojaves contributed the Cry, a mourning ceremony. However, the Utes and Mexicans were aggressive slave raiders, and the Navajos also stole women, children, and horses (Malouf and Malouf 1945).

To the north and northwest, the Shoshone and Las Vegas Southern Paiutes intermarried and cooperated economically. The Las Vegas and Chemehuevi had amicable contact with California peoples as well, and the Chemehuevi, once part of the Las Vegas Southern Paiutes, became allies of the Mojave and Quechan in their wars with the Cocopa (although they were intermittently at war with the Mojave). The Chemehuevi took on many Mojave traits, such as floodplain farming, certain crops, earth-covered houses, an emphasis on dreams, a complex associated with warfare, vocabulary, and features of the song cycles (Laird 1976). They regularly hunted in Hualapai country, as well as in the territory of the Yavapai, with whom they intermarried and traded (ibid.).

By the late 1700s Navajo, Ute, and New Mexican slave traders had begun to prey on Southern Paiute children and young adults to meet the demand for forced labor in Spanish settlements. Anglo-Americans began to trade goods for horses and then for Indian children. Upon reaching California, slave traders sold children for more horses or trade goods; they captured more Paiutes on their return trip, selling these children in New Mexico. The proximity of the Old Spanish Trail, a major trade route linking Santa Fe with California, made spring an especially dangerous season for the Southern Paiutes: by this time of year, winter stores of food had run out, leaving everyone in such a weakened physical condition that they had little strength to flee. Well aware of this fact, many slave traders timed their raids accordingly. Fearing for their families, Southern Paiute bands were forced to stay in seclusion far away from the richest farmland in their territory, a practice that led to malnourishment and increased rates of disease. By 1830 wagon trains were passing regularly through their country.

In 1852 the Utah territorial legislature outlawed the Spanish Trail slave trade, but by that time the Mormons had arrived and had colonized the area south of Salt Lake City. Claiming that American Indians were Lamanites, whose ancestors they considered to be one of the lost tribes of Israel, the Mormons began buying Paiute children as indentured servants, whom they then converted to their religion. Mormons quickly encroached into traditional Paiute territory, first that of the Cedar City band, then into the Arizona Strip, appropriating water sources as well as land.

By the 1870s most Paiutes (except for the Uinkarets and Kaibab) were either on reservations or were concentrated around the Anglo settlements, and by the beginning of the twentieth century additional reservations had been established besides the Moapa Reserve (Euler 1966:98). The Paiutes had lost most of their traditional land to miners, ranchers, farmers, and, in Arizona, to the Navajos, and their population had declined sharply because of diseases introduced by outsiders. Although they continued their foraging and farming, they no longer had control of enough territory to meet their subsistence needs, and many were forced to work as farmhands, ranch hands, or domestics. Others sold their crafts, especially basketry; the San Juan Paiutes raised sheep and goats (Bunte and Franklin 1994:428).

Aboriginal Southern Paiute Culture

Subsistence and Material Culture

Primarily foragers who hunted large and small game animals, birds, and fish, and gathered over a hundred plant species, Southern Paiute groups lived in terrain that ranged from the high Colorado Plateaus through basin-and-range canyonland and into the Mojave Desert (Fowler 1966:15–16). Such a range in elevation meant changes in rainfall and temperature that were reflected in a wide range of local resources. Depending upon the ecological zones that lay within a band's territory, their resources might include fish (important to the Panguitch Lake group), piñon nuts, cactus fruits and stems, or mescal crowns. Efficient use of resources required tremendous knowledge, because each plant was only available for a short period each year. Living semi-nomadically, each group moved within its territory with the seasons as the people gathered material from both lower deserts and high plateaus.

In summer they gathered seeds, fruits, and berries, and those who farmed shared their harvest with others who did not. While some stayed to complete the collection and storage of crops, others left for the mountains to begin gathering piñon nuts. The fall harvest of yucca fruits, piñon nuts, and deer made this the time of greatest abundance as well as a time of great mobility, for the people were constantly moving back and forth from high to low country and from spot to spot to collect and hunt where the resources were most plentiful. They cached piñon nuts and hunted large game in the mountains, while returning to the valleys for communal rabbit drives. Other small game animals included the squirrel, chipmunk, wood rat, mouse, dove, quail, and duck, while large game animals were antelope, bighorn sheep, and deer (SPC 1995). As much food as possible was stored because spring famine was a common occurrence; nearly all groups identified starvation foods (foods that they normally did not prefer but resorted to only out of necessity) (Kelly and Fowler 1986:370–71). Some chose to winter at higher elevations, where fuel was plentiful and stores of piñon nuts were at hand, while others, who did not rely on pine nuts, preferred the foothills or protected canyons where agave was abundant and caves could be used as dwellings.

Puebloan and Southern Paiute prehistoric pottery dating from around A.D. 1150 shows that the two groups shared sites (Euler 1964:379), which means that they probably also shared subsistence information (Stoffle and Evans 1978:4). In order to use the greatest possible range of plants and animals, many Southern Paiute groups added cultivation to their annual round of food gathering. To increase new growth and seed production, they burned grasslands, cultivated seed-producing plants such as amaranth, and transplanted mesquite and wild grapes (Stoffle and Dobyns 1983).

The Spanish explorer-missionary Silvestre Velez de Escalante, who traveled through their country in 1776, observed the Southern Paiutes' irrigated fields of corn and squash on river banks and plains (Bolton 1950:205). The Southern Paiute have often mistakenly been classified as hunter-gatherers because most of their territory was not explored by European Americans until after contact had disrupted their traditional subsistence patterns. They actually practiced casual agriculture, planting fields but relying primarily on their annual round of hunting and gathering for subsistence. Leaving the elderly to watch the fields, most of the camp went on their usual collecting and hunting trips. A few Southern Paiute groups (Antarianunts, Panguitch, Kaiparowits) remained nonagricultural, but others, such as the Kaibab, Chemehuevi, Las Vegas, Moapa, Saint George, and Shivwits groups, practiced varying degrees of agriculture, raising such crops as red, white, yellow, and blue corn; winter wheat; semicultivated grasses; gourds; squash; and pumpkin (Kelly and Fowler 1986:371).

The people used bent willow boughs thatched with cedar bark and covered with earth to build conical or semi-conical winter houses with smoke holes and eastward-facing doorways (Watkins 1945), although a San Juan Southern Paiute described gabled houses with ridgepoles as typical (Stewart 1942:257). They slept outside in summer or built shades and circular windbreaks. The Chemehuevis built earth-covered dwellings similar to those of the Mojave, and the Cedar group began using Ute-influenced tipis as early as 1855 (Euler 1966:67). Some groups favored sweat lodges, which they borrowed from the Ute, Shoshone, Hualapai, and Navajo cultures.

Social and Political Organization

Because of the harsh environmental conditions that kept the Southern Paiutes from developing a sedentary lifestyle, they had little need to create a complex sociopolitical system, such as that required by large-scale irrigation societies. They had no overall tribal organization, and for the most part the subgroups north of the Colorado River were on friendly terms with each other. The Moapa, Shivwits, Saint George, and Pahranagat accused the Beaver, Cedar, Gunlock, and Panguitch of capturing women and children to sell as slaves, which fueled resentment but not resistance (Kelly and Fowler 1986:368). By 1900, although some gatherings held in connection with the Mourning Ceremony were almost pan–Southern Paiute (Kelly 1976:95; Sapir 1912), as late as the early 1930s groups knew little about the area farther away than the territory of the groups adjacent to their area (Kelly and Fowler 1986:369).

There are several identifiable subgroups, named primarily for the areas they occupied. Those in present-day Arizona are the San Juan, Kaibab, Uinkaret, and Shivwits. Those in Utah are the Antarianunts, Kapirowits, Panguitch, Beaver, Cedar, Gunlock, and Saint George. Those who live primarily in Nevada are the Panaca, Pahranagat, and Moapa (half of whose territory was in California). Finally, the Chemehuevi live in California. These groups, however, were not bands because they had no centralized political control or sense of solidarity among their members, nor did these groups spend any considerable length of time together as a cohesive unit.

Each of these subgroups was composed of anywhere from a few to many economic units or clusters, and each economic cluster had between one and ten households; in some cases, there might be as many as twenty individual households in one economic cluster (Kelly 1932). There was a tendency toward patrilocality after a temporary period of matrilocal residence immediately after marriage, with the nuclear family serving as the basic economic unit. These individual households tended to move together on hunting and gathering trips, following the same annual cycle and returning to the same spring or agricultural site.

Most large economic clusters had a headman who advised rather than led with authority. Known for his oratorical skills, a headman spoke early every morning, either from the doorway of his home or from a nearby hill, advising the people to treat each other well or shouting directions on how and where to hunt. He urged his people not to steal or fight and admonished thieves. Chosen by the elder men of the group after lengthy deliberations, the headman often belonged to the same family as the previous leader (Kelly and Fowler 1986:380).

Religion and World View

Both men and women shamans helped cure illness attributed to disease-object intrusion caused by a malevolent shaman or ghost; ghost intrusion; or soul loss (Kelly 1936). Usually appearing in the form of an animal that provided instructions and songs, one or more tutelaries gave power to an individual in a dream. Among the Chemehuevi and Las Vegas, a person could obtain such a dream by spending a night alone in one of several caves (Laird 1976:38). For the most part, the Southern Paiutes did not associate shamanism with datura (a plant known for its narcotic properties), as did some California groups, or perform cures while in a trance state, as was common throughout the Great Basin (Kelly and Fowler 1986:383). To heal soul loss, the shaman had to pursue and restore the wandering soul; to heal disease-object intrusion, he or she removed the object by sucking. Shamans specialized in the power to cure rattlesnake bites and wounds, ensure luck in hunting, control the weather, and aid in childbirth.

The Chemehuevi, Las Vegas, and Pahranagat, who had "dreamers" for large game, gave gifts to the mountain spirits for assistance in hunting (Kelly and Fowler 1986:370). Defined by songs with recurrent references to specific place-names, hunting rights for large game within certain tracts of Chemehuevi territory were inherited, and a man either had to have the proper song (which bestowed the rights) or had to be in the company of one who did, in order to hunt (Laird 1976:33). When hunters had been unsuccessful for a period of time, they asked a game dreamer-singer to direct them to a spot where they could find game. Men and women gathered at night, ate, and formed an incomplete circle about the singer, with hunters holding their bows across their bellies with fingers turned inward to simulate hooves (Kelly and Fowler 1986:384). Some groups sang to attract mountain sheep (Kelly 1932).

The Ghost Dance movement of the 1890s affected the western and northwestern Southern Paiutes, including the Chemehuevi, Las Vegas, Moapa, Panaca, and Pahranagat, while the Saint George had the dance as early as 1889 (Kroeber 1935:198). The Panaca were the first to learn the songs and procedures, and the Pahranagat and Moapa learned them through visiting the Panaca; the Moapa then dispersed the dance to the Chemehuevi and Las Vegas. Dreams brought supplementary songs to the songs that came with the Ghost Dance. Although songs held messages from dead relatives, whose return was promised through the dance along with the restoration of their land and resources, most songs followed the pattern of naming geographical features (Kelly and Fowler 1986:384). Men and women, especially young people, alternated in a circle facing inward with arms linked and moved clockwise in the Round Dance—also known as the harvest, pine nut, rabbit, or squaw dance—which was also the formation for Ghost Dances, and for the War-Incitement and Scalp Dances (ibid.).

Prosperous relatives of a deceased person gave a Mourning Ceremony, or Cry, related to the Mojave ceremony, from three months to a year after the death. Several families who had lost loved ones often shared the enormous outlay of food and goods required by the ceremony. Over a period of time families accumulated the buckskins, eagle feathers, rabbitskin blankets, nets, baskets, and weapons for the ceremonial burning.

By the early 1900s the Kaibab had adopted the Ute Bear Dance (Sapir 1930), and it spread westward to other Southern Paiute groups. Celebrated in early spring to conciliate the bear just beginning to awaken from winter hibernation, the Bear Dance is also a festive social occasion when women take the initiative by selecting their partners and directing the elements of the dance. Male singers provide the music on rasps, with the initial tremolo that begins all Bear Dance songs creating the noise of thunder that is believed to awaken the bear in his cave.

More Recent History and Contemporary Issues

Each group of Southern Paiutes was treated differently by the federal government. In 1872 the government established a reservation for all Southern Paiute at Moapa in southern Nevada; at the turn of the century, this was still their only protected land. Landless, many Utah Paiute lived marginal lives, scraping by on the outskirts of Mormon towns where townspeople gave them some work. In 1903 Congress granted official recognition to the Shivwits Reservation in Utah; several years after this, the Kaibab Southern Paiutes received a small reservation in Arizona. However, the lack of a secure resource base meant that most of the people in a Southern Paiute community had to work in nearby towns, an underemployed pool of unskilled rural labor. In 1911 the Las Vegas Southern Paiute Tribe also received federal recognition.

In 1965 the Southern Paiutes were awarded a court judgment for just over $7 million in compensation for land illegally taken from them. Groups with trust lands, such as the Moapa and Kaibab, allocated a large portion of the settlement to economic and social development to create employment for their members and income for their tribes. Utah Southern Paiute groups, "terminated" in 1954, established a legal corporation in the 1970s to reverse termination and to restore their trust lands, as well as developing economic enterprises. Termination entailed not only the loss of a land base—and the cultural identity that went with it—but also the loss of educational programs, government employment, and job training. It contributed to even greater poverty, a still lower standard of living, and an increased rate of disease, along with the loss of access to the Indian Health Service. Their federally recognized status was restored in 1980 after long legal battles, and five Utah-based groups united to form a larger tribal entity, the Paiute Indian Tribe of Utah. Of the three Southern Nevada Southern Paiute Tribes, the Moapa, Las Vegas, and Pahrump, only the last-named has not received recognition by the federal government, although it has initiated the process to become federally recognized. (The two reservations on which the Chemehuevi live are discussed in chapter 7 because of their long-term association with the Colorado River Mojaves.)

Few Navajos lived in the territory of the San Juan Southern Paiute people—northernmost Arizona above Monument Valley—until 1864, when the Paiutes gave refuge to those Navajos who managed to escape Kit Carson's troops. By the 1880s Navajo herds had begun to encroach on Paiute farms, and by 1884 this Paiute territory was subsumed within the Navajo Reservation. When the 1974 Navajo-Hopi Relocation Act opened the way for legal action, the San Juans filed a formal petition, which finally brought federal recognition to their communities in Arizona and Utah that lie within the Navajo Reservation. In 1990 the San Juan Southern Paiute Tribe finally received federal recognition as an independent tribe rather than as members of the Navajo Nation. They elect their own council and hire their own managers and directors (Fontana 1999:41).

Pipe Spring National Monument, Kaibab-Paiute Reservation, Arizona, 1999. Author photograph

It is the San Juan Paiutes who make most Navajo-style ceremonial baskets, commonly called wedding baskets; their distinctive pattern includes a broken circle of red with a black stepped design outlining it on both sides. Over the years, as fewer Navajo women produced these baskets because of the many ritual restrictions they were expected to follow while weaving them, Southern Paiute women, who had no taboos regarding the weaving process, began to make these baskets for the Navajos. Although they have no tribal museum, they sell their traditional baskets through the San Juan Southern Paiute Ying-Up Weavers Association (Fontana 1999:41).

Set against the Vermilion Cliffs, the Kaibab-Paiute Reservation is one of the more remote reservations in the Southwest. Located on the Arizona Strip, their reservation has as its northern boundary the southern Utah border. Until 1996 the Kaibab Paiutes owned and operated the now defunct Pipe Springs Resort; the principal attraction today is Pipe Spring National Monument with its well-preserved, nineteenth-century Mormon ranch (Fontana 1999:40–41).

Cultural Resource Management

In 1992 Southern Paiute people representing three federally recognized tribes—the Paiute Indian Tribe of Utah, the San Juan Southern Paiute Tribe, and the Kaibab Southern Paiute Tribe—began participating in a program called Glen Canyon Environmental Studies, which was initiated by the federal Bureau of Reclamation in 1982 (SPC 1995). The Southern Paiutes have conducted ethnographic research and investigated the impact of water releases on their cultural resources in an area known as the Colorado River Corridor, which extends 255 miles downstream from Glen Canyon Dam within Grand Canyon National Park.

In addition to conducting systematic research on cultural resources in the Colorado River Corridor, issuing reports summarizing research activities, and developing a cultural resource monitoring program, Southern Paiute representatives have also begun a youth environmental education program. The Bureau of Reclamation arranged for an interagency trip through the Grand Canyon in 1985, which laid the groundwork for a Southern Paiute Consortium youth program in experiential education. The program is designed to prepare Paiute youth to fulfill their tribal consortium's responsibilities for adaptive management of the Glen Canyon Dam and its impacts. The program focuses on concepts related to the water of the Colorado River, the geology of the Grand Canyon, the biology of the Colorado River Corridor, and the anthropology of the Southern Paiute people (SPC 1992).

In the past, Southern Paiute youth have not been encouraged to develop an interest in the sciences or in the combination of scientific and cultural knowledge. The tribal councils wanted to take advantage of this opportunity to involve youth in scientific study while maintaining and passing on tribal knowledge. Each tribal government appointed a tribal elder and four or five youths to represent them during the eleven-day Colorado River trip. The first-year participants, who were between the ages of eleven and sixteen, learned to record scientific data related to the environment as well as taking part in traditional activities conducted by Southern Paiute elders. One of the most interesting aspects of their research was identifying and exploring the impact of humans, plants, and animals within the Colorado River Corridor in ways that highlighted the complementarity and differences between scientific and traditional Southern Paiute ways of knowing (SPC 1992).

Ceremonies and Traditions Today

Different bands of the Southern Paiutes continue to celebrate three major rituals, the Girls' Puberty Ceremony, the First Childbirth Ceremony, and the Cry. The Girls' Puberty Ceremony, celebrated by the San Juan Southern Paiutes in a continuous tradition, includes the girl's isolation for four days at the time of her first menstruation, when elders of both sexes instruct her about the responsibilities of womanhood and the taboos she must observe during these four days. At sunrise she runs to the east, and at sunset, to the west. The ceremony ends on the morning of the fifth day.

Both men and women celebrate the First Childbirth Ceremony, during which the husband and wife receive instruction on proper parenting and observe dietary and behavioral taboos. After thirty days, the new parents bathe in cold water, have their faces painted with red ocher, have their hair clipped, and are fed a ritual meal (Bunte and Franklin 1994:432).

The Chemehuevis, who had adopted it from the Mojaves, introduced the Cry Ceremony to other Southern Paiute tribes sometime before 1870, and by 1890 this memorial ceremony had become an integral part of Southern Paiute ceremonial life for all groups except the San Juan Paiutes. Today this ceremony lasts only one or two nights, although traditionally it was longer, and is performed the night before a church funeral as well as a year or so later as a memorial. The host families sponsor a "giveaway" of valuables to the guests. Two groups of singers sing two song cycles, the Salt Songs and the Bird Songs, on the last night from sunset to sunrise, and between performances of songs friends and family pay their respects through emotional speeches honoring the deceased person.

Traditionally, Southern Paiute families passed on belief and ritual in a cycle of stories known as Coyote Tales or Winter Stories. These stories, peopled with animals that act like humans, set forth standards of behavior and provide explanations for the origins of the world, rituals, and traditional practices. Some Southern Paiute groups are videotaping their stories to save them for future generations, as well as using them in Southern Paiute cultural programs. San Juan storytellers still tell the ancient stories in traditional settings to family members of all ages. However, today most Southern Paiute children hear Coyote stories in English.

References and Further Reading

Bolton, Herbert E., ed. 1950. "Pageant in the Wilderness: The Story of the Escalante Expedition to the Interior Basin, 1776; Including the Diary and Itinerary of Father Escalante." *Utah Historical Quarterly* 18, nos. 1–4:1–265.

*Bunte, Pamela A., and Robert J. Franklin. 1987. *From the Sands to the Mountain: Change and Persistence in a Southern Paiute Community.* University of Nebraska Press, Lincoln. [A remarkably detailed history of the San Juan Southern Paiutes.]

———. 1994. "Paiute: Southern." In *Native America in the Twentieth Century: An Encyclopedia,* pp. 428–32, ed. Mary Davis. Garland Publishing, New York.

Euler, Robert C. 1964. "Southern Paiute Archaeology." *American Antiquity* 29, no. 3:379–81.

———. 1966. *Southern Paiute Ethnohistory.* University of Utah Press, Salt Lake City.

———. 1972. *The Paiute People.* Indian Tribal Series, Phoenix.

Fontana, Bernard L. 1999. *A Guide to Contemporary Southwest Indians.* Southwest Parks and Monuments Association, Tucson.

Fowler, Catherine S. 1966. *Environmental Setting and Natural Resources.* University of Utah Press, Salt Lake City.

Fowler, Catherine, and Nancy Parezo. 1996. "The N ŋgw·(Southern Paiutes): The People of the Northwestern Frontier." In *Paths of Life,* pp. 163–86. University of Arizona Press, Tucson.

*Franklin, Robert J., and Pamela A. Bunte. 1990. *The Paiute.* Chelsea House, New York. [Providing fine descriptions of contemporary Paiute life, this book is an excellent general source.]

*Holt, Ronald L. *Beneath These Red Cliffs: An Ethnohistory of the Utah Paiutes.* University of New Mexico Press, Albuquerque. [Carefully documented account of termination for the Utah Paiute.]

Jake, Lucille, Evelyn James, and Pamela Bunte. 1983. "The Southern Paiute Woman in a Changing Society." *Frontiers* 7, no. 1:44–49.

Kelly, Isabel T. 1932. "Ethnography of the Suprise Valley Paiute." *University of California Publications in American Archaeology and Ethnology* 31, no. 3:67–210. [Reprinted in 1965 by Krauss Reprint, New York.]

———. 1934. "Southern Paiute Bands. *American Anthropologist* 36, no. 4:548–60.

———. 1936. "Chemehuevi Shamanism." In *Essays in Anthropology Presented to A. L. Kroeber in Celebration of His Sixtieth Birthday,* pp. 129–42, ed. R. E. Lowie. University of California Press, Berkeley.

*———. 1976. *Southern Paiute Ethnography.* Garland Publishing, New York. [This book provides basic historical and ethnographic details.]

Kelly, Isabel T., and Catherine S. Fowler. 1986. "Southern Paiute." In *Handbook of North American Indians,* vol. 11: *Great Basin,* pp. 368–97.

*Knack, Martha C. 1980. *Life Is with People: Household Organization of the Contemporary Southern Paiute Indians.* Ballena Press, Socorro, N.Mex. [Set in the 1970s, this book provides a glimpse of terminated communities.]

Kroeber, Alfred. 1935. *Walapai Ethnography*. Memoirs of the American Anthropological Association 42. Menasha, Wis.

Laird, Carobeth. 1974. "Chemehuevi Religious Beliefs and Practices." *Journal of California Anthropology* 1, no. 1:19–25.

*———. 1975. *Encounters with an Angry God: Recollections of My Life with John Peabody Harrington*. Malki Museum Press, Banning, Calif. [Once the wife of famed linguist Harrington, Laird married a Chemehuevi, and writes from her firsthand knowledge.]

———. 1976. *The Chemehuevis*. Malki Museum Press, Banning, Calif.

———. 1977. "Behavioral Patterns in Chemehuevi Myths." In *Flowers of the Wind: Papers on Ritual, Myth, and Symbolism in California and the Southwest*, pp. 97–119, ed. Thomas Blackburn. Ballena Press Anthropological Papers 8. Socorro, N.Mex.

Malouf, Carling, and A. Arline Malouf. 1945. "The Effects of Spanish Slavery on the Indians of the Intermountain West." *Southwestern Journal of Anthropology* 1, no. 3:378–91.

Sapir, Edward. 1912. "The Mourning Ceremony of the Southern Paiutes." *American Anthropologist* 14, no. 1:168–69.

———. 1930. "Southern Paiute, A Shoshonean Language." *Proceedings of the American Academy of Arts and Sciences* 65 (June):1.

SPC. 1995. *ITUS, AUV, TE'EK (PAST, PRESENT, FUTURE): Managing Southern Paiute Resources in the Colorado River Corridor*. Report of work carried out under the Southern Paiute Consortium Cooperative Agreement with the Bureau of Reclamation, no. 4-FC-40–15260. Southern Paiute Consortium and Bureau of Applied Research in Anthropology, University of Arizona, September 1995.

———. 1998. *Nengwetevip: The Land, Resources and History of the Southern Paiute People*. CD-ROM. Southern Paiute Consortium, Fredonia, Ariz.

Stewart, Omer C. 1942. "Culture Element Distributions, XVIII: Ute–Southern Paiute." *Anthropological Records* 6, no. 4:231–356.

Stoffle, Richard, and Henry Dobyns. 1983. *Niagantu*. Cultural Resources Series Monograph 7. Nevada State Office, Bureau of Land Management, Reno.

Stoffle, Richard W., and Michael J. Evans. 1978. *Kaibab Paiute History: The Early Years*. Kaibab Paiute Tribe.

Watkins, Frances. 1945. "Moapa Paiute Winter Wickiup." *Masterkey* 19, no. 1:13–18.

Whiteford, Andrew Hunter. 1988. *Southwestern Indian Baskets: Their History and Their Makers*. School of American Research Press, Santa Fe.

Whiteford, Andrew Hunter, and Susan McGreevey, eds. 1985. *Translating Tradition, Basketry Arts of the San Juan Paiute*. Wheelwright Museum, Santa Fe.

Chapter 12   Conclusion

December 1998   Palm fronds glisten in the light of a new day, and trade winds carry the fragrant scent of plumeria through an open door. The air resonates with the songs of doves, the raucous cries of mynahs, and the delighted laughter of children, set against the constant sound of the sea as waves break on the beach. Molokai rises from the ocean to my right; just above the treetops on the left, the island of Lanai sits between sky and sea. From my fifth-floor room, I can see a broad expanse of sky and a horizon rimmed by ocean, a landscape whose stark simplicity reminds me of the Southwest.

Here, in Hawaii, the land is alive—even as volcanoes continue to create new land, the ocean is washing away existing areas—and songs portraying the mountains as living beings are played on pop radio stations. Hawaii is also remarkable for the degree to which different ethnic groups have blended with relative harmony: one-quarter of the total population is of part-Hawaiian descent. Hawaiian artist Herb Kane attributes this blending to the prevailing spirit of aloha, the acceptance of all who come in a spirit of goodwill and peace.

However, now that tourism has replaced agriculture as Hawaii's economic base, the aloha spirit and the culture from which it springs have become commodities on the world market. Saddened by this commercialization, I am pleasantly surprised to discover that the Kaanapali Beach Hotel, where we are staying, has an Office of Cultural Resources, staffed by people of Hawaiian ancestry. Sam Ako and Dee Coyle tell me about the hotel's twelve-year-old Project Po'okela (Hawaiian for "excellence"), through which employees attend classes on Hawaiian culture to better understand their own heritage and to share these traditional values with guests. The hotel also hosted and coordinated the activities of the Hawaiian Agencies and Organizations for the 1993 Commemoration of Queen Liliuokalani and the Overthrow of the Hawaiian Nation, which was celebrated throughout the state of Hawaii and was a rallying point for the Hawaiian sovereignty movement. Most tourists return home unaware of grim statistics showing that Hawaiians, among all Americans, have the shortest life expectancy and highest rates of death from such diseases as cancer and diabetes, the lowest rates of higher education, and the highest rates of incarceration (Blaisdell 1996:369). My old neighborhood on the slopes of Aliamanu crater is unrecognizable today, because local families, priced out of the real estate market—in the mid-1990s a very modest house cost $360,000 (Mast and Mast 1996:160)—must now build onto existing homes to accommodate married children and their offspring. Others are less fortunate: in 1997, on a drive along Oahu's North Shore, we encountered an encampment of homeless Hawaiians, living in tents and flying the Hawaiian flag upside down, the international sign of distress.

The Hawaiian sovereignty movement and that of Native American self-determination are local expressions of the global struggle for the rights of indigenous peoples. All over the world, native cultures are facing similar forms of dispossession and impoverishment. Although many of the concerns faced by Native Americans are unique by virtue of their relationship with the federal government, it is important to understand their struggle as part of a much broader, global movement for indigenous rights.

1995–2004: The International Decade of the World's Indigenous People

Often overlooked in discussions of human rights is the distinction between ethnic minorities (who no longer live in their homeland) and indigenous peoples (the original inhabitants of a region). By virtue of their aboriginal ties to the land on which they live, it is argued that indigenous peoples have an inherent right to ownership and control over the land and resources of their heritage. However, governments—especially those of newly independent countries that fear that tribal loyalties may take precedence over national loyalties—often describe tribal peoples as "national" or "ethnic" minorities in an effort to undermine their legitimate claims to local autonomy (Bodley 1999:61). Thus, it is important to distinguish between ethnic minorities, such as Hispanics and African Americans, and indigenous peoples, such as Native Americans, because the latter can claim inherent rights to the land on which they live.

Although never passive victims of expansion, indigenous peoples are mobilizing politically on a new scale, with regional, national, and international organizations. Furthermore, the rapid dissemination of information through the electronic mass media has made it increasingly difficult for countries to hide human rights violations. In 1975 the Sheshaht (Nootka) Indians hosted the first general assembly of the World Council of Indigenous Peoples (WCIP), attended by representatives of indigenous organizations from nineteen countries (Sanders 1977). The WCIP has official status as a nongovernmental organization (NGO) of the United Nations and has since expanded the scope of its organization to include more indigenous groups in various parts of the world. As part of the International Decade of the World's Indigenous People (1995–2004), the United Nations has approved a Declaration on the Rights of Indigenous Peoples. It is a complex document with forty-five articles endorsing the right of indigenous peoples to self-determination and control over territory and resources, and condemning all forms of ethnocide and genocide against them. The International Decade represents a heightened awareness within the international community of the rights of indigenous peoples. (See Quesenberry 1999:103–18.)

The loss of political autonomy means the loss of control over cultural as well as environmental resources. Thus, tourist agencies are able to exploit native cultures as exotic attractions by presenting an aestheticized and hegemonic portrayal of carefree natives, while ignoring the actual quality of life the people in that culture are experiencing today. Anthropologist John Bodley explains that tourists then "return home believing themselves to be 'experts' on the peoples they visited, but knowing little about the larger realities of land rights, discrimination, and economic exploitation"—an assumption that obscures the plight of indigenous peoples to an even greater degree (1999:131).

Today no area is isolated from the national and world political economy. This was especially evident to me in Hawaii, where despite the holiday season, hotels were not fully occupied because of the many Japanese tourists who had remained at home as a result of the decline in Asian financial markets. Native Americans are directly affected by the global economy through such factors as tourism, mineral prices, and agricultural prices. They also experience a trickle-down effect from the global economy, which affects the federal budget and the amount of money allocated for Indian programs. Caught between conflicting currents of state and federal allocations, tribes must compete with businesses and political action groups for their slice of the federal budget, which continues to decrease (Anders 1999:167).

Based on a capitalist world economy committed to production for sale and the maximization of profits instead of the replenishment of local needs, the modern world system is founded upon the extraction of resources and the promotion of markets. Previously, the dynamic between tribes and states enabled indigenous societies to keep their cultures more or less intact, but today the natural—and cultural—resources that ensured their autonomy have become commodities on the global market. Furthermore, the values upon which indigenous cultures are founded—relative social equality, communitywide control of resources, and especially the sense of stewardship based on a spiritual connection to the land and its resources—are antithetical to global-scale culture with its emphasis on consumerism and exploitation. (See Bodley 1999:7.)

Humans and their hominid ancestors have been on the planet for over 4 million years, yet it has taken less than 300 years—since the development of the fossil fuel–driven machines of the Industrial Revolution—to destroy the planet's natural resources and to make large areas of the world uninhabitable. No longer is it possible to dismiss as isolated cases the acid-induced destruction of Germany's Black Forest or the carcasses of beluga whales floating in the Saint Lawrence River. Although the spiritual and human costs of technological development have been enormous, it remains to be seen if governments will take a more humanistic stance by controlling the exploitation of their resources and protecting cultural diversity; to do so means they will have to override the free market system that now dominates the global economy.

Native American Sovereignty

Today Hawaiians and other indigenous peoples are struggling to gain parity with Native Americans whose tribes have treaties with the U.S. government that give them a unique relationship with the federal government. Established in the Constitution of the United States, this special relationship is based on the fact that Indian tribes are sovereigns and, at least in principle, enjoy a government-to-government relationship. (This is only true for "treaty tribes," those that actually have treaties with the U.S. government. In general, the United States stopped making treaties in 1871, except for then on-going negotiations.) Over time, however, their status changed from sovereign Indian nations to wards of the government, which led to considerable diminution of their jurisdiction. In the twentieth century, especially in the last quarter of the century, state and local governments enlarged their jurisdictional role at the expense of tribal jurisdiction. Tribes and their members, pointing out that they never voluntarily surrendered their sovereign powers and jurisdiction, often justifiably claim to retain far greater sovereign powers than local, state, and federal governments consider them to have (Clinton 1992:611).

Many powerful interests, such as big businesses, fish and game lobbies, and state and local groups, are constantly trying to erode Indian rights, especially those related to water, land, and economic issues. A good example of the effort to diminish Indian sovereignty through federal legislation came in 1997, when Sen. Slade Gorton (R-Washington), chair of the Senate Interior Appropriation Subcommittee, proposed that federal funds should be allocated to Indian tribes according to their wealth, thus punishing them for economic development, including the success of their gambling operations; he also proposed that to receive federal funding, a tribe would have to waive its sovereign immunity (Oswalt and

Neely 1999:506–7). Although the Senate rejected these proposals, Senator Gorton vows that he will continue to fight for them.

State and local governments resent federal protection of such Indian rights as the ability to tax, to partially control their subsistence resources, and to generate income through casino gambling. Indian gaming has ignited considerable conflict between tribal and state governments, primarily because states are afraid of losing revenue from their lotteries to Indian-run casinos. The struggle began in the 1980s, when the federal government began to cut back severely on funding to tribes. Tribes, especially those without sizable tax bases or natural resources, such as the Cabezon Band of Mission Indians of California, began to sell tobacco at cheaper prices and set up bingo enterprises. In response to court action against the Cabezon from neighboring Anglo communities, the federal government eventually enacted the 1988 Indian Gaming Regulatory Act. Designed to mediate between the economic interests of tribes and states, this act allocates regulatory jurisdiction over different classes of gaming among tribal, federal, and state governments. By 1994 Indian tribes operated over a hundred high-stakes bingo operations and more than sixty casinos in twenty-four states (Newton and Frank 1994:205). Although states voice concern over the infiltration of organized crime, the U.S. Department of Justice has concluded that this has not occurred (Maloney 1992).

Although Indian gaming is not a permanent or complete solution for tribal economic independence, it does continue to stimulate economic growth in many tribal communities, where gaming revenues are being used to create economic ventures that will become self-sustaining or where gaming revenues are used to improve housing, education, and medical care. Thanks to Indian gaming, tribes have been able to supplement underfunded and discontinued federal programs, to fund legal services and land acquisition projects, to establish loan programs for tribal businesses, and to provide employment, health, housing, and educational programs, including scholarships, for tribal members. Nevertheless, casino gaming has provided an easy outlet for tribal members who are compulsive gamblers, as well as exacerbated existing problems, such as alcoholism and drug use, domestic violence, and violent crime (Anders 1999:168).

A positive outcome of Indian gaming has been the formation of Native American coalitions. Concerned about the restriction of their sovereign powers, especially with regard to gaming operations, tribes have joined forces to create such organizations as the National Indian Gaming Association, a lobby comparable to other business and political action groups. Native Americans, in contrast to many other indigenous peoples who are just beginning to unite for common causes, are not new to the struggle for self-determination and have learned over time how to mobilize as an effective political force on a national level.

One of the most emotional issues facing Indians in the Southwest and elsewhere has been the return of ancestral remains and affiliated cultural items. In 1991 President Bush signed into law the Native American Graves Protection and Repatriation Act (NAGPRA), establishing a process for the return of Indian skeletal remains and artifacts from all public and private institutions that receive federal funding. Although most curators are sympathetic, understaffing makes a daunting task of compiling inventories and identifying the legitimate owners. Millions of potential problems exist, from difficulties over proving the cultural affiliation of unassociated funerary objects and sacred objects to the mistreatment of certain items. According to some Pueblo religious leaders, ceremonial dolls should not be classed with children's dolls (Stoffle and Evans 1994:30). There are also disagreements among tribes of different cultural backgrounds, as well as those within the same cultural background, over the cultural affiliation of human remains and objects. Yet the complexities of identifying these remains, consulting about their origin and ownership, and treating these remains in a culturally sensitive manner provide an opportunity for anthropologists, federal agencies, and Native Americans to work together in a spirit of good will, increasing mutual understanding.

Tribal groups have also joined forces to bring ancestral remains home: after their division into a series of eleven tribes in four states stretched over a thousand miles, the Southern Paiutes formed the Southern Paiute Consortium to speak with a single, powerful voice. (See Southwestern Tribal Peoples NAGPRA Conference 1997:102.) Together, they have been able to accomplish much, not only in the realm of repatriation but also in other areas, that they would not otherwise have been able to do.

While NAGPRA protects Indian interests by federal law, some tribes are also organizing at the state level to shape the public view of them. Mojave/Tohono O'odham John Lewis is the executive director of the Inter Tribal Council of Arizona, Inc., a private coalition that guards the cultural and political interests of nineteen federally recognized tribes. Excited about the major expansion of Phoenix's Heard Museum, Lewis says, "The Heard Museum expansion will really enhance Indian awareness not just in this state but throughout the country. We've had an on-going relationship with the Heard, and we'll be collaborating even more" (1999:81–82). The museum's outreach manager, a Delaware Indian, sees the doubling of the museum space as an opportunity for Indian people to be able to shape the views the public has about them to an even greater degree than was possible previously.

Threats to Native American Survival

The statistics for Native Americans are as staggering as those for Hawaiians in the areas of health, education, and economics. Thirty-three percent of Indians die before they reach the age of forty-five, in contrast to 11 percent for the U.S. population, and Indians and Alaska Natives are much more likely to die from accidents (120 deaths per 100,000 versus less than 40 deaths per 100,000 for all ethnic groups in the United States), chronic liver disease and cirrhosis, suicide, and homicide; they also have a much higher incidence of diabetes and gallbladder disease (Garrett 1994:233–37). The health of American Indians is worse than that of the U.S. population by almost every indicator; as this population, which is younger by almost eight years than the U.S. population, is growing rapidly (from 524,000 in 1960 to nearly 2 million in 1990 [Oswalt and Neely 1999: 505–6]), these health issues present a tremendous challenge. American Indians also lag behind the general population with respect to higher education, even though more of them are pursuing college degrees today.

Native Americans are the poorest of the poor, with the income gap between white households and Indian households growing from 37 percent in 1979 to 54 percent in 1989; in most respects, they are more disadvantaged than African Americans (Snipp 1994: 175–79). In 1990 over half of all Native Americans and Alaska Natives had incomes below the poverty line (U.S. Dept. of Commerce). Reservation unemployment can be as high as 80 percent, and in 1996 only 28 percent of Indians with jobs earned over $7,000 annually (Rushlo 1997). Facing many of the same challenges as developing nations, tribes must decide whether to lease their land to corporations, to develop natural areas, or to leave it as it is. Economic development on reservations presents one of the greatest threats to Native American survival.

In much the same way that their natural resources have become commodities on the world market, Native American cultural resources have also become marketable items. Some of this cultural knowledge, especially dealing with plants, medicine, and arts, has commercial value; according to the concept of indigenous intellectual property rights, each group has the right to determine how this knowledge and its products should be used and the appropriate level of compensation for such use. Of major concern to native peoples the world over is the appropriation by nonnatives of their stories, designs, and rituals; this kind of exploitation in the fine arts is exemplified by German-born artist Sibylle Szaggars, who uses post-abstract expressionism to interpret Hopi katsinam, earning as much as $23,000 apiece for her canvases (Williams 1995:130).

Tribal and Individual Resilience

Statistics, however, do not tell the entire story. On both tribal and individual levels, Native Americans remain rooted and resilient. Once described as "a vanishing race," they have survived on this continent at least thirty times longer than non-Indians. At the start of the twenty-first century, the native peoples of the Southwest are developing their own solutions to the challenges they face.

The Southwest Indian Center Diabetes Prevention Program at Zuni offers a ray of hope in the battle against diabetes, the debilitating disease that touches the lives of nearly every indigenous person in the world today. Stunned when the new dialysis unit at the pueblo was immediately overwhelmed by demand for its services, Zuni Norman Cooeyate, who coordinates the diabetes program, developed a holistic program based not only on lifestyle changes, such as diet and exercise, but also on religious practices, so that all aspects of Zuni life are integrated and drawn upon for the management of this disease (Hill 1997:30–31). Zuni tribal members also developed the Zuni Wellness Center, which has received national recognition as one of the most successful grass-roots programs among Native American tribes. Fitness instructors from Zuni lead aerobics classes, circuit weight training, and cardiovascular classes on a daily basis and teach people about proper nutrition. The program manager of the center, Zuni Carlton Albert, attributes the program's success to the fact that, instead of outsiders, tribal members initiated and supported the endeavor (ibid., 30).

Navajo Larry Holiday, an educator at Monument Valley High School, explains the dilemma facing Native Americans: "We cannot ignore our own ways without losing our moorings, our sense of self, of *hózhǫ́*, but we cannot survive in this economy, in this country, without accommodating our knowledge to the demands of the predominant culture" (Clemens et al. 1995:62). Concerned that their students would lack computer skills, educators at the school successfully tried an educational graphics software program called LOGO to use Navajo weaving to teach computer design and mathematics skills, such as geometry.

Too often Native Americans experience a sense of numbing alienation when they enter the work force and find themselves in a sea of non-Indian faces. Santa Clara Pueblo Louis Baca says that he "wanted to turn around and walk out. The corporate environment and lack of other brothers and sisters, Indian people, was an environment that made me feel like this isn't where I belong" (Evans 1996:27). Instead of giving up, Baca brought his company, computer giant Intel Corporation, together with the American Indian Science and Engineering Society (AISES), the Santa Fe Indian School, and the Gila River Community in Arizona. Responding to the needs of both school systems, Intel representatives worked with them to create an approach based on computer labs located in tribal communities, to be used as learning centers for students, teachers, parents, and elders; these labs will also serve as a tribal communication center and provide opportunities to help preserve the cultures of the communities.

What sees people through the challenges of facing two diametrically opposed worlds? For college student Alisha Antonio from Laguna Pueblo, the "yearly religious ceremonies get me through the toughest times, gently cleansing and healing for a new day. That kind of nourishment indeed overfills my soul" (1998:97). Overwhelmed by an alien environment for which they have no preparation, many Indian students drop out after a year or two of college. However, many wait awhile, gathering their energies while they earn money, and eventually try again. "I had no idea college would be so time-consuming. I didn't have the study skills or the discipline to carry my learning outside of the classroom," says Hopi/ Santa Clara Paul Kabotie (Wakshul 1998:42), who failed at his first two attempts at the University of New Mexico. After working for two years, he returned to earn his degree in computer science and, after working for thirteen years in the corporate world, founded Kabotie Software Technology in 1997. Living away from his community was the hardest thing he ever had to do, but "if I had gone home right after college, I would've done disservice to myself and my tribe" (ibid., 43–44).

Paul Kabotie is also remarkable in overcoming alcoholism. Often not apparent in statistics of Indian alcoholism is that many Native Americans reach a turning point in their lives when a life-changing experience sets them on the road to sobriety (Levy and Kunitz 1974). Kabotie's came when he was twenty-two, after a decade of drinking. His father, also an alcoholic, reclaimed his life after a car accident sent him into intensive rehabilitation; during this time, his father "talked to me sincerely and openly about his disease and about things in the community I had never seen before—dysfunction in the community and in our home. He opened my eyes to so many things . . . how easy it is to be lulled into alcoholism and how insidious the disease is. . . . That was the turning point for me" (ibid., 41). Kabotie advises young people not to accept the dysfunction in their communities: "You may not be able to change others in your communities, but you can vow to change your own actions and make sure you don't go down that road" (ibid., 42).

The Navajo-Ute flutist, R. Carlos Nakai, also stresses the importance of a strong personal philosophy: "In the traditional way you go out there and . . . build on your worldly experiences . . . you build on . . . communication . . . with elders. And you build a personal philosophy. . . . If you don't have a personal philosophy of what you *intend* to do in the world you'll get out there and begin drinking, and you'll lose sight of your path" (Simonelli 1992:24 [emphasis in original]).

Santa Clara Pueblo Dr. Greg Cajete, an educator and private consultant who operates his own business, sees alcoholism as one of "the spiritual ills which befall traditional people once they lose their direct connection to spiritual ecology. Tewa people call this state of unwhole, unwise existence *pingeh heh* . . . split thought or thinking, being foolish and doing things with only half your mind" (1993:52–53). He points out, "It is not only Indian people who must heal this split in themselves" (ibid.).

Facing the Twenty-First Century

Native American societies had been responding to changing conditions for centuries before Europeans ever set foot on the North American continent. Today American Indians remain rooted and resilient in the land; this sure sense of identity enables them to face the challenges that lie ahead. Hopi Al Qöyawayma explains that the ability to meet change successfully is an inherent part of his heritage: "Out of our family clan, the Coyote Clan, it was said that we would be the generation to meet the new world and make changes—that was our ancient role as the Coyote Clan—to be those who go before" (1998: 86). He continues to shape the future by channeling his creative skills into technology as well as art: he holds the patents worldwide on inertial guidance systems, used in passenger and military planes, and builds on his twenty-year body of fine ceramic work based on his Hopi roots.

R. Carlos Nakai believes, "The tradition of being a native person isn't tied to what happened in the 1700s or the 1800s, but what's going on with us *right* now, in the waning years of the twentieth century. What kinds of new songs, what kinds of new stories, what kinds of experiences are we going to record and add to the vast compendium of oral tradition that travels with us?" (Simonelli 1992:18 [emphasis in original]).

Al Qöyawayma and R. Carlos Nakai think of themselves as not only being part of their native communities but also as part of the larger, global community. Nakai says, "I consider myself *of service to the greater community,* besides the extended family of my culture, of my tribe, of my own people in general. There are many human beings out there from various cultures" (ibid., 21 [emphasis in original]). Rina Swentzell, Santa Clara architectural historian, shares this global perspective: "What does remain as a hope in the end is that we all—Indian, non-Indian, artists, non-artists, rural or urban—desire that genuine experience of oneness with the breath of life that forms the world we live in" (1998:64). It is that sense of connection, with the land, with ourselves, and with each other, that will sustain and nurture all of us in the years ahead.

References and Further Reading

For current issues viewed from the Native American perspectives, *Native Peoples* and *Winds of Change* magazines are excellent.

Anders, Gary C. 1999. "Indian Gaming: Financial and Regulatory Issues." In *Contemporary Native American Political Issues,* pp. 163–73, ed. Troy R. Johnson. Altamira Press, Walnut Creek, Calif.

Antonio, Alisha. 1998. "Life's Reflection." *Winds of Change* 13, no. 4:97.

*Blaisdell, Kekuni. 1996. "Sovereignty." In *Autobiography of Protest in Hawaii,* pp. 363–73, ed. Robert H. Mast and Anne B. Mast. University of Hawai'i Press, Honolulu. [This book contains a variety of perspectives regarding the Hawaiian sovereignty movement and the rights to which native Hawaiians should be entitled. Lack of proper management in instituting land distribution by the Hawaiian Homes Commission is also discussed.]

Bodley, John. 1999. *Victims of Progress.* 4th ed. Mayfield Publishing, Mountain View, Calif.

Cajete, Greg. 1993. "An Enchanted Land: Spiritual Ecology and a Theology of Place." *Winds of Change* 8, no. 2:50–55.

Clemens, Herbert, Don Mose, and Eli Spanier. 1995. "*Ndahoo'aah:* Relearning and New Learning." *Winds of Change* 10, no. 4:60–63.

Clinton, Robert N. 1992. "Sovereignty and Jurisdiction." In *Native America in the Twentieth Century: An Encyclopedia*, pp. 605–11, ed. Mary Davis. Garland Publishing, New York.

Evans, Lara. 1996. "Creating Alliances: Pathways to Leadership." *Winds of Change* 11, no. 2:26–30.

Garrett, J. T. 1994. "Health." In *Native America in the Twentieth Century: An Encyclopedia*, pp. 233–37, ed. Mary Davis. Garland Publishing, New York.

*Getches, David H. 1985. "Alternative Approaches to Land Claims: Alaska and Hawaii." In *Irredeemable America: The Indians' Estate and Land Claims*, pp. 301–35, ed. Imre Sutton. University of New Mexico Press, Albuquerque. [This article explains that the rights to which native Hawaiians are entitled are a question of morality as well as legality because pre-contact Hawaii was a kingdom with a system of established land tenure.]

Hill, Mary Anne. 1997. "The Curse of Frybread: The Diabetes Epidemic in Indian Country." *Winds of Change* 12, no. 3:26–31.

Kunitz, Stephen, and Jerrold Levy. 1974. "Changing Ideas of Alcohol Use among Navajo Indians." *Quarterly Journal of Studies on Alcohol* 35:243–59.

Levy, Jerrold, and Stephen Kunitz. 1974. *Indian Drinking: Navajo Practices and Anglo-American Theories*. Wiley-Interscience, New York.

Lewis, John. 1999. Quoted in "Have You Heard?" *Native Peoples* 12, no. 2:80–82.

Maloney, Paul L. 1992. Statement of Paul L. Maloney, senior counsel for policy, Criminal Division, before the Senate Committee on Indian Affairs, 18 March.

Mast, Robert H., and Anne B. Mast, eds. 1996. *Autobiography of Protest in Hawaii*. University of Hawai'i Press, Honolulu.

Newton, Nell Jessup, and Shawn Frank. 1994. "Gaming." In *Native America in the Twentieth Century: An Encyclopedia*, pp. 205–7, ed. Mary Davis. Garland Publishing, New York.

Oswalt, Wendell H., and Sharlotte Neely. 1999. *This Land Was Theirs: A Study of Native Americans*. 6th ed. Mayfield Publishing, Mountain View, Calif.

Qöyawayma, Al. 1998. "Al Qöyawayma." *Winds of Change* 13, no. 1:86.

Quesenberry, Stephen V. 1999. "Recent United Nations Initiatives." In *Contemporary Native American Indian Political Issues*, pp. 103–18, ed. Troy R. Johnson. Altamira Press, Walnut Creek, Calif.

Rushlo, Michelle. 1997. "State's Job Boom Stops at Reservations." *Arizona Republic*, 14 May.

Sanders, Douglas E. 1977. *The Formation of the World Council of Indigenous Peoples*. IWGIA Document 29. IWGIA, Copenhagen.

Simonelli, Richard. 1992. "A Conversation with Native Flutist R. Carlos Nakai." *Winds of Change* 7, no. 4:16–26.

Snipp, C. Matthew. 1994. "Economic Conditions." In *Native America in the Twentieth Century: An Encyclopedia*, pp. 175–79, ed. Mary Davis. Garland Publishing, New York.

Stoffle, Richard W., and Michael J. Evans. 1994. "To Bury the Ancestors: A View of NAGPRA." *Practicing Anthropology* 16, no. 3:29–32.

Southwestern Tribal Peoples NAGPRA Conference. 1997. Sponsored by the Museum of Indian Arts and Culture/Laboratory of Anthropology, a Division of the Museum of New Mexico, Santa Fe, 9–10 October.

*Swentzell, Rina. 1998. Essay in *Pueblo Artists: Portraits*, pp. 9–16, ed. Toba Pato Tucker. Museum of New Mexico Press, Santa Fe. [This inspiring book presents intimate portraits of young as well as older artists.]

Szasz, Margaret Connell. 1994. "Educational Policy." In *Native America in the Twentieth Century: An Encyclopedia* pp. 182–85, ed. Mary Davis. Garland Publishing, New York.

U.S. Dept. of Commerce, Bureau of the Census. 1991. *1990 Census of Population and Housing.* Government Printing Office, Washington, D.C.

Wakshul, Barbra. 1998. "Overcoming Adversity and Soaring." *Winds of Change* 13, no. 4:40–45.

Williams, Cat. 1995. "The Indian Problem: Mass Media Images Create Stereotypes and False Impressions." *Indian Country Today* (Rapid City, S.D.), 6 July.

Tribal Addresses and Phone Numbers

The Apaches

Jicarilla Apache Tribe, P.O. Box 507, Dulce, NM 85728; tel. 505-759-3242.

Mescalero Apache Tribe, P.O. Box 227, Mescalero, NM 88340; tel. 505-671-4494.

San Carlos Apache Tribe, P.O. Box "O", San Carlos, AZ 85550; tel. 520-475-2361.

Tonto Apache Tribe, No. 30 Tonto Apache Reservation, Payson, AZ 85541;
  tel. 520-474-5000.

White Mountain Apache Tribe, Fort Apache Indian Reservation, P.O. Box 700,
  Whiteriver, AZ 85941; tel. 520-338-4346.

The Navajo

Navajo Nation, P.O. Box 9000, Window Rock, AZ 86515; tel. 520-871-6352.

The O'odham

Ak-Chin Indian Community, 42507 W. Peters and Nall Rd., Maricopa, AZ 85239;
  tel. 520-568-2618.

Gila River Indian Community, P.O. Box 97, Sacaton, AZ 85247; tel. 520-562-3311.

Salt River Pima-Maricopa Indian Community, Route 1, Box 216, Scottsdale, AZ 85256;
  tel. 602-941-7277.

Tohono O'odham Nation, P.O. Box 837, Sells, AZ 85634; tel. 520-383-2221.

The Pascua Yaqui

Pascua Yaqui Tribe, 7474 S. Camino de Oeste, Tucson, AZ 85746; tel. 520-883-5000.

The Pueblos

Acoma Pueblo, P.O. Box 309, Acomita, NM 87034; tel. 505-552-6604.

Cochiti Pueblo, P.O. Box 70, Cochiti, NM 87072; tel. 505-465-2245.

Hopi Tribe, P.O. Box 123, Kykotsmovi, AZ 86039; tel. 520-734-2441.

Isleta Pueblo, P.O. Box 1270, Isleta, NM 87022; tel. 505-869-3111.

Jemez Pueblo, P.O. Box 100, Jemez, NM 87024; tel. 505-834-7359.

Laguna Pueblo, P.O. Box 194, Laguna, NM 87026; tel. 505-552-6654.

Nambe Pueblo, Route 1, Box 117-BB, Santa Fe, NM 87501; tel. 505-455-2036.

Picuris Pueblo, P.O. Box 127, Penasco, NM 87533; tel. 505-587-2519.

Pojoaque Pueblo, Route 11, Box 71, Santa Fe, NM 87501; tel. 505-455-2278.

Sandia Pueblo, P.O. Box 6008, Bernalillo, NM 87004; tel. 505-867-3317.

San Felipe Pueblo, P.O. Box 4339, San Felipe, NM 87001; tel. 505-867-3381.

San Ildefonso Pueblo, Route 5, P.O. Box 315-A, Santa Fe, NM 87501; tel. 505-455-2273.

San Juan Pueblo, P.O. Box 1099, San Juan, NM 87566; tel. 505-852-4400.

Santa Ana Pueblo, 2 Dove Rd., Bernalillo, NM 87004; tel. 505-867-3301.

Santa Clara Pueblo, P.O. Box 580, Espanola, NM 87532; tel. 505-753-7330.

Santo Domingo Pueblo, P.O. Box 99, Santo Domingo, NM; tel. 505-465-2214.

Taos Pueblo, P.O. Box 1846, Taos, NM 87571; tel. 505-758-9593.

Tesuque Pueblo, Route 5, Box 360-T, Santa Fe, NM 87501; tel. 505-983-2667.

Zia Pueblo, General Delivery, San Ysidro, NM 87053; tel. 505-867-3304.

Zuni Pueblo, P.O. Box 339, Zuni, NM 87327; tel. 505-782-4481.

The River Yumans

Chemehuevi Indian Tribe, P.O. Box 1976, Chemehuevi Valley, CA 92362; tel. 760-858-4301.

Cocopah Tribe, Ave. G and Co. Fifteenth, Somerton, AZ 85350; tel. 520-627-2061.

Colorado River Indian Tribes, Rt. 1, Box 23-B, Parker, AZ 85344; tel. 520-669-9211.

Fort Mojave Indian Tribe, 500 Merriman Ave., Needles, CA 92363; tel. 760-326-4591.

Fort Yuma Quechan Tribe, P.O. Box 11352, Yuma, AZ 85366; tel. 760-572-0213.

The Southern Paiutes

Kaibab Paiute Tribe, HC 65, Box 2, Fredonia, AZ 86022; tel. 520-643-7245.

San Juan Southern Paiute Tribe, P.O. Box 1989, Tuba City, AZ 86045; tel. 520-283-4589.

The Upland Yumans

Fort McDowell Yavapai Tribe, P.O. Box 17779, Fountain Hills, AZ 85269;
tel. 602-837-5121.

Havasupai Tribe, P.O. Box 10, Supai, AZ 85435; tel. 520-448-2731.

Hualapai Tribe, P.O. Box 179, Peach Springs, AZ 86434; tel. 520-769-2216.

Yavapai-Apache Nation, 3435 Shaw Ave., P.O. Box 1188, Camp Verde, AZ 86322;
tel. 520-567-3649.

Yavapai-Prescott Indian Tribe, 530 E. Merritt, Prescott, AZ 86301;
tel. 520-445-8790

Index